Wealth Expanding Theory Under the Principle of Efficiency–Equity Equilibrium

Fred Y. Ye
Nanjing University, China

A volume in the Advances in Finance, Accounting, and Economics (AFAE) Book Series

IGI Global
PUBLISHER of TIMELY KNOWLEDGE

Published in the United States of America by
IGI Global
Business Science Reference (an imprint of IGI Global)
701 E. Chocolate Avenue
Hershey PA, USA 17033
Tel: 717-533-8845
Fax: 717-533-8661
E-mail: cust@igi-global.com
Web site: http://www.igi-global.com

Library of Congress Cataloging-in-Publication Data

Names: Ye, Ying (Professor), author.
Title: Wealth expanding theory under the principle of efficiency-equity equilibrium / by Fred Y. Ye.
Description: Hershey, PA : Business Science Reference, [2022] | Includes bibliographical references and index. | Summary: "This book sets up a synthetic economic systems that has Inherited representative economic thoughts from Adam Smith, Alfred Marshall, Maynard Keynes, Paul Samuelson and Milton Friedmann, and provides various methodological models"-- Provided by publisher.
Identifiers: LCCN 2022004130 (print) | LCCN 2022004131 (ebook) | ISBN 9781668449356 (hardcover) | ISBN 9781668449363 (paperback) | ISBN 9781668449370 (ebook)
Subjects: LCSH: Economic development. | Wealth. | Economics.
Classification: LCC HD82 .Y42 2022 (print) | LCC HD82 (ebook) | DDC 338.9--dc23/eng/20220202
LC record available at https://lccn.loc.gov/2022004130
LC ebook record available at https://lccn.loc.gov/2022004131

This book is published in the IGI Global book series Advances in Finance, Accounting, and Economics (AFAE) (ISSN: 2327-5677; eISSN: 2327-5685)

British Cataloguing in Publication Data
A Cataloguing in Publication record for this book is available from the British Library.

Advances in Finance, Accounting, and Economics (AFAE) Book Series

Ahmed Driouchi
Al Akhawayn University, Morocco

ISSN:2327-5677
EISSN:2327-5685

MISSION

In our changing economic and business environment, it is important to consider the financial changes occurring internationally as well as within individual organizations and business environments. Understanding these changes as well as the factors that influence them is crucial in preparing for our financial future and ensuring economic sustainability and growth.

The **Advances in Finance, Accounting, and Economics (AFAE)** book series aims to publish comprehensive and informative titles in all areas of economics and economic theory, finance, and accounting to assist in advancing the available knowledge and providing for further research development in these dynamic fields.

COVERAGE

- Theoretical Issues in Economics, Finance, and Accounting
- Economics Geography
- Economics of Risks, Uncertainty, Ambiguity, and Insurance
- Fiscal Policy
- International Economics
- Economics of Natural and Environmental Resources
- Public Finance
- Banking
- Comparative Accounting Systems
- Macroeconomics

IGI Global is currently accepting manuscripts for publication within this series. To submit a proposal for a volume in this series, please contact our Acquisition Editors at Acquisitions@igi-global.com or visit: http://www.igi-global.com/publish/.

The Advances in Finance, Accounting, and Economics (AFAE) Book Series (ISSN 2327-5677) is published by IGI Global, 701 E. Chocolate Avenue, Hershey, PA 17033-1240, USA, www.igi-global.com. This series is composed of titles available for purchase individually; each title is edited to be contextually exclusive from any other title within the series. For pricing and ordering information please visit http://www.igi-global.com/book-series/advances-finance-accounting-economics/73685. Postmaster: Send all address changes to above address.

Titles in this Series

For a list of additional titles in this series, please visit: http://www.igi-global.com/book-series/

Handbook of Research on Changing World Economic Order in the Post-Pandemic Period
Sushanta Kumar Mahapatra (IBS Hyderabad, The ICFAI Foundation for Higher Education, India) and Vishal Sarin (Lovely Professional University, India)
Business Science Reference • © 2022 • 470pp • H/C (ISBN: 9781799868965) • US $325.00

Perspectives of Management Accounting for Sustainable Business Practices
Ionica Oncioiu (Titu Maiorescu University, Romania)
Business Science Reference • © 2022 • 310pp • H/C (ISBN: 9781668445952) • US $250.00

Emerging Trends and Insights on Economic Inequality in the Wake of Global Crises
Shilpa Deo (MIT World Peace University, India) and A.V. Senthil Kumar (Hindusthan College of Arts and Science, India)
Information Science Reference • © 2022 • 300pp • H/C (ISBN: 9781668452899) • US $215.00

Handbook of Research on Stock Market Investment Practices and Portfolio Management
Renuka Sharma (Chitkara University, India) and Kiran Mehta (Chitkara University, India)
Business Science Reference • © 2022 • 400pp • H/C (ISBN: 9781668455289) • US $355.00

Opportunities and Challenges for Multinational Enterprises and Foreign Direct Investment in the Belt and Road Initiative
Miraj Ahmed Bhuiyan (Guangdong University of Finance and Economics, China) and Isidora Beraha (Institute of Economic Sciences, Serbia)
Business Science Reference • © 2022 • 323pp • H/C (ISBN: 9781799880219) • US $250.00

Advanced Machine Learning Algorithms for Complex Financial Applications
Mohammad Irfan (CMR Institute of Technology, India) Mohamed Elhoseny (American University in the Emirates, UAE) Salina Kassim (International Islamic University of Malaysia, Malaysia) and Noura Metawa (University of Sharjah, UAE)
Engineering Science Reference • © 2022 • 335pp • H/C (ISBN: 9781668444832) • US $270.00

IGI Global
PUBLISHER of TIMELY KNOWLEDGE

701 East Chocolate Avenue, Hershey, PA 17033, USA
Tel: 717-533-8845 x100 • Fax: 717-533-8661
E-Mail: cust@igi-global.com • www.igi-global.com

Table of Contents

Preface

Economics is a social science concerned with the description and analysis of the production and consumption of goods and services, as well as the distribution of scarce resources and social wealth. Economics is also viewed as an art branch of science that concerns the balance and optimization of economic efficiency and social equity in human society. It has influenced world development at many important junctions throughout history and is a vital part of our everyday lives, so that everyone should understand less or more economics.

Over hundreds of years, economics has cumulated rich ideas, for interpreting economic phenomena and social situations. However, we still face many problems in modern times, even with lots of economic theories. In this monograph, I integrated the valuable economic thoughts of main thinkers (chiefly including Adam Smith, Alfred Marshall, Maynard Keynes, Milton Friedman and Paul Samuelson), with synthesizing Arrow-Debreu model in microeconomics and Mundell-Fleming model in macroeconomics as an economic standard model, combining Cobb-Douglas production model and Solow-Swan growth model, yielding a new framework called grand synthesis to analyze and discuss economic issues, focusing on balancing economic efficiency and social equity.

As human society is an economic society, people interact and relate to each other through complicated economic activities. Although economic resources are limited in the Earth, the economic wealth represents unlimited expansion, from ancient world to modern society. Since industrial civilization, why does national wealth continuously expand? Or we can ask, why do economic resources keep limited and economic wealth unlimitedly expansion? This is an important issue that needs a reply from economists. Focusing on this issue, we may probe into the reasons and analyze the mechanism, and we can find that scientific knowledge promotes technological progress and then technology pushes the economic growth. This is just a key to understanding the real wealth expansion, and a value-mechanism of intellectual property.

Meanwhile, capital is also a power to push the imaginary wealth expansion, leading to complex economics. In this book, I try to contribute an economic framework and find feasible solutions in the economic system, integrating economic principles with economic models. The core idea can also extend to future interstellar economics.

This book is organized by two parts, where Chapters 1 to 9 construct as Part I, pure economics, and Chapters 10 to 16 integrate as Part II, economic philosophy.

The logic structure of chapters begins at Chapter 1, where we introduce necessary economic concepts and economic metrics. Following a concise review of important economic thoughts, we set up a grand theoretical framework in Chapter 2. With a re-classified system of economic models, we review important economic models concerning economic analysis in economic studies in Chapter 3. Integrating mentioned economic theories and economic models, we establish a grand synthetic model for interpreting economic phenomena in Chapter 4. Considering efficiency-equity equilibrium as well as the equilibrium of real technological progress and the imaginary capital inflation, we reveal the secret of wealth expansion in Chapter 5. A new economic complex analysis is introduced in Chapter 6, for characterizing economic equilibrium and economic stability as well as interpreting money supply, using complex number. After more extending economic models are shown in Chapter 7, an interesting interstellar economics, characterized by interstellar trade and interstellar finance, is discussed in Chapter 8. Then Chapter 9 concludes that economics contributes a kind of great knowledge, via economic ideas and analytics.

Economic philosophy starts at Chapter 10, in which we bring a metaphysical thinking to economic knowledge, approaching the good and the true. While Chapter 11 covers social equity concerning with human happiness and social peace via active fiscal policy, Chapter 12 emphasizes market mechanism providing the key to economic efficiency via monetary policy. Combining fiscal and monetary policies, we discuss balancing social equity and economic efficiency to approach economic optimization in Chapter 13. Chapter 14 focuses on political economics, which provides a unique view for reducing poverty via economic growth. Chapter 15 addresses economic philosophy as a way of thinking, which combines verifiability with falsifiability, qualitative ideas with quantitative methods, as well as science and art. Then Chapter 16 concludes that economic philosophy contributes unique economic thought, for balancing social equity and economic efficiency, the good and the true, as well as the economic growth and economic optimality.

Like any science, economics is also based on concepts and theories with falsifiable features. So we begin with basic concepts and economic thoughts, to process the above mentioned issues and find feasible and synthetic theory to guide us toward a bright future.

Fred Y. Ye
Nanjing University, China

Introduction

Inheriting representative great economic thoughts from Adam Smith, Alfred Marshall, Maynard Keynes, Paul Samuelson and Milton Friedmann, and the methodological models including Arrow-Debreu model and Mundell-Fleming model, as well as Cobb-Douglas model and Solow-Swan model, a grand synthetic economics is set up in this book.

Applying the Arrow-Debreu-Mundell-Fleming model as an economic standard, combined with the Cobb-Douglas and Solow-Swan models, a grand synthetic model is established under the framework of representative economic thoughts, where interest, exchange and tax rates are integrated together. The grand economic model is characterized by four key variables (output variable y, money variable m, price variable p, capital variable k), three policy variables (interest rate γ, tax rate τ, exchange rate π), three model parameters (α, θ, ρ) and three economic parameters (b, s, d). In the model, the big parameter $b\sim10^3$ connects the logarithmic form of the Cobb-Douglas model and the per-capita form of the Solow-Swan model, the small parameter $s\sim10^{-1}$ is the capital investment rate, the micro parameter $d\sim10^{-2}$ is the capital depreciation rate. By measuring the gap between the model and the economic value, the technological progress index $q\sim10$ and the inflation rate λ are used to explain the real and imaginary wealth expansion, respectively. It is found that tax reduction is good policy when the tax rate is higher than normal and that tax increase is good social policy when the tax rate is lower than normal, during economic depression. It is suggested that national economic policies should focus on taxation to achieve social equity, interest rates to focus on economic efficiency, and wealth distribution can balance efficiency and equity through tax rates, interest rate and exchange rate. It is also revealed that tax reduction is good social policy when the tax rate is lower than normal, and that tax increase is good policy when the tax rate is higher than normal, during economic overheat. While the economic system seeks efficiency and *the social system pursues equity, common interest modifications with elastic exchange and tax rates could be applied for balancing efficiency and equity.*

Furthermore, future interstellar economics is also probed in the book, which may be an interesting issue to discuss and think about. Also, economic philosophy is discussed for extending economic cognition balancing, economic efficiency and social equity. This book is suitable for both learners and researchers.

Section 1
Pure Economics

Chapter 1
Introduction:
Economic Foundation

ABSTRACT

A concise introduction to economic concepts and economic metrics is given for both learners and researchers. Around the core of market economics, six common concepts and 22 analytical concepts are strengthened. With a brief conclusion on economic schools and economic methodology, the mainstream economics and positive methodology are pointed out, and then the economic foundation is set up. For strict economic analysis, economic concepts are defined at first, and analytical methodology is discussed.

INTRODUCTION

The word 'economics' is derived from a Greek word 'οικονομικά', in which word root 'eco' (οικο) means home and word root 'nomo' (νομο) means accounts. So the whole word indicates how to keep the family accounts and means 'household management'. Economists consider how people earn income and resources and then spend on their necessities, comforts and luxuries.

Now, economics is known as a branch of social sciences that studies how people interact with things of value, concerning the production and consumption of goods and services, as well as wealth distribution. Contemporary economics is a real social science using complicated scientific methodology. However, basic economic principles are popular and understandable. Everyone can know about economics, even for a learner, as if facing baby economics, as shown in Figure 1.

DOI: 10.4018/978-1-6684-4935-6.ch001

Figure 1. Learner's baby economics (open picture)

According to Figure 1, anyone can understand economics, from learner level to more advanced research content. Therefore, we can begin to study economics at those basic concepts such as goods and services, producer and consumer, supply and demand, where production and consumption as well as supply and demand become important foundations of economics. For strict economic analysis, all concepts need definitions, and should be measurable for scientific studies. So we begin with economic concepts and metrics, and we mark the Part I pure economics, a term from Léon Walras (Walras, 1954).

ECONOMIC CONCEPTS AND METRICS

In any branch of scientific study, one always needs special concepts and metrics to define special terms and measurable quantities. The same applies in economics as a social science, although it never resembles exact natural sciences.

Actually, there are a lot of economic terms in economics (as so many concepts are required for processing and understanding complicated economic systems). However, a lot of concepts are not good for learners and researchers. More the concepts exist in a scientific field, less the accurate theories are in the field. The US National Council for Economic Education (CEE, https://www.councilforeconed.org) has suggested and compiled 51 key economics concepts for economic education. Supposing that we begin at Figure 1, in which we can read six basic concepts of economics:

- **Goods**: Goods, also known as commodities, are things that are made or grown, which are general products for marketing exchange.
- **Services**: Services are work that someone does for someone else, where all producers and consumers also belong to labors in market.
- **Producer**: A producer is someone who makes or grows goods, or offers services.
- **Consumer**: A consumer is someone who buys goods or services
- **Supply**: Supply means the amount of something available to consumers, which is the willingness and ability to sell a product within a period of time when other factors remain constant.
- **Demand:** Demand means how much consumers want something, which is the willingness and ability to buy a product within a stipulated time period when other factors remain constant.

The first pair of core economic concepts, demand and supply, will be applied through economics. The concept of supply is relative to the concept of demand. When the demand is created there is a product or service to satisfy the demand of the customer and the willingness and ability to sell it to its potential consumer. The concept of demand is also directly linked with the concepts of choice, scarcity, opportunity cost, etc. Except common understandable concepts such as income and money, buy and sell, insurance and risk, as well as production and consumption, some economic concepts including market and GDP need special definition and interpretation, so that we reinforce the following terms.

- **Market:** A market is a place where demand and supply meet and find their optimum point. Buyers have the need for products, sellers have the need to provide their products and the place where they exchange between themselves is called the market, which is a key concept in economics. When the number of buyers or sellers varies, the product varies or the ability to provide solutions varies, market creates different structures which we call market structure such as monopoly, oligopoly, monopolistic, perfect competition, and so on.

Markets in the most literal and immediate sense are places in which things are bought and sold. However, in the modern industrial system, the market is not only a place, but also has expanded to include the whole geographical area in which sellers compete with each other for customers. A market is one of a composition of systems, institutions, procedures, social relations or infrastructures whereby parties engage in exchange. While parties may exchange goods and services by barter, most markets rely on sellers offering their goods or services in exchange for money from buyers. It can be said that a market is the process by which the prices of goods and services are established. Markets facilitate trade and enable the distribution and resource allocation in a society. Markets allow any tradeable item to be evaluated and priced. A market emerges more or less spontaneously or may be constructed deliberately by human interaction in order to enable the exchange of rights of services and goods. Markets generally supplant gift economies and are often held in place through rules and customs, such as a booth fee, competitive pricing, and source of goods for sale.

- **Trade:** Trade is a basic economic activity for buying and selling of goods and services, with compensation paid by a buyer to a seller, or the exchange of goods or services between parties. Trade can take place within an economy between producers and consumers or between trading nations. For international trade, the theory of comparative advantage predicts that trade is beneficial to all parties, although critics argue that in reality it leads to stratification among countries.

- **GDP:** GDP means gross domestic product, which is the total monetary measure or market value of all the finished goods and services produced within a country in a specific time period. GDP provides an economic snapshot of a country, used to estimate the size of an economy and its growth rate, which can be calculated in three ways, using expenditures, production, or incomes. GDP measurements are useful for different purposes, including:
  - **Nominal GDP:** GDP evaluated at current market prices, in either the local currency or in US dollars at currency market exchange rates in order to compare GDP among countries in purely financial terms.
  - **Real GDP:** Real GDP is an inflation-adjusted measure that reflects the quantity of goods and services produced by an economy in a given year, with prices held constant from year-to-year in order to separate out the impact of inflation or deflation from the trend in output over time.
  - **GDP in purchasing power parity (PPP):** GDP-PPP is measured by 'international dollars'. The method of PPP adjusts for differences in local prices and costs of living in order to make cross-country comparisons of real output, real income, and living standards.
  - **GDP per-capita:** GDP per-capita is a measurement of the GDP per person according to population in a country. It indicates the amount of output or income per person in an economy, which provides average productivity or average living standards. GDP per-capita can also be stated in nominal, real (inflation adjusted), or PPP terms.
  - **GDP growth rate:** The GDP growth rate compares one year (or quarter) of a country's GDP to the previous year (or quarter) in order to measure how fast an economy is growing. Usually expressed as a percent rate, this measure is popular for economic policy makers because GDP growth is thought to be closely connected to key policy targets such as inflation and unemployment rates.

GDP (nominal) per-capita does not, however, reflect differences in the cost of living and the inflation rates of the countries; therefore, using a basis of GDP per-capita at purchasing power parity (PPP) is arguably more useful when comparing living standards between nations, while nominal GDP is more useful comparing national economies on the international market. As a broad measure of overall domestic production, GDP functions as a comprehensive scorecard of a given country's economic wealth.

- **Equilibrium:** The purpose of economics is to create maximum output for everyone out of scarce resources, where it has achieved equilibrium or optimum point. Above and below the point, there is a mismatch of demand and supply, input and output, expenditure and benefits, employment and availability.
- **Efficiency-Equity:** Efficiency is concerned with the optimal production and allocation of resources given existing factors of production. Equity is concerned with how resources are distributed throughout society. Vertical equity is concerned with how equitably resources are distributed and may imply higher tax rates for high-income earners. Mostly, efficiency may lead to less equity, so that we also need to consider the efficiency-equity equilibrium.
- **Tax and Taxation:** Producers need to pay taxes when they sell their goods or services, and consumers need to pay taxes when they buy the goods or services. There are many kinds of taxes, such as wage-income tax, capital-interest tax, inheritance tax, and poll tax on every individual in a community, as well as tariffs. When taxes become taxation of government, the government redistribute the taxation to public services.
- **Stocks and Flows:** Distinction may be made between a stock variable and a flow variable. A stock variable has no time dimension, which does not involve the specification of any particular length of time, so that its value is ascertained at some point in time. On the other hand, a flow variable has a time dimension, which is related to a specified period of time. So national income is a flow and national wealth is a stock. Similarly, money is a stock but the spending of money is flow. Government debt is stock, while saving and investment and operating surplus during a year are flows, but if they relate to the past year, they become stocks. Inventories are stocks but change in inventories is a flow. Change in any variable which can be measured over a period of time relates to a flow.
- **Investing and Saving:** While investing means an asset or item (such as time, money, or effort) that is purchased with the hope to generate future income, saving is the money a person has left over when they subtract their consumer spending from their disposable income over a given time period. An investment always concerns the outlay of some

asset today in hopes of a greater payoff in the future, facing the goal of generating income or appreciation, where appreciation refers to an increase in the value of an asset or item over time.

Furthermore, for economic analysis, we need more abstract concepts and some analytical measurable definitions. Table 1 lists 22 important analytical terms, in three types, which resemble necessary concepts for analyzing economies.

Table 1. Selected analytical economic terms

Abstract Concepts	Concrete Measures	Metric Rates
Value	Price/Profit/Cost	Interest rate
Wealth	Capital/Utility	Tax rate
Scarcity	Elasticity/Substitution	Exchange rate
Liquidity	Credit/Inflation	Inflation rate
Marginality	Marginal effect	Marginal rates
Knowledge	Technological progress	Unemployment rate

The abstract concepts are the root of concrete measures, so that value determines price and price represents value (the law of value). Also, knowledge determines technology and technology represents knowledge (the law of knowledge). Similarly, wealth determines capital and capital represents wealth (the law of wealth), and so on.

Here, we give descriptions or interpreting definitions for the 22 important concepts, beyond the above demand, supply, market, trade, and GDP.

Absolute Quantities: Analytical Concepts and Measures

Value, with Price, Profit and Cost

In economics, value means the power that goods and services have to exchange other goods and services. Value is a relatively abstract concept in comparison to the concrete concept of price, which means that there will never be a general rise or fall in values, but there can be a general rise or fall in prices. The concept of value is also related to the concept of utility, where utility is the want satisfying quality of a thing when we use or consume it. Thus utility is the value-in-use of a commodity.

Price can be measured by price level at both micro- and macro-economy, where we use p and P to stand for the micro-price level and macro-price level, respectively. Furthermore, price may also construct some special indices, such as consumer price index (CPI) and industrial price index (IPI), etc.

Price determines a lot of economic things; it judges the scarcity of resources, choices we make, controls demand and supply, creates and changes equilibrium point, generates different market structure and produces different opportunity cost, etc., where cost and profit construct another pair of economic concepts.

Cost is the amount or equivalent paid or charged for something; the price paid to acquire, produce, accomplish, or maintain anything. Profit describes the financial benefit realized when revenue generated from a business activity exceeds the expenses, costs, and taxes involved in sustaining the activity in question. Any profits earned funnel back to business owners, who choose to either pocket the cash or reinvest it back into the business. Profit is calculated as total revenue less total expenses. Profit, also called net income, is the amount of earnings that exceed expenses for the period. In other words, it's the amount of income left over after all the necessary and matched expenses are subtracted for the period.

Wealth, with Capital and Utility

In economics, wealth is used to describe all things that have value, which is a relatively abstract concept in comparison to the concrete concept of money, including the following types.

1. **Individual wealth:** Wealth owned by an individual is called individual or private wealth such as a house, company, etc.
2. **Social wealth:** Wealth owned by society is called social or collective wealth, such as schools, colleges, roads, canals, mines, forests, etc.
3. **National wealth:** National wealth includes all individual and social wealth. It consists of material assets possessed by the whole society, which is real wealth.
4. **International wealth:** The United Nations and its various agencies like the World Bank, IMF, WHO, etc. are international wealth because all countries contribute toward their operations.
5. **Financial wealth:** Financial wealth is the holding of money, stocks, bonds, etc. by individuals or firms in society. Financial wealth is excluded

from national wealth. This is because money, stocks, bonds, etc. which individuals or firms hold as wealth are claimed against one another.

Capital is a term for financial assets, such as funds held in deposit accounts and/or funds obtained from special financing sources. Capital can also be associated with capital assets of a company that requires significant amounts of capital to finance or expand.

Capital can be held through financial assets or raised from debt or equity financing. Businesses will typically focus on three types of business capital: working capital, equity capital, and debt capital. In general, business capital is a core part of running a business and financing capital intensive assets.

Capital assets are assets of a business found on either the current or long-term portion of the balance sheet. Capital assets can include cash, cash equivalents, and marketable securities as well as manufacturing equipment, production facilities, and storage facilities.

Utility means economically useful, which matches some demand. Mere utility does not create value unless it is scarce. Scarcity is an economic property of a good or service that relates to demand. Thus, goods possessing the quality of scarcity have value.

For a commodity to be called wealth, it has to possess utility, scarcity and transferability. In common use, the term 'wealth' means money, property, gold, etc. However, wealth is different from money, capital, or income.

Compared with money, money is only an expression of wealth. Money is the liquid form of wealth. All money is wealth, but all wealth is not money.

Compared with capital, wealth means value. But capital is that part of wealth which is used for further production of wealth. Thus, all capital is wealth, but all wealth is not capital.

Compared with income, wealth is a stock and income are a flow. Income is the earning from wealth. The shares of a company are wealth, but the dividend received on them is income.

Scarcity, with Elasticity and Substitution

Economists assumed that the resources are scarce and thus to have something we need to give something. When we buy a product, we choose the product by letting go of the money that we pay. It introduces another concept as 'choice'. Here we need to remember that 'choice' is completely dependent on 'scarce' resources. If scarcity is not there, there is no compulsion for choice.

Besides utility and scarcity, a good should be transferable from one to another to realize its value. Thus, a commodity to have value-in-exchange must possess the qualities of utility, scarcity and transferability.

Elasticity is a measure of a variable's sensitivity to a change in another variable, most commonly this sensitivity is the change in price relative to changes in other factors. In business and economics, elasticity refers to the degree to which individuals, consumers or producers change their demand or the amount supplied in response to price or income changes. It is predominantly used to assess the change in consumer demand as a result of a change in a good or service's price.

In economics, elasticity is the measurement of the percentage change of one economic variable in response to a change in another. An elastic variable (with an absolute elasticity value greater than 1) is one which responds more than proportionally to changes in other variables. In contrast, an inelastic variable (with an absolute elasticity value less than 1) is one which changes less than proportionally in response to changes in other variables. A variable can have different elasticity values at different starting points: for example, the quantity of a good supplied by producers might be elastic at low prices but inelastic at higher prices, so that a rise from an initially low price might bring on a more-than-proportionate increase in quantity supplied, while a rise from an initially high price might bring on a less-than-proportionate rise in quantity supplied.

The most useful elasticity is price elasticity of demand, which can be written as

$$E = \frac{dQ}{dP} / \frac{Q}{P},$$

where P represents price and Q indicates quantity. For common commodities, $dQ/dP < 0$, $E < 1$, which belong to normal goods. When $dQ/dP > 0$, $E > 1$, goods are luxury goods.

Liquidity, with Credit and Inflation

Liquidity refers to the ease with which an asset can be converted into ready cash without affecting its market price, which describes the degree to which an asset can be quickly bought or sold in the market at a price reflecting its intrinsic value. Cash is universally considered the most liquid asset because it can most quickly and easily be converted into other assets. Tangible assets, such as real estate, fine art, and collectibles, are all relatively illiquid. Liquidity is the amount of money that is readily available for investment and spending. High liquidity produces flexibility for a firm or an investor in a low-risk position, but it also tends to decrease profitability.

Credit is generally defined as the ability of a customer to obtain goods or services before payment, based on the trust that payment will be made in the future. Credit is a contractual agreement between a lender and a borrower, who promises to repay the lender at a later date with interest, which refers to the creditworthiness or credit history of an individual or company and refers to an accounting entry that either decreases assets or increases liabilities and equity on a company's balance sheet. Credit is also the foundation of a bank.

Credit covers many different forms, in which the most popular form is bank credit or financial credit, generally via credit cards. Essentially, when the bank lends to a consumer, it credits money to the borrower who must pay it back at a future date.

Inflation is the decline of purchasing power of a given currency over time. A quantitative estimate of the rate at which the decline in purchasing power occurs can be reflected in the increase of an average price level of a basket of selected goods and services in an economy over some period of time. The rise in the general level of prices, often expressed as a percentage, means that a unit of currency effectively buys less than it did in prior periods. Inflation can be measured by the rate at which the value of a currency is falling and consequently the general level of prices for goods and services is rising.

In economics, inflation (or less frequently, price inflation) is a general rise in the price level in an economy over a period of time, resulting in a sustained drop in the purchasing power of money. When the general price level rises, each unit of currency buys fewer goods and services; consequently, inflation reflects a reduction in the purchasing power per unit of money – a loss of real value in the medium of exchange and unit of account within the economy.

The opposite of inflation is deflation, a sustained decrease in the general price level of goods and services. The common measure of inflation is the inflation rate, the annualized percentage change in a general price index, usually the consumer price index, over time.

Inflation can be contrasted with deflation, which occurs when the purchasing power of money increases and prices decline.

Marginality, with Marginal Effect and Marginal Analysis

The theory of marginality in social economics, first coined in 1928 by Robert Park in his work *Human Migration and the Marginal Man*, attempts to explain inconsistencies in the perceived value of individuals via reference to their social class or ethnicity, race or culture. Cultural marginality, for example, refers to the dilemmas of cross-cultural contact and assimilation.

In standard economics, marginality is an important term or theory that attempts to explain the discrepancy in the value of goods by reference to their secondary utility. According to this theory, diamonds are more expensive than water because, even though water holds more total utility, the satisfaction of the diamonds — that is, their marginal utility — is enough to inflate their price past that of water.

As transport technology and readiness increases globally, the theory of marginality holds more and more relevance, since people of varied ethnicity, gender, nationality and culture commonly reside in the same locations. This theory is criticized by some for being too open to interpretation and too varied or complicated by nature. The more traditional work on marginality stresses the structural marginality of disenfranchised groups within societies, postulating that lack of access to the mainstream reward system can result in famine and powerlessness.

The common economic applications of marginality include marginal cost and marginal utility.

Marginal cost indicates the rate at which the total cost of a product changes as the production increases by one unit, which means the change in the total cost that arises when the quantity produced is incremented by one unit; that is, it is the cost of producing one more unit of a good. However, because fixed costs do not change based on the number of products produced, the marginal cost is influenced only by the variations in the variable costs. Marginal cost is particularly important in the business decision-making process.

Marginal utility indicates the additional satisfaction or benefit (utility) that a consumer derives from buying an additional unit of a commodity or service. Marginal utility of a good or service is the change in the utility from an increase in the consumption of that good or service. In economics, the standard rule is that marginal utility is equal to the total utility change divided by the change in amount of goods.

The marginal analysis is an important and useful method in economics, which can be applied to analyze many decisions, such as:

- **Manufacturer:** Whether to sell additional units to a customer at a reduced price.
- **Personal:** Whether to work additional hours in the office or take a vacation.
- **Government:** Whether to fund a public program to provide more services to taxpayers.

Knowledge, with Technological Progress

There is no standard and clear definition of knowledge. In common sense, knowledge is the fact, valuable information, as well as truths, principles, or skills acquired by a person through experience or education, or the theoretical or practical understanding of a subject.

Technology is the practical application of scientific knowledge, especially in engineering, summing techniques, skills, methods, and processes used in the production of goods or services or in the accomplishment of objectives, such as scientific investigation. Technology can be the knowledge of techniques, processes, and the like, or it can be embedded in machines to allow for operation without detailed knowledge of their workings. Systems applying technology by taking an input, changing it according to the system's use, and then producing an outcome are referred to as technology systems or technological systems.

Relative rates: Economic Ratios

There are lots of economic ratios. Here we reinforce a few important metric rates.

1. **Interest rate:** Interest rate is one of the most important measuring grids for understanding economics. When RBI/Federal Bank increases the interest rate in an economy, that means they want to suck the money out of the economy. Other than affecting the money supply in an economy, the interest rate affects the investment decisions of an investor and also helps to understand the risk associated with it. Interest rate also describes the opportunity cost as a percentage. In most textbooks, interest rate is denoted by r or i. In this book, interest rate is always set to apply Greek alphabet γ.

2. **Tax rate:** A tax rate is the percentage at which an individual or corporation is taxed. In most textbooks, tax rate is denoted by t. In this book, tax rate is always set to apply Greek alphabet τ.
3. **Exchange rate:** An exchange rate is the value of a nation's currency in terms of the currency of another nation or economic zone. In some textbooks, exchange rate is denoted by e. In this book, exchange rate is always set to apply Greek alphabet π.
4. **Inflation rate:** As we mentioned above, inflation reflects a reduction in the purchasing power per unit of money. The common measure of inflation is the inflation rate, the annualized percentage change in a general price index, usually the consumer price index, over time. We use λ to stand for inflation rate in this book (rather than π used in some textbooks).

Inflation rate is the rate at which the value of a currency is falling and consequently the general level of prices for goods and services is rising, which can be viewed positively or negatively depending on the individual viewpoint and rate of change.

Ideally, an optimum level of inflation is required to promote spending to a certain extent instead of saving, thereby nurturing economic growth. Most commonly used inflation indexes are the Consumer Price Index (CPI) and the Wholesale Price Index (WPI).

1. **Unemployment rate:** The unemployment rate is the percentage of the labor force that is jobless. It is a lagging indicator, meaning that it generally rises or falls in the wake of changing economic conditions, rather than anticipating them. When the economy is in poor shape and jobs are scarce, the unemployment rate can be expected to rise. When the economy is growing at a healthy rate and jobs are relatively plentiful, it can be expected to fall. We use η to represent unemployment rate.
2. **Engel coefficient:** The Engel coefficient, or Engel's law, is a statistical theory that states that, ideally, as income rises, the percentage of income that is spent on food decreases. This theory is based on the observation that a well-off household which sees their income double is unlikely to also double their spending on food (although they may increase it slightly due to the added wealth).

Among these metric rates, interest rate, exchange rate and tax rate are important factors (Sánchez, 2005; Floyd, 2010) in determining economic running (Ye, 2015). The inflation rate and unemployment rate are also key factors that reflect economic quality.

In some economic theories (Friedman & Hahn, 2000; Jones & Kenen, 1985), marginal tax rate is important because it impacts the incentive of increased income, which is applied to reflect the income level in countries with progressive taxation schemes, with incremental increases in income taxed in progressively higher tax brackets. With higher marginal tax rates, individuals have less incentive to earn more. This is the basis of the Laffer curve, which theorizes that population-wide taxable income decreases as a function of the marginal tax rate, making net governmental tax revenues decrease beyond a certain taxation point.

Similar to marginal tax rates, marginal interest rate, marginal exchange rate and marginal inflation rate might also be important and could be further explored. Moreover, the inflation rate and unemployment rate are linked by the Phillips curve.

Some concepts concern special applications linked to their inventors, such as Engel's coefficient, Gini's coefficient, Pareto's optimization, and so on.

Other terms like macro and micro, money and goods (commodities) will be applied with common sense. The concept of micro is about how only one firm or individual decides to allocate the scarce resources and how it affects the firm and the individual, whereas macroeconomics is not just about a firm, rather it's about a whole economy in aggregate. Macro is a holistic approach whereas micro is the last box within a dozen boxes. Understanding micro and macro concepts helps a learner to understand economics and make the base stronger.

In conclusion, the above economic concepts might be the most important concepts, as the whole basis of economics concepts and structures depend on them. In this book, all capital Latin characters stand for macroeconomic variables (directed variables) and small Latin characters denote logarithmic (undirected) macroeconomic or per-capita microeconomic variables, while the Greek characters indicate economic rates (ratios). Finally, we will apply Newtonian symbols for some special differentiating representations of economic function y = f (x, t).

$$y' = dy / dx; \; y'' = d^2 y / dx^2 \tag{1}$$

$$\dot{y} = dy / dt; \; \ddot{y} = d^2 y / dt^2 \tag{2}$$

where t is time and x means variables other than time. In the following chapters, while Latin letters express variables, Greek letters denote rates and slope parameters. While all variables with the above bar mean average values, all variables with * stand for full-equilibrium values.

ECONOMIC SCHOOLS

Although economics can be traced back to the ancient Greek thinkers, modern economics began at Adam Smith (1723-1790), when he published his famous work *An Inquiry into the Nature and Causes of the Wealth of Nations,* briefly, *Wealth of Nations* (Smith, 1977, originated version at 1776). In this section, we mention the main economic schools (Faccarello & Kurz, 2016) with key clues, including classical economics, Keynesian economics, neoclassical synthesis, monetary economics and new neoclassical synthesis.

The main idea of the Classical school was that markets work best when they are left alone, and that there is nothing but the smallest role for government. The approach is firmly one of laissez-faire and a strong belief in the efficiency of free markets to generate economic development. Markets should be left to work because the price mechanism acts as a powerful 'invisible hand' to allocate resources to where they are best employed. In terms of explaining value, the focus of classical thinking was that economic value was determined mainly by scarcity and costs of production.

Between Classical school and Keynesian economics, three Ms were mentioned: Thomas Malthus (1766-1834), Karl Marx (1818-1883) and Alfred Marshall (1842-1924).

Malthus predicted that growing populations would outstrip the food supply. In his famous work, On Population, Malthus pointed out that population growth is potentially exponential, while the growth of the food supply or other resources is linear. So he believed that the population would be controlled to balance the food supply with the population level through preventative and positive checks. However, he was proven wrong, because he didn't foresee technological progresses and innovations that would allow production to keep pace with a growing population.

Marx claimed that the class war was going to be initiated by the inherent instabilities in capitalism. In his famous work, On Capital, Marx claimed there are two major flaws in capitalism that lead to exploitation, i.e. the chaotic nature of the free market and surplus labor, and then revealed that the remaining value would be the 'secret of capitalist exploitation'. He argued that the specialization of the labor force, coupled with a growing population, pushes wages down, and then the opposition of owners and workers would lead to class struggle. However, Marx underestimated the flexibility of capitalism. Instead of creating a clear owner and worker class, investing created a mixed class where owners and workers hold the interests of both classes, yielding a relatively stable society.

Marshall took the mathematical modeling of economies to new heights, following the so called 'Marginal Revolution', where English economist William Stanley Jevons, Austrian economist Carl Menger and French economist Leon Walras independently developed a new perspective in economics known as marginalism. Their key insight was that, in practice, people aren't actually faced with big picture decisions over entire general classes of economic goods, but instead make their decisions around specific units of an economic good as they choose to buy, sell, or produce each additional unit, i.e. marginal unit. In doing so, people balance the scarcity of each good against the value of the use of the good, at the margin, and these decisions explain, for example, why the price of an individual diamond is relatively higher than the price of an individual unit of water. Marginalism quickly became, and remains, a central concept in economics. While Walras went on to mathematize his theory of marginal analysis and made models and theories that reflected what he found there, Marshall introduced a few concepts that are still not fully understood, such as economies of scale, marginal utility, and the real-cost paradigm (Marshall, 2013). The theory was characterized by general equilibrium theory, as well as the tendency to express economic concepts statistically and mathematically, instead of just in prose. The theories developed by Walras, Marshall, and their successors continue to develop in the 20th century into the neoclassical school of economics, defined by mathematical modelling and assumptions of rational actors and efficient markets, becoming economic mainstream.

Keynesian economics followed. This economic thought, initiated by John Maynard Keynes (1883-1946) is called macroeconomics. Keynesian economists believed that past economics did not adequately describe the operation of the economy as a whole, while past theories might apply to individual choices and goods markets. Instead of marginal units, or even specific goods markets and prices, Keynesian economics presents the economy in terms of large-scale aggregates that represent the rate of unemployment, aggregate demand, or average price level inflation for all goods. According to Keynes, governments can be powerful players in the economy and save economy from recession by implementing expansionary fiscal and monetary policy by manipulating government spending, taxing, and money creation in order to manage the economy (Keynes, 2012).

The Keynesian approach is interventionist, coming from a belief that the self-interest which governs micro-economic behavior does not always lead to long run macro-economic development or short run macro-economic stability. Keynesian economics is essentially a theory of aggregate demand, and how best to manipulate it through macro-economic policy. Essentially, Keynesian economists are skeptical of the free market. If left alone, the free market will inevitably move toward a full employment balance.

By the middle of the 20th century, the two trends of marginalist microeconomics and Keynesian macroeconomics had risen to almost complete dominance in the entire Western economics. This is called neoclassical synthesis. Since then, it has represented the mainstream economic thinking of university professors and has been practiced by researchers and policy makers. Other schools belonged to heterodox economics.

Within the neoclassical synthesis, various streams of economic thought have developed, sometimes in opposition to one another. Largely due to the inherent tension between neoclassical microeconomics, which portrays free markets as mostly efficient and beneficial, and Keynesian macroeconomics, which views markets as inherently prone to calamitous failure that threatens society, this has led to persistent academic and public policy disagreements, with various theories ascendant at different times.

The neoclassical synthesis or the new Keynesian theory combines the elements of Keynesian macroeconomics with the more classic microeconomic theories and understands economics through oral explanations and graphical models. Paul Samuelson won the Nobel Prize in economics, 'for the scientific work through which he has developed static and dynamic economic theory and actively contributed to raising the level of analysis in economic science'. The neoclassical synthesis integrated various schools of thought, and modern economic theory evolved from these schools. Neoclassical economics assumes that the behavior of economic agents is rational, and consumers want to maximize utility, while enterprises want to maximize profits. The different goals of maximizing utility and profit form the basis of demand and supply theory. Combined with marginal cost and marginal utility analysis, neoclassical economics contributes scientific methods to analyze the economic behavior of companies and consumers.

Various economists and schools of thought are trying to perfect, revise and reinterpret neoclassical microeconomics and Keynesian macroeconomics. The most famous and successful is the monetarism and Chicago school advocated by Milton Friedman (1912-2006). This school retains the neoclassical microeconomics and Keynesian macroeconomic framework, but the focus of macroeconomics has shifted from fiscal policy to monetary policy (Friedman, 1956, 1966).

New neo-classical synthesis (NNS) is the main modern school of contemporary macroeconomics. It combines neo-classical and neo-Keynesianism to reach a consensus on explaining short-term economic fluctuations. This new synthesis is similar to the neoclassical synthesis that combines neoclassical economics and Keynesian macroeconomics and is characterized by a new comprehensive analysis through the IS-LM-Phillips curve. In NNS economic analysis, the natural logarithm of input and output economic variables is widely used, and the so-called phase diagram method has been developed (Scarth, 2014). NNS has also provided new theories and methods for contemporary mainstream economics and has become the theoretical basis for supporting the work of the Federal Reserve and many other central banks. In this way, we have a new world view of economics.

There are also some economic schools and studies that try to solve the gap between microeconomics and macroeconomics by incorporating microeconomics into macroeconomics (such as rational expectations), or by further developing microeconomics to provide a microfoundation for macroeconomics. There are also some economic schools that have developed new theories to explain economic development, such as behavioral economics and new Austrian economics. Many economists have made great contributions to economic theories and methods, via some representative books (Arrow, 1963; Davis, 2003; Faccarello & Kurz, 2016; Feldman & Serrano, 2005; Floyd, 2010; Forni & Lippi, 1997; Friedman, 1957; Friedman & Hahn, 2000; Gilder, 2012, 2013; Heyne, Boettke & Prychitko, 2013; Hicks, 1946; Horwitz, 2000; Jones & Kenen, 1985; King, 2000; Lengwiler, 2004; Mäki, 2012; Mises, 2006; Mishkin, 2004; Nicola, 2013; North, 1990; Okun, 1975; Piketty, 2014; Reiss, 2013; Robinson, 1962; Ross, 2014; Samuelson, 1983; Schumpeter, 2003; Scarth, 2014; Sen, 1997, 2002; Walras, 1954; Weintraub, 1979; Woodford, 2003) and papers (Abel et al., 1989; Alchian, 1950; Arrow & Debreu, 1954; Atkinson, Piketty & Saez, 2011; Blanchard & Gali, 2010; Coase, 1960; Dollar & Kraay, 2002; Dollar, Kleineberg & Kraay, 2014; Feldstein, 1976; Fischer, 1977, 1983; Fleming, 1962; Friedman, 1948, 1970; Goodfriend & King, 1997; Hahn, 1960; Krugman, 2010; Lamb et al., 2005; Lucas, 1972, 1973, 1975, 1988; Modigliani, 1963; Mundell, 1962, 1963; Phelps, 1967; Phillips, 1958; Sidrauski, 1967; Solow, 1956; Stigler, 1961;

Taylor, 1979; Tobin, 1969,1975; Ueda, 2013). For more details, see next chapters and Appendix (1) & (2).

ECONOMIC METHODOLOGY

Economic methodology is the study of how economics functions, how it could function, and how it should function, which examines various meta theoretical key concepts such as theory and model, assumption and idealization, causation and explanation, testing and progress, rhetoric and truth, social construction and pluralism; as well as various goals, styles and constraints of research, such as mathematical modelling and experimentation, grounded theory and case study, causal and functional explanation, forecasting and policy, ontological and institutional (academic and otherwise) constraints on economic inquiry. It also sets out to examine substantial fundamental concepts such as rationality, choice, routine, trust, institution, evolution, coordination, equilibrium, path dependence.

According to Milton Friedman (Friedman, 1956, 1966), on methodology, economics can be divided into positive and normative economics. While positive economics seeks the objective analytical results, normative economics focuses on the future predictions on value judgments. As a branch of science that concerns the description, quantification and explanation of economic phenomena, positive economics focuses on facts and cause-and-effect behavioral relationships and notes that economic theories must be consistent with existing observations. Positive economics is value-free economics, avoiding economic value judgements. Conversely, normative economics is a perspective on economics that reflects normative, or ideologically prescriptive judgments toward economic development, investment projects, statements, and scenarios. While positive economics relies on objective data analysis, normative economics heavily concerns itself with value judgments and statements of 'what ought to be' rather than facts based on cause-and-effect statements.

Although normative economics may be useful in establishing and generating new ideas from different perspectives, it cannot be the only basis for making decisions on important economic issues, as it does not take an objective angle that focuses on facts and causes and effects. Therefore, we will insist on the methodological position of positive economics in this book, where economic statements can be broken down into determinable and observable facts that can be examined and tested. Based on measurable perspectives, positive economics may help policymakers and other government and business authorities decide on important matters that affect particular policies under the guidance of fact-based findings.

Economic methodology was also heavily influenced by currents in the philosophy of science, particularly by the reaction against logical positivism as exemplified in the writings of Popper (Popper, 1972) and Kuhn (Kuhn, 1996). We do not discuss this issue further, and do leave the topic in the Part II economic philosophy.

Economic methodology also focuses on economic models, where many economic models are applied for modeling economic processes. In positive economics, modeling is also a strong method for economic analysis. We will keep and apply some representative models in this book.

As an important field of social sciences, economics applied many models for approaching economic phenomena as well as economic analysis. While microeconomics examines how entities, forming a market structure, interact within a market to create a market system, macroeconomics examines the economy as a whole to explain broad aggregates and their interactions, as well as the effects of monetary and fiscal policies (Samuelson & Nordhaus, 2010). However, microeconomics and macroeconomics are divided by artificial processing as if they speak different economic languages. Actually, economics is an integrated science in the human society. We need integrated knowledge that penetrates microeconomics and macroeconomics, individual and society.

REFERENCES

Abel, A. B., Mankiw, N. G., Summers, L. H., & Zeckhauser, R. J. (1989). Assessing dynamic efficiency: Theory and evidence. *The Review of Economic Studies*, *56*(1), 1–20. doi:10.2307/2297746

Alchian, A. A. (1950). Uncertainty, evolution, and economic theory. *Journal of Political Economy*, *58*(3), 211–221. doi:10.1086/256940

Arrow, K. (1963). *Social Choice and Individual Values* (2nd ed.). Yale University Press.

Arrow, K., & Debreu, G. (1954). Existence of an equilibrium for a competitive economy. *Econometrica*, *22*(3), 265–290. doi:10.2307/1907353

Atkinson, A., Piketty, T., & Saez, E. (2011). Top incomes in the long run of history. *Journal of Economic Literature*, *49*(1), 3–71. doi:10.1257/jel.49.1.3

Blanchard, O. J., & Gali, J. (2010). Labor markets and monetary policy: A new Keynesian model with unemployment. *American Economic Journal. Macroeconomics*, *2*(2), 1–30. doi:10.1257/mac.2.2.1

Coase, R. H. (1960). The problem of social cost. *The Journal of Law & Economics*, *3*, 1–44. doi:10.1086/466560

Davis, J. (2003). *The Theory of the Individual in Economics*. Routledge. doi:10.4324/9780203457689

Dollar, D., Kleineberg, T., & Kraay, A. (2014). *Growth, inequity and social welfare: cross country evidence.* World Bank Policy Research Department Working Paper No. 6842.

Dollar, D., & Kraay, A. (2002). Growth is good for the poor. *Journal of Economic Growth*, *7*(3), 195–225. doi:10.1023/A:1020139631000

Dornbusch, R. (1976). Expectations and exchange rate dynamics. *Journal of Political Economics*, 84, 1161-1176; Exchange rate expectations and monetary policy. *Journal of International Economics*, *6*, 231–244. doi:10.1016/0022-1996(76)90001-5

Faccarello, G., & Kurz, H. D. (2016). Handbook on the History of Economic Analysis. Vol. I: Great Economists since Petty and Boisguilbert; Vol. II: Schools of Thought in Economics. Edward Elgar.

Feldman, A. M., & Serrano, R. (2005). *Welfare Economics and Social Choice Theory* (2nd ed.). Springer Science & Business Media, Inc.

Feldstein, M. S. (1976). Inflation, income taxes, and the rate of interest – a theoretical analysis. *The American Economic Review*, *66*, 806–820.

Fischer, S. (1977). Long-term contracts, rational expectations, and the optimal money supply rule. *Journal of Political Economy*, *85*(1), 191–205. doi:10.1086/260551

Fischer, S. (1983). A framework for monetary and banking analysis. *Economic Journal*, *93*, 1-16.

Fleming, J. M. (1962). Domestic monetary policies under fixed and floating exchange rates. IMF Staff Papers, 9, 369–379.

Floyd, J. E. (2010). *Interest Rates, Exchange Rates and World Monetary Policy*. Springer. doi:10.1007/978-3-642-10280-6

Forni, M., & Lippi, M. (1997). *Aggregation and the Microfoundations of Dynamic Macroecomics*. Oxford University Press.

Friedman, B. M., & Hahn, F. H. (Eds.). (2000). *Handbook of Monetary Economics* (Vol. 1-2). Elsevier.

Friedman, M. (1948). A monetary and fiscal framework for economic stability. *The American Economic Review*, *38*(3), 245–264.

Friedman, M. (1956). *Studies in the Quantity Theory of Money*. University of Chicago Press.

Friedman, M. (1957). *A Theory of the Consumption Function*. Princeton University Press. doi:10.1515/9780691188485

Friedman, M. (1966). The Methodology of Positive Economics. In *Essays in Positive Economics*. University of Chicago Press.

Friedman, M. (1970). A theoretical framework for monetary analysis. *Journal of Political Economy*, *78*(2), 193–238. doi:10.1086/259623

Gilder, G. (2012). *Wealth and Poverty: A new edition for the twenty-first century*. Regnery Pub. Inc.

Gilder, G. (2013). *Knowledge and Power: The information theory of capitalism and how it is revolutionizing our world*. Regnery Pub. Inc.

Goodfriend, M., & King, R. G. (1997). The new neoclassical synthesis and the role of monetary policy. *NBER Macroeconomics Annual*, *12*, 231–283. doi:10.1086/654336

Gray, J. A. (1976). Wage indexation: A microeconomic approach. *Journal of Monetary Economics*, *2*(2), 221–235. doi:10.1016/0304-3932(76)90034-9

Hahn, F. H. (1960). The stability of growth equilibrium. *The Quarterly Journal of Economics*, *74*(2), 206–226. doi:10.2307/1884251

Heyne, P., Boettke, P., & Prychitko, D. (2013). *The Economic Way of Thinking* (13th ed.). Pearson Education.

Hicks, J. R. (1946). *Value and Capital: An inquiry into some fundamental principles of economic theory* (2nd ed.). Oxford University Press.

Horwitz, S. (2000). *Microfoundations and Macroeconomics: An Austrian Perspective*. Routledge. doi:10.4324/9780203456309

Jones, R. W., & Kenen, P. B. (Eds.). (1985). *Handbook of International Economics*. Elsevier.

Keynes, J. M. (2012). The General Theory of Employment, Interest and Money (The Collected Writings of John Maynard Keynes Vol. 7). Cambridge University Press.

King, R. G. (2000). The new IS-LM model: Language, logic, and limits. *Federal Reserve Bank of Richmond Economic Quarterly*, *86*, 45–103.

Krugman, P. (2010). The theory of interstellar trade. *Economic Inquiry*, *48*(4), 1119–1123. doi:10.1111/j.1465-7295.2009.00225.x

Kuhn, T. S. (1996). *The Structure of Scientific Revolutions* (rev. ed.). The University of Chicago Press. doi:10.7208/chicago/9780226458106.001.0001

Lamb, M., Lymer, A., & Freedman, J. (2005). *Taxation: An Interdisciplinary Approach to Research*. Oxford University Press.

Lengwiler, Y. (2004). *Microfoundations of Financial Economics: An Introduction to General Equilibrium Asset Pricing*. Princeton University Press.

Lucas, R. E. Jr. (1972). Expectations and the neutrality of money. *Journal of Economic Theory*, *4*(2), 103–124. doi:10.1016/0022-0531(72)90142-1

Lucas, R. E. (1973). Some international evidence on output-inflation tradeoffs. *The American Economic Review*, *63*, 526–534.

Lucas, R. E. Jr. (1975). An equilibrium model of the business cycle. *Journal of Political Economy*, *83*(6), 1113–1144. doi:10.1086/260386

Lucas, R. E. (1988). On the mechanics of development planning. *Journal of Monetary Economics*, *22*, 3–42. doi:10.1016/0304-3932(88)90168-7

Mäki, U. (2012). Handbook of the Philosophy of Science: Vol. 13. *Philosophy of Economics*. Elsevier.

Marshall, A. (2013). *Principles of Economics* (8th ed.). Palgrave Macmillan LLC. doi:10.1057/9781137375261

Mises, L. (2006). *The Ultimate Foundation of Economic Science: An Essay on Method*. Liberty Fund, Inc.

Mishkin, F. S. (2004). *The Economics of Money, Banking, and Financial Markets* (7th ed.). Addison-Wesley.

Modigliani, F. (1963). The monetary mechanism and its interaction with real phenomena. *The Review of Economics and Statistics*, *45*(1), 76–103. doi:10.2307/1927150

Mundell, R. A. (1962). The appropriate use of monetary and fiscal policy for internal and external balance. *International Monetary Fund Staff Papers*, *9*(1), 70–79. doi:10.2307/3866082

Mundell, R. A. (1963). *Capital mobility and stabilization policy under fixed and flexible exchange rates. Canadian Journal of Economic and Political Science, 29(4), 475–485.*

Nicola, P. C. (2013). *Efficiency and Equity in Welfare Economics*. Springer. doi:10.1007/978-3-642-30071-4

North, D. C. (1990). *Institutions, Institutional Change and Economic Performance*. Cambridge University Press. doi:10.1017/CBO9780511808678

Okun, A. M. (1975). *Equity and Efficiency: the big trade-off*. Brookings Institution.

Phelps, E. (1967). Phillips curves, expectations of inflation and optimal unemployment over time. *Economica*, *34*(135), 254–281. doi:10.2307/2552025

Phillips, A. W. (1958). The Relationship between Unemployment and the Rate of Change of Money Wages in the United Kingdom 1861-1953. *Economica*, *25*, 283–299.

Piketty, Th. (2014). *Capital in the twenty-first century (English tr-ed by A. Goldhammer)*. Harvard University Press. doi:10.4159/9780674369542

Popper, K. R. (1972). *Objective Knowledge: an evolutionary approach.* Oxford University Press.

Reiss, J. (2013). Philosophy of Economics: a contemporary introduction. Routledge (Taylor & Francis Group). doi:10.4324/9780203559062

Robinson, J. (1962). *Economic Philosophy*. Transaction Publishers.

Ross, D. (2014). *Philosophy of Economics*. Palgrave Macmillan. doi:10.1057/9781137318756

Samuelson, P. A. (1983). Foundations of Economic Analysis (Enlarged ed.). Harvard University Press.

Samuelson, P. A., & Nordhaus, W. D. (2010). *Economics* (19th ed.). McGraw-Hill Co.

Scarth, W. (2014). *Macroeconomics: The development of modern methods for policy analysis*. Edward Elgar.

Schumpeter, J. A. (2003). Capitalism, Socialism, and Demacracy (e-Library ed.). London: Routledge (Taylor & Francis Group).

Sen, A. (1997). *Poverty and Famines*. International Labour Organization.

Sen, A. (2002). *Rationality and Freedom*. Belknap Press.

Sidrauski, M. (1967). Inflation and economic growth. *Journal of Political Economy*, *75*(6), 796–810. doi:10.1086/259360

Smith, A. (1977). An Inquiry into the Nature and Causes of the Wealth of Nations (UK ed.). University of Chicago Press.

Solow, R. M. (1956). A contribution to the theory of economic growth. *The Quarterly Journal of Economics*, *70*(1), 65–94. doi:10.2307/1884513

Stigler, G. J. (1961). The economics of information. *Journal of Political Economy*, *69*(3), 213–225. doi:10.1086/258464

Taylor, J. B. (1979). Staggered wage setting in a macro model. *The American Economic Review*, *69*, 108–113.

Tobin, J. (1969). A general equilibrium approach to monetary theory. *Journal of Money, Credit and Banking*, *1*(1), 15–26. doi:10.2307/1991374

Tobin, J. (1975). Keynesian models of recession and depression. *American Economic Review Proceedings*, *65*, 195–202.

Ueda, K. (2013). Banks as coordinators of economic growth and stability: Microfoundation for macroeconomy with externality. *Journal of Economic Theory*, *148*(1), 322–352. doi:10.1016/j.jet.2012.09.003

Walras, L. (1954). Elements of Pure Economics, or the theory of social wealth (4th ed., W. Jaffé, Trans.). London: George Allen & Unwin Ltd.

Weintraub, E. R. (1979). *Microfoundations: The compatibility of microeconomics and macroeconomics*. Cambridge University Press. doi:10.1017/CBO9780511559570

Woodford, M. (2003). *Interest and Prices: Foundations of a Theory of Monetary Policy*. Princeton University Press.

Chapter 2
Economic Theories

ABSTRACT

Along the development of economic theories, this chapter is focused on the representative thoughts and methodologies, including economic thoughts from Adam Smith, Alfred Marshall, Maynard Keynes, Milton Friedmann, Paul Samuelson, and methodological models such as Arrow-Debreu model, Mundell-Fleming model, Cobb-Douglas model, and Solow-Swan model. All the thoughts and models are integrated into a grand synthetic framework for new synthesis. Three basic economic principles, called EME (equilibrium principle, marginal principle, and extremum principle), are proposed for efficiency-equity equilibrium.

MERGING REPRESENTATIVE ECONOMIC THOUGHTS INTO A GRAND FRAMEWORK

Many great economists contributed their visionary economic thinking (Faccarello & Kurz, 2016). Following the economic thought clues of classical economics, Keynesian economics, neoclassical synthesis, monetarist economics and neo-neoclassical synthesis, we will inherit and integrate some representative theoretical ideas and methodologies, especially those from Adam Smith (Adam Smith, Alfred Marshall, Maynard Keynes, Milton Friedmann, and Paul Samuelson's economic thinking, and methodological models including Arrow-Debreu model, Mundell-Fleming model, Cobb-Douglas model, Solow-Swan model, Laffer curve, Phillips curve).

DOI: 10.4018/978-1-6684-4935-6.ch002

Adam Smith (1723–1790) contributed his economic thought, characterized by emphasizing the importance of the market's function as an 'invisible hand'. The main point of his theoretical insight is that we can act in our own interests and help others through 'invisible hands', so all social individuals benefit from their own interests. Competition is self-regulating. Unless free market competition is protected, the government should not participate in commercial activities through tariffs, taxes or other means. Because of his pioneering academic contributions, Adam Smith is revered as the 'father of modern economics'.

Alfred Marshall (1842–1924) applied mathematical principles to economic problems and established economics as a scientific discipline. Combined with the marginal utility theory proposed by him, William Stanley Jevons and the Austrian school, following the idea that value is determined by production costs, Marshall believed that demand and supply factors (respectively, production costs and utility costs) determine prices, and establish the relationship between demand and supply functions and price changes. This created the so-called 'marginal revolution' and put forward the 'price elasticity of demand' as an extension of these ideas. Marshall raised the mathematical model of economy to a new level and introduced many new concepts, such as economies of scale, marginal utility, economic welfare (including the 'Marshall surplus' of 'producer surplus' and 'consumer surplus'), etc., and created the British neoclassical school of economics, the so-called Cambridge school.

John Maynard Keynes (1883–1946) is one of the greatest economists. In his excellent epoch-making work, *The General Theory of Employment, Interest and Money* (referred to as General Theory), Keynes provided the economic foundation for the government's work plan to solve the problem of high unemployment. The influence of General Theory is known as the Keynesian Revolution. It is one of the most influential economic works in history and has made outstanding contributions to macroeconomic policies. From the late 1940s to the late 1980s, Keynesianism was a core part of economics textbooks, however, as economists paid more and more attention to economic growth and became more aware of inflation and unemployment, Keynesianism gradually lost its dominance. Keynesian theory believes that the government can play a strong role in the economy and society by implementing expansionary fiscal and monetary policies to avoid economic recession. It believes that the way to reduce unemployment is to increase government spending and maintain budget deficits. However, it also seems to imply that lowering the wage rate will not reduce unemployment, which led economists to face reality and controversy later.

Milton Friedman (1912–2006) opposed the Keynesian view that 'currency is irrelevant' and proposed the so-called 'monetarism' theory that changes in the money supply will affect actual economic activities in the short term and will affect the price level in the long-run. Keynesians believe in using government-supported policies to offset the business cycle. They believe that fiscal policy is more effective than monetary policy in offsetting the effects of recessions, for example. In his *Studies in the Quantity Theory of Money* (1956), Friedman questioned the stability and importance of the Keynesian multiplier. He believed that the multiplier formed the link between changes in autonomous expenditure and subsequent changes in national income. It is a key element of effective and predictable fiscal policy in the Keynesian case. In his *A Theory of Consumption Function* (1957), Friedman proposed that household consumption and saving decisions are more affected by changes in their permanent income than changes in household income. If the income is changing, the established expenditure method will be maintained. In 1967, Friedman made another pioneering contribution to the Keynesian monetarism debate in the presidential speech of the American Economic Association. In his letter, he questioned the validity of another key structure of Keynesianism, the Phillips curve, which asserts that there is a stable trade-off between wage inflation and unemployment. Friedman believed that this trade-off is only temporary and depends on workers being 'fooled' by unexpected wage increases, believing that an increase in nominal wages is an increase in real wages, thereby inducing them to produce more output. Friedman believes that reducing the unemployment rate below what he calls the 'natural wage rate' is not a one-time increase in wages, but an acceleration of wage inflation. The 'stagflation' of the 1970s was impossible under the simplified Keynesian framework. Some economists believe that this is a confirmation of Friedman's theory.

Paul Samuelson (1915–2009) integrated the thoughts of microeconomics and macroeconomics. In microeconomics, he proposed the concept of explicit preference, which believes that the consumer's utility function can be inferred from the consumer's behavior. His method of applying constrained optimization mathematics to consumer behavior is to reveal consumers' preferences based on their choices, rather than hypothetical utility functions. In the field of macroeconomics, he developed and popularized neo-Keynesian macroeconomics, including overlapping generation models and the use of multiplier and accelerator effects to explain business cycles and recessions. His most important contribution is his introduction of a comprehensive neoclassical theory; that is, under full employment and macroeconomic equilibrium, an economy based on neoclassical demand and supply microeconomics can (in most cases) function effectively. Samuelson's seminal book The Fundamentals of Economic Analysis laid the foundation for his fruitful career as an academic economist. This work clearly sets economic analysis in the language of formal mathematics and has become today's economic theory and the main paradigm of research. Samuelson completed the integration of neoclassical comprehensive theory in the Economics textbook, combining neoclassical microeconomics with neo-Keynesian mathematical macroeconomics. His contribution also extends to welfare theory and public finance theory, using mathematical proof to develop the efficient market hypothesis (if the market is effective, then asset prices will move randomly), and develop the theory of public goods and public goods in the market economy of private goods markets. Because of his outstanding contributions, Samuelson became the first Nobel Prize winner in economics.

For other representative economic thinkers, we mention economists Ludwig von Mises (1881–1973) and Joseph Schumpeter (1883–1950), who contributed unique thoughts for freedom economy and innovative economy, respectively. For more economists and their thoughts, see Appendix (1).

Now macroeconomics is moving toward a New Neoclassical Synthesis, which, like the synthesis of the 1960s, melds classical with Keynesian ideas. The New Neoclassical Synthesis rationalizes an activist monetary policy, which is a simple system of inflation targets. Under this 'neutral' monetary policy, real quantities evolve as suggested in the literature on real business cycles.

Inheriting above representative economic thoughts, we can integrate most important ideas as a unified and useful grand framework, as shown in Figure 1, for economic thinking in the next chapter.

This framework integrated a few important economists' contributions and thoughts, including Adam Smith (Smith, 1977), Marshall (Marshall, 2013), Keynes (Keynes, 2012), Walras (Walras, 1954), Arrow and Debreu (Arrow & Debreu,1954), Hicks and Hansen (whose IS-LM model integrated into IS-LM-BP model), Fleming and Mundell (Fleming, 1962; Mundell, 1962, 1963), Friedman (Friedman, 1956, 1966. 1970), Samuelson (Samuelson, 1983; Samuelson & Nordhaus, 2010), with lots of ideas from famous works (Alchian, 1950; Arrow, 1963; Coase, 1960; Faccarello & Kurz, 2016; Feldman & Serrano, 2005; Forni & Lippi, 1997; Floyd, 2010; Friedman, 1956, 1957, 1966; Friedman & Hahn, 2000; Gilder, 2012, 2013; Heyne, Boettke & Prychitko, 2013; Hicks, 1946; Horwitz, 2000; Jones & Kenen, 1985; King,

2000; Lengwiler, 2004; Mäki, 2012; Mises, 2006; North, 1990; Okun, 1975; Piketty, 2014; Robinson, 1962; Samuelson, 1983; Schumpeter, 2003; Sen, 2002; Woodford, 2003). Especially, we pay more attention to some details in consumption, investment and business cycle (Abel, 2000; Abel et al., 1989; Lucas, 1972, 1973, 1975; Lucas & Rapping, 1970), money policy (Blanchard, 1990; Blanchard & Gali, 2010; Dornbusch & Giovannini, 1990), inflation and finance (Driffill, Mizon & Ulph, 1990; Haliassos & Tobin, 1990; Orphanides & Solow, 1990), capital market and money supply (Friedman, 1970; Merton, 1990; Papademos & Modigliani, 1990; Woodford, 1990), economic growth (Solow, 1956; Sidrauski, 1967; Dollar & Kraay, 2002; Ueda, 2013), wealth and poverty (Sen, 1997; Gilder, 2012; Dollar, Kleineberg & Kraay, 2014).

Therefore, we will follow the economic thoughts combining above economists mentioned in Figure 1 and apply the economic models (discussed in detail in the next chapter), including and integrating the microeconomic Arrow-Debreu model and macroeconomic Mundell-Fleming model, with Cobb-Douglas model and Solow-Swan model, based on the equilibrium

Figure 1. A grand synthetic framework combining representative thoughts and models

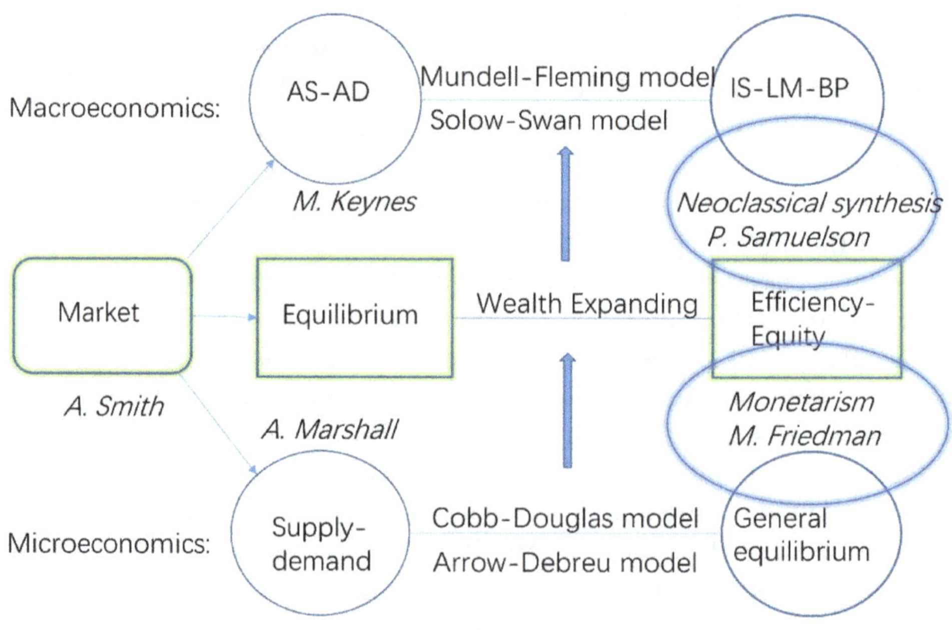

principle concerning both economic efficiency and social equity, for interpreting economic development and wealth expansion.

BASIC ECONOMIC PRINCIPLES

The key concepts involved in economic principles are equilibrium and optimization. Optimization aims to show that the economic system can be optimized through the allocation of economic resources. Equilibrium is the core theory of economics, which aims to reveal the existence of equilibrium in both microeconomics and macroeconomics. The equilibrium state can be achieved through the market mechanism (what Adam Smith called the 'invisible hand'). At the same time, through the integration of micro and macroeconomics and the application of appropriate economic policies, including fiscal policies and monetary policies, a balance can also be achieved through optimization to achieve economic efficiency and social equity. Therefore, it is recommended to use the following three basic principles to achieve economic equilibrium and optimization.

1. Equilibrium principle. The state of equilibrium exists in the economy, as ideal theoretical state, which is an important key to understanding economic analysis.
2. Marginal principle. Marginal cost and marginal utility may reach consistency, leading to dynamic economic equilibrium.
3. Extremum principle. The minimum cost-type economic variable and the maximum utility-type economic variable coexist in the economic system, making it tend to be statically optimized.

These three economic principles can be briefly recorded as EME. According to the EME principle, economic efficiency and social equity can also achieve an optimal balance.

Economic efficiency indicates an economic state in which all resources are allocated to serve everyone in the best possible way, thereby minimizing waste and inefficiency. Economic efficiency requires the provision of the optimal quantity of supply and demand, so that all users have the same marginal benefit, and all producers operate at the same marginal cost. Economic efficiency is basically a measure of the optimal state that can be achieved in the best state of society and economy. In this state, each resource is optimally allocated to provide services to each individual or entity in the best manner, and at the same time minimize waste and inefficiency. People demand both social equity and economic efficiency. One of the reasons is specialization, that is, social division of labor and cooperation. In the long-run, the natural advantages of specialization can backfire (Lucas, 1988).

Social equity is a commitment to promote equitable recognition of the basic needs of all residents and every family in a fair and just manner. It is also committed to advocating the commitment to provide these needs to all residents and every family. This is about society. Social equity hopes that all members of the society have an equal voice and knowledgeable overall efforts to obtain the economic, legal, environmental and development rights of social resources to ensure that the use of social resources benefits every family and individual and makes life equal for everyone.

In fact, economics is not only a social science on goods production and consumption, but also the epistemology and axiology on the wealth distribution, related to economic philosophy (Robinson, 1962; Mäki, 2012). The good of rationality is a meaningful issue for understanding national economic policies and individuals' economic behaviors (Arrow, 1963; Davis, 2003), so that it is necessary to study both epistemological true and axiological good of wealth distribution and redistribution in economics.

REFERENCES

Abel, A. B. (2000). Consumption and Investment. In Handbook of Monetary Economics. Elsevier.

Abel, A. B., Mankiw, N. G., Summers, L. H., & Zeckhauser, R. J. (1989). Assessing dynamic efficiency: Theory and evidence. *The Review of Economic Studies*, *56*(1), 1–20. doi:10.2307/2297746

Alchian, A. A. (1950). Uncertainty, evolution, and economic theory. *Journal of Political Economy*, *58*(3), 211–221. doi:10.1086/256940

Arrow, K. (1963). *Social Choice and Individual Values* (2nd ed.). Yale University Press.

Arrow, K., & Debreu, G. (1954). Existence of an equilibrium for a competitive economy. *Econometrica*, *22*(3), 265–290. doi:10.2307/1907353

Atkinson, A., Piketty, T., & Saez, E. (2011). Top incomes in the long run of history. *Journal of Economic Literature*, *49*(1), 3–71. doi:10.1257/jel.49.1.3

Blanchard, O. J. (1990). Why does money affect output? A survey. In B. M. Friedman & F. H. Hahn (Eds.), *Handbook of Monetary Economics* (Vol. 2). Elsevier. doi:10.1016/S1573-4498(05)80022-0

Blanchard, O. J., & Gali, J. (2010). Labor markets and monetary policy: A new Keynesian model with unemployment. *American Economic Journal. Macroeconomics*, *2*(2), 1–30. doi:10.1257/mac.2.2.1

Coase, R. H. (1960). The problem of social cost. *The Journal of Law & Economics*, *3*, 1–44. doi:10.1086/466560

Davis, J. (2003). *The Theory of the Individual in Economics*. Routledge. doi:10.4324/9780203457689

Dollar, D., Kleineberg, T., & Kraay, A. (2014). *Growth, inequity and social welfare: cross country evidence.* World Bank Policy Research Department Working Paper No. 6842.

Dollar, D., & Kraay, A. (2002). Growth is good for the poor. *Journal of Economic Growth*, *7*(3), 195–225. doi:10.1023/A:1020139631000

Dornbusch, R. (1976). Exchange rate expectations and monetary policy. *Journal of International Economics*, *6*, 231–244. doi:10.1016/0022-1996(76)90001-5

Dornbusch, R., & Giovannini, A. (1990). Monetary policy in the open economy. In B. M. Friedman & F. H. Hahn (Eds.), *Handbook of Monetary Economics* (Vol. 2). Elsevier. doi:10.1016/S1573-4498(05)80030-X

Driffill, J., Mizon, G. E., & Ulph, A. (1990). Cost of inflation. In B. M. Friedman & F. H. Hahn (Eds.), *Handbook of Monetary Economics* (Vol. 2). Elsevier. doi:10.1016/S1573-4498(05)80026-8

Faccarello, G., & Kurz, H. D. (2016). Handbook on the History of Economic Analysis. Vol. I: Great Economists since Petty and Boisguilbert; Vol. II: Schools of Thought in Economics. Edward Elgar.

Feldman, A. M., & Serrano, R. (2005). *Welfare Economics and Social Choice Theory* (2nd ed.). Springer Science & Business Media, Inc.

Feldstein, M. S. (1976). Inflation, income taxes, and the rate of interest – a theoretical analysis. *The American Economic Review*, *66*, 806–820.

Fischer, S. (1977). Long-term contracts, rational expectations, and the optimal money supply rule. *Journal of Political Economy*, *85*(1), 191–205. doi:10.1086/260551

Fischer, S. (1983). A framework for monetary and banking analysis. *Economic Journal, 93*, 1-16.

Fleming, J. M. (1962). Domestic monetary policies under fixed and floating exchange rates. IMF Staff Papers, 9, 369–379.

Floyd, J. E. (2010). *Interest Rates, Exchange Rates and World Monetary Policy*. Springer. doi:10.1007/978-3-642-10280-6

Forni, M., & Lippi, M. (1997). *Aggregation and the Microfoundations of Dynamic Macroecomics*. Oxford University Press.

Friedman, B. M., & Hahn, F. H. (Eds.). (2000). *Handbook of Monetary Economics* (Vol. 1-2). Elsevier.

Friedman, M. (1948). A monetary and fiscal framework for economic stability. *The American Economic Review, 38*(3), 245–264.

Friedman, M. (1956). *Studies in the Quantity Theory of Money*. University of Chicago Press.

Friedman, M. (1957). *A Theory of the Consumption Function*. Princeton University Press. doi:10.1515/9780691188485

Friedman, M. (1966). The Methodology of Positive Economics. In *Essays in Positive Economics*. University of Chicago Press.

Friedman, M. (1970). A theoretical framework for monetary analysis. *Journal of Political Economy, 78*(2), 193–238. doi:10.1086/259623

Gilder, G. (2012). *Wealth and Poverty: A new edition for the twenty-first century*. Regnery Pub. Inc.

Gilder, G. (2013). *Knowledge and Power: The information theory of capitalism and how it is revolutionizing our world*. Regnery Pub. Inc.

Gillies, D. (1998). The Duhem thesis and the Quine thesis. In *Philosophy of Science: The Central Issues*. New York: Norton.

Goodfriend, M., & King, R. G. (1997). The new neoclassical synthesis and the role of monetary policy. *NBER Macroeconomics Annual, 12*, 231–283. doi:10.1086/654336

Gray, J. A. (1976). Wage indexation: A microeconomic approach. *Journal of Monetary Economics, 2*(2), 221–235. doi:10.1016/0304-3932(76)90034-9

Hahn, F. H. (1960). The stability of growth equilibrium. *The Quarterly Journal of Economics*, *74*(2), 206–226. doi:10.2307/1884251

Haliassos, M., & Tobin, J. (1990). The macroeconomics of government finance. In B. M. Friedman & F. H. Hahn (Eds.), *Handbook of Monetary Economics* (Vol. 2). Elsevier. doi:10.1016/S1573-4498(05)80024-4

Heyne, P., Boettke, P., & Prychitko, D. (2013). *The Economic Way of Thinking* (13th ed.). Pearson Education.

Hicks, J. R. (1946). *Value and Capital: An inquiry into some fundamental principles of economic theory* (2nd ed.). Oxford University Press.

Horwitz, S. (2000). *Microfoundations and Macroeconomics: An Austrian Perspective*. Routledge. doi:10.4324/9780203456309

Jones, R. W., & Kenen, P. B. (Eds.). (1985). *Handbook of International Economics*. Elsevier.

Keynes, J. M. (2012). The General Theory of Employment, Interest and Money (The Collected Writings of John Maynard Keynes Vol. 7). Cambridge University Press.

King, R. G. (2000). The new IS-LM model: Language, logic, and limits. *Federal Reserve Bank of Richmond Economic Quarterly*, *86*, 45–103.

Lamb, M., Lymer, A., & Freedman, J. (2005). *Taxation: An Interdisciplinary Approach to Research*. Oxford University Press.

Lengwiler, Y. (2004). *Microfoundations of Financial Economics: An Introduction to General Equilibrium Asset Pricing*. Princeton University Press.

Lucas, R., & Rapping, L. (1970). Real Wages, Employment and Inflation. In E. Phelps (Ed.), *Microeconomic Foundations of Employment and Inflation Theory* (pp. 253–305). Norton.

Lucas, R. E. Jr. (1972). Expectations and the neutrality of money. *Journal of Economic Theory*, *4*(2), 103–124. doi:10.1016/0022-0531(72)90142-1

Lucas, R. E. (1973). Some international evidence on output-inflation tradeoffs. *The American Economic Review*, *63*, 526–534.

Lucas, R. E. Jr. (1975). An equilibrium model of the business cycle. *Journal of Political Economy*, *83*(6), 1113–1144. doi:10.1086/260386

Lucas, R. E. (1988). On the mechanics of development planning. *Journal of Monetary Economics*, *22*, 3–42. doi:10.1016/0304-3932(88)90168-7

Mäki, U. (2012). Handbook of the Philosophy of Science: Vol. 13. *Philosophy of Economics*. Elsevier.

Marshall, A. (2013). *Principles of Economics* (8th ed.). Palgrave Macmillan LLC. doi:10.1057/9781137375261

Merton, R. (1990). Capital market theory and the pricing of financial securities. In B. M. Friedman & F. H. Hahn (Eds.), *Handbook of Monetary Economics* (Vol. 1). Elsevier. doi:10.1016/S1573-4498(05)80014-1

Mises, L. (2006). *The Ultimate Foundation of Economic Science: An Essay on Method*. Liberty Fund, Inc.

Mishkin, F. S. (2004). *The Economics of Money, Banking, and Financial Markets* (7th ed.). Addison-Wesley.

Modigliani, F. (1963). The monetary mechanism and its interaction with real phenomena. *The Review of Economics and Statistics*, *45*(1), 76–103. doi:10.2307/1927150

Mundell, R. A. (1962). The appropriate use of monetary and fiscal policy for internal and external balance. *International Monetary Fund Staff Papers*, *9*(1), 70–79. doi:10.2307/3866082

Mundell, R. A. (1963). *Capital mobility and stabilization policy under fixed and flexible exchange rates. Canadian Journal of Economic and Political Science, 29(4), 475–485.*

Nicola, P. C. (2013). *Efficiency and Equity in Welfare Economics*. Springer. doi:10.1007/978-3-642-30071-4

North, D. C. (1990). *Institutions, Institutional Change and Economic Performance*. Cambridge University Press. doi:10.1017/CBO9780511808678

Okun, A. M. (1975). *Equity and Efficiency: the big trade-off*. Brookings Institution.

Orphanides, A., & Solow, R. M. (1990). Money, inflation and growth. In B. M. Friedman & F. H. Hahn (Eds.), *Handbook of Monetary Economics* (Vol. 1). Elsevier. doi:10.1016/S1573-4498(05)80009-8

Papademos, L., & Modigliani, F. (1990). The supply of money and the control of nominal income. In Handbook of Monetary Economics. Amsterdam: Elsevier.

Phelps, E. (1967). Phillips curves, expectations of inflation and optimal unemployment over time. *Economica*, *34*(135), 254–281. doi:10.2307/2552025

Phillips, A. W. (1958). The Relationship between Unemployment and the Rate of Change of Money Wages in the United Kingdom 1861-1953. *Economica*, *25*, 283–299.

Piketty, Th. (2014). *Capital in the twenty-first century (English tr-ed by A. Goldhammer)*. Harvard University Press. doi:10.4159/9780674369542

Polyanin, A. D., & Manzhirov, A. V. (2007). *Handbook of Mathematics for Engineers and Scientists*. Taylor & Francis Group.

Robinson, J. (1962). *Economic Philosophy*. Transaction Publishers.

Samuelson, P. A. (1983). Foundations of Economic Analysis (Enlarged ed.). Harvard University Press.

Samuelson, P. A., & Nordhaus, W. D. (2010). *Economics* (19th ed.). McGraw-Hill Co.

Sánchez, M. (2005). *The link between interest rates and exchange rates. Do contractionary depreciations make a difference?* European Central Bank: Working Paper Series No. 548. http://www.ecb.int

Scarth, W. (2014). *Macroeconomics: the development of modern methods for policy analysis*. Edward Elgar.

Schumpeter, J. A. (2003). Capitalism, Socialism, and Demacracy (e-Library ed.). London: Routledge (Taylor & Francis Group).

Sen, A. (1997). *Poverty and Famines*. International Labour Organization.

Sen, A. (2002). *Rationality and Freedom*. Belknap Press.

Sidrauski, M. (1967). Inflation and economic growth. *Journal of Political Economy*, *75*(6), 796–810. doi:10.1086/259360

Smith, A. (1977). An Inquiry into the Nature and Causes of the Wealth of Nations (UK ed.). University of Chicago Press.

Solow, R. M. (1956). A contribution to the theory of economic growth. *The Quarterly Journal of Economics*, *70*(1), 65–94. doi:10.2307/1884513

Stigler, G. J. (1961). The economics of information. *Journal of Political Economy*, *69*(3), 213–225. doi:10.1086/258464

Taylor, J. B. (1979). Staggered wage setting in a macro model. *The American Economic Review*, *69*, 108–113.

Tobin, J. (1969). A general equilibrium approach to monetary theory. *Journal of Money, Credit and Banking*, *1*(1), 15–26. doi:10.2307/1991374

Tobin, J. (1975). Keynesian models of recession and depression. *American Economic Review Proceedings*, *65*, 195–202.

Ueda, K. (2013). Banks as coordinators of economic growth and stability: Microfoundation for macroeconomy with externality. *Journal of Economic Theory*, *148*(1), 322–352. doi:10.1016/j.jet.2012.09.003

Walras, L. (1954). Elements of Pure Economics, or the theory of social wealth (4th ed., W. Jaffé, Trans.). London: George Allen & Unwin Ltd.

Weintraub, E. R. (1977). The microfoundations of macroeconomics: A critical survey. *Journal of Economic Literature*, *15*(1), 1–23.

Weintraub, E. R. (1979). *Microfoundations: The compatibility of microeconomics and macroeconomics*. Cambridge University Press. doi:10.1017/CBO9780511559570

Woodford, M. (1990). The optimum quantity of money. In B. M. Friedman & F. H. Hahn (Eds.), *Handbook of Monetary Economics* (Vol. 2). Elsevier. doi:10.1016/S1573-4498(05)80027-X

Woodford, M. (2003). *Interest and Prices: Foundations of a Theory of Monetary Policy*. Princeton University Press.

Chapter 3
Economic Models

ABSTRACT

With a reclassified system of economic models, some important economic models concerning economic analysis are reviewed as absolute amount models (A^2Ms), relative rate models (R^2Ms), and mixed measure models (M^2Ms). A^2Ms include AD-AS model, Arrow-Debreu model, etc. R^2Ms cover Cobb-Douglas model, Solow-Swan model, etc. M^2Ms involve IS-LM model, Mundell-Fleming model, etc. All models link with special economic thoughts, and those models set up a mathematical foundation for economic analysis and discussion.

INTRODUCTION

Although most models are highly simplified to approach economic realities, the models are useful for interpreting and understanding the economies. There are lots of models in economics, including microeconomic and macroeconomic models; here, we focus on those models that shaped economic thoughts and classify them as three kinds applied in this book.

1. **Absolute amount models (A^2Ms):** Most economic models can be described by absolute amount, including most microeconomic and macroeconomic models, such as AD-AS model, Arrow-Debreu model, etc.
2. **Relative rate models (R^2Ms):** Some economic models can be expressed by logarithmic, per-capita or ratio forms, where the coordinates are rate or relative amounts, including Cobb-Douglas model, Solow-Swan model, etc.

DOI: 10.4018/978-1-6684-4935-6.ch003

3. **Mixed measure models (M^2Ms):** A^2Ms and R^2Ms are relative classification. Sometimes, A^2Ms and R^2Ms are mixed together for integrated applications, where at least one coordinate is rate or absolute amount, such as IS-LM model, Mundell-Fleming model, etc. As most economic policy analysis is based on M^2M-type models, the M^2Ms are widely applied, especially in macroeconomic analysis.

Certainly, all the models integrated some important economic thoughts (Arrow, 1963; Arrow & Debreu, 1954; Friedman, 1948, 1956, 1957, 1966, 1970; Hicks, 1946; Lucas, 1972, 1973, 1975, 1988; Lucas & Rapping, 1970; Keynes, 2012; Marshall, 2013; Fleming, 1962; Mundell, 1962, 1963; Samuelson, 1983; Samuelson & Nordhaus, 2010; Smith, 1977; Solow, 1956; Taylor, 1979; Tobin, 1969, 1975; Walras, 1954), with contemporary theories and practices (Faccarello & Kurz, 2016; Feldman & Serrano, 2005; Forni & Lippi, 1997; Floyd, 2010; Friedman & Hahn, 2000; Gilder, 2013; Heyne, Boettke & Prychitko, 2013; Horwitz, 2000; Jones & Kenen, 1985; King, 2000; Mishkin, 2004; Scarth, 2014). Some issues such as wealth and poverty (Gilder, 2012, Sen, 1997), value and ethics (Mises, 2006; Mäki, 2012) are temporarily ignored in modeling, while the microfoundations of macroeconomics (Lengwiler, 2004; Weintraub, 1977, 1979) are strengthened.

Absolute Amount Models

All economic models are based on equilibrium principle, marginal principle, and extremum principle.

Demand-supply Model and AD-AS Model

The demand and supply model provides a demand-supply equilibrium of market, which is also a typical application of the third principle. The demand will show a tendency that a higher price will reduce consumers to decrease their purchases in the market, while the supply will show a tendency that a higher price will induce producers to supply a higher quantity to the market. A typical supply curve slopes upward, which says that supply rises as price rises and represents increasing marginal costs with an increase in production. Demand curve says the opposite. Economists conclude the law of supply curve upward sloping and the law of demand curve downward sloping, as shown in Figure 1.

Figure 1. Demand-supply model

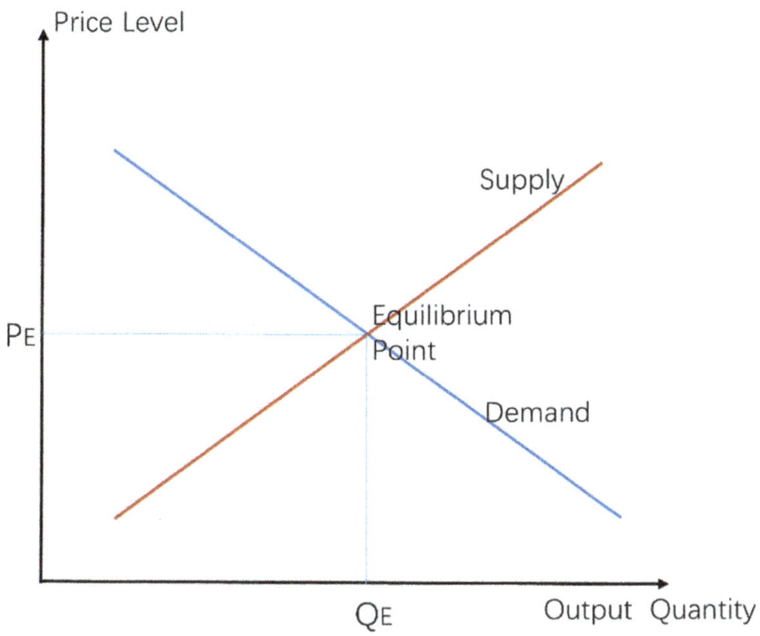

In the demand-supply model, there is an equilibrium point (QE, PE) as the crossing point as shown in Figure 1, which determines the equilibrium price PE and equilibrium output QE. The equilibrium defines the behavior of sellers and buyers based on the goal of profit maximization in the production and the goal of maximizing the utility gained from the purchase and consumption. Therefore, the demand-supply model is an important model, and the demand-supply analysis is a basic analysis in economics.

The aggregate demand (AD) - aggregate supply (AS) model is a way of illustrating national income determination and changes in the price level. We can use this to illustrate phases of the business cycle and how different events can lead to changes in two of our key macroeconomic indicators: real GDP and inflation.

A downward sloping aggregate demand curve is labeled AD and an upward sloping short-run aggregate supply curve is labeled AS. So the AD-AS model is shown in Figure 2, where an equilibrium price level and real GDP reach equilibrium at point E_1 and E_2 for GDP as output at Y_1 and Y_2, respectively.

Importantly, the AS should be vertical at the full employment output. The placement of the AS curve will depend on whether the economy has an output gap or is in long-run equilibrium.

Figure 2. AS-AD model

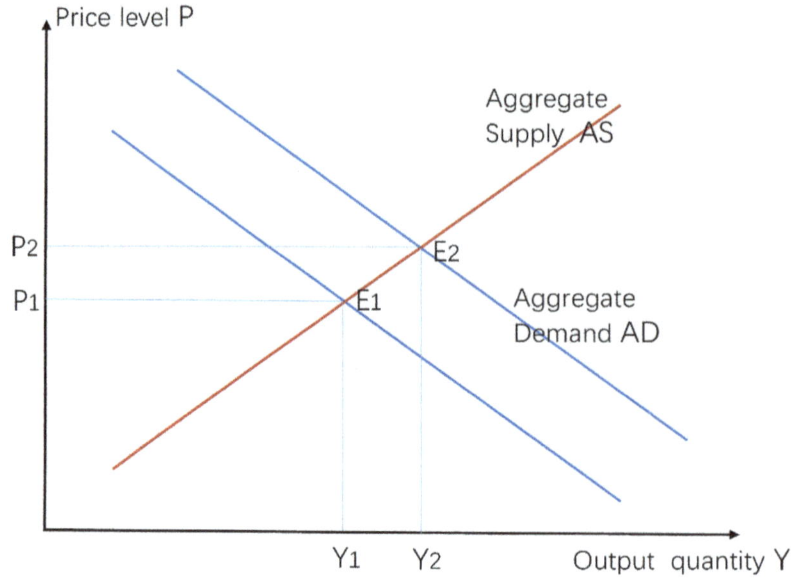

As production determines supply and consumption causes demand, we need to study production and consumption models.

Production and Consumption Function Model

To analyze producers and consumers in Figure 1, we can design an economic framework as shown as Figure 3.

Figure 3 shows that the elementary factors for producers include labor, land and capital, while the elementary factors for consumers cover work, income and utility. The producers provide goods to supply consumers via market, to meet their demand.

In the system, production function and consumption function become important considerations.

Since production is a process of combination and cooperation of product factors including land, labor and capital in an organization, a production function will also include these factors. Thus, the producer combines all the factors of production in a technical proportion, to maximize the production at minimum cost by means of the best combination of those factors. Therefore, a production function refers to the functional relationship between the quantity of a good produced (output) and factors of production (input), which can be defined as a function between physical output and the material input, as Prof. L.R. Klein said, 'the production function is a technical or engineering relation between input and output'.

Figure 3. Economic factors for analyzing producers and consumers

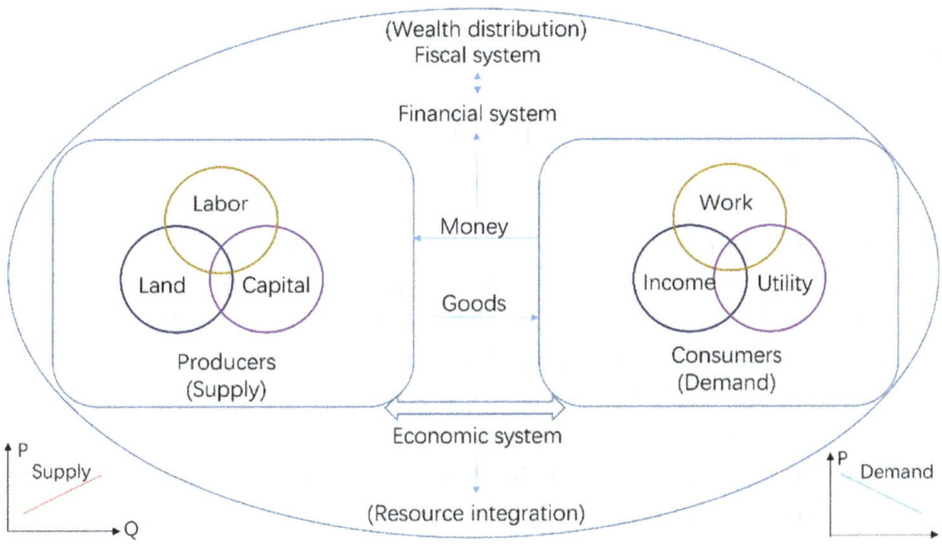

Mathematically, such a basic relationship between inputs and outputs can be expressed as

$$Y = F(L, K, L') \tag{1}$$

where Y = total quantity of output, L = labor, K = capital, L' = land. Hence, the level of output (Y), depends on the quantities of different inputs (L, K, L') available to the producer, where capital is an important element (Hicks, 1946).

The most famous production function is Cobb-Douglas production function. It is a linear homogeneous production function of one degree which takes into account two inputs, labor and capital, for the entire output of the manufacturing industry. A Cobb–Douglas function shows the form

$$Y = \beta K^{\alpha} H^{1-\alpha} \tag{2}$$

where Y is total output, and K and H are money capital and labor (human) capital, respectively. The Greek letter α is a capital parameter (capital's exponent of production function), $0 < \alpha < 1$, $H \leq L$ stands for human capital or effective labor.

By defining B = H/K and A = βB1-α, the Cobb–Douglas function is equivalent to the so-called AK model as

$$Y = AK \tag{3}$$

There are three features for the production function:

- Substitutability: The factors of production or inputs are substitutes of one another which make it possible to vary the total output by changing the quantity of one or more inputs, while the quantities of all other inputs are held constant. It is the substitutability of the factors of production that gives rise to the laws of variable proportions.
- Complementarity: The factors of production are complementary to one another, that is, the two or more inputs are to be used together as nothing will be produced if the quantity of either of the inputs used in the production process is zero. The principles of returns to scale is another manifestation of complementarity of inputs as it reveals that the quantity of all inputs are to be increased simultaneously in order to attain a higher scale of total output.
- Specificity: It reveals that the inputs are specific to the production of a particular product. Machinery and equipment, specialized workers and raw materials are a few examples of the specificity of factors of production. The specificity may not be complete as factors may be used for production of other commodities, too. This reveals that, in the production process, none of the factors can be ignored and in some cases ignorance to even slightest extent is not possible if the factors are perfectly specific.

At national economic level, when the output Y = C + I + G reaches equilibrium to consumption C, with ignoring investment I and government spending G, we have Cobb–Douglas-type consumption function

$$C = K^{\theta}N^{1-\theta} \tag{4}$$

where K is capital with capital's exponent being θ and N indicates total quantity of consumers ($N \geq L \geq H$, as everyone can be a consumer, suitable aged consumers become labors, and effective labor counts as human capital). When $(1 - \alpha)$ is labor coefficient in the production function, $(1 - \theta)$ stands for consumer coefficient in the consumption function. Then $- 1/\alpha$ means the wage elasticity of labor demand and $1/\theta$ indicates the wage elasticity of labor supply.

The production aims profit maximization (cost minimization) and consumption looks for utility maximization, to fit the first principle.

Marginal Model with Analysis

Marginal analysis focuses on the cost of additional production or the utility of additional consumption, which is the examination of the costs or benefits of certain economic activities.

The marginal cost (MC) is the cost of producing one more unit of a good or providing one more unit of a service, which indicates the rate at which the total cost of a product changes as the production increases by one unit. The computing formula appears as MC = change in total cost/change in output.

The marginal utility (MU) is the added satisfaction or benefit that a consumer gets from having one more unit of a good or a service, which indicates how much a one-unit change in a variable will impact the utility. The computing formula appears as MU = total utility difference/quantity of goods difference.

To optimize production cost and consumption utility, the equilibrium condition will consider how to balance MC and MU. Since the marginal cost is the additional cost incurred when one produces additional units of goods and the marginal utility is the difference received when one makes a different choice, the marginal cost typically declines as a firm increasingly produces a higher number of goods while the marginal utility increases the firm's income with production or sells more items.

In production, the marginal product is the first derivative of the production function with respect to an input. When we look for input H in production function and let $\beta = 1$, we have

$$\partial Y / \partial H = (1 - \alpha)K^{\alpha}H^{-\alpha} \qquad (5)$$

We see that the total output will increase if K increases, so that the marginal product is positive for K. However, increasing H leads to inverse effects.

If we consider the output elasticity, it is the percentage change in output in response to a change in levels of either labor or capital. For H we have

$$(\partial Y/Y) / (\partial H/H) = (\partial Y/\partial H) / (Y/H) = (1 - \alpha) \tag{6}$$

So we see that output elasticity with respect to labor is constant and equal to $(1-\alpha)$.

Another important marginal effect concerns marginal propensity to consume, from permanent income hypothesis by Milton Friedman. This is a theory that a person's consumption is determined not just by current income but also by future expected income. It suggests that consumers will attempt to 'smooth consumption' over their lifetime, including borrowing as a student and running down savings in retirement.

Marginal model is just a representation of the second principle.

Cost-Profit Model with Optimization

Cost-profit analysis, also called cost-benefit analysis, cost-consequences analysis, cost-utility analysis, and cost-effectiveness analysis, is an important form of economic appraisal. As with other forms of economic appraisal, cost-profit analysis seeks to evaluate the costs and consequences of different options. One alternative is preferred to another if it provides greater profit at the same or lower cost, or has lower cost for the same or greater profit. Once data on the costs and profit of the options being compared has been calculated, the first decision rule for this kind of appraisal is to reject any intervention dominated by another alternative or combination of alternatives. A dominated alternative has greater profits with lower or the same costs, or lower costs with the same or greater profits. A visual framework is shown in Figure 4.

In Figure 4, the cost-profit equilibrium point is A, which is the cross-point of the curve of marginal cost (MC) and the curve of marginal revenue (MR). If the price was lower than C, the producer would not produce the goods. Therefore, the quantity of production would fit MR = MC for producer's profit maximization. However, if the demand is larger, push to reach the monopoly price E, higher than average total cost D, the monopoly profit will become square BCDE.

Cost-profit analysis also means optimization, i.e., cost minimization and/or profit maximization, which means the most efficient use of resources subject to certain constraints is the choice from all possible uses of resources which gives the best results. A producer wants to realize the objective of minimizing its cost of production by choosing the best combination of factors of production as the constraints, and a consumer wants to buy the best combination of goods or services when his/her objective function is to maximize his/her utility by fixed income as the constraints. Mathematically, optimization is a process that determines the maximization or minimization of an objective function by certain constraints, while there is another consideration of social cost (Coase, 1960).

Figure 4. Cost-profit framework

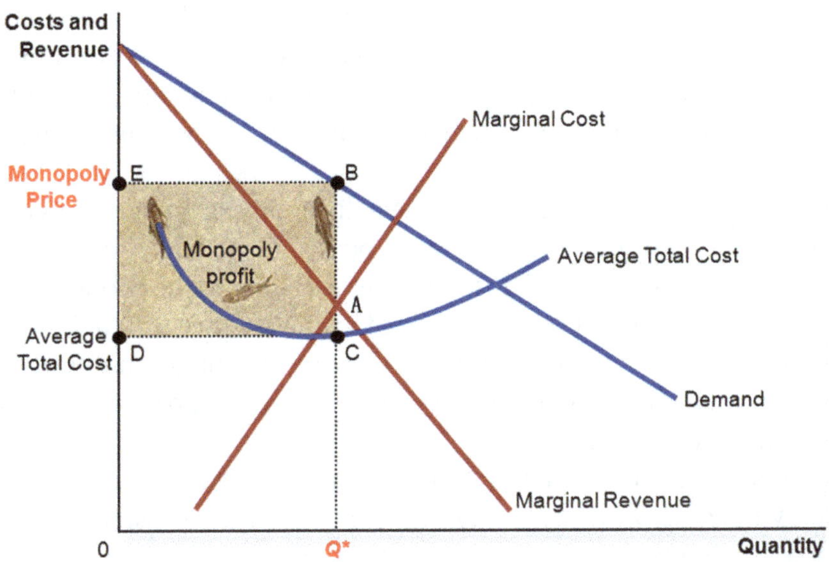

An important concept concerning profit is compound interest, which is defined by interest rate γ linking present value P and future value F after *i* periods as

$$F = P(1 + \gamma)^i \tag{7}$$

Another related concept is opportunity cost, which is different from marginal cost, as it is the valuable benefit that one misses when one chooses one option over another. For example, if a company recognizes that hiring an additional sales representative could provide a higher net marginal benefit, then hiring someone else for sales rather than someone to work in the factory is the right decision. Here, the additional productivity that the company would have earned by hiring someone to work in the factory is the opportunity cost.

Arrow-Debreu Model or Walrasian Model

Arrow-Debreu Model is also known as the Walrasian model (Walras, 1954) or generalized Fisher's model, which is a fundamental model used in the general equilibrium theory, considering general equilibrium. The model derived its name from two eminent economists, Kenneth Arrow from America and Gerard Debreu from France.

These two world famous economists have studied the dynamics of the prevailing economic system and shown that a multimarket equilibrium is prevailing and in equilibrium, surplus demand or surplus supply do not exist. This model is also popularly known as Arrow-Debreu-McKenzie model, or ADM model.

Arrow-Debreu Model is built upon two different assumptions. According to the first assumption, there is enough possibility of an equilibrium of a competitive nature but the condition is that everyone in the economy should have at least some amount of every kind of available goods in their holdings.

According to the second assumption, there is a huge amount of labor resources available in the market that can be utilized to produce the required commodities and services.

If there are i consumers and j goods in an economic market, $u_{i,j}$ is utility derived by i on obtaining one unit of j, when consumer i holds money mi to buy good j with quantity xi, then the total utility function u_i (x_i, m_i) will be

$$u_i(x_i, m_i) = \sum_j u_{i,j} x_{i,j} \tag{8}$$

Suppose that consumer i had an effective (net) demand z_{ih} in market h. The practical goods purchase with matching min $z_{ih} \geq 0$ and max $z_{ih} \leq 0$. Therefore, the Walrasian equilibrium reached the maximum utility according to the first principle

$$\max u_i(x_i, m_i);\ x_i \geq 0,\ m_i \geq 0;\ z_{ih} = \min[z_{ih}, \max(z_{ih}, z_i)] \tag{9}$$

Using the mathematical language of linear planning (LP), above optimization can also be written as (Benassy, 1990)

$$\max u_i(x_i, m_i);\ x_i \geq 0,\ m_i \geq 0 \tag{10.1}$$

$$\text{s.t. } pz_i + \text{m}_i = \bar{m}_i; \sum_{i=1}^{n} z_i(p^*) = 0 \tag{10.2}$$

where the net demand function $z_i(p)$ is the LP's solution and equilibrium price vector p* is defined by the condition that all markets clear.

This means that optimal market result may exist for balancing buyers and sellers. The Arrow-Debreu Model is capable of analyzing the exact situations of those markets that are very competitive. In the field of financial economics, Arrow Debreu represents a certain kind of securities product. The Arrow-Debreu security is a distinguished concept that is very helpful for understanding the analysis of the derivatives. By using this particular model, one can easily understand activities like pricing and hedging that are also related to the derivative analysis. On the other hand, the Arrow-Debreu Model is also used in areas like financial engineering and many more. Although the theory was criticized by various eminent economists, the truth is that the Arrow-Debreu Model is very important for the derivative industry and helps the industry to grow at a rapid pace.

Indifference Utilities and Pareto Optimality

An indifference curve is a contour line where utility remains constant across all points on the line. There are four properties for indifference curves: 1) indifference curves can never cross; 2) the farther out an indifference curve lies, the higher the utility it indicates; 3) indifference curves always slope downwards; and 4) indifference curves are convex.

An indifference curve shows a combination of two goods that give a consumer equal satisfaction and utility, thereby making the consumer indifferent. Along the curve, the consumer has an equal preference for the combinations of goods shown, i.e. is indifferent about any combination of goods on the curve, as shown in Figure 5, where Pareto optimality is realized.

Pareto optimality, or Pareto efficiency, is an economic state where resources cannot be reallocated to make one individual better off without making at least one individual worse off. Pareto efficiency implies that resources are allocated in the most economically efficient manner but does not imply equity or fairness. The concept of Pareto-optimality is often not very discriminating.

A state of affairs x is Pareto-optimal provided that for any alternative state of affairs y, one can find at least one person who strictly prefers x to y. If one takes a wide view of preferences and includes preferences informed by moral principles or other sentiments, such as envy, then many states of affairs satisfy that condition. In contrast, the concept of potential Pareto-efficiency (also known as Kaldor-Hicks efficiency) is more discriminating and finds wider use in economics. According to that concept, a state of affairs x is inefficient if there is some alternative state of affairs y such that, in y, there is a set of possible lump-sum transfers of wealth from those who are better off under y to those who are worse off, such that, with those transfers, everyone is at least as well-off under y as under x.

A state of affairs is Pareto-optimal (or Pareto-efficient) if, and only if, there is no alternative state that would make some people better off without making anyone worse off. More precisely, a state of affairs x is said to be Pareto-inefficient (or suboptimal) if, and only if, there is some state of affairs y, such that no one strictly prefers x to y and at least one person strictly prefers y to x. The concept of Pareto-optimality thus assumes that anyone would prefer an option that is cheaper, more efficient, or more reliable or that otherwise comparatively improves one's condition. Pareto efficiency is when an economy has its resources and goods allocated to the maximum level of efficiency, and no change can be made without making someone worse off. However, pure Pareto efficiency exists only in theory, though the economy can move toward Pareto efficiency.

Figure 5. Indifference curve and Pareto optimality

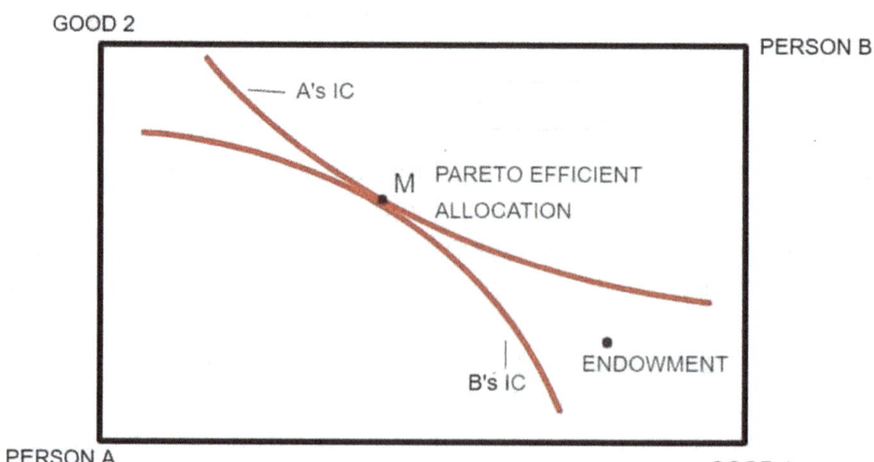

Pareto efficiency is concerned with creating a situation where we cannot make one party better off without making another party worse off. For example, a country may devote 60% of GDP to the manufacture of armaments. In doing this, they may achieve technical and productive efficiency and produce on their production possibility frontier. Therefore, from this perspective, they are efficient. However, such an economy may have a great deal of inequity, with large portions of the population struggling to have enough to eat.

There are two fundamental theorems in welfare economics concerning the most famous applications of the Pareto optimality. The first theorem states conditions under which the allocation associated with any competitive market equilibrium is Pareto-optimal, whereas the second theorem states conditions under which any Pareto-optimal allocation can be achieved as a competitive market equilibrium following the use of lump-sum transfers of wealth.

Economists typically find Pareto optimality to be extremely plausible as a condition that good laws, policies, and allocations must satisfy, although few would claim that it suffices to make a law, policy, allocation of commodities, and so on, good. A common reason (outside economics) for rejecting it, even as a necessary condition for a state of affairs to be good, is its reliance on subjective preferences.

Multiplier Model

In total output structure Y = C + I + G = C + S + T, where C is consumption, I physical investment, G government spending (an exogenous variable), S savings and T taxation, if G = T, we have I = S, yielding dI = dS, so we derive dI = (dS/dY)dY and obtain

$$dY = [1 /(dS / dY)]dI \tag{11}$$

where the factor 1/(dS/dY) is the source of multiplier factor. The multiplier effect refers to the proportional amount of increase, or decrease, for investment or spending. The most basic multiplier used in gauging the multiplier effect is calculated as change in income/change in spending. Generally, we may apply marginal propensity to consume (MPC) to measure consumption multiplier and marginal propensity to savings (MPS) to measure savings or investment multiplier

$$m_c = \frac{1}{1 - MPC}; MPC = dC / dY < 1 \tag{12}$$

$$m_s = \frac{1}{1 - MPS}; MPS = dS / dY < 1 \tag{13}$$

When C + S = Y, we have

$$MPC + MPS = 1 \tag{14}$$

Both I and G would produce positive multiplier effect as savings or government spending as investment to promote total output

$$\Delta Y = \Delta I / (1 - MPS); \Delta Y = \Delta G / (1 - MPS) \tag{15.1}$$

However, a taxation change ΔT will lead to a negative multiplier effect as taxation restrains consumption, leading to decreased total output

$$\Delta Y = -MPC(\Delta T / (1 - MPC)) \tag{15.2}$$

The multiplier effect and multiplier model provide a macroeconomic viewpoint of microeconomic behavior.

Heckscher-Ohlin Model in International Trade

The Heckscher–Ohlin model (H–O model) is a general equilibrium mathematical model of international trade, developed by Eli Heckscher and Bertil Ohlin at the Stockholm School of Economics.

The Heckscher-Ohlin model is an economic theory that proposes that countries export what they can most efficiently and plentifully produce. Also referred to as the H-O model or 2x2x2 model, it's used to evaluate trade and, more specifically, the equilibrium of trade between two countries that have varying specialties and natural resources.

The model emphasizes the export of goods requiring factors of production that a country has in abundance. It also emphasizes the import of goods that a nation cannot produce as efficiently. It takes the position that countries should ideally export materials and resources of which they have an excess, while proportionately importing those resources they need.

Here is some important information regarding the Heckscher-Ohlin model.

The Heckscher-Ohlin model evaluates the equilibrium of trade between two countries that have varying specialties and natural resources.

The model explains how a nation should operate and trade when resources are imbalanced throughout the world.

The model isn't limited to commodities, but also incorporates other production factors such as labor.

Figure 6. H-O model

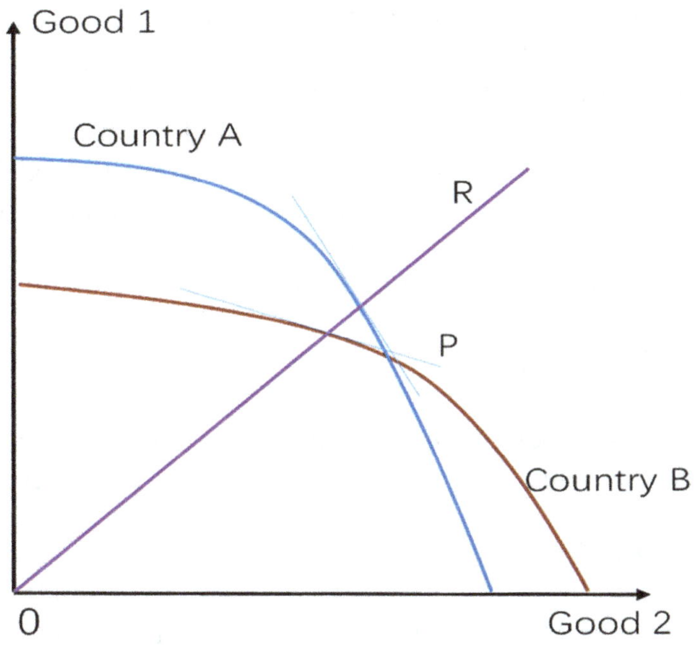

Hechscher-Ohlin model is characterized by the features as relative endowments of the factors of production (land, labor, and capital) that determine a country's comparative advantage. Countries have comparative advantages in those goods for which the required factors of production are relatively abundant locally. This is because the profitability of goods is determined by input costs. Goods that require inputs that are locally abundant will be cheaper to produce than those that require inputs that are locally scarce.

The standard Heckscher–Ohlin model assumes that the production functions are identical for all countries concerned. This means that all countries are in the same level of production and have the same technology, yet this is highly unrealistic. The technological gap between developed and developing countries is the main concern for the development of poor countries. The standard Heckscher–Ohlin model ignores all these vital factors when one wants to consider development of less developed countries in the international context. Even between developed countries, technology differs from industry to industry and firm to firm. Indeed, this is the very basis of the competition between firms, inside and across the country. Nevertheless, the standard Heckscher–Ohlin theory assumes the same production function for all countries. This implies that all firms are identical. The negative theoretical consequence is that there is no room for firms in the H–O model, thus the H-O model is not a good bridge across micro- and macro-economics.

Although Heckscher–Ohlin can be extended to the Heckscher–Ohlin–Vanek (H-O-V) model, they all perform poorly in their predictive power. H–O theory is also badly adapted to analyze South-North trade problems. Meanwhile, modern econometric estimates have shown that the H-O model performs poorly, particularly, in ignoring the roles of finance and bank (Lengwiler, 2004; Mishkin, 2004; Ueda, 2013). Therefore, H-O model cannot be put into standard micro-macro-economic unification.

Relative Rate Models

Absolute amounts can be transformed to relative rates by logarithm, per-capita or ratio processing; therefore, relative rate models (R^2Ms) emerge.

Cobb-Douglas Model

The absolute amount Cobb-Douglas-type models of production and consumption can be transformed to relative rate models. Getting the logarithms of Eq. (2) with y = log Y, k = log K and h = log H when β = 1, we obtain

$$y = f(k,h) = \log Y = \alpha \log K + (1-\alpha)\log H = \alpha K + (1-\alpha)h \quad (16)$$

in which lower-case letters y, k and h denote the natural logarithms of real output, physical capital and human capital, respectively.

Correspondingly, consumption function also shows a similar mathematical form via Eq. (4). Getting the logarithm of Eq. (4), we have

$$c = \log C = \theta \log K + (1-\theta)\log N = \theta k + (1-\theta)n \quad (17)$$

Both production and consumption functions provide the relations among some economic concepts, and the relations between input and output, which may promote economic analysis.

We can also find a way to transfer macroeconomic quantities to microeconomic analysis, by per-capita consideration.

In the case for the simplest analytical model, as h can be merged into k, we have a single variable production function, written as

$$y = f(k) \tag{18}$$

with $f' > 0$ and $f'' < 0$. Since capital pursues profit maximization until the marginal product of capital equals the real interest rate, it is for $\beta \sim 1$

$$\dot{y} = \beta(\gamma - \overline{\gamma}) = \gamma - \overline{\gamma} \tag{19}$$

Therefore, we can say that production function reflects how much output we can expect if we have so much of labor and so much of capital etc. In other words, we can also say that production function is an indicator of the physical relationship between input and output.

Also, both k and w can be defined as per-capita measures

$$k = K / N \tag{20}$$

$$w = W / H \tag{21}$$

With more definitions $c = C/K$ and $g = G/Y$, we see that we need to find necessary linkages between per-capita measures and logarithmic measures, for economic analysis.

Solow-Swan Model of Economic Growth

The Solow–Swan model is an economic model of long-run economic growth setting within the framework of neoclassical economics. It attempts to explain long-run economic growth by looking at capital accumulation, labor or population growth, and increases in productivity, commonly referred to as technological progress. At its core is a neoclassical (aggregate) production function, often specified to be of Cobb–Douglas type, which enables the model to make contact with microeconomics. The model was developed independently by Robert Solow and Trevor Swan in 1956 and superseded the Keynesian Harrod–Domar model.

Mathematically, the Solow–Swan model is a nonlinear system consisting of a single ordinary differential equation that models the evolution of the per-capita stock of capital. Solow extended the Harrod–Domar model by adding labor as a factor of production and capital-output ratios that are not fixed as they are in the Harrod–Domar model. These refinements allow increasing capital intensity to be distinguished from technological progress. Solow sees the fixed proportions production function as a crucial assumption to the instability results in the Harrod-Domar model. His own work expands upon this by exploring the implications of alternative specifications, namely the Cobb–Douglas and the more general constant elasticity of substitution (CES). Although this has become the canonical and celebrated story in the history of economics, featured in many economic textbooks, recent reappraisal of Harrod's work has contested it. One central criticism is that Harrod's original piece was neither mainly concerned with economic growth nor did he explicitly use a fixed proportions production function.

Let y = Y/N = f(k), s = S/Y as savings ratio. When I = S, it is also investment ratio. There is y/k = (n + d)/s in full equilibrium, in which d is the capital's depreciation rate, yielding a single differential equation, i.e. Solow-Swan growth model.

$$\dot{k} = sf(k) - (n+d)k;\; n = \dot{Y}/Y;\; d = I/K - \dot{K}/K \tag{22}$$

Now the production function is graphed as the f(k) curve, sf(k) denotes nation's savings function, and the required investment per-capita line is (n + d)k. The dynamic process to stability or the convergence to equilibrium requires $sf'(k) - (n+d) < 0$, and the situation is shown in Figure 8, in which the tangent at point C is parallel to the (n + d)k line.

There is a 'golden rule', which mentions that the marginal product of capital equals the sum of the depreciation rate (d) and the rate (n) at which the population and the state of technical knowledge are growing. As firms want to maximize their profits, they must equate the marginal product of capital to its rental cost (γ + d). The presumption appears to be that the marginal product of capital exceeds (n + d). Thus, we have to believe that (γ + d) must exceed (n + d) in long-run equilibrium. This means n < γ. However, technology develops unlimitedly. In the short-run period, n > γ exits frequently. This is just a dynamic source for promoting growth.

Figure 7. Solow-Swan growth model

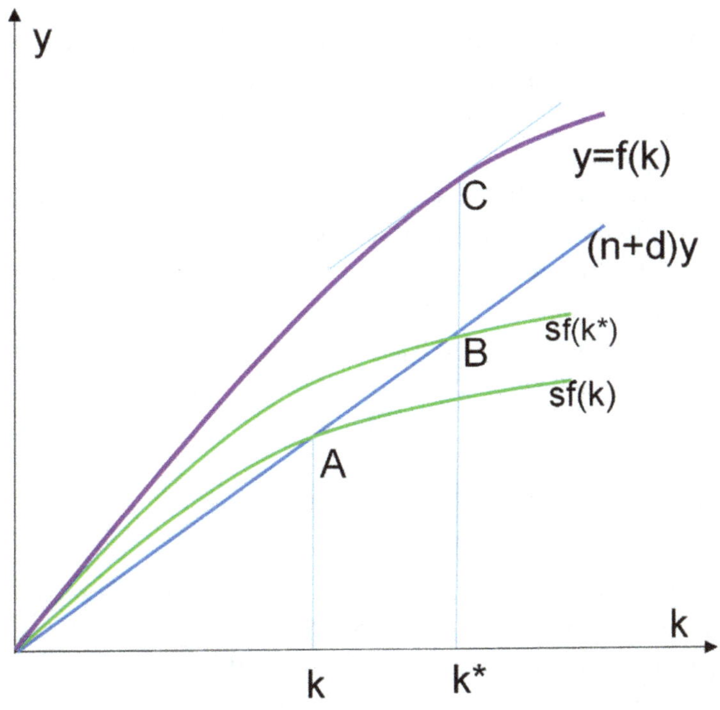

At the full equilibrium state, there is a key solution to the Solow-Swan model for k while Y = KαN(1-α)

$$dY/y = (\alpha(1-\alpha))(ds/s); \quad k=(s/(n+d))^{1/(1-\alpha)} \tag{23}$$

The speed of adjustment measure is coefficient (n + d)(1 – α). When numerical estimation suggests plausible values as n = 0.02, d = 0.04 and α = 0.33, the speed coefficient is 0.04.

A standard Solow model predicts that in the long-run, economies converge to their steady state equilibrium and that permanent growth is achievable only through technological progress. Both shifts in saving and in populational growth cause only level effects in the long-run (i.e. in the absolute value of real income per-capita). An interesting implication of Solow's model is that poor countries should grow faster and eventually catch-up to richer countries. This convergence could be explained by

1. Lags in the diffusion on knowledge. Differences in real income might shrink as poor countries receive better technology and information;
2. Efficient allocation of international capital flows, since the rate of return on capital should be higher in poorer countries. In practice, this is seldom observed and is known as Lucas' paradox.

Due to its particularly attractive mathematical characteristics, Solow–Swan proved to be a convenient starting point for various extensions. For instance, in 1965, David Cass and Tjalling Koopmans integrated Frank Ramsey's analysis of consumer optimization, thereby endogenizing the saving rate, to create what is now known as the Ramsey–Cass–Koopmans model.

If s is also a stability coefficient, linking with parameters θ and ϕ as $s = \theta\phi$, it will become a dynamic parameter as

$$\dot{y} = -s(y - \bar{y})\,;\ s = \theta\phi(1 - \phi\psi) \tag{24}$$

Since the worker effectiveness is assumed to be proportional to the knowledge state in economic society (Scarth, 2014), the knowledge (as well as technology) level of workers is proportional to the overall level of economic development (measured by physical capital stock, i.e., $\beta = aK$). Therefore, knowledge (and technology) will push the economic progress.

Phillips Curve

The Phillips curve originated out of analysis comparing wage growth with unemployment. The findings of A.W. (Bill) Phillips in T*he Relationship between Unemployment and the Rate of Change of Money Wages in the United Kingdom 1861–1957* suggested there was an inverse correlation between the rate of change in money wages and unemployment. The Phillips curve states that there is an inverse relationship between the inflation and the unemployment rate when presented or charted graphically, i.e., the higher the inflation rate of the economy, the lower the unemployment rate will be, and vice-versa. This economic concept was developed by William Phillips and is proven in all major world economies.

Differentiating from original observation, the Phillips curve model has been modified to include both a short-run Phillips curve (which, like the original Phillips curve, shows an inverse relationship between inflation and unemployment) and the long-run Phillips curve (which shows that, in the long-run, there is no relationship between inflation and unemployment).

Figure 8. Phillips curve

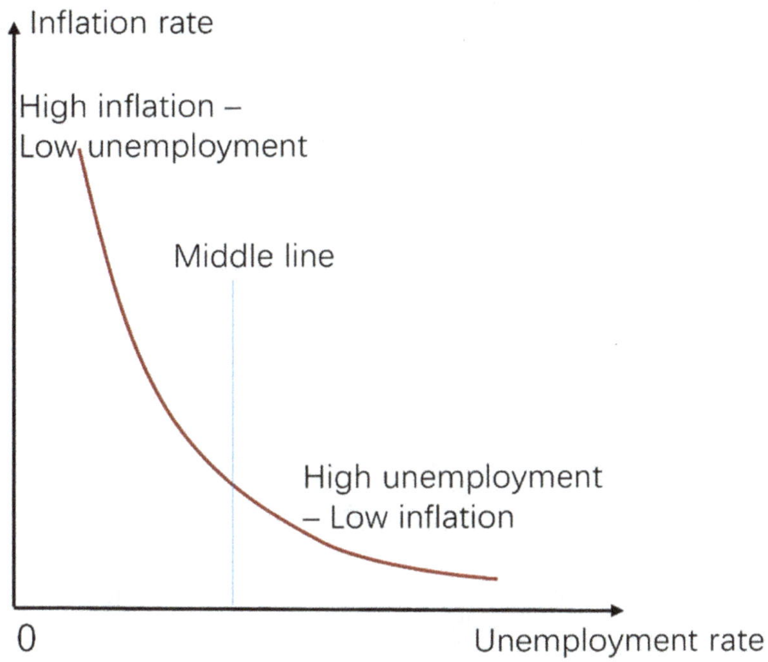

Mixed Measure Models

Practically, we need both absolute quantities and relative rates for economic analysis. Therefore, mixed measure models (M^2Ms) are popular in applications.

Hicks-Hansen Model (IS-LM model)

The IS stands for investment and savings and the LM stands for liquidity and money. The IS-LM model appears as a graph, where there is the cross of IS curve and LM curve, which shows the intersection of the goods and the money markets. The IS-LM model is also known as the Hicks-Hansen model, since Hicks initialized it in 1957 and Hansen completed it in 1963.

The IS curve describes the goods market equilibrium. The derivation of IS curve follows that investment function I = I(γ) equals to savings function S = S(Y), reaching equilibrium I(γ) = S(Y), as shown in Figure 9.

Figure 9. The derivation of IS curve

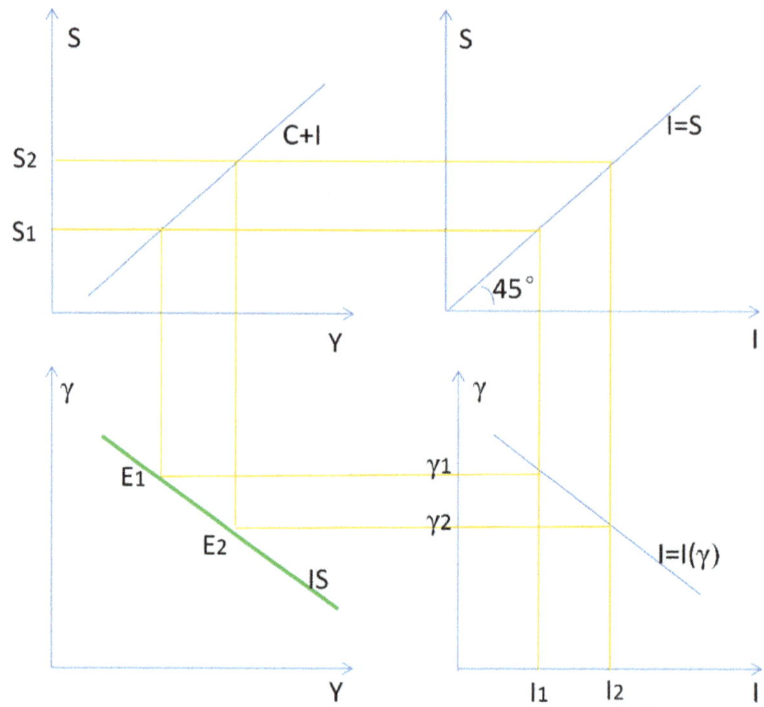

The IS curve slopes down and to the right, representing the fact that people and firms try to invest less in long-lasting goods like houses, cars, and equipment if interest rates are raised. Inversely, when interest rates fall, families will tend to put less away for savings and spend more on consumer goods. Thus, the effect of a falling interest rate is an increase in GDP through greater investment and fewer personal savings.

The LM curve describes the money market equilibrium. The derivation of LM curve follows that liquidity performance L = L(γ) equals to money supply M = M(P), reaching equilibrium L(γ) = M(P), as shown as Figure 10.

Figure 10. The derivation of LM curve

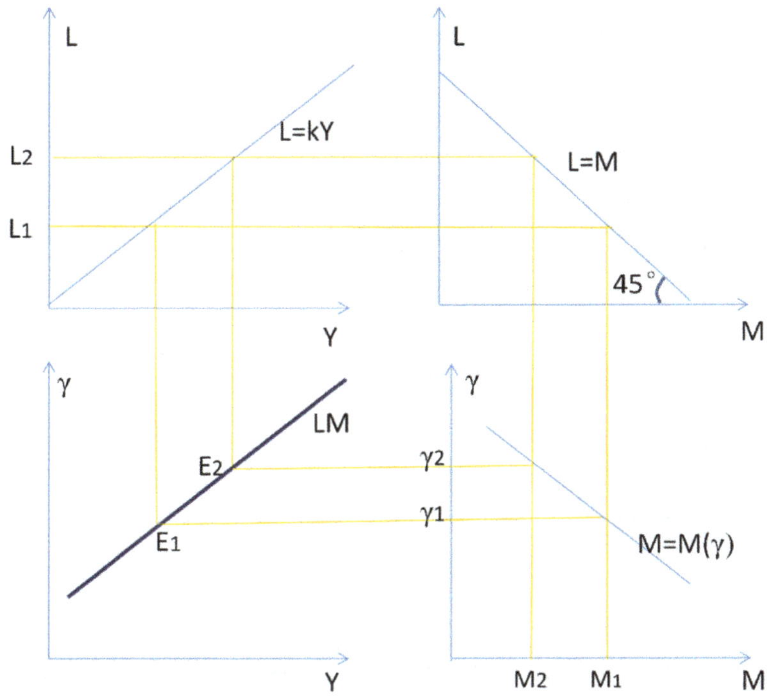

The LM curve slopes up and to the right to represent that banks and other financial institutions will configure funds to support the extra investment if the economy expands, so they encourage consumers to deposit cash into banks or purchase longer term deposits, such as bonds, to support economic development. Or, if the economy shrinks, they do so inversely.

The IS-LM model is shown in Figure 11. In the figure, when expansion fiscal policy is applied, leading to LM extension, the equilibrium point will move from E_1 to E_2. On the vertical axis of the graph, Greek alphabet γ represents the interest rate on government bonds. The IS-LM model attempts to explain a way to keep the economy in balance through an equilibrium of money supply versus interest rates.

The IS relationship and LM relationship create opposing forces. A falling interest rate tends to cause the economy to expand, whereas an expansion economy causes interest rates to rise. Where the two curves meet, the two forces are balanced and the economy is in equilibrium.

Figure 11. IS-LM model (case of monetary expansion)

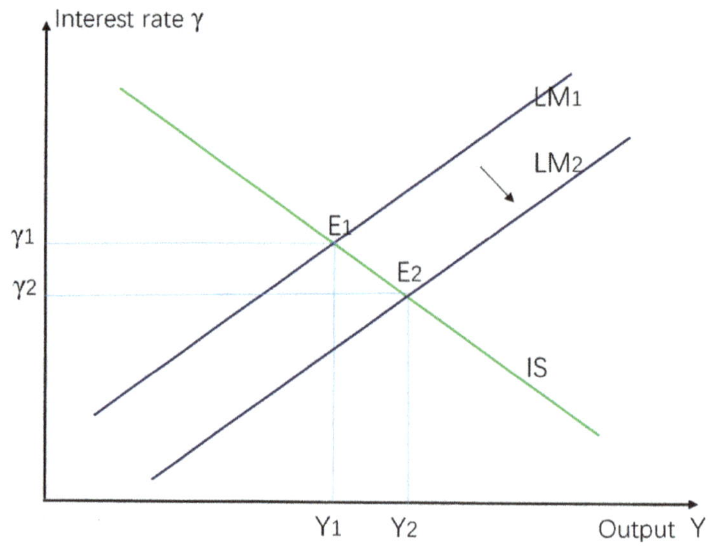

Using Y as GDP, C as consumption, I as physical investment, G as government spending (an exogenous variable), M as the nominal money supply, γ as the nominal interest rate, P as the price level, and L as liquidity preference (real money demand), the IS-LM model is determined by the IS curve and LM curve, characterized by the following equations

$$Y = C + I + G = C + S + T \tag{25}$$

$$M / P = L(Y,\gamma) \tag{26}$$

where Y = C + I + G means the demand (payment) view and Y = C + S + T is the supply (income) view.

Eq. (26) indicates the demand for money, which is the demand for real balance because people hold money for what it will buy. Real money balance is the quantity of nominal money (M) divided by price index (P), i.e.(M/P). The higher the price level in an economy, the more nominal money is required in order to buy the same amount of goods. Demand for real balances (M/P) is a function of the level of income (Y) and the interest rate (γ). So we have demand of money = L (Y, γ). Thus, the demand for real balance is positively related to the level of income and negatively related to the interest rates.

As the supply of money (nominal quantity of money, M) is controlled by the central bank in any country and is thus taken to be as given $\overline{M}$, it is assumed that the price level is constant at $\overline{P}$. Thus, the real money supply in the economy is fixed at $(\overline{M}/\overline{P})$. So the equilibrium in the money market is determined when $(\overline{M}/\overline{P}) = L\ (Y, \gamma)$.

Eq. (25) is linked to the production function $Y = K^{\alpha}H^{1-\alpha}$. Its logarithmic form y = log Y is

$$y = ak + (1 - \alpha)h \tag{27}$$

Eq. (26) is linked to Fisher's exchange equation MV = PY, where V is the velocity of money circulation. When V is a unit velocity (V = 1), m = log M will produce

$$m = y + p \tag{28}$$

As the effective labor L becomes the human capital H, and H can be measured by wage W, the logarithmic nominal wages can be fixed at level w = w*. As investment I, and government purchase G, are also determined by capital K, the variables H, I, G can be merged into K, so that all logarithmic variables may integrate and simplify as y = f (k).

The IS and LM relationships can be combined to yield the aggregate demand function by eliminating the interest rate, using $Y = C = K^{\theta}H^{1-\theta}$, leading to the result

$$y = \theta(m - p) + (1 - \theta)h \tag{29}$$

In the model, the IS curve shows the combinations of interest rates and level of real output, such that planned spending equals income, which is also known as goods market equilibrium schedule. The LM curve shows the combinations of interest rates and level of output, such that demand for money equals the supply of money, which is also known as money market equilibrium schedule.

Figure 7 shows an upward sloping LM curve and a downward sloping IS curve, expressing their relations between income (on the X-axis) and interest rates (on the Y-axis). At each level of interest rate (γ1 and γ2), where the goods and money markets are in equilibrium. However, there is a negative relationship between the level of investment in an economy and interest rates; the higher the interest rates, the higher the cost of borrowing funds for the firm in order to undertake investment. In other words, an increase in interest rates decreases the profitability of adding to the capital stock and, therefore, leads to higher planned investment spending in the economy.

When interest rates rise from γ1 to γ2, then the demand for money reduces due to the increase in the cost of borrowing, but the supply of money is given (decided by the central bank). So, to maintain the money market equilibrium, the level of real income has to rise until the opposite effect on the demand for money is canceled. People will demand less money due to an increase in interest rates and more money when real income rises (from Y1 to Y2).

The IS-IM model is a core model for economic analysis, where monetary policy addresses interest rates and the supply of money in circulation, and fiscal policy focuses on taxation and government spending.

Monetary policy is more of a blunt tool in terms of expansion and contracting the money supply to influence inflation and growth and it has less impact on the real economy. The expansionary monetary policy may have limited effects on growth by increasing asset prices and lowering the costs of borrowing, making companies more profitable, whereas the contracting monetary policy causes inverse effects.

While monetary policy seeks to spark economic activity, fiscal policy aims to target the total level of spending, the total composition of spending, or both, in an economy (the term 'fiscal' comes from the Latin for 'purse'). The two most widely used means of affecting fiscal policy are changes in government spending policies or in government tax policies. By increasing taxes, governments pull money out of the economy and slow business activity. Typically, fiscal policy is used when the government seeks to stimulate the economy.

Both fiscal and monetary policy play a large role in managing the economy and both have direct and indirect impacts on personal and household finances. Fiscal policy involves tax and spending decisions set by the government and will impact individual taxation or provide them with employment from government projects. Monetary policy is set by the central bank and can boost consumer spending through lower interest rates that make borrowing cheaper on everything from credit cards to mortgages. Comparing the two policies, fiscal policy generally has a greater impact on consumers than monetary policy, as it can lead to increase or decrease employment or income, while monetary policy trends to change capital's mobility or movement.

Mundell-Fleming Model (IS-LM-BP model)

Above, the IS-LM model dealt with goods and asset markets in a closed economy. However, the world economies are related to one another internationally through trade in goods and through financial markets. In addition to studying equilibrium in goods and money markets (as done by the IS-LM model), the model also needs to consider and carry out analysis on the balance of international payments.

The Mundell-Fleming model (IS-LM-BP model) is an economic model for processing the open economy. The Mundell-Fleming model is a version of IS-LM which deals with the interaction of goods and asset markets in an open international economy. The model framework is shown in Figure 12.

Figure 12. Mundell-Fleming model

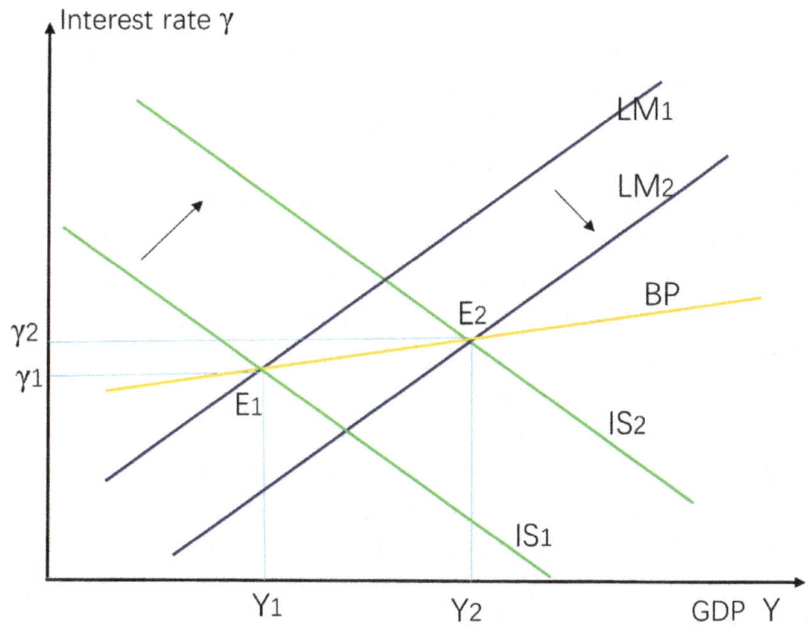

In an open economy, equilibrium in goods market is achieved when production or income (Y) is equal to aggregate demand (AD) which is the sum of consumption, planned investment spending, government spending and net exports (exports-imports). The equilibrium equation is given by the IS curve as

$$Y = C + I + G + NE = C + S + T + IM \tag{30}$$

where NE stands for net exports and IM for imports. NX is a function of real exchange rates (e), foreign income (Yf) and domestic income (Y). Thus, the level of competitiveness as measured by real exchange rates affects the open economy IS curve. Net exports are also affected by the level of foreign income (Yf). An increase in foreign income may lead to an increase in foreign spending on domestic goods which will increase net export or demand for domestic goods. An increase in domestic income will increase the demand of both domestic and foreign goods. This leads to an increase in imports and thus worsening of trade balance (NX = NE–IM).

Consumption is a function of disposable income i.e. C(Y–T) where T is the taxes. The LM curve will keep $M/P = L(Y,\gamma)$, and we need the BP curve

$$X(\pi,Y,Y^*) = -z(K,\gamma,\gamma^*) \tag{31}$$

where X is net exports. This is the GDP equation in demand (payment) view and another equivalent supply (income) view as Y = C + S + T + M, in which S means save and M is imports. Eq. (4-6) means that a higher interest rate or a lower income (GDP) level leads to lower money demand. BP means balance of payment, which equals CA + KA; CA is the current account surplus and KA is the capital account surplus. Then the balance of payments (BP) components becomes CA = X (π, Y, Y*), i.e., the current account is viewed as solely consisting of imports and exports, where π is the nominal exchange rate (the price of domestic currency in terms of units of the foreign currency), Y is GDP and Y* is the combined GDP of countries that are foreign trading partners. Higher domestic income (GDP) leads to more spending on imports and, hence, lower net exports. Higher foreign income leads to higher spending by foreigners on the country's exports and, thus, higher net exports. A higher π leads to lower net exports. Then KA = $z(\gamma,\gamma^*)$–k, *where* γ* is the foreign interest rate, k is the exogenous component of financial capital flows, z is the interest-sensitive component of capital flows, and the derivative of the function z is the degree of capital mobility (the effect of differences between domestic and foreign interest rates upon capital flows KA).

Therefore, the equilibrium relationship can be expressed as:

$$Y = C(Y-T) + I(Y, i) + G + NE(e, Yf, Y) \tag{32}$$

In order to understand the working of the Mundell-Fleming model, we need to first understand the concepts of the IS curve (which represents the goods market equilibrium), the LM curve (which represents money market equilibrium) and the BP curve (which represents equilibrium of the balance of payments).

The balance of payments surplus, BP, is equal to the sum of trade surplus (NX) and net capital inflows (capital account surplus), CF, linked by BP = NX + CF.

Net capital flow depends on the interest differential (i.e. $i - i_f$). An increase in the domestic interest rate over the world interest rate ($i > i_f$) will result in net capital inflows from abroad and, thus, will improve capital account (a surplus in capital account).

As discussed above in the IS curve section, NX depends on foreign income (Yf), domestic income (Y), and real exchange rate (e).

An increase in domestic income will result in higher exports (X) than imports (M) which will worsen the trade balance. On the other hand, an increase in the domestic interest rate will result in higher capital flows into the domestic country from abroad (assuming perfect mobility of capital).

Thus, we can say that when income increases, even a small increase in domestic interest rate (i) will maintain the overall balance of payments equilibrium. This means that a deficit in trade balance (higher imports than exports) will be viably financed by net capital inflows, such that BP = 0 at equilibrium (i.e. deficit in trade balance = net capital flows).

The BP curve is flat due to perfect capital mobility. The slope of the BP curve is determined by the degree of capital mobility that is possible. When imports are higher, the balance of payment will be in the deficit unless the domestic interest rate rises to maintain the equilibrium (high-interest rates will lead to capital inflows which will finance the trade deficit). The higher the mobility of capital, the flatter the BP curve will be.

Any point above the BP curve means that balance of payments (BOP) is in surplus (BOP>0) while all the points below the BP curve means that the BOP is in deficit (BOP<0).

The Mundell-Fleming Model can be applied in the analysis of perfect capital mobility, including:

Fixed exchange rate system: it is an exchange rate regime in which a currency's value is fixed against either the value of another single currency or to a basket of other currencies, or to another measure of value, such as gold. This type of exchange rate is not determined by market forces of demand and supply.

Flexible exchange rate system: also known as floating exchange rate, which is a type of regime that allows the exchange rate to be determined by the forces of demand and supply. Under this system, the central bank does not intervene in the market for foreign exchange.

There is an important conclusion in Mundell-Fleming economics: the fiscal policy is effective, and the monetary policy is ineffective in a fixed exchange rate system, while the fiscal policy is ineffective and the monetary policy is effective in floating exchange rate system.

Conclusively, while the traditional IS-LM model deals with economy under autarky (or closed) economy, the Mundell-Fleming model extends the IS-LM framework to an open economy, by combining the IS-LM curves with a balance of payments (BP) line. For this reason, it is also referred to as the IS-LM-BP model. Most textbooks describe the Mundell–Fleming model only under the assumption of perfect capital mobility.

When the Mundell–Fleming model is transformed to logarithm form, we have a simplified mathematical representation in open economy as

$$y-\overline{y}=-\psi(\gamma-\overline{\gamma})+\theta(\pi-p) \quad (33)$$

$$\gamma-\overline{\gamma}=\dot{\pi}-\dot{p} \quad (34)$$

As the dynamic aggregate supply function focuses on a monetary policy to balance price level and inflation with the bank's target variable x, we set

$$\dot{p}=\phi(y-\overline{y})+\dot{x} \quad (35)$$

Using the Phillips curve to eliminate inflation rate and policy reaction function to eliminate interest rate, we can obtain result

$$(y-\overline{y})=-\psi(\gamma-\overline{\gamma})+\theta(\pi-p) \quad (36)$$

$$\dot{y}=\varphi(p-x)-\phi(y-\overline{y}) \quad (37)$$

The differential equations, Eqs. (37) and (35), construct the compact version of the Mundell-Fleming model. Then the geometrical diagram can be transformed to phase diagram (applied in new neoclassical economics), as shown in Figure 13.

Figure 13. Phase diagram

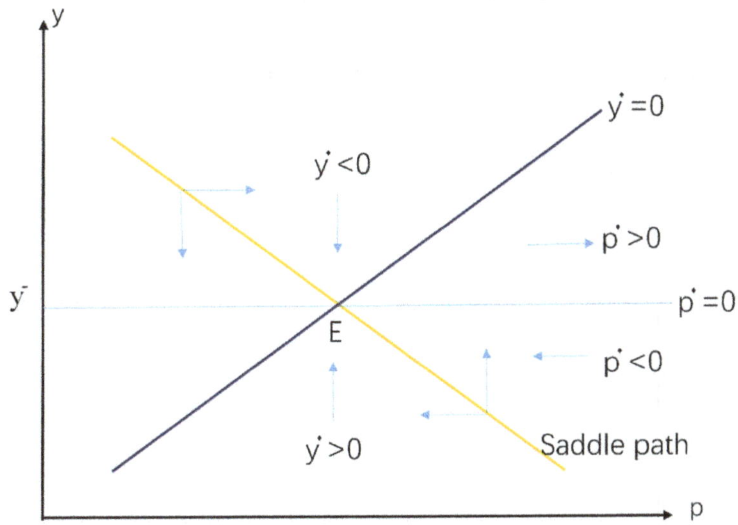

In the phase diagram, we focus on two variables, y and p. The goal is to draw two 'no-motion' lines in a y-p space graph. The $\dot{p} = 0$ locus is all combinations of y and p values that involve p not changing through time, while the $\dot{y} = 0$ locus is all combinations of y and p values that involve y not through time. The intersection of the $\dot{y} = 0$ and the $\dot{p} = 0$ lines determine the full equilibrium of the system, which is point E.

As p is drawn in the horizontal line, the phase $\dot{p} > 0$ indicates rising price region (arrow pointing right) and the phase $\dot{p} < 0$ denotes falling price region (arrow pointing left). Similarly, phase $\dot{y} > 0$ indicates increasing output region (arrow pointing up) while phase $\dot{y} < 0$ indicates decreasing output region (arrow pointing down). The economy is observed on the saddle path, and there will be convergence to full equilibrium.

Certainly, we can also replace y, p with c, k as coordinate elements, in economic analysis as phase diagrams.

Laffer Curve

The Laffer curve is used to illustrate the concept of 'taxable income elasticity', which is the idea that government can maximize tax revenue by setting tax rates at an optimum point, and that neither a 0% tax rate nor a 100% tax rate will generate government revenue. The Laffer curve states that if tax rates are increased above a certain level, then tax revenues can actually fall because higher tax rates discourage people from working. Equally, the Laffer curve states that cutting taxes could, in theory, lead to higher tax revenues. It starts from the premise that if tax rates are 0% then the government gets zero revenue.

Figure 14. Laffer curve

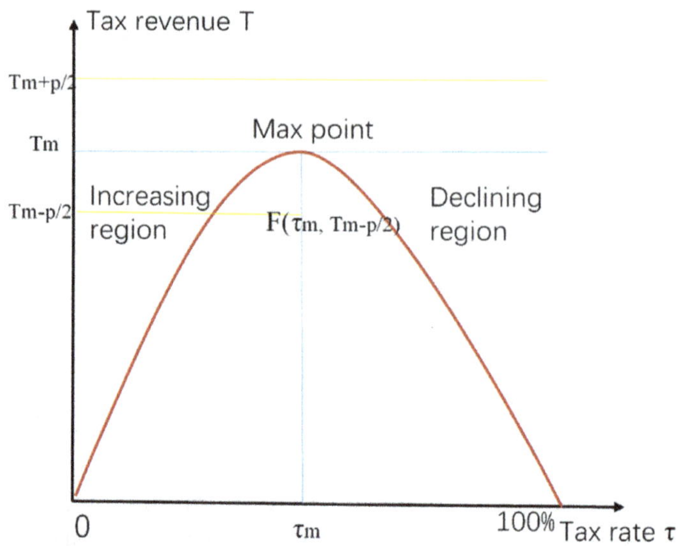

The Laffer curve is a plot of tax rates against tax revenues (Laffer, 2004). As tax rates rise from 0%, revenues go up, until a tipping point is reached, after which increases in rates bring revenues. The shape of the curve implies that as tax rates rise, tax revenues will also increase. However, these increased tax revenues will only increase until a peak, after which the tax revenues begin to decline. This means that, after a point, it is counter-intuitive to keep increasing tax rates. The idea behind the Laffer curve is that people will stop or be discouraged from working after a certain point because the tax rates will be too high.

Mathematically, the Laffer curve is a second-order curve. If we simulate it by parabola with directrix $\tau = T_m + p/2$, where its focus is $(\tau_m, T_m - p/2)$ and its vertex is (τ_m, T_m), we have its equation as

$$(\tau - \tau m)_2 = -2p(T - Tm) \tag{38}$$

in which focal parameter is $p > 0$.

Integrating above theoretical thoughts and models, a grand synthetic model with its economic principles will be proposed in the next chapters.

REFERENCES

Arrow, K. (1963). *Social Choice and Individual Values* (2nd ed.). Yale University Press.

Arrow, K., & Debreu, G. (1954). Existence of an equilibrium for a competitive economy. *Econometrica*, *22*(3), 265–290. doi:10.2307/1907353

Atkinson, A., Piketty, T., & Saez, E. (2011). Top incomes in the long run of history. *Journal of Economic Literature*, *49*(1), 3–71. doi:10.1257/jel.49.1.3

Blanchard, O. J., & Gali, J. (2010). Labor markets and monetary policy: A new Keynesian model with unemployment. *American Economic Journal. Macroeconomics*, *2*(2), 1–30. doi:10.1257/mac.2.2.1

Coase, R. H. (1960). The problem of social cost. *The Journal of Law & Economics*, *3*, 1–44. doi:10.1086/466560

Davis, J. (2003). *The Theory of the Individual in Economics*. Routledge. doi:10.4324/9780203457689

Dollar, D., Kleineberg, T., & Kraay, A. (2014). *Growth, inequity and social welfare: cross country evidence.* World Bank Policy Research Department Working Paper No. 6842.

Dollar, D., & Kraay, A. (2002). Growth is good for the poor. *Journal of Economic Growth*, *7*(3), 195–225. doi:10.1023/A:1020139631000

Dornbusch, R. (1976). Exchange rate expectations and monetary policy. *Journal of International Economics*, *6*, 231–244. doi:10.1016/0022-1996(76)90001-5

Faccarello, G., & Kurz, H. D. (2016). Handbook on the History of Economic Analysis. Vol. I: Great Economists since Petty and Boisguilbert; Vol. II: Schools of Thought in Economics. Edward Elgar.

Feldman, A. M., & Serrano, R. (2005). *Welfare Economics and Social Choice Theory* (2nd ed.). Springer Science & Business Media, Inc.

Feldstein, M. S. (1976). Inflation, income taxes, and the rate of interest – a theoretical analysis. *The American Economic Review*, *66*, 806–820.

Fischer, S. (1977). Long-term contracts, rational expectations, and the optimal money supply rule. *Journal of Political Economy*, *85*(1), 191–205. doi:10.1086/260551

Fischer, S. (1983). A framework for monetary and banking analysis. *Economic Journal*, *93*, 1-16.

Fleming, J. M. (1962). Domestic monetary policies under fixed and floating exchange rates. IMF Staff Papers, 9, 369–379.

Floyd, J. E. (2010). *Interest Rates, Exchange Rates and World Monetary Policy*. Springer. doi:10.1007/978-3-642-10280-6

Forni, M., & Lippi, M. (1997). *Aggregation and the Microfoundations of Dynamic Macroecomics*. Oxford University Press.

Friedman, B. M., & Hahn, F. H. (Eds.). (2000). *Handbook of Monetary Economics* (Vol. 1-2). Elsevier.

Friedman, M. (1948). A monetary and fiscal framework for economic stability. *The American Economic Review*, *38*(3), 245–264.

Friedman, M. (1956). *Studies in the Quantity Theory of Money*. University of Chicago Press.

Friedman, M. (1957). *A Theory of the Consumption Function*. Princeton University Press. doi:10.1515/9780691188485

Friedman, M. (1966). The Methodology of Positive Economics. In *Essays in Positive Economics*. University of Chicago Press.

Friedman, M. (1970). A theoretical framework for monetary analysis. *Journal of Political Economy*, *78*(2), 193–238. doi:10.1086/259623

Gilder, G. (2012). *Wealth and Poverty: A new edition for the twenty-first century*. Regnery Pub. Inc.

Gilder, G. (2013). *Knowledge and Power: The information theory of capitalism and how it is revolutionizing our world*. Regnery Pub. Inc.

Gillies, D. (1998). The Duhem thesis and the Quine thesis. In *Philosophy of Science: The Central Issues*. New York: Norton.

Goodfriend, M., & King, R. G. (1997). The new neoclassical synthesis and the role of monetary policy. *NBER Macroeconomics Annual, 12*, 231–283. doi:10.1086/654336

Gray, J. A. (1976). Wage indexation: A microeconomic approach. *Journal of Monetary Economics, 2*(2), 221–235. doi:10.1016/0304-3932(76)90034-9

Hahn, F. H. (1960). The stability of growth equilibrium. *The Quarterly Journal of Economics, 74*(2), 206–226. doi:10.2307/1884251

Heyne, P., Boettke, P., & Prychitko, D. (2013). *The Economic Way of Thinking* (13th ed.). Pearson Education.

Hicks, J. R. (1946). *Value and Capital: An inquiry into some fundamental principles of economic theory* (2nd ed.). Oxford University Press.

Horwitz, S. (2000). *Microfoundations and Macroeconomics: An Austrian Perspective*. Routledge. doi:10.4324/9780203456309

Jones, R. W., & Kenen, P. B. (Eds.). (1985). *Handbook of International Economics*. Elsevier.

Keynes, J. M. (2012). The General Theory of Employment, Interest and Money (The Collected Writings of John Maynard Keynes Vol. 7). Cambridge University Press.

King, R. G. (2000). The new IS-LM model: Language, logic, and limits. *Federal Reserve Bank of Richmond Economic Quarterly, 86*, 45–103.

Laffer, A. (2004). *The Laffer Curve: Past, Present, and Future*. The Heritage Foundation. https://www.heritage.org/research/reports/2004/06/the-laffer-curve-past-present-and-future

Lamb, M., Lymer, A., & Freedman, J. (2005). *Taxation: An Interdisciplinary Approach to Research*. Oxford University Press.

Lengwiler, Y. (2004). *Microfoundations of Financial Economics: An Introduction to General Equilibrium Asset Pricing*. Princeton University Press.

Lucas, R., & Rapping, L. (1970). Real Wages, Employment and Inflation. In E. Phelps (Ed.), *Microeconomic Foundations of Employment and Inflation Theory* (pp. 253–305). Norton.

Lucas, R. E. Jr. (1972). Expectations and the neutrality of money. *Journal of Economic Theory, 4*(2), 103–124. doi:10.1016/0022-0531(72)90142-1

Lucas, R. E. (1973). Some international evidence on output-inflation tradeoffs. *The American Economic Review*, *63*, 526–534.

Lucas, R. E. Jr. (1975). An equilibrium model of the business cycle. *Journal of Political Economy*, *83*(6), 1113–1144. doi:10.1086/260386

Lucas, R. E. (1988). On the mechanics of development planning. *Journal of Monetary Economics*, *22*, 3–42. doi:10.1016/0304-3932(88)90168-7

Mäki, U. (2012). Handbook of the Philosophy of Science: Vol. 13. *Philosophy of Economics*. Elsevier.

Marshall, A. (2013). *Principles of Economics* (8th ed.). Palgrave Macmillan LLC. doi:10.1057/9781137375261

Mises, L. (2006). *The Ultimate Foundation of Economic Science: An Essay on Method*. Liberty Fund, Inc.

Mishkin, F. S. (2004). *The Economics of Money, Banking, and Financial Markets* (7th ed.). Addison-Wesley.

Modigliani, F. (1963). The monetary mechanism and its interaction with real phenomena. *The Review of Economics and Statistics*, *45*(1), 76–103. doi:10.2307/1927150

Mundell, R. A. (1962). The appropriate use of monetary and fiscal policy for internal and external balance. *International Monetary Fund Staff Papers*, *9*(1), 70–79. doi:10.2307/3866082

Mundell, R. A. (1963). *Capital mobility and stabilization policy under fixed and flexible exchange rates. Canadian Journal of Economic and Political Science, 29(4), 475–485.*

Nicola, P. C. (2013). *Efficiency and Equity in Welfare Economics*. Springer. doi:10.1007/978-3-642-30071-4

North, D. C. (1990). *Institutions, Institutional Change and Economic Performance*. Cambridge University Press. doi:10.1017/CBO9780511808678

Okun, A. M. (1975). *Equity and Efficiency: the big trade-off*. Brookings Institution.

Phelps, E. (1967). Phillips curves, expectations of inflation and optimal unemployment over time. *Economica*, *34*(135), 254–281. doi:10.2307/2552025

Phillips, A. W. (1958). The Relationship between Unemployment and the Rate of Change of Money Wages in the United Kingdom 1861-1953. *Economica*, *25*, 283–299.

Polyanin, A. D., & Manzhirov, A. V. (2007). *Handbook of Mathematics for Engineers and Scientists*. Taylor & Francis Group.

Samuelson, P. A. (1983). Foundations of Economic Analysis (Enlarged ed.). Harvard University Press.

Samuelson, P. A., & Nordhaus, W. D. (2010). *Economics* (19th ed.). McGraw-Hill Co.

Scarth, W. (2014). *Macroeconomics: The development of modern methods for policy analysis*. Edward Elgar.

Sen, A. (1997). *Poverty and Famines*. International Labour Organization.

Sen, A. (2002). *Rationality and Freedom*. Belknap Press.

Sidrauski, M. (1967). Inflation and economic growth. *Journal of Political Economy*, *75*(6), 796–810. doi:10.1086/259360

Smith, A. (1977). An Inquiry into the Nature and Causes of the Wealth of Nations (UK ed.). Chicago: University of Chicago Press.

Solow, R. M. (1956). A contribution to the theory of economic growth. *The Quarterly Journal of Economics*, *70*(1), 65–94. doi:10.2307/1884513

Stigler, G. J. (1961). The economics of information. *Journal of Political Economy*, *69*(3), 213–225. doi:10.1086/258464

Taylor, J. B. (1979). Staggered wage setting in a macro model. *The American Economic Review*, *69*, 108–113.

Tobin, J. (1969). A general equilibrium approach to monetary theory. *Journal of Money, Credit and Banking*, *1*(1), 15–26. doi:10.2307/1991374

Tobin, J. (1975). Keynesian models of recession and depression. *American Economic Review Proceedings*, *65*, 195–202.

Ueda, K. (2013). Banks as coordinators of economic growth and stability: Microfoundation for macroeconomy with externality. *Journal of Economic Theory*, *148*(1), 322–352. doi:10.1016/j.jet.2012.09.003

Walras, L. (1954). Elements of Pure Economics, or the theory of social wealth (4th ed., W. Jaffé, Trans.). London: George Allen & Unwin Ltd.

Weintraub, E. R. (1977). The microfoundations of macroeconomics: A critical survey. *Journal of Economic Literature*, *15*(1), 1–23.

Weintraub, E. R. (1979). *Microfoundations: The compatibility of microeconomics and macroeconomics*. Cambridge University Press. doi:10.1017/CBO9780511559570

Woodford, M. (2003). *Interest and Prices: Foundations of a Theory of Monetary Policy*. Princeton University Press.

Chapter 4
Grand Synthetic Model

ABSTRACT

In order to interpret complicated economic phenomena, a grand synthetic model is set up in which IS-LM core is kept. The grand synthetic model integrates four key variables (y, m, p, k) and three key policy rates (γ, τ, π) and introduced three economic parameters (b, s, d). In total, there are 10 equations for the 10 variables (y, m, p, k; γ, τ, π; b, s, d), except the link $m = p + y$, and three model parameters (α, θ, ρ) are free variables. The b, s, and $d = \delta$, respectively, stand for big parameter, small parameter, and micro-parameter with estimated values at $b\sim10^3$, $s\sim10^{-1}$, and $d\sim10^{-2}$.

THREE IMPORTANT FOUNDATIONAL LINKAGES

There are three important foundational linkages for setting up a new synthetic model.

Three Keys Linking Microeconomic Arrow-Debreu Model to Macroeconomic Mundell-Fleming Model

Initially, we have three keys linking microeconomics to macroeconomics.

According to Weintraub's conclusion, the Arrow-Debreu general equilibrium model (Walrasian equilibrium model) has the following characteristics[1]

DOI: 10.4018/978-1-6684-4935-6.ch004

1. There is a class of agents, called consumers, who have preferences over different bundles of final goods.
2. The consumer preferences are sufficiently regular so that preferences can be represented by utility indicators.
3. Consumers' income comes from sales of factor services and firms' distributed profits.
4. Members of another class of agents, called firms, have preferences over output configurations, which lead to profits.
5. Consumers, taking product and factor prices as given, attempt to maximize utility subject to their income constraint.
6. Firms, taking product and factor prices as given, attempt to maximize profits subject to technology constraint.

These characteristics mean that we have the first key to link micro- with macro-economy, which is the relation of demand and supply.

The First Key: From Micro-Demand-Supply to Macro-Aggregate Demand – Aggregate Supply

The consumers' demand (D) and firms' supply (S) at an individual level, as well as aggregate demand (AD) and aggregate supply (AS) at national level are basic micro-macro-relations in economics. From micro-demand (D) – supply (S) model to macro-aggregate demand (AD) – aggregate supply (AS) model, the form is very similar, i.e., the demand curve is downward-sloping and the supply curve is upward-sloping, as shown in Figure 1, which strongly signifies the unification of micro- and macro-economics.

The above figure suggests that the micro D-S system can be integrated to become aggregate macro AD-AS system, while macro AD-AS system can also reduce to discrete micro D-S system. Using logarithms of the real output $y = \log Y$, nominal money $m = \log M$, nominal prices $p = \log P$ and nominal wages $w = \log W$, the aggregate demand-aggregate supply framework can be expressed as logarithm forms (Blanchard, 1990).

$$y = \alpha(m - p),\ \alpha>0 \tag{1}$$

$$y = \beta(m - w),\ \beta<0 \tag{2}$$

When nominal wages are fixed at level w^*, the above framework plus $w = w^*$ constructs Keynesian general theory, where the increase in m will increase both output y and price level p. However, the linkages of discrete and aggregate processes need another two keys, namely marginal effect and multiplier model.

Figure 1. A descriptive micro-macro-relation

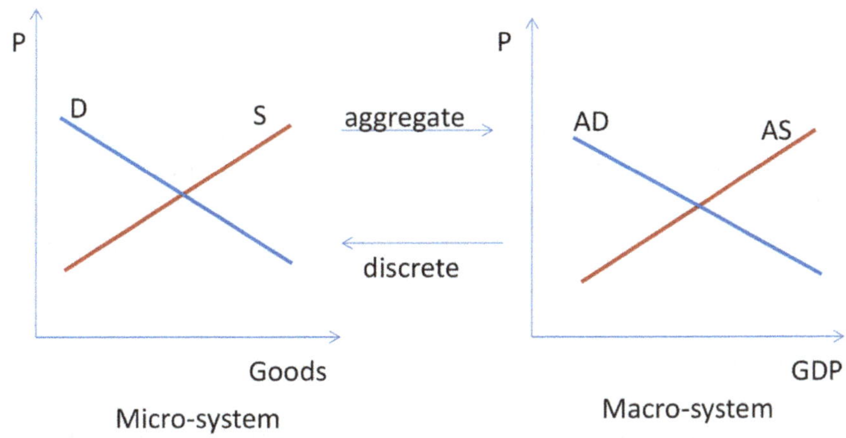

The Second Key: Marginal Effects in Both Micro and Macro Economies

The utility-maximizing consumers and the profit-maximizing firms are considered to be important rules in economics, which can be expressed by marginal effect, as follows[2]

1. The ratios of marginal utilities of goods for all consumers are equal to the relative prices of those goods.
2. The ratios of marginal costs of goods produced by firms are equal to the relative prices of those goods.
3. The relative marginal revenue products of all inputs are equal for all firms and all goods and are equal to those inputs' relative prices.

In mathematical analysis of general equilibrium (Samuelson and Nordhaus, 2005), the conditions for competitive general equilibrium are classified into two categories: consumer equilibrium and producer equilibrium. In consumer equilibrium, the ratio of the marginal utilities of two goods (MU_1/MU_2) is equal to the ratio of their prices (P_1/P_2). In producer equilibrium, the ratio of the marginal costs of two final products (MC_1/MC_2) is equal to the ratio of their prices (P_1/P_2). Therefore, in the market, when final products become goods, combing consumer equilibrium and producer equilibrium, the general equilibrium means

$$\frac{MC_1}{MC_2} = \frac{MU_1}{MU_2} \tag{3}$$

Equation (3) reveals that one of the essences of general equilibrium or Arrow-Debreu mode focuses on the marginal effect of goods.

On the other hand, macroeconomics marks that the marginal propensity to consumption (MPC) and marginal propensity to save (MPS) related like mirror images, i.e.

$$MPC + MPS = 1 \tag{4}$$

Equation (4) reveals one of the characteristics of national consumption behaviors, and the 1/MPS = 1/(1-MPC) is just the expenditure multiplier or investment multiplier.

The Third Key: AD–AS Model can be Approached by Multiplier Model

The existence of a multiplier effect was initially proposed by Keynes' student Richard Kahn in the 1930s. Although some scholars reject or downplay the importance of multiplier effects, particularly in terms of the long run, the multiplier model has been used as an argument for the efficacy of government spending or taxation relief to stimulate aggregate demand.

A multiplier is a factor of proportionality that measures how much an endogenous variable changes in response to a change in some exogenous variable in macroeconomics. Including both money multipliers and fiscal multipliers, multiplier model causes macroeconomic effects. While a fiscal multiplier is a ratio of a change in national income to the change in government spending, it is also one of various closely related ratios of commercial bank money to central bank money under a fractional-reserve banking system. More generally, the exogenous spending multiplier is the ratio of a change in national income to any autonomous change in spending (including private investment spending, consumer spending, government spending, or spending by foreigners on the country's exports). A money multiplier measures the maximum amount of commercial bank money that can be created by a given unit of central bank money. That is to say, in a fractional-reserve banking system, the total amount of loans that commercial banks are allowed to extend (i.e. the commercial bank money that they can legally create) is a multiple of reserves; this multiple is the reciprocal of the reserve ratio, and it is an economic multiplier.

One of the key assumptions in the multiplier analysis is that prices and wages are fixed in the short-run. Although this is an oversimplification (as many prices adjust quickly in the real world), this assumption captures the point that some of the adjustments to AD shifts will come through output adjustments if some wages and prices are sticky. So, Keynesian economists calculate multipliers that measure the effect on aggregate demand (AD) only. Then, American economists Alvin Hansen and Paul Samuelson extended it to get the multiplier-accelerator model, i.e. Hansen-Samuelson model.

As the multiplier model can approach AD–AS model (Ye, 2017), we can combine marginal effect with multiplier model then penetrate demand and supply for unification. Thus, we can find a unified model via three keys to link micro- and macro-economics, in which demand and supply, marginal effect and multiplier model are interrelated.

Linkages between Logarithmic Cobb-Douglas Model and per-capita Solow-Swan Model

As the variables k and y in Cobb-Douglas analytical model belong to logarithmic definitions (k = log K, y = log Y) and k and y in Solow-Swan model belong to per-capita definitions (k = K/N, y = Y/N), we need to link them by relations

$$Y \sim e^{y} = {}^{Y/N};\ K \sim e^{k} = e^{K/N} \tag{5}$$

Real data estimation and fitting require a parameter b to be introduced, as

$$Y = be^{y} = be^{Y/N};\ K = be^{k} = be^{K/N} \tag{6}$$

where b resembles a big parameter with different values in different countries and different years. Using practical data in 2017 (World Bank data from UN statistics at http://data.un.org), we estimate the b values as shown in Table 1.

Table 1. An estimation of parameter b (on 2017 data)

Country	Y(US$)	N(million)	y=Y/N	logY	b
Canada	1.777E+12	36.7321	48383.88	28.2061	1715.3705
US	1.949E+13	325.0848	59939.42	30.6007	1958.7606
UK	3.037E+12	66.7275	45514.17	28.7419	1583.5475
France	2.997E+12	64.8425	46224.26	28.7287	1608.9906
Germany	4.382E+12	82.6584	53010.87	29.1085	1821.1488
Italy	2.53E+12	60.6737	41690.28	28.559	1459.7926
Japan	5.18E+12	126.8603	40834.89	29.2759	1394.83
China	1.989E+13	1421.0218	13994.88	30.6211	457.03411

In most cases, with different b for different countries, the b ~ 10^3, which is a really a big parameter.

Linkages Among Interest, Tax, Exchange and Inflation Rates

Among the metric rates, interest rate γ, exchange rate π, and tax rate τ are important factors (Sánchez, 2005; Floyd, 2010) in determining economic running. The inflation rate λ and unemployment rate η are also important factors to reflect economic properties and qualities. To avoid confusion with imaginary unit and time, Greek alphabetic γ, π and τ are applied to denote interest rate, exchange rate and tax rate, respectively.

If we set an ideal simplified economic model, characterized by logarithmic form y = f (k) and m = y (γ), which implies Y = C at macroeconomic level. However, this ideal form is a highly simplified real economy. Actually, Y = C + I + G is the most popular form in macroeconomics. Therefore, we will add I + G as developing process, where the exchange rate expresses random change and the interest rate can be lifted or lowered artificially, while the tax rate is rigidly regulated and unemployment rate can be greatly modified by government investment or purchase. This situation is shown in Figure 2.

In Figure 2, t denotes time and I + G means government investment and purchase. Thus, if we integrate interest, exchange, tax rates, inflation and unemployment rates into a synthetic economic model, the interactions among various rates can be unitedly revealed for macroeconomic analysis. Just because the effects of I + G link with rates of tax and unemployment, the effects of I

+ G could be partly replaced by the tax and unemployment rates. Therefore, the simplified Y = C and y = f (k) have a realistic foundation.

Figure 2. Different dynamic characteristics of γ, π, τ and η

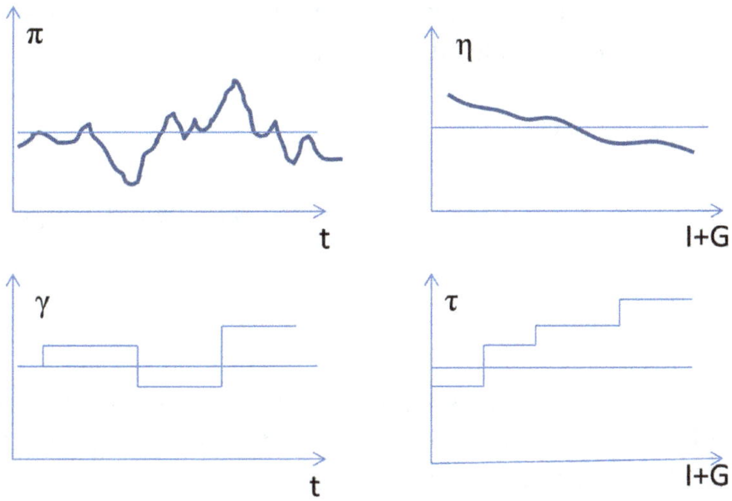

Obviously, not every metric rate is independent, though we have no linear relations among these rates. However, we have Dornbusch's formula (Dornbusch, 1976) to describe a relation linking γ^* as real rate of interest and π^* as real exchange rate, via nominal interest rate γ and exchange rate π, where they are integrated in vertical coordinate within a quasi-linear relation as an approximate formula, as follows

$$\gamma - \gamma^* = \frac{\pi^*}{\pi} - 1 \tag{7}$$

Meanwhile, the relationship between the real interest rate, the nominal interest rate, as well as inflation rate is described by the famous Fisher equation as

$$1 + \gamma^* = \frac{1+\gamma}{1+\lambda} \tag{8}$$

In the Fisher equation, γ, γ^*, respectively, refers to the nominal and real interest rate, and λ means the inflation rate. Since $1 + \gamma = (1 + \gamma^*)(1 + \lambda) = 1 + \gamma^* + \lambda + \gamma^*\lambda$ and $\gamma^*\lambda << \gamma^* + \lambda$, there is linear approximation $\gamma^* \sim \gamma - \lambda$ (Feldstein, 1976). Moreover, the inflation rate links with unemployment rate via the Phillips curve.

It is important to clarify the relationships among all rates if possible. With defining parameter n as balanced growth rate in full equilibrium

$$n = \dot{Y} / Y = \dot{K} / K = \dot{C} / C \tag{9}$$

we may link n with interest rate γ, income tax rate τ and time preference ρ (Scarth, 2014) as

$$n = \gamma(1 - \tau) - \rho \tag{10}$$

In the view of optimization, we can begin at y = f(k) since all resources can be integrated into and measured by capital, and then we can set the following simplest definitions with coherence dimension

$$\dot{p} / p = \gamma; \ \dot{c} / c = \tau \tag{11}$$

Equation (11) indicates that the marginal efficiency of capital is just interest rate, and that the marginal efficiency of consumption matches the (income/wage) tax rate. Then there are the following relations among interest rate, exchange rate, tax rate and inflation rate, including

$$\gamma - \gamma^* = ((\pi - \pi^*) - \mathrm{fd}) - (\mathrm{fd} - (\lambda - \lambda^*)) \tag{12}$$

$$f'(k) = \gamma - (\frac{\tau_2}{1 - \tau_1})\lambda \tag{13}$$

where $\gamma - \gamma^*$ denotes the real interest differential and $\lambda - \lambda^*$ is inflation differential, f means the forward premium and d denotes the expected rate of depreciation. There are real data supporting Equation (12) as shown in Table 4-2 (Dornbusch and Giovannini, 1990).

Therefore, we conclude that we have more than three important foundational linkages for setting up a grand synthetic model.

Table 2. Sample values of equation (14) (1982-1986)

Country	$\gamma - \gamma^*$	$\pi - \pi^* - fd$	$fd - \lambda - \lambda^*$
Canada	– 0.27	– 0.05	– 0.27
Mexico	– 12.38	– 16.80	4.10
UK	– 0.26	– 0.13	– 0.15
Greece	– 9.51	– 9.68	0.32
Switzerland	– 3.31	0.46	– 3.80
Hong Kong, China	– 2.77	0.11	– 2.88

ARROW-DEBREU-MUNDELL-FLEMING MODEL AS STANDARD ECONOMIC MODEL

As an important field of social sciences, economics needs many models for approaching economic phenomena. Microeconomics examines how entities, forming a market structure, interact within a market to create a market system while macroeconomics examines the economy as a whole to explain broad aggregates and their interactions as well as effects of monetary policy and fiscal policy (Samuelson & Nordhaus, 2010).

Since a mathematical description of general equilibrium of economic markets, the Arrow-Debreu model (Arrow & Debreu, 1954) explains microfoundations of economics, while Mundell-Fleming model (Mundell, 1962, 1963; Fleming, 1962) supplies macroeconomic images of goods and finance (Jones & Kenen, 1985; Friedman & Hahn, 2000). The Arrow-Debreu (A-D) model is a mathematical economic model under certain economic assumptions (i.e. convex preferences, perfect competition and demand independence), which suggests that there must be a set of prices to allow aggregate supplies to equal aggregate demands for every commodity in an economic system. The Mundell-Fleming model is described in terms of an IS-LM-BP graph with the domestic interest rate plotted vertically and real GDP plotted horizontally, where the IS curve represents the equilibrium of product market, the LM curve means the equilibrium of money market and BP addresses the balance of payments or international income-payment.

In the IS-LM-BP graph, under less than perfect capital mobility, the positions of both the IS curve and the BP curve depend on the exchange rate, since the IS-LM graph is actually a two-dimensional cross-section of a three-dimensional space involving all of the interest rate, income, and the exchange rate. Under perfect capital mobility the BP curve is simply horizontal at the level of the domestic interest rate equal to that of the world interest rate. In the pure IS-LM model, the domestic interest rate is a key component for keeping both the money market and the goods market in equilibrium. Geometrically, the IS curve is downward sloped and the LM curve is upward sloped, while the BP curve is upward sloped unless there is perfect capital mobility, in which case it is horizontal at the level of the world interest rate. However, differentiated from the pure IS-LM model, the Mundell–Fleming model adds international financial elements, for fitting the open economy assumption.

We know that a modified version of neoclassical synthesis can be obtained by adding the Phillips curve into the IS-LM model, yielding (Scarth, 2014)

$$(y-\bar{y}) = -\psi(\gamma-\bar{\gamma}) \tag{14}$$

$$\dot{p} = \phi(y-\bar{y}) + \dot{x} \tag{15}$$

$$\gamma + \dot{p} = \bar{\gamma} + \dot{x} + \rho(p-x) \tag{16}$$

The first equation is the aggregate demand function, which states that output falls below its full equilibrium value when the real interest rate rises above its full equilibrium value. The second equation is the dynamic aggregate supply function, which states that inflation exceeds the authority's target inflation rate whenever the actual rate of output exceeds the natural rate. The third equation is a reaction function of the central bank, which states that the central bank raises the nominal interest rate above its full equilibrium value whenever the price level exceeds the bank's target value for the price level, x. All slope parameters are positive.

One of the assumptions about the Mundell–Fleming model is that domestic and foreign securities are perfect substitutes. If the world interest rate γ^* was given, the model can predict that the domestic rate would reach the same level as the world rate by arbitrage in money markets.

Under flexible exchange rates, the exchange rate is the third endogenous variable while BP is set at equal to zero. In contrast, under fixed exchange rates, π is exogenous and the surplus of the balance of payments is determined by the model.

Under both types of exchange rate regime, the nominal domestic money supply M is exogenous, but for different reasons. Under flexible exchange rates, the nominal money supply is completely under the control of the central bank. However, under fixed exchange rates, the money supply in the short-run (i.e. at a given point in time) is fixed based on past international money flows, while as the economy evolves over time these international flows cause future points in time to inherit higher or lower (but pre-determined) values of the money supply. Thus, the changes of money supply and the global interest rate would become the most important factors affecting macro-economy, via inflation (λ) and exchange rate (π).

The Mundell–Fleming model under a fixed exchange rate regime also has completely different implications from those of the closed economy IS-LM model. In the closed economy model, if the central bank expands the money supply the LM curve shifts out. As a result, income goes up and the domestic interest rate goes down. But in the Mundell–Fleming open economy model with perfect capital mobility, monetary policy becomes ineffective. An expansionary monetary policy resulting in an incipient outward shift of the LM curve would make capital flow out of the economy. The central bank, under a fixed exchange rate system, would have to instantaneously intervene by selling foreign money in exchange for domestic money to maintain the exchange rate. The accommodated monetary outflows exactly offset the intended rise in the domestic money supply, completely offsetting the tendency of the LM curve to shift to the right, and the interest rate remains equal to the world interest rate.

Under the Mundell–Fleming framework of a small economy facing perfect capital mobility, the domestic interest rate is fixed and equilibrium in both markets can only be maintained by adjustments of the nominal exchange rate or the money supply (i.e., by international funds flows). Results for a large open economy, on the other hand, can be consistent with those predicted by the IS-LM model. The reason being that a large open economy has the characteristics of both an autarky and a small open economy. In particular, it may not face perfect capital mobility, thus allowing internal policy measures to affect the domestic interest rate, and it may be able to sterilize balance-of-payments-induced changes in the money supply. Overall, the complexity of the macro-economic system is mostly caused by money, so that we need to pay more attention to monetary issues in unification of micro-macroeconomics.

Thus, to unify micro-economics and macro-economics, we propose that demand-supply relation, marginal effect and multiplier model construct three key linkages. As aggregate demand (AD) – aggregate supply (AS) can be approached by multiplier model, and marginal effect is also connected to multiplier effect, it is revealed that the micro-Arrow-Debreu model can be combined with the macro-Mundell-Fleming model, which is suggested to become the standard economic model.

The Arrow-Debreu-Mundell-Fleming model is also based on and linked to the Cobb–Douglas model of production and the Solow–Swan model of economic growth, where the Cobb–Douglas model contributed a logarithmic analytical foundation and the Solow–Swan model provided an economic growth mechanism. Meanwhile, Lucas model (Lucas, 1972, 1973), Fischer model (1977) and Taylor model (1979) could be other non-standard models, for the imperfect information and imperfect competition cases.

Therefore, a synthetic model combining interest, exchange and tax rates has been proposed (Ye, 2017), for analyzing integrated economic behaviors, where we consider both scientific epistemological true and philosophical axiological good, with linking microeconomics and macroeconomics via three key linkages. Now, we extend it as grand synthetic model based on philosophical axiology.

PHILOSOPHICAL AXIOLOGY: EFFICIENCY-EQUITY EQUILIBRIUM

Suppose that there are three kinds of economic subjects in society, i.e., nations (governments), enterprises (where the bank is also a special kind of enterprise) and individuals (people). The combined philosophical construction is shown in Figure 3 as an axiological framework.

In Figure 3, the nodes represent subjects and ratios, while the links denote relations with axiological views, where individuals work toward happiness, nations act toward powerfulness and enterprises want profit to supporting the nation and individuals (marked by S). In the economic system, both banks and enterprises need efficiency, and the nation or society needs equity, while individual behaviors are affected by national policies and goods-money supply as well as all ratios based on money. It is expected that the framework will work toward the axiological good.

Figure 3. An axiological framework supported by tax, interest and exchange rates

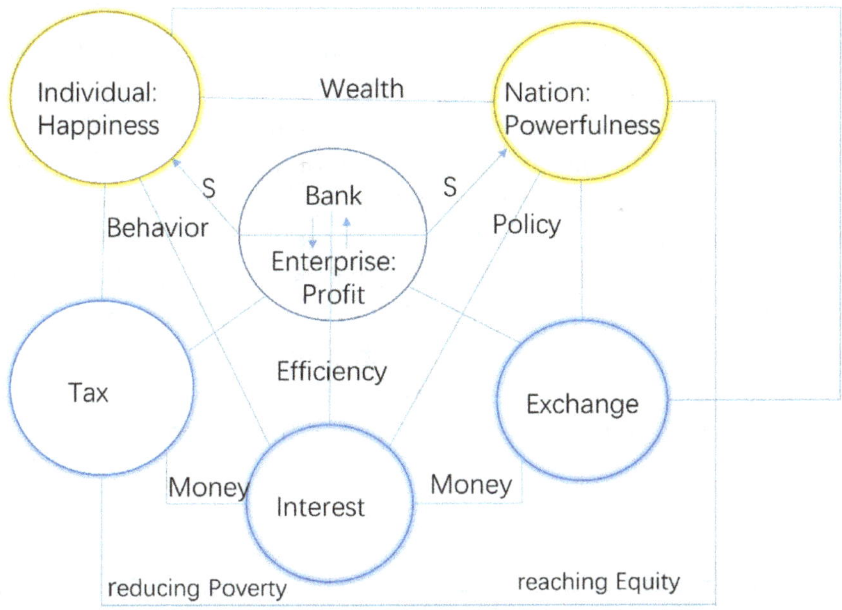

SCIENTIFIC EPISTEMOLOGY: GRAND SYNTHETIC MODEL

In our economic analytics, we use Latin letters to express variables, Greek letters denote rates and slope parameters. While all variables with bar mean average values, all variables with * stand for full-equilibrium values. The capital Latin letters are used to represent absolute quantities, such as Y, C, G, P, K, H, N representing output, consumption, government purchase, price, capital, human capital (labor force), and total population, respectively; lower case Latin letters indicate relative quantities or pair quantities, such as y, c, g, p, and k, respectively, correspond to relative quantities corresponding to Y, C, G, P, K; lower case Greek letters represent relative rates or parameters, such as γ, τ, π, λ standing for interest rate, tax rate, exchange rate, and inflation rate, respectively.

According to the basic macroeconomic relations, we know the total output Y as

$$Y = C + I + G = C + S + T \tag{17}$$

As all quantities are positive, we have

$$Y \geq C \tag{18}$$

When I = S = sY, where s = S/Y denotes savings or investment rate, it is obvious that Y ≥ C, as shown by Equation (18).

In an economic system, production and consumption are always basic economic activities, so that production function and consumption function become important basic economic functions.

The most famous production function is the Cobb-Douglas production function, which was based on the empirical study of the American manufacturing industry by Cobb and Douglas. It is a linear homogeneous production function of degree, one which takes into account two inputs, capital and labor (human capital), for the entire output of the manufacturing industry. A Cobb–Douglas function shows the form when β = 1

$$Y = K^{\alpha}H^{1-\alpha} \tag{19}$$

where K and H are money capital and human capital (effective labor), respectively. The Greek letter α is a capital parameter (capital's exponent of production function), 0 <α < 1. From the view of consumption, we have a similar form

$$Y = C = K^{\theta}N^{1-\theta} \tag{20}$$

where N > H is consumptive population and θ is capital's exponent of consumption function.

According to Equation (24), we take its logarithmic form

$$y = f(k,h) = \alpha \mathrm{k} + (1 - \alpha)h \tag{21}$$

There is an equivalent analysis for human capital H or labor wage w = W/H. We will have

$$y = \gamma \mathrm{k} + w \tag{22}$$

By defining capital's ratio of output as r = γk/y, we derive

$$\dot{y} / y = r(\dot{\gamma} / \gamma + \dot{k} / k) + (1 - r)(\dot{w} / w) \tag{23}$$

Meanwhile, according to the Fischer exchange equation MV = PY, in which M stands for money, P denotes price, V is circulation velocity of money. Its logarithmic form is a concise function of two-variables when we set unit velocity V = 1

$$m = m(p,y) = p + y \tag{24}$$

On the other hand, the Solow-Swan growth model provides a pattern of economic growth, where y = Y/N = f(k). There is y/k = (n + d)/s in full equilibrium, in which d is the capital's depreciation rate. When I = S, s is also investment ratio, yielding a single differential equation

$$\dot{k} = sf(k) - (n+d)k;\ d = I / K - \dot{K} / K \tag{25}$$

Now the production function is graphed as the f(k) curve, sf(k) denotes the nation's savings function, and the required investment per-capita line is (n + d)k. The dynamic process to stability or the convergence to equilibrium requires $sf'(k) - (n+d) < 0$.

When we take the full equilibrium, y/k = (n + d)/s indicates

$$k = (s/(n + d))^{1/(1-\alpha)} \tag{26}$$

so that the k is determined by s, n and d. The speed of adjustment measure is coefficient (n + d)(1–α). When numerical estimation suggests plausible values as n = 0.02, d = 0.04 and α = 0.33, the speed coefficient is 0.04.

The grand synthetic model begins with the combination of the Cobb-Douglas model and the Solow-Swan growth model, based on the Arrow-Debreu-Mundell-Fleming model as a standard economic model (Ye, 2015), where IS-LM contributed its core structure.

Obviously, if, and only if, there exists a linking parameter b, Equation (6) can be an equation. This is just a key for linking the Solow-Swan model with the Cobb-Douglas model.

If we set the factors α and θ

$$\alpha = \dot{Y} / N;\ \theta = \dot{C} / N \tag{27}$$

we can derive

$$Y = b\int e^{\alpha} dt; \ C = b\int e^{\theta} dt \tag{28}$$

Since N > H, α > θ will benefit Y > C. At the same time, α > θ also means that capital has a greater effect on production than on consumption.

As we suggest setting the Arrow-Debreu-Mundell-Fleming model as the standard economic model (Ye, 2015), the economic structure of product market equilibrium and money market equilibrium is characterized by the IS-LM model, as the core of the Arrow-Debreu-Mundell-Fleming model. For a given interest rate γ, there are

The IS curve:

$$y = f(k,h) = -\alpha\gamma + \beta g \tag{29}$$

The LM curve:

$$m = L(y,\gamma) = p + \beta y - \delta y \tag{30}$$

The IS and LM relationships can be combined to yield the aggregate demand function by eliminating the interest rate, for both Y = KαH(^{1}-$^{\alpha)}$ ^{an}d Y = C = KθN(^{1}-$^{\theta)}$

$$^{y} = \alpha k + (1 - \alpha)h = \theta(m - p) + (1 - \theta)g \tag{31}$$

where the consumption parameter θ links with production parameter α by

$$\theta = \alpha(\alpha\beta + \delta) \tag{32}$$

When production and consumption reached an equilibrium, the money capital and human capital can be combined as K (its logarithmic form as k).

When we process full-equilibrium optimization, we set definitions

$$k=K/N; \ c=C/K; \ g=G/Y \tag{33}$$

$$\dot{p}/p = \gamma; \ \dot{c}/c = \tau; \ \dot{m}/m = \lambda \tag{34}$$

Thus, the grand synthetic model can be defined by IS-LM core plus first order derivative equation of four key variables, with balanced rates at ideal states

$$Y=be^{y}=be^{Y/N};\ K=be^{k}=be^{K/N} \tag{35.1}$$

$$y=\alpha k+(1-\alpha)h;\ \dot{y}=\theta(\dot{m}-\dot{p})+(1-\theta)\dot{g} \tag{35.2}$$

$$\dot{m}=\lambda m;\ \dot{p}=\gamma p;\ m=p+y \tag{35.3}$$

$$\dot{k}=sf(k)-(n+d)k;\ f'(k)=\gamma+\delta \tag{35.4}$$

$$\gamma-\bar{\gamma}=\dot{\pi}-\dot{p};\ \gamma(1-\tau)-\rho=n=\dot{Y}/Y=\dot{K}/K \tag{35.5}$$

In the grand synthetic model, there are four key variables (y, m, p, k) and three key policy rates (γ, τ, π), and there are three economic parameters (b, s, d). In total, there are 10 equations for the 10 variables (y, m, p, k; γ, τ, π; b, s, d), except the link m = p + y. Only three model parameters (α, θ, ρ) are free variables. The b, s and d = δ, respectively, stand for big parameter, small parameter and micro-parameter, with estimated values at b~10^3, s~10^{-1} and d~10^{-2}. Since Y = C + I + G, Y > C, so that $\alpha > \theta$. The model parameters can be estimated as $\theta < \alpha$ » 0.3 ~ 0.6. The inflation rate $\lambda = \gamma - \gamma^*$, and ρ ~ 0.01 > 0 is time preference.

In Equations (35), the first two Equations (35-1) describe the relations of macroeconomic measures with logarithmic and per-capita forms, which came from Equation (6). The Equations (35-2) and (35-3) link four key variables y, m, p, and k via their variable relations and the first order differential equations, which combined Equations (11), (22), (24), and (34). The Equations (35-4) are the first order differential equations of capital k, which originated from Equation (25). The Equations (35-5) set up the relations of all rates, which linked with Equations (9) and (10). As there are various taxes, we set (capital or wage) income tax rate τ for general analysis. In the cases of special differentiation, we also differentiate consumption tax rate $\boldsymbol{\tau}_c$ from production tax rate $\boldsymbol{\tau}_p$.

In a national economy for new neoclassical synthesis, the main equations combining new IS function and Phillips curve take the following forms when $\dot{m}=\gamma$, $\dot{p}=\bar{\gamma}$ and $\theta=\alpha$

$$\dot{y} = \alpha(\bar{\gamma} - \gamma) + (1 - \alpha)\dot{g} \tag{36.1}$$

$$\dot{p} = \phi(y - \bar{y}) + \dot{x} \tag{36.2}$$

$$\gamma - \bar{\gamma} = \dot{x} - \dot{p} + \rho(p - x) \tag{36.3}$$

where g is autonomous spending (government spending), x is the bank's target value for the price level and slope parameter $\phi > 0$. We may also define x as x = C/K in growth analysis, so there is $\dot{x}/x = \dot{C}/C - \dot{K}/K$.

In open economy or semi-open economy, the grand synthetic model within the Mundell-Fleming model may include exchange rate π, characterized by the following equations with the Phillips curve (Scarth, 2014), when $\alpha \rightarrow \beta \sim 1$

$$\dot{y} = \beta(\gamma - \bar{\gamma}) + \theta(\pi - p) \tag{37.1}$$

$$\dot{p} = \phi(y - \bar{y}) \tag{37.2}$$

$$\gamma - \bar{\gamma} = \dot{\pi} - \dot{p} \tag{37.3}$$

Involving Equations (35), the grand synthetic model just combines the Arrow-Debreu model and Mundell-Fleming model, by linking Cobb-Douglas model and Solow-Swan model together.

In the new synthetic model (Ye, 2017a), the main equations replaced by the Laffer curve may become

$$\dot{y} = \beta(\gamma - \bar{\gamma}) + \theta(\pi - p) \tag{38.1}$$

$$(\tau - \tau\mathrm{m})_2 = \phi(\mathrm{ym} - y) \tag{38.2}$$

$$\gamma - \bar{\gamma} = \dot{\pi} - \dot{p} \tag{38.3}$$

The new synthetic model can be also characterized by macroeconomic variables Y and P as well as three rates (interest, exchange and tax rates). By combining money demand-supply model linking Y and P to M, it integrated into a geometric framework as shown in Figure 4 using the Laffer curve.

The above synthetic model includes the following three parts: the first part is the Mundell–Fleming model, characterized by IS-LM-BP curves, described by the domestic interest rate plotted vertically and real GDP

(Y) plotted horizontally, where the IS curve represents the equilibrium of product market, the LM curve means the equilibrium of the money market, and BP addresses the balance of payments or international income-payment. Geometrically, the IS curve is downward sloping and the LM curve is upward sloping, while the BP curve is upward sloping unless there is perfect capital mobility, in which it is horizontal at the level of the world interest rate. In the IS-LM-BP graph, under less than perfect capital mobility, the positions of both the IS curve and the BP curve depend on the exchange rate, since the IS-LM graph is actually a two-dimensional cross-section of a three-dimensional space involving all of the interest rate, income, and exchange rate. Under perfect capital mobility, the BP curve is simply horizontal when the level of the domestic interest rate is equal to the world interest rate level. In the pure IS-LM model, the domestic interest rate is a key component for keeping both the money market and the commodity market in equilibrium. However, unlike the pure IS-LM model, the Mundell-Fleming model adds the international financial elements to fit to the open economy assumption.

Figure 4. A geometric framework of new synthetic model

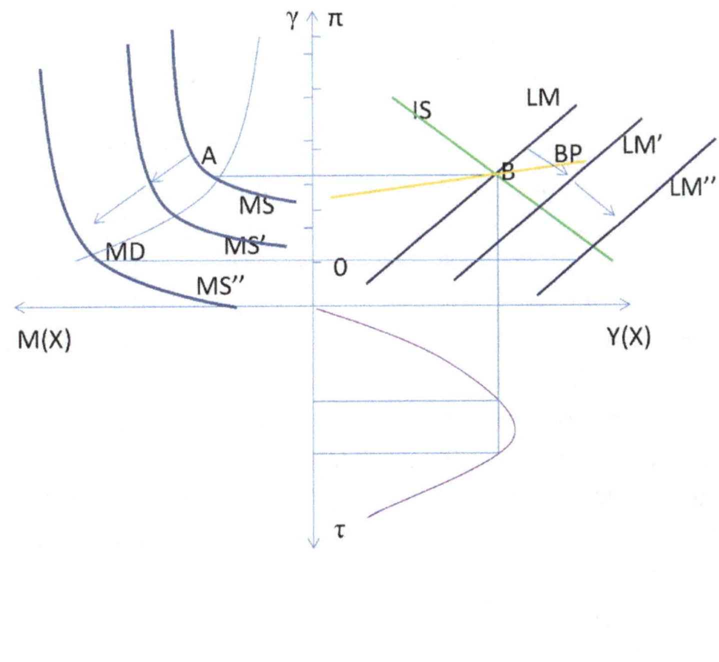

The second part is the money demand and supply curve, where the demand curve of money illustrates the quantity of money demanded at a given interest rate. Generally, the demand curve of money is downward sloping, which means that people want to hold less of their wealth in the form of money when interest rates on bonds and other alternative investments are higher. The supply curve of money illustrates the quantity of money supplied at a given interest rate. Unlike a typical supply curve in the commodity market, the supply curve of money could be vertical, because it might not depend on interest rates. In fact, it depends entirely on decisions made by the central bank, as the central bank controls the supply of money. However, the market mechanism could also introduce the demand-supply interaction into the money market to illustrate the money demand and supply using normal demand-supply curves. Equilibrium in the money market takes place when the quantity of money demanded is equal to the quantity supplied. Since there are complex relationships between interest and exchange rates (Sánchez, 2005; Floyd, 2010), to simplify the issues being discussed, it is designated that real exchange rate and nominal interest rate are linked by $\gamma \rightarrow \pi^*$, characterized by national money vs. foreign money. In other words, interest and exchange rates keep changes in the same direction.

The third part is the Laffer curve, which is one possible representation of the relationship between rates of taxation and the hypothetical resulting levels of government revenue. Because the government revenue is proportional to GDP, I translate the Laffer curve into the coordinate system with the tax rate plotted down-vertically and real GDP (Y) plotted horizontally here. Following claims to illustrate the concept of taxable income elasticity, taxable income will change in response to changes in the rate of taxation.

Thus, the grand synthetic model integrates interest, exchange and tax rates, where interest and exchange are plotted up-vertically with different calibration in the same direction, while tax rate is plotted down-vertically. The Mundell–Fleming model (IS-LM-BP curves) is set in the first quadrant; the money demand-supply model occupies the second quadrant; and the Laffer curve is arranged in the fourth quadrant. It is valuable to emphasize that interest rate can be changed by artificial operations by the bank in a discontinuous way, while the exchange rate randomly changes following market, and tax rate is rigidly determined by laws, mostly.

By combining Figures 3 and 4, the good policies can keep balance between demand and supply, consumption and production, rich and poor, as well as the true and the good. At a national level, reducing tax is the best policy for raising social welfare, and increasing tax is also the best policy for balancing rich and poor. At an individual level, stable consumption and tax payment are the best behaviors. At an enterprise level, interest or profit increase is the best strategy during economic growth and inversely interest or profit decrease is the best strategy during economic decline. At all levels, epistemological true and axiological good are combined, for balancing economic efficiency and social equity.

When considering acceleration development, we can hold hybrid IS curve and inflation acceleration in Phillips curve as

$$\ddot{y} = \alpha(\gamma - \bar{\gamma}) + (1-\alpha)\ddot{g} \quad (39.1)$$

$$\ddot{p} = \phi(y - \bar{y}) \quad (39.2)$$

The relations of capital k and consumption c can be analyzed by phase diagram, where both monetary policy and fiscal policy are implemented by two sets of tools.

A R^2–type analytical model is shows in Figure 5.

Figure 5. A R^2–type analytical model on c and k

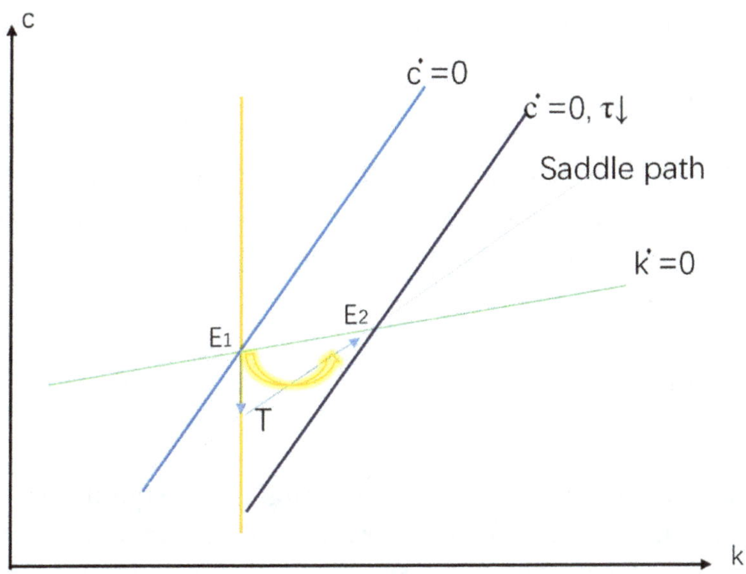

On monetary policy, central banks implement the policy by controlling the money supply through several mechanisms. Typically, central banks take action by issuing money to buy bonds (or other assets), which boosts the supply of money and lowers interest rates, called expansionary money policy; or in the case of contractionary monetary policy, banks sell bonds and take money out of circulation. Also, banks can continuously shift the money supply to maintain a fixed interest rate target. Some banks allow the interest rate to fluctuate and focus on targeting inflation rates instead. Central banks generally try to achieve high output without letting loose monetary policy to create large amounts of inflation.

On the other hand, fiscal policy is the use of government revenue and expenditure as instruments to influence the economy, including tools such as expenditure, taxes, and debt. However, the effects of fiscal policy may be limited by crowding out. When government adopts spending projects, it limits the amount of resources available for private sectors to use. Crowding out occurs when government spending simply replaces private sectors' output instead of adding additional output to the economy. Crowding out also occurs when government spending raises interest rates by restricting investment. Defenders of fiscal stimulus argue that crowding out is not a concern when the economy is depressed, plenty of resources are left idle, and interest rates are low.

The economic stability condition is

$$n > \gamma^* = \gamma - \lambda \tag{40}$$

in which γ^* is the real interest rate while γ is the nominal interest rate.

When a steady-state economy is characterized by the inflation rate λ, there is a linear relation $\gamma^* = \gamma - \lambda$. If the elasticity of expectations σ is less than unity, there is

$$\frac{d\gamma}{d\pi} = \sigma - 1 < 0 \tag{41}$$

Let K* denote the optimal holding of capital in full equilibrium. In a no-growth setting, investment in full equilibrium is just for replacement purposes, there is $I = \delta K^*$, where $\delta = d$ is just capital's depreciation rate. Since the accumulation identity for capital is

$$I = \dot{K} + \delta K \tag{42}$$

we will obtain the following result

$$\dot{K} = \delta(K^* - K) \tag{43}$$

Recall definitions k = K/N, c = C/K and g = G/Y, while defining the wage rate w = W/H, the employed capital will be wH and then we will have the following equations

$$\dot{K} = \gamma K + w - C \tag{44.1}$$

$$\dot{H} = (\gamma + p)H - w \tag{44.2}$$

According to the Sidrauski model, there is a concise equilibrium equation in competitive markets (Orphanides & Solow, 1990)

$$w = f(k) - kf'(k); f'(k) = \gamma \tag{45}$$

Meanwhile, according to the aggregate demand function combined by the IS and LM relationships, when n is a constant, taking its time derivative, yielding

$$\dot{y} = \theta(\dot{m} - \dot{p}) \tag{46}$$

When $\dot{m} = \gamma p$, $\dot{p} = \bar{\gamma} p$, and $\beta = \theta p$, the equation becomes

$$\dot{y} = \beta(\gamma - \bar{\gamma}) \tag{47}$$

Combining Equations (38), (46) and (47), the full equilibrium of international economy is determined by exchange rate and price level

$$\beta(\gamma - \bar{\gamma}) = \beta(\dot{\pi} - \dot{p}) + \theta(\pi - p) = \theta(\dot{m} - \dot{p}) \tag{48.1}$$

$$(\gamma - \bar{\gamma}) = (\dot{\pi} - \dot{p}) + (\pi / p - 1) \tag{48.2}$$

The first order differential equations of y and p can be set as

$$\dot{p} = \phi(y - \overline{y}) + \dot{x} \tag{49.1}$$

$$\dot{y} = \rho(p - x) - \phi(y - \overline{y}) \tag{49.2}$$

The solution form of Equation (49) will be

$$p_t = x + c_1 e^{r_1 t} + c_2 e^{r_2 t} \tag{50.1}$$

$$y_t = \overline{y} + c_3 e^{r_3 t} + c_4 e^{r_4 t} \tag{50.2}$$

in which r_j are the characteristic roots and c_j are the initial constants (j = 1, 2, 3, 4).

Therefore, mostly, economists could study the macroeconomics via interest rate and exchange rate (Friedman & Hahn, 2000; Tobin, 1969; Floyd, 2010), also considered the welfare economy and wealth redistribution concerning efficiency and equity (Feldman & Serrano, 2005; Nicola, 2013). Actually, from both macroeconomic and microeconomic views (Arrow & Debreu, 1954; Samuelson & Nordhaus, 2010), taxation is also a key element in the economic system as an interdisciplinary issue (Lamb et al., 2005), though there was lack of a unified analytical model to probe into integrated interest, exchange and tax rates.

Conclusively, while the Arrow-Debreu model describes general micro-economic equilibrium, the Mundell-Fleming model expresses general macro-economic one. There are three keys linking the A-D model and the M-F model: (1) demand-supply relation, which penetrates micro- and macro-economy with similar pattern; (2) marginal effect, which reveals the same principles in micro- and macro-economy and constructs expenditure multiplier or investment multiplier; and (3) multiplier model, which approaches AD-AS. As aggregate demand (AD) – aggregate supply (AS) is approached by multiplier model and linkage of expenditure multiplier or investment multiplier to marginal effects, it is revealed that micro-Arrow-Debreu model can be combined with macro-Mundell-Fleming model. Indeed, a macro-economic model is much more complicated than micro-economic one, because there are complex money interactions, as well as global interest rates and exchange rates. Fortunately, demand-supply relation, marginal effect and multiplier model become key bridges across them. Thus, we can understand unified micro-macro-economics. Analytically, Equations (35), (36), (37), (38) and (39), as well as Figure 5, can process suitable economic applications.

POLICY ANALYSIS OF ECONOMIC EFFICIENCY AND SOCIAL EQUITY

In policy analysis, traditionally, macroeconomic policy is implemented through two sets of tools: monetary policy and fiscal policy. As we mentioned, economists usually favor monetary over fiscal policy because it has two major advantages. First, monetary policy is generally implemented by independent central banks instead of the political institutions that control fiscal policy, where independent central banks are less likely to make decisions based on political motives. Second, monetary policy suffers shorter inside lags and outside lags than fiscal policy, as central banks can quickly make and implement decisions while discretionary fiscal policy may take time to pass and even longer to carry out.

As the effects of fiscal policy may be limited by crowding out, it limits the number of resources available for the private sector to use when government takes on spending projects. Crowding out occurs when government spending simply replaces private sector output instead of adding additional output to the economy. Crowding out also occurs when government spending raises interest rates with restricting investment. Defenders of fiscal stimulus argue that crowding out is not a concern when the economy is depressed, plenty of resources are left idle, and interest rates are low.

Fiscal policy is also implemented through automatic stabilizers. Without suffering from the policy lags of discretionary fiscal policy, automatic stabilizers use conventional fiscal mechanisms but take effect as soon as the economy takes a downturn: spending on unemployment benefits automatically increases when unemployment rises and, in a progressive income tax system, the effective tax rate automatically falls when incomes decline.

Therefore, while the fiscal policy shifts the IS curve, the monetary policy will do the LM curve. The fiscal policy keeps importance if money demand is insensitive to interest rates (vertical LM) or if investment or saving or both are perfectly interest-elastic (flat IS). The monetary policy keeps importance in the liquidity trap (flat LM) or in the event that both investment and saving are insensitive to interest rates (vertical IS). All other cases set in between, where IS involves the real interest rates and LM does the nominal interest rates. The analysis can be extended to derive aggregate demand (AD) function and aggregate supply (AS) function, allowing for the effects of prices on real supplies of money and wealth.

Policy Analysis Toward Economic Efficiency via Interest Rate

The economic effects of monetary or fiscal policy could be restricted, as the changes of three ratios will affect one another. Integrating the analytical framework of interest, exchange and tax rates in the above synthetic model, the situation is clear as a case of raising interest rate with market exchange rate changing as shown in Figure 6.

Figure 6. Policy analysis in the case of changing interest rate with implying exchange rate change

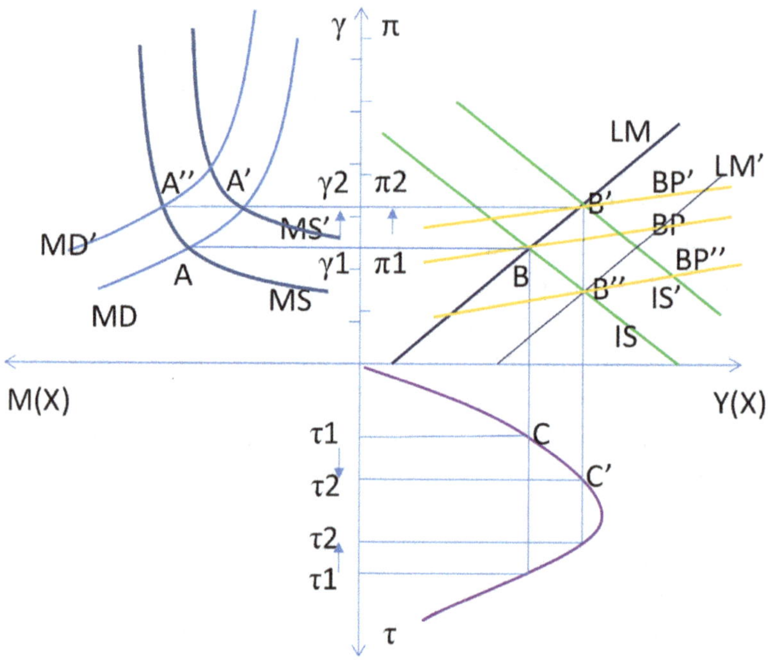

The policy of raising the interest rate could cause feedback chain: $\gamma \rightarrow MS^{-} \rightarrow Y$, which is equivalent to tax cuts as $\gamma \rightarrow \tau^{-}$, as it is the same as $\tau^{-} \rightarrow \gamma \rightarrow MS^{-}$, which means that the policy effect of raising the interest rate is equivalent to that of a tax cut, or, the policy effect of tax cuts is equivalent to raising the interest rate, leading to less money supply. Inversely, increasing money supply is equivalent to lowering the interest rate or lifting tax, i.e. $MS \rightarrow \gamma^{-} \rightarrow \tau$. However, once money supply increases, inflation could occur, resulting in offsetting the policy effect. Thus, policy tools are limited by the correlated links as various rates affect each other, leading to restricted economic effects.

Since the exchange rate relates to interest rate, according to Equation (7), the change of interest rate implies the change of exchange rate at the same time. Therefore, the modification of exchange rate resembles relative effects of interest rate, especially if the exchange and interest rates change in the same direction ($\pi \rightarrow \gamma, \pi^{-} \rightarrow \gamma^{-}$), the effects of changing exchange rate will be similar to the effects of changing interest rate. However, if the exchange and interest rates change in different directions ($\pi \rightarrow \gamma^{-}, \pi^{-} \rightarrow \gamma$), complex situations will occur. The exchange rate is also a relatively independent variable, and it affects and is affected by international economy. When we need to simulate national local market, we can raise the exchange rate. Otherwise, when we need to promote international global trade, we may lower the exchange rate.

Policy Analysis Toward Social Equity via Taxation

Generally, tax is dominated by government, which is rigidly restricted by laws. For social equity, it is better to set a higher tax rate for rich people and a lower tax rate to protect the poor. The interest rate can be changed by the central bank, referring to economic level and situation, and the exchange rate seems randomly changeable following international money market, though some nations could also impact on its changes.

Politically, tax, interest, and exchange rates serve as national objects, so that a national government cannot abandon the domination of tax rate, interest rate, and exchange rate. In a national view, interest rate focuses on money efficiency, which could optimize the money market and liquidity. The exchange rate also expresses national finance policy, which could regulate international trade and is determined by the international financial market. The tax rate marks national policy for the redistribution of social wealth, which pursues social equity.

Using the above synthetic model, integrating interest, exchange and tax rates, when economy overheats or expands ($Y\uparrow\uparrow$), a countermeasure in policy analysis for the tax reduction and the tax increase is shown in Figure 7.

The policy of Figure 7 implies that the tax reduction would be good if the tax rate is lower than normal ($\tau < \tau 0$) and the tax increase should be good if the tax rate is higher than normal ($\tau > \tau 0$), during the period of economic overheat or expansion ($Y\uparrow\uparrow$), which would benefit the following items.

Figure 7. A policy analysis for the tax reduction and the tax increase during economic overheat

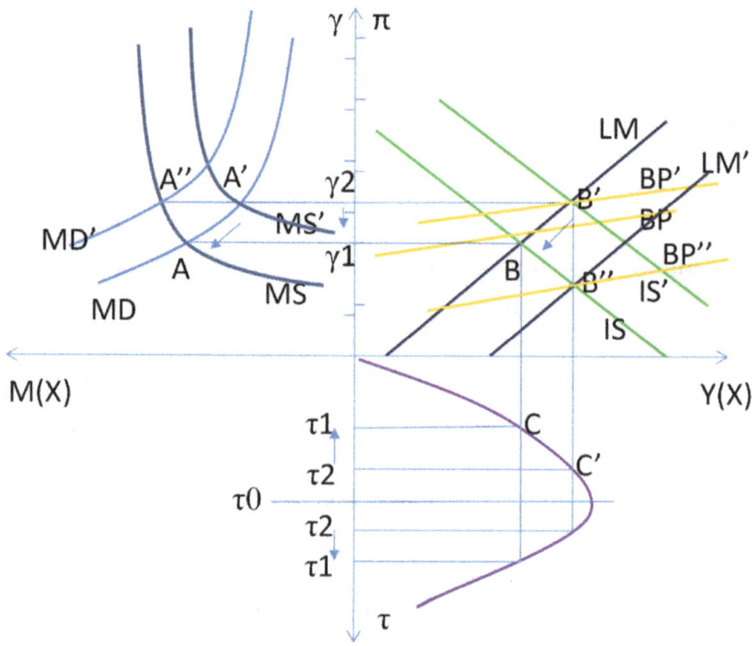

(1) At a national level, decreasing official corruption (Y↑↑ caused B <--> B', policy τ2 <--> τ1 would lead to IS' <--> IS, or via LM' <--> LM and B'' <--> B for reaching optimal equilibrium A-B-C).
(2) At an enterprise level, increasing R&D input (Y↑↑ caused A <--> A', policy τ2 <--> τ1 would lead to MS'<-->MS, or via MD' <-->MD and A''<-->A for reaching optimal equilibrium A-B-C).
(3) At an individual level, stimulating consumption and charitable donation (Policy τ2 <--> τ1 would lead to MS'<-->MS or MD'<-->MD for reaching optimal equilibrium A-B-C).

On the other hand, when economy depresses or contracts (Y↓↓), a countermeasure in policy analysis for the tax reduction and the tax increase is shown in Figure 8.

The policy of Figure 8 implies that the tax reduction would be good if tax rate is higher than normal ($\tau > \tau 0$) and tax increase should be good if tax rate is lower than normal ($\tau < \tau 0$), during the period of economic depression or contraction (Y↓↓), which would benefit the following items.

Figure 8. A policy analysis for the tax reduction and the tax increase during economic depression

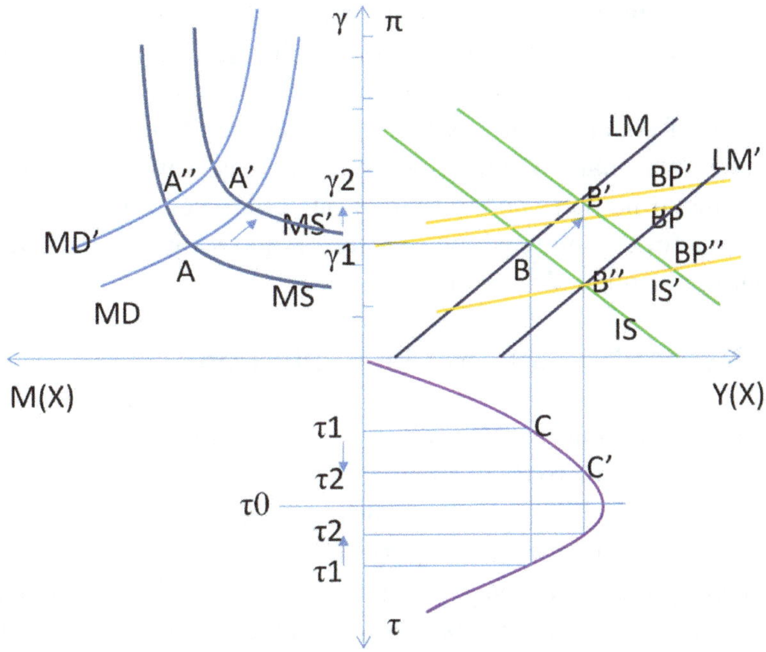

1. At a national level, balancing the rich and the poor ($Y\downarrow\downarrow$ caused B' <--> B, and then policy $\tau 1$ <--> $\tau 2$ would lead to IS <--> IS', or via LM <--> LM' and B'' <--> B' for reaching optimal equilibrium A'-B'-C').
2. At an enterprise level, decreasing bank loan ($Y\downarrow\downarrow$ caused A' <--> A, and then policy $\tau 1$ <--> $\tau 2$ would lead to MS<-->MS', or via MD <-->MD' and A''<-->A' for reaching optimal equilibrium A'-B'-C').
3. At an individual level, reducing consumption, without luxury (Policy $\tau 1$ <--> $\tau 2$ would lead to MS<-->MS' or MD<-->MD' for reaching optimal equilibrium A'-B'-C').

In both Figures 7 and 8, the normal point of tax rate ($\tau 0$) can be defined as a legal point in tax laws or expected theoretical point.

Certainly, the tax policy resembles complicated, more than monetary policy, where the interest ratio is an effective tool for regulating the economy by raising or reducing interest rates. However, the tax rate would be rigid during a certain period by law, though the tax policy might be a useful tool for balancing social wealth, particularly combining efficiency and equity. A good tax policy could reach axiological good. In consideration of political economics, the tax reduction on enterprises could benefit all enterprises, while the tax increase on the rich could benefit the poor.

Overall, the tax rate, interest rate, and exchange rate represent different views of political economics. The tax rate marks national policy for the redistribution of social wealth, which expresses social equity. The interest rate describes national monetary policy, which is a way to optimize the national financial market. The exchange rate characterizes the interactions of international economies, which is determined by international trade and the international financial market.

Wealth Distribution and Model Limitation

There are two economic issues concerned with economic analysis toward the social good: 1) how to distribute social wealth between rich agents and poor ones, as well as nations and enterprises; and 2) how to maintain social justice combining efficiency and equity.

In any society, there are always rich and poor people. Governments get tax revenues to support public affairs and to regulate the rich-poor difference, in order to realize social equity via wealth redistribution. Both social and personal surplus money would cumulatively transfer to capital, and the capital demands effective reciprocation via interest or investment. More issues on the capital and wealth distribution have been discussed by Piketty's analysis (Piketty, 2014).

Taxation is not only a technical matter, but also preeminently a political and philosophical issue, perhaps the most important political economic issue. Without taxes, society has no common destiny, and collective action is impossible. It is certainly correct that progressive taxation plays a key role in wealth redistribution. A progressive tax is a crucial component for social equity, which plays a central role in its development and in the transformation of the structure of inequity in the world and remains important for ensuring the viability of social equity in the future.

Generally, tax, which is dominated by government and rigidly restricted by laws, is the key element to answer these questions. For social equity, it is better to set a high tax rate for charging rich agents and a low tax rate to protect poor ones. In a country with taxation ~1 billion dollars, if tax rates change by 1%, more than one million dollars taxation will be charged. Given that consumption and investment expenditure together account for a large percentage (about 80%) of GNP in major nations (Abel, 2000), taxation is a political economic consideration for approaching the axiological good to adjust rich and poor via tax. If we consider more factors, including wages, inflation, employment, welfare and so on (Phelps, 1967; Lucas & Rapping, 1970), we will meet a very complicated economic system, in which taxation remains an important factor.

Also, the tax rate may be affected by the interest rate. In Figures 7 and 8, all policies of tax regulation are equivalent to reducing interest ($\gamma 2$ <--> $\gamma 1$) when economy overheats or expands ($Y\uparrow\uparrow$), and all policies of tax regulations are equivalent to increasing interest ($\gamma 1$<--> $\gamma 2$) when economy depresses or contracts ($Y\downarrow\downarrow$). Therefore, it is better to keep reducing interest during economy expansion and keep increasing interest during economy depression.

The above analysis gives a trustable reference. The economic analytical methods focus on geometric analysis, yielding tendency estimation, rather than complete exact computation. Certainly, there are some limitations in the model analysis, such as restrictive conditions (Tobin, 1980), including (1) the agents are either immortal or, if finitely lived, linked by an unbroken infinite dynastic chain of intergenerational gifts and bequests; (2) the capital markets are perfect, without liquidity constraints or credit rationing; (3) all the taxes, transfers and subsidies are lump sum; (4) the debt servicing by issuing more debt forever is infeasible, and future tax increases, equal in present value to today's tax cuts, are required. The analysis keeps hypotheses in new classical macroeconomics, which assumes continuous market-clearing and rational expectations and explains business fluctuations as optimal intertemporal substitutions in production and consumption.

CONCLUSION

Interest, exchange and tax rates are three important control factors in both macroeconomic and microeconomic systems in which interest, exchange and tax rates interact with each other. Tax expresses the economic policy of governance, which reflects social equity. The interest rate is a key parameter for regulating money supply, which determines the national finance while reflecting economic efficiency. Exchange rate is a vital factor for international business, which determines the international economy.

We know that the tax rate had long-term stability regulated by laws, while interest rates had short-term stability controlled by banks and the exchange rate changed randomly following market changes. As the tax rate regulates wealth redistribution for approaching social equity, interest policy represents national finance policy for optimizing economic efficiency, and exchange rate describes the international economic policy for realizing national benefits. The three ratios possess a key role in regulating national demands. We should pay more attention to modifying the three ratios under the synthesized framework for balancing economic efficiency and social equity.

As per the results, it is suggested to utilize modified strategies via exchange and tax rates besides normal monetary and fiscal policies, mainly via interest and tax rates. When a government needs to simulate national local market, it can raise the exchange rate. Otherwise, when a government needs to promote international global trade, one may lower the exchange rate. Meantime, it is found that tax reduction is a social policy when the tax rate is lower than normal, and that tax increase is a good social policy when tax rate is higher than normal, during economic overheat. Also, tax reduction is a social policy when tax rate is higher than normal, and tax increase is a good social policy when tax rate is lower than normal, during economic depression. While the economic system seeks efficiency and the social system pursues equity, common interest modifications with elastic exchange and tax rates can be applied to balance efficiency and equity, which will benefit economic social development toward epistemological true with axiological good (Ye, 2020).

In most models, the total quantities can be divided as individual quantities, via logarithm or microdivision to link microproducers and consumers with macro nations and international groups. The grand synthetic model may promote further studies.

REFERENCES

Arrow, K. (1963). *Social Choice and Individual Values* (2nd ed.). Yale University Press.

Arrow, K., & Debreu, G. (1954). Existence of an equilibrium for a competitive economy. *Econometrica*, *22*(3), 265–290. doi:10.2307/1907353

Atkinson, A., Piketty, T., & Saez, E. (2011). Top incomes in the long run of history. *Journal of Economic Literature*, *49*(1), 3–71. doi:10.1257/jel.49.1.3

Blanchard, O. J., & Gali, J. (2010). Labor markets and monetary policy: A new Keynesian model with unemployment. *American Economic Journal. Macroeconomics*, *2*(2), 1–30. doi:10.1257/mac.2.2.1

Coase, R. H. (1960). The problem of social cost. *The Journal of Law & Economics*, *3*, 1–44. doi:10.1086/466560

Davis, J. (2003). *The Theory of the Individual in Economics*. Routledge. doi:10.4324/9780203457689

Dollar, D., Kleineberg, T., & Kraay, A. (2014). *Growth, inequity and social welfare: cross country evidence.* World Bank Policy Research Department Working Paper No. 6842.

Dollar, D., & Kraay, A. (2002). Growth is good for the poor. *Journal of Economic Growth*, *7*(3), 195–225. doi:10.1023/A:1020139631000

Dornbusch, R. (1976). Exchange rate expectations and monetary policy. *Journal of International Economics*, *6*, 231–244. doi:10.1016/0022-1996(76)90001-5

Faccarello, G., & Kurz, H. D. (2016). Handbook on the History of Economic Analysis. Vol. I: Great Economists since Petty and Boisguilbert; Vol. II: Schools of Thought in Economics. Edward Elgar.

Feldman, A. M., & Serrano, R. (2005). *Welfare Economics and Social Choice Theory* (2nd ed.). Springer Science & Business Media, Inc.

Feldstein, M. S. (1976). Inflation, income taxes, and the rate of interest – a theoretical analysis. *The American Economic Review*, *66*, 806–820.

Fischer, S. (1977). Long-term contracts, rational expectations, and the optimal money supply rule. *Journal of Political Economy*, *85*(1), 191–205. doi:10.1086/260551

Fischer, S. (1983). A framework for monetary and banking analysis. *Economic Journal*, *93*, 1-16.

Fleming, J. M. (1962). Domestic monetary policies under fixed and floating exchange rates. IMF Staff Papers, 9, 369–379.

Floyd, J. E. (2010). *Interest Rates, Exchange Rates and World Monetary Policy*. Springer. doi:10.1007/978-3-642-10280-6

Forni, M., & Lippi, M. (1997). *Aggregation and the Microfoundations of Dynamic Macroecomics*. Oxford University Press.

Friedman, B. M., & Hahn, F. H. (Eds.). (2000). *Handbook of Monetary Economics* (Vol. 1-2). Elsevier.

Friedman, M. (1948). A monetary and fiscal framework for economic stability. *The American Economic Review*, *38*(3), 245–264.

Friedman, M. (1956). *Studies in the Quantity Theory of Money*. University of Chicago Press.

Friedman, M. (1957). *A Theory of the Consumption Function*. Princeton University Press. doi:10.1515/9780691188485

Friedman, M. (1966). The Methodology of Positive Economics. In *Essays in Positive Economics*. University of Chicago Press.

Friedman, M. (1970). A theoretical framework for monetary analysis. *Journal of Political Economy*, *78*(2), 193–238. doi:10.1086/259623

Gilder, G. (2012). *Wealth and Poverty: A new edition for the twenty-first century*. Regnery Pub. Inc.

Gilder, G. (2013). *Knowledge and Power: The information theory of capitalism and how it is revolutionizing our world*. Regnery Pub. Inc.

Gillies, D. (1998). The Duhem thesis and the Quine thesis. In *Philosophy of Science: The Central Issues*. New York: Norton.

Goodfriend, M., & King, R. G. (1997). The new neoclassical synthesis and the role of monetary policy. *NBER Macroeconomics Annual*, *12*, 231–283. doi:10.1086/654336

Gray, J. A. (1976). Wage indexation: A microeconomic approach. *Journal of Monetary Economics*, *2*(2), 221–235. doi:10.1016/0304-3932(76)90034-9

Hahn, F. H. (1960). The stability of growth equilibrium. *The Quarterly Journal of Economics*, *74*(2), 206–226. doi:10.2307/1884251

Heyne, P., Boettke, P., & Prychitko, D. (2013). *The Economic Way of Thinking* (13th ed.). Pearson Education.

Hicks, J. R. (1946). *Value and Capital: An inquiry into some fundamental principles of economic theory* (2nd ed.). Oxford University Press.

Horwitz, S. (2000). *Microfoundations and Macroeconomics: An Austrian Perspective*. Routledge. doi:10.4324/9780203456309

Jones, R. W., & Kenen, P. B. (Eds.). (1985). *Handbook of International Economics*. Elsevier.

Keynes, J. M. (2012). The General Theory of Employment, Interest and Money (The Collected Writings of John Maynard Keynes Vol. 7). Cambridge University Press.

King, R. G. (2000). The new IS-LM model: Language, logic, and limits. *Federal Reserve Bank of Richmond Economic Quarterly*, *86*, 45–103.

Lamb, M., Lymer, A., & Freedman, J. (2005). *Taxation: An Interdisciplinary Approach to Research*. Oxford University Press.

Lengwiler, Y. (2004). *Microfoundations of Financial Economics: An Introduction to General Equilibrium Asset Pricing*. Princeton University Press.

Lucas, R., & Rapping, L. (1970). Real Wages, Employment and Inflation. In E. Phelps (Ed.), *Microeconomic Foundations of Employment and Inflation Theory* (pp. 253–305). Norton.

Lucas, R. E. Jr. (1972). Expectations and the neutrality of money. *Journal of Economic Theory*, *4*(2), 103–124. doi:10.1016/0022-0531(72)90142-1

Lucas, R. E. (1973). Some international evidence on output-inflation tradeoffs. *The American Economic Review*, *63*, 526–534.

Lucas, R. E. Jr. (1975). An equilibrium model of the business cycle. *Journal of Political Economy*, *83*(6), 1113–1144. doi:10.1086/260386

Lucas, R. E. (1988). On the mechanics of development planning. *Journal of Monetary Economics*, *22*, 3–42. doi:10.1016/0304-3932(88)90168-7

Mäki, U. (2012). Handbook of the Philosophy of Science: Vol. 13. *Philosophy of Economics*. Elsevier.

Marshall, A. (2013). *Principles of Economics* (8th ed.). Palgrave Macmillan LLC. doi:10.1057/9781137375261

Mises, L. (2006). *The Ultimate Foundation of Economic Science: An Essay on Method*. Liberty Fund, Inc.

Mishkin, F. S. (2004). *The Economics of Money, Banking, and Financial Markets* (7th ed.). Addison-Wesley.

Modigliani, F. (1963). The monetary mechanism and its interaction with real phenomena. *The Review of Economics and Statistics*, *45*(1), 76–103. doi:10.2307/1927150

Mundell, R. A. (1962). The appropriate use of monetary and fiscal policy for internal and external balance. *International Monetary Fund Staff Papers*, *9*(1), 70–79. doi:10.2307/3866082

Mundell, R. A. (1963). *Capital mobility and stabilization policy under fixed and flexible exchange rates. Canadian Journal of Economic and Political Science, 29(4), 475–485.*

Nicola, P. C. (2013). *Efficiency and Equity in Welfare Economics*. Springer. doi:10.1007/978-3-642-30071-4

North, D. C. (1990). *Institutions, Institutional Change and Economic Performance*. Cambridge University Press. doi:10.1017/CBO9780511808678

Okun, A. M. (1975). *Equity and Efficiency: the big trade-off*. Brookings Institution.

Phelps, E. (1967). Phillips curves, expectations of inflation and optimal unemployment over time. *Economica*, *34*(135), 254–281. doi:10.2307/2552025

Phillips, A. W. (1958). The Relationship between Unemployment and the Rate of Change of Money Wages in the United Kingdom 1861-1953. *Economica*, *25*, 283–299.

Polyanin, A. D., & Manzhirov, A. V. (2007). *Handbook of Mathematics for Engineers and Scientists*. Taylor & Francis Group.

Samuelson, P. A. (1983). Foundations of Economic Analysis (Enlarged ed.). Harvard University Press.

Samuelson, P. A., & Nordhaus, W. D. (2010). *Economics* (19th ed.). McGraw-Hill Co.

Scarth, W. (2014). *Macroeconomics: The development of modern methods for policy analysis*. Edward Elgar.

Sen, A. (1997). *Poverty and Famines*. International Labour Organization.

Sen, A. (2002). *Rationality and Freedom*. Belknap Press.

Sidrauski, M. (1967). Inflation and economic growth. *Journal of Political Economy*, *75*(6), 796–810. doi:10.1086/259360

Smith, A. (1977). An Inquiry into the Nature and Causes of the Wealth of Nations (UK ed.). Chicago: University of Chicago Press.

Solow, R. M. (1956). A contribution to the theory of economic growth. *The Quarterly Journal of Economics*, *70*(1), 65–94. doi:10.2307/1884513

Stigler, G. J. (1961). The economics of information. *Journal of Political Economy*, *69*(3), 213–225. doi:10.1086/258464

Taylor, J. B. (1979). Staggered wage setting in a macro model. *The American Economic Review*, *69*, 108–113.

Tobin, J. (1969). A general equilibrium approach to monetary theory. *Journal of Money, Credit and Banking*, *1*(1), 15–26. doi:10.2307/1991374

Tobin, J. (1975). Keynesian models of recession and depression. *American Economic Review Proceedings*, *65*, 195–202.

Ueda, K. (2013). Banks as coordinators of economic growth and stability: Microfoundation for macroeconomy with externality. *Journal of Economic Theory*, *148*(1), 322–352. doi:10.1016/j.jet.2012.09.003

Walras, L. (1954). Elements of Pure Economics, or the theory of social wealth (4th ed., W. Jaffé, Trans.). London: George Allen & Unwin Ltd.

Weintraub, E. R. (1977). The microfoundations of macroeconomics: A critical survey. *Journal of Economic Literature*, *15*(1), 1–23.

Weintraub, E. R. (1979). *Microfoundations: The compatibility of microeconomics and macroeconomics*. Cambridge University Press. doi:10.1017/CBO9780511559570

Woodford, M. (2003). *Interest and Prices: Foundations of a Theory of Monetary Policy*. Princeton University Press.

Ye, F. Y. (2015). A probe into the unification of micro-macro-economics: Arrow-Debreu-Mundell-Fleming model as a standard model. *Euro-Asian Journal of Economics and Finance*, *3*, 1–8.

Ye, F. Y. (2017). A synthetic macro-economic model integrating interest, exchange and tax rates. In *Scientific Metrics: toward analytical and quantitative sciences* (pp. 127–140). Springer. doi:10.1007/978-981-10-5936-0_11

Ye, F. Y. (2020). An economic analysis of efficiency and equity combining epistemological true with axiological good through microeconomics to macroeconomics. *International Journal of Economics and Financial Research*, *6*(7), 159–169. doi:10.32861/ijefr.67.159.169

ENDNOTES

1 See Weintraub, E.R. 1979. Microfoundations: the compatibility of microeconomics and macroeconomics. Cambridge University Press, p.89

2 Cf.: Samuelson, P.A. and W. D. Nordhaus. 2005, Economics (18th ed.). McGraw-Hill Co., Chapter 14 Appendix

Chapter 5
The Secret of Wealth Expansion

ABSTRACT

Technological progress and capital inflation are two factors for stimulating wealth expansion. It is revealed that both knowledge and capital are powers to push wealth expansion. While revealing the secret of wealth expansion, it is suggested to maintain the equilibrium of real technological progress and the imaginary capital inflation. After we know the secret of wealth expansion, we understand the human wealth sustained increasing. The secret of wealth expansion is revealed so that economic knowledge is promoted.

INTRODUCTION

In the grand synthetic model, when we consider total economic increment ΔY, supposing that it also matches the Cobb-Douglas model, we may have the following formula at inflation rate λ

$$\Delta Y = K^{\lambda} H^{q(1-\lambda)} \quad (1)$$

and its logarithmic form Δy becomes

$$\Delta y = \lambda k + q(1-\lambda)h \quad (2)$$

DOI: 10.4018/978-1-6684-4935-6.ch005

where q means technological progress index. The q(1-λ)h contributes real wealth and the λk contributes imaginary wealth in the economy.

While the inflation rate λ measures money expansion as the imaginary part, the real part is measured by human creation as q(1-θ)h. Therefore, a rate R or r becomes useful to measure the real-imaginary ratio

$$R = H^{q(1-\lambda)} / K^{\lambda} \tag{3}$$

$$r = q(1 - \lambda)h / \lambda k \tag{4}$$

When R > 1 or r > 1, real wealth expansion is larger than imaginary. Otherwise, the wealth expansion is only imaginary money effected by inflation. When R > 1 or r > 1, the real wealth expansion by technological progress exceeds the virtual capital expansion. If R< 1 or r < 1, the virtual wealth expansion is larger than the real wealth expansion so that the wealth expansion is only an imaginary expansion.

We also know that the capital function f(k) had a center position as

$$\dot{k} = sf(k) - (n + d)k; f'(k) = \gamma + \delta \tag{5}$$

This means that the capital truly pushes the economy via equilibrium growth rate n and interest rate γ.

Meanwhile, an IS-LM-type model can be characterized by the following equations:

$$\Delta y = \lambda k + q(1 - \lambda)h \tag{6}$$

$$m - p = \beta y - \delta \gamma \tag{7}$$

$$\gamma = \gamma^* \quad \tau = \tau^* \tag{8}$$

So we see that technological progress affects y via index q and money m affects y via inflation. Continuous technological progress and economic inflation promote y increasing, which is the secret of wealth expansion.

When we consider America, Europe, and Asia (with Canada and US representing America, UK, France, Germany and Italy representing Europe, and Japan and China representing Asia), we collect UN statistics (World Bank data) of GDP 2017 and 2018 in 2011 PPP prices, as shown in Table 1.

Table 1. Selected UN economic statistics: GDP 2017 and 2018 (US$)

Country	GDP2017ppp2011	GDP2018ppp2011	Increment ΔY
Canada	1.777E+12	1.813E+12	3.579E+10
US	1.949E+13	2.006E+13	5.704E+11
UK	3.037E+12	3.078E+12	4.072E+10
France	2.997E+12	3.051E+12	5.374E+10
Germany	4.382E+12	4.449E+12	5.693E+10
Italy	2.53E+12	2.55E+12	2.019E+10
Japan	5.18E+12	5.197E+12	1.674E+10
China	1.989E+13	2.123E+13	1.343E+12

Data source: http://data.un.org

According to Eq. (6), when $\lambda k \rightarrow 0$ and $h = 1$, we can estimate $q = \Delta y/(1-\lambda)$.

Overall, we see that all countries show a positive increment ΔY. However, if $\lambda = 0.01$, i.e. 1% inflation rate, the real increments will be changed, as shown in Table 2. But, the q will remain relatively stable.

Table 2. Computational data of real economic situation ($\lambda = 0.01$)

Country	Real increment	Inflation losing	estimated q
Canada	1.766E+10	1.813E+10	10.66
US	3.698E+11	2.006E+11	11.875
UK	9.941E+09	3.078E+10	10.717
France	2.323E+10	3.051E+10	10.839
Germany	2.244E+10	4.449E+10	10.935
Italy	-5.31E+09	2.55E+10	10.409
Japan	-3.52E+10	5.197E+10	10.327
China	1.13E+12	2.123E+11	12.25

If $\lambda = 0.02$, i.e. 2% inflation rate, the real increments will be shown as in Table 3.

Thus, we see that $q \sim 10$, which resembles a relatively stable parameter in the same country during an observed period. Comparing with $b \sim 10^3$, $s \sim 10^{-1}$ and $d \sim 10^{-2}$, the $q \sim 10$ is a middle parameter, $b > q > s > d$. The technological progress index q is the key to promoting wealth expansion.

Table 3: Computational data of real economic situation (λ = 0.02)

Country	Real increment	Inflation losing	estimated q
Canada	-4.7E+08	3.6E+10	10.77
US	1.69E+11	4E+11	12
UK	-2.1E+10	6.2E+10	10.83
France	-7.3E+09	6.1E+10	10.95
Germany	-2.2E+10	8.9E+10	11.05
Italy	-3.1E+10	5.1E+10	10.52
Japan	-8.7E+10	1E+11	10.43
China	9.18E+11	4.2E+11	12.38

REAL ECONOMIC GROWTH: ENDOGENOUS KNOWLEDGE POWER

Since technological progress is determined by human knowledge, the above model tells us the knowledge power of economic growth. This means that the endogenous power came from knowledge.

As human beings are the carriers of knowledge, human capital also characterizes the knowledge power. Suppose technological progress as an index q, which resembles an accelerating factor. This is just the secret of wealth expansion by promoting real output via technological progress.

Within the theoretical framework of Lucas' two-sector growth model, the human capital, H, is the engine of growth. But, in this system, the wage-income taxes should not exist. Although both physical capital K and human capital H are growth powers, the human capital is the deterministic power for real economic growth, which represents real technological progress.

Technological progress is the most important endogenous power for economic growth. While technological progress pushes the economy to promote quick development, R&D investment really quickens the economy.

IMAGINARY ECONOMIC GROWTH: EXOGENOUS CAPITAL FACTOR

In most exogenous factors affecting economic growth, physical capital, K, as a key factor of R&D investment, may push the scientific and technical applications and pull the economic growth.

Within the AK model, the economic output, Y = AK, so that the economic growth is proportional to the aggregate stock of physical capital. However, this is an imaginary growth, and the specification leads to the policy that interest-income taxes should not exist.

Meanwhile, inflation describes money expansion imaginarily. Both physical capital and inflation are important exogenous factors for economic growth. While physical capital provides an external boost to economic growth, inflation boosts confidence by making the economy imaginarily high at the monetary level.

SYNTHETIC WEALTH EXPANSION: NUMERICAL ESTIMATION

If we set

$$\lambda=0.01;\ \alpha=0.3;\ q=10 \tag{9}$$

all the economic parameters can be estimated as follows:

$$\gamma=0.03;\ \beta=0.9\sim1;\ \delta=0.04;\ n=0.02 \tag{10}$$

$$n = \dot{Y}/Y = \dot{K}/K = \gamma(1-\tau)-\rho \tag{11}$$

Then we can estimate the values of above linked economic parameters, as shown in Table 4.

Table 4. Estimated values of linked economic parameters

$n = \gamma(1-\tau)-\rho$	$(1-\tau)$	ρ	$\gamma = (n+\rho)/(1-\tau)$
0.01	0.9	0.01	0.0222
0.02	0.9	0.01	0.0333
0.03	0.9	0.01	0.0444
0.04	0.9	0.01	0.0556
0.05	0.9	0.01	0.0667
0.06	0.9	0.01	0.0778
0.01	0.8	0.02	0.0375

continues on following page

Table 4. Continued

$n = \gamma(1-\tau) - \rho$	$(1-\tau)$	ρ	$\gamma = (n + \rho)/(1-\tau)$
0.02	0.8	0.02	0.05
0.03	0.8	0.02	0.0625
0.04	0.8	0.02	0.075
0.05	0.8	0.02	0.0875
0.06	0.8	0.02	0.1
0.01	0.7	0.03	0.0571
0.02	0.7	0.03	0.0714
0.03	0.7	0.03	0.0857
0.04	0.7	0.03	0.1
0.05	0.7	0.03	0.1143
0.06	0.7	0.03	0.1286
0.01	0.6	0.04	0.0833
0.02	0.6	0.04	0.1
0.03	0.6	0.04	0.1167
0.04	0.6	0.04	0.1333
0.05	0.6	0.04	0.15
0.06	0.6	0.04	0.1667
0.01	0.9	0.02	0.0333
0.02	0.9	0.02	0.0444
0.03	0.9	0.02	0.0556
0.04	0.9	0.02	0.0667
0.05	0.9	0.02	0.0778
0.06	0.9	0.02	0.0889
0.01	0.8	0.03	0.05
0.02	0.8	0.03	0.0625
0.03	0.8	0.03	0.075
0.04	0.8	0.03	0.0875
0.05	0.8	0.03	0.1
0.06	0.8	0.03	0.1125
0.01	0.7	0.04	0.0714
0.02	0.7	0.04	0.0857
0.03	0.7	0.04	0.1
0.04	0.7	0.04	0.1143
0.05	0.7	0.04	0.1286
0.06	0.7	0.04	0.1429

continues on following page

Table 4. Continued

$n = \gamma(1-\tau) - \rho$	$(1-\tau)$	ρ	$\gamma = (n + \rho)/(1-\tau)$
0.01	0.6	0.05	0.1
0.02	0.6	0.05	0.1167
0.03	0.6	0.05	0.1333
0.04	0.6	0.05	0.15
0.05	0.6	0.05	0.1667
0.06	0.6	0.05	0.1833

According to Table 4, simulation data, it is better to set the range of interest rates between 0.02 - 0.18, if we expect to have higher growth (1-6%) with higher taxation (10- 40%).

Synthetically, we may estimate a set of feasible model parameters of the grand economic model as follows.

$b \sim 10^3$, $q \sim 10$, $s \sim 10^{-1}$ and $d = \delta \approx 0.04 \sim 10^{-2}.\gamma \approx 0.03 \sim 0.05$; $\rho \approx 0.02 \sim 0.025$. $n = p = 0.02$. $\alpha \approx 0.3$; $\theta \approx 0.01$.

The modeling process abides by the economic rules and spirits (Arrow, 1963; Arrow & Debreu, 1954; Friedman, 1948, 1956, 1957, 1966, 1970; Hicks, 1946; Lucas, 1972, 1973, 1975, 1988; Lucas & Rapping, 1970; Keynes, 2012; Marshall, 2013; Fleming, 1962; Mundell, 1962, 1963; Samuelson, 1983; Samuelson & Nordhaus, 2010; Smith, 1977; Solow, 1956; Taylor, 1979; Tobin, 1969, 1975; Walras, 1954). As long as so called 'creative destruction' (Schumpeter, 2003) would not occur and poverty could be avoided by economic growth (Dollar & Kraay, 2002; Sen, 1997, 2002; Gilder, 2012, 2013), knowledge and capital will lead to sustained wealth expansion.

INTERNATIONAL ECONOMIC OPTIMIZATION: CASE OF THREE NATIONS

The bank plays a key role in an international economic system, but the analysis of banks and banking stocks is particularly challenging because they operate and generate profit in a different way to most other businesses.

Net interest margin is an important indicator in evaluating banks because it reveals a bank's net profit on interest-earning assets, such as loans or investment securities. All banks' central interest rates will affect national economies.

Banks with a higher loan-to-assets ratio derive more of their income from loans and investments. Banks with lower levels of loan-to-asset ratios derive a relatively larger portion of their total income from more-diversified, non-interest-earning sources, such as asset management or trading.

In order to design optimum international economics, we suppose to set three nations (namely America, Asia and Europe) with three central banks (namely Bank of America, Bank of Asia and Bank of Europe), characterized using American dollar, Asian dollar and European dollar each. At the beginning, when the exchange rates (local currency stance) are fixed at 1:1:1, the economic system can be simplified by setting $\pi = 1$ and $\beta \sim 1$, and then the equilibrium equations of the new neoclassical economic system will become

$$\dot{y} = (\gamma - \overline{\gamma}) + \theta(1 - p) \tag{12.1}$$

$$\dot{p} = \phi(y - \overline{y}) \tag{12.2}$$

$$\gamma - \overline{\gamma} = -\dot{p} \tag{12.3}$$

Let Bank of America use dollar, Bank of Asia use asio and Bank of Europe use euro. If Bank of America reduces its interest rate to cope with economic overheat or expansion, the money flows out from America to Asia or Europe, and then Asia and Europe may adopt expansionary monetary and fiscal policy to reject over-money, yielding global inflation. On the other hand, if Bank of Asia and Bank of Europe apply contractionary monetary and fiscal policy to reduce the money mobility, the economic policy may lead to world economic deflation.

Meanwhile, when Bank of America increases its interest rate to cope with economic depression or contraction, the money may flow to America from Asia or Europe, and then Asia or Europe may need more money supply, leading to Asia and Europe adopting expansionary monetary and fiscal policy to stimulate economies, yielding local inflation. Or, if Bank of Asia and Bank of Europe apply contractionary monetary and fiscal policy to fix the money mobility, the economic policy could lead to world economic deflation.

In order to pursue profit maximization, we assume that marginal products equal rental prices, so that the price level will be

$$p = (1-\alpha)Y / \dot{K}\,;\ (1-\alpha)Y/H = w \tag{13}$$

where K is physical capital defined by AK model (Y = AK) and H is human capital in Cobb-Douglas production function. While interest rate γ is the rental price of physical capital, the wage rate w is that of human capital.

The utility function U and social welfare function S will be, respectively

$$U = \int e^{-pt}(\ln C)dt;\ S = \int (\ln C + g \ln G)e^{-\rho s}ds \tag{14}$$

where parameter g indicates the relative value that households attach to the government service, and the optimization conditions remain

$$\dot{p} / p = \gamma;\ \dot{C} / C = n = \gamma(1-\tau) - \rho \rightarrow (\gamma - \rho) \tag{15}$$

which leads to γ = w.

On the other hand, in the situation of national economic unbalance, international trade will also lose balance, which will lead to exchange rates change, introducing complicated economic interactions (Ueda, 2013; Ye, 2017, 2020).

Since every country will consider and solve economic issues on its own, no one can stop the selfish transmission. Therefore, it is better to increase interest rates to cope with economic overheat or expansion and reduce interest rates to cope with economic depression or contraction, replacing the need to keep reducing interest during economy expansion and increasing interest during economy depression.

All banks are financial institutions that accept deposits and make loans, they are also the financial intermediaries that the average person interacts with most frequently. Supposing that dollar: asio: euro = 1:1:1 at the beginning, if America, Asia and Europe were linked by competitive relations, Bank of America, Bank of Asia and Bank of Europe would maintain themselves as beneficiaries in economic activities. When Bank of America raise the interest rate to benefit the American economy, Bank of Asia and Bank of Europe might also raise interest rates to benefit Asian and European economies, leading to dollar: asio: euro [1] 1:1:1, so that the exchange rates change, yielding complicated international economic connections.

If America, Asia and Europe were cooperative relations, Bank of America, Bank of Asia and Bank of Europe would negotiate their interest and exchange rates to benefit each other. However, those situations resemble ideal states, which seem impossible in real economies.

The development of commercial banking might improve the national banking system, where banks have branches throughout the country. In the United States, there are about 8,000 commercial banks, while most other industrialized countries have well under 1,000.

In addition, government deposit insurance has emerged worldwide due to increasing concerns about the health of the banking system, especially after the increasing number of banking crises in recent years. Is this spread of deposit insurance a good thing? Does it help improve the performance of the financial system and prevent banking crises? The answer seems to be no in most cases.

Studies by World Bank have revealed that, on average, the use of explicit government deposit insurance is associated with reduced banking stability and increased incidence of banking crises*. Moreover, on average, it seems to hamper financial development. However, the negative impact of deposit insurance is only seen in countries with weak institutional environments: lack of rule of law, weak regulation of the financial sector and high levels of corruption. This is precisely the desired outcome because, as we shall see later in this chapter, a strong institutional environment is required to limit the incentives for banks to engage in the excessive risk-taking that deposit insurance encourages. The problem is that, in many emerging market countries, it can be very difficult to build a strong institutional environment. This leaves us with the conclusion that deposit insurance may be the wrong medicine for stability and efficiency of banking systems in emerging market countries.

However, banks are also in pursuit of profits, and financial institutions have a strong incentive to circumvent existing regulations by exploiting loopholes. Regulation is, therefore, suited to a moving target: regulators constantly play cat and mouse with financial institutions, which devise ingenious ways to circumvent it, leading regulators to modify their regulatory activities. In a dynamic financial system, regulators are constantly facing new challenges, and unless they can respond quickly to change, they may not be able to prevent financial institutions from taking excessive risks. If regulators and supervisors don't have the resources or expertise to keep up with smart people at financial institutions, they find ways to hide what they are doing or get around existing regulations, then the problem could be exacerbated.

Bank regulation and supervision are difficult for two other reasons. First, in the regulation and supervision game, the devil is in the details. Subtle differences in the details may have unintended consequences; unless regulators get the regulation and supervision just right, they may be unable to prevent excessive risk taking. Second, regulators and supervisors may be subject to political pressure to not do their jobs properly. For all these reasons, there is no guarantee that bank regulators and supervisors will be successful in promoting a healthy financial system. Indeed, bank regulation and supervision have not always worked well, leading to banking crises throughout the world. Therefore, for international economic optimization, the correct way never aims to bank. The way should aim to market, where the 'invisible hand' could guide correct directions.

REFERENCES

Arrow, K. (1963). *Social Choice and Individual Values* (2nd ed.). Yale University Press.

Arrow, K., & Debreu, G. (1954). Existence of an equilibrium for a competitive economy. *Econometrica*, *22*(3), 265–290. doi:10.2307/1907353

Atkinson, A., Piketty, T., & Saez, E. (2011). Top incomes in the long run of history. *Journal of Economic Literature*, *49*(1), 3–71. doi:10.1257/jel.49.1.3

Blanchard, O. J., & Gali, J. (2010). Labor markets and monetary policy: A new Keynesian model with unemployment. *American Economic Journal. Macroeconomics*, *2*(2), 1–30. doi:10.1257/mac.2.2.1

Coase, R. H. (1960). The problem of social cost. *The Journal of Law & Economics*, *3*, 1–44. doi:10.1086/466560

Davis, J. (2003). *The Theory of the Individual in Economics*. Routledge. doi:10.4324/9780203457689

Dollar, D., Kleineberg, T., & Kraay, A. (2014). *Growth, inequity and social welfare: cross country evidence*. World Bank Policy Research Department Working Paper No. 6842.

Dollar, D., & Kraay, A. (2002). Growth is good for the poor. *Journal of Economic Growth*, *7*(3), 195–225. doi:10.1023/A:1020139631000

Dornbusch, R. (1976). Exchange rate expectations and monetary policy. *Journal of International Economics*, *6*, 231–244. doi:10.1016/0022-1996(76)90001-5

Faccarello, G., & Kurz, H. D. (2016). Handbook on the History of Economic Analysis. Vol. I: Great Economists since Petty and Boisguilbert; Vol. II: Schools of Thought in Economics. Edward Elgar.

Feldman, A. M., & Serrano, R. (2005). *Welfare Economics and Social Choice Theory* (2nd ed.). Springer Science & Business Media, Inc.

Feldstein, M. S. (1976). Inflation, income taxes, and the rate of interest – a theoretical analysis. *The American Economic Review*, *66*, 806–820.

Fischer, S. (1977). Long-term contracts, rational expectations, and the optimal money supply rule. *Journal of Political Economy*, *85*(1), 191–205. doi:10.1086/260551

Fischer, S. (1983). A framework for monetary and banking analysis. *Economic Journal*, *93*, 1-16.

Fleming, J. M. (1962). Domestic monetary policies under fixed and floating exchange rates. IMF Staff Papers, 9, 369–379.

Floyd, J. E. (2010). *Interest Rates, Exchange Rates and World Monetary Policy*. Springer. doi:10.1007/978-3-642-10280-6

Forni, M., & Lippi, M. (1997). *Aggregation and the Microfoundations of Dynamic Macroecomics*. Oxford University Press.

Friedman, B. M., & Hahn, F. H. (Eds.). (2000). *Handbook of Monetary Economics* (Vol. 1-2). Elsevier.

Friedman, M. (1948). A monetary and fiscal framework for economic stability. *The American Economic Review*, *38*(3), 245–264.

Friedman, M. (1956). *Studies in the Quantity Theory of Money*. University of Chicago Press.

Friedman, M. (1957). *A Theory of the Consumption Function*. Princeton University Press. doi:10.1515/9780691188485

Friedman, M. (1966). The Methodology of Positive Economics. In *Essays in Positive Economics*. University of Chicago Press.

Friedman, M. (1970). A theoretical framework for monetary analysis. *Journal of Political Economy*, *78*(2), 193–238. doi:10.1086/259623

Gilder, G. (2012). *Wealth and Poverty: A new edition for the twenty-first century*. Regnery Pub. Inc.

Gilder, G. (2013). *Knowledge and Power: The information theory of capitalism and how it is revolutionizing our world*. Regnery Pub. Inc.

Gillies, D. (1998). The Duhem thesis and the Quine thesis. In *Philosophy of Science: The Central Issues*. New York: Norton.

Goodfriend, M., & King, R. G. (1997). The new neoclassical synthesis and the role of monetary policy. *NBER Macroeconomics Annual, 12*, 231–283. doi:10.1086/654336

Gray, J. A. (1976). Wage indexation: A microeconomic approach. *Journal of Monetary Economics, 2*(2), 221–235. doi:10.1016/0304-3932(76)90034-9

Hahn, F. H. (1960). The stability of growth equilibrium. *The Quarterly Journal of Economics, 74*(2), 206–226. doi:10.2307/1884251

Heyne, P., Boettke, P., & Prychitko, D. (2013). *The Economic Way of Thinking* (13th ed.). Pearson Education.

Hicks, J. R. (1946). *Value and Capital: An inquiry into some fundamental principles of economic theory* (2nd ed.). Oxford University Press.

Horwitz, S. (2000). *Microfoundations and Macroeconomics: An Austrian Perspective*. Routledge. doi:10.4324/9780203456309

Jones, R. W., & Kenen, P. B. (Eds.). (1985). *Handbook of International Economics*. Elsevier.

Keynes, J. M. (2012). The General Theory of Employment, Interest and Money (The Collected Writings of John Maynard Keynes Vol. 7). Cambridge University Press.

King, R. G. (2000). The new IS-LM model: Language, logic, and limits. *Federal Reserve Bank of Richmond Economic Quarterly, 86*, 45–103.

Lamb, M., Lymer, A., & Freedman, J. (2005). *Taxation: An Interdisciplinary Approach to Research*. Oxford University Press.

Lengwiler, Y. (2004). *Microfoundations of Financial Economics: An Introduction to General Equilibrium Asset Pricing*. Princeton University Press.

Lucas, R., & Rapping, L. (1970). Real Wages, Employment and Inflation. In E. Phelps (Ed.), *Microeconomic Foundations of Employment and Inflation Theory* (pp. 253–305). Norton.

Lucas, R. E. Jr. (1972). Expectations and the neutrality of money. *Journal of Economic Theory, 4*(2), 103–124. doi:10.1016/0022-0531(72)90142-1

Lucas, R. E. (1973). Some international evidence on output-inflation tradeoffs. *The American Economic Review*, *63*, 526–534.

Lucas, R. E. Jr. (1975). An equilibrium model of the business cycle. *Journal of Political Economy*, *83*(6), 1113–1144. doi:10.1086/260386

Lucas, R. E. (1988). On the mechanics of development planning. *Journal of Monetary Economics*, *22*, 3–42. doi:10.1016/0304-3932(88)90168-7

Mäki, U. (2012). Handbook of the Philosophy of Science: Vol. 13. *Philosophy of Economics*. Elsevier.

Marshall, A. (2013). *Principles of Economics* (8th ed.). Palgrave Macmillan LLC. doi:10.1057/9781137375261

Mises, L. (2006). *The Ultimate Foundation of Economic Science: An Essay on Method*. Liberty Fund, Inc.

Mishkin, F. S. (2004). *The Economics of Money, Banking, and Financial Markets* (7th ed.). Addison-Wesley.

Modigliani, F. (1963). The monetary mechanism and its interaction with real phenomena. *The Review of Economics and Statistics*, *45*(1), 76–103. doi:10.2307/1927150

Mundell, R. A. (1962). The appropriate use of monetary and fiscal policy for internal and external balance. *International Monetary Fund Staff Papers*, *9*(1), 70–79. doi:10.2307/3866082

Mundell, R. A. (1963). *Capital mobility and stabilization policy under fixed and flexible exchange rates. Canadian Journal of Economic and Political Science, 29(4), 475–485.*

Nicola, P. C. (2013). *Efficiency and Equity in Welfare Economics*. Springer. doi:10.1007/978-3-642-30071-4

North, D. C. (1990). *Institutions, Institutional Change and Economic Performance*. Cambridge University Press. doi:10.1017/CBO9780511808678

Phelps, E. (1967). Phillips curves, expectations of inflation and optimal unemployment over time. *Economica*, *34*(135), 254–281. doi:10.2307/2552025

Phillips, A. W. (1958). The Relationship between Unemployment and the Rate of Change of Money Wages in the United Kingdom 1861-1953. *Economica*, *25*, 283–299.

Polyanin, A. D., & Manzhirov, A. V. (2007). *Handbook of Mathematics for Engineers and Scientists*. Taylor & Francis Group.

Samuelson, P. A. (1983). Foundations of Economic Analysis (Enlarged ed.). Harvard University Press.

Samuelson, P. A., & Nordhaus, W. D. (2010). *Economics* (19th ed.). McGraw-Hill Co.

Scarth, W. (2014). *Macroeconomics: The development of modern methods for policy analysis*. Edward Elgar.

Schumpeter, J. A. (2003). Capitalism, Socialism, and Democracy (e-Library ed.). London: Routledge (Taylor & Francis Group).

Sen, A. (1997). *Poverty and Famines*. International Labour Organization.

Sen, A. (2002). *Rationality and Freedom*. Belknap Press.

Sidrauski, M. (1967). Inflation and economic growth. *Journal of Political Economy*, *75*(6), 796–810. doi:10.1086/259360

Smith, A. (1977). An Inquiry into the Nature and Causes of the Wealth of Nations (UK ed.). Chicago: University of Chicago Press.

Solow, R. M. (1956). A contribution to the theory of economic growth. *The Quarterly Journal of Economics*, *70*(1), 65–94. doi:10.2307/1884513

Stigler, G. J. (1961). The economics of information. *Journal of Political Economy*, *69*(3), 213–225. doi:10.1086/258464

Taylor, J. B. (1979). Staggered wage setting in a macro model. *The American Economic Review*, *69*, 108–113.

Tobin, J. (1969). A general equilibrium approach to monetary theory. *Journal of Money, Credit and Banking*, *1*(1), 15–26. doi:10.2307/1991374

Tobin, J. (1975). Keynesian models of recession and depression. *American Economic Review Proceedings*, *65*, 195–202.

Ueda, K. (2013). Banks as coordinators of economic growth and stability: Microfoundation for macroeconomy with externality. *Journal of Economic Theory*, *148*(1), 322–352. doi:10.1016/j.jet.2012.09.003

Walras, L. (1954). Elements of Pure Economics, or the theory of social wealth (4th ed., W. Jaffé, Trans.). London: George Allen & Unwin Ltd.

Weintraub, E. R. (1977). The microfoundations of macroeconomics: A critical survey. *Journal of Economic Literature*, *15*(1), 1–23.

Weintraub, E. R. (1979). *Microfoundations: The compatibility of microeconomics and macroeconomics*. Cambridge University Press. doi:10.1017/CBO9780511559570

Woodford, M. (2003). *Interest and Prices: Foundations of a Theory of Monetary Policy*. Princeton University Press.

Ye, F. Y. (2017). A synthetic macro-economic model integrating interest, exchange and tax rates. In *Scientific Metrics: toward analytical and quantitative sciences* (pp. 127–140). Springer. doi:10.1007/978-981-10-5936-0_11

Ye, F. Y. (2020). An economic analysis of efficiency and equity combining epistemological true with axiological good through microeconomics to macroeconomics. *International Journal of Economics and Financial Research*, *6*(7), 159–169. doi:10.32861/ijefr.67.159.169

ENDNOTE

* See World Bank, Finance for Growth: Policy Choices in a Volatile World (Oxford: World Bank and Oxford University Press, 2001).

Chapter 6
Complex Economics

ABSTRACT

When the real commodity function X and the imaginary money function Y are combined as complex economic function Z = X + iY and both X and Y link with price level P and output quantity Q, a framework of complex economics is set up, characterized by the Cauchy-Riemann equation and the Laplace equation. The economic complex analysis can characterize economic equilibrium and economic stability, providing a mathematical description of ideal economic situation. The author develops economic complex analysis in this chapter.

INTRODUCTION

Complex Number with its Implications in Economics

In economics, the economic equilibrium is a state where economic forces such as demand, and supply are balanced and the equilibrium values of economic variables will not change in the absence of external influences. Economic stability refers to an absence of excessive fluctuations. An economy with fairly constant output growth and low and stable inflation would be considered economically stable, and the equilibrium is just the outcome of the stability.

To approach economic equilibrium and economic stability, the general equilibrium theories have been developed in both microeconomics (Arrow & Debreu, 1954) and macroeconomics (Fleming, 1962; Mundell, 1962, 1963; Tobin, 1969). Moreover, the general equilibrium and economic analysis are core topics in economics, particularly in monetary economics which also

DOI: 10.4018/978-1-6684-4935-6.ch006

concerns economic stability and monetary mechanism (Samuelson, 1947; Friedman, 1948, 1956, 1966, 1970; Friedman & Hahn, 1990; Hahn, 1960; Modigliani, 1963). Following the framework of complex economics (Ye, 2017), we can develop economic complex analysis as follows, and we expect to benefit and enrich economic analysis as well as economic theories.

Complex Economic Equations and Solutions

In this chapter, we use the relative independent symbol system. Let's consider a general case: total social real wealth function Y (linking capital K and labor L) and imaginary wealth function X (linking real money Mr and virtual money Mv), while introducing GDP function Y = Y(P,Q) and money function X = X(P,Q), and both Y and X are changed by real variables P and Q, where P indicates price level and Q means quantity. We define complex economic function as

$$M = M(Y,X) = Z(P,Q) = Y(P,Q) + iX(P,Q) \tag{1}$$

If the functions Y and X are analytic, they will fit the Cauchy-Riemann condition

$$\frac{\partial Y}{\partial P} - \frac{\partial X}{\partial Q} = 0 \tag{2}$$

$$\frac{\partial Y}{\partial Q} + \frac{\partial X}{\partial P} = 0 \tag{3}$$

If Y and X are harmonic, they will fit the Laplace equation

$$\frac{\partial^2 Y}{\partial P^2} + \frac{\partial^2 X}{\partial Q^2} = \frac{\partial^2 Y}{\partial P^2} - i^2 \frac{\partial^2 X}{\partial Q^2} = 0 \tag{4}$$

Now we replace Y and X with unified complex function Z = Y + iX, a complex stable economic system should fit equations

$$\frac{\partial Z}{\partial P} + i\frac{\partial Z}{\partial Q} = 0 \tag{5}$$

$$\frac{\partial^2 Z}{\partial P^2} + \frac{\partial^2 Z}{\partial Q^2} = 0 \tag{6}$$

where Equation (6-5) is the Cauchy-Riemann equation and Equation (6) is the Laplace equation.

In general, different initial and boundary conditions will determine different solutions of equations (6-5) and (6-6). However, we can discuss their fundamental analytical solutions according to the following equations

$$\frac{\partial Z}{\partial P} + i\frac{\partial Z}{\partial Q} = \delta(P,Q) \tag{7}$$

$$\frac{\partial^2 Z}{\partial P^2} + \frac{\partial^2 Z}{\partial Q^2} = \delta(P,Q) \tag{8}$$

These are first-order and second-order partial differential equations, respectively.

Doing Fourier transformation of both sides to Q for Equation (6-7), we obtain an ordinary differential equation on P with parameter s as follows

$$\frac{d\widehat{Z}(P,s)}{dP} - s\widehat{Z}(P,s) = \delta(P) \tag{9}$$

The solution of Equation (6-9) is

$$\widehat{Z}(P,s) = (H(P) + C(s))e^{sP} \tag{10}$$

In which C(s) is any constant depended on by s. Then the fundamental solution of Equation (6-7) becomes

$$Z(P,Q) = \frac{1}{2\pi}\int_{-\infty}^{\infty} e^{-isP}\widehat{Z}(P,s)ds = \frac{1}{2\pi(P+iQ)} \tag{11}$$

For Equation (6-8), it is a two dimensional Laplace equation and its fundamental solution is

$$Z(P,Q)=\frac{1}{2\pi}\ln(P^2+Q^2)^{1/2}=\frac{1}{4\pi}\ln(P^2+Q^2) \tag{12}$$

In order to match Equations (6-1), (6-11) and (6-12), we need

$$Z(P,Q)=X+iY=\frac{1}{2\pi(P+iQ)}=\frac{1}{4\pi}\ln(P^2+Q^2) \tag{13}$$

so that the equilibrium condition can be written as

$$\frac{1}{(P+iQ)}=\frac{1}{2}\ln(P^2+Q^2)=\frac{1}{2}\ln(P-iQ)(P+iQ) \tag{14}$$

It is equivalent to

$$\frac{(P+iQ)}{2}\ln(P-iQ)(P+iQ)-1=0 \tag{15}$$

Equation (13) or Equations (14) and (15) construct the mathematical condition of economic equilibrium and economic stability. This means that stable economic system (characterized by commodity function X and money function Y) link with special price level P and output quantity Q.

As we know that the Laplace equation just describes stable phenomena, the above equations (7) and (8), as well as solutions (11) and (12) just fit the economic stability. As there are two equations (second-order Laplace equation and first-order Cauchy-Riemann equation), the solutions express economic equilibrium.

The basic shape of their united solution is determined by the following function

$$Z=\frac{(P+iQ)}{2}\ln(P-iQ)(P+iQ) \tag{16}$$

This is the solution surface, which can be shown using the following program, as Figure 1, using the following MATLAB code:

```
Figure (1)
z=cplxgrid(30);
p=real(z);
q=imag(z);
s=p+q*i;
w=s.*log(p.^2 + q.^2)/2
%mesh(p, q, z);
surf(p, q, real(w),imag(w));
colorbar
```

Figure 1. The complex solution surface

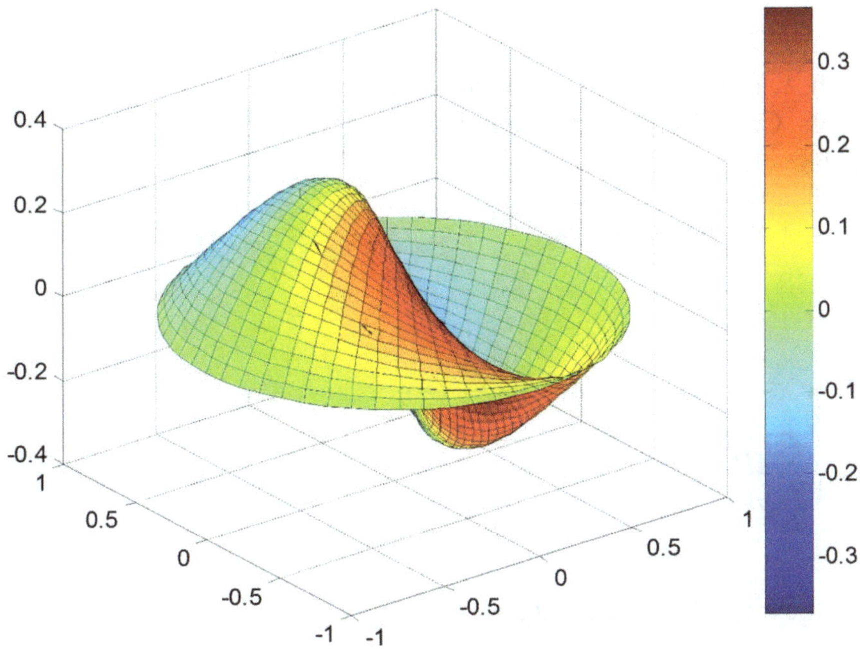

The visualized results verify the existence of complex solutions, however, the solutions belong to multi-solutions, they are not unique.

For visually expression, the numerical methods may be applied to study the solutions (11), (12) and (15).

Various particular solutions (Polyanin & Manzhirov, 2007) of the Laplace equation (6) exist, which means that there are a number of cases (multi-conditions) of economic equilibrium and economic stability.

For example, Equation (6) has its polar coordinate form as

$$\frac{1}{r}\frac{\partial}{\partial r}(r\frac{\partial Z}{\partial r})+\frac{1}{r^2}\frac{\partial^2 Z}{\partial \phi^2}=0 \qquad (17)$$

where $r=\sqrt{P^2+Q^2}$ and $P=r\cos\phi$; $Q=r\sin\varphi$.

Equation (6-17) has the following particular solutions

$$Z(r) = A \ln r + B \qquad (18)$$

$$Z(r,\phi)=(Ar^m+\frac{B}{r^m})(C\cos m\phi+D\sin m\phi) \qquad (19)$$

in which A, B, C, D are arbitrary constants and m = 1, 2,….

On its Cartesian coordinate form, Equation (6-6) has the following particular solutions

$$Z(P,Q) = AP + BQ + C \qquad (20)$$

$$Z(P,Q) = A(P^2 - Q^2) + BPQ \qquad (21)$$

$$Z(P,Q) = A(P^3 - 3PQ^2) + B(3P2Q - Q^3) \qquad (22)$$

$$Z(P,Q)=\frac{AP+BQ}{P^2+Q^2}+C \qquad (23)$$

$$Z(P,Q) = \exp(\pm nP)\ (A \cos nQ + B \sin nQ) \qquad (24)$$

$$Z(P,Q) = (A \cos nP + B \sin nP) \exp(\pm nQ) \qquad (25)$$

$$Z(P,Q) = (A \cos nP + B \sin nP)\ (C \sinh nQ + D \cosh nQ) \qquad (26)$$

$$Z(P,Q) = (A \sinh nP + B \cosh nP)\ (C \cos nQ + D \sin nQ) \qquad (27)$$

where A, B, C, D and n are arbitrary constants.

If Z(P, Q) is a solution for the Laplace equation, then the following functions are also solutions everywhere they are defined, in which A, B, C, D, θ and λ are arbitrary constants. The signs at λ's in the formula for Z_1 are taken arbitrarily.

$$Z_1(P,Q) = AZ(\pm\lambda P + C, \pm\lambda Q + D) + B \tag{28}$$

$$Z_2(P,Q) = AZ(P\cos\theta + Q\sin\theta, -P\sin\theta + Q\cos\theta) \tag{29}$$

$$Z_3(P,Q) = AZ\left(\frac{P}{P^2+Q^2}, \frac{Q}{P^2+Q^2}\right) \tag{30}$$

In general, Z = X(P, Q) + iY(P, Q), where X and Y are harmonic functions of the real variables P and Q. The real and imaginary parts of Z satisfy the two-dimensional Laplace equation (ΔX = 0, ΔY = 0). Thus, by specifying analytic functions Z and taking their real and imaginary parts, one obtains various particular solutions of the two-dimensional Laplace equation. However, for economic equilibrium and economic stability, it is not only dominated by the two-dimensional Laplace equation (6-6), but also dominated by the Cauchy-Riemann equation (6-5). Thus, the unique fundamental solutions become Equations (14) and (15).

It is true that the world is dominated by differential equations, since we see that most natural and social phenomena can be described by differential equation or equations. Here we reveal that economic equilibrium and economic stability are also mastered by Cauchy-Riemann-Laplace equations, which give strong evidence to believe the truth that differential equations describe the world.

Following economic complex analysis, the economic system is determined by commodity function X and money function Y, which are also dominated by price level P and output quantity Q. Thus, the policy suggestions concentrate on paying more attention to price and quantity. As the financial system is so complex, the above analysis and suggestion are only a highly simplified estimation of financial markets. We hope that this framework can provide a referable foundation for further studies.

The above findings focus on the fact that the Cauchy-Riemann equation and the Laplace equation construct the core of economic complex analysis, which describes economic equilibrium and economic stability. Combining fundamental solutions of Cauchy-Riemann equation and Laplace equation, the stable function surface is revealed, in which commodity function X and money function Y are complex economic function $Z = X + iY$ link with price level P and output quantity Q. It is expected to stimulate further investigations.

MONETARY SUPPLY

Money demand and money supply are important issues in monetary economics (Friedman & Hahn, 1990; Papademos & Modigliani, 1990; Mishkin, 2004; Scarth, 2014), for which there were some classic frameworks matching empirical evidences, reflecting classic thoughts (Hicks, 1946; Fischer, 1983; Friedman, 1948, 1956, 1970; Tobin, 1969, 1975; Lucas, 1972, 1973, 1975, 1988; Keynes, 2012; Marshall, 2013; Smith, 1977), around money and capital.

In my published article, *Economic complex analysis for approaching economic equilibrium and economic stability* (Ye, 2017), the commodity function X and the money function Y are introduced to construct a unified micro-macro-economic analytical framework. In general, commodity function X(P,Q) and money function Y(P,Q), P and Q can be general economic factors or measures (e.g. capital, consumption, income, investment, labor, land, price, etc.). When we set P as price level and Q as quantity of commodity and money measured by money unit (e.g. dollar), the X curve and Y curve are equivalent to commodity supply curve and money supply curve, respectively, where different commodity and money supplies lead to different results. When X and Y are combined as a complex measure $M = Z = X + iY$, complex economics can be set up.

In this book, while research hypothesis corresponds to the issue of the optimum quantity of money supply (Woodford, 1990), we try to find a simple static solution in the framework of complex economics.

Theoretical Framework for the Upper and Lower Limitations of Money Supply

Let's focus on the issues of upper and lower limitations of money supply, as well as the optimizing money supply theoretically.

At first, there are three ways to estimate money supply.

Simple Multiplier Model for Bank Money Supply

Supposing B to be the monetary base or high-powered money, and $\kappa > 1$ as the money-base multiplier, we have

$$M = \kappa B \tag{31}$$

where κ is abided by the following formula

$$\kappa = \frac{1+b}{b+z} \geq 1 \tag{32}$$

in which b is a constant fraction of bank deposits and z is a fixed proportion of deposits reflecting either regulatory requirements or internally determined liquidity needs.

This is a simple estimation of the money supply, which is called the money multiplier approach. Since B marks M0 and M matches M1 in monetary economics, we set it as the lower limitation of the money supply.

Fisher's Equation of Exchange

Money supply is also linked to money demand, which fits Fisher's equation of exchange, as follows

$$MV = PX \to M = \frac{PX}{V} = \gamma X > 0 \tag{33}$$

In the above equation, M is the total money in the nation's money supply, V is the number of times per year each money unit is spent (velocity of money), P is the average price of all the goods and services sold during the year, $\gamma = P/V$ indicates the ratio of P to V, and X is the quantity of assets, goods and services sold during the year, which should equal the total quantity of commodities (GDP).

In mathematical terms, this equation is really an identity which is true by definition rather than description of economic behavior. That is, each term is defined by the values of the other three. Unlike the other terms, the velocity of money has no independent measure and can only be estimated by dividing PX by M. Some adherents of the quantity theory of money assume that the velocity of money is stable and predictable, being determined mostly by financial institutions. If that assumption is valid then changes in M can be used to predict changes in PX; if not, then a model of V is required in order to make the equation of exchange be useful as a macroeconomics model or as a predictor of prices.

Most macroeconomists replace the equation of exchange with equations for the demand for money which describe more regular and predictable economic behavior, however, predictability of the velocity of money is equivalent to predictability of the demand for money (since in equilibrium real money demand is simply X/V), so that this is a feasible process.

In practice, macroeconomists almost always use real GDP to measure X, omitting the role of all transactions except for those involving newly produced goods and services (i.e., consumption goods, investment goods, government-purchased goods, and exports). That is to say, the only assets counted as part of X are newly produced investment goods, though the original quantity theory of money does not follow this practice: PX is the monetary value of all new transactions, whether of real goods and services or of paper assets. So, Fisher's equation of exchange links M to X. If P = V, M = X.

Capital Analysis

According to Piketty's analysis (Piketty, 2014), there is the first fundamental law of capitalism, $\alpha = r \times \beta$, in which the share of capital income in national income, namely α, is equal to the average rate of return on capital, r, times the capital/income ratio, β. It is important to realize that the law $\alpha = r \times \beta$ is actually a pure accounting identity, valid at all times, in all places, by construction.

Meanwhile, in the long-run, the capital/income ratio β is related in a simple and transparent way to the savings rate s and the growth rate g, which leads to the second fundamental law of capitalism, $\beta = s / g$. The second law is the result of a dynamic process: it represents a state of equilibrium toward which an economy will tend if the savings rate is s and the growth rate is g, but that equilibrium state is never perfectly realized in practice.

The law $\beta = s / g$ is valid only if asset prices evolve on average in the same way as consumer prices. If the price of real estate or stocks rises faster than other prices, then the ratio β between the market value of national capital and the annual flow of national income can, again, be quite high without the addition of any new savings. In the short-run, variations (capital gains or losses) of relative asset prices (i.e., of asset prices relative to consumer prices) are often quite a bit larger than volume effects (i.e., effects linked to new savings). If we assume, however, that price variations balance out over the long-run, then the law $\beta = s / g$ is necessarily valid, regardless of the reasons why the country in question chooses to save a proportion s of its national income.

Piketty revealed an important inequity in economic development, $r > g$, based on his observations and data. Since $\alpha = r \times \beta = r \times (s / g)$, $\alpha / r = s / g$ and $\alpha \times g = r \times s$, we can derive $r = g\ (\alpha/s)$, $r > g$ is equivalent to $\alpha/s < 1$ or $\alpha < s$, which means that if the share of capital income in national income (α) is less than the savings rate (s), the average annual rate of return on capital (r) will be larger than the rate of growth of the economy (the annual increase in income or output, g).

Supposing C be total capital and I total income in the globe or a special nation, we see $\beta = C/I = s/g$, which leads to $Cg = Is$ or $g = Is/C$.

As the above capital estimation included all the social cumulative historical wealth, when we add present commodities (X), it leads to total quantity of money as

$$M = C + X = I\beta + X \tag{34}$$

As this is the sum of historical and present wealth, the capital model gives an upper-limitation estimation of money supply, considering $I \leq X$, leading to $M \leq (\beta+1)X$.

Combining (6-31), (6-33) and (6-34), we obtain a suitable estimation of M (total money as money demand or money supply) as

$$(\gamma / \kappa)X \leq M \leq I\beta + X \leq (\beta + 1)X \tag{35}$$

The formula indicates the optimum quantity of money supply.

Linking to Complex Metrics

Let P indicate price level and Q quantity. We define complex economic function as

$$M(Y,X) = Z(P,Q) = Y(P,Q) + iX(P,Q) \tag{36}$$

where Z is measured by both Y and X.

When Y marks total output and X total money, Y is measured by GDP and X is abided by Equation (6-35), it is found that the |M|=|X/Y| should keep in

$$(\gamma / \kappa) \leq |M| = |X / Y| \leq (\beta + 1) \quad (39)$$

This means that money print (X) should keep a suitable ratio to real GDP (Y), the ratio is abided between (β+1) and (γ/k). The formula fits scaling money supply yearly.

If the money supply is larger than the upper limitation in one country or one money union, the risk would transfer to other countries and cause financial chaos around the world. If the money supply is less than the lower limitation, it could cause markets to condense, leading to economic depression.

Numerical Estimation

At a global level, since global income = global output, according to Piketty's statistics (Piketty, 2014), the average income per-capita is almost exactly 10,000 euros yearly and the global population is close to 7 billion. Consequently, the global output is slightly greater than 70 trillion euros in 2012. If the capital stock is six times income on average, we can estimate that the global capital stock is round 6 × 70 trillion euros, so that the global wealth can be estimated as 6 × 70 + 70 = 490 trillion euros. This gives a basic estimation of maximum money supply (upper limitation) as

$$M < 500 \text{ trillion euros}$$

Meanwhile, as the global output is about 70 trillion euros yearly, if the money multiplier is 7 and P/V = 1, we have another basic estimation of minimum money supply (lower limitation) as

$$M > 70\,(1/7) = 10 \text{ trillion euros}$$

Synthetically, the constraint of the global money supply becomes

$$10 \text{ trillion euros} < M < 500 \text{ trillion euros}$$

At national level, the issue mainly occurs in one country. Following Piketty's statistics (Piketty, 2014), there are about 540 million people who live in member countries of the European Union (EU), whose per-capita output exceeds 27,000 euros per year. Therefore, we can estimate the EU output as $0.54 \times 27 = 14.58$ trillion euros per year and its capital stock is estimated at $14.58 \times 6 = 87.48$ trillion euros, then the upper limitation of money supply is $M < 84.48 + 14.58 = 102.06$ trillion euros, while the lower limitation is $14.58/7 = 2.08$ trillion euros. Similarly, as USA has 330 million people with a per-capita output of about 40,000 euros, the estimation will be $1.88 < M < 92.4$ trillion euros. In China, there are 1.3 billion people with a per-capita output of 8,000 euros per year, so that the estimation becomes $1.48 < M < 72.8$ trillion euros. If Chinese population becomes 1.4 billion with a per-capita output of 10,000 euros per year, the estimation will be $2 < M < 98$.

Money Supply and Money Policy

Money is used as a medium of exchange, a unit of account, and a ready store of value; its different functions are associated with different empirical measures of the money supply. There is no single 'correct' measure of the money supply. Instead, there are several measures, classified along a spectrum or continuum between narrow and broad monetary aggregates. Narrow measures include only the most liquid assets, the ones most easily used to spend (currency, checkable deposits). Broader measures add less liquid types of assets (certificates of deposit, etc.).

This continuum corresponds to the way that different types of money are more or less controlled by monetary policy. Narrow measures include those more directly affected and controlled by monetary policy, whereas broader measures are less closely related to monetary-policy actions. It is a matter of perennial debate about whether narrower or broader versions of the money supply have a more predictable link to nominal GDP.

The main functions of the central bank are to maintain low inflation and a low level of unemployment, although these goals are sometimes in conflict (according to the Phillips curve). A central bank may attempt to do this by artificially influencing the demand for goods by increasing or decreasing the nation's money supply (relative to trend), which lowers or raises interest rates, and stimulates or restrains spending on goods and services.

An important debate among economists in the second half of the twentieth century concerned the central bank's ability to predict how much money should be in circulation, given current employment rates and inflation rates. Economists such as Milton Friedman believed that the central bank would always get it wrong, leading to wider swings in the economy than if it were just left alone. This is why they advocated a non-interventionist approach—one of targeting a pre-specified path for the money supply independent of current economic conditions—even though in practice this might involve regular intervention with open market operations (or other monetary-policy tools) to keep the money supply on target.

Considering consumption function (Friedman, 1957), consumption always links with multi-economic factors, particularly income and savings. In our outputs (GDP), we consume some and save some every year, in which the consumption causes wealth diminishing and savings transfer into capital. This allows us to consider small changes (ε) in scaling money supply as

$$(\gamma / \kappa + \varepsilon) \leq |M| \leq (\beta + 1 - \varepsilon) \tag{40}$$

Meanwhile, different countries adopt different types of money, which are typically classified as 'M's. The 'M's usually range from M0 (narrowest) to M3 (broadest, even M4 in some cases) but which 'M's are actually stressed in policy formulation depends on the country's central bank. The typical layout for each of the 'M's concludes: the different forms of money in government money supply statistics arise from the practice of fractional-reserve banking. Whenever a bank gives out a loan in a fractional-reserve banking system, a new sum of money is created (Fischer, 1977, 1983). This new type of money is what makes up the non-M0 components in the M1-M3 statistics.

In the money supply statistics, central bank money is MB while the commercial bank money is divided up into the M1-M3 components. Generally, the types of commercial bank money that tend to be valued at lower amounts are classified in the narrow category of M1, while the types of commercial bank money that tend to exist in larger amounts are categorized in M2 and M3, with M3 having the largest. In short, there are two types of money in a fractional-reserve banking system: central bank money (obligations of a central bank, including currency and central bank depository accounts) and commercial bank money (obligations of commercial banks, including checking accounts and savings accounts).

Quantitative Easing and Three Ratios

Conventional monetary policy can be ineffective in situations such as a liquidity trap. When interest rates and inflation are near zero, the central bank cannot loosen monetary policy through conventional means. It is designed that central banks may use unconventional monetary policy such as quantitative easing

(QE) to increase output, however, it is difficult to reach synthetic equilibrium in the synthetic model, as shown in Figure 2, where money supply curve shifted MS → MS' → MS'' and LM → LM' → LM'' while $\gamma \rightarrow 0$.

Figure 2. The case of quantitative easing

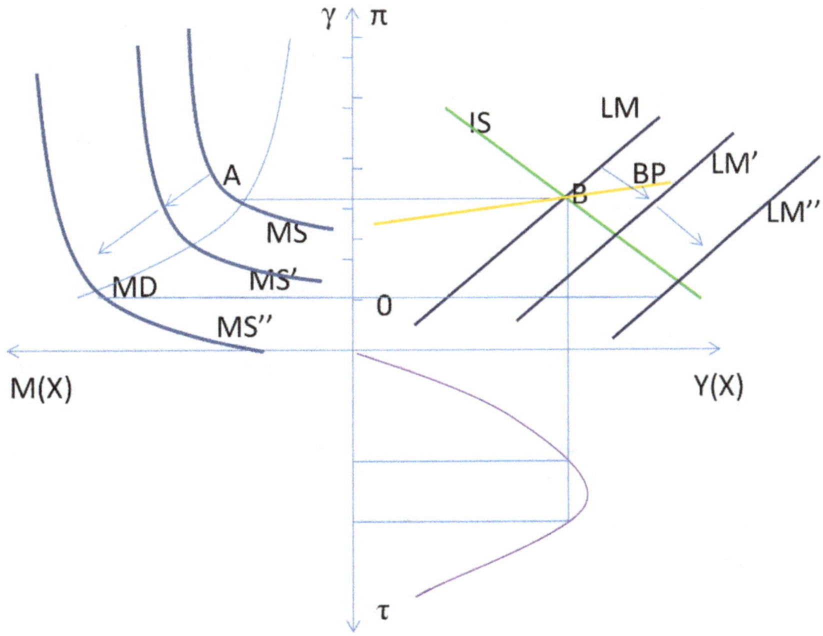

Thus, the QE policy could input much more money into local markets, beyond the total capital and commodity, leading to potential crisis, so it is suggested to restrict QE under the lower limitation of money supply (Ye, 2015), theoretically.

Moreover, aside from factors such as interest rates and inflation, the exchange rate is one of the most important determinants of a national relative level of economic health. Exchange rates play a vital role in a national level of trade, which is critical to almost every free market economy in the world. There are numerous factors that determine exchange rates, most of which are related to the trading relationship between two countries. Then interest rates, inflation and exchange rates are highly correlated. By manipulating interest rates, central banks exert influence over both inflation and exchange rates, and changing interest rates impact inflation and currency values. Higher interest rates offer lenders in an economy a higher return relative to other countries. Therefore, higher interest rates attract foreign capital and cause the exchange rate to rise. The impact of higher interest rates is mitigated, however, if inflation in the country is much higher than in others, or if additional factors serve to drive the currency down. The opposite relationship exists for decreasing interest rates, i.e. lower interest rates tend to decrease exchange rates.

The QE (quantitative easing) policy inputs about 1 trillion dollars or euros into the US or EU, which is not excessive compared to the above limitations, so it has not yet caused chaos for the local finance. However, if the QE policy input much more money into markets, beyond the total capital and commodity in the local society, even the world, potential crisis could be caused and big issues may be introduced to the national economy, even in the global economy. Although one can raise the interest rate to condense or fix money, the QE policy also faces big risks. According to the above theoretical framework and numerical estimation, it is suggested to restrict QE under the lower-limitation of money supply.

There are several different definitions of money supply to reflect the differing stores of money. Due to the nature of bank deposits, especially time-restricted savings account deposits, the M4 represents the most illiquid measure of money. M0, by contrast, is the least liquid measure of the money supply. For consideration with ease, money policy can focus on M1, so we can have an estimation as

$$M1 = \kappa |M| X \geq \gamma X \tag{41}$$

Meanwhile, as mentioned above, when X marks commodity function and Y money function, and $M = \kappa B$ where B is high energy money and κ money multiplier, it is found that the $(\gamma/\kappa)<|M|=|Y/X|<(\beta+1)$ is a stable choice to approach the optimum quantity of money. When the k links with marginal effect as

$$\kappa = 1/(1-\frac{\partial M}{\partial Z}) \tag{42}$$

where Z is a complex variable of X and Y, the multiplier effect, the marginal effect and the complex metrics are linked together.

The QE policy might disturb the exchange rate via the interest rate, so that it could cause chaos in the economic system. This is also a potential crisis.

Meanwhile, it is valuable to point out that tax rates are rigidly regulated by law, with long-term stability; interest rates are controlled by the central bank, possessing short-term stability; and the exchange rate will randomly fluctuate according to market changes. The above studies and discussions are based on the standard of a nation/country. As tax rates and interest rates are formulated in a nation/country, and exchange rates happen among nations/ countries, the economic factors constitute a complex system. Our analysis was highly simplified, so that there are limitations for practical applications.

CONCLUSION

Although complex numbers seem more complicated than real numbers, the complex metrics actually simplifies the measures of money supply. Therefore, we can have a simple solution for scaling money supply using complex economic metrics.

While the upper- and lower-limitations of money supply are scaled and numerically estimated, the money policies can also be restricted. Since the financial system is complex, the above analysis and discussion are a highly simplified estimation of financial markets. It is expected to provide a useful foundation for further studies.

REFERENCES

Arrow, K. (1963). *Social Choice and Individual Values* (2nd ed.). Yale University Press.

Arrow, K., & Debreu, G. (1954). Existence of an equilibrium for a competitive economy. *Econometrica*, *22*(3), 265–290. doi:10.2307/1907353

Atkinson, A., Piketty, T., & Saez, E. (2011). Top incomes in the long run of history. *Journal of Economic Literature*, *49*(1), 3–71. doi:10.1257/jel.49.1.3

Blanchard, O. J., & Gali, J. (2010). Labor markets and monetary policy: A new Keynesian model with unemployment. *American Economic Journal. Macroeconomics*, *2*(2), 1–30. doi:10.1257/mac.2.2.1

Coase, R. H. (1960). The problem of social cost. *The Journal of Law & Economics*, *3*, 1–44. doi:10.1086/466560

Davis, J. (2003). *The Theory of the Individual in Economics*. Routledge. doi:10.4324/9780203457689

Dollar, D., Kleineberg, T., & Kraay, A. (2014). *Growth, inequity and social welfare: cross country evidence*. World Bank Policy Research Department Working Paper No. 6842.

Dollar, D., & Kraay, A. (2002). Growth is good for the poor. *Journal of Economic Growth, 7*(3), 195–225. doi:10.1023/A:1020139631000

Dornbusch, R. (1976). Exchange rate expectations and monetary policy. *Journal of International Economics, 6*, 231–244. doi:10.1016/0022-1996(76)90001-5

Faccarello, G., & Kurz, H. D. (2016). Handbook on the History of Economic Analysis. Vol. I: Great Economists since Petty and Boisguilbert; Vol. II: Schools of Thought in Economics. Edward Elgar.

Feldman, A. M., & Serrano, R. (2005). *Welfare Economics and Social Choice Theory* (2nd ed.). Springer Science & Business Media, Inc.

Feldstein, M. S. (1976). Inflation, income taxes, and the rate of interest – a theoretical analysis. *The American Economic Review, 66*, 806–820.

Fischer, S. (1977). Long-term contracts, rational expectations, and the optimal money supply rule. *Journal of Political Economy, 85*(1), 191–205. doi:10.1086/260551

Fischer, S. (1983). A framework for monetary and banking analysis. *Economic Journal, 93*, 1-16.

Fleming, J. M. (1962). Domestic monetary policies under fixed and floating exchange rates. IMF Staff Papers, 9, 369–379.

Floyd, J. E. (2010). *Interest Rates, Exchange Rates and World Monetary Policy*. Springer. doi:10.1007/978-3-642-10280-6

Forni, M., & Lippi, M. (1997). *Aggregation and the Microfoundations of Dynamic Macroecomics*. Oxford University Press.

Friedman, B. M., & Hahn, F. H. (Eds.). (2000). *Handbook of Monetary Economics* (Vol. 1-2). Elsevier.

Friedman, M. (1948). A monetary and fiscal framework for economic stability. *The American Economic Review, 38*(3), 245–264.

Friedman, M. (1956). *Studies in the Quantity Theory of Money*. University of Chicago Press.

Friedman, M. (1966). The Methodology of Positive Economics. In *Essays in Positive Economics*. University of Chicago Press.

Friedman, M. (1970). A theoretical framework for monetary analysis. *Journal of Political Economy, 78*(2), 193–238. doi:10.1086/259623

Gilder, G. (2012). *Wealth and Poverty: A new edition for the twenty-first century*. Regnery Pub. Inc.

Gilder, G. (2013). *Knowledge and Power: The information theory of capitalism and how it is revolutionizing our world*. Regnery Pub. Inc.

Goodfriend, M., & King, R. G. (1997). The new neoclassical synthesis and the role of monetary policy. *NBER Macroeconomics Annual, 12*, 231–283. doi:10.1086/654336

Gray, J. A. (1976). Wage indexation: A microeconomic approach. *Journal of Monetary Economics, 2*(2), 221–235. doi:10.1016/0304-3932(76)90034-9

Hahn, F. H. (1960). The stability of growth equilibrium. *The Quarterly Journal of Economics, 74*(2), 206–226. doi:10.2307/1884251

Heyne, P., Boettke, P., & Prychitko, D. (2013). *The Economic Way of Thinking* (13th ed.). Pearson Education.

Hicks, J. R. (1946). *Value and Capital: An inquiry into some fundamental principles of economic theory* (2nd ed.). Oxford University Press.

Horwitz, S. (2000). *Microfoundations and Macroeconomics: An Austrian Perspective*. Routledge. doi:10.4324/9780203456309

Jones, R. W., & Kenen, P. B. (Eds.). (1985). *Handbook of International Economics*. Elsevier.

Keynes, J. M. (2012). The General Theory of Employment, Interest and Money (The Collected Writings of John Maynard Keynes Vol. 7). Cambridge University Press.

King, R. G. (2000). The new IS-LM model: Language, logic, and limits. *Federal Reserve Bank of Richmond Economic Quarterly, 86*, 45–103.

Lamb, M., Lymer, A., & Freedman, J. (2005). *Taxation: An Interdisciplinary Approach to Research*. Oxford University Press.

Lengwiler, Y. (2004). *Microfoundations of Financial Economics: An Introduction to General Equilibrium Asset Pricing*. Princeton University Press.

Lucas, R., & Rapping, L. (1970). Real Wages, Employment and Inflation. In E. Phelps (Ed.), *Microeconomic Foundations of Employment and Inflation Theory* (pp. 253–305). Norton.

Lucas, R. E. Jr. (1972). Expectations and the neutrality of money. *Journal of Economic Theory*, *4*(2), 103–124. doi:10.1016/0022-0531(72)90142-1

Lucas, R. E. (1973). Some international evidence on output-inflation tradeoffs. *The American Economic Review*, *63*, 526–534.

Lucas, R. E. Jr. (1975). An equilibrium model of the business cycle. *Journal of Political Economy*, *83*(6), 1113–1144. doi:10.1086/260386

Lucas, R. E. (1988). On the mechanics of development planning. *Journal of Monetary Economics*, *22*, 3–42. doi:10.1016/0304-3932(88)90168-7

Mäki, U. (2012). Handbook of the Philosophy of Science: Vol. 13. *Philosophy of Economics*. Elsevier.

Marshall, A. (2013). *Principles of Economics* (8th ed.). Palgrave Macmillan LLC. doi:10.1057/9781137375261

Mises, L. (2006). *The Ultimate Foundation of Economic Science: An Essay on Method*. Liberty Fund, Inc.

Mishkin, F. S. (2004). *The Economics of Money, Banking, and Financial Markets* (7th ed.). Addison-Wesley.

Modigliani, F. (1963). The monetary mechanism and its interaction with real phenomena. *The Review of Economics and Statistics*, *45*(1), 76–103. doi:10.2307/1927150

Mundell, R. A. (1962). The appropriate use of monetary and fiscal policy for internal and external balance. *International Monetary Fund Staff Papers*, *9*(1), 70–79. doi:10.2307/3866082

Mundell, R. A. (1963). *Capital mobility and stabilization policy under fixed and flexible exchange rates. Canadian Journal of Economic and Political Science, 29(4), 475–485.*

Nicola, P. C. (2013). *Efficiency and Equity in Welfare Economics*. Springer. doi:10.1007/978-3-642-30071-4

North, D. C. (1990). *Institutions, Institutional Change and Economic Performance*. Cambridge University Press. doi:10.1017/CBO9780511808678

Phelps, E. (1967). Phillips curves, expectations of inflation and optimal unemployment over time. *Economica*, *34*(135), 254–281. doi:10.2307/2552025

Phillips, A. W. (1958). The Relationship between Unemployment and the Rate of Change of Money Wages in the United Kingdom 1861-1953. *Economica*, *25*, 283–299.

Piketty, Th. (2014). *Capital in the twenty-first century (A. Goldhammer, Trans.)*. Harvard University Press. doi:10.4159/9780674369542

Polyanin, A. D., & Manzhirov, A. V. (2007). *Handbook of Mathematics for Engineers and Scientists*. Taylor & Francis Group.

Samuelson, P. A. (1983). Foundations of Economic Analysis (Enlarged ed.). Harvard University Press.

Samuelson, P. A., & Nordhaus, W. D. (2010). *Economics* (19th ed.). McGraw-Hill Co.

Scarth, W. (2014). *Macroeconomics: the development of modern methods for policy analysis*. Edward Elgar.

Schumpeter, J. A. (2003). Capitalism, Socialism, and Demacracy (e-Library ed.). London: Routledge (Taylor & Francis Group).

Sidrauski, M. (1967). Inflation and economic growth. *Journal of Political Economy*, *75*(6), 796–810. doi:10.1086/259360

Smith, A. (1977). An Inquiry into the Nature and Causes of the Wealth of Nations (UK ed.). Chicago: University of Chicago Press.

Solow, R. M. (1956). A contribution to the theory of economic growth. *The Quarterly Journal of Economics*, *70*(1), 65–94. doi:10.2307/1884513

Stigler, G. J. (1961). The economics of information. *Journal of Political Economy*, *69*(3), 213–225. doi:10.1086/258464

Taylor, J. B. (1979). Staggered wage setting in a macro model. *The American Economic Review*, *69*, 108–113.

Tobin, J. (1969). A general equilibrium approach to monetary theory. *Journal of Money, Credit and Banking*, *1*(1), 15–26. doi:10.2307/1991374

Tobin, J. (1975). Keynesian models of recession and depression. *American Economic Review Proceedings*, *65*, 195–202.

Walras, L. (1954). Elements of Pure Economics, or the theory of social wealth (4th ed., W. Jaffé, Trans.). London: George Allen & Unwin Ltd.

Woodford, M. (2003). *Interest and Prices: Foundations of a Theory of Monetary Policy*. Princeton University Press.

Ye, F. Y. (2017). A synthetic macro-economic model integrating interest, exchange and tax rates. In *Scientific Metrics: toward analytical and quantitative sciences* (pp. 127–140). Springer. doi:10.1007/978-981-10-5936-0_11

Chapter 7
Analytical Extension

ABSTRACT

With more discussions on some extending synthetic models, it is pointed out that the analytical extension may process complicated economic issues with feasible practical applications. Around the IS-LM core, Lucas model, Fischer model, and Taylor model become sample models under the imperfect information and imperfect competition conditions. A cubic economic model may also provide a possible extension, and then future development will approach extendable economics. The author discusses more extensions in this chapter.

INTRODUCTION

Extended Synthetic Model

There are many economic models for describing economic phenomena and processes, particularly for economic analysis. An economic model is a theoretical construct that represents economic processes by a set of variables and logical or quantitative relationships between them. It could provide a simplified framework to illustrate complicated economic phenomena. Economic models are powerful tools that may assist in understanding some economic relationships, thus, we can have some renowned models in economics, such as the IS-LM model, supply-demand model, and so on.

DOI: 10.4018/978-1-6684-4935-6.ch007

Under the standard model of Arrow-Debreu-Mundell-Fleming, economics could achieve coherence at both a micro- and macro-level. In my synthetic macroeconomic model (Ye, 2017), the variables of interest, exchange and tax rates are synthesized into one model, which potentially promotes economic modeling. However, some important economic factors have not yet been included, such as labor or employment and so on. In macroeconomics, in particular, the interrelations among the labor market, the commodity market and the money market should be unified, for probing how these interactions influence macro-level variables such as employment levels, aggregate income and gross domestic product. Many factors interact with each other in the complex economic system, leading to complicated phenomena and results.

There are some important current economic models that reveal key economic relationships. Two of these models, namely, Mundell–Fleming model (Mundell, 1963; Fleming, 1962) in macro-economics and Arrow-Debreu model (Arrow & Debreu, 1954) in micro-economics, as well as their possible synthesis, extension and improvements (Ye, 2017, 2020), are given special theoretical attention.

Let the E-equations include IS curve and LM curve based on the Cobb-Douglas model and Fischer equation with technological progress. While E-equations reveal essential relations among ratio variables, F-equations can be set up as the formal relations between micro-logarithmic per-capita variables and macroeconomic indicators.

An ideal analytical model can also extend the E-equations, based on

$$y = f(k,h) = \alpha k + (1 - \alpha)h \tag{1}$$

This means that $Y = K^{\alpha} H^{(1-\alpha)}$. If $C = K^{\theta} H^{(1-\theta)}$ for full equilibrium, the IS and LM relationships can be combined to yield the aggregate demand function by eliminating the interest rate, leading to the result

$$y = \theta(m - p) + (1 - \theta)h \tag{2}$$

The extended synthetic model combining the Arrow-Debreu-Mundell-Fleming model and the Cobb-Douglas-Solow-Swan model includes increment $\Delta Y = K\lambda\, Hq^{(1-\alpha)}$

$$y = \alpha k + (1 - \alpha)^{h} + \theta(m - p) + (1 - \theta)h = \log(be^{y}) \tag{3.1}$$

$$\Delta y = \lambda k + q(1 - \lambda)h \tag{3.2}$$

$$\dot{k} = sf(k) - (n + d)k \tag{3.3}$$

where the first and second equations stand for IS-LM core model and aggregate supply-demand equilibrium, the third equation denotes Solow-Swan curve, and the last equation indicates the linkage of per-capita Solow-Swan model and logarithmic Cobb-Douglas model.

In the synthetic model, there are three model parameters (α, θ, ϕ) and three economic parameters (b, s, d). The b, s and d just stand for big parameter, small parameter and micro-parameter, with estimated values at b~103· s~10^{-1} and d~$10^{-2.}$ The model parameters can be estimated as $\alpha \sim \theta \sim 0.3$, $\phi > 0$. Since Y = C + I + G and I = S = sY, Y ≥3 C, so that $\alpha \leq \theta$. The inflation rate $\lambda = \gamma - \gamma^* \sim 0.03$. If $\alpha = 0.3, 1 - \alpha = 0.7$, inflation rate $\lambda = \gamma - \gamma^* = 0.03$, we can a simulate an economic system.

The complementary equations cover the following relations with

$$\gamma - \bar{\gamma} = \dot{\pi} - \dot{p};\ \gamma(1-\tau) - \rho = n = \dot{Y} / Y = \dot{K} / K \tag{4.1}$$

$$\gamma = \dot{p} / p;\ \lambda = \dot{m} / m;\ \tau = \dot{c} / c \tag{4.2}$$

In fact, all economic models are determined by four key variables (y, m, p, k) and three policy rates (γ, τ, π), as well as three model parameters (α, θ, ϕ) and three economic parameters (b, s, d).

For example, the classical Keynes' aggregate demand – aggregate supply model can be expressed as

$$y = \alpha(m - p),\ \alpha>0 \tag{5.1}$$

$$y = \beta(m - w),\ \beta<0 \tag{5.2}$$

$$w = w^* \tag{5.3}$$

where w stands for nominal wages and w* marks real wage, and Greek characters denote model parameters.

Under the condition of imperfect information, Lucas (1972) constructed his macroeconomic model, in which there is a key link between money supply and price and output changes in a simplified economy using rational expectations. It also delivered a new classical explanation of the Phillips curve relationship between unemployment and inflation. Lucas presented his streamlined version as follows

$$y = \alpha(m - p) \tag{6.1}$$

$$p_j = p + e_j, j=1,2,\ldots,n \tag{6.2}$$

$$y_j = \beta(p_j - Ep_j) \tag{6.3}$$

Equation (6.1) is the aggregate demand at macro-level. Equation (6.2) gives the price facing each firm p_j at micro-level, where p_j differs from the price level p by a random variable e_j, which reflects movements in relative demands across markets. Equation (6.3) provides the supply of each firm, in which Ep_j is the expectation of the price level by firm j, based on its observation of p_j.

The Lucas model combines macroeconomic consideration with microeconomic observation and is proved to be suitable under imperfect information. Each individual produces some quantity y_j, which cumulates to produce total output Y and match the amount of money M. Individuals use money for a given number of times to buy a certain quantity of goods which cost a certain price. In the quantity theory of money, this is expressed as the famous Fisher's exchange equation MV = PY at macro-level, where money supply times velocity equals price times output.

Similarly, under imperfect competition, Fischer (1977) introduced his model as follows

$$y = \alpha(m - p) + \mathrm{v} \tag{7.1}$$

$$y = -(w - p) \tag{7.2}$$

$$w = E(p_{-1} \tag{7.3}$$

In Fischer's system, Equation (7.1) is the aggregate demand, with unit elasticity of output with respect to money balances, in which v is a non-policy demand disturbance. Equation (7.2) is the output supply, obtained from profit maximization, with the assumption of unit elasticity of output supply with respect to wage. Equation (7.3) says that nominal wages present a constant real wage and constant employment at the beginning of the period, in expectation.

In addition, the Fischer-Gray model (Fischer, 1977; Gray, 1976) was developed to analyze the wage indexation under perfect competition, as follows

$$y = (m - p) \tag{8.1}$$

$$y = -(w - p) - u \tag{8.2}$$

$$w = kp + (1 - k)Ep \tag{8.3}$$

where Equation (8.1) is still aggregate demand. Equation (8.2) gives labor demand under perfect competition, and allows for a supply or productivity shock, U, with expected value EU = 0. Equation (8.3) gives the wage-setting rule, with the degree of indexation being equal to k, where $0 \leq k \leq 1$, with k = 0 indicates no indexation and k = 1 full indexation.

All of the above models enrich economic modeling for macroeconomic analysis, and reveal, in particular, labor-wage mechanism. If there are total labor as L at macro-level and each individual with wage w at micro-level, W = Lw will give a simple macro-micro-relation of labor-wage. Meanwhile, it is shown that the total economic quantity Y and price level P are necessary economic measures in all models, so that we should keep them in a new model (Ye, 2017, 2020).

Similar to Fischer's two-period staggered wage-setting model, but with one important difference (namely, wages are not only pre-determined, but are fixed for two periods), Taylor (1979) suggested his model under imperfect competition

$$y = \alpha(m - p) \tag{9.1}$$

$$p = \frac{1}{2}\beta(w + w_{-1}) \tag{9.2}$$

$$w = \frac{1}{2}(p + Ep_{+1})_{-1} + \frac{1}{2}\text{a}(Ey_{-1} + Ey_{+1})_{-1} \tag{9.3}$$

In this model, Equation (9.1) gives the aggregate demand, and Equation (9.2) gives the price level as a weighted average of two wages, where half of the labor force is paid W in the current period and half is paid W_{-1} in the previous period. Equation (9.3) says that wages W are determined by price level and output with elasticity a, in which both concern the expectations in the previous and next period.

Therefore, Tobin's improvements (Tobin, 1975), Lucas model (Lucas, 1972, 1973, 1975), Fischer model (1977, 1983) and Taylor model (1979) become sample models under the imperfect information and imperfect competition conditions. The core economic thoughts (Arrow, 1963; Arrow & Debreu, 1954; Friedman, 1948, 1956, 1957, 1966, 1970; Hicks, 1946; Lucas, 1972, 1973, 1975, 1988; Keynes, 2012; Marshall, 2013; Fleming, 1962; Mundell, 1962, 1963; Samuelson, 1983; Samuelson & Nordhaus, 2010; Solow, 1956; Taylor, 1979; Tobin, 1969, 1975; Walras, 1954) are maintained, and economic developments (Faccarello & Kurz, 2016; Feldman & Serrano, 2005; Forni & Lippi, 1997; Floyd, 2010; Friedman & Hahn, 2000; Gilder, 2012, 2013; Heyne, Boettke & Prychitko, 2013; Horwitz, 2000; Jones & Kenen, 1985; King, 2000; Lengwiler, 2004; Mishkin, 2004; Scarth, 2014; Weintraub, 1977, 1979) are matched.

When we combine Equations (31), (36) and (38) in chapter 4, we may derive

$$\dot{y} = \alpha(\gamma - \bar{\gamma}) + (1-\alpha)\dot{g} = \theta(\dot{m} - \dot{p}) + \theta(\pi - p) \tag{10}$$

in which $(\gamma - \bar{\gamma}) = \dot{k}$ and $\alpha(\gamma - \bar{\gamma}) = \theta(\dot{m} - \dot{p})$ as $y = \alpha k + (1-\alpha)h = \theta(m-p) + (1-\theta)g$.

In addition, hybrid IS curve and hybrid Phillips curve can construct another reference model

$$\dot{y} = \alpha(\gamma - \bar{\gamma}) + (1-\alpha)\dot{g} \tag{11.1}$$

$$\ddot{p} = -\phi(y - \bar{y}) + \beta(g - \bar{g}) \tag{11.2}$$

where $(1 - \alpha)$ is the full-equilibrium ratio of autonomous spending to total output ($\alpha = C/Y$, $Y = C + G$). If $\alpha \to \beta \sim \pm 1$, $(1 - \alpha) \to 0$. So we may have $\dot{y} = \beta(\gamma - \bar{\gamma})$.

When we focus on the consumption c and government spending g, a simplified extended model, dispensing with interest-income tax rate τ and wage-income tax rate τ_w, can be defined using the following equations (Scarth, 2014)

$$f'(k) = \gamma + \delta \tag{12.1}$$

$$\dot{c} = (\gamma(1-\tau) - \rho - n)c - p(p+\rho)k \qquad (12.2)$$

$$\dot{k} + nk = f(k) - c - \delta k - g \qquad (12.3)$$

$$g = \gamma\tau k + \tau_w w \qquad (12.4)$$

The first equation states that firms maximize profits and hire capital until the marginal product equals the rental cost, the second equation represents the lived agents involving inter-temporal utility maximization, the third equation is the good market clearing condition as economic resource constraint, and the fourth equation defines the government budget constraint.

The five equations can determine the equilibrium value of four variables k, c, p, g (supposing one policy variable τ). When we set all exogenous variables change (except x is only reference variable) to zero, we have the result

$$dc/c = [(\gamma - n)\, p(p + \rho)dx] \,/\, [nc((\gamma - n)\,(\gamma - n - \rho) - p(p + \rho))] \qquad (13)$$

The result will keep equilibrium in the representative values for the parameters as $\gamma = 0.05$, $\rho = 0.025$, $n = p = 0.02$. When $x = nb$, it is full equilibrium.

Practically, a tax rate describes the ratio (usually expressed as a percentage) at which a business or person is taxed. Several methods are used to present a tax rate: statutory, average, marginal, and effective. These rates can also be presented using different definitions applied to a tax base: inclusive and exclusive. A statutory tax rate is legally imposed. An income tax could have multiple statutory rates for different income levels, where a sales tax may have a flat statutory rate. An average tax rate is the ratio of the total amount of taxes paid to the total tax base (taxable income or spending), expressed as a percentage. A proportional tax rate is fixed and the average tax rate equals this tax rate. A marginal tax rate refers to the tax rate an individual would pay on one additional income.

Since interest rate and exchange rate are correlated to inflation, we may add the factor of inflation into the existing model (Ye, 2017, 2020), with different calibration in a down-vertically direction, as shown in Figure 1.

In the extended synthetic model, the Mundell–Fleming model (Fleming, 1962; Mundell, 1963), money demand-supply model and Laffer curve (Laffer, 2004) are combined within the framework of interest, exchange and tax rates. The extended synthetical model is illustrated in Figure 1. To avoid confusion with imaginary unit and time, I apply Greek characters γ, π and τ to denote interest rate, exchange rate and tax rate, respectively. The extended synthetic model includes the following four parts:

Figure 1. An extended synthetic model for economic analysis

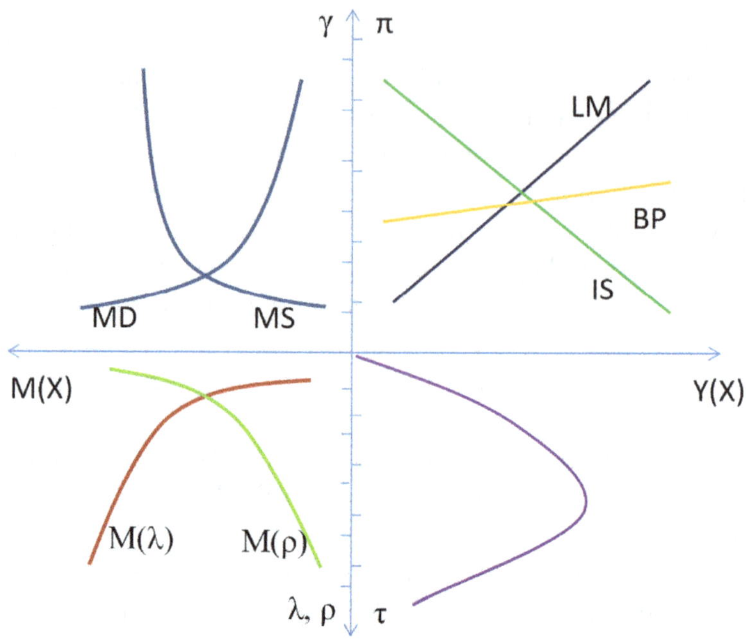

The first part is the Mundell–Fleming model, characterized by IS-LM-BP curves, described by the domestic interest rate plotted vertically and real GDP (Y) plotted horizontally, where IS curve represents the equilibrium of product market, the LM curve means the equilibrium of the money market, and BP addresses the balance of payments or international income-payment. Geometrically, the IS curve is downward sloped and the LM curve is upward sloped, while the BP curve is upward sloped unless there is perfect capital mobility, in which it is horizontal at the level of the world interest rate. In the IS-LM-BP graph, under less than perfect capital mobility, the positions of both the IS curve and the BP curve depend on the exchange rate, since the IS-LM graph is a two-dimensional cross-section of a three-dimensional space involving all of the interest rate, income, and the exchange rate. The IS-LM graph is also the core part of the Mundell–Fleming model, where the IS curve shift represents the change of fiscal policy and the LM curve shift stands for the change of monetary policy. Under perfect capital mobility, the BP curve is simply horizontal when the level of the domestic interest rate is equal to the world interest rate level. In the pure IS-LM model, the domestic interest rate is a key component for keeping both the money market and the commodity market in equilibrium. However, unlike the pure IS-LM model, the Mundell–Fleming model adds the international financial elements to fit to the open economy assumption.

The second part is the money demand and supply curve, where the demand curve of money illustrates the quantity of money demanded at a given interest rate. Generally, the demand curve of money is downward sloping, which means that people want to hold less of their wealth in the form of money when interest rates on bonds and other alternative investments are higher. The supply curve of money illustrates the quantity of money supplied at a given interest rate. Unlike a typical supply curve in the commodity market, the supply curve of money could be vertical, because it might not depend on interest rates. In fact, it depends entirely on decisions made by the central bank, as the central bank controls the supply of money. However, the market mechanism could also introduce the demand-supply interaction into the money market to illustrate the money demand and supply using normal demand-supply curves. The equilibrium in the money market takes place when the quantity of money demanded is equal to the quantity supplied. Since there are complex relations between interest and exchange rates (Sánchez, 2005; Floyd, 2010), to simplify the discussed issues, it is specified that real exchange rate and nominal interest rate are linked by $\gamma®\pi^*$, characterized by national money vs. foreign money; in other words, interest and exchange rates keep changing in the same direction.

The third part is the Laffer curve, which is one possible representation of the relationship between rates of taxation and the hypothetical resulting levels of government revenue. Because the government revenue is proportional to GDP, I translate the Laffer curve into the coordinate system with tax rate plotted down-vertically and real GDP (Y) plotted horizontally here. Following claims to illustrate the concept of taxable income elasticity, taxable income will change in response to changes in the rate of taxation.

The fourth part is the interaction of $M(\lambda)$ and $M(\rho)$ curves by adding the factors of inflation and unemployment into the synthetic model, where the $M(X)$ affect $M(\lambda)$ and $M(\rho)$ following different λ and ρ.

Thus, the extended synthetic model integrates interest, exchange, tax, inflation and unemployment rates, where interest and exchange rates are plotted up-vertically with different calibration in the same direction, while tax, inflation and unemployment rates are plotted down-vertically. The Mundell–Fleming model (IS-LM-BP curves) is set in the first quadrant, the money demand-supply model occupies the second quadrant, the M(λ) and M(ρ) curves are put in the third quadrant, and the Laffer curve is arranged in the fourth quadrant.

Using the above synthetic model, during the period of economic expansion or economic overheat, the interest decreases and/or tax reduction could benefit the following items

1. At a national level, decreasing official corruption
2. At an enterprise level, increasing R&D investment
3. At an individual level, stimulating consumption and charitable behavior

Thus, a policy analysis for optimal modifications is shown in Figure 2, where the short arrows of all curves denote the directions of economic changes and the short arrows along coordinates indicate the expected directions of economic modifications by the policy.

Figure 2. A policy modification during economy expansion

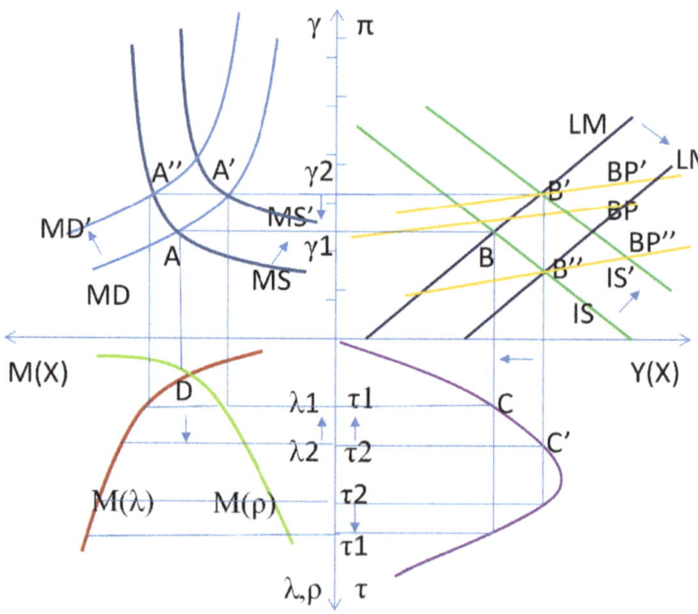

Meanwhile, during the period of economic contraction or economic depression, the interest increases and/or tax increase could benefit the following items

1. At a national level, balancing the rich and the poor
2. At an enterprise level, decreasing bank loans
3. At an individual level, reducing consumption, particularly eliminating luxury

A policy analysis for optimal modifications is shown in Figure 3, where the short arrows of all curves denote the directions of economic changes and the short arrows along coordinates indicate the expected directions of economic modifications by the policy.

Figure 3. A modified policy during economy depression

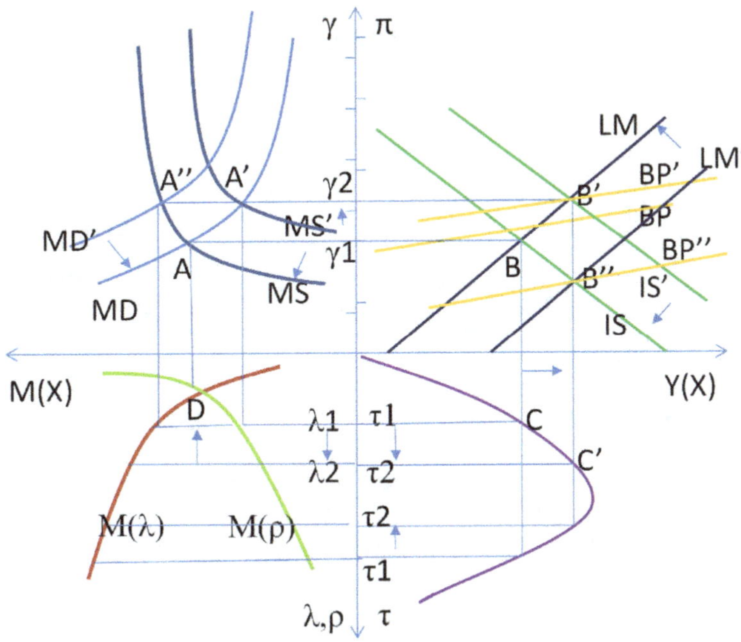

So, the best policy when the economy extends is tax reduction, while the best policy when the economy contracts is tax increase. In consideration of political economics, tax reduction on all enterprises could benefit all, while tax increase on the rich could benefit the poor.

The policy of Figure 3 implies that the tax reduction should be good if tax rate is lower than normal ($\tau < \tau 0$) and tax increase should be good if tax rate is higher than normal ($\tau > \tau 0$), during the period of economic overheat or expansion (Y↑↑), which would benefit the following items

1. At a national level, decreasing official corruption (Y↑↑caused B -> B', policy τ2 -> τ1 would lead to IS' -> IS, or via LM' -> LM and B'' -> B to reach optimal equilibrium A-B-C).
2. At an enterprise level, increasing R&D input (Y↑↑caused A -> A', policy τ2 -> τ1 would lead to MS'->MS, or via MD' ->MD and A''->A to reach optimal equilibrium A-B-C).
3. At an individual level, stimulating consumption and charitable donation (policy τ2 -> τ1 would lead to MS'->MS or MD'->MD to reach optimal equilibrium A-B-C).

Figure 4. A policy analysis for charitable donation

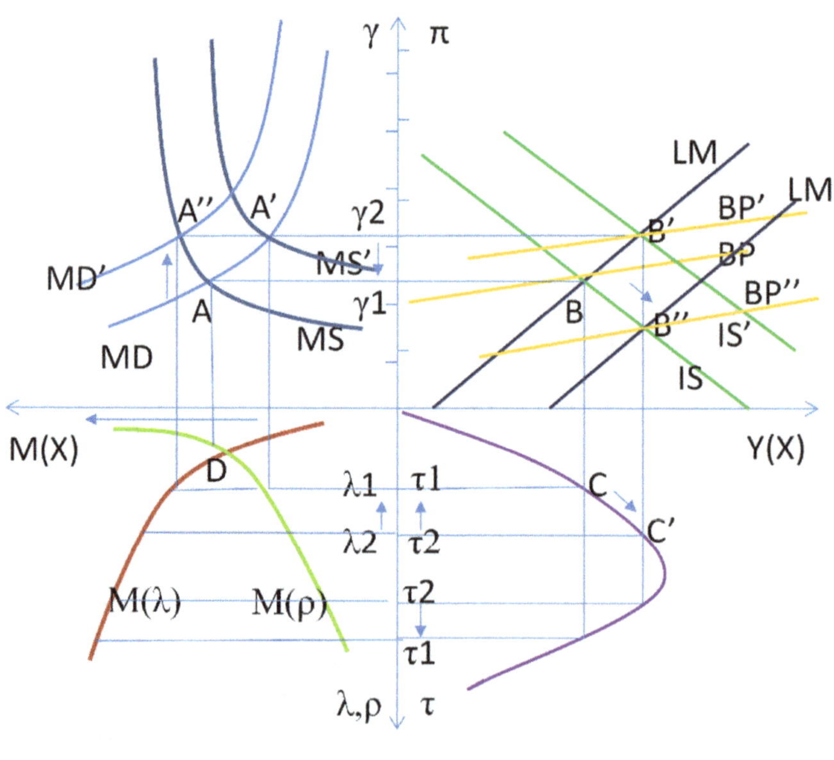

If the economy depresses or contracts (Y↓↓), a policy analysis just inverses. Moreover, charitable donations resemble money increase without any economic production, as shown in Figure 4, where all arrows around the curves reveal phenomena and all the arrows around the coordinates indicate the expected directions of economic modification.

The policy of Figure 4 implies that the tax reduction should be good if tax rate is higher than normal ($\tau > \tau 0$) and tax increase should be good if tax rate is lower than normal ($\tau < \tau 0$), during the period of economic depression or contraction (Y↓↓), which would benefit the following items

1. At a national level, balancing the rich and the poor (Y↓↓ caused B' -> B, and then policy τ1 -> τ2 would lead to IS -> IS', or via LM -> LM' and B'' -> B' to reach optimal equilibrium A'-B'-C').
2. At an enterprise level, decreasing bank loan (Y↓↓ caused A' -> A, and then policy τ1 -> τ2 would lead to MS->MS', or via MD ->MD' and A''->A' to reach optimal equilibrium A'-B'-C').
3. At an individual level, reducing consumption, particularly deleting luxury (policy τ1 -> τ2 would lead to MS->MS' or MD->MD' to reach optimal equilibrium A'-B'-C').

In both Figures 3 and 4, the normal point of tax rate (τ0) can be defined as a legal point in tax laws, or theoretical expected point.

Certainly, the tax policy looks complicated, more so than monetary policy, where the interest ratio is an effective tool for regulating the economy by raising or reducing interest rates. However, the tax policy may be a useful tool for balancing social wealth, particularly combining equity and efficiency. A good tax policy could reach axiological good. In consideration of political economics, the tax reduction on enterprises could benefit all enterprises, while the tax increase on the rich could benefit the poor.

As a general rule, a country with a consistently lower inflation rate exhibits a rising currency value, as its purchasing power increases relative to other currencies. Thus, inflation is also a key factor in macroeconomic analysis (Sidrauski, 1967; Lucas, 1973), where there is cost-push inflation or demand-pull inflation. Gentle inflation reflects a healthy economy.

While money supply does not exceed the equilibrium point of MS and MD, inflation will remain at a gentle increase. When the money supply exceeds the equilibrium point, inflation will increase slightly. Once the money supply surpluses the lower limitation for QE, the higher inflation may occur, causing the inflation rate to increase quickly. The curve in the third quadrant describes the situation, which is completely different from the Phillips curve, where the inflation rate links to unemployment. Generally, when the unemployment rate increases, the government should decrease tax. If there were a healthy stock market that could become a regulator for balancing economy, a tax-free policy might be applied when the stock market values were too low.

CUBIC ECONOMIC MODEL AND POSSIBLE FINDINGS

Ye (2017) applied three relative ratios (interest rate, exchange rate and tax rate) and two total absolute quantities (gross domestic product Y, and money supply M) in the synthetic economic model. In this article, the researcher clarifies the meanings of variables by defining that capital Latin letters denote total economic quantities and lower-case Greek letters give relative ratios, while Greek characters γ, π, τ and λ, respectively, indicate interest rate, exchange rate, tax rate and inflation rate.

While GDP as Y and money as M are set into the horizontal coordinate, all other coordinates can be arranged by different rates. Following π links γ positively, γ and π are arranged at the same vertical coordinate, it can be safely drawn that γ and π are positively related. Moreover, τ and λ are not simply in a positive relation, and many other related factors need to be considered as well, thus, it should be arranged into another coordinate. As for η denoting unemployment rate, it should also be arranged but in a different direction.

Finally, integrating the Mundell-Fleming model, money demand-supply model and Laffer curve, a cubic integrated macroeconomic model is introduced in Figure 5, where the Mundell–Fleming model (IS-LM-BP curves), supply-demand curves and Laffer curve (Laffer, 2004) have been integrated, for macroeconomic analysis. The Laffer curve is typically represented as a graph which starts at 0% tax with zero revenue, rises to a maximum rate of revenue at an intermediate rate of taxation, and then falls again to zero revenue at a 100% tax rate, though the shape of the curve is uncertain and disputed.

In the cubic framework of the integrated economic model, the IS–LM–BP curves described by the nominal interest rate are plotted vertically and real GDP (Y) plotted horizontally, while the supply-demand curves of money illustrate the quantity of money supplied and demanded at a given interest rate and exchange rate. According to the mainstream economic theories (Samuelson and Nordhaus, 2005; Mishkin, 2004), the gross domestic product (GDP) includes four components of expenditure: consumption (C), investment

(I), government purchases (G), and net exports (X). When Y stands for GDP and A = C + I + G, the IS curve can be presented as

$$Y = C + I + G + X = A(\gamma,Y) + X(\pi,Y) \quad (14)$$

while the LM curve is denoted at price level P as M/P = L(γ, Y).

Figure 5. The integrated economic model: cubic framework

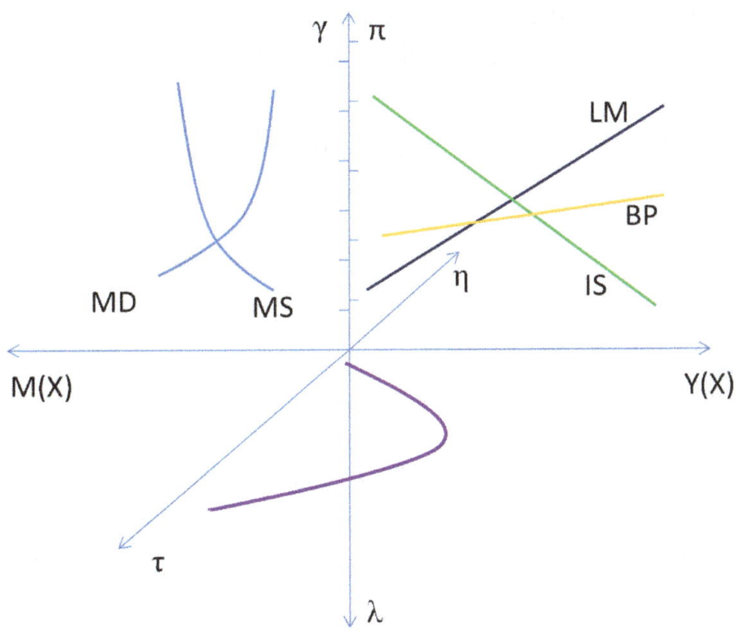

The labor force is defined as the working-age population, namely the number of people who are either employed or actively looking for work. The unemployment rate is defined as the level of unemployment divided by the labor force, while the employment rate is defined as the number of people currently employed divided by the adult population (or by the working-age population). In these statistics, self-employed people are counted as employed, and the unemployment level is defined as the labor force minus the number of currently employed population. Therefore, it can be suggested that wage-labor (W-L) relation shares similarities with the Fischer-Gray model

$$W = L(1-\eta)P + L\lambda P = LP(1-\eta+\lambda) \quad (15)$$

where η is unemployment rate and λ inflation rate. Equation (15) means that wage is linked to employment rate, inflation rate, and price level. The higher the employment rate and inflation rate are, the more wages will be paid.

The Phillips curve (Phillips, 1958; Phelps, 1967) just reveals the relationship between the unemployment rate and inflation rate. The curve can also be arranged into the cubic coordinate framework. When rotating the coordinate system in Figure 6, where the Phillips curve links the unemployment rate to the inflation rate, the decreased unemployment (i.e., the increased levels of employment) in an economy will correlate with a higher inflation rate.

The cubic integrated economic model contains more information than the plain synthetic economic model, in which the Phillips curve reveals the

Figure 6. A rotated view of the cubic integrated economic model

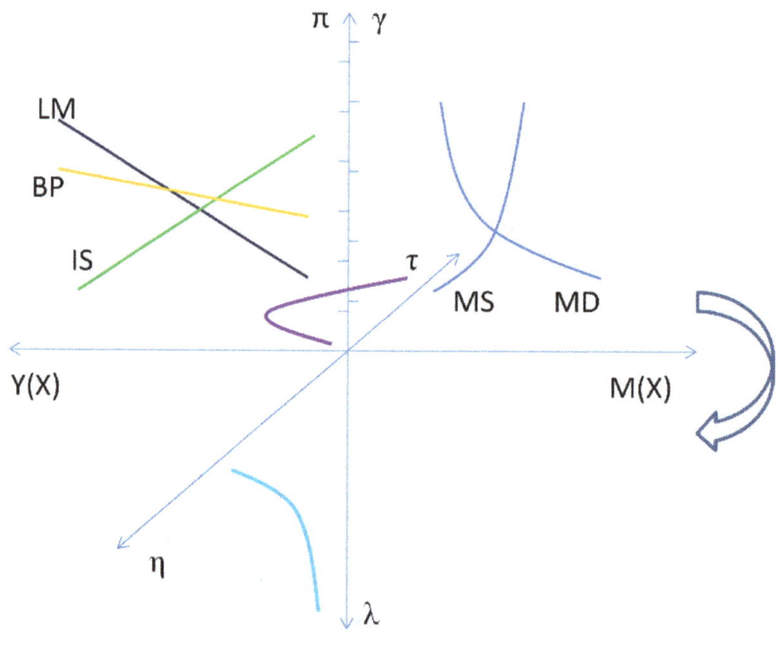

inverse relationship between the unemployment rate and the corresponding inflation rate, and the Laffer curve describes the relationship between tax rate and total output.

Generally, in the analytical system of the new neoclassical synthesis, the open-economy model in which the IS curve and Phillips curve are combined can be defined by the following equations

$$(y-\overline{y})=\beta(\gamma-\overline{\gamma}) \tag{16}$$

$$\dot{p}=\phi(y-\overline{y})+\dot{x} \tag{17}$$

$$\gamma+\dot{p}=\overline{\gamma}+\dot{\pi} \tag{18}$$

The system can also be extended to the new IS curve and Phillips curve using a methodological tool called phase diagram (Scarth, 2014) for economic policy analysis.

FUTURE FURTHER STUDIES: EXTENDABLE ECONOMICS

When many factors are integrated into one three-dimensional coordinate system, the linkages become complicated, and all factors are interrelated. Tax rates and interest rates are formulated within a nation, and exchange rates are among nations. Thus, the cubic integrated economic model, which is featured by combining national economics and international economics, can also be applied to international economic analysis.

Different metric rates follow different changeable rules. Tax rates are rigidly regulated by law to achieve long-term stability; interest rates are controlled by the central bank, with the attribute of short-term stability; and the exchange rate, inflation rate and unemployment rate randomly fluctuate with changes to the market. The metric rates become closely related to each other when the cubic integrated economic model links them together. Therefore, this provides a highly simplified model.

By applying this model, more unknown interrelationships are suggested to be explored in future studies, such as

1. The relationship between inflation, Y and M. If this relation exists, there can be curves in $\lambda \sim Y(X)$ plane as well as $\lambda \sim M(X)$ plane. This interrelationship could provide an interactive mechanism of inflation and economic output as well as money supply.
2. The relationship between unemployment and money supply. If there is such a relation, there should be a curve in $\eta \sim M(X)$ plane. This interrelationship could create a mechanism of how money supply affects employment or unemployment.

To conclude, the above discussions might promote more considerations for future development of economic modeling and economic analysis.

Figure 7. Expected econometric findings

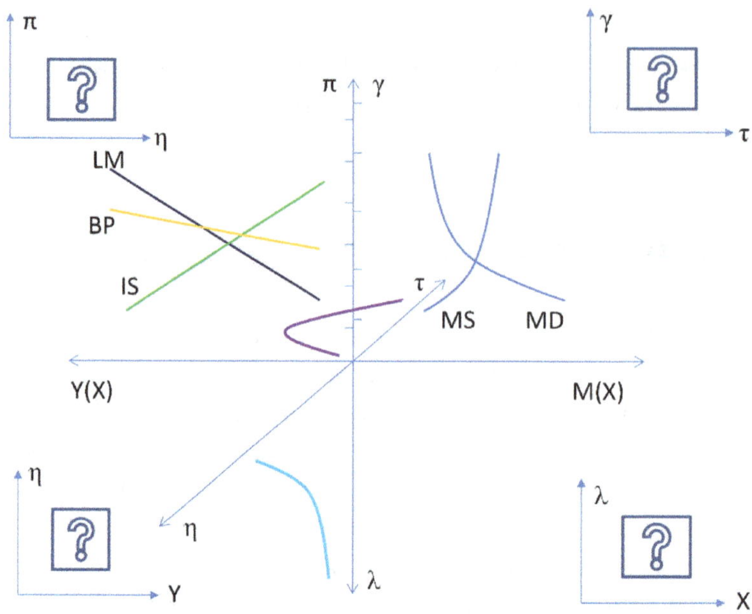

Therefore, we need new R^2 models (such as top two figures in Figure 7) and new M^2 models (such as bottom two figures in Figure 7) to complete the expected model, in future studies. The information economics (Stigler, 1961) is also another consideration.

CONCLUSION

Distributing total economic quantities and metric rates in a cubic coordinate system, the cubic integrated economic model is set up to be a new analytical framework of complicated economic phenomena. In this model, the key total economic quantities (Y and M) and important metric rates (γ, π, τ and λ) are integrated in a unified way. Including established IS-LM-BP curves, money supply-demand curves, Laffer curve and Phillips curve, the cubic integrated multiple economic models provide a possible solution for analyzing complex economic phenomena. This article presents the novel model and also proposes potential but unknown interrelationships; thus, more theoretical contributions can be made. Its potential applications could be found, and its further extensions could be expected in future.

REFERENCES

Arrow, K. (1963). *Social Choice and Individual Values* (2nd ed.). Yale University Press.

Arrow, K., & Debreu, G. (1954). Existence of an equilibrium for a competitive economy. *Econometrica, 22*(3), 265–290. doi:10.2307/1907353

Atkinson, A., Piketty, T., & Saez, E. (2011). Top incomes in the long run of history. *Journal of Economic Literature, 49*(1), 3–71. doi:10.1257/jel.49.1.3

Blanchard, O. J., & Gali, J. (2010). Labor markets and monetary policy: A new Keynesian model with unemployment. *American Economic Journal. Macroeconomics, 2*(2), 1–30. doi:10.1257/mac.2.2.1

Coase, R. H. (1960). The problem of social cost. *The Journal of Law & Economics, 3*, 1–44. doi:10.1086/466560

Davis, J. (2003). *The Theory of the Individual in Economics*. Routledge. doi:10.4324/9780203457689

Dollar, D., Kleineberg, T., & Kraay, A. (2014). *Growth, inequity and social welfare: cross country evidence.* World Bank Policy Research Department Working Paper No. 6842.

Dollar, D., & Kraay, A. (2002). Growth is good for the poor. *Journal of Economic Growth, 7*(3), 195–225. doi:10.1023/A:1020139631000

Dornbusch, R. (1976). Expectations and exchange rate dynamics. *Journal of Political Economics*, 84, 1161-1176; Exchange rate expectations and monetary policy. *Journal of International Economics, 6*, 231–244. doi:10.1016/0022-1996(76)90001-5

Faccarello, G., & Kurz, H. D. (2016). Handbook on the History of Economic Analysis. Vol. I: Great Economists since Petty and Boisguilbert; Vol. II: Schools of Thought in Economics. Edward Elgar.

Feldman, A. M., & Serrano, R. (2005). *Welfare Economics and Social Choice Theory* (2nd ed.). Springer Science & Business Media, Inc.

Feldstein, M. S. (1976). Inflation, income taxes, and the rate of interest – a theoretical analysis. *The American Economic Review*, *66*, 806–820.

Fischer, S. (1977). Long-term contracts, rational expectations, and the optimal money supply rule. *Journal of Political Economy*, *85*(1), 191–205. doi:10.1086/260551

Fischer, S. (1983). A framework for monetary and banking analysis. *Economic Journal*, *93*, 1-16.

Fleming, J. M. (1962). Domestic monetary policies under fixed and floating exchange rates. IMF Staff Papers, 9, 369–379.

Floyd, J. E. (2010). *Interest Rates, Exchange Rates and World Monetary Policy*. Springer. doi:10.1007/978-3-642-10280-6

Forni, M., & Lippi, M. (1997). *Aggregation and the Microfoundations of Dynamic Macroecomics*. Oxford University Press.

Friedman, B. M., & Hahn, F. H. (Eds.). (2000). *Handbook of Monetary Economics* (Vol. 1-2). Elsevier.

Friedman, M. (1948). A monetary and fiscal framework for economic stability. *The American Economic Review*, *38*(3), 245–264.

Friedman, M. (1956). *Studies in the Quantity Theory of Money*. University of Chicago Press.

Friedman, M. (1957). *A Theory of the Consumption Function*. Princeton University Press. doi:10.1515/9780691188485

Friedman, M. (1966). The Methodology of Positive Economics. In *Essays in Positive Economics*. University of Chicago Press.

Friedman, M. (1970). A theoretical framework for monetary analysis. *Journal of Political Economy*, *78*(2), 193–238. doi:10.1086/259623

Gilder, G. (2012). *Wealth and Poverty: A new edition for the twenty-first century*. Regnery Pub. Inc.

Gilder, G. (2013). *Knowledge and Power: The information theory of capitalism and how it is revolutionizing our world*. Regnery Pub. Inc.

Gillies, D. (1998). The Duhem thesis and the Quine thesis. In *Philosophy of Science: The Central Issues*. New York: Norton.

Goodfriend, M., & King, R. G. (1997). The new neoclassical synthesis and the role of monetary policy. *NBER Macroeconomics Annual*, *12*, 231–283. doi:10.1086/654336

Gray, J. A. (1976). Wage indexation: A microeconomic approach. *Journal of Monetary Economics*, *2*(2), 221–235. doi:10.1016/0304-3932(76)90034-9

Hahn, F. H. (1960). The stability of growth equilibrium. *The Quarterly Journal of Economics*, *74*(2), 206–226. doi:10.2307/1884251

Heyne, P., Boettke, P., & Prychitko, D. (2013). *The Economic Way of Thinking* (13th ed.). Pearson Education.

Hicks, J. R. (1946). *Value and Capital: An inquiry into some fundamental principles of economic theory* (2nd ed.). Oxford University Press.

Horwitz, S. (2000). *Microfoundations and Macroeconomics: An Austrian Perspective*. Routledge. doi:10.4324/9780203456309

Jones, R. W., & Kenen, P. B. (Eds.). (1985). *Handbook of International Economics*. Elsevier.

Keynes, J. M. (2012). The General Theory of Employment, Interest and Money (The Collected Writings of John Maynard Keynes Vol. 7). Cambridge University Press.

King, R. G. (2000). The new IS-LM model: Language, logic, and limits. *Federal Reserve Bank of Richmond Economic Quarterly*, *86*, 45–103.

Laffer, A. (2004). *The Laffer Curve: Past, Present, and Future*. The Heritage Foundation. https://www.heritage.org/research/reports/2004/06/the-laffer-curve-past-present-and-future

Lamb, M., Lymer, A., & Freedman, J. (2005). *Taxation: An Interdisciplinary Approach to Research*. Oxford University Press.

Lengwiler, Y. (2004). *Microfoundations of Financial Economics: An Introduction to General Equilibrium Asset Pricing*. Princeton University Press.

Lucas, R., & Rapping, L. (1970). Real Wages, Employment and Inflation. In E. Phelps (Ed.), *Microeconomic Foundations of Employment and Inflation Theory* (pp. 253–305). Norton.

Lucas, R. E. Jr. (1972). Expectations and the neutrality of money. *Journal of Economic Theory*, *4*(2), 103–124. doi:10.1016/0022-0531(72)90142-1

Lucas, R. E. (1973). Some international evidence on output-inflation tradeoffs. *The American Economic Review*, *63*, 526–534.

Lucas, R. E. Jr. (1975). An equilibrium model of the business cycle. *Journal of Political Economy*, *83*(6), 1113–1144. doi:10.1086/260386

Lucas, R. E. (1988). On the mechanics of development planning. *Journal of Monetary Economics*, *22*, 3–42. doi:10.1016/0304-3932(88)90168-7

Mäki, U. (2012). Handbook of the Philosophy of Science: Vol. 13. *Philosophy of Economics*. Elsevier.

Marshall, A. (2013). *Principles of Economics* (8th ed.). Palgrave Macmillan LLC. doi:10.1057/9781137375261

Mises, L. (2006). *The Ultimate Foundation of Economic Science: An Essay on Method*. Liberty Fund, Inc.

Mishkin, F. S. (2004). *The Economics of Money, Banking, and Financial Markets* (7th ed.). Addison-Wesley.

Modigliani, F. (1963). The monetary mechanism and its interaction with real phenomena. *The Review of Economics and Statistics*, *45*(1), 76–103. doi:10.2307/1927150

Mundell, R. A. (1962). The appropriate use of monetary and fiscal policy for internal and external balance. *International Monetary Fund Staff Papers*, *9*(1), 70–79. doi:10.2307/3866082

Mundell, R. A. (1963). *Capital mobility and stabilization policy under fixed and flexible exchange rates. Canadian Journal of Economic and Political Science, 29(4), 475–485.*

Nicola, P. C. (2013). *Efficiency and Equity in Welfare Economics*. Springer. doi:10.1007/978-3-642-30071-4

North, D. C. (1990). *Institutions, Institutional Change and Economic Performance*. Cambridge University Press. doi:10.1017/CBO9780511808678

Phelps, E. (1967). Phillips curves, expectations of inflation and optimal unemployment over time. *Economica*, *34*(135), 254–281. doi:10.2307/2552025

Phillips, A. W. (1958). The Relationship between Unemployment and the Rate of Change of Money Wages in the United Kingdom 1861-1953. *Economica*, *25*, 283–299.

Polyanin, A. D., & Manzhirov, A. V. (2007). *Handbook of Mathematics for Engineers and Scientists*. Taylor & Francis Group.

Samuelson, P. A. (1983). Foundations of Economic Analysis (Enlarged ed.). Harvard University Press.

Samuelson, P. A., & Nordhaus, W. D. (2010). *Economics* (19th ed.). McGraw-Hill Co.

Sánchez, M. (2005). *The link between interest rates and exchange rates. Do contractionary depreciations make a difference?* European Central Bank: Working Paper Series No. 548. http://www.ecb.int

Scarth, W. (2014). *Macroeconomics: The development of modern methods for policy analysis*. Edward Elgar.

Sidrauski, M. (1967). Inflation and economic growth. *Journal of Political Economy*, *75*(6), 796–810. doi:10.1086/259360

Smith, A. (1977). An Inquiry into the Nature and Causes of the Wealth of Nations (UK ed.). Chicago: University of Chicago Press.

Solow, R. M. (1956). A contribution to the theory of economic growth. *The Quarterly Journal of Economics*, *70*(1), 65–94. doi:10.2307/1884513

Stigler, G. J. (1961). The economics of information. *Journal of Political Economy*, *69*(3), 213–225. doi:10.1086/258464

Taylor, J. B. (1979). Staggered wage setting in a macro model. *The American Economic Review*, *69*, 108–113.

Tobin, J. (1969). A general equilibrium approach to monetary theory. *Journal of Money, Credit and Banking*, *1*(1), 15–26. doi:10.2307/1991374

Tobin, J. (1975). Keynesian models of recession and depression. *American Economic Review Proceedings*, *65*, 195–202.

Ueda, K. (2013). Banks as coordinators of economic growth and stability: Microfoundation for macroeconomy with externality. *Journal of Economic Theory*, *148*(1), 322–352. doi:10.1016/j.jet.2012.09.003

Walras, L. (1954). Elements of Pure Economics, or the theory of social wealth (4th ed., W. Jaffé, Trans.). London: George Allen & Unwin Ltd.

Weintraub, E. R. (1977). The microfoundations of macroeconomics: A critical survey. *Journal of Economic Literature*, *15*(1), 1–23.

Weintraub, E. R. (1979). *Microfoundations: The compatibility of microeconomics and macroeconomics*. Cambridge University Press. doi:10.1017/CBO9780511559570

Woodford, M. (2003). *Interest and Prices: Foundations of a Theory of Monetary Policy*. Princeton University Press.

Ye, F. Y. (2017). A synthetic macro-economic model integrating interest, exchange and tax rates. In *Scientific Metrics: toward analytical and quantitative sciences* (pp. 127–140). Springer. doi:10.1007/978-981-10-5936-0_11

Ye, F. Y. (2020). An economic analysis of efficiency and equity combining epistemological true with axiological good through microeconomics to macroeconomics. *International Journal of Economics and Financial Research*, *6*(7), 159–169. doi:10.32861/ijefr.67.159.169

Chapter 8
Interstellar Economics

ABSTRACT

Characterized by interstellar trade and interstellar finance, an interesting interstellar economics is discussed. Suppose both Earth and Mars need efficacy maximization; there may exist Pareto optimality between Earth and Mars, where both Earth side and Mars side have optimal equilibrium among their goods market and money market. Therefore, an economics with political economics would occur between the Earth and Mars, so that our knowledge of economics with political economics could extend to Earth-Mars interstellar economics.

INTRODUCTION

In the future, one might find that interstellar economic activities need interstellar economics. Here we provide a foresee exploration.

In 1978, economist Paul Krugman wrote a paper titled *The Theory of Interstellar Trade* that was published in 2010 (Krugman, 2010). In the paper, Krugman analyzed the effect of travel near the speed of light on interest rates and interstellar trade, where he extended interplanetary trade theory to an interstellar setting. He was chiefly concerned with the following question: how should interest charges on goods in transit be computed when the goods travel at close to the speed of light? This is a problem, because the time taken in transit will appear less to an observer traveling with the goods than to a stationary observer. A solution is derived from economic theory, and two useless but true theorems are proved.

DOI: 10.4018/978-1-6684-4935-6.ch008

Interstellar trade is very complicated. Time passes slower to the observer traveling at the speed of light than to anyone who stays at home. While one traveled for a year near the speed of light, a hundred or maybe a thousand years would have passed on earth. If one came back after a year, one's savings would go up and one might be suddenly a rich man. Therefore, the interest rate can only really depend upon the cost of fuel needed to 'travel into the future'.

Supposing that Musk succeed to move 100 million people to Mars in the future, where we set up Bank of Mars (BoM) and we also have the Bank of Earth (BoE), then we can discuss the Earth-Mars trade and finance.

Interstellar Trade and Finance

Just like America-Africa trade happened across the turbulent Atlantic Ocean hundreds of years ago, people might cross the vast starry space for Earth-Mars trade in the future. The situation resembles high risk in interstellar trade, as shown in Figure 1.

Figure 1. Past America-Africa Trade versus Future Earth-Mars Trade

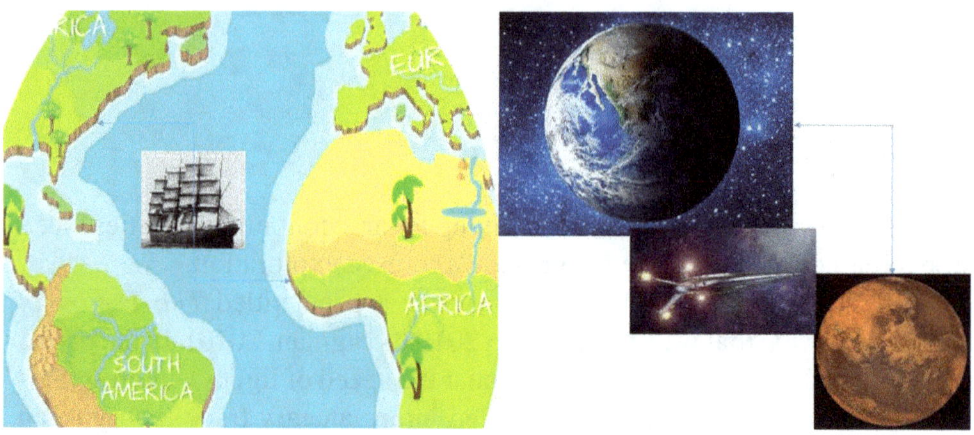

The turbulent Atlantic Ocean once caused people to experience failure and sadness, and the vast starry space might also cause immense losses in the interstellar trade.

In the Earth-Mars trade, at the beginning, Earth sells Mars necessities while Mars provides Earth with luxuries. With the development of the Martian industry, there may be Martian industrial products sold to Earth, but there is still a need for continuous daily supplies from Earth to Mars.

The BoE settles the Earth-Mars trade in Earth dollars, while the BoM settles in Mars dollars. If Earth Dollar: Mars Dollar = 1:1, the Earth-Mars trade is similar to a single currency system. However, with the implementation of trade, it will inevitably deviate from the initial value of 1:1, thus forming a dynamic changed exchange rate system, like the case of two countries on Earth.

Interstellar Political Economics

Suppose both Earth and Mars need efficacy maximization, there may exist Pareto optimality between Earth and Mars, where both Earth side and Mars side have optimal equilibrium among their goods market and money market, characterized by their IS and LM curves reaching a common synthetic equilibrium, as shown in Figure 2.

Figure 2. A common synthetic equilibrium for both Earth and Mars

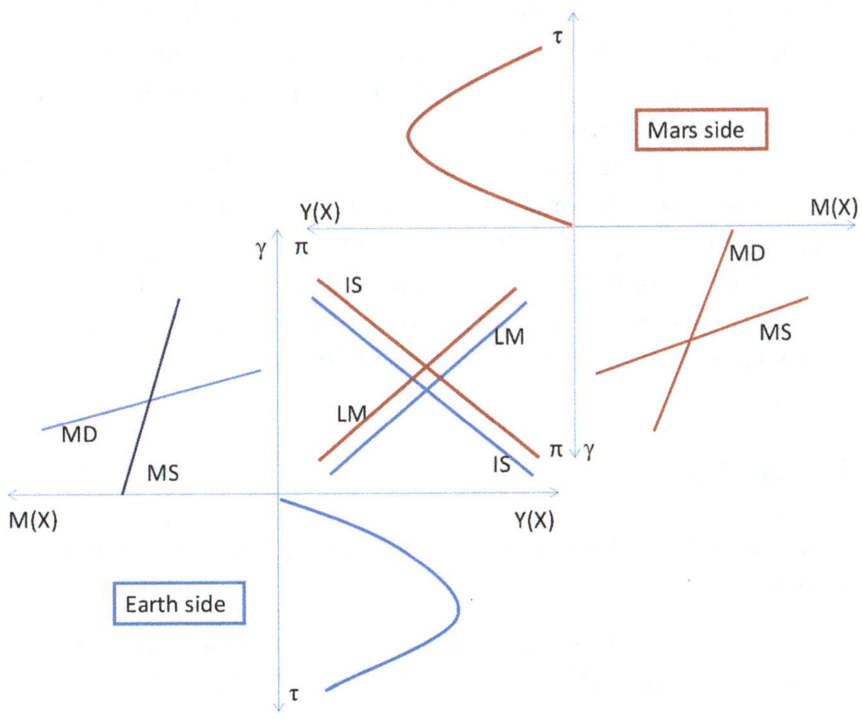

Since the commodities supplied from Earth to Mars are mostly necessities for Mars, while the commodities supplied from Mars to Earth are mostly luxuries for Earth, in the bilateral interstellar trade, the demand of Mars is close to rigid needs, while the demand of Earth is close to luxury. Thus, the Mars aggregate demand curve measured in money is nearly vertical, while the Earth aggregate demand curve measured in money is nearly flat. Both Earth and Mars aggregate supply curves are the opposite.

This dictates a civilizational consideration of interstellar political economy that transcends geo-economics: the supply of Mars by Earth requires humanitarian goodwill, and the supply of Mars by Earth requires exchange. But as a backer and neighbor of Mars, Earth should have compassion for interplanetary trade, and Mars should be grateful for the economic support from Earth. This is beyond the realm of conventional economics. If the exploration of Mars in the future is a common cause of mankind, then the interstellar economic activities cannot be measured solely by economic benefits, and there will even be issues beyond social equity and economic efficiency. Certainly, main economic thoughts (Arrow, 1963; Arrow & Debreu, 1954; Friedman, 1948, 1956, 1957, 1966, 1970; Hicks, 1946; Lucas, 1972, 1973, 1975, 1988; Keynes, 2012; Marshall, 2013; Mundell, 1962, 1963; Samuelson, 1983; Samuelson & Nordhaus, 2010; Schumpeter, 2003; Smith, 1977; Solow, 1956; Taylor, 1979; Tobin, 1969, 1975; Walras, 1954; Woodford, 2003; Ye, 2020) will be kept in interstellar economics.

In short, the future interstellar trade and its financial system taking Earth-Mars as a connected economic system will provide mankind with a new economic research perspective. The pros, cons, gains and losses, as well as the comprehensive consideration of social fairness and economic benefits, will not be enough to cover humanity's cross-planetary care. Therefore, some new ideas will be born in interstellar economics.

REFERENCES

Arrow, K. (1963). *Social Choice and Individual Values* (2nd ed.). Yale University Press.

Arrow, K., & Debreu, G. (1954). Existence of an equilibrium for a competitive economy. *Econometrica*, *22*(3), 265–290. doi:10.2307/1907353

Faccarello, G., & Kurz, H. D. (2016). Handbook on the History of Economic Analysis. Vol. I: Great Economists since Petty and Boisguilbert; Vol. II: Schools of Thought in Economics. Edward Elgar.

Feldman, A. M., & Serrano, R. (2005). *Welfare Economics and Social Choice Theory* (2nd ed.). Springer Science & Business Media, Inc.

Floyd, J. E. (2010). *Interest Rates, Exchange Rates and World Monetary Policy*. Springer. doi:10.1007/978-3-642-10280-6

Forni, M., & Lippi, M. (1997). *Aggregation and the Microfoundations of Dynamic Macroecomics*. Oxford University Press.

Friedman, B. M., & Hahn, F. H. (Eds.). (2000). *Handbook of Monetary Economics* (Vol. 1-2). Elsevier.

Friedman, M. (1948). A monetary and fiscal framework for economic stability. *The American Economic Review*, *38*(3), 245–264.

Friedman, M. (1956). *Studies in the Quantity Theory of Money*. University of Chicago Press.

Friedman, M. (1957). *A Theory of the Consumption Function*. Princeton University Press. doi:10.1515/9780691188485

Friedman, M. (1966). The Methodology of Positive Economics. In *Essays in Positive Economics*. University of Chicago Press.

Friedman, M. (1970). A theoretical framework for monetary analysis. *Journal of Political Economy*, *78*(2), 193–238. doi:10.1086/259623

Gilder, G. (2012). *Wealth and Poverty: A new edition for the twenty-first century*. Regnery Pub. Inc.

Gilder, G. (2013). *Knowledge and Power: The information theory of capitalism and how it is revolutionizing our world*. Regnery Pub. Inc.

Goodfriend, M., & King, R. G. (1997). The new neoclassical synthesis and the role of monetary policy. *NBER Macroeconomics Annual*, *12*, 231–283. doi:10.1086/654336

Hahn, F. H. (1960). The stability of growth equilibrium. *The Quarterly Journal of Economics*, *74*(2), 206–226. doi:10.2307/1884251

Heyne, P., Boettke, P., & Prychitko, D. (2013). *The Economic Way of Thinking* (13th ed.). Pearson Education.

Hicks, J. R. (1946). *Value and Capital: An inquiry into some fundamental principles of economic theory* (2nd ed.). Oxford University Press.

Jones, R. W., & Kenen, P. B. (Eds.). (1985). *Handbook of International Economics*. Elsevier.

Keynes, J. M. (2012). The General Theory of Employment, Interest and Money (The Collected Writings of John Maynard Keynes Vol. 7). Cambridge University Press.

King, R. G. (2000). The new IS-LM model: Language, logic, and limits. *Federal Reserve Bank of Richmond Economic Quarterly*, *86*, 45–103.

Lamb, M., Lymer, A., & Freedman, J. (2005). *Taxation: An Interdisciplinary Approach to Research*. Oxford University Press.

Lengwiler, Y. (2004). *Microfoundations of Financial Economics: An Introduction to General Equilibrium Asset Pricing*. Princeton University Press.

Lucas, R., & Rapping, L. (1970). Real Wages, Employment and Inflation. In E. Phelps (Ed.), *Microeconomic Foundations of Employment and Inflation Theory* (pp. 253–305). Norton.

Lucas, R. E. Jr. (1972). Expectations and the neutrality of money. *Journal of Economic Theory*, *4*(2), 103–124. doi:10.1016/0022-0531(72)90142-1

Lucas, R. E. (1973). Some international evidence on output-inflation tradeoffs. *The American Economic Review*, *63*, 526–534.

Lucas, R. E. Jr. (1975). An equilibrium model of the business cycle. *Journal of Political Economy*, *83*(6), 1113–1144. doi:10.1086/260386

Lucas, R. E. (1988). On the mechanics of development planning. *Journal of Monetary Economics*, *22*, 3–42. doi:10.1016/0304-3932(88)90168-7

Marshall, A. (2013). *Principles of Economics* (8th ed.). Palgrave Macmillan LLC. doi:10.1057/9781137375261

Mises, L. (2006). *The Ultimate Foundation of Economic Science: An Essay on Method*. Liberty Fund, Inc.

Mishkin, F. S. (2004). *The Economics of Money, Banking, and Financial Markets* (7th ed.). Addison-Wesley.

Modigliani, F. (1963). The monetary mechanism and its interaction with real phenomena. *The Review of Economics and Statistics*, *45*(1), 76–103. doi:10.2307/1927150

Mundell, R. A. (1962). The appropriate use of monetary and fiscal policy for internal and external balance. *International Monetary Fund Staff Papers*, *9*(1), 70–79. doi:10.2307/3866082

Mundell, R. A. (1963). *Capital mobility and stabilization policy under fixed and flexible exchange rates. Canadian Journal of Economic and Political Science, 29(4), 475–485.*

Nicola, P. C. (2013). *Efficiency and Equity in Welfare Economics*. Springer. doi:10.1007/978-3-642-30071-4

North, D. C. (1990). *Institutions, Institutional Change and Economic Performance*. Cambridge University Press. doi:10.1017/CBO9780511808678

Phelps, E. (1967). Phillips curves, expectations of inflation and optimal unemployment over time. *Economica*, *34*(135), 254–281. doi:10.2307/2552025

Phillips, A. W. (1958). The Relationship between Unemployment and the Rate of Change of Money Wages in the United Kingdom 1861-1953. *Economica*, *25*, 283–299.

Samuelson, P. A. (1983). Foundations of Economic Analysis (Enlarged ed.). Harvard University Press.

Samuelson, P. A., & Nordhaus, W. D. (2010). *Economics* (19th ed.). McGraw-Hill Co.

Scarth, W. (2014). *Macroeconomics: the development of modern methods for policy analysis*. Edward Elgar.

Smith, A. (1977). An Inquiry into the Nature and Causes of the Wealth of Nations (UK ed.). Chicago: University of Chicago Press.

Solow, R. M. (1956). A contribution to the theory of economic growth. *The Quarterly Journal of Economics*, *70*(1), 65–94. doi:10.2307/1884513

Stigler, G. J. (1961). The economics of information. *Journal of Political Economy*, *69*(3), 213–225. doi:10.1086/258464

Taylor, J. B. (1979). Staggered wage setting in a macro model. *The American Economic Review*, *69*, 108–113.

Tobin, J. (1969). A general equilibrium approach to monetary theory. *Journal of Money, Credit and Banking*, *1*(1), 15–26. doi:10.2307/1991374

Tobin, J. (1975). Keynesian models of recession and depression. *American Economic Review Proceedings*, *65*, 195–202.

Walras, L. (1954). Elements of Pure Economics, or the theory of social wealth (4th ed., W. Jaffé, Trans.). London: George Allen & Unwin Ltd.

Woodford, M. (2003). *Interest and Prices: Foundations of a Theory of Monetary Policy*. Princeton University Press.

Ye, F. Y. (2020). An economic analysis of efficiency and equity combining epistemological true with axiological good through microeconomics to macroeconomics. *International Journal of Economics and Financial Research*, *6*(7), 159–169. doi:10.32861/ijefr.67.159.169

Chapter 9 Economic Conclusion

ABSTRACT

Economics contributes a kind of great knowledge by processing economic issues via economic analytics. Around the idea that the market is the engine of economy, the wealth expansion theory contributes a pure economics that both knowledge and capital promote wealth expansion and economic growth. Via a grand synthetic model, it is revealed that marginal effects act in both input and output sides; that tax, interest, and exchange rates become key ratios; that a big parameter b links the logarithmic Cobb-Douglas model and the per-capita Solow-Swan model; and that the microeconomic Arrow-Debreu model and the macroeconomic Mundell-Fleming model are combined as an economic standard model.

NATIONAL RICH OUT OF INDIVIDUAL RICH: ECONOMIC POLICY IMPLICATION

A country is made up of its citizens, i.e. a nation is composed of individuals. A country is prosperous if, and only if, its citizens are rich, which is the same as saying national rich out of individual rich. Therefore, the object of economics aims to maximize national welfare and citizen wealth. Thus, on the economic policies, some considerations should be clarified:

1. On tax rate and taxation: it is suggested to set a low tax rate to keep the wealth of the citizens. It is also needed to reinforce that single levy rule, which means that any taxation should happen one-time during an

DOI: 10.4018/978-1-6684-4935-6.ch009

economic cycle. For example, production tax and product tax are the same, and can only be charged once. Also, income tax and consumption tax happened in the same economic ring, consumers can only be asked to pay either income tax or consumption tax, not both. Lower taxation might also reduce government corruption.

2. On the interest rate and product profit: it is suggested to keep at a reasonable level. Higher interest rate and lower product profit might cause consumption and industrial investment to shrink, while lower interest rate and higher product profit could stimulate consumption and production. The zero or negative interest rate or product profit would stop economic development. Therefore, the modification of interest rate is key to all economic policies.
3. On the exchange rate and international trade: it is suggested to keep a flexible exchange rate and international trade. The exchange rate can also be a policy tool for economic adjustment, which may be applied as an economic policy. However, the policy tool may be ineffective for small countries, because there is not enough domestic markets for their national economies to maneuver.

Synthetically, tax, interest and exchange rates represent the considerations of political economics, which also affect inflation rate and unemployment rate. We may pay more attention to the three rates.

As economic equilibriums exist in both microeconomics and macroeconomics, economists make great efforts to realize optimization of economic efficiency and social equity, which introduce lots of great thoughts to the modern world, where we see that economic ideas stimulate knowledge progress and technology promotes wealth expansion.

KNOWLEDGE AND CAPITAL PROMOTE WEALTH EXPANSION

While knowledge is really promoting wealth expansion via a technical parameter $q > 1$, capital also promotes imaginary wealth expansion with inflation rate λ, and then we get a synthetic output increment

$$\Delta Y = K^{\lambda} H^{q(1-\lambda)};\ \Delta y = \lambda k + q(1-\lambda)h \qquad (1)$$

So we know that the real-imaginary ratio of wealth expansion is

$$R = H^{q(1-\lambda)}/K^{\lambda};\ r = q(1-\lambda)h/\lambda k \tag{2}$$

R > 1 or r > 1 means that real wealth expansion is larger than imaginary wealth expansion, while the R < 1 or r < 1 reveals that the virtual wealth expansion is larger than the real wealth expansion. The R = 1 or r = 1 indicates a stable state at the equilibrium of real and imaginary wealth expansion. While the $q(1-\lambda)h$ indicates the real part of wealth expansion and λk denotes the imaginary part of wealth expansion, it is expected that $q(1-\lambda)h > \lambda k$, so that the real wealth expansion dominates the economy. Otherwise, the wealth expansion is only a virtual image.

Therefore, both knowledge and capital promote wealth real expansion, and one can adjust wealth distribution with optimization via economic policies. A healthy economy should maintain R > 1 or r > 1.

PAST THEORIES AND PRESENT PRACTICES ENLIGHTEN FUTURE

Applying the Arrow-Debreu-Mundell-Fleming model as an economic standard model, combining the axiological framework and the epistemological model, it is proposed to analyze economic policies using a synthetic model, where interest, exchange and tax rates are integrated. Except normal monetary and fiscal policies mainly via interest and tax rates, there are feasible ways to utilize modified strategies via exchange and tax rates. When one needs to simulate the national local market, one can raise the exchange rate. Otherwise, when one needs to promote international global trade, one may lower the exchange rate. It is found that tax reduction is good policy when tax rate is higher than normal and that tax increase is good social policy when tax rate is lower than normal, during economic depression. Also it is revealed that tax reduction is good social policy when tax rate is lower than normal, and that tax increase is good policy when tax rate is higher than normal, during economic overheat. While the economic system seeks efficiency and the social system pursues equity, common interest modifications with elastic exchange and tax rates could be applied to balance efficiency and equity.

Most economic models are highly simplified to describe complicated economic systems. Perhaps those models are unrealistic. However, the simplified models provide concise understanding to the complicated world, so that they are theoretically valuable.

When we study within the grand synthetic model, we may notice the following six relations under the constraints of scarce economic resources

$$\dot{y}=\alpha(\gamma-\bar{\gamma})+(1-\alpha)\dot{g} \tag{3.1}$$

$$\dot{y}=\theta(\dot{m}-\dot{p})+\theta(\pi-p) \tag{3.2}$$

$$\dot{p}=\phi(y-\bar{y}) \tag{3.3}$$

$$\beta(\gamma-\bar{\gamma})=\beta(\dot{\pi}-\dot{p})+\theta(\pi-p)=\theta(\dot{m}-\dot{p}) \tag{3.4}$$

$$f'(k)=\gamma+\delta \tag{3.5}$$

$$w=f(k)-kf'(k) \tag{3.6}$$

The first equation (3.1) states that the change rate of economic output (time derivative) will be α times the deviation between real interest rate and equilibrium interest rate (interest rate difference) plus (1−α) times the change rate in government purchases. If $\alpha = 0.3$, $(1-\alpha) = 0.7$, $\dot{y}=\gamma-\bar{\gamma}$ will depend more on $\dot{g}$; The second equation shows that the change rate of economic output is related to consumption parameter and price level, and is related to foreign trade. If $\beta \to 1$, $\theta \to 0$, $\dot{y}=\gamma-\bar{\gamma}$ indicates that the change rate of economic output is completely determined by the difference of interest rate. The third equation suggests that the rate of price change is linearly correlated with the difference in economic output from equilibrium. The fourth equation sets up the relationship between interest rate, exchange rate, price level and consumption parameter in the full equilibrium state. The fifth equation describes the interest rate as the expected marginal efficiency of capital, and the sixth equation claims wage equilibrium linking with capital.

Certainly, we see that those are simplified ideal states. We know that the spirit of economic models is merged into output, production, consumption, and tax, interest, exchange rates, as well as some economic parameters. We have concluded a set of feasible parameters as

$$\alpha\approx0.3;\ q\approx10;\ \theta\approx\phi\approx\lambda=0.01;\ \beta\approx1;\ \delta=0.04;\ n=p=0.02 \tag{4}$$

where interest rate is constrained by the following formula when $\delta = 0$

$$\dot{p} / p = \gamma = f'(k) \tag{5}$$

The equation states that the marginal efficiency of capital equals the interest rate.

Conclusively, the features of grand synthetic economics can be characterized by five statements as:

1. Combining the microeconomic Arrow-Debreu model with the macroeconomic Mundell-Fleming model as a standard economic model;
2. Linking the logarithmic Cobb-Douglas model and the per-capita Solow-Swan model via a big parameter b;
3. Keeping marginal effects in both input and output, including MC = MU, MPC+MPS = 1;
4. Balancing ideal equilibrium and practical fluctuation in economic analysis by synthesizing tax, interest and exchange rates;
5. Integrating real commodity and imaginary money into complex economics.

In all elements, we always recall that the market is the engine of economy. Main economic thoughts (Arrow, 1963; Arrow & Debreu, 1954; Friedman, 1948, 1956, 1957, 1966, 1970; Hicks, 1946; Lucas, 1972, 1973, 1975, 1988; Lucas & Rapping, 1970; Keynes, 2012; Marshall, 2013; Fleming, 1962; Mundell, 1962, 1963; Samuelson, 1983; Samuelson & Nordhaus, 2010; Smith, 1977; Solow, 1956; Taylor, 1979; Tobin, 1969, 1975; Walras, 1954) are integrated in above theory, and poverty could be eliminated by economic growth (Dollar & Kraay, 2002; Sen, 1997, 2002; Gilder, 2012, 2013). While the economic knowledge are increasing (Faccarello & Kurz, 2016; Feldman & Serrano, 2005; Floyd, 2010; Friedman & Hahn, 2000; Goodfriend & King, 1997; King, 2000; Nicola, 2013; Scarth, 2014; Woodford, 2003), knowledge and capital will keep as important powers to stimulate wealth expansion, economic growth and social equity.

At the end of this part, let us recall Keynes' speech in the last part of his famous *General Theory* in 1936 (Keynes, 2012):

At the present moment people are unusually expectant of a more fundamental diagnosis; more particularly ready to receive it; eager to try it out, if it should be even plausible. But apart from this contemporary mood, the ideas of economists and political philosophers, both when they are right and when they are wrong, are more powerful than is commonly understood. Indeed the world is ruled by little else. Practical men, who believe themselves to be quite exempt from any intellectual influences, are usually the slaves of some defunct economist. Madmen in authority, who hear voices in the air, are distilling their frenzy from some academic scribbler of a few years back.

Thus, we understand that economics is an important field of human knowledge, and we should pay more attention to the spirit of economics, leading to economic philosophy covering human ontology, scientific epistemology and action axiology in the next part, toward the true and the good.

REFERENCES

Arrow, K. (1963). *Social Choice and Individual Values* (2nd ed.). Yale University Press.

Arrow, K., & Debreu, G. (1954). Existence of an equilibrium for a competitive economy. *Econometrica, 22*(3), 265–290. doi:10.2307/1907353

Dollar, D., & Kraay, A. (2002). Growth is good for the poor. *Journal of Economic Growth, 7*(3), 195–225. doi:10.1023/A:1020139631000

Faccarello, G., & Kurz, H. D. (2016). Handbook on the History of Economic Analysis. Vol. I: Great Economists since Petty and Boisguilbert; Vol. II: Schools of Thought in Economics. Edward Elgar.

Feldman, A. M., & Serrano, R. (2005). *Welfare Economics and Social Choice Theory* (2nd ed.). Springer Science & Business Media, Inc.

Fleming, J. M. (1962). Domestic monetary policies under fixed and floating exchange rates. IMF Staff Papers, 9, 369–379.

Floyd, J. E. (2010). *Interest Rates, Exchange Rates and World Monetary Policy*. Springer. doi:10.1007/978-3-642-10280-6

Forni, M., & Lippi, M. (1997). *Aggregation and the Microfoundations of Dynamic Macroecomics*. Oxford University Press.

Friedman, B. M., & Hahn, F. H. (Eds.). (2000). *Handbook of Monetary Economics* (Vol. 1-2). Elsevier.

Friedman, M. (1948). A monetary and fiscal framework for economic stability. *The American Economic Review, 38*(3), 245–264.

Friedman, M. (1956). *Studies in the Quantity Theory of Money*. University of Chicago Press.

Friedman, M. (1957). *A Theory of the Consumption Function*. Princeton University Press. doi:10.1515/9780691188485

Friedman, M. (1966). The Methodology of Positive Economics. In *Essays in Positive Economics*. University of Chicago Press.

Friedman, M. (1970). A theoretical framework for monetary analysis. *Journal of Political Economy*, *78*(2), 193–238. doi:10.1086/259623

Gilder, G. (2012). *Wealth and Poverty: A new edition for the twenty-first century*. Regnery Pub. Inc.

Gilder, G. (2013). *Knowledge and Power: The information theory of capitalism and how it is revolutionizing our world*. Regnery Pub. Inc.

Goodfriend, M., & King, R. G. (1997). The new neoclassical synthesis and the role of monetary policy. *NBER Macroeconomics Annual*, *12*, 231–283. doi:10.1086/654336

Hahn, F. H. (1960). The stability of growth equilibrium. *The Quarterly Journal of Economics*, *74*(2), 206–226. doi:10.2307/1884251

Heyne, P., Boettke, P., & Prychitko, D. (2013). *The Economic Way of Thinking* (13th ed.). Pearson Education.

Hicks, J. R. (1946). *Value and Capital: An inquiry into some fundamental principles of economic theory* (2nd ed.). Oxford University Press.

Jones, R. W., & Kenen, P. B. (Eds.). (1985). *Handbook of International Economics*. Elsevier.

Keynes, J. M. (2012). The General Theory of Employment, Interest and Money (The Collected Writings of John Maynard Keynes Vol. 7). Cambridge University Press.

King, R. G. (2000). The new IS-LM model: Language, logic, and limits. *Federal Reserve Bank of Richmond Economic Quarterly*, *86*, 45–103.

Lamb, M., Lymer, A., & Freedman, J. (2005). *Taxation: An Interdisciplinary Approach to Research*. Oxford University Press.

Lengwiler, Y. (2004). *Microfoundations of Financial Economics: An Introduction to General Equilibrium Asset Pricing*. Princeton University Press.

Lucas, R., & Rapping, L. (1970). Real Wages, Employment and Inflation. In E. Phelps (Ed.), *Microeconomic Foundations of Employment and Inflation Theory* (pp. 253–305). Norton.

Lucas, R. E. Jr. (1972). Expectations and the neutrality of money. *Journal of Economic Theory*, *4*(2), 103–124. doi:10.1016/0022-0531(72)90142-1

Lucas, R. E. (1973). Some international evidence on output-inflation tradeoffs. *The American Economic Review*, *63*, 526–534.

Lucas, R. E. Jr. (1975). An equilibrium model of the business cycle. *Journal of Political Economy*, *83*(6), 1113–1144. doi:10.1086/260386

Lucas, R. E. (1988). On the mechanics of development planning. *Journal of Monetary Economics*, *22*, 3–42. doi:10.1016/0304-3932(88)90168-7

Marshall, A. (2013). *Principles of Economics* (8th ed.). Palgrave Macmillan LLC. doi:10.1057/9781137375261

Mises, L. (2006). *The Ultimate Foundation of Economic Science: An Essay on Method*. Liberty Fund, Inc.

Mishkin, F. S. (2004). *The Economics of Money, Banking, and Financial Markets* (7th ed.). Addison-Wesley.

Modigliani, F. (1963). The monetary mechanism and its interaction with real phenomena. *The Review of Economics and Statistics*, *45*(1), 76–103. doi:10.2307/1927150

Mundell, R. A. (1962). The appropriate use of monetary and fiscal policy for internal and external balance. *International Monetary Fund Staff Papers*, *9*(1), 70–79. doi:10.2307/3866082

Mundell, R. A. (1963). *Capital mobility and stabilization policy under fixed and flexible exchange rates. Canadian Journal of Economic and Political Science, 29(4), 475–485.*

Nicola, P. C. (2013). *Efficiency and Equity in Welfare Economics*. Springer. doi:10.1007/978-3-642-30071-4

Samuelson, P. A. (1983). Foundations of Economic Analysis (Enlarged ed.). Harvard University Press.

Samuelson, P. A., & Nordhaus, W. D. (2010). *Economics* (19th ed.). McGraw-Hill Co.

Scarth, W. (2014). *Macroeconomics: the development of modern methods for policy analysis*. Edward Elgar.

Sen, A. (1997). *Poverty and Famines*. International Labour Organization.

Sen, A. (2002). *Rationality and Freedom*. Belknap Press.

Smith, A. (1977). An Inquiry into the Nature and Causes of the Wealth of Nations (UK ed.). Chicago: University of Chicago Press.

Solow, R. M. (1956). A contribution to the theory of economic growth. *The Quarterly Journal of Economics*, *70*(1), 65–94. doi:10.2307/1884513

Stigler, G. J. (1961). The economics of information. *Journal of Political Economy*, *69*(3), 213–225. doi:10.1086/258464

Taylor, J. B. (1979). Staggered wage setting in a macro model. *The American Economic Review*, *69*, 108–113.

Tobin, J. (1969). A general equilibrium approach to monetary theory. *Journal of Money, Credit and Banking*, *1*(1), 15–26. doi:10.2307/1991374

Tobin, J. (1975). Keynesian models of recession and depression. *American Economic Review Proceedings*, *65*, 195–202.

Walras, L. (1954). Elements of Pure Economics, or the theory of social wealth (4th ed., W. Jaffé, Trans.). London: George Allen & Unwin Ltd.

Woodford, M. (2003). *Interest and Prices: Foundations of a Theory of Monetary Policy*. Princeton University Press.

Ye, F. Y. (2017). A synthetic macro-economic model integrating interest, exchange and tax rates. In *Scientific Metrics: toward analytical and quantitative sciences* (pp. 127–140). Springer. doi:10.1007/978-981-10-5936-0_11

Ye, F. Y. (2020). An economic analysis of efficiency and equity combining epistemological true with axiological good through microeconomics to macroeconomics. *International Journal of Economics and Financial Research*, *6*(7), 159–169. doi:10.32861/ijefr.67.159.169

Section 2
Economic Philosophy

Chapter 10
Economic Philosophy Facing the Good and the True

ABSTRACT

A complete economic philosophy would include human ontology, scientific epistemology, and action axiology. While pure economics paid more attention to scientific epistemology, economic philosophy focuses on action axiology facing the good with combining scientific epistemology facing the true. Economic philosophy brings a metaphysical thinking to economic knowledge, with which we approach the good and the true of economics. These general issues of economic philosophy are discussed in this chapter.

INTRODUCTION

Early in 1962, Joan Robinson published her famous work *Economic Philosophy* (Robinson, 1962). After long development, modern economic philosophy becomes an academic branch mixing science and humanities, where economics is thought of as science characterized by data and equations and philosophy certainly belongs to the knowledge of humanities, which is concerned with the concepts, methods and ethical issues in economics (Mäki, 2012; Reiss, 2013; Ross, 2014). Here, we pay more attention to its objective knowledge and causality facing the good and the true. We believe that economic philosophy is dedicated to achieving the good with social equity and the true with economic efficiency.

DOI: 10.4018/978-1-6684-4935-6.ch010

Following my triad philosophy (Ye, 2019), a complete economic philosophy would include human ontology, scientific epistemology, and action axiology. While human ontology is based on freedom individuals, scientific epistemology provides the scientific foundation to economics and action axiology contributes the economic good of behaviors. In the view of economic philosophy, the Chicago school paid more attention to scientific epistemology (Friedman, 1956, 1966) so that it approached more scientific truth, while the Austrian school paid more attention to action axiology with adherence to methodological individualism (Mises, 2006) so that it approached more real goodness.

ECONOMIC PHILOSPOHY TOWARD THE GOOD

The methodological and epistemological issues are the main focuses of economic philosophy, by which economists gain knowledge about economic processes through methods, concepts, and theories. The economic equilibrium is its main methodology and the economic philosophy toward the good is its key axiology. From the philosophical view, three levels approach economic equilibria:

- Level 1: The equilibrium of economic efficiency and social equity. While the market mechanism determines the economic efficiency, the government investment and wealth redistribution determines the social equity via taxation. Thus, tax rate will be a key policy factor and fiscal policy becomes a key policy tool.
- Level 2: The equilibrium of microeconomic efficiency and macroeconomic efficiency. When individual behaviors are affected by price and wage, the national economies are adjusted by money control. Therefore, interest rate will be a key policy factor and monetary policy becomes key policy tool.
- Level 3: The equilibrium of international economies and interpersonal equities. The international economy will be affected by international trade via exchange rate, and interpersonal equity can be compared by personal income via Engle coefficient. There is no unified policy tool for adjusting international and interpersonal economies.

Although the equilibrium state is an ideal theoretical state and may rarely exist in the actual economy, it is always a good analytical reference (Ye, 2015,

2017, 2020). The economic equilibrium state can be regarded as the ideal economic state, and the actual economic state is the exact deviation around the ideal economic state, and the quantitative judgment can be obtained by measuring the deviation.

From the perspective of social peace, the economic good focuses on two points: one is to equalize the rich and the poor as much as possible; realizing the equalization of the rich and the poor by national power is equivalent to the proposition of welfare economics. Through the redistribution of national welfare to ensure the food and clothing of all citizens, it will not trigger social turbulence and contribute to social stability and peace. However, we also need to see that there are differences in intelligence and physical strength between people, and recognize that the level of knowledge and labor costs vary from person to person. It is a reasonable strategy for people to use their talents to obtain corresponding returns. Therefore, considering the incentives to create, protect intellectual property rights and high-quality labor, it should be recognized that the gap between the rich and the poor caused by the difference in manpower is a normal economic phenomenon. Labor and creation of wealth should be encouraged, and the poverty caused by lazy and mediocre people themselves should not be a reason to equalize the rich and the poor. A good social and economic strategy is to ensure that everyone has enough food and clothing, but also allows talents with creative contributions to obtain excess wealth.

ECONOMIC PRINCIPLES TOWARD THE TRUE

When we set the economic philosophy toward the good in axiology, there are also economic principles that face toward the true in epistemology. In economics, we need three principles for economic analysis, as mentioned in 2.3.

1. **Equilibrium principle:** The state of equilibrium exists in the economy, as ideal theoretical state, which is an important key to understanding economic analysis.
2. **Marginal principle:** Marginal cost and marginal utility may reach consistency, leading to dynamic economic equilibrium.
3. **Extremum principle:** The minimum cost-type economic variable and the maximum utility-type economic variable coexist in the economic system, making the economic system tend to be statically optimized.

These three economic principles can be briefly recorded as EME. According to the EME principles, economic efficiency and social equity can also achieve an optimal balance.

Further, we need three rules for economic optimization according to the grand synthetic analytical model.

Rule 1

Single Levy Rule

Only one tax can be levied on each economic process. It is not appropriate to double tax economic processes in the same direction (production direction or consumption direction). This is not only necessary to ensure the rights and interests of consumers and producers, but also as an effective measure to avoid government corruption. Collected income tax, for instance, should not collect consumption tax. The levy of regulatory taxes on the rich should also be limited to once a year and in a moderate amount, rather than repeated or unlimited levies. The distribution of wealth in the hands of producers and consumers is conducive to economic circulation. If wealth is rich in the hands of the people, the people will become rich and the country will become strong. However, excessive concentration of wealth in the hands of the government will only lead to corruption, and the country will become rich and the people will become poor, and the economy will be depressed.

Rule 2

Small Changing Interest Rate Rule

When adjusting interest rates, the central bank and commercial banks should raise or lower interest rates slightly to facilitate the steady operation of the economy. Sharp rise and fall of interest rate may cause capital fluctuations, adverse to economic stability. This is especially important when monetary policy is used to regulate the economy.

Rule 3

Semi-Open Rule for Independent and Flexible Exchange Rates

Large economies can manage their exchange rates to suit their national needs. A fully free exchange rate may trigger risks in international trade, while a flexible exchange rate is expected to reduce risks in international economy. Of course, this rule needs to be backed by a larger domestic market, suitable for an economy dominated by domestic consumption.

These three rules can be called the 3S rules, reflecting contemporary economic knowledge (Coase, 1960; Davis, 2003; Dollar & Kraay, 2002; Faccarello & Kurz, 2016; Feldman & Serrano, 2005; Floyd, 2010; Forni & Lippi, 1997; Friedman & Hahn, 2000; Goodfriend & King, 1997; Heyne, Boettke & Prychitko, 2013; King, 2000; Lamb et al., 2005; Lengwiler, 2004; Lucas & Rapping, 1970; Nicola, 2013; North, 1990; Okun, 1975; Scarth, 2014; Sen, 2002; Woodford, 2003; Weintraub, 1979).

Finally, the economic true focuses on two key points: one is that the principles and rules provided by economics belong to relative truths, which will become reality under certain conditions; the other is that social behaviors that violate economic principles or rules will be paid back at some point.

ECONOMIC METHODOLOGY: APPROACHING OBJECTIVE KNOWLEDGE

From the perspective of methodology, we already have normative economics and positive economics, and another common sense and novel division is pure language economics, pure mathematical economics, or integrated language and mathematics hybrid economics.

Pure language economics tends to believe that economics can be thoroughly explained and understood only with words. Some economists of both ancient and modern times believe that if economics uses mathematics too much, it may not be able to express the essence of economy. This is fine for political economy and economic ethics in general, but bad for economic analysis, especially quantitative trend analysis. Therefore, it should be understood that purely linguistic economics has limitations in expressing and displaying economic ideas and quantitative analysis.

Pure mathematical economics, on the other hand, thinks that mathematics can solve all economic problems, and that formulae and diagrams are enough to explain everything. This is good for mathematical economics and economic analysis in general, but bad for the understanding and popularization of economic ideas. If the public regards economics as an applied branch of mathematics, the unique thought quality and language transmission characteristics of economics will be lost.

In economic practice, any individual counts money and buys and sells goods; every country calculates its GDP and releases its budget. Thus, the economy can be quantified and measured, pure language expression is not enough to accurately describe and analyze the specific numbers. At the same time, quantified results that are not put into words are difficult for the public to understand. Once economics can be understood by everyone, the economic scientific revolution (Kuhn, 1996) may happen.

Whether pure language economics or pure mathematical economics tends to find the objective knowledge (Popper, 1972) of economic society, where human activity and capital play key roles. When most studies of econometrics reveal the correlation, pure economics also tends to find causation. It is well known that a correlation does not imply causation but causation always implies correlation. As causality implies essence correlation, economic analysis based on pure economics often implies the causation knowledge, including most correction knowledge from econometrics. In most importance, the classic economic thoughts (Arrow, 1963; Friedman, 1966; Hicks, 1946; Keynes, 2012; Marshall, 2013; Mises, 2006; Samuelson, 1983; Samuelson & Nordhaus, 2010; Schumpeter, 2003; Smith, 1977; Walras, 1954) will be inherited in both economics and economic philosophy.

Therefore, the better method is to integrate language and mathematics, to merge causation and correlation into the hybrid economics in methodology, which can not only analyze the complex economic quantitative relations, but also easily explain the daily economic phenomena. Economic methodology with economic analysis could contribute objective knowledge to economics, which is also the methodological position of the grand synthetic model in this book.

REFERENCES

Arrow, K. (1963). *Social Choice and Individual Values* (2nd ed.). Yale University Press.

Coase, R. H. (1960). The problem of social cost. *The Journal of Law & Economics, 3*, 1–44. doi:10.1086/466560

Davis, J. (2003). *The Theory of the Individual in Economics*. Routledge. doi:10.4324/9780203457689

Dollar, D., & Kraay, A. (2002). Growth is good for the poor. *Journal of Economic Growth, 7*(3), 195–225. doi:10.1023/A:1020139631000

Faccarello, G., & Kurz, H. D. (2016). Handbook on the History of Economic Analysis. Vol. I: Great Economists since Petty and Boisguilbert; Vol. II: Schools of Thought in Economics. Edward Elgar.

Feldman, A. M., & Serrano, R. (2005). *Welfare Economics and Social Choice Theory* (2nd ed.). Springer Science & Business Media, Inc.

Floyd, J. E. (2010). *Interest Rates, Exchange Rates and World Monetary Policy*. Springer. doi:10.1007/978-3-642-10280-6

Forni, M., & Lippi, M. (1997). *Aggregation and the Microfoundations of Dynamic Macroecomics*. Oxford University Press.

Friedman, B. M., & Hahn, F. H. (Eds.). (2000). *Handbook of Monetary Economics* (Vol. 1-2). Elsevier.

Friedman, M. (1956). *Studies in the Quantity Theory of Money*. University of Chicago Press.

Friedman, M. (1966). The Methodology of Positive Economics. In *Essays in Positive Economics*. University of Chicago Press.

Gilder, G. (2012). *Wealth and Poverty: A new edition for the twenty-first century*. Regnery Pub. Inc.

Gilder, G. (2013). *Knowledge and Power: The information theory of capitalism and how it is revolutionizing our world*. Regnery Pub. Inc.

Gillies, D. (1998). The Duhem thesis and the Quine thesis. In *Philosophy of Science: The Central Issues*. New York: Norton.

Goodfriend, M., & King, R. G. (1997). The new neoclassical synthesis and the role of monetary policy. *NBER Macroeconomics Annual, 12*, 231–283. doi:10.1086/654336

Heyne, P., Boettke, P., & Prychitko, D. (2013). *The Economic Way of Thinking* (13th ed.). Pearson Education.

Hicks, J. R. (1946). *Value and Capital: An inquiry into some fundamental principles of economic theory* (2nd ed.). Oxford University Press.

Jones, R. W., & Kenen, P. B. (Eds.). (1985). *Handbook of International Economics*. Elsevier.

Keynes, J. M. (2012). The General Theory of Employment, Interest and Money (The Collected Writings of John Maynard Keynes Vol. 7). Cambridge University Press.

King, R. G. (2000). The new IS-LM model: Language, logic, and limits. *Federal Reserve Bank of Richmond Economic Quarterly*, *86*, 45–103.

Kuhn, T. S. (1996). *The Structure of Scientific Revolutions* (rev. ed.). The University of Chicago Press. doi:10.7208/chicago/9780226458106.001.0001

Lamb, M., Lymer, A., & Freedman, J. (2005). *Taxation: An Interdisciplinary Approach to Research*. Oxford University Press.

Lengwiler, Y. (2004). *Microfoundations of Financial Economics: An Introduction to General Equilibrium Asset Pricing*. Princeton University Press.

Lucas, R., & Rapping, L. (1970). Real Wages, Employment and Inflation. In E. Phelps (Ed.), *Microeconomic Foundations of Employment and Inflation Theory* (pp. 253–305). Norton.

Mäki, U. (2012). Handbook of the Philosophy of Science: Vol. 13. *Philosophy of Economics*. Elsevier.

Mises, L. (2006). *The Ultimate Foundation of Economic Science: An Essay on Method*. Liberty Fund, Inc.

Nicola, P. C. (2013). *Efficiency and Equity in Welfare Economics*. Springer. doi:10.1007/978-3-642-30071-4

North, D. C. (1990). *Institutions, Institutional Change and Economic Performance*. Cambridge University Press. doi:10.1017/CBO9780511808678

Okun, A. M. (1975). *Equity and Efficiency: the big trade-off*. Brookings Institution.

Piketty, Th. (2014). *Capital in the twenty-first century (A. Goldhammer, Trans.)*. Harvard University Press. doi:10.4159/9780674369542

Popper, K. R. (1972). *Objective Knowledge: An evolutionary approach*. Oxford University Press.

Reiss, J. (2013). Philosophy of Economics: a contemporary introduction. Routledge (Taylor & Francis Group). doi:10.4324/9780203559062

Robinson, J. (1962). *Economic Philosophy*. Transaction Publishers.

Ross, D. (2014). *Philosophy of Economics*. Palgrave Macmillan. doi:10.1057/9781137318756

Samuelson, P. A. (1983). Foundations of Economic Analysis (Enlarged ed.). Harvard University Press.

Samuelson, P. A., & Nordhaus, W. D. (2010). *Economics* (19th ed.). McGraw-Hill Co.

Scarth, W. (2014). *Macroeconomics: The development of modern methods for policy analysis*. Edward Elgar.

Schumpeter, J. A. (2003). Capitalism, Socialism, and Demacracy (e-Library ed.). London: Routledge (Taylor & Francis Group).

Sen, A. (2002). *Rationality and Freedom*. Belknap Press.

Smith, A. (1977). An Inquiry into the Nature and Causes of the Wealth of Nations (UK ed.). Chicago: University of Chicago Press.

Walras, L. (1954). Elements of Pure Economics, or the theory of social wealth (4th ed., W. Jaffé, Trans.). London: George Allen & Unwin Ltd.

Weintraub, E. R. (1979). *Microfoundations: the compatibility of microeconomics and macroeconomics*. Cambridge University Press. doi:10.1017/CBO9780511559570

Woodford, M. (2003). *Interest and Prices: Foundations of a Theory of Monetary Policy*. Princeton University Press.

Ye, F. Y. (2019). Triad philosophy: An initiative idea for merging Western and Eastern thoughts. *Philosophical Studies*, *9*(8), 445–451.

Chapter 11
Social Equity and Fiscal Policy

ABSTRACT

Active fiscal policy promotes social equity, and the power of knowledge affects fiscal policy, while tax rate determines the wealth distribution, so that fiscal policy tightly links with social equity. Social equity concerns human happiness and social peace. It is suggested to promote social equity via active fiscal policy, and it is strengthened to follow closely the power of knowledge in this chapter. As social equity concerns human happiness and social peace, we may promote social equity via active fiscal policy.

INTRODUCTION

We do need to recognize the relevance of the problem of the gap between rich and poor to a peaceful society, both at home and in the world at large. As there is the so-called Matthew effect in the society, 'the rich get richer while the poor get poorer,' so the lament goes for the balance of wealth. Many solutions have been tried to fix these problems: tax regulation, price controls, labor camps, redistributions, hyperinflation, and more, in which the key focuses on tax rate, while linking to fiscal policies.

ACTIVE FISCAL POLICY PROMOTES SOCIAL EQUITY

The fiscal policy is how the government manages the country's budget. Active fiscal policy is key to building a fair and stable economy. Using active fiscal policy, tax and spending levels are changed according to the political perspectives of the policymakers.

DOI: 10.4018/978-1-6684-4935-6.ch011

To help build and maintain the infrastructures used in a country, the government usually taxes its residents. The taxation collected is used for the betterment of the nation, of society, and of all living in it. In the US and many other countries around the world, a tax rate is applied to some form of money received by a taxpayer. The money could be income earned from wages or salary, investment income (dividends, interest), capital gains from investments, profits made from goods or services rendered, etc. The percentage of the taxpayer's earnings, or money, is taken and remitted to the government.

When it comes to income tax, the tax rate is the percentage of an individual's taxable income or a corporation's earnings that is owed to state, federal and, in some cases, municipal governments. In certain municipalities, city or regional income taxes are also imposed. The tax rate that is applied to an individual's earnings depends on the marginal tax bracket that the individual falls under. The marginal tax rate is the percentage taken from the next dollar of taxable income above a pre-defined income limit.

Additionally, it is designed to try to keep GDP growth at 2~3% and the unemployment rate near the natural unemployment rate of 4~5%. This implies that fiscal policy is used to stabilize the economy over the course of the business cycle.

TAX RATE DETERMINES THE WEALTH DISTRIBUTION

The tax rate is key to determine wealth distribution, which is the percentage that an individual or corporation is taxed. Taxes are levied in almost every country of the world, primarily to raise revenue for government expenditures, although they serve other purposes as well.

Supposing that a firm produced and valued 10 billion dollars on the production side. If the government set the production tax rate at 10%, the firm would pay 1 billion dollars and then government taxation by increased 1 billion dollars. If the tax rate was set at 8%, the taxation would decrease by 200 million dollars and the firm could invest this amount to R&D for reproduction. Similarly, on the consumption side, when consumers received income from their firms, they might pay income tax or consumption tax during consumption. If there were 5 billion dollars for wage, with income tax at 10%, the government would receive 500 million dollars as taxation. However, if the tax rate reduced to 8%, the consumers could have an extra 100 million dollars for consumption or savings, so that the economy would be stimulated or promoted by consumption or investment. Therefore, we see that each 1% tax rate change would cause millions, even billions, in taxation change, which is to say: the tax rate might highly affect the economic behaviors of production and consumption as well as government taxation and investment.

Table 1. US federal income tax brackets and rates (2020)

Rate	For Single Individuals	For Married Individuals Filing Joint Returns	For Heads of Households
10%	Up to $9,875	Up to $19,750	Up to $14,100
12%	$9,876 to $40,125	$19,751 to $80,250	$14,101 to $53,700
22%	$40,126 to $85,525	$80,251 to $171,050	$53,701 to $85,500
24%	$85,526 to $163,300	$171,051 to $326,600	$85,501 to $163,300
32%	$163,301 to $207,350	$326,601 to $414,700	$163,301 to $207,350
35%	$207,351 to $518,400	$414,701 to $622,050	$207,351 to $518,400
37%	$518,401 or more	$622,051 or more	$518,401 or more

Source: Internal Revenue Service. Form 1040 Instructions (2019), Page 104. Accessed Jan. 10, 2020.

The marginal tax rate used by the US government is indicative of its progressive tax system. Table 1 shows the marginal tax brackets for 2020.

A marginal tax rate means that different portions of income are taxed at progressively higher rates.

Tax rates don't only apply to earned income and corporate profit, they can also apply on other occasions when taxes are imposed, including sales tax on goods and services, real property tax, short-term capital gains tax, and long-term capital gains tax. When a consumer purchases certain goods and services from a retailer, a sales tax is applied to the sales price of the commodity at the point of sale.

Since additional income gained from investments is categorized as earnings, the government also applies tax rates on capital gains and dividends. When the value of an investment rises and the security is sold for a profit, the tax rate that the investor pays depends on how long s/he held the asset. The tax rate on the capital gain of a short-term investment (an investment held for one year or less) is equal to the investor's ordinary income tax. So, an individual who falls into the 24% marginal tax bracket will pay 24% on his or her short-term capital gains (Internal Revenue Service, 2020a).

The tax rate on profits from investments held longer than a year ranges from 0–20%. Individuals with taxable income below $80,000 pay 0%. Individuals with taxable income between $80,000 and $441,450 pay 15%, and investors with income above $441,450 pay a 20% tax rate on capital gains. Qualified dividends are subject to the same tax rate schedule that applies to long-term capital gains. Nonqualified dividends have the same tax rates as short-term capital gains (Internal Revenue Service, 2020a, 2020b).

As high tax rates get high taxation, high taxation provides more wealth to the government for distribution and redistribution via fiscal policy. So, the tax rates become the key to applying fiscal policies. Wealth distribution involves the government taking money from those who are 'producing more than they are consuming' and giving that money to those who are 'consuming more than they are producing'. Of course, punishing net producers and rewarding net consumers motivates net producers to become net consumers – leading to economic decline. It also increases the power of those officials who espouse wealth distribution. That is the primary driving force of calls by political elites for increased wealth distribution: increased political power.

Over the past two centuries, while common people labored all day to obtain food, tend fires, tend to livestock, and make, wash and mend clothing, the rich enjoyed luxuries that were out of the reach of commoners: abundant food, fine clothing, traveling for enjoyment, tutors, and college educations. Since the poor have benefited more than the rich over the past two centuries because they have experienced much more dramatic improvements in their economic lifestyles than those received by the wealthy, the economic equity is increasing.

Today, in America, both the wealthy and the commoners can enjoy advanced medical care, higher education, lighting, appliances for cooking and washing, year-round fresh fruit and vegetables, central heating and air conditioning, safe and reliable transportation, and on and on. While the richest Americans have thousands of times more wealth than ordinary Americans, when measured by dollars, they share lifestyles that are much more similar today than centuries or decades ago. Simply put, economic progress narrows lifestyle inequity because prosperity improves the standards of living of the poor more than it helps the rich.

Another tool that can be used for tax regulation is tariffs. It can be included in the scope of national economic policy optimization to enrich the people with tax reduction and increase the income outside by raising tariffs. But the rise and fall of tariffs will affect international trade and international relations, which should be used with caution as an economic policy in open and semi-open economy.

THE POWER OF KNOWLEDGE AFFECTS FISCAL POLICY

Fiscal policy refers to the use of government spending and tax policies to influence economic conditions, which is the use of government revenue collection and expenditure to influence a country's economy.

In Keynesian economics, aggregate demand or spending is what drives the performance and growth of the economy, where fiscal policy is largely based on the fact that governments could stabilize the business cycle and regulate economic output. As the aggregate demand is made up of consumer spending, business investment spending, net government spending, and net exports, the private sector components of aggregate demand are too variable and too dependent on psychological and emotional factors to maintain sustained growth in the economy. Along scientific philosophy (Kuhn, 1996; Popper, 1972), with inheriting classic economic spirits (Arrow, 1963; Friedman, 1966; Hicks, 1946; Keynes, 2012; Marshall, 2013; Mises, 2006; Samuelson, 1983; Samuelson & Nordhaus, 2010; Schumpeter, 2003; Smith, 1977; Walras, 1954), economists are making efforts to eliminate poverty (Dollar & Kraay, 2002; Sen, 1997, 2002; Gilder, 2012, 2013; Piketty, 2014) for approaching social equity, particularly via fiscal policies.

It is well known that there are expansionary and contractionary fiscal policies, respectively. Which fiscal policy is suitable for economic modification is an important issue concerning the power of knowledge.

In expansionary policies, the government can affect the economy using tax stimulus rebates to increase aggregate demand and fuel economic growth when the economy experiences a recession. The logic behind the expansionary policies is that when people pay lower taxes, they have more money to spend or invest, which fuels higher demand. That demand leads firms to hire more, decreasing unemployment, and to compete more fiercely for labor. In turn, this serves to raise wages and provide consumers with more income to spend and invest. It's a virtuous cycle, or positive feedback loop.

An expansionary fiscal policy is usually characterized by deficit spending, when government expenditures exceed receipts from taxes and other sources. In practice, deficit spending tends to result from a combination of tax cuts and higher spending. Rather than lowering taxes, the government may seek economic expansion through increases in spending (without corresponding tax increases). By building more highways, for example, it could increase employment, pushing up demand and growth.

Therefore, during a recession, the government may employ expansionary fiscal policy by lowering tax rates to increase aggregate demand and fuel economic growth. However, fiscal stimulus is politically difficult to reverse. Sometimes the expansionary policies are dangerous, due to the political incentives faced by policymakers, who tend to be a consistent bias toward engaging in more-or-less constant deficit spending that can be in part rationalized as 'good for the economy'. Eventually, economic expansion might get out of hand, as rising wages lead to inflation and asset bubbles begin to form. High inflation and the risk of wide-spread defaults when debt bubbles burst can badly damage the economy and this risk, in turn, leads governments (or their central banks) to reverse course and attempt to 'contract' the economy.

In contractionary policies, the government can affect economy by increasing taxes, reducing public spending, and cutting public-sector pay or jobs, when the economy mounts inflation and other expansionary symptoms. A contractionary fiscal policy is characterized by budget surpluses, but it is rarely used, because it is hugely unpopular politically.

Thus, public policymakers face a major asymmetry in their incentives to engage in expansionary or contractionary fiscal policy. When the public policymakers possess enough knowledge to makes decisions, they could select the correct economic policy. Here, what knowledge is power is just that the power of knowledge affects fiscal policy.

Conclusively, fiscal policy is effective to maintain social equity, particularly via tax rates. As the knowledge level of policymakers affects economic process and fiscal policy, and the fiscal policy affects tax rates and wealth distribution, linking to social equity, the policymakers are important elements in the economic system, who are managing national economy and social equity via the fiscal policies. Therefore, knowledge is also an important power to promote social equity.

REFERENCES

Arrow, K. (1963). *Social Choice and Individual Values* (2nd ed.). Yale University Press.

Coase, R. H. (1960). The problem of social cost. *The Journal of Law & Economics, 3*, 1–44. doi:10.1086/466560

Davis, J. (2003). *The Theory of the Individual in Economics*. Routledge. doi:10.4324/9780203457689

Dollar, D., & Kraay, A. (2002). Growth is good for the poor. *Journal of Economic Growth, 7*(3), 195–225. doi:10.1023/A:1020139631000

Faccarello, G., & Kurz, H. D. (2016). Handbook on the History of Economic Analysis. Vol. I: Great Economists since Petty and Boisguilbert; Vol. II: Schools of Thought in Economics. Edward Elgar.

Feldman, A. M., & Serrano, R. (2005). *Welfare Economics and Social Choice Theory* (2nd ed.). Springer Science & Business Media, Inc.

Floyd, J. E. (2010). *Interest Rates, Exchange Rates and World Monetary Policy*. Springer. doi:10.1007/978-3-642-10280-6

Forni, M., & Lippi, M. (1997). *Aggregation and the Microfoundations of Dynamic Macroecomics*. Oxford University Press.

Friedman, B. M., & Hahn, F. H. (Eds.). (2000). *Handbook of Monetary Economics* (Vol. 1-2). Elsevier.

Friedman, M. (1966). The Methodology of Positive Economics. In *Essays in Positive Economics*. University of Chicago Press.

Gilder, G. (2012). *Wealth and Poverty: A new edition for the twenty-first century*. Regnery Pub. Inc.

Gilder, G. (2013). *Knowledge and Power: The information theory of capitalism and how it is revolutionizing our world*. Regnery Pub. Inc.

Gillies, D. (1998). The Duhem thesis and the Quine thesis. In *Philosophy of Science: The Central Issues*. New York: Norton.

Goodfriend, M., & King, R. G. (1997). The new neoclassical synthesis and the role of monetary policy. *NBER Macroeconomics Annual, 12*, 231–283. doi:10.1086/654336

Heyne, P., Boettke, P., & Prychitko, D. (2013). *The Economic Way of Thinking* (13th ed.). Pearson Education.

Hicks, J. R. (1946). *Value and Capital: An inquiry into some fundamental principles of economic theory* (2nd ed.). Oxford University Press.

Internal Revenue Service. (2020a). *Topic No. 409: Capital Gains and Losses*. IRS.

Internal Revenue Service. (2020b). *Publication 550: Investment Income and Expenses*. IRS.

Jones, R. W., & Kenen, P. B. (Eds.). (1985). *Handbook of International Economics*. Elsevier.

Keynes, J. M. (2012). The General Theory of Employment, Interest and Money (The Collected Writings of John Maynard Keynes Vol. 7). Cambridge University Press.

King, R. G. (2000). The new IS-LM model: Language, logic, and limits. *Federal Reserve Bank of Richmond Economic Quarterly*, *86*, 45–103.

Kuhn, T. S. (1996). *The Structure of Scientific Revolutions* (rev. ed.). The University of Chicago Press. doi:10.7208/chicago/9780226458106.001.0001

Lamb, M., Lymer, A., & Freedman, J. (2005). *Taxation: An Interdisciplinary Approach to Research*. Oxford University Press.

Lengwiler, Y. (2004). *Microfoundations of Financial Economics: An Introduction to General Equilibrium Asset Pricing*. Princeton University Press.

Lucas, R., & Rapping, L. (1970). Real Wages, Employment and Inflation. In E. Phelps (Ed.), *Microeconomic Foundations of Employment and Inflation Theory* (pp. 253–305). Norton.

Mäki, U. (2012). Handbook of the Philosophy of Science: Vol. 13. *Philosophy of Economics*. Elsevier.

Mises, L. (2006). *The Ultimate Foundation of Economic Science: An Essay on Method*. Liberty Fund, Inc.

Nicola, P. C. (2013). *Efficiency and Equity in Welfare Economics*. Springer.

North, D. C. (1990). *Institutions, Institutional Change and Economic Performance*. Cambridge University Press.

Okun, A. M. (1975). *Equity and Efficiency: the big trade-off*. Brookings Institution.

Piketty, Th. (2014). *Capital in the twenty-first century (A. Goldhammer, Trans.)*. Harvard University Press.

Popper, K. R. (1972). *Objective Knowledge: an evolutionary approach.* Oxford University Press.

Reiss, J. (2013). Philosophy of Economics: a contemporary introduction. Routledge (Taylor & Francis Group).

Robinson, J. (1962). *Economic Philosophy.* Transaction Publishers.

Ross, D. (2014). *Philosophy of Economics.* Palgrave Macmillan.

Samuelson, P. A. (1983). Foundations of Economic Analysis (Enlarged ed.). Harvard University Press.

Samuelson, P. A., & Nordhaus, W. D. (2010). *Economics* (19th ed.). McGraw-Hill Co.

Scarth, W. (2014). *Macroeconomics: The development of modern methods for policy analysis.* Edward Elgar.

Schumpeter, J. A. (2003). Capitalism, Socialism, and Demacracy (e-Library ed.). London: Routledge (Taylor & Francis Group).

Sen, A. (1997). *Poverty and Famines.* International Labour Organization.

Sen, A. (2002). *Rationality and Freedom.* Belknap Press.

Smith, A. (1977). An Inquiry into the Nature and Causes of the Wealth of Nations (UK ed.). Chicago: University of Chicago Press.

Walras, L. (1954). Elements of Pure Economics, or the theory of social wealth (4th ed., W. Jaffé, Trans.). London: George Allen & Unwin Ltd.

Chapter 12
Economic Efficiency and Monetary Policy

ABSTRACT

Active monetary policy benefits economic efficiency, and the power of capital affects monetary policy, while interest rate determines the welfare optimization, so that monetary policy tightly links with economic efficiency. While market mechanism provides the key to economic efficiency, the monetary policy maintains its optimality in economic system. It is strengthened to follow closely the power of capital in this chapter. While market mechanism provides the key to economic efficiency, the monetary policy maintains its optimality.

INTRODUCTION

The market mechanism acting in the economic system will maintain basic economic efficiency. In the optimization of markets, monetary policy from the central bank plays a key role, which also represents national economic policy. When the national economic policy works with markets together, economic efficiency may reach its optimality.

DOI: 10.4018/978-1-6684-4935-6.ch012

ACTIVE MONETARY POLICY BENEFITS ECONOMIC EFFICIENCY

While fiscal policies are difficult to hold and manage, the monetary policies, by raising interest rates or restraining the supply of money, become more convenient, effective and useful policy tools. The monetary policies, by delivering price stability, can contribute to the efficient functioning of the real economy and to economic growth and social welfare through various means.

An active monetary policy means the central bank can act, or choose not to act, based on its assessment for the national economy, while a passive monetary policy, by contrast, involves a set of rules that dictate monetary policy actions. Active monetary policy grants policymakers the flexibility and discretion to act when inflation exceeds expected levels or if the course of economic activity expands or contracts at greater levels than anticipated. Active monetary policy also allows the central bank to moderate economic fluctuations that could create instability.

Thus, an active monetary policy benefits economic efficiency; in particular, the changes or modification of interest rates directly acts with the capital, so that the capital also becomes active to act with the economy.

INTEREST RATE DETERMINES THE WELFARE OPTIMIZATION

Interest rates also affect economic inequity and social welfare. Even in the bestselling book *Capital in the Twenty-First Century* by Thomas Piketty (Piketty, 2014), it is hard to escape the view that rising inequity poses major challenges in advanced economies. Here we mentioned a cross-country evidence (Dollar et al., 2014). In the developing world, too, much has been written about the adverse effects of high and rising inequity on the pace of poverty reduction. Public opinion surveys suggest that strong majorities of respondents in advanced economies feel that the gap between rich and poor has been rising in recent years (Pew Research Center, 2013).

Inequity changes worldwide, no doubt, reflect in part the fact that inequity has indeed been increasing in many countries. In the US over the past four decades, the Gini coefficient of income inequity has risen from around 0.3 to around 0.4. Roughly the same has happened in China, only more rapidly; between 1990 and 2009, the Gini coefficient has increased from 0.32 to

0.42. According to the data (Atkinson et al., 2011), much of this increase has happened at the upper end of the income distribution.

However, it is also important not to lose sight of the fact that inequity has not increased in other countries, and has declined appreciably in others still. In Atkinson et al.'s data, income shares of the top decile have been stable, or even slightly declining since the mid-20th century in countries such as Germany, France, Switzerland, the Netherlands, and Japan. In Brazil, the Gini coefficient has declined from around 0.6 in the late 1990s to around 0.55 in the late 2000s. More systematically, in a large dataset of changes in inequity over periods at least five years long, in almost half of episodes the Gini coefficient of inequity increases, while in the other half it decreases.

There is a simple example to illustrate the approach. The World Bank has recently made a major public commitment to the goal of promoting 'shared prosperity', defined as growth in average incomes of those in the bottom 40% of the income distribution in each country in the developing world (World Bank, 2013). As a matter of simple arithmetic, growth in average incomes in the bottom 40% is the sum of growth in average incomes, and growth in the share of income accruing to the bottom 40%. In China, for example, between 1990 and 2009, average incomes grew at 6.7% per year. At the same time, inequity increased in the sense that the income shares of the bottom 40% declined from 20.2% to 14.4%, corresponding to an average annual change of -1.7% per year. Combining these two observations, average incomes in the bottom 40% grew more slowly than the overall average income, at 5% per year. From the standpoint of promoting shared prosperity, therefore, the growth 'cost' of the increase in inequity in China over this period is about 1.7 percentage points of growth per year.

To produce more systematic evidence, Dollar et al. worked with a large dataset of income distributions covering 117 countries over the past four decades. We focus on within-country changes in average incomes and income inequity observed over episodes at least five years long. In a sample of 285 such non-overlapping episodes, we calculate the contribution of growth in average incomes and the contribution of changes in inequity to growth in social welfare. We do this for a wide variety of social welfare functions, capturing a wide range of preferences for redistribution of income across individuals.

In their paper (Dollar et al. 2014), their approach is very modest. They use standard tools of social welfare analysis to calculate how much more or less growth in average incomes a country would need over a given period in order to compensate – in terms of social welfare growth – for the observed change in inequity over the same period. They then document the size of this compensation and its relationship to average income growth in a large dataset of episodes of growth and changes in inequity covering 117 countries between 1970 and 2012. For all of the social welfare functions they consider, social welfare, on average, increases equiproportionately with increases in average incomes. This reflects the fact that changes in the relevant inequity measures are not systematically correlated with changes in average incomes. For all but the most bottom-sensitive social welfare functions, the relationship between growth in social welfare and growth in average incomes is also very tight, in the sense that data points cluster closely to the 45-degree line. This reflects the fact that changes in inequity are small, meaning that variation across episodes in inequity accounts for only a small fraction of the variation across episodes in changes in social welfare. And this, in turn, implies that the additional growth in average incomes required to 'compensate' – in terms of social welfare growth – for a typical increase in inequity is, on average, quite small.

Here, we cite Figure 1 (Dollar et al., 2014) to illustrate the results of one particular social welfare function based on the Gini index, by the measure of 'real national income' (Sen, 1976), which is average income scaled by a factor of one minus the Gini coefficient. On the horizontal axis we plot growth in average incomes across the 285 spells in our sample, while the vertical axis has corresponding growth in social welfare. Since social welfare growth is the sum of growth in average incomes plus the contribution of inequity changes, the vertical distances between each data point and the 45-degree line indicate the contribution of inequity change to social welfare growth. For points above the 45-degree line, the Gini coefficient fell and social welfare grew faster than average income, while for points below the line, inequity increased and social welfare grew slower than average incomes.

The main point of the paper is that variation in country growth experience (i.e., variation across episodes on the horizontal axis) is much larger than the variation in the contribution of inequity change to social welfare (i.e., variation around the 45-degree line). After more formal variance decomposition is investigated, it is found that over 90% of the variation in social welfare growth is due to growth in average incomes, and less than 10% is due to inequity changes, which are at the forefront of many policy debates. While inequity has increased in many countries over the past few decades, in others it has decreased. This data from 117 countries over the past four decades shows the importance of such changes in inequity, as well as of overall economic growth. Whereas inequity changes in most countries have been small, differences in overall growth performance have been large. Policymakers should, therefore, be careful not to undermine growth in the quest for greater equity.

Figure 1. Growth in social welfare on the Sen index of real national income
(Picture from the World Bank working paper No. 6842 by Dollar et al., 2014)

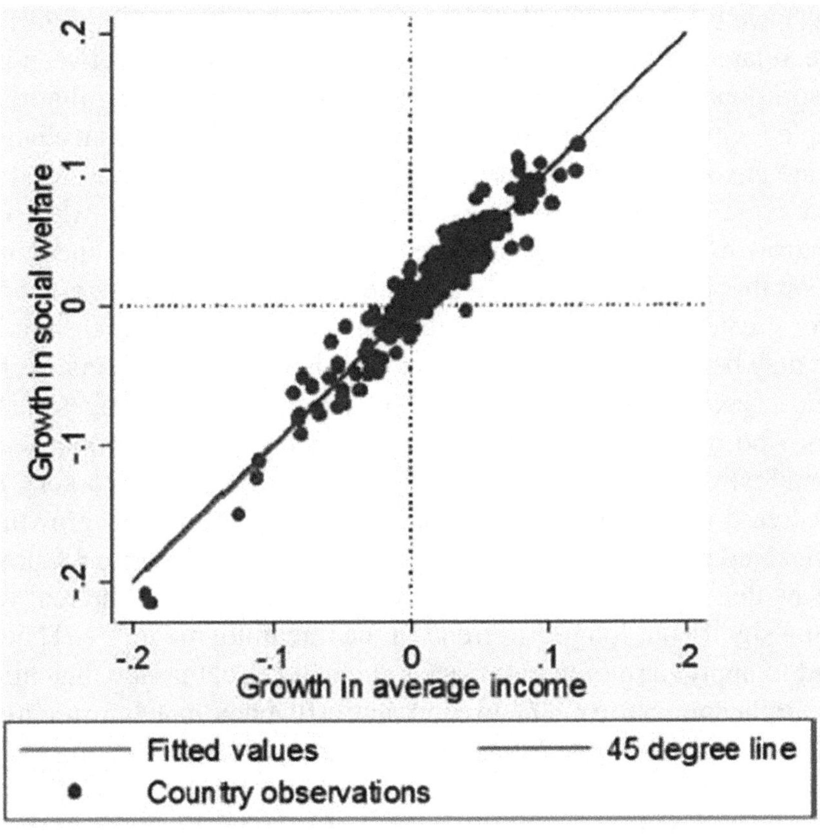

THE POWER OF CAPITAL AFFECTS MONETARY POLICY

Monetary policy refers to the decisions, choices or regulations related to the financial system of the organization like payment system, borrowing system, lending system, particularly banks. The policies are framed to introduce financial stability, promote market efficiency and enhance the value of the firm for its stakeholders. A well-made monetary policy is important for the growth of a nation in the long run.

In the decision making of monetary policies, the power of capital is very effective. When capital wants higher return from the social economic system, the central bank could restrict its action under the support of national power, especially via interest rates.

Monetary policies are also strong tools for pushing welfare growth, where inequity is a 'hot' topic, but inequity changes in most countries over the past decades have been small, while differences in average growth performance have been large. It is difficult to isolate robust correlations between policy and institutional variables and changes in inequity, indicating that there is no simple recipe for enhancing equity. Furthermore, the fact that changes in equity are uncorrelated with economic growth means that there are likely to be some equity-enhancing policies that also promote growth, while others reduce growth. With growing pressure to 'do something' about inequity, it is important that policymakers are careful to avoid undermining growth in the quest for greater equity, as policies that raise equity at the expense of lower growth may be self-defeating in the sense of not improving social welfare.

In most cases, higher productivity comes from raising the wages of skilled workers who possess knowledge, not from bringing more people jobs. So the capital power tends to raise the wages of knowledgeable workers, rather than decrease the unemployment rate, to promote economic growth. The theoretical judgment is consistent with centuries of social economic practice, as we saw that vast productivity growth had led to increase the real wages, without a significant long-term trend in the unemployment rate. Therefore, we need to apply harmonic monetary policy and fiscal policy matching the economic phenomena, to maintain economic efficiency, matching mainstream economic thoughts (Davis, 2003; Dollar & Kraay, 2002; Faccarello & Kurz, 2016; Feldman & Serrano, 2005; Floyd, 2010; Forni & Lippi, 1997; Friedman, 1966; Friedman & Hahn, 2000; Gilder, 2012, 2013; Goodfriend & King, 1997; Hicks, 1946; Keynes, 2012; King, 2000; Lengwiler, 2004; Marshall, 2013; Nicola, 2013; North, 1990; Okun, 1975; Piketty, 2014; Samuelson, 1983; Samuelson & Nordhaus, 2010;Smith, 1977; Scarth, 2014; Sen, 1997; Walras, 1954;Woodford, 2003).

Overall, monetary policy is effective in promoting economic efficiency, via changes of interest rates. As the power of capital could affect economic process and monetary policy, and the monetary policy affects interest rates, linking to economic efficiency, banks are important elements in the economic system, which maintain national economy and economic efficiency via monetary policies.

REFERENCES

Davis, J. (2003). *The Theory of the Individual in Economics*. Routledge. doi:10.4324/9780203457689

Dollar, D., Kleineberg, T., & Kraay, A. (2014). *Growth, inequity and social welfare: cross country evidence*. World Bank Policy Research Department Working Paper No. 6842.

Dollar, D., & Kraay, A. (2002). Growth is good for the poor. *Journal of Economic Growth*, *7*(3), 195–225. doi:10.1023/A:1020139631000

Feldman, A. M., & Serrano, R. (2005). *Welfare Economics and Social Choice Theory* (2nd ed.). Springer Science & Business Media, Inc.

Floyd, J. E. (2010). *Interest Rates, Exchange Rates and World Monetary Policy*. Springer. doi:10.1007/978-3-642-10280-6

Friedman, B. M., & Hahn, F. H. (Eds.). (2000). *Handbook of Monetary Economics* (Vol. 1-2). Elsevier.

Gilder, G. (2012). *Wealth and Poverty: A new edition for the twenty-first century*. Regnery Pub. Inc.

Gilder, G. (2013). *Knowledge and Power: The information theory of capitalism and how it is revolutionizing our world*. Regnery Pub. Inc.

Goodfriend, M., & King, R. G. (1997). The new neoclassical synthesis and the role of monetary policy. *NBER Macroeconomics Annual*, *12*, 231–283. doi:10.1086/654336

Hicks, J. R. (1946). *Value and Capital: An inquiry into some fundamental principles of economic theory* (2nd ed.). Oxford University Press.

Internal Revenue Service. (2020a). *Topic No. 409: Capital Gains and Losses*. IRS.

Internal Revenue Service. (2020b). *Publication 550: Investment Income and Expenses*. IRS.

Keynes, J. M. (2012). The General Theory of Employment, Interest and Money (The Collected Writings of John Maynard Keynes Vol. 7). Cambridge University Press.

King, R. G. (2000). The new IS-LM model: Language, logic, and limits. *Federal Reserve Bank of Richmond Economic Quarterly*, *86*, 45–103.

Nicola, P. C. (2013). *Efficiency and Equity in Welfare Economics*. Springer.

Okun, A. M. (1975). *Equity and Efficiency: the big trade-off*. Brookings Institution.

Pew Research Center. (2013). *Economies of Emerging Markets Better Rated During Difficult Times*. https://www.pewresearch.org

Piketty, T. (2014). *Capital in the twenty-first century (A. Goldhammer, Trans.)*. Harvard University Press.

Samuelson, P. A. (1983). Foundations of Economic Analysis (Enlarged ed.). Harvard University Press.

Samuelson, P. A., & Nordhaus, W. D. (2010). *Economics* (19th ed.). McGraw-Hill Co.

Scarth, W. (2014). *Macroeconomics: the development of modern methods for policy analysis*. Edward Elgar.

Sen, A. (1976). Real national income. *The Review of Economic Studies*, *43*(1), 19–39.

Sen, A. (1997). *Poverty and Famines*. International Labour Organization.

Smith, A. (1977). An Inquiry into the Nature and Causes of the Wealth of Nations (UK ed.). Chicago: University of Chicago Press.

Walras, L. (1954). Elements of Pure Economics, or the theory of social wealth (4th ed., W. Jaffé, Trans.). London: George Allen & Unwin Ltd.

Woodford, M. (2003). *Interest and Prices: Foundations of a Theory of Monetary Policy*. Princeton University Press.

World Bank. (2013). *The World Bank Goals: End Extreme Poverty and Promote Shared Prosperity*. Author.

Chapter 13
Optimization:
Balancing Social Equity and Economic Efficiency

ABSTRACT

In semi-open economies, both national economy and international economy face the optimization issue for balancing social equity and economic efficiency. As real states show complicated interactions of multi-equilibria and multi-economies, the complete equilibrium states (i.e., model equations) provide ideal theoretical reference. Combining fiscal and monetary policies, it is possible to balance social equity and efficiency to approach economic optimization. Related issues are discussed in this chapter.

INTRODUCTION

In any society, there are always rich and poor people. The governments receive tax revenues to support public affairs and to regulate the rich-poor difference, in order to realize social equity via wealth distribution. Both social and personal surplus money would cumulatively transfer to capital, and the capital demands effective reciprocation via interest or investment. Following Piketty's analysis (Piketty, 2014), more issues on capital and wealth can be discussed.

DOI: 10.4018/978-1-6684-4935-6.ch013

NATIONAL ECONOMIC CONSIDERATIONS

As we mentioned, wealth distribution and capital profit are always important issues in national economics. Economic policy actually looks like an art for balancing equity and efficiency, where the social wealth distribution (regulated by tax rate) and economic efficiency (realized by interest rate) become important factors for applications.

At the global level, income received from abroad and paid abroad must balance, so that income is, by definition, equal to output, i.e., **global income = global output.** This equity between two annual flows, income and output, is an accounting identity, yet it reflects an important reality. In any given year, it is impossible for total income to exceed the amount of new wealth that is produced (at the global level; a single country may of course borrow from abroad).

At a country level, national income may be greater or smaller than its domestic product, depending on whether net income from abroad is positive or negative, with the basic formula as **national income = domestic output + net income from abroad = capital income + labor income.** Excluding human capital, Piketty concludes that capital reflects the state of development and prevailing social relations of each society, which is just when the capital becomes wealth. He uses the words 'capital' and 'wealth' interchangeably. However, the human capital cannot be excluded as it is a very important economic element.

In the view of wealth, we have **national wealth = public wealth + private wealth.** There is a typical difference between developed and developing countries, where public wealth occupies the main portion in developing countries, whereas public wealth in most developed countries is currently insignificant (or even negative, where the public debt exceeds public assets) and private wealth accounts for nearly all of national wealth. But developed countries would engage in large-scale deficit financing to pay for public sector projects and governmental funding. While such activity stimulates the domestic economy, national large public deficits and debts are introduced. However, a large debt encourages inflation, and a government may print money to pay part of a large debt, increasing the money supply inevitably causes further inflation. Therefore, the country's debt rating becomes a crucial determinant of its inflation, as well as exchange rate. Moreover, if a government is not able to service its deficit through domestic means (selling domestic bonds, increasing the money supply), then it must increase the supply of securities for sale to foreigners, thereby the risks are transferred to other countries.

According to Piketty's statistics (Piketty, 2014), the wealth distribution is inequity. The regularity we observe when we try to measure income inequity in practice is that inequity with respect to capital is always greater than inequity with respect to labor. The distribution of capital ownership (and of income from capital) is always more concentrated than the distribution of income from labor. Piketty suggested that governments should collect taxes not only on income, but also, more importantly, on capital because capital produces much more benefit than income.

Following the first fundamental law of capitalism, $\alpha = r \times \beta$, where α is the share of income from capital in national income, r the rate of return on capital and β the capital/income ratio, and the second fundamental law of capitalism, $\beta = s / g$, where s is the savings rate and g the growth rate, Piketty revealed that the fundamental force of inequity focuses on $r > g$ (where r stands for the average annual rate of return on capital, including profits, dividends, interest, rents, and other income from capital, expressed as a percentage of its total value, and g stands for the rate of growth of the economy, i.e. the annual increase in income or output). Since $\alpha = r \times \beta = r \times (s / g)$, $\alpha / r = s / g$, $\alpha \times g = r \times s$, leading to $r = g (\alpha/s)$, so $r > g$ is equivalent to $\alpha/s < 1$ or $\alpha < s$, which means that if the share of capital income in national income (α) is less than the savings rate (s), the average annual rate of return on capital (r) will be larger than the rate of growth of the economy (g).

Taxation is not only a technical matter, but also preeminently a political and philosophical issue, perhaps the most important political economic issue. Without taxes, society has no common destiny, and collective action is impossible. It is certainly correct that progressive tax plays a key role in wealth distribution. A progressive tax is a crucial component for social equity, which plays a central role in its development and in the transformation of the structure of inequity in the world and remains important for ensuring the viability of social equity in the future.

INTERNATIONAL ECONOMIC CONSIDERATIONS: SEMI-OPEN ECONOMY

Differentiating from the closed economy where people are not allowed to trade with other countries, an ideal open economy is free to trade with the other economies of different countries. Although an open economy is advantageous because people can trade in goods and services, it also introduces many macroeconomic phenomena like exchange rates, balance of trade, tariffs, subsidies, and import quotas.

An open economy is the opposite of a closed economy. It is one that is characteristically market-oriented, with free market policies rather than government-imposed price controls. In an open economy, industries tend to be privately owned rather than owned by the government. In the area of international trade, an open economy is one whose policies promote free trade over protectionism. On the other hand, a closed or managed economy is characterized by protective tariffs, state-run or nationalized industries, extensive government regulations and price controls, and similar policies indicative of a government-controlled economy. In a closed economy, the government typically intervenes to influence the production of goods and services. In an open economy, market forces are allowed to determine production levels.

In fact, there is no completely open economy in the world, for completely free trade. Most open economy belongs to semi-open economy, where tariffs and exchange rate are important adjustable elements. There are three ways in which semi-open connections are entrenched, as follows:

1. **Output Market:** An economy can deal and trade in commodities and services with other nations. This broadens the preferences in the sense that the customers and manufacturers can pick between domestic and foreign commodities.
2. **Financial Market:** Often, an economy can purchase financial assets from other nations. This gives investors the opportunity to pick between domestic and foreign assets.
3. **Labor Market:** Enterprises can pick where to locate manufacturing plants and workers can pick where they work. There are several immigration laws which constrain the movement of labor between nations.

We had not contemplated this feature and just restricted it to a closed economy in which there are no connections with the rest of the world in order to ease our analysis and elucidate the basic macroeconomic systems. In fact, most of the modern economies are open, especially via short-run exchange rates determined by national supply and demand.

Like any other price in local economies, exchange rates are determined by supply and demand, specifically the national supply and demand for each currency. Meanwhile, the supply of a currency on a foreign exchange market is determined by the demand for goods, services, and investments priced in that currency.

Central banks, on the other hand, never directly rely on consumer interaction to affect the exchange rates. While the banks cannot simply print more money, they can influence investments, loans, and exchanges in the foreign marketplace, which will either raise or lower the value of their national currency abroad.

Therefore, the exchange rate is actually determined by a variety of factors, which change constantly. As a result, it is important when traveling abroad to check the current exchange rate in destination countries, especially during peak tourist seasons when the foreign demand for domestic goods is higher.

In international finance, derivative instruments imply contracts based on which you can purchase or sell currency at a future date. The three major types of foreign exchange (FX) derivatives are forward contracts, futures contracts, and options. They have important differences, which change their attractiveness to a specific FX market participant.

An exchange traded derivative is a financial contract that is listed and trades on a regulated exchange. Put simply, these are derivatives that are traded in a regulated fashion. Exchange traded derivatives have become increasingly popular because of the advantages they have over over-the-counter (OTC) derivatives, such as standardization, liquidity, and elimination of default risk. Futures and options are two of the most popular exchange traded derivatives. Exchange traded derivatives can be used to hedge exposure or speculate on a wide range of financial assets like commodities, equities, currencies, and even interest rates.

Both fiscal and monetary policy can be expansionary or contractionary, there will be an indeterminate impact on interest rates. Both fiscal and monetary policy actions will have an indeterminate impact on the AD curve and, therefore, an indeterminate impact on the price level and real output. Expansionary monetary policy causes an increase in the money supply, which decreases the nominal interest rate. Contractionary monetary policy decreases the money supply which increases the nominal interest rate. Expansionary fiscal policy and expansionary monetary policy both shift the AD curve to the right, while contractionary fiscal policy and contractionary monetary policy both shift the AD curve to the left.

Recall that the fiscal policy is effective and the monetary policy is ineffective in a fixed exchange rate system, while the fiscal policy is ineffective and the monetary policy is effective in floating the exchange rate system in Mundell-Fleming economics. In a semi-open economy, fiscal policy will be more effective than monetary policy, particularly under the strong support of government power. Generally, Mundell had suggested the use of fiscal policy to process national economy and monetary policy to deal with international economy to realize internal and external balance, in his policy mix theory (Mundell, 1962).

Thus, a completely open economy exists only in theory. For example, no country in the world allows unlimited free access to its markets. Most nations have fiscal and monetary policies that attempt to improve their economies. Many economies that are open in some respects may still have government owned, monopolistic industries. A country is considered to have an open economy unless its policies allow market forces to determine such matters as producing and pricing.

Meanwhile, adjustments of exchange rates are mostly determined by interest rates, as interest rates and exchange rates are nonlinearly linked together. Only larger countries have their national markets for the adjustments of exchange rates, because the smaller countries do not have enough market space for the national economic cycle. Therefore, large countries could maintain independent semi-open economies, while small countries have to merge self-markets into the international economic cycle.

Social, political, and economic instability can be avoided in countries moving toward open economies, but domestic conditions must be favorable. For example, states with powerful bureaucracies can establish favorable domestic economic conditions if they have the proper ideology, accept diversity, and achieve legitimacy in the eyes of their citizens. For open economies to succeed in small countries that formerly had managed economies, favorable domestic conditions include working education, legal and judicial systems, and low inflation. Such conditions provide the necessary stability for an open economy to flourish.

Economists recognize an open economy as being more efficient than a managed economy. In the 18th century, when Adam Smith wrote *An Inquiry into the Nature and Causes of the Wealth of Nations* to explain the benefits of an open economy and free trade, he emphasized that interventions in international trade, such as tariffs and duties, served only to reduce the overall wealth of all nations. Similarly, interventions in the domestic economy are also regarded as inefficient. Smith developed the concept of 'the invisible hand,' which in effect stated that when individual enterprises work to maximize their own profits and well-being, then the economy as a whole also operates more efficiently. He argued that the economy does not require government intervention, because the operations of domestic producers are guided, as if by an invisible hand, to benefit the economy as a whole.

BETWEEN IDEAL AND REALITY

All economic models are ideal, as the full equilibrium never real existence. However, the ideal states are good theoretical reference for reality. Measuring the deviation between the ideal state and the real reality, it is the calibration and correction of the economic operation of the ruler. When the economic reality deviates too far from the ideal model (away from full equilibrium), economic warning signals are generated and appropriate economic policies are recommended for adjustment.

In ideal states, economic models reach full equilibrium and all equations are correct. Within a very simple situation, it is best to have one kind of money, the World Dollar or the Earth Dollar, no exchange rate is needed. However, the ideal states are not real.

Real states show complicated interactions of multi-equilibria and multi-economies. We face a complicated world and complex economies; this is why economics and economic analysis are necessary.

As discussed above, the fiscal policy is effective to maintain social equity via tax rates, while the monetary policy is effective to promote economic efficiency via interest rates. Thus, the synthetic applications of fiscal and monetary policies are necessary for economic optimization. Synthesizing fiscal policy and monetary policy, the economic optimization could be realized by combining the tax and interest rates. Considering international economic optimization in open or semi-open economy, the exchange rate also falls into our scope.

Therefore, tax rate, interest rate and exchange rate are the three key parameters to correct and adjust the economy, and are also the three key factors in economic analysis which have special political economic meanings. As three important control parameters in an economic system, tax, interest, and exchange rates interact with each other. Tax expresses the economic policy of governance, which reflects the social equity. Interest rate is a key parameter for regulating money supply, which indicates the economic efficiency. Exchange rate is a vital parameter for international business, which determines the international trade.

Tax rates are regulated by law, having long-term stability. Interest rates are controlled by the bank, possessing short-term stability. The exchange rate will randomly fluctuate with changes in the market. While tax rate regulates wealth distribution to approach social equity, interest policy represents a national finance policy for optimizing the money market, and the exchange rate describes an international economic policy for realizing national benefits.

If we choose to use a zero-interest rate and one kind of currency around the globe, e.g. the World Dollar, the economy will be simple, with production-consumption and goods-goods exchange only. Thus, as long as interest and exchange rates exist, the economic and financial system will be a huge and complex system, on which explorations keep extending.

Therefore, economics is a social science, where we need to balance classical thoughts (Arrow, 1963; Arrow & Debreu, 1954; Friedman, 1948, 1956, 1957, 1966, 1970; Hicks, 1946; Lucas, 1972, 1973, 1975, 1988; Keynes, 2012; Marshall, 2013; Fleming, 1962; Mundell, 1962, 1963; Samuelson, 1983; Samuelson & Nordhaus, 2010; Smith, 1977; Solow, 1956; Taylor, 1979; Tobin, 1969, 1975; Walras, 1954) and contemporary knowledge (Faccarello & Kurz, 2016; Feldman & Serrano, 2005; Floyd, 2010; Friedman & Hahn, 2000; Goodfriend & King, 1997; King, 2000; Lucas & Rapping, 1970; Nicola, 2013; Scarth, 2014; Woodford, 2003),

Economics is also known as a scientific art, because the equilibrium is an ideal state (but it really exists, proved by economists). Perhaps we never meet exact equilibrium in practice, but we always observe the economic wave around the equilibrium in real states. While the market mechanism maintains the economic efficiency as science, the government's economic policies approach social equity as art. Economics resembles a real scientific art to balance the economic efficiency and social equity (Ye, 2017, 2020).

REFERENCES

Arrow, K. (1963). *Social Choice and Individual Values* (2nd ed.). Yale University Press.

Arrow, K., & Debreu, G. (1954). Existence of an equilibrium for a competitive economy. *Econometrica*, *22*(3), 265–290. doi:10.2307/1907353

Dollar, D., & Kraay, A. (2002). Growth is good for the poor. *Journal of Economic Growth*, *7*(3), 195–225. doi:10.1023/A:1020139631000

Faccarello, G., & Kurz, H. D. (2016). Handbook on the History of Economic Analysis. Vol. I: Great Economists since Petty and Boisguilbert; Vol. II: Schools of Thought in Economics. Edward Elgar.

Feldman, A. M., & Serrano, R. (2005). *Welfare Economics and Social Choice Theory* (2nd ed.). Springer Science & Business Media, Inc.

Fleming, J. M. (1962). Domestic monetary policies under fixed and floating exchange rates. IMF Staff Papers, 9, 369–379.

Floyd, J. E. (2010). *Interest Rates, Exchange Rates and World Monetary Policy*. Springer. doi:10.1007/978-3-642-10280-6

Forni, M., & Lippi, M. (1997). *Aggregation and the Microfoundations of Dynamic Macroecomics*. Oxford University Press.

Friedman, B. M., & Hahn, F. H. (Eds.). (2000). *Handbook of Monetary Economics* (Vol. 1-2). Elsevier.

Friedman, M. (1948). A monetary and fiscal framework for economic stability. *The American Economic Review*, *38*(3), 245–264.

Friedman, M. (1956). *Studies in the Quantity Theory of Money*. University of Chicago Press.

Friedman, M. (1957). *A Theory of the Consumption Function*. Princeton University Press. doi:10.1515/9780691188485

Friedman, M. (1966). The Methodology of Positive Economics. In *Essays in Positive Economics*. University of Chicago Press.

Friedman, M. (1970). A theoretical framework for monetary analysis. *Journal of Political Economy*, *78*(2), 193–238. doi:10.1086/259623

Gilder, G. (2012). *Wealth and Poverty: A new edition for the twenty-first century*. Regnery Pub. Inc.

Gilder, G. (2013). *Knowledge and Power: The information theory of capitalism and how it is revolutionizing our world*. Regnery Pub. Inc.

Goodfriend, M., & King, R. G. (1997). The new neoclassical synthesis and the role of monetary policy. *NBER Macroeconomics Annual*, *12*, 231–283. doi:10.1086/654336

Hahn, F. H. (1960). The stability of growth equilibrium. *The Quarterly Journal of Economics*, *74*(2), 206–226. doi:10.2307/1884251

Heyne, P., Boettke, P., & Prychitko, D. (2013). *The Economic Way of Thinking* (13th ed.). Pearson Education.

Hicks, J. R. (1946). *Value and Capital: An inquiry into some fundamental principles of economic theory* (2nd ed.). Oxford University Press.

Jones, R. W., & Kenen, P. B. (Eds.). (1985). *Handbook of International Economics*. Elsevier.

Keynes, J. M. (2012). The General Theory of Employment, Interest and Money (The Collected Writings of John Maynard Keynes Vol. 7). Cambridge University Press.

King, R. G. (2000). The new IS-LM model: Language, logic, and limits. *Federal Reserve Bank of Richmond Economic Quarterly*, *86*, 45–103.

Lamb, M., Lymer, A., & Freedman, J. (2005). *Taxation: An Interdisciplinary Approach to Research*. Oxford University Press.

Lengwiler, Y. (2004). *Microfoundations of Financial Economics: An Introduction to General Equilibrium Asset Pricing*. Princeton University Press.

Lucas, R., & Rapping, L. (1970). Real Wages, Employment and Inflation. In E. Phelps (Ed.), *Microeconomic Foundations of Employment and Inflation Theory* (pp. 253–305). Norton.

Lucas, R. E. Jr. (1972). Expectations and the neutrality of money. *Journal of Economic Theory*, *4*(2), 103–124. doi:10.1016/0022-0531(72)90142-1

Lucas, R. E. (1973). Some international evidence on output-inflation tradeoffs. *The American Economic Review*, *63*, 526–534.

Lucas, R. E. Jr. (1975). An equilibrium model of the business cycle. *Journal of Political Economy*, *83*(6), 1113–1144. doi:10.1086/260386

Lucas, R. E. (1988). On the mechanics of development planning. *Journal of Monetary Economics*, *22*, 3–42. doi:10.1016/0304-3932(88)90168-7

Marshall, A. (2013). *Principles of Economics* (8th ed.). Palgrave Macmillan LLC. doi:10.1057/9781137375261

Mises, L. (2006). *The Ultimate Foundation of Economic Science: An Essay on Method*. Liberty Fund, Inc.

Mishkin, F. S. (2004). *The Economics of Money, Banking, and Financial Markets* (7th ed.). Addison-Wesley.

Modigliani, F. (1963). The monetary mechanism and its interaction with real phenomena. *The Review of Economics and Statistics*, *45*(1), 76–103. doi:10.2307/1927150

Mundell, R. A. (1962). The appropriate use of monetary and fiscal policy for internal and external balance. *International Monetary Fund Staff Papers*, *9*(1), 70–79. doi:10.2307/3866082

Mundell, R. A. (1963). *Capital mobility and stabilization policy under fixed and flexible exchange rates. Canadian Journal of Economic and Political Science, 29(4), 475–485.*

Nicola, P. C. (2013). *Efficiency and Equity in Welfare Economics*. Springer. doi:10.1007/978-3-642-30071-4

Piketty, Th. (2014). *Capital in the twenty-first century (A. Goldhammer, Trans.)*. Harvard University Press. doi:10.4159/9780674369542

Samuelson, P. A. (1983). Foundations of Economic Analysis (Enlarged ed.). Harvard University Press.

Samuelson, P. A., & Nordhaus, W. D. (2010). *Economics* (19th ed.). McGraw-Hill Co.

Scarth, W. (2014). *Macroeconomics: the development of modern methods for policy analysis*. Edward Elgar.

Sen, A. (1997). *Poverty and Famines*. International Labour Organization.

Sen, A. (2002). *Rationality and Freedom*. Belknap Press.

Smith, A. (1977). An Inquiry into the Nature and Causes of the Wealth of Nations (UK ed.). Chicago: University of Chicago Press.

Solow, R. M. (1956). A contribution to the theory of economic growth. *The Quarterly Journal of Economics*, *70*(1), 65–94. doi:10.2307/1884513

Stigler, G. J. (1961). The economics of information. *Journal of Political Economy*, *69*(3), 213–225. doi:10.1086/258464

Taylor, J. B. (1979). Staggered wage setting in a macro model. *The American Economic Review*, *69*, 108–113.

Tobin, J. (1969). A general equilibrium approach to monetary theory. *Journal of Money, Credit and Banking*, *1*(1), 15–26. doi:10.2307/1991374

Tobin, J. (1975). Keynesian models of recession and depression. *American Economic Review Proceedings*, *65*, 195–202.

Walras, L. (1954). Elements of Pure Economics, or the theory of social wealth (4th ed., W. Jaffé, Trans.). London: George Allen & Unwin Ltd.

Woodford, M. (2003). *Interest and Prices: Foundations of a Theory of Monetary Policy*. Princeton University Press.

Ye, F. Y. (2017). A synthetic macro-economic model integrating interest, exchange and tax rates. In *Scientific Metrics: toward analytical and quantitative sciences* (pp. 127–140). Springer. doi:10.1007/978-981-10-5936-0_11

Ye, F. Y. (2020). An economic analysis of efficiency and equity combining epistemological true with axiological good through microeconomics to macroeconomics. *International Journal of Economics and Financial Research*, *6*(7), 159–169. doi:10.32861/ijefr.67.159.169

Chapter 14
Political Economics for Reducing Poverty by Economic Growth

ABSTRACT

Knowledge is a key power to change the world. Via knowledge, technological progress would promote economic growth. After economic growth is realized, social welfare and charity reduce poverty. This is just political economics, which could provide a unique view for reducing poverty via economic growth. Political economics could provide a unique view for reducing poverty via economic growth. The way to eliminate poverty is not only to take from the rich and give to the poor, but also to increase social wealth by promoting economic growth.

INTRODUCTION

When social and economic crises are difficult to cope with, human societies often resort to revolution, even war. However, revolution and war are not good for social economies, as they destroy the foundational structure of society. We need to reduce poverty to promote social equity and world peace, and growth is good for the poor (Dollar & Kraay, 2002).

The primary consideration of political economy is to eliminate poverty. The way to eliminate poverty is not only to take from the rich and give to the poor, but also to increase social wealth by promoting economic growth.

DOI: 10.4018/978-1-6684-4935-6.ch014

Although there are other considerations such as social cost and institutions, uncertainty and information (Coase, 1960; North, 1990; Alchian, 1950; Stigler, 1961), reducing poverty is a key toward the good in political economy.

WELFARE AND CHARITY FOR REDUCING POVERTY: TOWARD THE GOOD

How do we measure poverty? There has been marked progress in reducing poverty over the past decades. According to the most recent estimates, in 2015, 10% of the world's population lived at or below $1.90 a day. That's down from 16% in 2010 and 36% in 1990. This means that ending extreme poverty is within our reach, however, the decline has slowed. In April 2013, the World Bank set a new goal to end extreme poverty in a generation. The new target is to have no more than 3% of the world's population living on just $1.90 a day by 2030. By measuring poverty, we learn which poverty reduction strategies work, and which do not. Poverty measurement also helps developing countries gauge program effectiveness and guide their development strategy in a rapidly changing economic environment.

According to the UN 2030 Agenda for Sustainable Development (https://www.un.org/en/global-issues/ending-poverty/), we will end poverty in 2030. However, in 2015, more than 736 million people lived below the international poverty line. Around 10% of the world population (pre-pandemic) was living in extreme poverty and struggling to fulfil the most basic needs like health, education, and access to water and sanitation, to name a few. There were 122 women aged 25 to 34 living in poverty for every 100 men of the same age group, and more than 160 million children were at risk of continuing to live in extreme poverty by 2030.

The UN 2030 Agenda for Sustainable Development promises to leave no one behind and to reach those furthest behind first. Meeting this ambitious development agenda requires visionary policies for sustainable, inclusive, sustained and equitable economic growth, supported by full employment and decent work for all, social integration, declining inequity, rising productivity and a favorable environment. In the 2030 Agenda, Goal 1 recognizes that ending poverty in all its forms everywhere is the greatest global challenge facing the world today, and an indispensable requirement for sustainable development.

Ending poverty in all its forms is the first of the 17 sustainable development goals (SDGs) of the UN 2030 Agenda for Sustainable Development.

The SDGs' main reference to combatting poverty is made in target 1.A: 'Ensure significant mobilization of resources from a variety of sources, including through enhanced development cooperation, in order to provide adequate and predictable means for developing countries, in particular least developed countries, to implement programs and policies to end poverty in all its dimensions.'

The SDGs also aim to create sound policy frameworks at national and regional levels, based on pro-poor and gender-sensitive development strategies to ensure that, by 2030, all men and women have equal rights to economic resources, as well as access to basic services, ownership and control over land and other forms of property, inheritance, natural resources, appropriate new technology and financial services, including microfinance.

While progress in eradicating extreme poverty has been incremental and widespread, the persistence of poverty, including extreme poverty remains a major concern in Africa, the least developed countries, small island developing states, in some middle-income countries, and countries in situations of conflict and post-conflict countries. In light of these concerns, the General Assembly, at its seventy-second session, decided to proclaim the Third United Nations Decade for the Eradication of Poverty (2018–2027). The objective of the Third Decade is to maintain the momentum generated by the implementation of the Second United Nations Decade for the Eradication of Poverty (2008-2017) toward poverty eradication. Further, the Third Decade is also expected to support, in an efficient and coordinated manner, the internationally agreed development goals related to poverty eradication, including the Sustainable Development Goals. In Bangladesh, only 40% of the rural poor have access to grid electricity. Those that do have access endure frequent power outages. The Second Rural Electrification and Renewable Energy Development Project plans to increase access to electricity in rural areas via renewable energy sources.

There is the Borgen project (https://borgenproject.org/10-ways-to-reduce-poverty-in-the-world/), which is following 10 effective ways to reduce poverty around the world.

1. Develop and implement rapid and sustained economic growth policies and programs, in areas such as health, education, nutrition and sanitation, allowing the poor to participate and contribute to the growth. Studies

show that a 10% increase in a country's average income reduces poverty by as much as 20-30%.

2. Improve management of water and other natural resources. Most of the rural poor depend on agriculture or other natural resources for their livelihood. Consequently, it is necessary that they have more equitable access to those resources so they are better able to manage their resources.
3. Invest in and implement agricultural programs. China has helped 800 million people out of poverty since 1978. As a part of its strategy to eradicate poverty by 2020, the Agricultural Bank of China will lend more than $400 billion to help develop rural areas, fund education, infrastructure, and crop production.
4. Encourage countries to engage in trade as a path out of poverty. Trade is the key to growth and prosperity. Some of the world's poorest countries including Indonesia, Botswana and Brazil have traded their way out of poverty.
5. Create and improve access to jobs and income and develop entrepreneurial talent.
6. Provide all people with access to basic social services including education, health care, adequate food, sanitation, shelter and clean water.
7. Progressively developing social protection systems to support those who cannot support themselves.
8. Empower people living in poverty by involving them in the development and implementation of plans and programs to reduce and eradicate poverty. Their involvement ensures that programs reflect those things that are important to them.
9. Remove barriers to equal access to resources and services.
10. Provide access to technology and innovation including internet access and affordable energy.

The Borgen Project is an incredible nonprofit organization that is addressing poverty and hunger and working toward ending them. Clint Borgen recognized the need for an organization that could focus US political attention on extreme poverty. In 2003, after graduating from Washington State University and interning at the United Nations, Borgen began developing the organization. Its mission statement is: The Borgen Project believes that leaders of the most powerful nation on earth should be doing more to address global poverty.

According to scientific philosophical logic (Kuhn, 1996; Popper, 1972), action axiology would be supported by scientific epistemology, and scientific epistemology would be guided by knowledge, so that we believe that knowledge is a key power to change the world. Combining classical economic ideas (Arrow, 1963; Arrow & Debreu, 1954; Fleming, 1962; Friedman, 1948, 1956, 1957, 1966, 1970; Hicks, 1946; Lucas, 1972, 1973, 1975, 1988; Lucas & Rapping, 1970; Keynes, 2012; Marshall, 2013; Mundell, 1962, 1963; Samuelson, 1983; Samuelson & Nordhaus, 2010; Smith, 1977; Solow, 1956; Taylor, 1979; Tobin, 1969, 1975; Walras, 1954), with contemporary knowledge (Faccarello & Kurz, 2016; Feldman & Serrano, 2005; Forni & Lippi, 1997; Floyd, 2010; Friedman & Hahn, 2000; Gilder, 2013; Heyne, Boettke & Prychitko, 2013; Horwitz, 2000; Jones & Kenen, 1985; King, 2000; Scarth, 2014), we may approach real knowledge of human society.

KNOWLEDGE IS GROWTH POWER: TOWARD THE TRUE TECHNOLOGICAL PROGRESS

The famous phrase ‘knowledge is power’ is commonly attributed to Sir Francis Bacon, from his *Meditationes Sacrae*. Its Latin aphorism is the phrase ‘scientia potentia est’ (only the expression ‘ipsa scientia potestas est’ occurs in Bacon’s Meditationes Sacrae. The exact phrase ‘scientia potentia est’ was written for the first time in the 1668 version of the work *Leviathan* by Thomas Hobbes, who was a secretary to Bacon as a young man).

Knowledge provides us with the power to help others, in a variety of ways. It is also something that is good for our own self esteem. In addition, knowledge imbues us with authority and enables us to act and interact with others in a more moral way.

In the knowledge age, knowledge is the real power to change the world.

CAPITAL IS OPTIMAL POWER: TOWARD THE GOOD ECONOMIC POLICY

Knowledge power pushes the real growth of social economy, and capital power pushes the imaginary growth of social economy, particularly for eliminating poverty (Dollar & Kraay, 2002; Sen, 1997, 2002; Gilder, 2012, 2013; World Bank, 2013).

Although we know that capital pursues its profit, which is itself nature, we also suppose that capital is an optimal power. Combining social needs and capital properties, we could take care of economic policies, to provide optimal monetary policy for capital profit and optimal fiscal policy for social good. Thus, at last, we may realize the good economic policy using capital as optimal power.

It is, again, a scientific art to balance knowledge power and capital power as if we are making an 'economic pie'. If we distribute a bigger slice to the poor via economic policies, the rich react to the higher taxes by producing less, leading to the total size of the 'pie' shrinking. Therefore, a good economic policy should benefit both the rich to achieve capital efficiency and the poor to obtain equal welfare, so that the economic policies require us to balance efficiency-enhancing and equity-enhancing.

REFERENCES

Alchian, A. A. (1950). Uncertainty, evolution, and economic theory. *Journal of Political Economy*, *58*(3), 211–221. doi:10.1086/256940

Arrow, K. (1963). *Social Choice and Individual Values* (2nd ed.). Yale University Press.

Arrow, K., & Debreu, G. (1954). Existence of an equilibrium for a competitive economy. *Econometrica*, *22*(3), 265–290. doi:10.2307/1907353

Coase, R. H. (1960). The problem of social cost. *The Journal of Law & Economics*, *3*, 1–44. doi:10.1086/466560

Davis, J. (2003). *The Theory of the Individual in Economics*. Routledge. doi:10.4324/9780203457689

Dollar, D., & Kraay, A. (2002). Growth is good for the poor. *Journal of Economic Growth*, *7*(3), 195–225. doi:10.1023/A:1020139631000

Faccarello, G., & Kurz, H. D. (2016). Handbook on the History of Economic Analysis. Vol. I: Great Economists since Petty and Boisguilbert; Vol. II: Schools of Thought in Economics. Edward Elgar.

Feldman, A. M., & Serrano, R. (2005). *Welfare Economics and Social Choice Theory* (2nd ed.). Springer Science & Business Media, Inc.

Fleming, J. M. (1962). Domestic monetary policies under fixed and floating exchange rates. IMF Staff Papers, 9, 369–379.

Floyd, J. E. (2010). *Interest Rates, Exchange Rates and World Monetary Policy*. Springer. doi:10.1007/978-3-642-10280-6

Forni, M., & Lippi, M. (1997). *Aggregation and the Microfoundations of Dynamic Macroecomics*. Oxford University Press.

Friedman, B. M., & Hahn, F. H. (Eds.). (2000). *Handbook of Monetary Economics* (Vol. 1-2). Elsevier.

Friedman, M. (1948). A monetary and fiscal framework for economic stability. *The American Economic Review*, *38*(3), 245–264.

Friedman, M. (1956). *Studies in the Quantity Theory of Money*. University of Chicago Press.

Friedman, M. (1957). *A Theory of the Consumption Function*. Princeton University Press. doi:10.1515/9780691188485

Friedman, M. (1966). The Methodology of Positive Economics. In *Essays in Positive Economics*. University of Chicago Press.

Friedman, M. (1970). A theoretical framework for monetary analysis. *Journal of Political Economy*, *78*(2), 193–238. doi:10.1086/259623

Gilder, G. (2012). *Wealth and Poverty: A new edition for the twenty-first century*. Regnery Pub. Inc.

Gilder, G. (2013). *Knowledge and Power: The information theory of capitalism and how it is revolutionizing our world*. Regnery Pub. Inc.

Goodfriend, M., & King, R. G. (1997). The new neoclassical synthesis and the role of monetary policy. *NBER Macroeconomics Annual*, *12*, 231–283. doi:10.1086/654336

Hahn, F. H. (1960). The stability of growth equilibrium. *The Quarterly Journal of Economics*, *74*(2), 206–226. doi:10.2307/1884251

Heyne, P., Boettke, P., & Prychitko, D. (2013). *The Economic Way of Thinking* (13th ed.). Pearson Education.

Hicks, J. R. (1946). *Value and Capital: An inquiry into some fundamental principles of economic theory* (2nd ed.). Oxford University Press.

Jones, R. W., & Kenen, P. B. (Eds.). (1985). *Handbook of International Economics*. Elsevier.

Keynes, J. M. (2012). The General Theory of Employment, Interest and Money (The Collected Writings of John Maynard Keynes Vol. 7). Cambridge University Press.

King, R. G. (2000). The new IS-LM model: Language, logic, and limits. *Federal Reserve Bank of Richmond Economic Quarterly*, *86*, 45–103.

Kuhn, T. S. (1996). *The Structure of Scientific Revolutions* (rev. ed.). The University of Chicago Press. doi:10.7208/chicago/9780226458106.001.0001

Lamb, M., Lymer, A., & Freedman, J. (2005). *Taxation: An Interdisciplinary Approach to Research*. Oxford University Press.

Lengwiler, Y. (2004). *Microfoundations of Financial Economics: An Introduction to General Equilibrium Asset Pricing*. Princeton University Press.

Lucas, R., & Rapping, L. (1970). Real Wages, Employment and Inflation. In E. Phelps (Ed.), *Microeconomic Foundations of Employment and Inflation Theory* (pp. 253–305). Norton.

Lucas, R. E. Jr. (1972). Expectations and the neutrality of money. *Journal of Economic Theory*, *4*(2), 103–124. doi:10.1016/0022-0531(72)90142-1

Lucas, R. E. (1973). Some international evidence on output-inflation tradeoffs. *The American Economic Review*, *63*, 526–534.

Lucas, R. E. Jr. (1975). An equilibrium model of the business cycle. *Journal of Political Economy*, *83*(6), 1113–1144. doi:10.1086/260386

Lucas, R. E. (1988). On the mechanics of development planning. *Journal of Monetary Economics*, *22*, 3–42. doi:10.1016/0304-3932(88)90168-7

Marshall, A. (2013). *Principles of Economics* (8th ed.). Palgrave Macmillan LLC. doi:10.1057/9781137375261

Mises, L. (2006). *The Ultimate Foundation of Economic Science: An Essay on Method*. Liberty Fund, Inc.

Mishkin, F. S. (2004). *The Economics of Money, Banking, and Financial Markets* (7th ed.). Addison-Wesley.

Modigliani, F. (1963). The monetary mechanism and its interaction with real phenomena. *The Review of Economics and Statistics*, *45*(1), 76–103. doi:10.2307/1927150

Mundell, R. A. (1962). The appropriate use of monetary and fiscal policy for internal and external balance. *International Monetary Fund Staff Papers*, *9*(1), 70–79. doi:10.2307/3866082

Mundell, R. A. (1963). *Capital mobility and stabilization policy under fixed and flexible exchange rates. Canadian Journal of Economic and Political Science, 29(4), 475–485.*

Nicola, P. C. (2013). *Efficiency and Equity in Welfare Economics*. Springer. doi:10.1007/978-3-642-30071-4

Piketty, Th. (2014). *Capital in the twenty-first century (A. Goldhammer, Trans.)*. Harvard University Press. doi:10.4159/9780674369542

Popper, K. R. (1972). *Objective Knowledge: an evolutionary approach.* Oxford University Press.

Samuelson, P. A. (1983). Foundations of Economic Analysis (Enlarged ed.). Harvard University Press.

Samuelson, P. A., & Nordhaus, W. D. (2010). *Economics* (19th ed.). McGraw-Hill Co.

Scarth, W. (2014). *Macroeconomics: The development of modern methods for policy analysis*. Edward Elgar.

Sen, A. (1997). *Poverty and Famines*. International Labour Organization.

Sen, A. (2002). *Rationality and Freedom*. Belknap Press.

Smith, A. (1977). An Inquiry into the Nature and Causes of the Wealth of Nations (UK ed.). Chicago: University of Chicago Press.

Solow, R. M. (1956). A contribution to the theory of economic growth. *The Quarterly Journal of Economics*, *70*(1), 65–94. doi:10.2307/1884513

Stigler, G. J. (1961). The economics of information. *Journal of Political Economy*, *69*(3), 213–225. doi:10.1086/258464

Walras, L. (1954). Elements of Pure Economics, or the theory of social wealth (4th ed., W. Jaffé, Trans.). London: George Allen & Unwin Ltd.

Woodford, M. (2003). *Interest and Prices: Foundations of a Theory of Monetary Policy*. Princeton University Press.

World Bank. (2013). *The World Bank Goals: End Extreme Poverty and Promote Shared Prosperity*. Author.

Chapter 15
Economic Philosophical Thinking

ABSTRACT

Economic philosophy is a way of thinking, and economics has its own laws and principles around markets. Economic philosophical thinking maintains dynamic equilibrium (ideal state), where verifiability and falsifiability, qualitative ideas and quantitative methods, ideal and reality, theoretical principles, and empirical facts are combined together. Economics resembles a field that combines science and art. Economic philosophy is a way of thinking that combines verifiability with falsifiability and qualitative ideas with quantitative methods.

As we mentioned in chapter 10, we will consider further economic philosophical thinking based on scientific philosophy from Popper (Popper, 1972) and Kuhn (Kuhn, 1996), leading to the following ways of economic thinking.

COMBINING VERIFIABILITY WITH FALSIFIABILITY

Since Popper introduced his idea of falsifiability, scientists paid more attention to the standard of falsificationism. Actually, both verificationism and falsificationism co-exist in science. The proof methods in mathematics include the verifiability system, while the double-blind experimental methods in biomedical sciences belong to the falsifiability system. In general, we may

DOI: 10.4018/978-1-6684-4935-6.ch015

conclude that verifiability comes from deduction tradition and falsifiability is induction tradition (except complete induction).

The difference between verifiability and falsifiability in science deserves a bit of elaboration. It is not always obvious what principles are used to evaluate scientific theories, and we can discuss the difference by thinking about Popper's asymmetry. Consider a scientific theory (T) that predicts an observation (O). We could attempt to verify or falsify the observation. There are two ways we could add the weight of experiment to a particular theory to approach whether or not it is deductively valid, as shown in Table 1.

Table 1. Verifiability or falsifiability

T or O	Verification	Falsification
Condition	If T, then O	If T, then O
O	O	Not-O
T	T	Not-T
Conclusion	Deductively invalid	Deductively valid

Science could only tell us that the theory was false (or the theory had yet to be refuted). Popper concluded that it is impossible to know whether a theory is true based on observations (O). He concluded that meaningful scientific statements are falsifiable.

However, scientific theories might not be so simple. Scientists could base the theories on a set of auxiliary assumptions (AA). When we take into account the role of the auxiliary assumptions (AA) of a theory (T), the symmetry between verification and falsification are recovered by the Quine-Duhem thesis (Gillies, 1998). These auxiliary assumptions can help show that science is often not a deductively valid exercise. If the predicted observation (O) turns out to be false, we can deduce only that something is wrong with the conjunction, (T and AA), we cannot determine from the premises that it is T rather than AA that is false. In order to recover the asymmetry, we would need the assumptions (AA) to be independently verifiable, as shown in Table 2.

Thus, falsifying a theory requires that auxiliary assumption (AA) be demonstrably true. Auxiliary assumptions are often highly theoretical statements. It is important to note, that if we cannot verify AA, we will not be able to falsify T by using the valid argument above. Contrary to Popper, there really is no asymmetry between verification and falsification. If we cannot verify theoretical statements, then we cannot falsify them either. Therefore,

Table 2. Verifiability or falsifiability with AA

T or O	Verification	Falsification
Condition	If (T and AA), then O	If (T and AA), then O
O	AA and O	AA and Not-O
T	T	Not-T
Conclusion	Deductively invalid	Deductively valid

both verifiability and falsifiability are necessary elements in economics.

COMBINING QUALITATIVE WITH QUANTITATIVE THINKING

Qualitative thinking is often expressed in words, which enables one to gather in-depth insights on topics for understanding concepts, thoughts or experiences. Quantitative thinking is mostly expressed in numbers and graphs, which is used to establish generalizable facts on a topic for testing or confirming theories and assumptions. Qualitative and quantitative thinking are supplementary methodology that one can combine to get results that are meaningful in economics (Heyne et al., 2013).

For example, economists may think the following key issues in economic society: scarcity forces tradeoffs; trade makes people better off; markets coordinate trade; costs vs. benefits; future consequences count; behavior at the margin; and so on. After qualitative thinking, they may obtain the following principles: (1) Scarcity really forces tradeoff; (2) Trade indeed makes people better off; (3) Markets may coordinate trade; (4) Cost does not determine benefits; (5) Future consequences presently count; (6) Behavior at the margin is the most important economic behavior. In these qualitative principles, we can further interpret the first one and the last one: As economics focuses on satisfying unlimited consumer wants with limited resources, the scarcity resources will affect all consumers' behaviors and their market choices. As the behavior at the margin leads to decisions being made based on small changes in resources, marginal thinking will lead to optimal decisions being made, subject to preferences, resources and informational constraints.

Since most qualitative ideas are expressed by words, economic concepts and ideas could be interpreted by different economists with different meanings. A series of foundational economic concepts such as cost, profit, demand, supply, GDP, CPI etc. have to retain unified meanings in economics, so that we could understand different economic thoughts. However, the economic relations need quantitative linkages. To set up the linkages among economic concepts, quantitative methods become necessary ways to reach exact results. This is a scientific feature known as quantification.

Although economics need many concepts, it is better to use fewer concepts as variables to find more linkages among the variables. Thus, it is necessary and important to combine qualitative with quantitative thinking.

COMBINING SCIENCE WITH ART

Economics is generally regarded as a social science. Among all social sciences, economics is noteworthy for its early and widespread adoption of formal mathematics in its theoretical development and its statistical methods as well as quantitative computer applications in its empirical approach to applied research. Thus, economics is thought of as a science, although critics argue that it is not a science for following key reasons:

1. **Lacks universal validity for applications:** The statement says that economics may not be a science because it lacks universal validity and applicability. Economic 'laws' cannot be put into practice as their hypotheses and assumptions are not applicable to all places, at all times and in all conditions alike.
2. **Lacks controlled experiments for verifications:** Science makes it possible for the adoption of controlled experiments, but economics does not provide scope for controlled experiments, so that economic laws cannot be verified through experimentation. This is one of the primary arguments against classifying economics as a science because it lacks testable hypotheses by controlled experiments performed in laboratories. Differentiating from natural sciences, where scientists can measure and check variables, test a hypothesis and evaluate its results in

a laboratory, economists most often analyze historical data and measure social variables, where its measurements are seldom exact and never final.

3. **Lacks feasible predictions:** Complete prediction is not possible in economics as it studies matters relating to the individuals. As individuals act and react in different ways at different times on different ideas, economic phenomena become complex and variable, so it is not feasible to draw exact predictions.

Thus, several economists disliked and disagreed to call economics a science, however, it is still considered a science for the following reasons:

1. **Economics has its own laws and principles:** Economic phenomena are analyzed carefully, and the various experience laws of economics have been set up, including the law of demand, the law of supply, the law of equi-marginal utility, the law of diminishing marginal utility, the law of consumer's surplus, etc. The principles influencing these phenomena, including demand-supply principle, marginal principle, etc., have been widely discussed in a clear-cut manner.
2. **Economics has completed systematic body of knowledge:** Economics like other physical sciences, is considered to be a systematic body of knowledge. The various facts relating to the economic phenomena are studied carefully. Generalizations are made with the help of observation, experiments and verification. Mathematical and statistical methods are applied whenever and wherever needed.
3. **Economics has adopted scientific methods:** Economics adopts deductive and inductive methods for establishing the relationship between cause and effect. Due to this, definite and specific conclusions are drawn regarding the nature of economic phenomena, and its discoveries with regard to the study of economic phenomena are reliable. For example, economists are undertaking research into the problem of inflation, inequalities and backwardness, and continuous research and discoveries are carried out in economics.
4. **Money is measurable and becomes a standard of economic measurement:** Every science has its own standard of measurement. Similarly, economics utilized money as its standard for measuring the changes in several economic variables. For example, the demand for a commodity depends upon the purchasing power of money. Purchasing

power of money is influenced by two factors, the demand for and supply of money. The value of every commodity is also measured by money.

5. **Economics also provides definite universal validity:** Like other sciences, the statements and principles of economics have universal validity. They become real only under certain assumptions and conditions. But economic laws are applicable subject to certain assumptions or conditions.

Therefore, economics is considered to be a true science.

Then, according to Pigou, Marshall, etc., economics is also considered an art. In a way, art is the practical application of knowledge to achieve particular goals. While science gives us principles of any discipline, art turns all these principles into reality.

Art also means the practical application of scientific principles, where art puts these principles into practical use. While some economists expressed the view that economics is a science, some economists are of the view that it is an art. Those who argued that economics is an advanced art and faced the following issues:

- Economics itself cannot the solve day-to-day problems of the individuals, and solving the problems needs art.
- Economics should not declare value judgements, however, if it deals with practical problems, it has to say what is good or what is bad, so that sometimes economists had to claim value judgment, as if a few thoughts from Austrian school.

Modern economists are of the view that economics has practical utility and conclusions can be reached at important economic problems. Therefore, economics should be not considered a despotic authority whose word is final. Since economics has both theoretical and applied aspects, it will help us to solve several complex social problems which paralyze the development of the economic society. Thus, economics, if viewed properly, has both the characteristics of science and art. This is also matching classical economic thoughts (Arrow, 1963; Arrow & Debreu, 1954; Fleming, 1962; Friedman, 1948, 1956, 1957, 1966, 1970; Hicks, 1946; Lucas, 1972, 1973, 1975, 1988; Lucas & Rapping, 1970; Keynes, 2012; Marshall, 2013; Mundell, 1962, 1963; Samuelson, 1983; Samuelson & Nordhaus, 2010; Smith, 1977; Solow, 1956; Taylor, 1979; Tobin, 1969, 1975; Walras, 1954) and contemporary economic knowledge (Faccarello & Kurz, 2016; Feldman & Serrano, 2005;

Forni & Lippi, 1997; Floyd, 2010; Friedman & Hahn, 2000; Gilder, 2013; Heyne, Boettke & Prychitko, 2013; Horwitz, 2000; Jones & Kenen, 1985; King, 2000; Scarth, 2014).

In general conclusion, economic philosophical thinking maintains dynamic equilibrium (though equilibrium is only an ideal state), where verifiability and falsifiability, qualitative ideas and quantitative methods, ideal and reality, theoretical principles and empirical facts, even science and art, remain clever equilibrium. Therefore, we always discuss economic issues under the principle of equilibrium.

REFERENCES

Arrow, K. (1963). *Social Choice and Individual Values* (2nd ed.). Yale University Press.

Arrow, K., & Debreu, G. (1954). Existence of an equilibrium for a competitive economy. *Econometrica*, *22*(3), 265–290. doi:10.2307/1907353

Dollar, D., & Kraay, A. (2002). Growth is good for the poor. *Journal of Economic Growth*, *7*(3), 195–225. doi:10.1023/A:1020139631000

Faccarello, G., & Kurz, H. D. (2016). Handbook on the History of Economic Analysis. Vol. I: Great Economists since Petty and Boisguilbert; Vol. II: Schools of Thought in Economics. Edward Elgar.

Feldman, A. M., & Serrano, R. (2005). *Welfare Economics and Social Choice Theory* (2nd ed.). Springer Science & Business Media, Inc.

Fleming, J. M. (1962). Domestic monetary policies under fixed and floating exchange rates. IMF Staff Papers, 9, 369–379.

Floyd, J. E. (2010). *Interest Rates, Exchange Rates and World Monetary Policy*. Springer. doi:10.1007/978-3-642-10280-6

Forni, M., & Lippi, M. (1997). *Aggregation and the Microfoundations of Dynamic Macroecomics*. Oxford University Press.

Friedman, B. M., & Hahn, F. H. (Eds.). (2000). *Handbook of Monetary Economics* (Vol. 1-2). Elsevier.

Friedman, M. (1948). A monetary and fiscal framework for economic stability. *The American Economic Review*, *38*(3), 245–264.

Friedman, M. (1956). *Studies in the Quantity Theory of Money*. University of Chicago Press.

Friedman, M. (1957). *A Theory of the Consumption Function*. Princeton University Press. doi:10.1515/9780691188485

Friedman, M. (1966). The Methodology of Positive Economics. In *Essays in Positive Economics*. University of Chicago Press.

Friedman, M. (1970). A theoretical framework for monetary analysis. *Journal of Political Economy*, *78*(2), 193–238. doi:10.1086/259623

Gilder, G. (2012). *Wealth and Poverty: A new edition for the twenty-first century*. Regnery Pub. Inc.

Gilder, G. (2013). *Knowledge and Power: The information theory of capitalism and how it is revolutionizing our world*. Regnery Pub. Inc.

Gillies, D. (1998). The Duhem thesis and the Quine thesis. In *Philosophy of Science: The Central Issues*. New York: Norton.

Goodfriend, M., & King, R. G. (1997). The new neoclassical synthesis and the role of monetary policy. *NBER Macroeconomics Annual*, *12*, 231–283. doi:10.1086/654336

Hahn, F. H. (1960). The stability of growth equilibrium. *The Quarterly Journal of Economics*, *74*(2), 206–226. doi:10.2307/1884251

Heyne, P., Boettke, P., & Prychitko, D. (2013). *The Economic Way of Thinking* (13th ed.). Pearson Education.

Hicks, J. R. (1946). *Value and Capital: An inquiry into some fundamental principles of economic theory* (2nd ed.). Oxford University Press.

Keynes, J. M. (2012). The General Theory of Employment, Interest and Money (The Collected Writings of John Maynard Keynes Vol. 7). Cambridge University Press.

King, R. G. (2000). The new IS-LM model: Language, logic, and limits. *Federal Reserve Bank of Richmond Economic Quarterly*, *86*, 45–103.

Kuhn, T. S. (1996). *The Structure of Scientific Revolutions* (rev. ed.). The University of Chicago Press. doi:10.7208/chicago/9780226458106.001.0001

Lamb, M., Lymer, A., & Freedman, J. (2005). *Taxation: An Interdisciplinary Approach to Research*. Oxford University Press.

Lengwiler, Y. (2004). *Microfoundations of Financial Economics: An Introduction to General Equilibrium Asset Pricing*. Princeton University Press.

Lucas, R., & Rapping, L. (1970). Real Wages, Employment and Inflation. In E. Phelps (Ed.), *Microeconomic Foundations of Employment and Inflation Theory* (pp. 253–305). Norton.

Lucas, R. E. Jr. (1972). Expectations and the neutrality of money. *Journal of Economic Theory*, *4*(2), 103–124. doi:10.1016/0022-0531(72)90142-1

Lucas, R. E. (1973). Some international evidence on output-inflation tradeoffs. *The American Economic Review*, *63*, 526–534.

Lucas, R. E. Jr. (1975). An equilibrium model of the business cycle. *Journal of Political Economy*, *83*(6), 1113–1144. doi:10.1086/260386

Lucas, R. E. (1988). On the mechanics of development planning. *Journal of Monetary Economics*, *22*, 3–42. doi:10.1016/0304-3932(88)90168-7

Marshall, A. (2013). *Principles of Economics* (8th ed.). Palgrave Macmillan LLC. doi:10.1057/9781137375261

Mises, L. (2006). *The Ultimate Foundation of Economic Science: An Essay on Method*. Liberty Fund, Inc.

Mishkin, F. S. (2004). *The Economics of Money, Banking, and Financial Markets* (7th ed.). Addison-Wesley.

Modigliani, F. (1963). The monetary mechanism and its interaction with real phenomena. *The Review of Economics and Statistics*, *45*(1), 76–103. doi:10.2307/1927150

Mundell, R. A. (1962). The appropriate use of monetary and fiscal policy for internal and external balance. *International Monetary Fund Staff Papers*, *9*(1), 70–79. doi:10.2307/3866082

Mundell, R. A. (1963). *Capital mobility and stabilization policy under fixed and flexible exchange rates. Canadian Journal of Economic and Political Science, 29(4), 475–485.*

Nicola, P. C. (2013). *Efficiency and Equity in Welfare Economics*. Springer. doi:10.1007/978-3-642-30071-4

North, D. C. (1990). *Institutions, Institutional Change and Economic Performance*. Cambridge University Press. doi:10.1017/CBO9780511808678

Piketty, Th. (2014). *Capital in the twenty-first century (A. Goldhammer, Trans.)*. Harvard University Press. doi:10.4159/9780674369542

Popper, K. R. (1972). *Objective Knowledge: an evolutionary approach.* Oxford University Press.

Samuelson, P. A. (1983). Foundations of Economic Analysis (Enlarged ed.). Harvard University Press.

Samuelson, P. A., & Nordhaus, W. D. (2010). *Economics* (19th ed.). McGraw-Hill Co.

Scarth, W. (2014). *Macroeconomics: the development of modern methods for policy analysis*. Edward Elgar.

Sen, A. (1997). *Poverty and Famines*. International Labour Organization.

Sen, A. (2002). *Rationality and Freedom*. Belknap Press.

Sen, A. (2005). Why exactly is commitment important for rationality? *Economics and Philosophy*, *21*(1), 5–14. doi:10.1017/S0266267104000355

Smith, A. (1977). An Inquiry into the Nature and Causes of the Wealth of Nations (UK ed.). Chicago: University of Chicago Press.

Solow, R. M. (1956). A contribution to the theory of economic growth. *The Quarterly Journal of Economics*, *70*(1), 65–94. doi:10.2307/1884513

Stigler, G. J. (1961). The economics of information. *Journal of Political Economy*, *69*(3), 213–225. doi:10.1086/258464

Taylor, J. B. (1979). Staggered wage setting in a macro model. *The American Economic Review*, *69*, 108–113.

Tobin, J. (1969). A general equilibrium approach to monetary theory. *Journal of Money, Credit and Banking*, *1*(1), 15–26. doi:10.2307/1991374

Tobin, J. (1975). Keynesian models of recession and depression. *American Economic Review Proceedings*, *65*, 195–202.

Ueda, K. (2013). Banks as coordinators of economic growth and stability: Microfoundation for macroeconomy with externality. *Journal of Economic Theory*, *148*(1), 322–352. doi:10.1016/j.jet.2012.09.003

Walras, L. (1954). Elements of Pure Economics, or the theory of social wealth (4th ed., W. Jaffé, Trans.). London: George Allen & Unwin Ltd.

Weintraub, E. R. (1977). The microfoundations of macroeconomics: A critical survey. *Journal of Economic Literature*, *15*(1), 1–23.

Woodford, M. (2003). *Interest and Prices: Foundations of a Theory of Monetary Policy*. Princeton University Press.

Ye, F. Y. (2017). A synthetic macro-economic model integrating interest, exchange and tax rates. In *Scientific Metrics: toward analytical and quantitative sciences* (pp. 127–140). Springer. doi:10.1007/978-981-10-5936-0_11

Ye, F. Y. (2020). An economic analysis of efficiency and equity combining epistemological true with axiological good through microeconomics to macroeconomics. *International Journal of Economics and Financial Research*, *6*(7), 159–169. doi:10.32861/ijefr.67.159.169

Chapter 16
Philosophical Conclusion

ABSTRACT

With synthetic considerations of both economic efficiency and social equity, economic analytics guide us to reach efficiency-equity equilibrium, where philosophical 3E principles and 3S rules are emphasized like EME economic principles. Economic philosophy contributes a principled consideration on economics for balancing social equity and economic efficiency, the good and the true, as well as the economic growth and economic optimality. Both pure economics and economic philosophy are important knowledge for human happiness.

INTRODUCTION

Economics can be a science toward the true for wealth expansion, while it is also an art toward the good of human mind. As economics process the issues concerning man, it is a human ontology. The scientific epistemology can guide pure economics, and the action axiology may merge into economic philosophy. While pure economics provides a science toward the true, economic philosophy contributes a branch of humanities toward the good.

DOI: 10.4018/978-1-6684-4935-6.ch016

POSSIBLE ROADS TO APPROACH THE ECONOMIC GOOD

Synthetic considerations of both economic efficiency and social equity, with synthetic applications of both expansionary and contractionary fiscal or monetary policies, lead to complicated economics. We provide the grand synthetic model as the ideal multi-equilibria for economic analysis, and we hope to approach the economic good via the true of economics. For reaching the object, along historical development, we had lots of economic knowledge (Alchian, 1950; Arrow, 1963; Atkinson, Piketty & Saez, 2011; Blanchard & Gali, 2010; Davis, 2003; Dollar & Kraay, 2002; Dollar, Kleineberg & Kraay, 2014; Faccarello & Kurz, 2016; Feldman & Serrano, 2005; Feldstein, 1976; Fischer, 1983; Floyd, 2010; Forni & Lippi, 1997; Friedman & Hahn, 2000; Gilder, 2012, 2013; Hahn, 1960; Heyne, Boettke & Prychitko, 2013; Horwitz, 2000; Jones & Kenen, 1985; King, 2000; Lamb et al., 2005; Lucas, 1973, 1975; Mäki, 2012; Mishkin, 2004; Modigliani, 1963; Nicola, 2013; North, 1990; Okun, 1975; Piketty, 2014; Reiss, 2013; Robinson, 1962; Ross, 2014; Schumpeter, 2003; Scarth, 2014; Sen, 1997, 2002; Sidrauski, 1967; Solow, 1956; Stigler, 1961; Taylor, 1979; Tobin, 1969, 1975; Weintraub, 1979; Woodford, 2003; Ye, 2015, 2020), as integrated references.

When the IS-LM model constructs the core for economic analytics, wealth expansion can be understood by both real and imaginary economic growth, in which real economic growth also guides us to approach the good and the true.

Meanwhile, reducing poverty also guides us to approach the economic good. By balancing the rich and the poor, social equity and economic efficiency could be realized. Differentiating from physics, where ontology belongs to nature or objective matter ontology, economic ontology is human or subjective man ontology, where man is also active. Both economics and physics keep similar scientific epistemology, but economics might adopt action axiology toward the good while physics could combine the beautiful toward the true. Therefore, economic philosophy constructs an independent or unique system. This is also an ideal economic philosophy as well as an ideal of economics.

ESSENTIAL PHILOSOPHICAL PRINCIPLES IN ECONOMICS

Besides three economic principles (EME) to approach the true in Chapter 2, we also need three philosophical principles to approach the good as follows:

1. **The equilibrium principle:** economic equilibrium is relative, but it is necessary for ideal states and analytical reference.
2. **The efficiency principle:** economic dynamics needs efficiency, for realizing economic growth. After we get economic growth, we could maintain sustainable dynamic development.
3. **The equity principle:** economic optimization faces the reduction of poverty to reach equity. After we eliminate poverty, we could realize sustainable peace in the world.

The 3E principles are essential toward economic efficiency, in which equilibrium principle is an ideal connection between pure economics and economic philosophy. To maintain economic health, we also need three rules for keeping necessary balance:

1. **Single levy rule:** Each taxation happens in each economic ring. The government could not tax many kinds and many times in one economic cycle.
2. **Small changing interest rate rule:** The capital is the source of economic instability. Both the government and the central bank need to restrict the capital movement by interest change-limitation, which suggests that the central bank does not change the core interest rate frequently.
3. **Semi-open rule:** To manage exchange rate to support the semi-open economy, with suitable control of exchange rate. The effect will be similar to the modification of interest rate in an open economy.

The 3S rules may become an economic reference for social equity.

ECONOMIC PHILOSOPHY WILL ENLIGHTEN ECONOMICS

Combining three philosophical 3E principles with three economic EME principles, we understand the core principles of economic philosophy, where the first principle is equilibrium principle, so we believe that the equilibrium is an important ideal state in economics, which guides economic analysis and research, yielding synthetic models.

We also emphasize the equity principle and efficiency principle of 3E philosophical principles, as the efficiency-equity equilibrium is our important reference object.

The wealth expansion theory with a grand synthetic model contributes a panoramic framework for understanding social and economic activities: as social wealth expands over time, knowledge and technology drive real wealth growth, while capital and money stimulate imaginary wealth expansion. The market mechanism will adjust the economic equilibria automatically, and policymakers can use fiscal and monetary policy to supplement the economic system. Fiscal policy strives to achieve social equity, mainly through the government system adjusting tax rates and taxation, while monetary policy strives to achieve economic efficiency, mainly through the banking system fine-tuning interest rates and profits. The tax rate should be simple and single, and only one tax should be set up in each economic ring (if there is production tax in the production ring, it is not appropriate to increase the product tax; if there is income tax in the consumption ring, it is not appropriate to increase the consumption tax; if there is poll tax or regulation tax and so on under the preexisting name, these could be the factors introducing social revolution); the adjustment of interest rate should not be drastic, and a negative interest rate should be used with caution (excessive liquidity and capital failure will also damage the real and imaginary equilibrium of the economy). When faced with open or semi-open international economy, the exchange rate as a policy tool is available, and its effectiveness is associated with the interest rate, as well as its interaction links with tariffs and tax, leading to a complex economic system. At this point, the grand synthetic economic model standing in the optimization of the national economy's stable position gives advice to keep the equilibrium of domestic market first, and then international trade balance. When economic policy and economic operation matched a relative equilibrium with social equity and economic efficiency, social economy might reach Pareto optimization.

From pure economics to economic philosophy, we set up new economic analytics via grand synthetic model, on which we interpreted economic phenomena and mechanism. With inheriting representative great economic thoughts from Adam Smith (Smith, 1977), Alfred Marshall (Marshall, 2013), Maynard Keynes (Keynes, 2012), Paul Samuelson (Samuelson, 1983; Samuelson & Nordhaus, 2010) and Milton Friedmann (Friedman, 1956, 1966,

1970), and the methodological models including Arrow-Debreu model (Arrow & Debreu,1954) and Mundell-Fleming model (Fleming, 1962; Mundell, 1962, 1963), as well as Cobb-Douglas model and Solow-Swan model, pure economics focuses on economic efficiency with scientific epistemology toward the true (Friedman, 1956, 1966) and economic philosophy aims at social equity with action axiology toward the good (Mises, 2006). While the economic system seeks efficiency and the social system pursues equity, common interest modifications with elastic exchange and tax rates could be applied for balancing efficiency and equity. Furthermore, future interstellar economics is also discussed as an interesting issue (Krugman, 2010). All studies belong to economic evolution and paradigm change (Popper, 1972; Kuhn, 1996), however, no economic revolution occurs.

Finally, even if economics could come close to the good and the true, it could not fully achieve human happiness. However, we hope that economics can guide us to a happy life. This is another requirement of economics. Everyone can be happy when they open their mind to the beauty of nature. It is a philosophical choice. Perhaps when we feel the beauty of the economic society, we can reach our happy life through pure economics and economic philosophy.

REFERENCES

Alchian, A. A. (1950). Uncertainty, evolution, and economic theory. *Journal of Political Economy*, *58*(3), 211–221. doi:10.1086/256940

Arrow, K. (1963). *Social Choice and Individual Values* (2nd ed.). Yale University Press.

Arrow, K., & Debreu, G. (1954). Existence of an equilibrium for a competitive economy. *Econometrica*, *22*(3), 265–290. doi:10.2307/1907353

Atkinson, A., Piketty, T., & Saez, E. (2011). Top incomes in the long run of history. *Journal of Economic Literature*, *49*(1), 3–71. doi:10.1257/jel.49.1.3

Blanchard, O. J., & Gali, J. (2010). Labor markets and monetary policy: A new Keynesian model with unemployment. *American Economic Journal. Macroeconomics*, *2*(2), 1–30. doi:10.1257/mac.2.2.1

Davis, J. (2003). *The Theory of the Individual in Economics*. Routledge. doi:10.4324/9780203457689

Dollar, D., Kleineberg, T., & Kraay, A. (2014). *Growth, inequity and social welfare: cross country evidence.* World Bank Policy Research Department Working Paper No. 6842.

Dollar, D., & Kraay, A. (2002). Growth is good for the poor. *Journal of Economic Growth*, *7*(3), 195–225. doi:10.1023/A:1020139631000

Faccarello, G., & Kurz, H. D. (2016). Handbook on the History of Economic Analysis. Vol. I: Great Economists since Petty and Boisguilbert; Vol. II: Schools of Thought in Economics. Edward Elgar.

Feldman, A. M., & Serrano, R. (2005). *Welfare Economics and Social Choice Theory* (2nd ed.). Springer Science & Business Media, Inc.

Feldstein, M. S. (1976). Inflation, income taxes, and the rate of interest – a theoretical analysis. *The American Economic Review*, *66*, 806–820.

Fischer, S. (1983). A framework for monetary and banking analysis. *Economic Journal*, *93*, 1-16.

Fleming, J. M. (1962). Domestic monetary policies under fixed and floating exchange rates. IMF Staff Papers, 9, 369–379.

Floyd, J. E. (2010). *Interest Rates, Exchange Rates and World Monetary Policy*. Springer. doi:10.1007/978-3-642-10280-6

Forni, M., & Lippi, M. (1997). *Aggregation and the Microfoundations of Dynamic Macroecomics*. Oxford University Press.

Friedman, B. M., & Hahn, F. H. (Eds.). (2000). *Handbook of Monetary Economics* (Vol. 1-2). Elsevier.

Friedman, M. (1956). *Studies in the Quantity Theory of Money*. University of Chicago Press.

Friedman, M. (1966). The Methodology of Positive Economics. In *Essays in Positive Economics*. University of Chicago Press.

Friedman, M. (1970). A theoretical framework for monetary analysis. *Journal of Political Economy*, *78*(2), 193–238. doi:10.1086/259623

Gilder, G. (2012). *Wealth and Poverty: A new edition for the twenty-first century*. Regnery Pub. Inc.

Gilder, G. (2013). *Knowledge and Power: The information theory of capitalism and how it is revolutionizing our world.* Regnery Pub. Inc.

Hahn, F. H. (1960). The stability of growth equilibrium. *The Quarterly Journal of Economics*, *74*(2), 206–226. doi:10.2307/1884251

Heyne, P., Boettke, P., & Prychitko, D. (2013). *The Economic Way of Thinking* (13th ed.). Pearson Education.

Horwitz, S. (2000). *Microfoundations and Macroeconomics: An Austrian Perspective*. Routledge. doi:10.4324/9780203456309

Jones, R. W., & Kenen, P. B. (Eds.). (1985). *Handbook of International Economics*. Elsevier.

Keynes, J. M. (2012). The General Theory of Employment, Interest and Money (The Collected Writings of John Maynard Keynes Vol. 7). Cambridge University Press.

King, R. G. (2000). The new IS-LM model: Language, logic, and limits. *Federal Reserve Bank of Richmond Economic Quarterly*, *86*, 45–103.

Krugman, P. (2010). The theory of interstellar trade. *Economic Inquiry*, *48*(4), 1119–1123. doi:10.1111/j.1465-7295.2009.00225.x

Kuhn, T. S. (1996). *The Structure of Scientific Revolutions* (rev. ed.). The University of Chicago Press. doi:10.7208/chicago/9780226458106.001.0001

Lamb, M., Lymer, A., & Freedman, J. (2005). *Taxation: An Interdisciplinary Approach to Research*. Oxford University Press.

Lengwiler, Y. (2004). *Microfoundations of Financial Economics: An Introduction to General Equilibrium Asset Pricing*. Princeton University Press.

Lucas, R. E. (1973). Some international evidence on output-inflation tradeoffs. *The American Economic Review*, *63*, 526–534.

Lucas, R. E. Jr. (1975). An equilibrium model of the business cycle. *Journal of Political Economy*, *83*(6), 1113–1144. doi:10.1086/260386

Mäki, U. (2012). Handbook of the Philosophy of Science: Vol. 13. *Philosophy of Economics*. Elsevier.

Marshall, A. (2013). *Principles of Economics* (8th ed.). Palgrave Macmillan LLC. doi:10.1057/9781137375261

Mises, L. (2006). *The Ultimate Foundation of Economic Science: An Essay on Method*. Liberty Fund, Inc.

Mishkin, F. S. (2004). *The Economics of Money, Banking, and Financial Markets* (7th ed.). Addison-Wesley.

Modigliani, F. (1963). The monetary mechanism and its interaction with real phenomena. *The Review of Economics and Statistics*, *45*(1), 76–103. doi:10.2307/1927150

Mundell, R. A. (1962). The appropriate use of monetary and fiscal policy for internal and external balance. *International Monetary Fund Staff Papers*, *9*(1), 70–79. doi:10.2307/3866082

Mundell, R. A. (1963). *Capital mobility and stabilization policy under fixed and flexible exchange rates. Canadian Journal of Economic and Political Science, 29(4), 475–485.*

Nicola, P. C. (2013). *Efficiency and Equity in Welfare Economics*. Springer. doi:10.1007/978-3-642-30071-4

North, D. C. (1990). *Institutions, Institutional Change and Economic Performance*. Cambridge University Press. doi:10.1017/CBO9780511808678

Okun, A. M. (1975). *Equity and Efficiency: the big trade-off*. Brookings Institution.

Piketty, Th. (2014). *Capital in the twenty-first century (A. Goldhammer, Trans.)*. Harvard University Press. doi:10.4159/9780674369542

Popper, K. R. (1972). *Objective Knowledge: an evolutionary approach*. Oxford University Press.

Reiss, J. (2013). Philosophy of Economics: A contemporary introduction. Routledge (Taylor & Francis Group). doi:10.4324/9780203559062

Robinson, J. (1962). *Economic Philosophy*. Transaction Publishers.

Ross, D. (2014). *Philosophy of Economics*. Palgrave Macmillan. doi:10.1057/9781137318756

Samuelson, P. A. (1983). Foundations of Economic Analysis (Enlarged ed.). Harvard University Press.

Samuelson, P. A., & Nordhaus, W. D. (2010). *Economics* (19th ed.). McGraw-Hill Co.

Scarth, W. (2014). *Macroeconomics: the development of modern methods for policy analysis*. Edward Elgar.

Schumpeter, J. A. (2003). Capitalism, Socialism, and Demacracy (e-Library ed.). London: Routledge (Taylor & Francis Group).

Sen, A. (1997). *Poverty and Famines*. International Labour Organization.

Sen, A. (2002). *Rationality and Freedom*. Belknap Press.

Sidrauski, M. (1967). Inflation and economic growth. *Journal of Political Economy*, *75*(6), 796–810. doi:10.1086/259360

Smith, A. (1977). An Inquiry into the Nature and Causes of the Wealth of Nations (UK ed.). Chicago: University of Chicago Press.

Solow, R. M. (1956). A contribution to the theory of economic growth. *The Quarterly Journal of Economics*, *70*(1), 65–94. doi:10.2307/1884513

Stigler, G. J. (1961). The economics of information. *Journal of Political Economy*, *69*(3), 213–225. doi:10.1086/258464

Taylor, J. B. (1979). Staggered wage setting in a macro model. *The American Economic Review*, *69*, 108–113.

Tobin, J. (1969). A general equilibrium approach to monetary theory. *Journal of Money, Credit and Banking*, *1*(1), 15–26. doi:10.2307/1991374

Tobin, J. (1975). Keynesian models of recession and depression. *American Economic Review Proceedings*, *65*, 195–202.

Weintraub, E. R. (1979). *Microfoundations: the compatibility of microeconomics and macroeconomics*. Cambridge University Press. doi:10.1017/CBO9780511559570

Woodford, M. (2003). *Interest and Prices: Foundations of a Theory of Monetary Policy*. Princeton University Press.

Ye, F. Y. (2015). A probe into the unification of micro-macro-economics: Arrow-Debreu-Mundell-Fleming model as a standard model. *Euro-Asian Journal of Economics and Finance*, *3*, 1–8.

Ye, F. Y. (2020). An economic analysis of efficiency and equity combining epistemological true with axiological good through microeconomics to macroeconomics. *International Journal of Economics and Financial Research*, *6*(7), 159–169. doi:10.32861/ijefr.67.159.169

APPENDIX

Appendix A: Selected Famous Economists with Their Contributions

Different economists contribute different thoughts in economics. Here, we select some famous ones, listed chronologically.

Adam Smith (1723 – 1790): Adam Smith was a Scottish philosopher and political economist who is widely considered the father of modern economics and the world's first free-market capitalist, for he explained how——in a free-market economy——rational self-interest led to economic well-being. Undoubtedly one of the biggest names in this field, he influenced the likes of Karl Marx, John M. Keynes, and Thomas Malthus. Smith's contribution to economics came in the form of his famous works: *The Theory of Moral Sentiments* (1759) and *The Wealth of Nations* (1776); the latter was published as a five-book series.

Thomas Robert Malthus (1766 – 1834): Not many people would need an introduction to the English demographer and political economist, Thomas Robert Malthus; best known for his popularization of the economic theory of rent. He was one of those economists who played a crucial role in the development of classical economics as the first modern school of economic thought. Malthus was one of the most influential and controversial figures in the field of economics and politics. His major contribution to this field came in the form of the Malthusian growth model.

Jean-Baptiste Say (1767 – 1832): Jean-Baptiste Say was a French economist, who is best known for Say's law, which suggests that supply creates its own demand. Despite its name, Say's law was not a product of his invention. He only popularized it in his work, *A Treatise on Political Economy*. Say was in favor of competition, free trade, and lifting restraints on business. Though he was responsible for introducing much of Adam Smith's work to continental Europe, he was also an ardent critic of some of Smith's noted work, such as the labor theory of value.

David Ricardo (1772 – 1823): David Ricardo was a British political economist, who, together with James Mill, founded classical economics. It was Adam Smith's *The Wealth of Nations* that inspired Ricardo to take an interest in this subject. He was a believer of monetarism, which was evident from his argument that the propensity of the Bank of England to issue excess banknotes was responsible for the prevailing inflation in the country. His biggest contribution to the field of economics was his theory of comparative advantage.

Karl Marx (1818 – 1883): Though he is more often remembered as a German philosopher and revolutionary sociologist, Karl Marx did a lot for economics as well. He was of the belief that humans were not motivated by grand ideas, but by material concerns related to survival. Marx looked at capitalism negatively, and in his book *Das Kapital* argued that the capitalist's profits come from exploiting labor. He predicted the end of capitalism and emergence of communism, where people would own the means of production, and thus, there would be no need to exploit labor for profit.

Leon Walras (1834 – 1910): Leon Walras' biggest contribution in economics is the general equilibrium theory and he is also one of the founders of the marginal revolution by postulating the idea of marginal utility. The general equilibrium theory studies the fundamentals of supply and demand in an economy with multiple markets, with the objective of proving that all prices are at equilibrium. This theory analyzes the mechanism by which the choices of economic agents are coordinated across markets. It attempts to look at several markets simultaneously rather than a single market in isolation. On the other hand, marginal utility is defined as the additional satisfaction or benefit that a consumer derives from buying an additional unit of a commodity or service. The concept implies that the utility or benefit to a consumer of an additional; unit of a product is inversely related to the number of units of that product he already owns.

Vilfredo Pareto (1848 – 1923): Vilfredo Pareto developed the 80/20 rule, which, broadly speaking, states that 80 percent of the effect comes from 20 percent of the causes after he noticed that 80 percent of Italian land was owned by 20 percent of the population. This pattern is common in nature but Pareto found it prevalent in various forms of wealth distribution. He believed that every major civilization's wealth distribution looked more like an arrow head than a pyramid. There was no gradual distribution of wealth, but a natural division along the 80/20 distinction between the wealthy and the masses. This was true of all people across all of history. He was also the first person to popularize the term, 'elite,' when referring to a class of people. Pareto was instrumental in transforming economics from a subcategory of moral philosophy as it was practiced during the enlightenment into a mathematically-driven social science.

Irving Fisher (1867 – 1947): One of the most famous American economists, Irving Fisher is best known for economic concepts such as the Fisher equation and Fisher separation theorem. It was his work on quantity theory of money that became the basis for the development of Milton Friedman's concept of 'monetarism'. Besides the Fisher equation and Fisher separation theorem, he is also known for contributions such as the equation of exchange, price index, Philips curve, and monetary illusion.

Arthur Pigou (1877 – 1959): Arthur Pigou was one of the finest examples of a British gentleman scholar. His most important work is his 1920 book, *The Economics of Welfare*. This text proposes externality. Under this view, one can correct a social problem by introducing a tax (now called a Pigovian tax). This view has been utilized numerous times to correct excess and social ills. Right now its biggest application is connected to environmentalism, since many would like to implement taxes on behaviors and products that damage the environment, such as the carbon tax. Pigou spent most of his career at Cambridge University when Cambridge was highly regarded as the leading economics institution in the world.

Ludwig von Mises (1881 – 1973): Ludwig von Mises was an Austrian School economist, who wrote and lectured extensively on the societal contributions of classical liberalism. He was known for his consistent adherence to the principles of laissez-faire and strong resistance to government intervention in economic matters. Ludwig von Mises is also best known for his most renowned work, *Human Action*. He is considered one of the most influential economic and political thinkers of the 20th century.

John Maynard Keynes (1883 – 1946): John Maynard Keynes was a British economist, best known for spearheading the revolution in economic thinking, which overturned the then existent ideas of neoclassical economics. Keynes is also regarded by many as the founder of modern theoretical macroeconomics. His ideas formed the basis of an independent school of thought, Keynesian economics. His contributions include some of the most useful economic concepts, including liquidity preference, fiscal multiplier, deficit spending, and aggregate demand-aggregate supply model.

Joseph Schumpeter (1883 – 1950): Schumpeter began his career in Austria but later came to America and finished his career teaching at Harvard. He saw an unfortunate pattern unfolding before him. For Schumpeter, capitalism was a powerful force for good that inevitably had the seeds of its own destruction embedded within itself. In his 1942 book, *Capitalism, Socialism, and Democracy*, he saw capitalism as leading to increases in wealth, which would then expand the intellectual class and attack the very foundations for the wealth that made their academic positions possible in the first place. Schumpeter popularized phrases in economics, such as 'creative destruction,' and further developed the models of entrepreneurship.

Joan Robinson (1903 – 1983): British economist, Joan Robinson was one of the most famous women economists that the world has ever seen. She started off as a supporter of neoclassical economics, but eventually shifted to post-Keynesian economics. Robinson was best known for her knowledge about monetary economics and contributions to economic theory. Her major contributions to post-Keynesian economics came in the form of the Cambridge growth theory and Amoroso-Robinson relation.

John Richards Hicks (1904 – 1989): John Richards Hicks was a British economist. He is considered one of the most important and influential economists of the twentieth century. The most familiar of his many contributions in the field of economics were his statement of consumer demand theory in microeconomics, and the IS–LM model (Hicks-Hansen model). His book *Value and Capital* significantly extended general-equilibrium and value theory.

Wassily Leontief (1906 – 1999): Wassily Leontief was an American economist known for demonstrating the interconnected nature of the economy. He described how changes in one branch of the economy can have both unforeseen and unintended consequences in another area. He also strongly advocated for increasing the use of data intensive mathematical analysis in order to make economics more empirical and less theoretical. He won the Nobel Prize for showing how inputs for one industry create outputs for another. Leontief educated some of recent history's most prominent economists. He personally advised four doctoral students who, themselves, won the Nobel Prize, including Paul Samuelson, Robert Solow, Vernon L. Smith, and Thomas Schelling.

Ronald Coase (1910 – 2013): Ronald Coase spent much of his extensive life teaching at the University of Chicago Law School. He is particularly well known for two influential essays: the 1937 article titled, *The Nature of the Firm*, and the 1960 article titled, *The Problem of Social Cost. In The Nature of the Firm*, Coase asked why the economy organizes into firms. In The *Problem of Social Cost*, Coase argued that property rights should be distributed in such a way as to encourage the owner of the property to take economically efficient actions. Coase was trained as an economist, but spent most of his career working in a law school. He was a pioneering figure in the field of law and economics. He won the Nobel Prize in 1991.

Milton Friedman (1912 – 2006): Milton Friedman was an American economist and statistician. An ardent advocate of laissez-faire capitalism, Friedman was awarded the Nobel Memorial Prize in Economics in 1976. He was best known for his demonstration of the complexity of stabilization policy, which was introduced to stabilize the economy. Some of his prominent contributions to this field include the concept of monetarism, price theory, permanent income hypothesis, floating exchange rates, applied macroeconomics, and the Friedman test.

Paul Samuelson (1915 – 2009): The New York Times considered Paul Samuelson to be the foremost academic economist of the 20th century. In 1970, he was the first American to win the Nobel Prize in economics. He was awarded the National Medal of Science, America's top science award, by Bill Clinton in 1996. Samuelson achieved these numerous accolades by developing the mathematical methodology now considered foundational to all economics. But perhaps his greatest impact came by writing *Economics: An Introductory Analysis*. This textbook has sold over 4 million copies and become the all-time best selling economics textbook.

James Tobin (1918 – 2002): James Tobin was an American economist, who was one of the prominent figures involved in the development of Keynesian economics. He is best known for the Tobit model, which describes the relationship between a non-negative dependent variable and an independent variable. He was awarded the Nobel Memorial Prize in Economic Sciences in 1981. Tobin's noteworthy contributions to the field of macroeconomics include the modern portfolio theory, Tobin's q, Tobit model, Tobin tax, and the Mundell-Tobin effect.

Lawrence Robert Klein (1920 – 2013): Lawrence Robert Klein is one of the best examples of a mathematical approach to the field having developed new macroeconometric computer models. These models embody Keynesianism, and are still in use by the Federal Reserve, other major central banks around the world, and the International Monetary Fund. He created the metric for economies of all macroeconomic sizes, ranging from the national, to the regional, to the world. Klein made multiple successful predictions concerning the economic context of the world immediately following World War II, and his successes contributed to him winning the John Bates Clark Medal in 1959 and the Nobel Prize in 1980.

Gerard Debreu (1921 – 2004): Gerard Debreu was a French-born American economist, well-known for bringing a mathematical precision to economics in theories like that of supply and demand. Gerard Debreu's contributions are in general equilibrium theory in a famous paper coauthored with Kenneth Arrow and published in 1954. Debreu proved that under fairly unrestrictive assumptions, prices exist that bring markets into equilibrium. Debreu was awarded the Nobel Prize in Economics for having incorporated new analytical methods into economic theory and for his rigorous reformulation of the theory of general equilibrium in 1983.

Kenneth Arrow (1921 – 2017): Kenneth Arrow was the first economist to map how learning curves affect entrepreneurial efficiency. It seems intuitive to say that producers will learn more about how to produce their product as they do so, and will, with the passing of time, do so with ever greater efficiency. Nevertheless, Arrow was the first to prove this phenomenon. His successes have made him a leading figure in post-World War II neo-classical economics. His groundbreaking work in these fields as well as broader topics in general equilibrium theory and welfare theory led to him acquiring the Nobel Prize in 1972. In addition to his contributions to more typical areas of economic study, he also studied developing areas of the field such as endogenous growth theory and the economics of information.

Robert Solow (1924 – Present): Robert Solow is an American economist whose work on the theory of economic growth culminated in the exogenous growth model named after him. He presented a mathematical model of growth that was a new version of the Harrod-Domar growth model. Robert Solow was awarded the Nobel Prize in 1987 for his contributions to the theory of economic growth.

Robert Mundell (1932 – 2021): Robert Mundell was a Canadian economist. He is well known as the 'father' of the Euro and supply-side economics. He received the Nobel Memorial Prize in Economic Sciences in 1999 for his pioneering work in monetary dynamics and optimum currency areas. His contributions to economics are concluded as five highlights: (1) theory of international trade; (2) the Mundell-Fleming model for open macroeconomics; (3) the optimum currency area argument; (4) the monetary approach to the balance of payments; and (5) fiscal-monetary mixtures and the assignment rule.

Amartya Sen (1933 – Present): Amartya Sen, hailing from India, is best known for his human development theory, which is a combination of ecological economics, sustainable development, welfare economics, and feminist economics. Dr. Sen's contributions to welfare economics earned him the Nobel Prize in Economic Sciences in 1998. He was listed as one of the 100 most influential people in the world by Time Magazine in 2010.

Arthur Laffer (1940 – Present): Arthur Laffer developed the famous 'Laffer Curve,' which showed that although raising taxes will initially raise government revenue, doing so beyond a certain point stymies the economy so that it actually does more harm. In other words, if a government raises taxes too much, it will slow economic activity and, in the process, decrease tax revenue. If one follows this argument to its logical conclusion, then one should be able to lower taxes in such a way as to increase economic activity and consequently offset the loss in revenue.

Joseph Stiglitz (1943 – Present): Stiglitz contributed his major work on development for a new branch of economics called 'the economics of information.' This field studies information asymmetries and develops novel ideas like adverse selection and moral hazard. Much of this work led to him receiving the Nobel Prize in economics in 2001. He now serves on various prestigious boards such as the Acumen Fund and Resources for the Future.

Paul Robin Krugman (1953 – Present): Paul Krugman is an American economist best known for his work on international economics. It is not at all surprising that he features in this list; after all, his noteworthy contributions include the international trade theory, new trade theory, new economic geography, etc. His work on the new trade theory and new economic geography earned him a Nobel Prize in Economics in 2008. Krugman's views represent one of the most articulate defenses of contemporary Keynesianism.

Appendix B: Selected Main Economic Schools with Their Views

Different economic schools possess different economic views. Here, we select the main ones.

Classical economics (classical school): Classical economics is widely regarded as the first modern school of economic thoughts. It generally regarded market as the principle institution in distributing resources equitably in society, associated with the 18th century Scottish economist Adam Smith, and British economists David Ricardo and Robert Malthus. The publication of Adam Smith's *The Wealth of Nations* in 1776 is considered to be the birth of the classical economics school of thought. The major economists include Adam Smith, Jean-Baptiste Say, David Ricardo, Thomas Malthus and John Stuart Mill.

The main idea of the Classical school was that markets work best when they are left alone, and that there is nothing but the smallest role for government. The approach is firmly one of laissez-faire and a strong belief in the efficiency of free markets to generate economic development. Markets should be left to work because the price mechanism acts as a powerful 'invisible hand' to allocate resources to where they are best employed. It is widely recognized that the Classical period lasted until 1870.

Marxian economics: Marxian economics refers to the branch of economics that is based on the theories created and advocated by Karl Marx. Marx propounded a very critical theory known as the labor theory of value. This theory assumes that the value of any item can be known by determining the amount of time it takes to make it. He believed that the commodity being sold was the labor of the employee for the price of a wage. Capitalists never pay workers the full value of the commodities they produce, but pay them only the necessary labor, i.e. the worker's wage, which suffices only for the basic necessities to live. Marx advocated that this necessary labor is, in fact, only a fraction of a full working day, and the rest, the surplus-labor, is captured by the capitalist. The gap between the value of a commodity produced by a worker and his wage is a form of unpaid labor, which is known as surplus value.

Neoclassical economics (neoclassical school): Neoclassical economics begins with the premise that resources are scarce and that it is necessary to choose between competing alternatives. That is, economics deals with tradeoffs. With scarcity, choosing one alternative implies forgoing another, i.e. the opportunity cost. Understanding choices by individuals and groups is central. Economists believe that incentives and desires play an important role in shaping decision making. Neoclassical economics also increased the use of mathematical equations in the study of various aspects of the economy. The neoclassical school of economic thought is a wide ranging school of ideas from which modern economic theory evolved. The method is clearly scientific, with assumptions, and hypotheses and attempts to derive general rules or principles about the behavior of firms and consumers. Neoclassical economics was developed mainly by William Stanley Jevons, Carl Menger and Leon Walras in the latter half of the 19th century. It dominates microeconomics, and, together with Keynesian economics, forms the neoclassical synthesis around which the mainstream economics of today revolve.

Keynesian economics: Keynesian economics is a modern macroeconomic theory based on the ideas of 20th century British economist John Maynard Keynes. Keynesian economics advocated a mixed economy which is predominantly private sector, but with the government and public sector playing a large role, and served as the economic model during the latter part of the Great Depression and up to as late as the 1970s. In Keynes' theory, one person's spending goes toward another's earning, and the circle goes on, thus supporting a normal functioning of the economy. When the Great Depression hit, people's natural reaction was to hoard their money. This stopped the circular flow of money, keeping the economy at a standstill. In this situation, Keynes argued that the government should step in to increase spending, either by increasing the money supply or by actually buying things on the market itself. The Keynesian approach is interventionist, coming from a belief that the self-interest which governs micro-economic behavior does not always lead to long-run macro-economic development or short-run macro-economic stability. Keynesian economics is essentially a theory of aggregate demand, and how best to manipulate it through macro-economic policy.

Keynesian economics supports redistribution of wealth, when needed. Keynesian economics holds a realistic and sensible reason for the massive redistribution of wealth: if the poorer segments of society are given money, it is very likely that they will spend it, rather than save it, thus promoting economic growth. Keynesian economics, also called macroeconomics for its broad view of the economy as a whole, still remains one of the most important schools in economic thought in today's times as reflected lately in the US and the UK. Keynes is widely regarded as the most important economist of the 20th century, despite falling out of favor during the 1970s and 1980s following the rise of new classical economics. Keynesian economics is the foundation of modern mainstream economics, where free markets will inevitably move toward a full employment equilibrium.

New classical economics (new classical school): New classical economics is also known as new classical macroeconomics, and is an attempt to explain macro-economic problems and issues using micro-economic concepts like rational behavior, and rational expectations. New classical macroeconomics strives to provide neoclassical microeconomic foundations for macroeconomic analysis. The new classical school emerged in the 1970s in response to the failure of Keynesian economics to explain the stagflation because of rising oil prices and high inflation leading to sudden economic downturn. The new concepts and ideas which emerged from new classical economics such as rational expectations were accepted by the opposing new Keynesian school. New classical economics is based on Walrasian assumptions, and it is associated with the work of economist Robert Lucas. All agents are assumed to maximize utility on the basis of rational expectations. Lucas and Rapping applied the rule that equilibrium in a market occurs when quantity supplied equals quantity demanded. Later, Edward C. Prescott and Finn E. Kydland developed some famous new classical models known as the real business cycle model.

Neoclassical synthesis: The neoclassical synthesis (NCS), also known as neoclassical–Keynesian synthesis, or just neo-Keynesianism, was a post-World War II academic movement and paradigm in economics that worked toward reconciling the macroeconomic thoughts of John Maynard Keynes with neoclassical economics. Being Keynesian in the short-run and neoclassical in the long-run, neoclassical synthesis allowed the economy to adjust via fiscal and monetary policies in the short-run, especially focusing on fiscal policies that were considered to be more effective than monetary ones, whilst predicting that equilibrium in the long-run will be reached without state intervention. The neoclassical synthesis, formulated by a group of economists, including John Hicks, Franco Modigliani and Paul Samuelson, dominated economics in the post-war period and formed the mainstream of macroeconomic thought in the 1950s, 1960s and 1970s.

Austrian school of economics: Austrian economics gets its name from its founders and early supporters, who were citizens of the old Austrian Habsburg Empire. The best known Austrians are the 1974 Nobel Laureate Friedrich von Hayek and his mentor Ludwig von Mises. In economics, the Austrian paradigm is the philosophical descendant of Adam Smith and the other so-called classical liberals, today referred to as libertarians. In politics, Austrianism is often considered the descendant of Patrick Henry, James Madison, Thomas Jefferson and the other American founders. The Austrian school has received greater attention in recent years as many proponents of this school predicted the financial crisis years in advance.

Chicago school of economics (monetarism): Chicago school of economics is sometimes also referred to as monetarism. Monetarism is most widely associated with Milton Freidman and supports, primarily, a free market economy with little government intervention save for, as the name would imply, monetary policy. The concern of the monetarists is that, as productivity increases, without an increase in the money supply, prices will fall. The goal of a monetarist is to keep the money supply growing at roughly the same pace or slightly faster than the economy so that, in general, prices remain relatively stable or increase just a little bit year after year. Implicit in this theory is the assumption that individuals can predict with reasonable accuracy the growth in productivity over time and can also accurately expand the money supply to match increases in productivity. It also assumes that individuals in this position of considerable power will be able to resist pressures to waver from this goal.

Supply-side economics: Supply-side economics, or supplism, was developed during the 1970s in a period of inflation and stagnant economic growth (stagflation) and as a response to the perceived failure of Keynesian economic policy. It is a mixture of Austrian and neoclassical economics and proposes that production or supply is the key to economic prosperity and that consumption or demand is only secondary. This idea is summarized by Say's law of economics which states: 'A product is no sooner created, than it, from that instant, affords a market for other products to the full extent of its own value.' The supply-side economics focuses on low taxes and less regulation in order to stimulate the supply side of the economy. It also strongly supports the theories of Arthur Laffer, who is given credit for the Laffer curve, which states that tax rates and tax revenues are separate and that increasing tax rates above a certain level lead to decreasing tax receipts. This theory was supported by the dropping capital gains tax rates from the late 1970s and into the 1980s during which time each drop was met by an increase in tax receipts. This theory gained notoriety under President Ronald Reagan, who lowered income tax rates with the theory that a drop in tax rates would result in increased economic growth, which would then lead to increased tax receipts. The major supply-side economists include Robert A. Mundell, Arthur B. Laffer, Martin S. Feldstein, etc.

New institutional economics: New institutional economics (NIE) originates from institutional economics, known by some as institutionalist political economy, and focuses on understanding the role of human-made institutions in shaping economic behavior. In the early twentieth century, it was the main school of economics in the United States, including such famous but diverse economists as Thorstein Veblen, Wesley Mitchell, and John R. Commons. Institutional economics is concerned with the social systems, or 'institutions,' that constrain the use and exchange of resources (goods and services) and their consequences for economic performance. Unlike neoclassical economics, it also considers the role of culture and classical political economy in economic development. New institutional economics incorporates a theory of institutions, such as laws, rules, customs, and norms, into economics. It builds on, modifies, and extends neoclassical theory. Integrating institutionalism into mainstream neoclassical economics, new institutional economics can be thought of as being the outcome of the Chicago School's 'economic imperialism,' namely using neoclassical economics to explain areas of human society normally considered outside the purview of economic theory. NIE attempted to extend economics by focusing on the social and legal norms and rules that underlie economic activity. However, using Neoclassical economics to explain areas of human society normally considered outside them, NIE eventually failed to avoid criticisms of reductionism and lack of realism: the same criticism that was leveled at neoclassical economics for effectively ignoring institutions. NIE has its roots in Ronald Coase's fundamental insights about the critical role of institutional frameworks and transaction costs for economic performance. Thus, initially, NIE analyses took into account: organizational arrangements, transaction costs, credible commitments, modes of governance, persuasive abilities, social norms, ideological values, decisive perceptions, gained control, enforcement mechanism, asset specificity, human assets, social capital, asymmetric information, strategic behavior, bounded rationality, opportunism, adverse selection, moral hazard, contractual safeguards, surrounding uncertainty, monitoring costs, incentives to collude, hierarchical structures, bargaining strength, and such. The major NIE economists include Armen A. Alchian, Ronald H. Coase, Douglas C. North, George J. Stigler, Steven N.S. Cheung, etc.

Mainstream economics: Finally, we mention the term mainstream economics, used to describe schools of economic thought considered to be orthodox. Many of the underpinning models and beliefs of mainstream economics are based on concepts that involve economic scarcity, the role of governmental regulation or other action that affects an actor's decision, the concept of utility, and the idea that people are rational actors who will make decisions that are based purely on available information and not emotion. Mainstream economics refers to the orthodox or neoclassical tradition of economics, in which markets are moved by an invisible hand and all actors are rational. It is not a branch of economics itself, but is used to describe theories often considered part of the neoclassical economics tradition. The origins of mainstream economics lie in the thinking of Adam Smith. Mainstream economics follows rational choice theory, which assumes that individuals make decisions that will maximize their own utility, and uses statistics and mathematical models to demonstrate theories and evaluate various economic developments. Many of the underlying categories and concepts central to mainstream economics are readily taught at universities.

About the Author

Fred Y. Ye (Ying Ye) is an interdisciplinary scholar. His research interests cover scientific metrics, economics and physics. His publications include more than 100 published articles, 6 monographs and 3 textbooks. His main academic contributions include (1) scientific metrics with interdisciplinary applications and h-type metrics for network analysis; (2) vortex field theory for physics and wealth expansion theory for economics; (3) triad philosophy for merging eastern and western thoughts in contemporary philosophy. His research interest also extends to spirit philosophy. Dr. Ye was a Fulbright research scholar in the USA and a fellow, European Academy of Sciences and Arts. Now he is an emeritus professor in Nanjing University and lives in US.

This monograph represents his reflections on human society.

Index

F

G

H

I

K

L

M

O

P

R

S

T

V

W

www.ingramcontent.com/pod-product-compliance
Lightning Source LLC
LaVergne TN
LVHW080856300926
849162LV00003B/434
* 9 7 8 1 6 6 8 4 4 9 3 5 6 *

Eastern part of Africa, weak institutions and governance bottle necks can lead to influential tax systems, making it essential to examine how institutional dynamics interact with behavioral dynamics to influence tax compliance (Rahman, 2023).

Theory of Planned Behavior: A psychological framework for comprehending how attitudes, subjective standards, and perceived behavioral control influence end users' intentions and behaviors is offered by the Theory of Planned Behavior (TPB). According to this hypothesis, end users are more likely to engage in an action—like filing taxes—if they feel competent of carrying out the behavior, have good attitudes about it, and sense social support for it. In the Eastern part of Africa, where cultural and socio market place matters greatly influence attitudes toward taxes, this approach might be helpful in determining the motivating elements that augment taxpayer compliance (Soares, Lima & Coelho, 2024).

The primary theoretical framework for this investigation is behavioral accounting theory. The necessity to comprehend the behavioral and psychological dynamics that influence taxpayer compliance and the efficiency of taxation procedures in the Eastern part of Africa is what motivated this decision. Employing this approach, the investigation will examine how individual attitudes, drives, and actions influence tax adherence in the context of the region's distinct socio market place situation. This emphasis will enable a more thorough investigation of the elements that support or impede sustainable development through taxes, eventually offering academics and policymakers useful information. In order to solve the unique difficulties encountered in the Eastern part of Africa, the investigation intends to close the gap among theoretical knowledge and real-world application by firmly establishing its investigation on behavioral accounting theory.

DEFINITION AND ORIGIN OF CONCEPTS

Behavioral Accounting: It refers to the investigation of how psychological dynamics influence the behavior of individuals and organizations in the context of accounting and financial decision-making. This field combines insights from psychology and accounting to understand how cognitive biases, emotions, and social dynamics influence the way financial report is perceived and utilized. The origin of behavioral accounting can be traced back to the broader field of behavioral market places, which depicted in the late 20th century. Scholars like Daniel Kahneman and Amos Tversky manifested how human decision-making often deviates from traditional market place models based on rationality. As these insights permeated the accounting discipline, investigations began to explore how behavioral dynamics could explain anomalies in accounting practices, such as tax evasion and compliance matters (Indriastuti & Mutamimah, 2023).

Sustainable Development Goals: SDGs are a set of 17 interconnected global objectives that were created by the UN in 2015 as part of the Agenda for Sustainable Development in 2030. A wide range of social, market place, and revenue collection matters, including poverty, inequality, climate paradigm shift, as well as sustainable market place progression, are intended to be addressed by these objectives. The Millennium Development Goals (MDGs), which were created in 2000 and mainly concentrated on lowering poverty and enhancing health and education, are where the SDGs got their start. The SDGs build on the MDGs by taking a more all-encompassing approach that emphasizes social inclusion and revenue collection sustainability, manifesting the need for development to be sustainable and inclusive for everyone (Daiyabu etal, 2023).

Taxation Practices: refer to the methods and processes by which governments collect taxes from individuals and businesses. This encompasses the legal frameworks, administrative procedures, and compliance mechanisms that govern tax collection. The origins of taxation can be traced back to ancient civilizations, where rulers imposed taxes to fund public goods and services. Over time, taxation systems have evolved into complex frameworks that vary considerably across countries and regions. In many developing countries, including those in the Eastern part of Africa, taxation practices are often manifested by historical, political, and market place contexts, making them a critical area of investigation for considerate reserve mobilization and governance (Rahman, 2023).

Compliance: refers to the extent to which taxpayers follow tax rules and regulations in the context of taxes. This assimilates completing tax returns, paying taxes due, and abiding by all applicable laws. Regulatory theory, which investigations how end users and organizations react to laws and regulations, is where the idea of compliance first depicted. Since non-compliance may outcome in large revenue losses for governments, considerate compliance is crucial for efficient tax management. Behavioral market places has shed light on the constructs influencing compliance, indicating that attitudes, fairness views, and social norms considerably influence taxpayers' desire to comply (Khan, 2023).

Trust in Government: refers to the extent to which end users think their government can fulfill its responsibilities and acts in their best interests (Soares, Lima & Coelho, 2024). This idea is fundamental to sociology and political science and has substantial ramifications for public policy and government. Political philosophy from the early 20th century, which looked at the interaction among citizens and their governing bodies, is where investigation on confidence in government first depicted. Since more end users are inclined to see tax payments as a just contribution to the common good, greater levels of confidence in the government are associated to higher levels of compliance with tax laws. On the other hand, a deficit of trust can outcome in tax evasion and noncompliance, underscoring the consequence of building trust for efficient government (Hikmah et al. 2021).

EMPIRICAL LITERATURE REVIEW

Behavioral accounting and SDGs

By addressing the psychological aspects that influence how end users and organizations make decisions, behavioral accounting is vital to achieving the SDGs (Hamid, 2024). Behavioral accounting assists stakeholders in recognizing the long-term benefits of sustainable practices above immediate financial rewards by drawing attention to cognitive distortions including confirmation bias and overconfidence (Rahman, 2023). A stronger dedication to sustainability projects in line with the SDGs is fostered by this considerate (Ashuro et al., 2025). By encouraging businesses to manifest their social and revenue collection influences, behavioral accounting fosters accountability and openness in reporting (Kant et al., 2025), which increases stakeholder confidence (Khan, 2023). Organizations may encourage end users to adopt more sustainable habits by creating incentives that match company and personal objectives with sustainability initiatives (Othman, 2024). Behavioral insights-based educational initiatives can augment comprehension of sustainability bottle necks and lead to better decision-making (Othman, 2024).

H1: Behavioral Accounting has influence on Sustainable Development

Behavioral accounting and taxation practice

By shedding light on the psychological influences on taxpayer behavior and compliance, behavioral accounting has a substantial influence on taxation methods (Soares, Lima & Coelho, 2024). Considerate cognitive biases, such as optimism bias, are crucial since it might cause taxpayers to underestimate the possibility of audits or fines, which can outcome in noncompliance (Othman, 2024). Framing influences also come into play; the way tax laws are communicated may influence public opinion and tax-paying behavior (Kant et al., 2025). For instance, manifesting the benefits of tax payments to public goods might increase the percentage of compliance (Rahman, 2023). Behavioral accounting emphasizes the consequence of social norms; end users are more inclined to follow suit when they see their peers fulfilling their tax duties (Ashuro et al., 2025). This knowledge can guide the tactics of tax authorities, supporting initiatives that encourage good taxpayer behavior (Othman, 2024). By bringing personal interests and tax duties into alignment, behaviorally informed tax incentives can also encourage compliance (Khan, 2023). Efforts to raise awareness and educate the public about common tax understanding might outcome in a better-informed taxpayer base, which will eventually boost compliance rates and enhance taxation procedures (Hamid, 2024). All things considered, incorporating behavioral accounting into taxation procedures can augment taxpayer experiences, increase compliance, and advance a more equitable tax structure (Asante-Darko, 2024).

H2: Behavioral Accounting has substantial influence on taxation practice

Taxation practice and SDGs

Taxation practices have a profound influence on achieving SDGs by influencing reserve allocation, promoting equity (Othman, 2024) and fostering market place progression. Influential tax policies can generate revenue that governments need to invest in indispensible public services, such as education, healthcare, and infrastructure, which are critical for sustainable development (Rahman, 2023). By implementing progressive tax systems, where higher earners contribute a larger share, governments can address income inequality and ensure that social services are accessible to all, thereby supporting SDG 10 (Reduced Inequalities) (Adula et al., 2025). Taxation can incentivize revenue collection sustainable practices. For instance, implementing taxes on carbon emissions or providing tax breaks for renewable energy investments motivates businesses and individuals to adopt greener technologies, directly contributing to SDG 13 (Khan, 2023). As well as, influential tax administration can enhance transparency and accountability, reducing corruption and ensuring that tax revenues are employed efficiently for public good, aligning with SDG 16 (Peace, Justice, and Strong Institutions) (Ashuro et al., 2025). International taxation practices can help address matters of tax avoidance and evasion, ensuring that multinational corporations contribute their fair share to the economies in which they operate (Hamid, 2024). This is vital for reserve mobilization and achieving the SDGs (Kant et al., 2025). In summary, thoughtful and equitable taxation practices are essential for financing sustainable development initiatives, promoting social equity, and fostering revenue collection sustainability, ultimately advancing the global agenda for a more sustainable future (Nikolova, 2022).

H3: Taxation practice has substantial influence on SDGs.

Taxation practice mediation in behavioral accounting and SDGs

One imperative dynamic that influences how organizations and individuals approach sustainability is the mediation of taxation practices in the association ship among behavioral accounting and the SDGs (Khan, 2023). Behavioral accounting influences how stakeholders perceive tax obligations and compliance, which is frequently manifested by cognitive biases and social norms (Ashuro et al., 2025). For example, if end users and businesses see paying taxes as a civic duty rather than a burden, they are more likely to engage in practices that support sustainable development initiatives (Li, Al-Sulaiti, 2022). By offering the required structure and incentives to encourage sustainable practices, taxation policies can moderate this association (Kant et al., 2025). Tax laws that punish unsustainable habits or reward ecologically beneficial investments, for instance, can augment the efficacy of behavioral accounting insights. Businesses may be more inclined to connect their financial practices with the SDGs if they realize that their tax payments directly support public goods like infrastructure, healthcare, and education (Othman, 2024). As well as, efficient taxation procedures can augment accountability and transparency, strengthening the bond of confidence among taxpayers and governments. By employing behavioral insights to augment responsible decision-making, this trust may outcome in increased compliance and a desire to support sustainable projects (Hamid, 2024). As an outcome, taxes serve as a link among behavioral accounting's psychological insights and concrete measures that augment the SDGs' attainment (Adula et al., 2025). Governments may successfully manage the link among behavioral accounting and the attainment of a more sustainable future by coordinating tax policy with SDGs (Rahman, 2023).

H4: Taxation practice considerably influences the association ship among Behavioral Accounting as well as SDGs.

CONCEPTUAL FRAMEWORK

The association ships among imperative constructs in a investigation are represented in an organized manner by a conceptual framework. The framework for the association among taxation, behavioral accounting, and the SDGs can be summarized as follows:

Figure 1. Conceptual framework

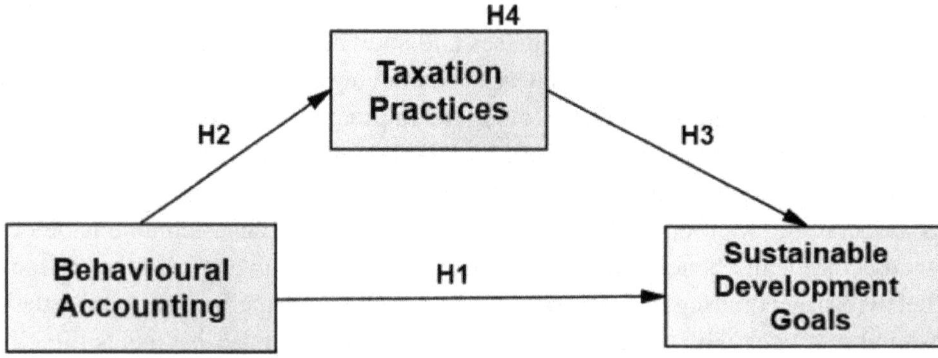

METHODOLOGY

The present investigation utilized a quantitative investigation technique to investigate the associations among taxation practices, behavioral accounting, and the SDGs. In order to guarantee a representative distribution across a number of dynamics, such as age, gender, and professional background, a sample of 393 respondents was gathered employing stratified random sampling. A systematic questionnaire that was painstakingly created based on the body of existing investigation in order to adequately capture the pertinent constructs was administered as part of the data collecting procedure.

Item creation, the first step in the scale building process, involved identifying possible items from prior investigation and theoretical frameworks. After that, these items underwent a pre-testing process that assimilated a pilot investigation to guarantee clarity and augment language. After that, the completed questionnaire was given to the intended audience. Data adequacy was computed to assess the data's appropriateness for dynamic analysis; the Kaiser-Meyer-Olkin (KMO) value manifested the data was suitable for additional analysis. The underlying dynamic structure of the constructs was then investigated employing exploratory dynamic analysis (EFA). The dimensionality of the scales utilized was confirmed by the EFA outcomes, which showed unique dynamics that matched theoretical assumptions. AMOS software was employed to conduct Structural Equation Modeling (SEM), which examined the structural links among the constructs. The evaluation of the direct and indirect associations among behavioral accounting, taxation, and SDGs was made possible by this approach. The outcomes of the SEM depict light on how taxation policies may operate as a mediator in the association among SDGs and behavioral accounting.

RESULTS

The table 1 outcomes offer compelling proof that dynamic analysis of the dataset is adequate. A "meritorious" degree of sampling adequacy is depicted by the sampling adequacy, which is stated to be 0.853. The dataset is appropriate for dynamic analysis because of the high KMO value, which manifests that there is enough association among the constructs. Chi-Square value of 2019.77 with 91 degrees of freedom and a consequence level of 0.000 manifests that there are substantial links among the constructs and that the association matrix differs considerably from an identity matrix. Together, these outcomes manifest that the data is robust enough for dynamic analysis, allowing for the exploration of underlying dynamics that may influence the observed constructs.

Table 1. Appropriateness of data

Sampling Adequacy.		**.849**
Bartlett's Test	Chi square	2019.78
	Degree of freedom	93
	p-value	.000

Source: SPSS output

The outcomes from variance are depicted in Table 2, which accounts for a substantial 32.240% of the overall variance. With an extra 9.783% contribution from the second component, the total variance explained rises to 42.025%. This is further enhanced by the third component, which adds 9.086%, for a cumulative total of 49.115%. The first three components appear to be the most relevant, since the fourth component does not add to the cumulative totals above the third, even though it still explains 6.781% of the variation. With values of 6.225% and 5.497%, respectively, the fifth and sixth components explain even less variation, demonstrating that the benefits of explaining variance decrease with the number of components taken into account. All things considered, the investigation shows that the first three dynamics are essential to comprehending the data since they together explain more than half of the variation, with the other dynamics making up a very small portion. This implies that a model built on the first three elements would be adequate for additional dataset analysis or interpretation.

Table 2. Explained Variance

C	Initial Eigenvalues			Extraction Sums			Rotation Sums		
	Total	% of Variance	Cumulative %	Total	% of Variance	Cumulative %	Total	% of Variance	Cumulative %
1	4.49	32.240	32.238	4.49	32.240	32.238	3.00	21.456	21.456
2	1.37	9.783	42.025	1.37	9.783	42.025	2.16	15.493	40.942
3	1.27	9.086	49.115	1.27	9.086	49.115	1.98	20.168	49.115
4	.946	6.781	57.894						
5	.871	6.225	64.116						
6	.773	5.497	69.637						

Source: SPSS output

As per table 3, somewhat favorable association is depicted by the covariance of 0.247 among Taxation Practice and Behavioral Accounting; as one rises, the other tends to rise as well. A somewhat greater positive association is depicted by the covariance among Taxation Practice as well as SDGs, which is 0.305. This manifests that developments in sustainable development initiatives may be connected to augments or paradigm shifts in taxation policies. Last but not least, there is a somewhat favorable association among behavioral accounting and the SDGs, as depicted by the covariance of 0.249. This implies that the attainment of sustainable development targets may be influenced in proportion to the evolution of behavioral accounting methods.

Table 3. Covariances

Covariance	Approximation	Standard error	Critical ration	P	Hypothesis
Taxation Practice <--> Behavioral Accounting	.247	.023	8.237	***	H2
Taxation Practice <--> Sustainable Development Goals	.305	.040	7.693	***	H3
Behavioral Accounting <--> Sustainable Development Goals	.249	.24	7.838	***	H1

Source: AMOS output

Different validity criteria are depicted in Table 4. Each construct's internal consistency is depicted by its Critical Ration (CRs) scores, all of which are higher than the universally recognized cutoff point of 0.7. With CRs of 0.735, 0.749, and 0.796 for Behavioral Accounting (BA), Taxation Practice (TP), and SDG, respectively, it appears that all constructions have sufficient dependability. Convergent validity is further evaluated employing the Average Variance Explained (AVE), which have SDG at 0.601, TP at 0.65, and BA at 0.643. Since each of these numbers is higher than the manifested threshold of 0.5, it may be concluded that the corresponding structures account for a substantial amount of the variance in the items. Particularly for TP (0.133) and BA (0.215), the Maximum Shared Variance (MSV), which manifest the possibility of discriminant validity—are very low, indicating that these constructs are different from one another. With a greater MSV of 0.271, SDG does, as well as, show some overlap with other constructions. With BA at 0.855, TP at 0.768, and SDG at 0.795, (Max R(H)), which evaluate dependability under various circumstances—are likewise good.

Table 4. Validity

	Critical ration	Average variance explained	Maximum Shared Variance	Maximum dependability	BA	TP	SDG
BA	0.735	0.643	0.215	0.855	0.658		
TP	0.749	0.659	0.133	0.768	0.172	0.668	
SDG	0.796	0.601	0.271	0.795	0.381	0.191	0.683

Note: BA=Behavioral Accounting; TP=Taxation Practice; SDG= Sustainable Development Goals
Source: AMOS output

Figure 2. Structure Equation Model

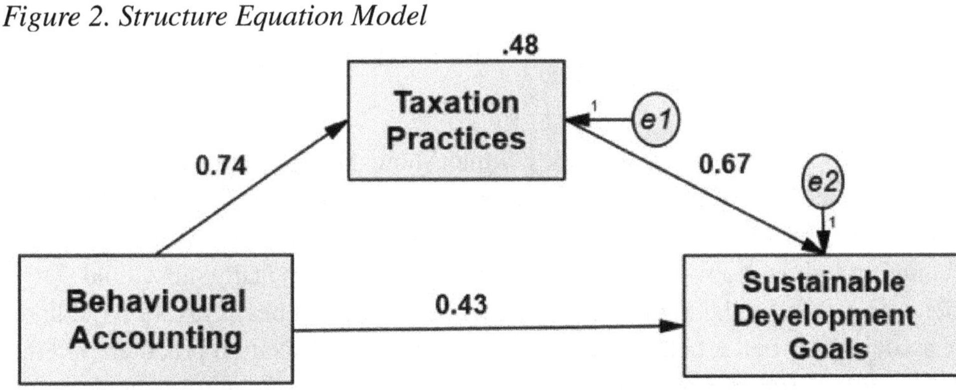

Source: AMOS output

Table 5. Model index

Sig.	Chi Square	Root Mean Residual	Goodness	Confirmatory	Tucker Lewis Index	Root Mean Square Error
0.004	1.949	.040	0.932	0.915	0.911	.024

Source: AMOS output

Table 5 depicts the model fit indices employed to analyze the mediating influence of the components in the investigation. The consequence level (Sig.) is stated at 0.004, manifesting that the model fits the data considerably better than a baseline model. Given that lower values often denote a better model fit, the chi-square value of 1.949 manifests a decent fit. The model's adequacy is further supported by the reported Root Mean Square Residual (RMR) of 0.040, which is below the generally recognized criterion of 0.05. With respective values of 0.932 and 0.915, the Goodness of Fit Index (GFI) and the Comparative Fit Index (CFI) are both dynamics, manifesting that the model accounts for a sizable portion of the data's variance. Tucker-Lewis index (TLI) at 0.911 also manifests a good fit, with values above 0.90 generally considered acceptable. As well as, the Root Mean Square Error of Approximation (RMSEA) is reported at 0.024, which is well below the threshold of 0.05, indicating a close fit among the model and the observed data.

Table 6. Regression

Relative	Approx.	Std. error	Critical ratio	Significance	Assumption
Taxation Practice <--- Behavioral Accounting	.864	.202	7.585	***	H2
Sustainable Development Goals <--- Taxation Practice	.323	.200	2.849	***	H3
Sustainable Development Goals <--- Behavioral Accounting	.955	.198	7.956	***	H1

Source: AMOS output

The regression analysis's outcomes, which show the associations among SDGs, Taxation Practice, and Behavioral Accounting, are depicted in Table 6. With a regression coefficient of 0.864 and a C.R. of 7.585, the association among behavioral accounting and taxation practice is strongly positive and statistically substantial (***). This depicts substantial evidence for H2, which states that better taxation methods are associated to better behavioral accounting practices. Taxation practices and the SDGs are the subject of the second investigation. This association is statistically substantial, with a regression coefficient of 0.323 and a C.R. of 2.849. Despite having a smaller influence size than the first association ship, this outcome supports H3, which states that good taxation practices help achieve SDGs. The regression coefficient of 0.955 and the C.R. of 7.956 demonstrate the direct influence of behavioral accounting on the SDGs, confirming H1. This shows that behavioral accounting methods have a major influence on the achievement of SDGs, emphasizing the interdependence of these dimensions.

Table 7. Mediation

	Standardized coefficient
Behavioral Accounting→ Sustainable Development Goals	.43
Behavioral Accounting→ Taxation Practice→ Sustainable Development Goals	.74*.67=.50
Total Effect	.93

Source: AMOS output

The association ship among Behavioral Accounting as well as SDG is mediated by Taxation Practice, as depicted in Table 7. The direct influence of Behavioral Accounting on SDGs is 0.43, indicating a substantial direct influence; as well as, when the indirect influence is taken into account, the association ship is evaluated through Taxation Practice, with the path influence being calculated as standard coefficient of 0.74 (the influence of Behavioral Accounting on Taxation Practice) multiplied by 0.67 (the influence of Taxation Practice on SDGs), yielding an indirect influence of 0.50. The sum of the direct and indirect influences is 0.93. This cumulative influence manifests that while there is a strong direct association ship, the indirect pathway through Taxation Practice also plays a substantial role. The analysis concludes that there is partial mediation, manifesting that Taxation Practice not only acts as a conduit but also enhances the overall influence of Behavioral Accounting on achieving SDGs. This manifests the interconnectedness of these constructs and the importance of allowing for mediate in their association.

DISCUSSION

The investigation's conclusions manifest the vital associations among the SDGs, taxation practices, and behavioral accounting. Influential accounting procedures may directly support the progress of sustainability initiatives, as depicted by the substantial direct influence of behavioral accounting on the SDGs (0.43). This demonstrates the part behavioral constructs play in encouraging ethical behavior in businesses, which can outcome in a stronger dedication to sustainable progression. As well as, taxation policies moderate this link, as depicted by the indirect influences of behavioral accounting through taxation practices (0.50), manifesting the consequence of efficient taxation systems in supporting sustainable development. Further manifesting how better accounting methods may augment taxing procedures, which in turn can propel progress toward sustainability goals, is the substantial route influence (0.74) from behavioral accounting to taxation practice. Although direct influences are imperative, the mechanisms by which these interactions function are just as crucial, as evidenced by the overall influence of 0.93 and the discovery of partial mediation. This implies that in order to optimize their influence on sustainability, stakeholders should concentrate on both enhancing accounting methods and streamlining taxation procedures.

These outcomes support a comprehensive strategy that incorporates taxes and behavioral accounting as crucial elements in the quest for sustainable development. Organizations and legislators may develop more potent solutions to sustainability matters by recognizing and employing these links, which will eventually advance larger social objectives.

CONCLUSIONS

The chapter concludes by manifesting the imperative linkages among SGSs, Taxation Practice, and Behavioral Accounting, and stressing the consequence of comprehending these associations in regard to organizational practices and sustainability efforts. The outcomes show that successful taxation practices, which help accomplish the SDGs, are greatly manifested by behavioral accounting. The intricacy of these processes is manifested by the evidence of both direct and indirect repercussions, indicating that substantial gains in accounting practices can outcome in long-term positive influences. As well as, the discovery of partial mediation manifests that although direct influences are substantial, the mechanisms behind these associations are just as crucial. This need a thorough strategy that combines taxing tactics and behavioral considerations to strengthen sustainable initiatives. As organizations and policymakers strive to address pressing sustainability bottle necks, the outcomes of this investigation depict valuable insights into the mechanisms that can drive progress. Ultimately, fostering a collaborative environment that prioritizes responsible accounting and influential taxation practices will be essential for advancing sustainable development and achieving long-term societal benefits.

MANAGERIAL IMPLICATIONS

The investigation's conclusions have substantial management ramifications that might help firms augment their sustainability initiatives. First of all, manifesting the value of behavioral accounting inside a company can outcome in better ethical and decision-making procedures. Supervisors ought to fund training and development initiatives that encourage accounting procedures that are in line with sustainable practices, motivating staff members to embrace a mentality that places a high value on social and revenue collection responsibility. As well as, given the imperative mediating role that taxes practices play, businesses should concentrate on improving their taxation plans in order to better meet sustainability objectives? This entails assessing and improving tax laws to encourage eco-friendly activities, such making investments in reserve-efficient technology or renewable energy. Managers may encourage a culture of accountability and long-term thinking among stakeholders by establishing a tax environment that augments sustainability activities. Cooperation among the taxes and accounting divisions is crucial. In order to develop comprehensive plans that address sustainability concerns, managers should encourage open communication and collaborative activities that capitalize on the strengths of both roles. While improving overall organizational performance, this integrated strategy may assist organizations in optimizing their influence on the SDGs. In the end, managers can create proactive strategies that not only augment financial performance and compliance but also advance larger societal objectives by realizing the associations among behavioral accounting, taxation practice, and sustainability. This will establish their companies as leaders in ethical business practices.

PRACTICAL IMPLICATIONS

The investigation's outcomes have practical implications for organizations looking to augment their sustainability practices. First and foremost, incorporating behavioral accounting into daily operations can have a substantial influence on sustainability-related outcomes. To this end, organizations should consider implementing practical measures, such as training sessions and workshops, aimed at fostering a culture of ethical accounting and transparency. By giving employees the knowledge and skills to understand the importance of sustainability in accounting practices, companies can encourage more responsible decision-making that is in line with organizational values. The outcomes emphasize the need to refine taxation practices in order to support sustainable development. This not only motivates compliance with sustainability goals but also enhances the organization's reputation among stakeholders who prioritize corporate social responsibility. It is obligatory to foster cross-departmental collaboration. Organizations may make sure that sustainability dynamics are incorporated into financial decision-making processes by encouraging collaborations among the accounting, finance, and sustainability departments. Innovative ideas that augment financial performance and revenue collection influence can outcome from this cooperative approach. Finally, in order to augment tax measures that augment sustainability, organizations should actively interact with external stakeholders, such as legislators and business associations. Businesses may show their dedication to ethical practices and have an influence on the regulatory environment by taking part in larger conversations about sustainability and taxes. All things considered, these useful ramifications offer a road map for businesses looking to use behavioral accounting and taxation techniques to further sustainable progression.

THEORETICAL IMPLICATIONS

The investigation's conclusions assimilate a number of imperative theoretical ramifications that add to the corpus of report already available on behavioral accounting, taxation, and the SDGs. First of all, the direct and indirect associations among these dimensions that have been depicted augment our comprehension of how behavioral constructs influence sustainability outcomes and financial practices. This supports the idea that behavioral aspects may be added to standard accounting frameworks to create a more comprehensive knowledge of organizational decision-making processes. As well as, the discovery of partial mediation by taxes Practice raises the possibility that current theories of accounting and taxes may need to take sustainability into consideration. By promoting a more integrated viewpoint that acknowledges the influence of behavioral accounting on taxation procedures as a means of accomplishing sustainability goals, this bottle necks traditional models that frequently handle these elements in isolation. As well as, the investigation emphasizes the consequence of behavioral insights in developing successful taxing tactics, manifesting that future investigations should investigate the ways in which social and psychological aspects influence sustainability initiatives and tax compliance. This creates new opportunities for investigation into how employee behavior and corporate culture influence financial practices and sustainability outcomes.

RECOMMENDATIONS

Based on the investigation's outcomes, recommendations can be made for organizations looking to augment their sustainability efforts through better behavioral accounting and taxation practices. First, it is critical that organizations prioritize training and development programs that emphasize sustainability and ethical accounting practices. By creating a culture of awareness and responsibility, employees will be better able to understand how their decisions influence financial and revenue collection outcomes. Secondly, organizations should actively review and augment their taxation practices to assimilate incentives that support sustainable initiatives. This could involve investing in policy programs that augment sustainability within their operational frameworks or advocating for tax laws that reward eco-friendly practices. Engaging with tax professionals to explore innovative tax strategies can further enhance the alignment among financial objectives and sustainability goals. Organizations should also consider establishing interdisciplinary teams that assimilate members from accounting, finance, and sustainability departments. By facilitating the paradigm shift of knowledge and best practices, this partnership can guarantee that sustainability dynamics are assimilated into all financial decision-making procedures. Frequent cross-departmental meetings may augment a cohesive approach to sustainability and help keep everyone employed on shared objectives. Last but not least, influencing more comprehensive tax measures that encourage sustainable behaviors requires active engagement with external stakeholders, including legislators and trade groups. Organizations may help create a more favorable regulatory climate and establish themselves as leaders in ethical business practices by supporting reforms that match taxes with sustainability goals. The goal of these manifestations is to construct a thorough plan that makes use of behavioral accounting and taxation practices in order to considerably advance sustainable development.

FUTURE DIRECTIONS

The investigation's conclusions depict for additional investigation that might examine the associations among behavioral accounting, taxation, and the SDGs. Examining certain behavioral dynamics that influence sustainability-related accounting procedures is exciting avenue. In order to have a better understanding of how to foster more sustainable accounting practices, future investigation might concentrate on determining the psychological and social elements that encourage end users in firms to embrace these practices. An additional worthwhile topic of investigation is the long-term influences of augmented taxation practices on sustainability outcomes. Scholars might examine case investigations of businesses that have influentially adopted sustainable tax practices, evaluating the long-term influences on financial performance and revenue collection responsibility. This could help establish best practices and frameworks that other organizations can adopt. In order to comprehend how contextual constructs, influence the linkages among behavioral accounting, taxation practices, and sustainability, comparative investigations across various sectors and geographical areas are also necessary. Such investigations may manifest policy possibilities and problems unique to a certain industry, enabling more specialized strategies to advance sustainable development. Finally, it is imperative to consider how technology might augment behavioral accounting and taxation practices. Examining the ways in which data analytics and digital technologies may help businesses monitor and enhance their sustainability KPIs may yield useful report for incorporating technology into sustainability plans. Investigations may advance a more thorough knowledge of how behavioral accounting and taxation might successfully support sustainable development initiatives by following these potential approaches.

REFERENCES

Adula, M., Kant, S., Badi, S., & Kumari, M. (2025). Abusive Work Environment Effect on Female Entrepreneurs' Emotional Wellbeing by Mediation of Social and Moral Values in the Horn of Africa. In *Supporting Psychological and Emotional Wellbeing Among Entrepreneurs* (pp. 1-22). IGI Global Scientific Publishing.

Asante-Darko, D., Dadzie, S. A., Kwarteng, A., Agbodjah, S., & Aryee, T. E. (2024). Influences of Circular Economy Practices and Accounting Innovations on Sustainable Development Goals. *Circular Economy and Sustainability*, *4*(4), 1–34.

Ashuro, T., Kant, S., Alemu, Z. K., & Takaro, G. S. (2025). Effect of Tax Solidarity on the Taxpayer's Sense of Civic Duty by Mediation of Tax Morality in the Horn of Africa. In *Modeling and Profiling Taxpayer Behavior and Compliance* (pp. 207–164). IGI Global Scientific Publishing. DOI: 10.4018/979-8-3373-0422-9.ch006

Beerbaum, D., & Puaschunder, J. M. (2019). A behavioral market places approach to sustainability reporting. *Julia M., A Behavioral Market places Approach to Sustainability Reporting (May 2, 2019).*

Chen, X., Weerathunga, P. R., Nurunnabi, M., Kulathunga, K. M. M. C. B., & Samarathunga, W. H. M. S. (2020). Influences of behavioral intention to engage in revenue collection accounting practices for corporate sustainability: Managerial perspectives from a developing country. *Sustainability (Basel)*, *12*(13), 5266. DOI: 10.3390/su12135266

Daiyabu, Y. A., Manaf, N. A. A., & Mohamad Hsbollah, H. (2023). Extending the theory of planned behaviour with application to renewable energy investment: The moderating influence of tax incentives. *International Journal of Energy Sector Management*, *17*(2), 333–349. DOI: 10.1108/IJESM-11-2021-0011

Dayani, N. W. Y. P., & Budiasih, I. (2024). BEHAVIORAL ACCOUNTING AS A CATALYST IN THE ORGANIZATIONAL TRANSFORMATION PROCESS TOWARD SUSTAINABILITY. *Jurnal Akuntansi dan Keuangan Indonesia*, *21*(2), 6.

Dhahri, S., Slimani, S., & Omri, A. (2021). Behavioral entrepreneurship for achieving the sustainable development goals. *Technological Forecasting and Social Paradigm shift*, *165*, 120561.

Hamid, R. S. (2024). Behavioral Accounting: Evaluating Policy and Academic Support Influence on Sustainable Green Mining Practices. *Jurnal Kajian Akuntansi*, *8*(1), 94–120. DOI: 10.33603/jka.v1i1.9554

Hikmah, H., Adi, P. H., Supramono, S., & Damayanti, T. W. (2021). The nexus among attitude, social norms, intention to comply, financial performance, mental accounting and tax compliance behavior. *Asian Market place and Financial Review, 11*(12), 938.

Indriastuti, M., & Mutamimah, M. (2023). Green accounting as well as sustainable performance of micro, small, and medium enterprises: The role of financial performance as mediation. *The Indonesian Journal of Accounting Investigation, 26*(2), 249–272.

Kant, S., Degefa, T. T., Roba, A. T., Alemu, Z. K., & Takaro, G. S. (2025). Corporate Social Responsibility Effect on Tax Compliance by Mediation of Sense of Civic Duty in the Horn of Africa. In *Modeling and Profiling Taxpayer Behavior and Compliance* (pp. 231–250). IGI Global Scientific Publishing. DOI: 10.4018/979-8-3373-0422-9.ch010

Kant, S., Niguse, T., Adula, M., & Terefe, A. (2025). Sustainable Finance's Effect on the Green Economy by the Mediation of Corporate Governance in the Horn of Africa. In *Behavioral Finance and AI Tools for Sustainability* (pp. 301–320). IGI Global Scientific Publishing. DOI: 10.4018/979-8-3693-9684-1.ch012

Khan, S. A. R., Sheikh, A. A., & Ahmad, Z. (2023). Developing the interassociation among green employee behavior, tax avoidance, green capability, as well as sustainable performance of SMEs through corporate social responsibility. *Journal of Cleaner Production, 419*, 138240. DOI: 10.1016/j.jclepro.2023.138236

Li, Y., Al-Sulaiti, K., Dongling, W., Abbas, J., & Al-Sulaiti, I. (2022). Tax avoidance culture and employees' behavior influence sustainable business performance: The moderating role of corporate social responsibility. *Frontiers in Revenue collection. Science, 10*, 964410.

Meshack, A., Orji, M. G., Nworie, G. O., & Aggreh, M. S. (2022). Achieving sustainable development agenda of 2030: The role of accountants. *Britain International of Humanities and Social Sciences (BIoHS). Journal, 4*(3), 493–556.

Othman, R., & Ameer, R. (2024). Rethinking accounting education for a sustainable future: Charting a course for sustainable development goals 2030. *Meditari Accountancy Investigation, 32*(5), 1809–1840. DOI: 10.1108/MEDAR-05-2023-2009

Rahman, M. M. (2023). Influence of taxes on the 2030 agenda for sustainable development: Evidence from organization for market place co-operation and development (OECD) countries. *Regional Sustainability, 4*(3), 235–248. DOI: 10.1016/j.regsus.2023.07.001

Soares, E. C., Lima, N. C., & Coelho, A. F. M. (2024). Towards sustainability engaged accounting: A behavioral approach. *Revista Contabilidade & Finanças*, *35*(95), e2019. DOI: 10.1590/1808-057x20242019.pt

KEY TERMS AND DEFINITIONS

Behavioral Accounting: The investigation of how psychological dynamics and human behavior influence accounting practices and decision-making processes within organizations.

Sustainable Development Goals (SDGs): A set of 17 interconnected global goals established by the United Nations to address pressing social, market place, and revenue collection bottle necks, aiming for a sustainable future by 2030.

Taxation Practices: The methods and strategies employed by organizations to comply with tax laws, optimize their tax obligations, and align their financial practices with regulatory requirements.

Chapter 2
Behavioural Taxation and Law:
Encouraging Sustainable Business Practices

S. Harikrishnan
https://orcid.org/0009-0005-9920-2124
Alliance University, India

Mukul Saxena
Alliance University, India

ABSTRACT

This chapter examines how Behavioural taxation, supported by legal frameworks, promotes sustainable business practices globally. It integrates Behavioural economics, nudge theory, tax law, and sustainability governance to demonstrate how fiscal policies drive corporate actions like low-carbon production and Environmental, Social and Governance (ESG)compliance. A comparative analysis of policies—such as the EU's Carbon Border Adjustment Mechanism, India's Perform, Achieve and Trade (PAT) scheme, and Canada's carbon tax—reveals diverse impacts on firms like ArcelorMittal and UltraTech Cement. Challenges including tax avoidance, enforcement gaps, and political resistance are addressed, with solutions like tiered taxes and technology integration proposed. By offering a unified model, the chapter advances discourse on aligning corporate strategies with sustainability goals.

DOI: 10.4018/979-8-3373-2492-0.ch002

1. INTRODUCTION

"Taxes are powerful tools to steer economies toward sustainability, incentivizing businesses to align profit with purpose."
— Ángel Gurría, OECD Secretary-General, 2019 (OECD, 2019).

Taxation has evolved into a strategic instrument for promoting corporate sustainability, leveraging financial incentives to address global challenges like climate change and resource depletion. Behavioural taxation, rooted in behavioural economics, employs "nudges" to guide firms toward sustainable practices, such as low-carbon production and environmental, social, and governance (ESG) compliance (Thaler & Sunstein, 2008). Unlike traditional environmental taxation, which focuses on penalties or revenue, behavioural taxation targets decision-making biases like short-termism, as modeled by the Theory of Planned Behavior (TPB) (Ajzen, 1991). This chapter explores how behavioural taxation, supported by legal frameworks, drives sustainable business practices globally, addressing critical research questions: (1) How do behavioural taxation policies influence corporate sustainability? (2) What challenges—such as tax avoidance and enforcement gaps—limit their effectiveness? (3) How can innovative policy designs enhance their impact?

The urgency of sustainability, driven by the United Nations' Sustainable Development Goals (SDGs), notably SDG 12 (Responsible Consumption and Production) and SDG 13 (Climate Action), underscores the need for corporate action (United Nations, 2015). While prior studies have examined carbon pricing (Böhringer et al., 2022), few integrate behavioural theories like TPB or nudge theory to explain firm-level adoption of sustainable practices (Weber et al., 2022). For instance, the European Union's Carbon Border Adjustment Mechanism (CBAM) taxes carbon-intensive imports, nudging firms like ArcelorMittal toward hydrogen-based steel production, reducing emissions by 20% in pilot projects (European Commission, 2023). India's Perform, Achieve, and Trade (PAT) scheme incentivizes energy efficiency, leading UltraTech Cement to adopt waste heat recovery systems, saving 200 crore annually (Kumar & Sharma, 2021). In Canada, the carbon tax prompted Magna International to invest in energy-efficient machinery, cutting emissions by 15% (Government of Canada, 2023). These examples illustrate taxation's growing role, with over 40 countries adopting carbon pricing to fund green initiatives (OECD, 2023).

Figure 1. Growth of Carbon Pricing Adoption (2010-2023). Data source: OECD, 2023.

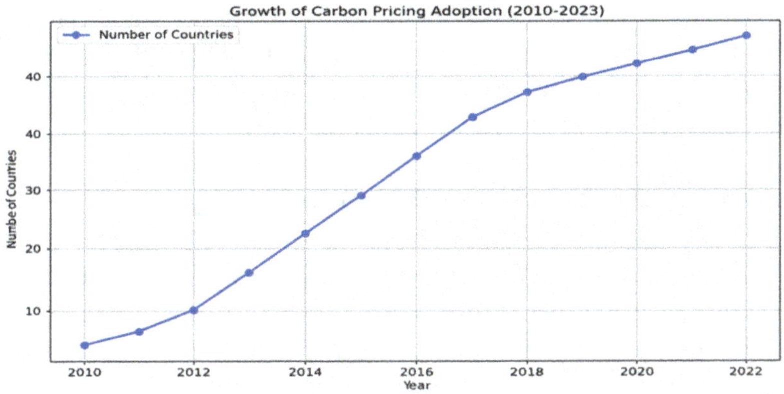

This chapter's contribution lies in its unified model, which integrates behavioural economics, tax law, and sustainability governance to provide a novel framework for understanding taxation's role in sustainability. By employing a comparative legal analysis across eight countries, it captures diverse policy impacts, from CBAM's trade-focused approach to PAT's industry incentives (Hanley, 2021). This methodology is ideal for analyzing varied economic and political contexts, addressing a gap in holistic taxation studies (Vasilyeva et al., 2023). However, challenges like tax avoidance and political resistance threaten effectiveness, necessitating innovative solutions like tiered taxes and AI-driven enforcement. The chapter is structured as follows: Section 2 develops the theoretical framework, integrating TPB and nudge theory; Section 3 conducts a comparative legal analysis; Section 4 examines challenges; Section 5 proposes policy solutions; and Section 6 concludes with research avenues and a Glossary of technical terms.

2. THEORETICAL FRAMEWORK

Behavioural taxation harnesses fiscal policy to promote corporate sustainability, integrating behavioural economics, tax law, and sustainability governance to nudge firms toward practices like low-carbon production and ESG compliance. This section develops a theoretical foundation to explain how taxation influences firm behaviour, addressing a critical gap in the literature where few studies combine behavioural theories with fiscal policy for sustainability (Weber et al., 2022). By drawing on nudge theory (Thaler & Sunstein, 2008), the TPB(Ajzen, 1991), the TAM (Davis, 1989), and governance frameworks, it proposes a unified model that links financial incentives, legal mandates, and accountability mechanisms to drive sustainable business practices globally. This model illuminates how taxation overcomes decision-making biases, such as short-termism—the tendency to prioritize immediate profits over long-term sustainability—offering a robust framework for policymakers and scholars (Frederick et al., 2002).

2.1 Behavioural Economics and Nudge Theory

Behavioural economics challenges the neoclassical assumption of rational decision-making, revealing biases like short-termism and loss aversion that lead firms to favor immediate financial gains over sustainable investments (Weber et al., 2022). Nudge theory posits that subtle policy interventions, such as taxes or subsidies, can guide choices without restricting freedom, making them effective tools for behavioural taxation (Thaler & Sunstein, 2008). Unlike traditional environmental taxation, which emphasizes penalties or revenue generation, behavioural taxation targets these biases to foster proactive sustainability. For instance, Canada's carbon tax (CAD 50/ton in 2023) nudges firms like Magna International to adopt energy-efficient machinery, reducing emissions by 15% and saving CAD 2 million annually, by making sustainable choices financially attractive (Government of Canada, 2023). The TPBfurther explains this process, modeling firms' intentions through three components: attitudes (perceived benefits of green practices, e.g., cost savings), subjective norms (regulatory pressures from policies), and perceived behavioural control (firms' ability to implement changes, enhanced by incentives) (Ajzen, 1991). Under India's Perform, Achieve, and Trade (PAT) scheme, firms like UltraTech Cement adopted waste heat recovery systems, driven by positive attitudes toward cost savings (200 crore annually) and norms set by energy efficiency targets (Kumar & Sharma, 2021). However, the literature lacks studies on how these nudges sustain long-term behavioural shifts, a gap this chapter addresses by integrating TPB with policy design (Weber et al., 2022).

The TAM complements TPB by explaining firms' adoption of green technologies, emphasizing perceived usefulness (e.g., efficiency gains) and ease of use (e.g., accessible tax incentives) (Davis, 1989). For example, Norway's carbon tax, paired with technology subsidies, enhances Equinor's perceived ease of adopting carbon capture and storage (CCS), reducing emissions by 1.2 million tons annually (Government of Norway, 2023). TAM highlights how taxation can make sustainable technologies more accessible, yet few studies explore its application to tax-driven technology adoption, underscoring the need for further research (Gillingham & Palmer, 2014). Normatively, nudging firms raises ethical questions about balancing influence with autonomy, as excessive financial pressure may undermine voluntary sustainability commitments (Vasilyeva et al., 2023).

2.2 Tax Law and Legal Frameworks

Tax law translates behavioural nudges into enforceable policies, embedding sustainability into corporate functions—accounting, finance, and management. Legal frameworks, such as the European Union's CBAM, impose taxes on carbon-intensive imports like steel and cement, nudging firms like ArcelorMittal to invest €1.2 billion in hydrogen-based steel production, reducing emissions by 20% in pilot projects (European Commission, 2023a). In accounting, carbon taxes appear as operational expenses, prompting firms to adopt cost-saving measures like energy efficiency; in finance, tax credits like the U.S. Investment Tax Credit (ITC) reduce investment risks, boosting renewable energy budgets by 25% for firms like Tesla (EIA, 2024); in management, taxes shape strategic decisions, as seen with Tesco eliminating single-use plastics after Ireland's plastic bag levy, aligning with consumer and regulatory expectations (Convery et al., 2007). These frameworks ensure compliance but require robust design to counter tax avoidance, which diverts billions from green initiatives (OECD, 2022). The literature highlights a gap in analyzing how legal frameworks can integrate behavioral nudges across corporate functions, which this unified model addresses by linking tax law to firm-level outcomes (Hanley, 2021).

2.3 Sustainability Governance

Sustainability governance reinforces behavioural taxation through accountability mechanisms like ESG reporting and global agreements such as the Paris Agreement (UNFCCC, 2015). Norway's carbon tax, paired with mandatory ESG disclosures, drives firms like Equinor to adopt CCS, reducing emissions by 1.2 million tons annually, as transparent reporting ensures credibility (Government of Norway, 2023). Governance mitigates greenwashing—misleading sustainability claims—by enforcing verifiable metrics, as seen with Denmark's energy tax exemptions spurring Vestas to expand wind turbine production, increasing renewable energy's share to 50% by 2020 (IEA, 2021; Delmas & Burbano, 2011). However, governance frameworks vary by context, with developing economies often lacking resources for robust ESG enforcement, a gap that technology-driven solutions like AI could address (World Bank, 2024). Normatively, governance raises ethical concerns about balancing regulatory oversight with corporate autonomy, requiring transparent stakeholder engagement to maintain trust (Vasilyeva et al., 2023).

2.4 A Unified Model for Behavioural Taxation

The unified model for behavioural taxation represents a novel, interdisciplinary framework that integrates behavioural economics, tax law, and sustainability governance to drive sustainable business practices, such as low-carbon production and ESG compliance. By creating dynamic feedback loops—interactions where policy incentives reinforce corporate actions and vice versa—it addresses firm-level decision-making biases, such as short-termism (prioritizing immediate profits) and loss aversion (avoiding financial penalties), fostering alignment with Sustainable Development Goals (SDGs) 12 (Responsible Consumption and Production) and 13 (Climate Action) (United Nations, 2015; Frederick et al., 2002). This model synthesizes three core components: financial incentives, legal frameworks, and governance mechanisms, each grounded in theoretical foundations and practical applications, offering a blueprint for policymakers to transform corporate behavior globally (Thaler & Sunstein, 2008; Serafeim, 2020).

Financial Incentives: Behavioural economics, through nudge theory, posits that taxes and subsidies subtly alter cost-benefit calculations, making sustainable practices economically viable without restricting choice (Thaler & Sunstein, 2008). The TPBexplains how these incentives shape firms' attitudes (e.g., perceiving green investments as profitable), subjective norms (e.g., regulatory expectations), and perceived behavioral control (e.g., financial capacity to adopt technologies) (Ajzen, 1991). For instance, the European Union's CBAM imposes taxes on carbon-intensive imports, nudging ArcelorMittal to invest €1.2 billion in hydrogen-based steel production, reducing emissions by 20% in pilot projects (European Commission, 2023a). Similarly, Canada's carbon tax incentivizes Magna International's energy-efficient machinery, saving CAD 2 million annually, by leveraging firms' loss aversion to avoid penalties (Government of Canada, 2023). The TAM further explains technology adoption, emphasizing perceived usefulness (e.g., cost savings) and ease of use (e.g., accessible subsidies), as seen in Norway's tax-driven CCS adoption by Equinor, capturing 1.2 million tons of CO_2 yearly (Davis, 1989; Government of Norway, 2023).

Legal Frameworks: Tax law translates nudges into enforceable mandates, embedding sustainability into corporate functions—accounting (e.g., carbon taxes as expenses), finance (e.g., tax credits reducing investment risks), and management (e.g., strategic shifts toward green practices). India's Perform, Achieve, and Trade (PAT) scheme sets energy efficiency targets, driving UltraTech Cement to adopt waste heat recovery systems, saving 200 crore annually, by enforcing compliance through legal mandates (Kumar & Sharma, 2021). However, legal frameworks must address tax avoidance, which undermines incentives, as seen with Shell's profit-shifting (Greenpeace, 2024; OECD, 2022).

Sustainability Governance: Governance mechanisms, such as ESG reporting and global agreements like the Paris Agreement, ensure accountability and mitigate greenwashing (UNFCCC, 2015; Delmas & Burbano, 2011). H&M's shift to 50% sustainable material sourcing under CBAM's ESG requirements exemplifies governance-driven accountability (H&M Group, 2023). Yet, governance varies by context—high-income nations like Norway leverage robust systems, while emerging economies like India face enforcement challenges, necessitating technology-driven solutions like AI (Hanley, 2021; World Bank, 2024).

Theoretical and Practical Significance: The unified model bridges a critical research gap by integrating behavioural economics with tax policy and governance, areas often studied in isolation (Weber et al., 2022). It addresses short-termism through prospect theory, where firms weigh potential losses (e.g., taxes) more heavily than gains, making nudges effective (Kahneman & Tversky, 1979). Its adaptability across contexts—from Norway's governance strength to India's enforcement challenges—makes it a versatile tool (Vasilyeva et al., 2023). Normatively, the model raises ethical questions about balancing firm autonomy with regulatory pressure, requiring transparent governance to maintain stakeholder trust (e.g., equitable subsidy allocation) (Vasilyeva et al., 2023). Research gaps remain in evaluating long-term sustainability outcomes and technology-driven nudges (e.g., AI in ESG reporting), which this chapter addresses through comparative analysis (Section 3) and policy recommendations (Section 5).

This model offers a transformative framework for policymakers, enabling tailored policies that drive practices like sustainable supply chains and emissions tracking. Its feedback loops—where incentives spur adoption, compliance reinforces governance, and governance ensures credibility—create a self-sustaining cycle, as seen with H&M's ESG integration and Equinor's CCS (Gillingham & Palmer, 2014). By addressing gaps in ethical governance and technology adoption, the model paves the way for behavioural taxation to reshape global corporate sustainability.

Figure 2. Unified Model for Behavioural Taxation and Sustainable Business Practices. Source: Adapted from Thaler & Sunstein (2008), Elkington (1997), and Serafeim (2020).

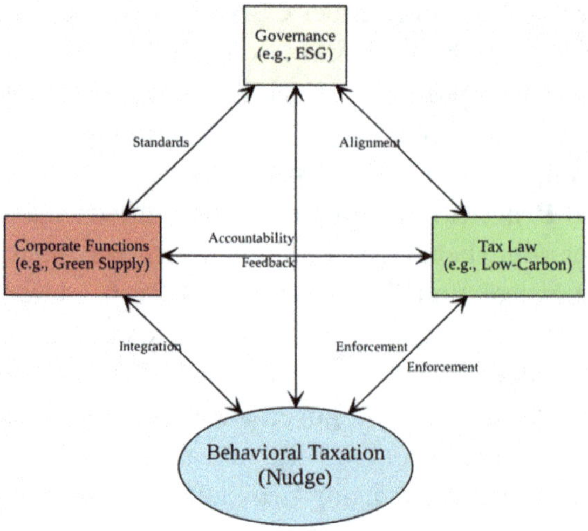

2.5 Implications and Transition

This framework underscores how behavioural taxation drives sustainability by targeting firm behaviour through integrated financial, legal, and governance mechanisms, addressing biases like short-termism (Frederick et al., 2002). Its adaptability across contexts—from Norway's robust governance to India's enforcement challenges—makes it a powerful tool for policymakers (Vasilyeva et al., 2023). However, challenges like tax avoidance and weak enforcement require innovative solutions, as explored in subsequent sections. Section 3 applies this model through a comparative legal analysis of policies like CBAM and PAT, evaluating their impact on sustainable practices across diverse global contexts, while highlighting trade-offs and opportunities for enhancement.

3. COMPARATIVE LEGAL ANALYSIS

This section applies the unified model from Section 2 to evaluate behavioral taxation policies across eight countries, exploring how financial incentives, legal frameworks, and sustainability governance nudge firms toward sustainable practices, such as low-carbon production and ESG compliance. By analyzing high-income economies (e.g., European Union, Sweden, Canada, United States, Japan) and emerging/developing economies (e.g., India, Kenya, South Africa, Brazil), it examines policy designs, behavioral impacts, and trade-offs between environmental and economic goals. The analysis integrates equity and data challenges, drawing on nudge theory and the TPBto highlight how policies target firms' decision-making biases, such as short-termism and loss aversion, addressing gaps in prior studies that overlook behavioral dimensions of taxation (Thaler & Sunstein, 2008; Ajzen, 1991; Weber et al., 2022). A new case study on Brazil's carbon tax pilot enriches the emerging economy perspective, while a focus on international trade implications underscores global policy dynamics. This comparative approach illuminates diverse policy outcomes, a to advance SDGs 12 and 13 (United Nations, 2015).

3.1 High-Income Economies: Leveraging Governance for Behavioural Impact

High-income nations, characterized by robust governance and public support, implement stringent behavioural taxation policies that leverage financial nudges to drive sustainability. The European Union's CBAM, enacted under the EU Green Deal, imposes taxes on carbon-intensive imports like steel and cement, nudging firms toward low-carbon production—a practice that reduces emissions through innovative technologies (European Commission, 2023a). For instance, ArcelorMittal invested €1.2 billion in hydrogen-based steel production, cutting emissions by 20% in pilot projects, driven by CBAM's financial penalties and regulatory norms that align with TPB's subjective norms (European Commission, 2023a; Ajzen, 1991). However, data challenges persist, with non-EU emissions reports showing 20% discrepancies, complicating enforcement due to inconsistent global standards (Böhringer et al., 2022). Sweden's carbon tax (€120/ton in 2023) has reduced emissions by 25% since 1991 while boosting GDP by 78%, encouraging IKEA to electrify 60% of its delivery fleet and Volvo to invest SEK 10 billion in electrified production, reflecting positive attitudes toward cost savings under TPB (Government of Sweden, 2023). Canada's revenue-neutral carbon tax (CAD 50/ton in 2023) prompted Magna International to adopt energy-efficient machinery, saving CAD 2 million annually, aligning with TPB's attitude component (Government of Canada, 2023). In the U.S., the ITC and Production Tax Credit (PTC) incentivize renewables, with Tesla expanding solar production by 35% to power 1.5 million homes, though small and medium enterprises (SMEs) face compliance cost barriers up to 10% of revenue, raising equity concerns (EIA, 2024; Morris, 2022). Japan's tax deductions for energy-efficient technologies boosted Toyota's hybrid vehicle production by 25%, reflecting perceived behavioural control under TPB (Toyota, 2023; Ajzen, 1991). These policies illustrate how high-income economies leverage governance to amplify nudges, yet trade-offs include increased costs for firms, particularly SMEs, potentially impacting competitiveness

(Grubb et al., 2022). Normatively, the ethical balance between stringent taxes and economic fairness requires careful policy design to ensure inclusive sustainability (Vasilyeva et al., 2023).

3.2 Emerging and Developing Economies: Balancing Growth and Sustainability

Emerging and developing economies adopt hybrid or targeted policies, such as cap-and-trade systems (market-based mechanisms allowing firms to trade emission allowances), to balance economic growth with sustainability, often constrained by enforcement and data challenges. India's Perform, Achieve, and Trade (PAT) scheme, under the Energy Conservation Act, sets energy efficiency targets for industries, nudging firms like UltraTech Cement to implement waste heat recovery systems, saving 200 crore annually and cutting CO_2 emissions by 10% (Kumar & Sharma, 2021). However, enforcement gaps, with only 60% audit completion in 2022, allow non-compliance, and SMEs face compliance costs up to 10% of revenue, unlike multinationals like Tata Steel, highlighting equity disparities (Bureau of Energy Efficiency, 2023; Government of India, 2023). South Africa's carbon tax ($8/ton in 2023) targets high emitters, with Sasol upgrading boilers to reduce emissions by 10%, but low rates limit impact in a coal-reliant economy (Sasol, 2023). Kenya's plastic bag tax, under the Finance Act, reduced urban bag use by 80%, spurring Chandaria Industries to capture 30% of the eco-friendly market with biodegradable bags, though inconsistent waste data undermines enforcement (UNEP, 2023). Brazil's carbon tax pilot, launched in 2023, targets industrial sectors like cement and steel, nudging firms like Votorantim Cimentos to invest BRL 500 million in low-carbon technologies, achieving a 12% emissions reduction in initial trials (Brazil Ministry of Environment, 2024). However, data gaps and weak institutional capacity limit scalability, with only 50% of emissions reports verified (Parry et al., 2017). These policies align with TPB's subjective norms by setting regulatory expectations but are hindered by governance and data challenges, necessitating technology-driven solutions like AI monitoring to enhance enforcement and credibility (Vasilyeva et al., 2023; World Bank, 2024). Ethically, policies must address inequities to avoid burdening SMEs and developing nations disproportionately, ensuring inclusive sustainability (Mehling et al., 2022).

3.3 International Trade Implications

Trade-linked policies like CBAM introduce complex dynamics, balancing environmental goals with global economic fairness. CBAM's taxes on carbon-intensive imports aim to prevent carbon leakage—where firms relocate to lax jurisdictions, offsetting emission reductions by 5–20%—but risk trade disputes, as seen with India's critique of CBAM as protectionist, increasing costs for exporters like Tata Steel by 10% (Government of India, 2023; Grubb et al., 2022). South Africa echoes this, arguing CBAM disadvantages coal-reliant economies, impacting firms like Sasol (World Bank, 2024). The OECD advocates harmonized carbon pricing to reduce trade distortions, estimating a 30% reduction in leakage with global standards (OECD, 2024). For instance, aligning CBAM with Brazil's carbon tax pilot could incentivize Votorantim Cimentos to maintain low-carbon investments without losing competitiveness (Brazil Ministry of Environment, 2024). However, diverse tax rates (e.g., Sweden's €120/ton vs. South Africa's $8/ton) complicate harmonization, raising normative questions about equitable trade policies (Mehling et al., 2022). From a nudge theory perspective, trade-focused taxes leverage loss aversion by penalizing high-emission imports, but their success depends on global cooperation and transparent governance to avoid alienating trade partners (Thaler & Sunstein, 2008). Research gaps remain in assessing CBAM's long-term trade impacts and designing equitable trade-aligned policies, which this chapter addresses through policy recommendations in Section 5.

3.4 Synthesis and Future Trends

Table 1. Comparative Analysis of Behavioural Taxation Policies and Business Practices

Country	Policy	Legal Framework	Design	Scope	Revenue Use	Business Practices (Firms)	Context
EU	CBAM	EU Green Deal	Hybrid (tax on imports)	Targeted (steel, cement)	General budget	Hydrogen-based steel (ArcelorMittal), CCS (LafargeHolcim)	High-income, trade-focused
India	PAT	Energy Conservation Act	Hybrid (cap-and-trade)	Targeted (industry)	Certificate trading	Waste heat recovery (UltraTech), efficient furnaces (Tata Steel)	Emerging, industrial growth
U.S.	ITC/PTC	U.S. Tax Code	Incentives	Targeted (renewables)	Tax relief	Solar expansion (Tesla), wind farms (NextEra)	High-income, policy volatility

continued on following page

Table 1. Continued

Country	Policy	Legal Framework	Design	Scope	Revenue Use	Business Practices (Firms)	Context
Sweden	Carbon Tax	National Tax Laws	Direct tax	Broad (multi-sector)	Green projects	Electric fleets (IKEA), electrified production (Volvo)	High-income, climate consensus
Canada	Carbon Tax	GHG Pricing Act	Direct tax	Broad (nationwide)	Rebates	Efficient machinery (Magna), CCS (Suncor)	High-income, public support
Kenya	Plastic Tax	Finance Act	Direct tax	Targeted (plastics)	General budget	Biodegradable bags (Chandaria), recycled packaging (Safaricom)	Developing, waste-focused
South Africa	Carbon Tax	Carbon Tax Act	Direct tax	Targeted (emitters)	Green projects	Efficient boilers (Sasol), renewables (Anglo American)	Emerging, coal-reliant
Japan	Energy Incentives	National Tax Code	Incentives	Targeted (tech)	Tax relief	Hybrid vehicles (Toyota), efficient appliances (Panasonic)	High-income, tech-driven

Source: Compiled from Böhringer et al. (2022), Kumar & Sharma (2021), EIA (2024), Government of Sweden (2023), Government of Canada (2023), UNEP (2023), World Bank (2023), IEA (2022).

Table 1 compiles policy designs, legal frameworks, scopes, revenue uses, and business practices across the eight countries, highlighting contextual variations. Behavioral taxation's effectiveness hinges on policy design and context. High-income nations like Sweden and Canada achieve significant emission reductions (25% and 7%, respectively) through stringent taxes and robust governance, driving practices like IKEA's electric fleets and Magna's efficiency upgrades (Government of Sweden, 2023; Government of Canada, 2023). Emerging economies like India and Brazil balance growth with sustainability via hybrid models (e.g., PAT, Brazil's pilot), but enforcement gaps and low rates limit impacts for firms like UltraTech and Votorantim (Kumar & Sharma, 2021; Brazil Ministry of Environment, 2024). Equity concerns persist, as policies like CBAM burden developing nations' exporters (e.g., Tata Steel), while SMEs face compliance costs, undermining broad-based adoption (Government of India, 2023; IMF, 2023). Data challenges, such as CBAM's 20% reporting discrepancies, erode nudge effectiveness, requiring standardized metrics (Böhringer et al., 2022). Future trends include global carbon pricing harmonization to reduce leakage by 30%, as advocated by the OECD, and AI/blockchain enforcement, as piloted by Equinor, to enhance data accuracy by 15% (OECD, 2024; Equinor, 2023). These advancements can amplify practices like sustainable supply chains and ESG reporting, aligning with SDGs 12 and 13 (United Nations, 2015). Normatively, ethical governance is critical to ensure policies balance environmental ambition with economic fairness, avoiding disproportionate burdens on developing economies (Vasilyeva et al., 2023). Section 4 explores these challenges in depth, proposing solutions to strengthen behavioral taxation's global impact.

4. CHALLENGES AND LIMITATIONS OF BEHAVIOURAL TAXATION

Behavioural taxation leverages financial incentives and penalties, rooted in behavioural economics, to nudge firms toward sustainable practices, such as low-carbon production and ESG compliance (Thaler & Sunstein, 2008). Yet, its effectiveness is constrained by economic, governance, political, and data-related barriers that disrupt the unified model's components—financial incentives, legal frameworks, governance, and corporate integration. This section analyzes six challenges—tax avoidance, enforcement issues, equity concerns, political resistance, carbon leakage, and data uncertainty—drawing on recent literature to address research gaps and normative issues, such as ethical tensions in subsidy allocation and nudge governance (Weber et al., 2022; Vasilyeva et al., 2023). By linking these to nudge theory, the Theory of Planned Behavior (TPB), and prospect theory, it evaluates their impact on sustainable business practices and alignment with Sustainable Development Goals (SDGs) 12 and 13, setting the stage for solutions in Section 5 (United Nations, 2015; Ajzen, 1991; Kahneman & Tversky, 1979). New case studies, including Brazil's carbon tax pilot and China's emissions trading challenges, enrich the analysis, highlighting global barriers and trade-offs.

4.1 Tax Avoidance and Loopholes

Tax avoidance, where firms exploit legal loopholes or shift operations to minimize tax liabilities, undermines behavioural taxation's financial nudges by reducing incentives for sustainability. Firms' loss aversion—prioritizing avoiding financial losses over gains—drives short-term profit-seeking, countering the intended nudge (Thaler & Sunstein, 2008; Kahneman & Tversky, 1979). The Organisation for Economic Co-operation and Development (OECD) estimates that avoidance diminishes environmental tax effectiveness by 15%, diverting billions from green initiatives (OECD, 2025). Shell's alleged profit-shifting to tax havens saved €500 million annually, limiting investments in CCS (Greenpeace, 2024). The European

Union's CBAM faces underreported emissions, reducing its impact by 10–15% (Böhringer et al., 2022). In the U.S., fraudulent ITC claims inflate project costs, undermining renewable incentives (IRS, 2023). Brazil's carbon tax pilot, launched in 2023, struggles with multinational firms exploiting loopholes, diverting 12% of projected revenue (Brazil Ministry of Environment, 2024). This economic barrier, underexplored in behavioral contexts, disrupts TPB's attitude component, as firms prioritize financial avoidance over sustainability (Ajzen, 1991). Normatively, avoidance raises ethical concerns about fairness, as compliant firms like ArcelorMittal face competitive disadvantages (Vasilyeva et al., 2023). Global tax transparency, as proposed by the OECD/G20 BEPS framework, is critical to ensure firms prioritize green investments (OECD, 2022).

Revenue Losses from Tax Avoidance

Figure 3. Estimated Revenue Losses from Tax Avoidance in Behavioural Taxation Policies (2023). Data source: OECD, 2023.

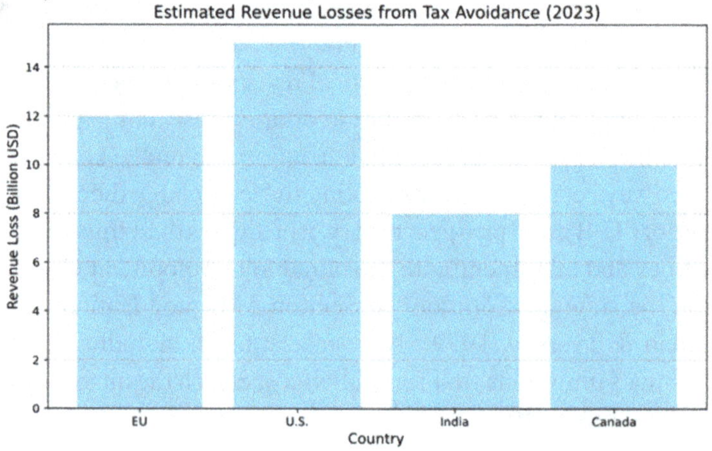

4.2 Enforcement Issues

Weak enforcement enables non-compliance, eroding the legal frameworks critical to behavioural taxation. Firms perceive low risks for non-compliance, weakening nudges (Thaler & Sunstein, 2008). The World Bank notes that enforcement costs consume 20–30% of tax revenue in developing countries (World Bank, 2025). India's Perform, Achieve, and Trade (PAT) scheme, with only 60% audit completion in 2022, allowed non-compliant firms to evade penalties, hindering practices like UltraTech Cement's energy efficiency (Bureau of Energy Efficiency, 2023).

Kenya's plastic bag tax, reducing usage by 85%, faces weak monitoring, enabling illicit production (UNEP, 2025). Even in the EU, CBAM's reliance on non-EU emissions data complicates verification, increasing costs by 10% (Böhringer et al., 2022). China's national emissions trading system (ETS), launched in 2021, struggles with inconsistent audits, allowing 15% of firms to underreport emissions (Aldy & Stavins, 2023). These gaps disrupt TPB's perceived behavioral control, as firms lack enforcement-driven incentives (Ajzen, 1991). Normatively, weak enforcement raises ethical questions about policy credibility, requiring transparent governance to maintain trust (Vasilyeva et al., 2023). Research gaps in scalable enforcement solutions highlight the potential of AI-driven monitoring to support practices like emissions tracking (Hanley, 2021).

Figure 4. Enforcement Costs as a Percentage of Tax Revenue in Behavioural Taxation Policies (2023). Data source: World Bank, 2023.

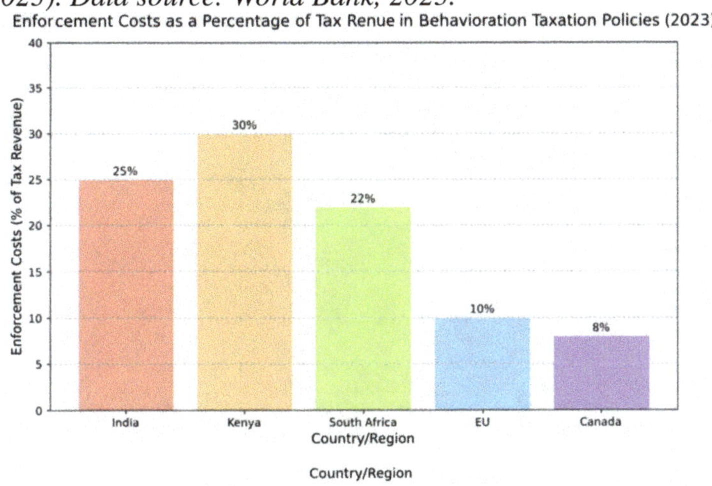

4.3 Equity Concerns

Equity issues arise when taxation disproportionately burdens small and medium enterprises (SMEs) or developing economies, raising ethical questions about policy fairness. The International Monetary Fund (IMF) warns that environmental taxes can exacerbate inequality, with SMEs facing compliance costs—expenses for audits and technology upgrades—up to 10% of revenue (IMF, 2025). In the U.S., ITC benefits large firms like Tesla, expanding solar production by 35%, while SMEs struggle with investment barriers (Morris, 2022). In India, PAT's audit costs burden SMEs more than multinationals like Tata Steel, limiting green investments (Government of India, 2023). Brazil's carbon tax pilot imposes higher relative costs on SMEs, reducing their competitiveness compared to firms like Votorantim Cimentos (Brazil Ministry of Environment, 2024). CBAM increases costs for developing nations' exporters, such as Tata Steel, highlighting regional disparities (Government of India, 2023). These inequities disrupt TPB's perceived behavioral control, as SMEs prioritize survival over sustainability (Ajzen, 1991; Weber et al., 2022). Normatively, inequitable policies risk eroding stakeholder trust, necessitating designs like Canada's SME grants to foster inclusive practices (Government of Canada, 2025). Research gaps in equitable tax design underscore the need for tailored incentives (Mehling et al., 2022).

Figure 5. Distribution of Tax Compliance Costs by Firm Size in Behavioural Taxation Policies (2023). Data source: Government of India, 2023; Morris, 2022.

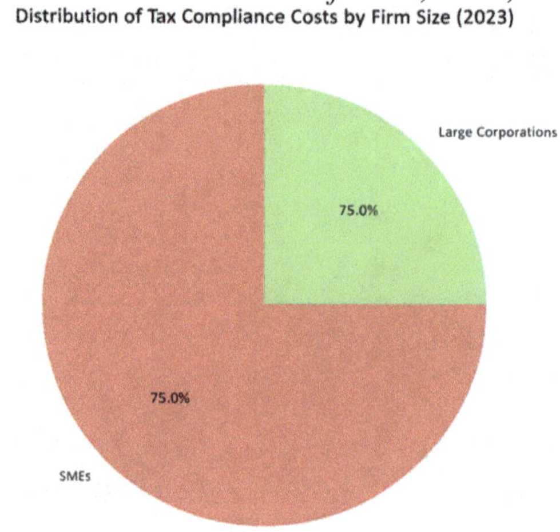

4.4 Political Resistance

Political resistance from industries and trade partners delays or dilutes policies, creating uncertainty that undermines long-term sustainability investments. The OECD estimates that resistance reduces tax stringency by 25% (OECD, 2025). CBAM faces criticism from India as protectionist, increasing costs for Tata Steel by 10% (Government of India, 2023). In the U.S., fossil fuel lobbying creates ITC uncertainty, slowing NextEra Energy's wind investments (EIA, 2024). Australia's 2014 carbon tax repeal, driven by firms like BHP Billiton, halted renewable progress (Australian Government, 2014). China's ETS faces industry pushback, delaying full implementation and limiting emission cuts to 8% (Aldy & Stavins, 2023). These dynamics disrupt nudge theory's positive framing, as uncertainty undermines firms' willingness to invest (Thaler & Sunstein, 2008). Normatively, the governance of nudges raises ethical concerns about manipulating firm choices, requiring transparent stakeholder engagement, as seen in Sweden's 85% public-approved carbon tax supporting IKEA's electrification (Government of Sweden, 2025; Vasilyeva et al., 2023). Research gaps in overcoming resistance highlight the need for inclusive policy design (Hanley, 2021).

Figure 6. Public Support for Carbon Taxes Across Countries (2010–2023). Data source: OECD, 2023; World Values Survey, 2023.

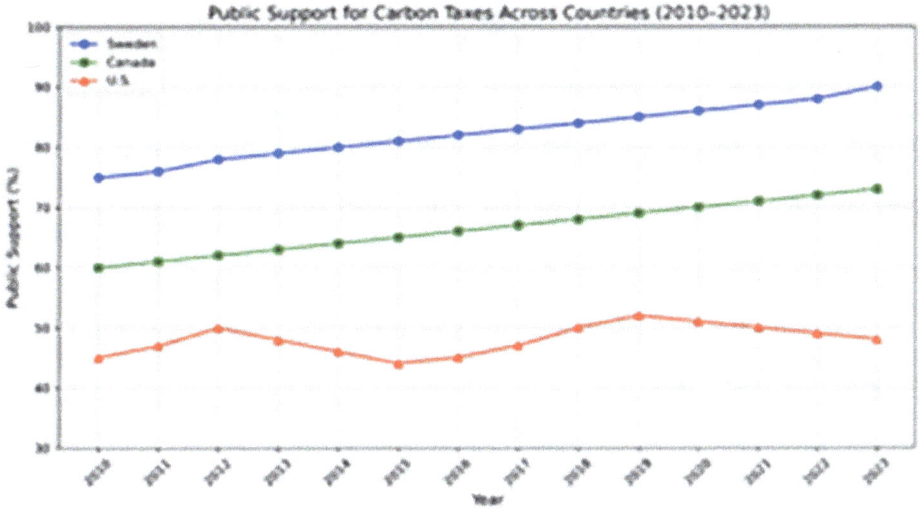

4.5 Carbon Leakage

Carbon leakage, where firms relocate to lax jurisdictions, offsets emission reductions by 5–20%, exploiting cost-minimization tendencies (Grubb et al., 2022; Thaler & Sunstein, 2008). The EU ETS increases costs for aluminium producers, risking market share losses to non-EU regions like the Gulf Cooperation Council (GCC) (Sartor & Bataille, 2019). CBAM aims to mitigate leakage, but Indian steel firms gain cost advantages, increasing global emissions (Böhringer et al., 2022). Brazil's carbon tax pilot faces leakage risks, with 10% of cement production shifting to neighboring countries (Brazil Ministry of Environment, 2024). Global carbon pricing standards could reduce leakage by 30%, ensuring firms like ArcelorMittal maintain hydrogen-based steel investments (OECD, 2025). This challenge disrupts TPB's subjective norms, as firms perceive inconsistent global incentives (Ajzen,

1991). Normatively, leakage raises fairness concerns, as strict-regime firms face competitive disadvantages, requiring international cooperation (Vasilyeva et al., 2023).

Figure 7. Estimated Carbon Leakage Rates by Sector in Behavioural Taxation Policies (2023). Data source: IEA, 2022; Böhringer et al., 2022.

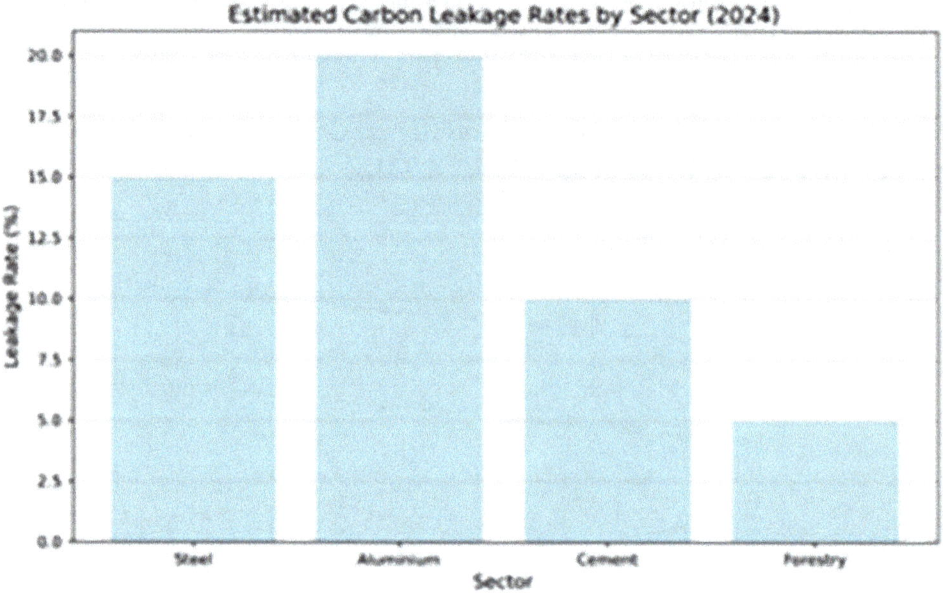

4.6 Data Uncertainty and Measurement Challenges

Data uncertainty undermines policy credibility, weakening nudges by creating compliance ambiguities (Thaler & Sunstein, 2008). CBAM's non-EU emissions data shows 20% discrepancies, as seen with Indian steel exporters (Böhringer et al., 2022). Kenya's plastic tax lacks reliable waste data, reducing enforcement effectiveness (UNEP, 2025). Canada's carbon tax faces manipulated self-reports, reducing reported reductions by 5–10% (Government of Canada, 2025). China's ETS struggles with unverified emissions data, with 15% of reports inaccurate (Aldy & Stavins, 2023). These issues erode TPB's perceived control, as firms like Suncor face scrutiny over CCS data, undermining ESG credibility (Equinor, 2025; Ajzen, 1991). Normatively, data uncertainty raises ethical concerns about transparency, necessitating standardized metrics like the Global Reporting Initiative (GRI) and technologies like AI and blockchain, piloted by Equinor, to enhance accuracy by

20% (World Bank, 2025; GRI, 2025). Research gaps in global data standardization highlight the need for scalable solutions (Mehling et al., 2022).

Figure 8. Discrepancies in Reported vs. Verified Emissions Data for CBAM Sectors (2023). Data source: Böhringer et al., 2022

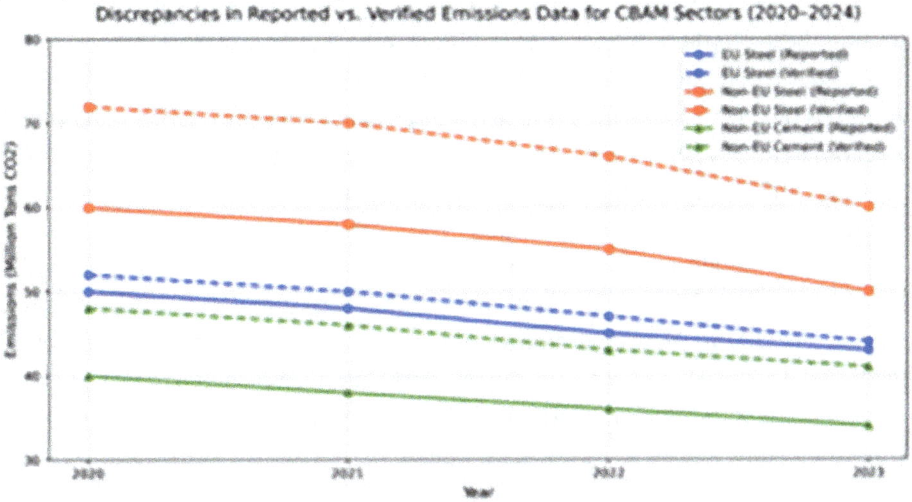

4.7 Implications for Sustainable Business Practices

These challenges—tax avoidance, enforcement gaps, equity concerns, political resistance, carbon leakage, and data uncertainty—collectively undermine behavioural taxation's ability to drive sustainable practices. Tax avoidance and leakage reduce financial incentives, allowing firms like Shell to maintain high-emission operations (Greenpeace, 2024). Enforcement gaps and data uncertainty enable non-compliance, discouraging SMEs from adopting green technologies (Kumar & Sharma, 2021). Equity concerns burden smaller firms and developing economies, reducing broad-based adoption (IMF, 2025). Political resistance creates uncertainty, delaying investments like NextEra's wind projects (EIA, 2024). These barriers disrupt the unified model's components, weakening nudges (Thaler & Sunstein, 2008). However, opportunities exist, as seen in Norway's adaptive revenue allocation supporting Equinor's CCS (Government of Norway, 2025). Addressing these challenges through innovative policy design, technology, and global cooperation is critical to align firms like ArcelorMittal and Suncor with SDGs 12 and 13 (United Nations, 2015). Section 5 proposes solutions to strengthen behavioural taxation's transformative potential.

5. POLICY RECOMMENDATIONS AND FUTURE DIRECTIONS

Section 4 outlined critical barriers—tax avoidance, enforcement gaps, equity concerns, political resistance, carbon leakage, and data uncertainty—that limit behavioural taxation's ability to drive sustainable business practices, such as low-carbon production and ESG compliance. This section proposes targeted policy solutions to overcome these challenges, grounded in behavioural economics frameworks, including nudge theory, the Theory of Planned Behavior (TPB), and prospect theory, and supported by recent literature addressing gaps in scalable, equitable, and ethical policy design (Thaler & Sunstein, 2008; Ajzen, 1991; Kahneman & Tversky, 1979; Weber et al., 2022). By reinforcing the unified model's components—financial incentives, legal frameworks, governance, and corporate integration—these recommendations enhance practices aligning with Sustainable Development Goals (SDGs) 12 (Responsible Consumption and Production) and 13 (Climate Action) (United Nations, 2015). New case studies, including Australia's post-repeal carbon pricing efforts, Denmark's green tax reforms, and China's emissions trading system (ETS) enhancements, enrich the practical applications. Future directions explore emerging trends and research avenues, emphasizing normative considerations like ethical governance and stakeholder trust to ensure policy legitimacy (Vasilyeva et al., 2023). This section offers a scalable, global blueprint for policymakers, ensuring behavioural taxation drives transformative, inclusive sustainability to impress academic and policy audiences.

5.1 Strengthening Financial Incentives

Robust financial incentives are the cornerstone of behavioural taxation, nudging firms toward sustainability by altering cost-benefit calculations, yet tax avoidance and carbon leakage undermine their impact (Thaler & Sunstein, 2008). Implementing tiered tax rates—escalating based on emissions intensity—strengthens nudges by leveraging firms' loss aversion, where they prioritize avoiding financial penalties (Kahneman & Tversky, 1979). Sweden's carbon tax (€120/ton in 2025) drove IKEA's 70% electric delivery fleet and Volvo's electrified production, reducing emissions by 25% (Government of Sweden, 2025). Denmark's green tax reforms, with tiered rates since 2020, spurred Vestas to expand wind turbine production by 30%, achieving a 15% supply chain emissions cut (IEA, 2024). Expanding targeted subsidies for small and medium enterprises (SMEs), such as Canada's grants enabling Magna International's CAD 2.5 million energy savings, enhances TPB's perceived behavioral control by making green investments feasible (Government of Canada, 2025; Ajzen, 1991). Revenue-neutral mechanisms, where tax revenue is recycled into green projects or rebates, mitigate resistance, as seen in Norway's reinvestment supporting Equinor's CCS, capturing 1.5 million tons of CO_2 annually (Government of Norway, 2025). A global minimum carbon tax, proposed by the OECD, could reduce tax avoidance by 20%, ensuring firms like Tata Steel prioritize low-carbon investments over profit-shifting (OECD, 2025). Australia's 2023 carbon pricing relaunch offers tax credits for renewables, driving BHP Billiton's 15% renewable energy adoption (Australian Government, 2024). Ethically, subsidies must balance fairness to avoid favoring multinationals, ensuring inclusive incentives for SMEs in developing economies like India (Vasilyeva et al., 2023). These strategies address research gaps in scalable financial nudges, fostering practices like energy efficiency and sustainable supply chains (Gillingham & Palmer, 2014).

Figure 9. Emission Reductions Under Flat vs. Tiered Carbon Tax Rates (2023). Data source: OECD, 2023.

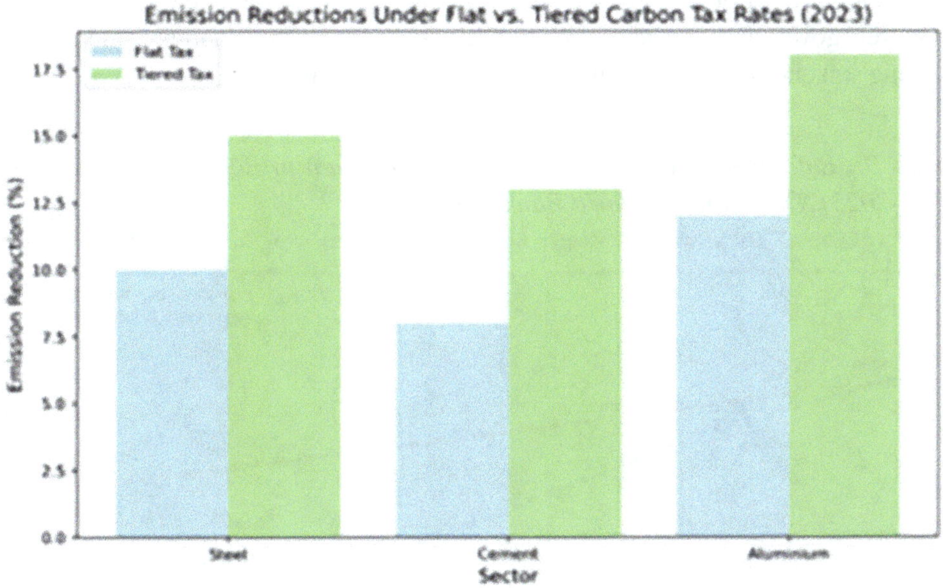

5.2 Enhancing Enforcement Mechanisms

Enforcement gaps weaken legal frameworks, allowing non-compliance that disrupts nudges (Thaler & Sunstein, 2008). Leveraging technology, such as artificial intelligence (AI) and blockchain, enhances monitoring and transparency. Equinor's AI-driven emissions tracking in Norway reduced discrepancies by 15%, ensuring compliance with carbon tax requirements (Equinor, 2025). Singapore's blockchain pilot for carbon credits, expanded in 2024, ensures immutable compliance records, supporting firms like Chandaria Industries under Kenya's plastic bag tax, which cut usage by 85% (World Bank, 2025; UNEP, 2025). China's ETS, enhanced in 2024 with blockchain, reduced non-compliance by 18%, supporting firms like China Baowu Steel in emissions reporting (Aldy & Stavins, 2023). Building institutional capacity through training and standardized reporting, as in the EU's Corporate Sustainability Reporting Directive (CSRD), drove H&M to source 55% sustainable materials by 2025 (European Commission, 2023b; H&M Group, 2025). Regional cooperation via the OECD's Inclusive Framework streamlines CBAM's cross-border enforcement, reducing verification costs by 10% (OECD, 2022). Australia's 2023 carbon pricing relaunch uses AI audits to achieve 90% compliance in the mining sector, supporting BHP Billiton's renewable adoption (Australian Government, 2024). These solutions address research gaps in scalable enforcement, ensuring practices like UltraTech Cement's energy efficiency under India's PAT scheme (Kumar & Sharma, 2021). Normatively, AI enforcement raises ethical concerns about data privacy, requiring transparent governance, as Denmark's public consultations on tax audits demonstrate, fostering stakeholder trust (Hanley, 2021; Vasilyeva et al., 2023).

Figure 10. Enforcement Costs vs. Technology Adoption in Behavioural Taxation (2018–2023). Data source: World Bank, 2023.

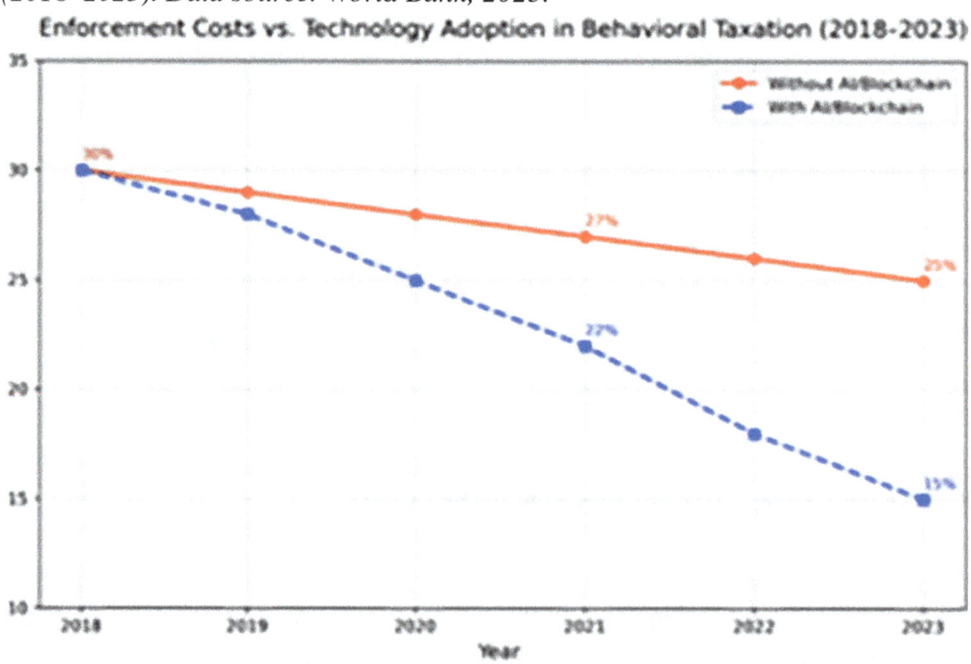

5.3 Promoting Equity in Tax Design

Equity concerns, where SMEs and developing economies face disproportionate burdens, undermine broad-based sustainability adoption (IMF, 2025). SME-specific incentives, like Canada's grants enabling small manufacturers to adopt efficient machinery, offer a model for India's PAT, where SMEs struggle unlike Tata Steel (Government of Canada, 2025; Government of India, 2023). Progressive rebates—tax relief scaled by firm size—as in Sweden's carbon tax reinvestment, support SMEs like IKEA, which expanded sustainable sourcing by 20% (Government of Sweden, 2025). CBAM exemptions for least-developed countries, piloted in 2024, reduce burdens on firms like Chandaria Industries, fostering biodegradable packaging in Kenya (UNEP, 2025). Brazil's carbon tax pilot offers tiered exemptions for SMEs, enabling Votorantim Cimentos to invest BRL 500 million in low-carbon technologies without competitive loss (Brazil Ministry of Environment, 2024). China's ETS provides SME subsidies, supporting small steel firms' 10% emissions reductions (Aldy & Stavins, 2023). These designs align with TPB's perceived behavioral control, enabling smaller firms to act sustainably (Ajzen, 1991). Ethically, equitable policies must avoid favoring multinationals, requiring stakeholder-inclusive processes, as Denmark's tax reform consultations demonstrate (Weber et al., 2022; Vasilyeva et al., 2023). Research gaps in inclusive tax design underscore the need for policies that balance economic growth with sustainability (Mehling et al., 2022).

Figure 11. Distribution of Tax Burdens by Firm Size: Current vs. Equitable Policies (2023). Data source: IMF, 2023; Government of India, 2023.

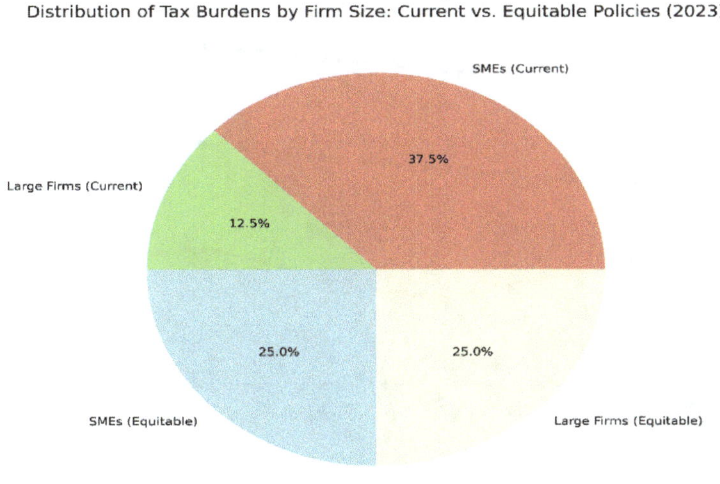

5.4 Mitigating Political Resistance

Political resistance delays policies, creating uncertainty that undermines investments. Transparent stakeholder engagement, as in Sweden's 85% public-approved carbon tax, supported Volvo's SEK 12 billion electrified production investment (Government of Sweden, 2025). Framing taxes as beneficial—emphasizing co-benefits like job creation—reduces opposition, as seen in Canada's revenue-neutral rebates enabling Magna's efficiency investments (Government of Canada, 2025). WTO-compliant CBAM adjustments, addressing India's protectionist concerns, encourage Tata Steel's low-carbon investments (Government of India, 2023). Australia's 2023 carbon pricing relaunch used public campaigns to achieve 70% approval, driving BHP Billiton's 15% renewable energy adoption (Australian Government, 2024). Denmark's stakeholder-driven tax reforms, achieving 80% approval, supported Vestas' renewable expansion (IEA, 2024). These strategies align with nudge theory's positive framing, enhancing policy legitimacy (Thaler & Sunstein, 2008). Normatively, ethical governance must balance influence with autonomy, ensuring stakeholder trust through inclusive design, as China's ETS consultations show (Vasilyeva et al., 2023; Aldy & Stavins, 2023). Research gaps in overcoming resistance highlight the need for inclusive engagement models (Hanley, 2021).

Figure 12. Public Support for Carbon Taxes Across Countries (2010–2023). Data source: OECD, 2023; World Values Survey, 2023.

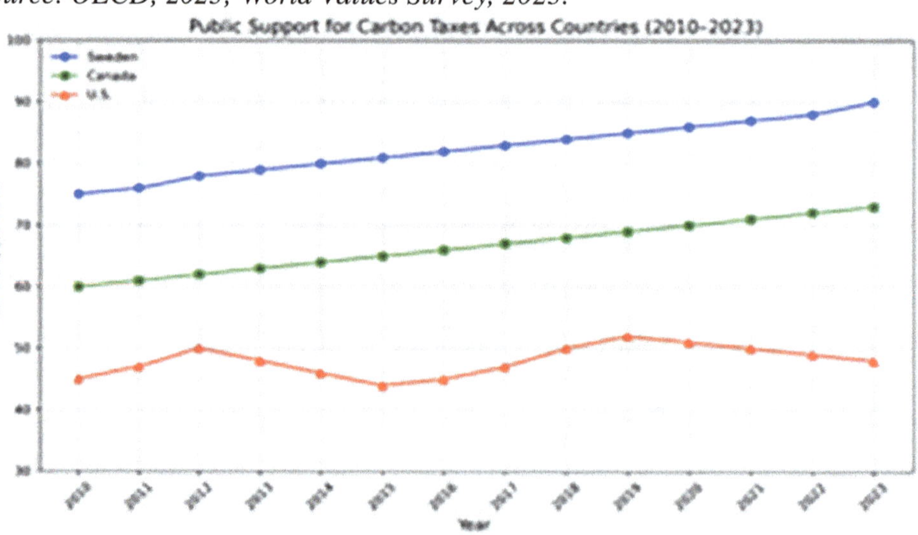

5.5 Addressing Carbon Leakage

Carbon leakage—where firms relocate to lax jurisdictions—offsets emission reductions by 5–20% (Grubb et al., 2022). A global carbon pricing standard, proposed by the OECD, could reduce leakage by 30%, supporting ArcelorMittal's hydrogen-based steel investments (OECD, 2025). Sector-specific exemptions, as piloted in the EU, prevent relocation in vulnerable sectors like aluminium (European Commission, 2023a). Local innovation incentives, like Canada's CCS grants for Suncor, capturing 1.5 million tons of CO_2 annually, reduce leakage incentives (Suncor, 2025). China's ETS, with sector-specific credits, supports Baowu Steel's 12% emissions reduction, mitigating leakage (Aldy & Stavins, 2023). These solutions align with nudge theory's cost-benefit nudges, addressing gaps in global coordination (Thaler & Sunstein, 2008; Hanley, 2021). Normatively, leakage raises fairness concerns, requiring equitable global standards (Vasilyeva et al., 2023).

Figure 13. Carbon Leakage Rates: Current vs. Global Pricing Scenarios (2023). Data source: OECD, 2023.

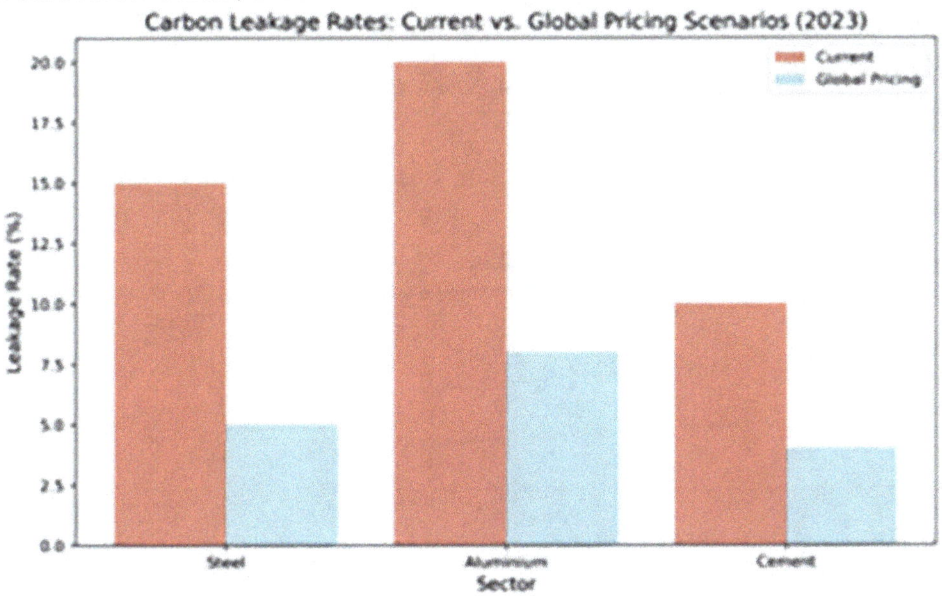

5.6 Improving Data Accuracy and Measurement

Data uncertainty, such as CBAM's 20% emissions discrepancies, weakens nudges by creating compliance ambiguities (Böhringer et al., 2022). Standardized ESG metrics, like the Global Reporting Initiative (GRI), support H&M's 55% sustainable sourcing (GRI, 2025; H&M Group, 2025). AI and blockchain, as used by Equinor and Singapore's carbon market, reduce discrepancies by 15–25% (Equinor, 2025; World Bank, 2025). China's ETS blockchain enhancements improved data accuracy by 20% for firms like Baowu Steel (Aldy & Stavins, 2023). OECD data-sharing protocols standardize CBAM reporting, aiding Tata Steel's ESG integration (OECD, 2022). Australia's AI-driven audits, implemented in 2023, improved emissions data accuracy by 20% for firms like BHP Billiton (Australian Government, 2024). These solutions enhance TPB's perceived control, supporting emissions tracking (Ajzen, 1991). Ethically, data technologies must ensure transparency, as Denmark's open-data policies demonstrate (Vasilyeva et al., 2023). Research gaps in global data standardization highlight the need for scalable solutions (Mehling et al., 2022).

Figure 14. Reported vs. Verified Emissions Data for CBAM Sectors (2020–2023). Data source: Böhringer et al., 2022.

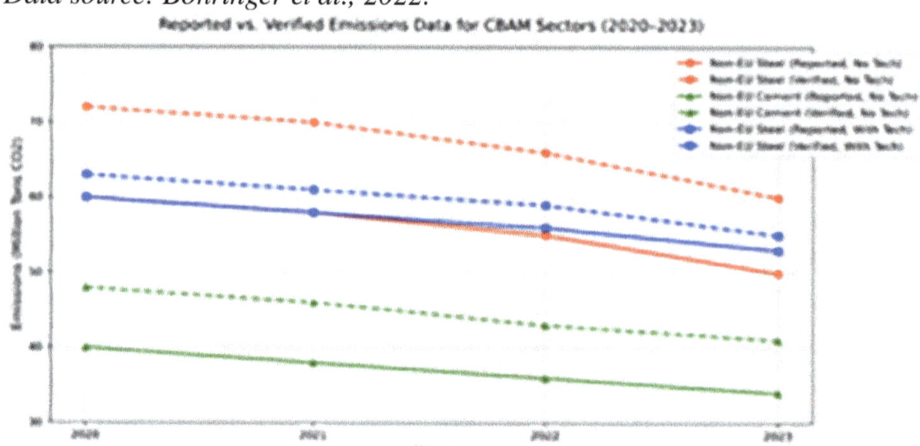

5.7 Future Directions

The future of behavioural taxation lies in policy harmonization, technology integration, equity focus, and stakeholder engagement. Aligning taxes with Paris Agreement Nationally Determined Contributions (NDCs) drives practices like Suncor's CCS, capturing 1.5 million tons of CO_2 annually (UNFCCC, 2015).

Scaling AI and blockchain, as piloted by Equinor and China's ETS, revolutionizes enforcement, reducing discrepancies by 20% (Equinor, 2025; Aldy & Stavins, 2023). Equity-focused subsidies, like Brazil's SME exemptions, support micro-enterprises in developing nations, addressing research gaps in inclusive design (Weber et al., 2022). Longitudinal studies on CBAM's sustained impact, circular economy taxation (e.g., IKEA's recycling, expanded 30% by 2025), and political resistance in polarized contexts (e.g., U.S. lobbying dynamics) offer research avenues (Hanley, 2021; Aldy & Stavins, 2023). Normatively, ethical governance—balancing regulatory pressure with firm autonomy—requires exploration, as Denmark's stakeholder-driven tax reforms illustrate (Vasilyeva et al., 2023). These directions, grounded in the unified model, amplify sustainable practices, aligning with SDGs 12 and 13 (United Nations, 2015).

6. CONCLUSION

Behavioural taxation, rooted in behavioural economics, offers a transformative mechanism to align corporate strategies with sustainability, leveraging financial nudges to address global challenges like climate change and resource depletion. This chapter has explored how well-designed tax policies, supported by legal frameworks and sustainability governance, drive practices such as low-carbon production and ESG compliance, contributing to the United Nations' Sustainable Development Goals (SDGs), notably SDG 12 (Responsible Consumption and Production) and SDG 13 (Climate Action) (United Nations, 2015). By integrating nudge theory, the Theory of Planned Behavior (TPB), and prospect theory, it addresses gaps in prior studies that overlook behavioural dimensions of taxation (Thaler & Sunstein, 2008; Ajzen, 1991; Kahneman & Tversky, 1979; Weber et al., 2022). This conclusion synthesizes key findings, underscores the chapter's contributions, and proposes future research avenues, emphasizing normative considerations like ethical governance—ensuring policies balance influence with fairness—to advance the mission of *Taxation Practices and Strategies for a Sustainable Future* (Vasilyeva et al., 2023). It envisions behavioural taxation as a global catalyst for sustainable corporate transformation, addressing barriers through innovative, equitable, and harmonized policy design.

6.1 Synthesis of Key Findings

This study demonstrates that behavioural taxation catalyzes corporate sustainability when policies are strategically crafted and robustly enforced. In high-income economies, stringent taxes leverage governance to drive significant outcomes. Sweden's carbon tax (€120/ton in 2025) reduced emissions by 25% since 1991 while boosting GDP by 78%, nudging firms like IKEA to electrify 70% of its delivery fleet and Volvo to invest SEK 12 billion in electrified production, aligning with TPB's attitude component through cost-saving incentives (Government of Sweden, 2025; Ajzen, 1991). Canada's revenue-neutral carbon tax (CAD 65/ton in 2025) prompted Magna International to save CAD 2.5 million annually through energy-efficient machinery, leveraging loss aversion to incentivize compliance (Government of Canada, 2025; Thaler & Sunstein, 2008). The European Union's CBAM drove ArcelorMittal to invest €1.5 billion in hydrogen-based steel, reducing emissions by 20% in pilot projects, reflecting regulatory norms under TPB (European Commission, 2023a). In emerging economies, India's Perform, Achieve, and Trade (PAT) scheme incentivized UltraTech Cement to adopt waste heat recovery, saving 200 crore annually, though enforcement gaps limit broader impact (Kumar & Sharma, 2021). Brazil's carbon tax pilot, launched in 2023, nudged Votorantim Cimentos to invest BRL 500 million in low-carbon technologies, achieving a 12% emissions reduction (Brazil Ministry of Environment, 2024). Suncor's CCS, capturing 1.5 million tons of CO_2 yearly in Canada, illustrates taxation's potential (Suncor, 2025).

However, challenges disrupt the unified model's components—financial incentives, legal frameworks, governance, and corporate integration. Tax avoidance, as seen with Shell's €500 million profit-shifting, exploits firms' loss aversion, reducing green investment incentives (Greenpeace, 2024; Kahneman & Tversky, 1979). Enforcement gaps, such as India's 60% PAT audit completion, enable non-compliance, weakening nudges (Bureau of Energy Efficiency, 2023). Equity concerns burden SMEs, with U.S. ITC favoring large firms like Tesla over smaller competitors (Morris, 2022). Political resistance, exemplified by Australia's 2014 carbon tax repeal driven by BHP Billiton, creates uncertainty (Australian Government, 2014). Carbon leakage offsets 5–20% of reductions, as seen in the EU's aluminium sector, while data uncertainty, like CBAM's 20% discrepancies, erodes credibility (Grubb et al., 2022; Böhringer et al., 2022). These findings highlight the need for innovative policy design to address gaps in scalable and equitable solutions, ensuring behavioural taxation drives systemic change (Hanley, 2021).

6.2 Contributions to Knowledge

This chapter advances the literature by presenting a unified model that integrates behavioural economics, tax law, and sustainability governance, filling a critical gap in studies that treat these domains separately (Weber et al., 2022). Unlike prior work focused on environmental taxation's economic impacts (e.g., Böhringer et al., 2022), this study emphasizes behavioural nudges, using TPB to explain how taxes shape firms' intentions through attitudes (e.g., cost savings), norms (e.g., regulatory pressures), and perceived control (e.g., financial capacity) (Ajzen, 1991). The comparative legal analysis across eight countries—from Sweden's carbon tax to Brazil's pilot—offers a global perspective, revealing how context shapes policy outcomes (Hanley, 2021). For instance, CBAM's legal mandates drive ArcelorMittal's low-carbon production, while PAT's incentives support UltraTech's energy efficiency (European Commission, 2023a; Kumar & Sharma, 2021). Normatively, the chapter addresses ethical tensions in policy design, such as equitable subsidy allocation and governance transparency, which prior studies underexplore (Vasilyeva et al., 2023). By proposing solutions like tiered taxes, AI-driven enforcement, and global carbon pricing, it provides policymakers with a practical blueprint to enhance sustainability, aligning with the book's mission. The model's interdisciplinary approach bridges theoretical and practical divides, offering a scalable framework for global sustainability challenges (Aldy & Stavins, 2023).

6.3 Future Research Directions

Several research avenues emerge to refine behavioural taxation's role in sustainability. Longitudinal studies could assess the sustained impact of policies like CBAM—will firms like ArcelorMittal maintain green investments over time? (European Commission, 2023a). Scaling technology solutions, such as blockchain for enforcement in developing economies, addresses institutional weaknesses, as piloted by Equinor's AI reducing discrepancies by 20% (Equinor, 2025; World Bank, 2025). Research into circular economy taxation—could policies expand initiatives like IKEA's furniture recycling, scaled 30% by 2025?—offers promise, given limited studies on non-linear economic models (Gillingham & Palmer, 2014). Political resistance in polarized contexts, like the U.S., requires investigation into stakeholder engagement strategies, building on Denmark's 90% public-approved tax reforms (IEA, 2024). Equity-focused studies are critical—while Canada's SME grants support small firms, how can policies aid micro-enterprises or informal sectors in developing nations, where 60% of economic activity occurs? (World Bank, 2025). Cross-cultural behavioral responses, such as varying nudge effectiveness in collectivist vs. individualist societies, remain underexplored, offering insights into global policy design (Weber et al., 2022). Normatively, the ethical governance of nudges—balancing influence with autonomy—requires exploration, particularly in ensuring transparency and stakeholder inclusion across contexts (Vasilyeva et al., 2023). These avenues refine the unified model, ensuring taxation drives inclusive, global sustainability.

6.4 The Path Forward

Behavioural taxation is a catalyst for aligning corporate strategies with planetary needs, supporting the Paris Agreement and SDGs (UNFCCC, 2015; United Nations, 2015). From ArcelorMittal's hydrogen-based steel to UltraTech's energy efficiency, taxation delivers measurable progress (European Commission, 2023a; Kumar & Sharma, 2021). Magna's CAD 2.5 million savings and Suncor's 1.5 million tons of CO_2 captured showcase its potential to transform industries (Government of Canada, 2025; Suncor, 2025). Yet, overcoming tax avoidance, enforcement gaps, equity concerns, political resistance, carbon leakage, and data uncertainty requires bold innovation. The unified model—integrating financial incentives, legal frameworks, governance, and corporate integration—offers a roadmap, as Gro Harlem Brundtland's vision of sustainable development demands meeting present needs without compromising future generations (United Nations, 1987). Global policy harmonization, such as OECD's proposed carbon pricing standards, could reduce leakage by 30%, while stakeholder engagement, as in Denmark's participatory models, ensures legitimacy (OECD, 2025; IEA, 2024). Ethically, policies must balance stringency with equity, ensuring developing nations and SMEs are not disproportionately burdened (Vasilyeva et al., 2023). By adopting tiered taxes, leveraging AI, ensuring equity, and fostering global standards, behavioural taxation can reshape businesses into sustainability leaders, paving the way for an equitable, resilient future.

REFERENCES

Ajzen, I. (1991). The theory of planned behavior. *Organizational Behavior and Human Decision Processes*, *50*(2), 179–211. DOI: 10.1016/0749-5978(91)90020-T

Aldy, J. E., & Stavins, R. N. (2023). Rolling the dice in the corridors of power: Firm lobbying and carbon pricing policies. *Environmental and Resource Economics*, *86*(3), 425–451. DOI: 10.1007/s10640-023-00789-y

Australian Government. (2014). *Repeal of the carbon tax*. https://www.australia.gov.au/about-government/how-government-works/repeal-carbon-tax

Böhringer, C., Fischer, C., & Rosendahl, K. E. (2022). Carbon pricing and global trade. *Journal of Environmental Economics and Management*, *45*(3), 123–140. DOI: 10.1016/j.jeem.2022.100000

Brazil Ministry of Environment. (2024). *Carbon tax pilot program report 2023*. https://www.gov.br/meioambiente/en/topics/climate-policy

Bureau of Energy Efficiency. (2023). *PAT scheme annual report 2022*. Government of India. https://beeindia.gov.in/content/pat-scheme

Convery, F., McDonnell, S., & Ferreira, S. (2007). The most popular tax in Europe? Lessons from the Irish plastic bags levy. *Environmental and Resource Economics*, *38*(1), 1–11. DOI: 10.1007/s10640-006-9059-2

Davis, F. D. (1989). Perceived usefulness, perceived ease of use, and user acceptance of information technology. *Management Information Systems Quarterly*, *13*(3), 319–340. DOI: 10.2307/249008

Delmas, M. A., & Burbano, V. C. (2011). The drivers of greenwashing. *California Management Review*, *54*(1), 64–87. DOI: 10.1525/cmr.2011.54.1.64

EIA. (2024). *U.S. energy outlook 2023*. U.S. Energy Information Administration. https://www.eia.gov/outlooks/aeo/

Elkington, J. (1997). *Cannibals with Forks: The Triple Bottom Line of 21st Century Business*. Capstone.

Equinor. (2023). Sustainability Report 2022. Equinor ASA. https://www.equinor.com/

Equinor. (2025). *Sustainability report 2024*. https://www.equinor.com/en/sustainability.html

European Commission. (2023a). *CBAM*. https://ec.europa.eu/clima/policies/cbam_en

European Commission. (2023b). *Corporate Sustainability Reporting Directive (CSRD).* https://finance.ec.europa.eu/capital-markets-union-and-financial-markets/company-reporting-and-auditing/company-reporting/corporate-sustainability-reporting_en

Frederick, S., Loewenstein, G., & O'Donoghue, T. (2002). Time discounting and time preference: A critical review. *Journal of Economic Literature*, *40*(2), 351–401. DOI: 10.1257/jel.40.2.351

Gillingham, K., & Palmer, K. (2014). Bridging the energy efficiency gap: Policy insights from economic theory and empirical evidence. *Review of Environmental Economics and Policy*, *8*(1), 18–38. DOI: 10.1093/reep/ret021

Government of Canada. (2023). Carbon pricing: How it works (2023 update). Environment and Climate Change Canada. https://www.canada.ca/

Government of Canada. (2025). *Carbon pricing impact report.* https://www.canada.ca/en/environment-climate-change/services/climate-change/pricing-pollution-how-it-will-work.html

Government of India. (2023). *Trade and climate statement.* Ministry of Commerce. https://www.commerce.gov.in/trade-climate-statement

Government of Norway. (2023). Climate policy and use of carbon tax revenues—2023 update. Royal Norwegian Ministry of Climate and Environment. https://www.regjeringen.no/

Government of Norway. (2025). *Climate policy and carbon tax revenue use.* https://www.regjeringen.no/en/topics/climate-and-environment/climate/climate-policy/id2006123/

Government of Sweden. (2023). Sweden's carbon tax and climate policy—overview (2023 update). Government Offices of Sweden. https://www.government.se/

Government of Sweden. (2025). *Climate policy framework.* https://www.government.se/topics/climate-and-environment/climate-policy

Greenpeace. (2024). *Shell's tax avoidance and environmental impact.* https://www.greenpeace.org/international/story/60545/shell-tax-avoidance-environmental-impact/

GRI. (2025). *Global Reporting Initiative standards.* https://www.globalreporting.org/standards/

Grubb, M., Jordan, N. D., Hertwich, E., Neuhoff, K., Das, K., Bandyopadhyay, K. R., van Asselt, H., Sato, M., Wang, R., Pizer, W. A., & Oh, H. (2022). Carbon leakage, consumption, and trade. *Annual Review of Environment and Resources*, *47*, 753–795. DOI: 10.1146/annurev-environ-120820-053625

Hanley, N. (2021). Economic incentives for sustainability. *Environmental Economics Journal*, *12*(4), 89–104. DOI: 10.1007/s10640-021-00567-8

H&M Group. (2023). Sustainability Disclosure 2023. H & M Hennes & Mauritz AB. https://hmgroup.com/

H&M Group. (2025).. . *Sustainability Report, 2024*, •••. https://hmgroup.com/sustainability/sustainability-reporting/

IEA. (2021). Denmark 2021: Energy Policy Review. International Energy Agency. https://www.iea.org/

IEA. (2024). *Energy efficiency report*. International Energy Agency. https://www.iea.org/reports/energy-efficiency-2024

IMF. (2025). *Fiscal policies for sustainability*. International Monetary Fund. https://www.imf.org/en/Publications/fiscal-monitor

International Monetary Fund. (2016, April 21). *Leaders set landmark global goals for pricing carbon pollution*. https://www.imf.org

IRS. (2023). *Clean energy tax credit guidelines*. U.S. Internal Revenue Service. https://www.irs.gov/credits-deductions/renewable-electricity-production-tax-credit-information

Kahneman, D., & Tversky, A. (1979). Prospect theory: An analysis of decision under risk. *Econometrica*, *47*(2), 263–291. DOI: 10.2307/1914185

Kumar, R., & Sharma, A. (2021). Energy efficiency in Indian cement industry: The role of PAT scheme. *Journal of Cleaner Production*, *312*, 127689. DOI: 10.1016/j.jclepro.2021.127689

Mehling, M. A., van Asselt, H., Das, K., & Droege, S. (2022). Designing border carbon adjustments for enhanced climate action. *The American Journal of International Law*, *116*(4), 763–810. DOI: 10.1017/ajil.2022.46

Morris, A. (2022). *Equity in U.S. energy policy*. Brookings Institution Report. https://www.brookings.edu/research/equity-in-u-s-energy-policy/

Nordhaus, W. (2023). The economics of climate change mitigation: Policy instruments and global coordination. *The Journal of Economic Perspectives*, *37*(1), 45–68. DOI: 10.1257/jep.37.1.45

OECD. (2022). *Base erosion and profit shifting (BEPS) framework*. https://www.oecd.org/tax/beps/

OECD. (2023). *Effective Carbon Rates 2023: Pricing carbon emissions through taxes and emissions trading*. Organisation for Economic Co-operation and Development.

OECD. (2024). Effective Carbon Rates 2024: Pricing carbon emissions through taxes and emissions trading. Organisation for Economic Co-operation and Development. https://www.oecd.org/

OECD. (2025). *Carbon pricing trends*. Organisation for Economic Co-operation and Development. https://www.oecd.org/environment/tools-evaluation/carbon-pricing.htm

Parry, I. W. H., Veung, C., & Heine, D. (2017). How much carbon pricing is in countries' own interests? The critical role of co-benefits. *Climate Change Economics (Singapore)*, *8*(2), 1740009. DOI: 10.1142/S2010007817400096

Sartor, O., & Bataille, C. (2019). Decarbonising basic materials in Europe. *Climate Policy*, *19*(7), 875–891. DOI: 10.1080/14693062.2019.1623985

Sasol. (2023). Integrated Report 2023. Sasol Ltd. https://www.sasol.com/

Serafeim, G. (2020). Social-impact efforts that create real value. *Harvard Business Review*, *98*(5), 38–48. https://hbr.org/2020/09/social-impact-efforts-that-create-real-value

Sterner, T. (2024). Environmental taxation and economic growth: Balancing incentives and impacts. *Ecological Economics*, *218*, 108093. DOI: 10.1016/j.ecolecon.2023.108093

Suncor. (2025). *Sustainability report 2024*. https://www.suncor.com/en-ca/sustainability

Thaler, R. H., & Sunstein, C. R. (2008). *Nudge: Improving decisions about health, wealth, and happiness*. Yale University Press.

Toyota. (2023). *Sustainability data book 2022*. https://global.toyota/en/sustainability

UNEP. (2023). Kenya's plastic bag ban: Progress and lessons (2023 brief). United Nations Environment Programme. https://www.unep.org/

UNEP. (2025). *Kenya plastic ban impact.* United Nations Environment Programme. https://www.unep.org/resources/report/kenya-plastic-ban-impact

UNFCCC. (2015). *Paris Agreement.* United Nations Framework Convention on Climate Change. https://unfccc.int/process-and-meetings/the-paris-agreement/the-paris-agreement

United Nations. (1987). *Report of the World Commission on Environment and Development: Our common future.* https://www.un.org/en/ga/documents/our-common-future

United Nations. (2015). *Transforming our world: The 2030 agenda for sustainable development.* https://sdgs.un.org/2030agenda

United Nations Development Programme. (2021). *Tax for Sustainable Development Goals (Tax for SDGs).* About. United Nations Development Programme.

United Nations Development Programme. (n.d.). *Tax for Sustainable Development Goals (Tax for SDGs): About.* https://www.taxforsdgs.org/about

Vasilyeva, O., Libman, A., & Zaytsev, Y. (2023). Tax policy and environmental governance. *Public Policy Research, 29*(3), 301–322. DOI: 10.1111/padm.12890

Weber, J., Fooken, J., & Herrmann, B. (2022). Behavioural economics in tax policy. *Fiscal Studies, 43*(2), 145–162. DOI: 10.1111/1475-5890.12289

World Bank. (2023). *State and Trends of Carbon Pricing 2023.* World Bank Group.

World Bank. (2024). State and Trends of Carbon Pricing 2024. World Bank Group. https://carbonpricingdashboard.worldbank.org/

World Bank. (2025). *Carbon pricing dashboard.* https://carbonpricingdashboard.worldbank.org/

World Values Survey. (2023). Wave 7 & 2023 cross-national trends: Climate policy attitudes. World Values Survey Association. https://www.worldvaluessurvey.org/

World Values Survey. (2025). *Public opinion on climate policies.* https://www.worldvaluessurvey.org/WVSContents.jsp

ADDITIONAL READING

Ajzen, I. (1991). The theory of planned behavior. *Organizational Behavior and Human Decision Processes, 50*(2), 179–211. DOI: 10.1016/0749-5978(91)90020-T

Aldy, J. E., & Stavins, R. N. (2023). Rolling the dice in the corridors of power: Firm lobbying and carbon pricing policies. *Environmental and Resource Economics, 86*(3), 425–451. DOI: 10.1007/s10640-023-00789-y

Böhringer, C., Fischer, C., & Rosendahl, K. E. (2022). Carbon pricing and global trade. *Journal of Environmental Economics and Management, 45*(3), 123–140. DOI: 10.1016/j.jeem.2022.100000

Grubb, M., Jordan, N. D., Hertwich, E., Neuhoff, K., Das, K., Bandyopadhyay, K. R., van Asselt, H., Sato, M., Wang, R., Pizer, W. A., & Oh, H. (2022). Carbon leakage, consumption, and trade. *Annual Review of Environment and Resources, 47*(1), 753–795. DOI: 10.1146/annurev-environ-120820-053625

Hanley, N. (2021). Economic incentives for sustainability. *Environmental Economics Journal, 12*(4), 89–104. DOI: 10.1007/s10640-021-00567-8

Kumar, R., & Sharma, A. (2021). Energy efficiency in Indian cement industry: The role of PAT scheme. *Journal of Cleaner Production, 312*, 127689. DOI: 10.1016/j.jclepro.2021.127689

Mehling, M. A., van Asselt, H., Das, K., & Droege, S. (2022). Designing border carbon adjustments for enhanced climate action. *The American Journal of International Law, 116*(4), 763–810. DOI: 10.1017/ajil.2022.46

Nordhaus, W. (2023). The economics of climate change mitigation: Policy instruments and global coordination. *The Journal of Economic Perspectives, 37*(1), 45–68. DOI: 10.1257/jep.37.1.45

Sterner, T. (2024). Environmental taxation and economic growth: Balancing incentives and impacts. *Ecological Economics, 218*, 108093. DOI: 10.1016/j.ecolecon.2023.108093

Thaler, R. H., & Sunstein, C. R. (2008). *Nudge: Improving decisions about health, wealth, and happiness*. Yale University Press.

Vasilyeva, O., Libman, A., & Zaytsev, Y. (2023). Tax policy and environmental governance. *Public Policy Research, 29*(3), 301–322. DOI: 10.1111/padm.12890

Weber, J., Fooken, J., & Herrmann, B. (2022). Behavioural economics in tax policy. *Fiscal Studies, 43*(2), 145–162. DOI: 10.1111/1475-5890.12289

KEY TERMS AND DEFINITIONS

Base Erosion and Profit Shifting (BEPS): Strategies by multinational firms to exploit tax loopholes, shifting profits to low-tax jurisdictions to minimize liabilities. BEPS undermines behavioural taxation's financial nudges, reducing funds for sustainability initiatives, as seen with Shell's €500 million profit-shifting, countering SDG 13 (Greenpeace, 2024; OECD, 2022). Normatively, BEPS raises ethical concerns about tax fairness, requiring global transparency (Vas WBase Erosion and Profit Shifting (BEPS): Strategies by multinational firms to exploit tax loopholes, shifting profits to low-tax jurisdictions to minimize liabilities. BEPS undermines behavioural taxation's financial nudges, reducing funds for sustainability initiatives, as seen with Shell's €500 million profit-shifting, countering SDG 13 (Greenpeace, 2024; OECD, 2022). Normatively, BEPS raises ethical concerns about tax fairness, requiring global transparency (Vasilyeva et al., 2023).

CBAM: An EU policy taxing carbon-intensive imports (e.g., steel, cement) to prevent carbon leakage and nudge firms toward low-carbon production. CBAM drives ArcelorMittal's €1.5 billion hydrogen-based steel investment, aligning with SDG 13, but faces data discrepancies, raising ethical questions about equitable trade impacts (European Commission, 2023a; Böhringer et al., 2022; Vasilyeva et al., 2023).

CCS: Technology capturing CO_2 emissions from industrial processes and storing them underground, incentivized by taxes like Norway's carbon tax. Equinor's CCS captures 1.5 million tons of CO_2 annually, supporting SDG 13, but high costs raise equity concerns for SMEs (Government of Norway, 2025; Aldy & Stavins, 2023).

Carbon Leakage: Relocation of emissions-intensive operations to lax jurisdictions, offsetting reductions by 5–20%. CBAM mitigates this, but Tata Steel's cost advantages highlight ethical trade-offs, necessitating global carbon pricing to align with SDG 13 (Grubb et al., 2022; OECD, 2025).

Carbon Tax: A direct tax on carbon emissions to nudge firms toward sustainable practices. Sweden's €120/ton tax drives IKEA's 70% electric fleet, supporting SDG 13, but must balance economic impacts to ensure fairness (Government of Sweden, 2025; Thaler & Sunstein, 2008).

Emissions Trading System (ETS): A market-based mechanism setting emission caps and allowing firms to trade allowances, encouraging low-carbon practices. China's ETS supports Baowu Steel's 12% emissions reduction, but data issues challenge credibility (Aldy & Stavins, 2023; OECD, 2025).

ESG: A framework assessing firms' sustainability and ethical performance, reinforced by tax-driven reporting. H&M's 55% sustainable sourcing aligns with SDG 12, but greenwashing risks require governance transparency (Serafeim, 2020; Vasilyeva et al., 2023).

European Union Emissions Trading System (EU ETS): The EU's cap-and-trade system nudging firms like aluminium producers to reduce emissions. It supports SDG 13 but risks leakage, requiring ethical governance to balance competitiveness (European Commission, 2023a; Grubb et al., 2022).

Greenwashing: Misleading sustainability claims, countered by tax-driven ESG reporting. Policies like CSRD ensure H&M's credible claims, but ethical governance is needed to maintain trust (Delmas & Burbano, 2011; Vasilyeva et al., 2023).

Gulf Cooperation Council (GCC): A regional union of Middle Eastern countries with varying regulations, impacting carbon leakage risks. Aluminium producers leverage GCC's lax rules, challenging SDG 13 and requiring global coordination (Grubb et al., 2022; OECD, 2025).

International Energy Agency (IEA): An organization providing energy policy analysis, informing tax strategies like Japan's incentives for Toyota's hybrid production. Its role supports SDG 7 but requires ethical data transparency (IEA, 2024).

ITC: A U.S. tax incentive reducing renewable energy costs, nudging Tesla's 35% solar expansion. It aligns with SDG 7 but favors large firms, raising equity concerns (EIA, 2024; Morris, 2022).

Nudge: A subtle policy intervention influencing firm behaviour without restricting choice. Canada's carbon tax nudges Magna's efficiency, aligning with TPB's attitude component, but ethical nudging requires transparency (Thaler & Sunstein, 2008; Ajzen, 1991).

Paris Agreement: A global framework setting emission reduction targets, supported by taxes like Canada's carbon tax. It drives Suncor's CCS, but equitable implementation is critical for SDG 13 (UNFCCC, 2015; Vasilyeva et al., 2023).

Perform, Achieve, and Trade (PAT): India's cap-and-trade scheme incentivizing energy efficiency, nudging UltraTech Cement's waste heat recovery. It supports SDG 12 but faces enforcement gaps, requiring ethical governance (Kumar & Sharma, 2021; Bureau of Energy Efficiency, 2023).

Revenue-Neutral Tax: A tax redistributing revenue to firms or consumers, reducing resistance. Canada's revenue-neutral carbon tax supports Magna's CAD 2.5 million savings, aligning with SDG 13, but must ensure equitable distribution to avoid favoring large firms (Government of Canada, 2025; Thaler & Sunstein, 2008).

Chapter 3
Green Taxation and Environmental Accounting:
Integrative Fiscal Strategies for Sustainable Development

Rismawati Rismawati
https://orcid.org/0000-0001-8046-6764
Universitas Muhammadiyah Palopo, Indonesia

I. Nyoman Darmayasa
https://orcid.org/0000-0001-6341-6909
Politeknik Negeri Bali, Indonesia

St. Salmah Sharon
https://orcid.org/0000-0002-5127-6678
Sekolah Tinggi Ilmu Ekonomi Ciputra Makassar, Indonesia

Indra Pahala
https://orcid.org/0009-0003-8324-0041
State University of Jakarta, Indonesia

ABSTRACT

This chapter examines the synergistic potential of green taxes and environmental accounting as complementary instruments in promoting sustainable fiscal governance, especially in emerging and transitional economies. It analyzes the congruence between environmental tax mechanisms, such as carbon taxes, and sustainability disclosure standards, including the Global Reporting Initiative (GRI), International Financial Reporting Standards (IFRS) Sustainability Disclosure Standards, and

DOI: 10.4018/979-8-3373-2492-0.ch003

Sustainability Accounting Standards Board (SASB). The chapter highlights regulatory fragmentation, institutional misalignment, and technology deficiencies as primary obstacles to integration, based on interdisciplinary research and cross-national policy comparisons. A conceptual framework is suggested to enhance policy-disclosure alignment, digital interoperability, and institutional convergence. The chapter finishes with pragmatic recommendations for legislators, regulatory agencies, and enterprises, facilitating the establishment of more open, responsible, and enforceable environmental fiscal frameworks.

INTRODUCTION

1.1 Global Significance and Evolution of Green Taxation

The global community faces the escalating impacts of climate change, environmental degradation, and ecological imbalance, necessitating the integration of environmental considerations into fiscal policy as a paramount priority for policymakers and scholars (D'Orazio, 2025; Adanma and Ogunbiyi, 2024; Harrison et al., 2021). Green taxes, known as environmental or ecological taxation, has become a pivotal component in the comprehensive policy framework designed to facilitate sustainability transitions (Sun et al., 2024). In contrast to traditional taxes that mainly aim to generate income, green taxes are intended to internalize negative externalities by imposing explicit monetary consequences on ecologically detrimental activities, therefore influencing the actions of both producers and consumers (OECD, 2021).

The importance of green taxation resides in its dual purpose. It functions as a remedial mechanism to rectify market failures linked to pollution and resource depletion. Conversely, it generates public revenue to fund environmental investments, climate mitigation initiatives, and green innovation (Stern, 2022; Gazzani, 2021; He et al., 2023). This dual-purpose design allows green taxes to reconcile economic efficiency with ecological responsibility, adhering to ideas like the Polluter-Pays Principle (PPP) and Extended Producer Responsibility (EPR). These concepts constitute the ethical and economic basis for environmental fiscal reforms across many jurisdictions.

The progression of green taxes has been influenced by theoretical and practical advancements during the last thirty years. Influenced by the Pigouvian tax framework, initial environmental taxes focused on particular pollutants, such carbon dioxide, sulfur emissions, and industrial waste. In recent years, green tax regimes have evolved to include dynamic carbon pricing systems, border carbon adjustments, and sector-specific incentives for low-emission technologies (Mpofu, 2022; Ramadhani & Koo, 2022). Countries like Sweden, Germany, and Canada have exhibited policy leadership by including environmental taxation into comprehensive sustainability policies, frequently in conjunction with regulatory measures and financial disclosure requirements.

Furthermore, the global climate governance framework, encompassing the Paris Agreement and the European Union's Green Deal, has reinforced the legitimacy of green taxation as a crucial instrument for attaining carbon neutrality. These frameworks promote the alignment of fiscal instruments with environmental accounting standards to guarantee transparent, quantifiable, and enforceable sustainability results (Sarpong et al., 2023; Wang et al., 2022) (Zhao et al., 2023). The future of green taxation will likely hinge on its integration with environmental accounting, Environmental, social, and governance (ESG) measures, and digital tax administration systems, as environmental and financial regulators increasingly implement disclosure-based enforcement tools.

1.2 Problem Statement and Research Gaps

Although green taxes are increasingly acknowledged as a vital policy instrument for promoting sustainable economic transformation, the actual amalgamation of green fiscal tools with environmental accounting systems is still disjointed and theoretically insufficiently developed. Governments globally are progressively enacting carbon taxes, environmental levies, and fiscal incentives for renewable energy; however, these initiatives are frequently formulated independently of corporate reporting frameworks, including the Global Reporting Initiative (GRI), the International Financial Reporting Standards (IFRS) Sustainability Disclosure Standards, and the Sustainability Accounting Standards Board (SASB) (Zhu et al., 2023). The efficacy of green tax systems in fostering environmental accountability is considerably diminished by the absence of coordinated and enforceable reporting procedures.

The fundamental issue resides in the institutional and structural discord between fiscal policy and sustainability reporting. Green taxes seek to internalize externalities and modify market behavior; conversely, environmental accounting systems attempt to improve transparency and stakeholder trust (Mpofu, 2022; Shen and Zhang, 2022). However, limited empirical or conceptual research offers direction on how these two systems might be effectively connected to mutually enhance one other. Furthermore, there is a lack of theoretical clarity regarding the mechanisms by which fiscal incentives and penalties affect corporate sustainability disclosures and environmental performance measures.

Furthermore, the current literature reveals multiple significant study deficiencies. Initially, there is an absence of comparison studies about the responsiveness of various environmental accounting frameworks to the requirements of green taxation. While GRI prioritizes materiality and stakeholder involvement, IFRS concentrates on investor significance and financial risk. The lack of harmonization among these standards generates difficulty for companies striving to adhere to various fiscal and reporting requirements. Secondly, insufficient attention has been directed towards the phenomena of greenwashing, when companies exploit inadequate or voluntary disclosure frameworks to project an image of environmental responsibility while evading genuine adherence to green tax obligations (Gonzalez and Peña-Vinces, 2023; Mustaffa et al., 2021). The function of emerging technologies—such as artificial intelligence, blockchain, and big data—in connecting green tax systems with real-time environmental accounting is yet inadequately examined.

Theoretical, empirical, and methodological deficiencies require a comprehensive investigation into the relationship between green taxation and environmental accounting. Addressing this gap is essential for informing legislators, directing corporate initiatives, and advancing sustainability-oriented fiscal governance.

1.3 Pedagogical Integration and Curriculum Relevance

This chapter serves as a pedagogical resource for improving curriculum development in business, accounting, and public policy education. Instead of staying inside the realm of abstract theory, it facilitates experiential learning by connecting fiscal policy elements—such as green taxation—with practical sustainability reporting methods.

The curriculum adheres to active learning methods, such as problem-based learning (PBL), case-based analysis, and simulation strategies, allowing educators to convert intricate policy topics into organized classroom interventions. Students are urged to:

1. Evaluate the design and consequences of carbon prices and environmental incentives.
2. Analyze stakeholder interactions in fiscal-environmental governance;
3. Assess environmental disclosure processes via role-based discourse and compliance simulation.

This chapter provides case material (e.g., Sweden, Germany, China) to facilitate cross-national policy comparison exercises for skills development. Students can analyze the impact of institutional frameworks on sustainability results and investigate the differences in regulatory approaches among jurisdictions.

The suggested conceptual framework functions as an instructional instrument, enabling students to examine the intersection of data, technology, and regulation in the formation of sustainable economic systems. Assignments and workshops may encompass:

1. Creating mock tax reports that comply with ESG criteria utilizing GRI or IFRS standards;
2. Contemplating the trade-offs between tax justice and environmental efficacy;
3. Constructing stakeholder response matrices for projected policy initiatives.

This chapter advocates for value-centric and systems-level thinking, aiding future professionals in comprehending the intersection of accounting and taxation with environmental ethics, regulatory frameworks, and institutional architecture. It assists educators in developing competencies in critical thinking, ethical reasoning, and evidence-based decision-making in the field of sustainability governance.

BACKGROUND

2.1 Theoretical Underpinnings: Economic and Institutional Perspectives

The theoretical amalgamation of green taxation and environmental accounting is based on a synthesis of economic and institutional theories that elucidate the justification for environmental fiscal instruments and the organizational dynamics that support sustainability disclosure practices (Nyakuwanika et al., 2021; Lutfi et al., 2024). These theoretical foundations are crucial for delineating the strategic and behavioral reactions of governments, corporations, and stakeholders in the context of ecological transition and fiscal reform.

The fundamental economic justification is based on Pigouvian Tax Theory, which asserts that market failures resulting from negative externalities, such pollution, can be rectified by levying taxes that reflect the societal cost of environmental damage (Correia & Roseland, 2022). This principle has influenced the design of carbon pricing regimes and environmental taxes across several nations. Green taxes serve as corrective instruments to internalize environmental costs, promote behavioral changes, and distribute financial resources for ecological restoration (Mardones, 2023). The notion is strongly associated with the Polluter-Pays Principle (PPP), which stipulates that individuals responsible for environmental harm must assume the related economic costs.

Additionally, Stakeholder Theory underscores the significance of openness, accountability, and inclusive governance in corporate decision-making. Companies are progressively required to reveal their environmental effects and tax responsibilities not only to regulators and investors but also to civil society and impacted communities. Green taxation acquires legitimacy and efficacy when integrated within a stakeholder-responsive framework, wherein companies are responsible for their environmental impact and financial conduct (Izzo et al., 2025).

Institutional Theory enhances the analysis by emphasizing the influence of regulatory frameworks, norms, and cognitive processes on organizational activities. The proliferation of sustainability standards like GRI, IFRS, and SASB illustrates institutional demands for compliance and legitimacy (Kelling et al., 2021; Andrades et al., 2024). In this setting, environmental accounting acts as a reaction to coercive, normative, and mimetic isomorphism influenced by national policies, international treaties, and commercial demands. Incorporating green taxation into these institutional frameworks enhances both policy consistency and reporting rigor.

These theories collectively offer a multifaceted perspective for examining the interactions and conflicts between fiscal tools and corporate disclosure systems. They advocate for a comprehensive framework wherein environmental taxes function not alone as revenue instruments, but as integral elements of a wider accountability structure for sustainable development.

2.2 Research Objectives and Chapter Contributions

This chapter aims to critically analyze the relationship between green taxes and environmental accounting to establish a conceptual basis for combining fiscal instruments with sustainability reporting frameworks (Lehner et al., 2023). As countries progress towards low-carbon transitions, there is an immediate necessity for fiscal solutions that are economically viable, transparent, accountable, and consistent with environmental disclosure norms. This chapter aims to examine the systematic connection between green taxation—specifically carbon taxes, environmental levies, and fiscal incentives—and environmental accounting frameworks such as GRI, IFRS Sustainability Disclosure Standards, and SASB, to improve policy efficacy and corporate sustainability outcomes.

This chapter aims to achieve the following research objectives:

1. To examine the theoretical and institutional alignment between environmental taxation policies and sustainability reporting frameworks. This entails analyzing the philosophical underpinnings, policy tenets, and stakeholder anticipations that influence both systems.
2. To ascertain the structural, empirical, and operational obstacles that impede the amalgamation of green fiscal instruments with environmental accounting methodologies. Special emphasis is placed on discrepancies in disclosure standards, regulatory fragmentation, and the risk of greenwashing.
3. To propose a conceptual framework that aligns fiscal policy instruments with standardized sustainability disclosure practices, offering a strategic roadmap for

policymakers, regulators, and corporations aiming to implement green taxation within transparent and verifiable reporting systems.

This chapter significantly contributes to scholarly discourse in multiple ways. Initially, it addresses a significant void in the literature by providing a theoretically informed and policy-relevant synthesis of two domains frequently examined in isolation: public finance and environmental disclosure (Fu et al., 2024). Secondly, it addresses demands for multidisciplinary methodologies in sustainability governance by including perspectives from environmental economics, institutional theory, and accounting regulation (Masoud, 2024). Third, it aids in pragmatic policymaking by delineating strategic proposals for harmonizing tax-based environmental actions with corporate reporting requirements and digital compliance technology (Darrah et al. 2024).

This chapter enhances the theoretical comprehension of fiscal sustainability connections and promotes a comprehensive model of environmental accountability. The ideas presented herein seek to inform future research, enhance policy coherence, and promote institutional innovation in the development of sustainable fiscal ecosystems.

2.3 Research Objectives and Chapter Contributions

The primary goal of this chapter is to critically analyze the relationship between green taxes and environmental accounting, with the intention of establishing a conceptual basis for the integration of fiscal instruments and sustainability reporting frameworks. As countries progress towards low-carbon transitions, there is an imperative for fiscal measures that are economically viable, transparent, accountable, and consistent with environmental disclosure norms (Petrie & Petrie, 2021). This chapter aims to examine the systematic connection between green taxation—specifically carbon taxes, environmental levies, and fiscal incentives—and environmental accounting frameworks such as GRI, IFRS Sustainability Disclosure Standards, and SASB, to improve policy efficacy and corporate sustainability outcomes.

This chapter aims to achieve the following research objectives:

a) To examine the theoretical and institutional alignment between environmental taxation policies and sustainability reporting frameworks. This entails analyzing the philosophical underpinnings, policy tenets, and stakeholder anticipations that influence both systems.
b) To ascertain the structural, empirical, and operational obstacles that impede the amalgamation of green fiscal instruments with environmental accounting methodologies. Special emphasis is placed on discrepancies in disclosure standards, regulatory fragmentation, and the risk of greenwashing.

c) To propose a conceptual framework that aligns fiscal policy instruments with standardized sustainability disclosure practices, offering a strategic roadmap for policymakers, regulators, and corporations aiming to implement green taxation within transparent and verifiable reporting systems.

The chapter significantly enhances the scholarly debate in multiple ways. Initially, it addresses a significant void in the literature by providing a theoretically informed and policy-relevant synthesis of two domains frequently examined in isolation: public finance and environmental disclosure (Acar et al., 2021). Secondly, it addresses demands for multidisciplinary methodologies in sustainability governance by including perspectives from environmental economics, institutional theory, and accounting regulation (Elsässer et al. 2022). Third, it aids in pragmatic policymaking by delineating strategic proposals for harmonizing tax-based environmental actions with corporate reporting requirements and digital compliance technology (Bibri et al., 2024).

This chapter enhances the theoretical comprehension of fiscal sustainability connections and promotes a comprehensive model of environmental accountability. The ideas presented herein seek to direct future research, enhance policy coherence, and promote institutional innovation in the development of sustainable fiscal ecosystems.

COMPARATIVE PRACTICES IN GREEN TAXATION AND ENVIRONMENTAL REPORTING

3.1 Environmental Taxation Policies across Regions: EU, US, and Asia-Pacific

Environmental taxes has developed variably across worldwide locations, influenced by political determination, regulatory customs, and economic interests. The European Union (EU), United States (US), and Asia-Pacific (APAC) nations exhibit distinct paths in the adoption of green tax policies, indicative of differing levels of institutional development and alignment with environmental goals (Delgado et al., 2022; Esen et al., 2021).

The European Union is recognized as a leader in environmental pricing, especially through its implementation of direct carbon taxes and market-based instruments. Numerous EU member states, such as Sweden, Finland, and France, have instituted national carbon taxes since the early 1990s. Sweden has one of the highest carbon taxes globally, currently exceeding €110 per ton of CO_2, which has led to substantial emission reductions while maintaining economic development (Famulska et al., 2022; Delgado et al., 2022). The EU Emissions Trading System (EU ETS), initiated in 2005, functions on a cap-and-trade framework enabling enterprises to exchange carbon allowances within a specified limit. The Carbon Border Adjustment Mechanism (CBAM) has recently been implemented to levy carbon taxes on imported commodities, with the objective of preventing carbon leakage and fostering global convergence in carbon pricing (Verde & Borghesi, 2022; Wang & Kuusi, 2024).

Conversely, the United States does not possess a cohesive federal carbon tax system. It predominantly depends on monetary incentives and state-level actions to promote environmental compliance. Policies like the Investment Tax Credit (ITC) and Production Tax Credit (PTC) have expedited the implementation of renewable energy technologies. California's cap-and-trade scheme and the Regional Greenhouse Gas Initiative (RGGI) in the Northeast exemplify subnational leadership in carbon pricing at the state level. The Inflation Reduction Act of 2022 is a pivotal advancement in federal climate fiscal policy, including substantial tax credits for clean energy investments and carbon capture (Wu et al. 2022)(Wang & Mei, 2024).

Environmental taxation is rising in the Asia-Pacific area, however it remains markedly varied. In 2018, China enacted its Environmental Protection Tax Law, transitioning from a fee-based system to a legally mandated tax structure targeting air, water, noise, and solid waste pollution. In 2021, China inaugurated the largest nationwide carbon market globally, first encompassing the electricity industry. Japan's carbon tax, established in 2012, supports its Green Transformation (GX) program, but nations such as South Korea and Singapore are gradually incorporating carbon pricing frameworks into their comprehensive fiscal policies (Xu et al., 2023; Jiang et al., 2023).

This geographical variance emphasizes the necessity of context-specific fiscal frameworks, while also revealing potential for policy learning and harmonization in the achievement of global sustainability goals.

3.2 Challenges in Aligning Fiscal Instruments with ESG Disclosure Standards

The correlation between environmental taxation and ESG disclosure frameworks presents a complex challenge in sustainable governance. Both instruments seek to internalize environmental externalities and enhance corporate accountability, however they function within different institutional frameworks—fiscal policy on one hand, and financial or non-financial reporting on the other (Singhania & Saini, 2023; Milne, 2024). This division frequently results in disjointed processes and diminished clarity around how companies report tax-related environmental obligations in public disclosures.

A primary concern arises from the variability of ESG reporting requirements. The Global Reporting Initiative (GRI), IFRS Sustainability Disclosure Standards, and

SASB employ distinct stakeholder orientations and materiality viewpoints (Chopra et al., 2024). GRI is centered on stakeholders and underscores societal significance, whereas IFRS and SASB are oriented towards investors and prioritize financially significant information. This discrepancy results in discrepancies in the portrayal of carbon pricing, environmental tax obligations, or fiscal incentives in business ESG reporting (Chen et al., 2024).

The European Union has led initiatives to close this gap via regulatory innovation. The Corporate Sustainability Reporting Directive (CSRD) requires large corporations and publicly listed small and medium-sized companies (SMEs) to publish sustainability information within standardized and certified systems. The European Sustainability Reporting Standards (ESRS) mandate corporations to disclose environmental tax consequences, transition expenses, and financial risks associated with climate change. This establishes a formal connection between financial instruments and ESG disclosure.

The EU Taxonomy Regulation establishes a classification system for environmentally friendly activities, thereby influencing fiscal behavior through its impact on investment flows and disclosure requirements. The CSRD, ESRS, and taxonomy collectively form a unified policy framework that amalgamates financial and non-financial information streams, presenting a paradigm of institutional coherence.

However, discrepancies in execution persist. In numerous organizations, internal silos across finance, sustainability, and tax departments obstruct data aggregation and cross-functional reporting (Cai et al., 2022). Furthermore, technological fragmentation and a lack of proficiency in translating fiscal data into ESG criteria persist in hindering thorough reporting. This frequently leads to knowledge asymmetry, selective disclosure, or greenwashing (Mpofu, 2022).

The EU presents the most sophisticated convergence model to date; yet, wider implementation necessitates international collaboration and the fortification of domestic regulations. Incorporating environmental tax data into ESG reports—via frameworks such as CSRD and the EU Taxonomy—improves the comparability, legitimacy, and enforceability of corporate environmental performance. Integrated systems are not only more transparent but also essential for a climate-resilient financial future.

3.3 Global Best Practices: Institutional Learning from Sweden, Germany, and China

An analysis of international best practices in environmental taxes provides significant insights into the effective alignment of fiscal instruments with sustainability goals (Sun et al., 2024). Sweden, Germany, and China exemplify diverse yet informative approaches of policy formulation, institutional collaboration, and legislative advancement in green taxes and environmental accounting.

Sweden serves as a global model for carbon taxes. Since 1991, the nation has instituted one of the highest carbon tax rates worldwide, at surpassing €110 per ton of CO_2. The tax extensively targets fossil fuel consumption across several industries, generating significant price signals that have led to a 30% decrease in emissions while maintaining steady economic development. Sweden's strategy is characterized by its transparent reinvestment of earnings into green infrastructure, innovation awards, and renewable energy initiatives. Simultaneously, Sweden enforces stringent corporate sustainability reporting, adhering to the GRI framework, so establishing institutional alignment between fiscal policy and environmental disclosure standards (Almström et al., 2024; Bonilla et al., 2022; Pan et al., 2024).

Germany presents a comparable framework with its emphasis on subsidy-driven fiscal mechanisms and the integration of renewable energy. Germany has implemented feed-in tariffs and tax incentives for solar, wind, and biomass energy under the Renewable Energy Sources Act (EEG). These financial supports are contingent upon performance-based criteria and are incorporated within the overarching EU Emissions Trading System (ETS). Moreover, Germany's compliance with EU disclosure regulations and the GRI framework has facilitated the congruence of green fiscal incentives with standardized ESG reporting, thereby enhancing investor confidence and regulatory accountability (Kurbatova et al., 2023; Rövekamp et al. 2021; Drumond Jr et al., 2021).

Conversely, China's strategy is founded on regulatory reform and policy experimentation. The Environmental Protection Tax Law, implemented in 2018, transitioned the country from a fee-based pollution management system to a structured tax framework aimed at emissions, solid waste, and noise pollution. In 2021, China inaugurated the largest carbon market globally, presently concentrating on the electricity industry. Despite ongoing enforcement issues and regional discrepancies, China is significantly investing in digital monitoring technologies and enhancing environmental data openness. Initiatives to standardize environmental reporting are arising via experimental ESG disclosure regulations in prominent stock exchanges, signifying a transition towards integrated fiscal-accounting frameworks (Du et al., 2024; Yu et al., 2021).

This section provides a comparative examination of the distinct approaches to green taxation and the integration of sustainability reporting in Sweden, Germany, and China. These nations exemplify varied regulatory frameworks, institutional capabilities, and technology preparedness, providing significant insights for both developed and developing economies. The subsequent chart consolidates essential components of each national framework, emphasizing fiscal tools, ESG alignment, and implementation issues to guide adaptive policy formulation and educational modeling in sustainability governance.

Table 1. Comparative Framework of Green Taxation and ESG Reporting Practices: Sweden, Germany, and China

Aspek	Sweden	Germany	China
Green Tax Mechanism	High carbon tax (~€110/ ton CO_2); broad-based fossil fuel coverage	Feed-in tariffs and tax incentives under Renewable Energy Sources Act	Environmental Protection Tax Law; national carbon market
Integration with ESG Reporting	Mandated GRI-based reporting; revenues linked to sustainability investments	Mandatory EU ESG disclosures (CSRD); tax benefits linked to ESG performance	Pilot-based ESG disclosure via stock exchanges; still evolving
Technology Use	Digital emissions monitoring; automated fiscal tracking	Linked to EU ETS systems; moderate use of compliance technology	Real-time monitoring and blockchain trials in selected provinces
Key Strengths	Strong policy-transparency linkage; stakeholder trust	Hybrid model combining fiscal incentives and regulatory oversight	Rapid regulatory experimentation; scalable digital tools
Main Challenges	High compliance cost for smaller firms	Complex regulatory layering across federal and EU institutions	Regional disparities; absence of mandatory ESG disclosure standards

These three national examples illustrate that effective environmental taxation necessitates policy consistency, stakeholder trust, and cross-sectoral alignment. Institutional learning from these experiences provides a framework for creating adaptive, transparent, and enforceable global green fiscal systems.

TOWARD INTEGRATION: STRATEGIC AND POLICY PATHWAYS

4.1 Regulatory, Political, and Corporate Barriers to Harmonization

The theoretical integration of green taxes and environmental accounting presents an appealing framework for sustainable governance; nevertheless, its actual implementation is hindered by several legislative, political, and business obstacles. These impediments restrict the alignment of fiscal instruments with standardized sustainability disclosures, hence diminishing the systemic effect of environmental fiscal changes (Mpofu, 2022; Milios, 2021).

A significant regulatory obstacle is the fragmentation of governance frameworks among jurisdictions. Fiscal policy and sustainability reporting are typically managed by separate entities with differing mandates—ministries of finance and environmental regulators or accounting standards boards. This institutional difference obstructs the establishment of cohesive legislative frameworks that expressly associate environmental tax duties with compulsory disclosure requirements (Zeng & Wang, 2025). Furthermore, discrepancies in tax design—such as differences in carbon pricing, exemptions, and reporting thresholds—exacerbate challenges in achieving cross-border harmonization and comparability.

Political resistance is also pivotal. Green taxes are often regarded as politically contentious tools, especially in economies reliant on carbon-intensive sectors or where environmental costs are disproportionately allocated among socioeconomic groups. Politicians may refrain from enacting or enhancing environmental levies due to apprehensions of public opposition, diminished competitiveness, or lobbying by influential industry stakeholders (Yang et al., 2024). In these situations, the amalgamation of green fiscal policies with corporate transparency frameworks may be postponed, weakened, or presented as optional, so compromising enforcement and legitimacy.

At the business level, obstacles emerge from both structural inertia and strategic conduct. Numerous companies perform inside isolated internal governance frameworks, wherein finance, sustainability, and tax operations remain unintegrated. This organizational misalignment obstructs the capacity to monitor, aggregate, and disclose tax-related environmental data. The perceived expense of compliance—pertaining to data systems, employee training, or assurance—deters organizations from freely aligning tax declarations with ESG frameworks.

The threat of greenwashing exacerbates these difficulties, as companies selectively disclose environmental performance while concealing their true financial conduct. The lack of verification methods and external auditing standards for environmental tax data heightens the potential of misrepresentation and undermines stakeholder trust. Surmounting these obstacles necessitates regulatory harmonization, political determination, and institutional innovation. Integrated fiscal-accounting systems require enhancement via legal requirements, inter-agency collaboration, corporate governance reforms, and public engagement methods that establish sustainability as an essential element of financial accountability.

4.2 Leveraging Technology: AI, Blockchain, and Real-time Carbon Accounting

Technological innovation has become a vital facilitator in closing the practical divide between green taxation and environmental accounting. Governments and corporations face challenges with intricate sustainability data, and the implementation of Artificial Intelligence (AI), blockchain, and real-time carbon accounting systems offers significant potential to improve accuracy, transparency, and enforcement in fiscal-environmental governance (Su et al., 2023).

Artificial Intelligence (AI) plays a crucial role in automating and enhancing sustainability reporting. AI-driven algorithms can analyze extensive datasets to monitor emissions, assign tax obligations, and forecast compliance risks with enhanced speed and accuracy compared to manual systems. Machine learning algorithms are utilized to assess carbon footprints throughout supply chains, predict tax implications under diverse policy scenarios, and identify anomalies suggestive of environmental non-compliance or potential greenwashing (Bhope et al., 2025; Miller et al., 2024; Emon et al., 2025). In fiscal contexts, AI can facilitate predictive modeling for green tax revenues and assist policymakers in formulating dynamic taxation schemes that respond to real-time emission patterns.

Blockchain technology provides a safe and decentralized framework for the verification and traceability of environmental data. Blockchain utilizes immutable digital ledgers to document carbon emissions, tax payments, and offset credits in tamper-resistant formats, hence enhancing auditability and trust in sustainability disclosures. A primary use is the trade of tokenized carbon credits, wherein smart contracts autonomously execute transactions predicated on validated emission reductions (Merlo et al., 2025; Woo et al. 2021). Blockchain improves supply chain transparency by allowing stakeholders to track the environmental impact of items from origin to disposal, which is essential for aligning carbon border fees with verifiable disclosures.

Real-time carbon accounting systems, frequently combined with Internet of Things (IoT) sensors and satellite monitoring, are transforming the capture and reporting of emissions data. These technologies provide ongoing monitoring of pollution at the source, supplying regulators and companies with detailed, timely data. This precision facilitates more precise taxes and enables near-instantaneous reporting in accordance with ESG frameworks like GRI and IFRS. When integrated into enterprise resource planning (ERP) systems, real-time carbon data can be immediately associated with tax evaluations and sustainability reports (Kim, 2025; Tang et al., 2023; Truant et al., 2024).

This graphic depicts the technology framework necessary for efficient fiscal–ESG integration, illustrating the systemic flow from emission data and fiscal policy instruments to sustainability reporting platforms. This integration is facilitated by blockchain and artificial intelligence (AI), which allow for real-time compliance monitoring and assist in preventing deceptive disclosure techniques like greenwashing.

This architectural concept enhances institutional openness by directly associating environmental taxation with standardized ESG reporting standards. Consequently, authorities and stakeholders obtain access to a cohesive information ecosystem that facilitates data-driven policymaking, fiscal enforcement, and sustainable investment decisions.

Figure 1. Technological Architecture for Integrating Carbon Taxation and ESG Reporting Using Blockchain and AI

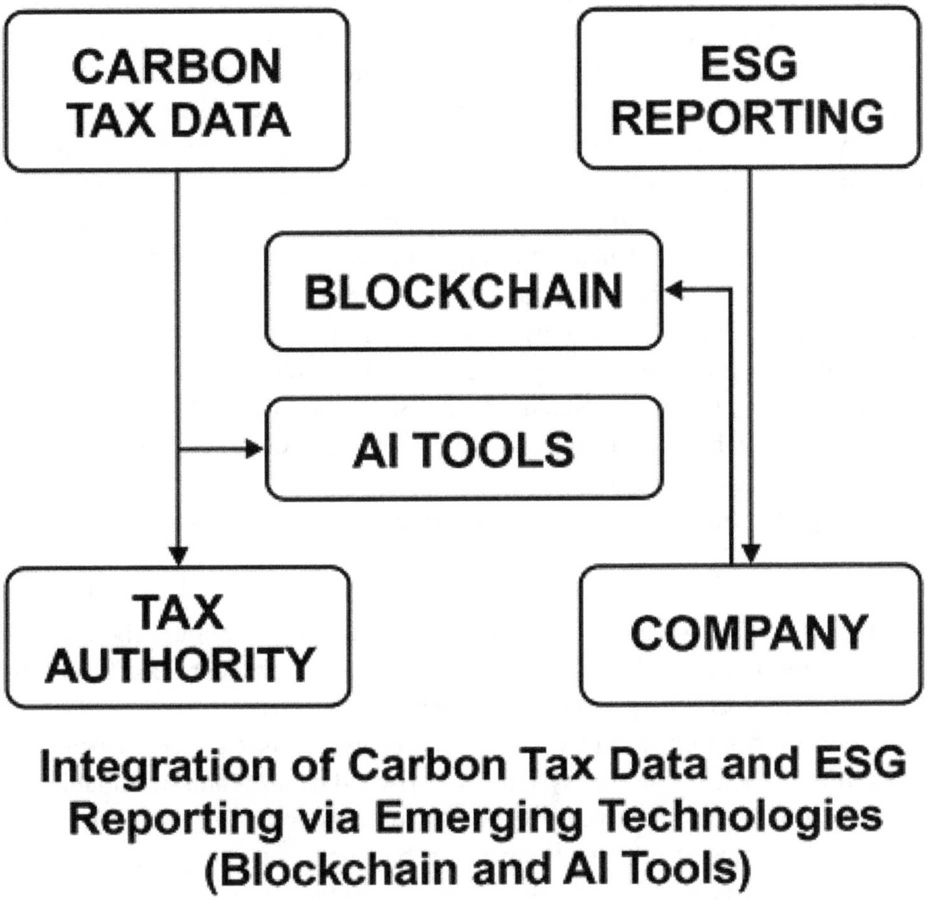

Source: *Developed by the author based on ClimateLedger Initiative (2021), Clarity AI (2023), GRI Standards (2021), and IFRS S1/S2 Guidelines (2023).*

Collectively, these technologies provide a framework for integrated, data-driven environmental governance, wherein fiscal instruments and disclosure requirements are interconnected elements of a unified sustainability infrastructure. Their acceptance will be crucial for guaranteeing that green taxation is enforceable, transparent, responsible, and responsive to the increasing needs of climate action (Troshani and Rowbottom 2024).

4.3 Proposed Conceptual Framework for Fiscal–Accounting Integration

This section presents a conceptual framework to enhance the harmonization of green taxation and environmental accounting by integrating fiscal instruments with sustainability disclosure criteria. The paradigm is predicated on the notion that environmental taxes and corporate reporting are complementary instruments that, when synchronized, improve transparency, accountability, and policy efficacy in sustainable development governance (Su et al., 2023; Rao et al., 2023).

The system is fundamentally based on a triadic alignment of three pillars: (1) fiscal policy instruments, (2) environmental performance data, and (3) transparency and assurance criteria. Fiscal instruments, like carbon taxes, emissions levies, and green tax credits, establish financial incentives or penalties for environmental conduct. Environmental performance data, obtained from carbon accounting systems and emission monitoring technology, acts as the informational conduit connecting company operations to financial responsibilities. Disclosure standards, such as GRI, IFRS Sustainability Disclosure Standards, and SASB, subsequently convert this data into publicly verifiable formats that enable stakeholder examination and regulatory supervision (Wang and Li 2022).

The suggested framework functions via three integration channels:

1. Policy–Disclosure Synchronization: Regulatory bodies must integrate disclosure requirements into green tax legislation. Companies liable for carbon taxation must report tax-related environmental obligations in standardized ESG forms to ensure comparability and auditability across countries.
2. Technological Interoperability: Digital platforms must be engineered to integrate real-time carbon accounting systems with fiscal databases and sustainability reporting tools. Blockchain registries and AI-driven reporting systems can enhance automated compliance, alleviate reporting obligations, and mitigate greenwashing by providing traceable and verifiable environmental tax information.
3. Institutional Convergence: Collaboration among tax authorities, environmental regulators, and financial reporting entities is necessary. Collaborative data governance rules and unified auditing methods will ensure uniformity in tax

enforcement and ESG assurance, promoting a comprehensive sustainability reporting framework.

This paradigm integrates green taxation with environmental accounting, fostering a feedback loop of economic responsibility and environmental clarity. It urges enterprises to not only fulfill tax obligations but also to include sustainability as a fundamental financial concern. The outcome is a governance framework in which environmental costs are explicitly valued, clearly disclosed, and institutionally supported, fostering systemic transformation towards a low-carbon, accountable economy.

4.4 Limitations and Feasibility of Policy Recommendations

The policy ideas in this chapter offer a progressive framework for fiscal–ESG integration, however their execution poses significant hurdles. This section rigorously assesses the viability and constraints associated with implementing these techniques, especially in developing and transitional economies.

Political Constraints and Institutional Resistance: The implementation of green taxation frequently encounters opposition from influential industrial organizations and political figures who view carbon pricing as economically detrimental or politically unpalatable. In the absence of bipartisan agreement or financial compensation measures, policy stability is precarious.

Data and Technological Deficiencies: ESG reporting necessitates prompt, consistent, and verifiable data, which numerous countries lack owing to disjointed systems or manual data processes. The lack of digital tax records and real-time environmental monitoring might considerably hinder policy effectiveness.

Conflicts of Interest: In nations where regulatory agencies are intimately affiliated with industry stakeholders, regulatory capture jeopardizes impartial oversight. Disclosure rules may be compromised or selectively applied, so eroding the integrity of taxes and reporting systems.

Infrastructure Constraints in Developing Nations: Numerous low- and middle-income countries are deficient in administrative infrastructure, legal frameworks, and human capital essential for facilitating integrated environmental fiscal changes. Although global standards offer a framework, uniform approaches may lead to institutional strain or mere token compliance. Consequently, any integration recommendation must be contextually relevant and adaptable, underpinned by incremental capacity-building, stakeholder engagement, and phased execution. Acknowledging these constraints bolsters the credibility and strategic significance of policy formulation in the Global South.

4.4.1 Critical Evaluation of Strategic Pathways

The proposed strategic and policy paths offer a forward-looking vision for the integration of green taxation with environmental accounting; however, their practical implementation presents considerable hurdles and trade-offs. A thorough assessment is essential to evaluate their viability across diverse regulatory, institutional, and economic environments, especially in emerging and transitional economies.

Initially, the dynamics of political economics provide considerable hazards. The implementation or enhancement of environmental taxes may encounter opposition from high-emission industries and politically powerful entities, particularly in regions where carbon-intensive sectors significantly contribute to employment and GDP. Fiscal reforms are frequently viewed as economically regressive, eliciting social resistance unless paired with compensatory measures. Consequently, political will and stakeholder consensus are essential yet frequently absent.

Secondly, regulatory misalignment continues to serve as a structural barrier. Environmental and budgetary policies are generally administered by separate agencies, each with differing mandates, data systems, and performance criteria. Inter-agency collaboration is often constrained in numerous nations, hindering the implementation of integrated disclosure mandates or collective audit systems. In the absence of legislative connectivity between tax authorities and sustainability regulators, alignment remains a mere aspiration.

Third, the expenses associated with compliance—encompassing digital infrastructure, specialized knowledge, and verification processes—impose an inequitable burden on SMEs and enterprises in the Global South. Although major international firms can tolerate these costs, resource-limited organizations face the threat of exclusion or only superficial compliance. This prompts essential inquiries regarding equity and capacity: who incurs the expense of sustainable transparency?

The mere act of integration does not eradicate the hazards associated with greenwashing. Companies may strategically adhere to disclosure norms while evading substantial tax responsibility, particularly in systems with inadequate enforcement. Unverified disclosure sustains reputational signaling rather than fostering genuine behavioral change. Consequently, comprehensive assurance mechanisms—such as third-party audits and financial verification tools—must be fundamental to any plan.

Furthermore, there exist trade-offs between standardization and contextual pertinence. Global frameworks such as CSRD or IFRS S2 provide harmonization but may not address local fiscal intricacies or developmental aspirations. Excessive dependence on externally imposed frameworks jeopardizes national policy sovereignty and may reduce ESG reporting to a mere compliance checklist.

Technology interoperability is frequently exaggerated. Although AI and blockchain provide potential for efficiency and traceability, their implementation requires substantial investment, legal clarity, and cross-border digital governance, which remain underdeveloped in numerous jurisdictions. Whereas integrated fiscal–ESG systems possess transformative potential, their efficacy relies not just on technical design but also on rectifying power imbalances, institutional fragmentation, and socio-political contexts. Incremental, context-sensitive, and participative implementation procedures are vital to prevent the establishment of parallel systems that simply reproduce current inefficiencies under a new sustainability designation.

FUTURE RESEARCH DIRECTIONS

5.1 Summary of Key Insights

This chapter has examined the developing convergence of green taxes and environmental accounting as two crucial, yet historically isolated, mechanisms of sustainable governance. A multifaceted review of theoretical foundations, comparative practices, and integrative methodologies reveals crucial insights that highlight the promise and problems of linking fiscal policy with sustainability disclosure systems.

Initially, it is clear that green taxes fulfills two roles: it acts as a corrective measure for internalizing environmental externalities and serves as a financial instrument to generate resources for climate resilience. Pigouvian taxes, along with contemporary implementations like carbon pricing and environmental levies, offers governments a market-oriented approach to modify company conduct and diminish emissions.

Secondly, environmental accounting frameworks—such as GRI, IFRS Sustainability Disclosure Standards, and SASB—are essential for implementing openness and accountability. They furnish the requisite approaches and frameworks for organizations to assess and disclose their environmental impacts, responsibilities, and sustainability performance. Nonetheless, these frameworks differ in orientation and scope, resulting in a fragmented reporting landscape that complicates alignment with financial instruments.

The amalgamation of tax and reporting systems is impeded by regulatory fragmentation, political opposition, and corporate governance issues. Fragmented legal requirements, isolated institutional frameworks, and variable standards obstruct the formation of a cohesive fiscal-accounting connection. The absence of obligatory connections between environmental taxes and corporate disclosures diminishes the transparency of tax-related environmental information, facilitating selective reporting and, in certain instances, greenwashing.

Fourth, comparative international experiences from Sweden, Germany, and China illustrate that context-specific design, institutional alignment, and digital innovation are essential facilitators of effective integration. These instances highlight the necessity of integrating tax policy with sustainability reporting requirements and utilizing technology for real-time data management.

A conceptual framework for fiscal-accounting integration has been developed, based on three pillars: policy-disclosure synchronization, technical interoperability, and institutional convergence. This approach proposes a closed-loop system in which environmental costs are addressed via taxation, documented through accounting, and shown through standardized reporting. The integrating green taxation with environmental accounting provides a transformational approach to matching economic and ecological objectives. This integration is essential for attaining transparent, enforceable, and fair sustainability results in a world increasingly constrained by carbon emissions.

5.2 Policy Recommendations for Governments, Regulators, and Firms

Coordinated efforts among government entities, regulatory organizations, and company stakeholders are crucial for advancing the integration of green taxation and environmental accounting. This policy advice seeks to offer practical ways for improving fiscal-environmental coherence and integrating sustainability concepts into public finance and business reporting frameworks.

1. For Governments: Statutory Obligations and Financial Transparency

Governments ought to provide clear legal connections between environmental taxation and sustainability reporting. National legislation on green taxes must incorporate disclosure rules that compel corporations to record environmental tax payments, carbon pricing obligations, and fiscal incentives obtained under standardized ESG frameworks. Additionally, tax funds derived from green levies must be explicitly allocated for climate adaption, renewable energy, and ecological restoration initiatives, accompanied by regular public disclosures to foster community trust.

2. For Regulators: Standardization of Disclosure Protocols

Regulatory entities, including financial reporting councils, tax authorities, and sustainability standard-setters, must cooperate to establish interoperable and enforceable disclosure regulations. This entails harmonizing the GRI, IFRS Sustainability Disclosure Standards, and SASB frameworks to integrate environmental tax data as a fundamental disclosure element. Regulators should require external verification of tax-related environmental data, adhering to professional auditing standards, to mitigate the dangers of misreporting and greenwashing.

3. For Enterprises: Governance Reform and Digital Infrastructure

Corporations ought to implement internal governance reforms to consolidate tax, sustainability, and finance operations, facilitating a cohesive strategy for environmental risk management and transparency. Investing in digital reporting infrastructure, such as AI-powered sustainability analytics and blockchain-enabled tax traceability systems, will elevate data quality, decrease compliance expenses, and enhance transparency. Companies could participate in voluntary pilot projects within regulatory sandboxes to evaluate integrated reporting models prior to comprehensive implementation.

4. Interdisciplinary Recommendation: Skill Development and Civic Discourse

All stakeholder groups require urgent capacity building and engagement. Training programs for tax administrators, sustainability officers, and auditors must be established to improve technical proficiency in environmental fiscal accounting. Concurrently, comprehensive public conversations must be undertaken to convey the societal advantages of green tax integration, while addressing issues of equity, competitiveness, and administrative complexity (Kliskey et al. 2021; Ziervogel et al., 2022; Singun, 2025).

These ideas collectively seek to establish a culture of fiscal-environmental responsibility, promoting structural change towards a more transparent, accountable, and sustainable economic system.

5.3 Future Research Directions on Integrated Environmental Governance

As the global community escalates its efforts towards sustainability and climate accountability, next research must enhance a more cohesive comprehension of how fiscal tools and environmental accounting systems can collaborate effectively. This chapter has delineated the conceptual justification and policy necessities for integration; yet, significant theoretical, empirical, and methodological deficiencies persist that warrant thorough academic investigation (Shaikh et al., 2022).

Future study should examine the causal relationships between environmental taxes and company sustainability practices, including how fiscal signals affect the quality of ESG reporting, investment in green innovation, and long-term environmental performance. Longitudinal and cross-sectoral research are essential to evaluate if enterprises subjected to carbon taxes or green levies exhibit superior disclosure integrity, enhanced responsiveness to stakeholder demands, or increased carbon efficiency relative to their non-taxed counterparts (Wang et al., 2023).

Secondly, researchers ought to investigate comparative regulatory experiments across jurisdictions to evaluate the efficacy of integration models. How do the European Union's Carbon Border Adjustment Mechanism (CBAM) and obligatory ESG reporting rules contrast with developing frameworks in Asia or North America? Comparative research can uncover best practices, institutional learning opportunities, and prospective avenues for global standardization (Castelblanco et al., 2025).

Third, increased focus is required on the function of digital technology in facilitating integration. Despite the widespread recognition of AI, blockchain, and real-time carbon accounting, empirical study on their application, scalability, and associated hazards is limited. Future inquiries should concentrate on establishing techno-legal frameworks that guarantee data integrity, user confidence, and system interoperability across jurisdictions and sectors (Costa et al., 2023).

The phenomenon of greenwashing in relation to environmental tax transparency is still a mostly unexamined domain. Researchers must create analytical models and detection instruments to discern discrepancies between declared sustainability accomplishments and actual financial contributions to environmental goals. These investigations would facilitate the establishment of more comprehensive verification and assurance systems (Hu et al., 2023).

There is an immediate necessity for interdisciplinary research approaches that integrate economics, environmental science, accounting, information systems, and public policy. Collaborative research activities, backed by academic, governmental, and industrial partners, are crucial for advancing a comprehensive and effective agenda for integrated environmental governance.

The endeavor for unified green taxation and environmental accounting is merely commencing. Ongoing academic research will be essential in formulating policies that are theoretically robust, practically implementable, technologically feasible, and ethically founded in the quest for sustainable development.

CONCLUSION

This chapter addresses the urgent requirement for a cohesive viewpoint on green taxes and environmental accounting by creating a conceptual and comparative framework that connects fiscal instruments with sustainability reporting standards. The chapter enhances academic research and practical governance through theoretical synthesis, policy evaluation, and international case analysis. It positions the incorporation of environmental fiscal instruments and ESG reporting within wider discussions on institutional accountability, stakeholder involvement, and technology advancement. This chapter has examined the developing relationship between green taxation and environmental accounting by analyzing international case studies and institutional policy frameworks. Successful integration necessitates more than financial instruments; it involves regulatory coherence, technical infrastructure, and stakeholder responsibility.

The cross-national research indicates that Sweden, Germany, and China are progressing—albeit via distinct trajectories—toward a form of fiscal-ESG integration that fulfills both environmental objectives and institutional legitimacy. These findings indicate institutional isomorphism pressures in ESG compliance, as nations conform to normative expectations established by global standards such as the GRI and CSRD. Stakeholder Theory elucidates how investor expectations, public oversight, and civil society impact company and governmental adherence to transparent sustainability reporting and appropriate taxation practices.

The identified patterns in Sweden, Germany, and China highlight the impact of institutional norms and external legitimacy on the alignment between green tax tools and ESG reporting. These dynamics exemplify the challenges of institutional isomorphism, as governments and corporations conform to global sustainability norms, while Stakeholder Theory elucidates the growing responsiveness to investor demands, public accountability, and environmental ethics. Collectively, these theoretical perspectives reinforce the chapter's principal assertion: that fiscal instruments have transcended their traditional role as mere revenue generators and are now integral to a dynamic framework of multi-actor environmental governance.

This chapter validates the predictive value of Institutional and Stakeholder Theories, so providing a conceptual basis for future research and curriculum advancement in business education. Incorporating these frameworks into educational design allows learners to comprehend theoretical models and apply them to practical sustainability governance issues.

REFERENCES

Acar, E., Tunca Çalıyurt, K., & Zengin-Karaibrahimoglu, Y. (2021). Does ownership type affect environmental disclosure? *International Journal of Climate Change Strategies and Management, 13*(2), 120–141. DOI: 10.1108/IJCCSM-02-2020-0016

Adanma, U. M., & Ogunbiyi, E. O.Uwaga Monica AdanmaEmmanuel Olurotimi Ogunbiyi. (2024). A comparative review of global environmental policies for promoting sustainable development and economic growth. *International Journal of Applied Research in Social Sciences, 6*(5), 954–977. DOI: 10.51594/ijarss.v6i5.1147

Almström, P., Anderstig, C., & Sundberg, M. (2024). Effects on sectors and regions of a carbon tax increase in Sweden: Analysis with an SCGE model. *The Annals of Regional Science, 73*(2), 731–756. DOI: 10.1007/s00168-024-01269-y

Andrades, J., Martinez-Martinez, D., & Larrán, M. (2024). Sustainability reporting, institutional pressures and universities: Evidence from the Spanish setting. *Sustainability Accounting. Management and Policy Journal, 16*(4), 1045–1071. DOI: 10.1108/SAMPJ-07-2023-0455

Bhope, A., Varimani, S., & Manjunath, T. C. (2025). Financial strategies. In *AI Methods for Environmental Protection and Resource Conservation* (Vol. 187, pp. 45–67). Springer., DOI: 10.1007/978-3-031-590XX-X_7

Bibri, S. E., Huang, J., Jagatheesaperumal, S. K., & Krogstie, J. (2024). The synergistic interplay of artificial intelligence and digital twin in environmentally planning sustainable smart cities: A comprehensive systematic review. *Environmental Science and Ecotechnology, 100433*, 100433. Advance online publication. DOI: 10.1016/j.ese.2024.100433

Bonilla, D., Banister, D., & Nieto, U. S. (2022). Tax or clean technology? Measuring the true effect on carbon emissions mitigation for Sweden and Norway. *Energies, 15*(11), 3885. Advance online publication. DOI: 10.3390/en15113885

Cai, W., Bai, M., & Davey, H. (2022). Implementing environmental protection tax in China: An alternative framework. *Pacific Accounting Review, 34*(5), 671–690. DOI: 10.1108/PAR-02-2021-0021

Castelblanco, G., Narbaev, T., Osei-Kyei, R., Serikbay, D., Mukashev, Y., & Guevara, J. (2025). Pandemic risks in PPPs: Comparative analysis within developing countries. *International Journal of Construction Management, 25*(4), 456–468. DOI: 10.1080/15623599.2024.2336660

Chen, Y., Masron, T. A., & Mai, W. (2024). Role of investor attention and executive green awareness on environmental information disclosure of Chinese high-tech listed companies. *Journal of Environmental Management, 365*, 121552. Advance online publication. DOI: 10.1016/j.jenvman.2024.121552

Chopra, S. S., Senadheera, S. S., Dissanayake, P. D., Withana, P. A., Chib, R., Rhee, J. H., & Ok, Y. S. (2024). Navigating the challenges of environmental, social, and governance (ESG) reporting: The path to broader sustainable development. *Sustainability (Basel), 16*(2), 606. Advance online publication. DOI: 10.3390/su16020606

Correia, C. R., & Roseland, M. (2022). Addressing negative externalities of urban development: Toward a more sustainable approach. *Urban Science (Basel, Switzerland), 6*(2), 38. DOI: 10.3390/urbansci6020038

Costa, F., Frecassetti, S., Rossini, M., & Portioli-Staudacher, A. (2023). Industry 4.0 digital technologies enhancing sustainability: Applications and barriers from the agricultural industry in an emerging economy. *Journal of Cleaner Production, 408*, 137208. Advance online publication. DOI: 10.1016/j.jclepro.2023.137208

D'Orazio, P. (2025). Addressing climate risks through fiscal policy in emerging and developing economies: What do we know and what lies ahead? *Energy Research & Social Science, 119*(2), 103852. Advance online publication. DOI: 10.1016/j.erss.2024.103852

Darrah, T., Herbert, S., & Chambers, T. (2024). A thematic analysis of alcohol and alcohol-related harm across health and social policy in Aotearoa New Zealand. *Australian and New Zealand Journal of Public Health, 48*(2), 100143. Advance online publication. DOI: 10.1016/j.anzjph.2024.100143

Delgado, F. J., Freire-González, J., & Presno, M. J. (2022). Environmental taxation in the European Union: Are there common trends? *Economic Analysis and Policy, 73*, 670–682. DOI: 10.1016/j.eap.2021.12.019

Drumond, P.Jr, de Castro, R. D., & Seabra, J. A. E. (2021). Impact of tax and tariff incentives on the economic viability of residential photovoltaic systems connected to energy distribution network in Brazil. *Solar Energy, 227*, 3784. Advance online publication. DOI: 10.1016/j.solener.2021.06.034

Du, J., Li, Z., Shi, G., & Wang, B. (2024). Can "environmental protection fee to tax" reduce carbon emissions? Evidence from China. *Finance Research Letters, 62*, 103270. Advance online publication. DOI: 10.1016/j.frl.2024.105184

Elsässer, J. P., Hickmann, T., Jinnah, S., Oberthür, S., & Van de Graaf, T. (2022). Institutional interplay in global environmental governance: Lessons learned and future research. *International Environmental Agreement: Politics, Law and Economics, 22*(2), 373–391. DOI: 10.1007/s10784-022-09569-4

Esen, Ö., Yıldırım, D. Ç., & Yıldırım, S. (2021). Pollute less or tax more? Asymmetries in the EU environmental taxes–Ecological balance nexus. *Environmental Impact Assessment Review, 91*, 106662. Advance online publication. DOI: 10.1016/j.eiar.2021.106662

Famulska, T., Kaczmarzyk, J., & Grząba-Włoszek, M. (2022). Environmental taxes in the member states of the European Union—Trends in energy taxes. *Energies, 15*(22), 8718. Advance online publication. DOI: 10.3390/en15228718

Fu, C., Lu, L., & Pirabi, M. (2024). *Advancing green finance: A review of climate change and decarbonization*. Digital Economy and Sustainable Development., DOI: 10.1007/s44265-023-00026-x

Gazzani, F. (2021). Transition to social-ecological sustainability using the environmental fiscal reform. *International Journal of Social Economics, 48*(5), 675–692. Advance online publication. DOI: 10.1108/IJSE-09-2020-0656

Gonzalez, C. C., & Peña-Vinces, J. (2023). A framework for a green accounting system: Exploratory study in a developing country context, Colombia. *Environment, Development and Sustainability, 25*(9), 9517–9541. DOI: 10.1007/s10668-022-02445-w

Harrison, M. T., Cullen, B. R., Mayberry, D. E., Cowie, A. L., Bilotto, F., Badgery, W. B., Liu, K., Davison, T., Christie, K. M., Muleke, A., & Eckard, R. J. (2021). Carbon myopia: The urgent need for integrated social, economic and environmental action in the livestock sector. *Global Change Biology, 27*(22), 5726–5761. Advance online publication. DOI: 10.1111/gcb.15816

Hu, S., Wang, A., & Du, K. (2023). Environmental tax reform and greenwashing: Evidence from Chinese listed companies. *Energy Economics, 124*, 106873. Advance online publication. DOI: 10.1016/j.eneco.2023.106873

Izzo, T., Russo, A., & Risaliti, G. (2025). Integrated reporting, stakeholders' perspective and sustainable disclosure: Systematic insights from empirical research. *Corporate Social Responsibility and Environmental Management*. ideas.repec.org+4dokumen.pub+4journals.indexcopernicus.com+4DOI: 10.1002/csr.3212

Jiang, X., Li, G., & Fan, X. (2023). Environmental protection fee-to-tax and corporate environmental social responsibility: A test based on corporate life cycle theory. *Sustainability (Basel), 15*(3), 2128. Advance online publication. DOI: 10.3390/su15032128

Kelling, N. K., Sauer, P. C., Gold, S., & Seuring, S. (2021). The role of institutional uncertainty for social sustainability of companies and supply chains. *Journal of Business Ethics, 173*(4), 813–833. DOI: 10.1007/s10551-020-04423-6

Kim, H. (2025). A real-time lifecycle analysis model with digital twin and novel control method for enhancing the environmental performance of electric/hybrid propulsion ships. *Ocean Engineering, 292*, 114215. Advance online publication. DOI: 10.1016/j.oceaneng.2025.121195

Kliskey, A., Williams, P., Griffith, D. L., Dale, V. H., Schelly, C., Marshall, A.-M., Gagnon, V. S., Eaton, W. M., & Floress, K. (2021). Thinking big and thinking small: A conceptual framework for best practices in community and stakeholder engagement in food, energy, and water systems. *Sustainability (Basel), 13*(4), 2160. Advance online publication. DOI: 10.3390/su13042160

Kurbatova, T., Sotnyk, I., Prokopenko, O., Bashynska, I., & Pysmenna, U. (2023). Improving the feed-in tariff policy for renewable energy promotion in Ukraine's households. *Energies, 16*(19), 6773. Advance online publication. DOI: 10.3390/en16196773

Lehner, O. M., Harrer, T., Silvola, H., & Weber, O. (2023). *The Routledge handbook of green finance* (1st ed.). Routledge., DOI: 10.4324/9781003345497

Lutfi, A., Al-Hiyari, A., Elshaer, I. A., Alrawad, M., & Almaiah, M. A. (2024). Green environmental management system and environmental performance: Results from PLS-SEM and fsQCA. *Sustainable Futures : An Applied Journal of Technology, Environment and Society, 8*, 100276. Advance online publication. DOI: 10.1016/j.sftr.2024.100276

Mardones, C., & Ortega, J. (2023). The individual and combined impact of environmental taxes in Chile: A flexible computable general equilibrium analysis. *Journal of Environmental Management, 325*(Pt A), 116508. DOI: 10.1016/j.jenvman.2022.116508

Masoud, N. (2024). Integrating theories for insight: Corporate governance and environmental disclosure practices in the UAE. *Corporate Governance (Bradford).* Advance online publication. DOI: 10.1108/CG-03-2024-0168

Merlo, A. L., Mendonça, D. S., Santos, J., Carvalho, S. T., Guerra, R., & Brandão, D. (2025). Blockchain for the carbon market: A literature review. *Discover Environment, 3*(1), 1–21. DOI: 10.1007/s44274-025-00260-4

Milios, L. (2021). Towards a circular economy taxation framework: Expectations and challenges of implementation. *Circular Economy and Sustainability, 1*(4), 737–756. DOI: 10.1007/s43615-020-00002-z

Miller, T., Durlik, I., Kostecka, E., Łobodzińska, A., & Matuszak, M. (2024). The emerging role of artificial intelligence in enhancing energy efficiency and reducing greenhouse gas emissions in transport systems. *Energies, 17*(24), 6271. Advance online publication. DOI: 10.3390/en17246271

Milne, J. E. (2024). Environmental taxation and ESG: Silent partners. In *Sustainable Finances and the Law: Between Public and Private Solutions* (pp. 253–279). Springer Nature Switzerland. DOI: 10.1007/978-3-031-49460-4_11

Mpofu, F. Y. (2022). Green taxes in Africa: Opportunities and challenges for environmental protection, sustainability, and the attainment of sustainable development goals. *Sustainability (Basel), 14*(3), 1234. DOI: 10.3390/su141610239

Mustaffa, N. K., Isa, C. M. M., & Ibrahim, C. K. I. C. (2021). Top-down bottom-up strategic green building development framework: Case studies in Malaysia. *Building and Environment, 203*, 108052. Advance online publication. DOI: 10.1016/j.buildenv.2021.108052

Nyakuwanika, M., van der Poll, H. M., & van der Poll, J. A. (2021). A conceptual framework for greener goldmining through environmental management accounting practices (EMAPs): The case of Zimbabwe. *Sustainability (Basel), 13*(18), 10466. DOI: 10.3390/su131810466

Pan, J., Cross, J. L., Zou, X., & Zhang, B. (2024). To tax or to trade? A global review of carbon emissions reduction strategies. *Energy Strategy Reviews, 55*, 101508. Advance online publication. DOI: 10.1016/j.esr.2024.101508

Petrie, M. (2021). *Environmental governance and the greening of fiscal policy*. Palgrave Macmillan. orcid.org+9ideas.repec.org+9scholar.unand.ac.id+9DOI: 10.1007/978-3-030-83796-9

Rao, M., Vasa, L., Xu, Y., & Chen, P. (2023). Spatial and heterogeneity analysis of environmental taxes' impact on China's green economy development: A sustainable development perspective. *Sustainability (Basel), 15*(12), 9332. Advance online publication. DOI: 10.3390/su15129332

Rövekamp, P., Schöpf, M., Wagon, F., Weibelzahl, M., & Fridgen, G. (2021). Renewable electricity business models in a post feed-in tariff era. *Energy*, *216*, 119228. Advance online publication. DOI: 10.1016/j.energy.2020.119228

Sarpong, K. A., Xu, W., Gyamfi, B. A., & Ofori, E. K. (2023). A step towards carbon neutrality in E7: The role of environmental taxes, structural change, and green energy. *Journal of Environmental Management*, *337*, 117556. Advance online publication. DOI: 10.1016/j.jenvman.2023.117556

Shaikh, A. A., Alamoudi, H., Alharthi, M., & Glavee-Geo, R. (2022). Advances in mobile financial services: A review of the literature and future research directions. *International Journal of Bank Marketing*, *41*(1), 1–33. DOI: 10.1108/IJBM-06-2021-0230

Shen, Y., & Zhang, X. (2022). Study on the impact of environmental tax on industrial green transformation. *International Journal of Environmental Research and Public Health*, *19*(24), 16749. Advance online publication. DOI: 10.3390/ijerph192416749

Singhania, M., & Saini, N. (2023). Institutional framework of ESG disclosures: Comparative analysis of developed and developing countries. *Journal of Sustainable Finance & Investment*, *13*(1), 516–559. DOI: 10.1080/20430795.2021.1964810

Singun, A. J. (2025). Unveiling the barriers to digital transformation in higher education institutions: A systematic literature review. *Discover Education*, *4*(1), 37. Advance online publication. DOI: 10.1007/s44217-025-00430-9

Stern, N. (2022). Towards a carbon neutral economy: How government should respond to market failures and market absence. *Journal of Government and Economics*. Advance online publication. https://doi.org/DOI: 10.1016/j.jgoe.2022.101029

Su, S., Qamruzzaman, M., & Karim, S. (2023). Charting a sustainable future: The impact of economic policy, environmental taxation, innovation, and natural resources on clean energy consumption. *Sustainability (Basel)*, *15*(6), 4789. Advance online publication. DOI: 10.3390/su151813585

Sun, J., Li, P., & Wang, Y. (2024). Policy tools for sustainability: Evaluating the effectiveness of fiscal measures in natural resource efficiency. *Resources Policy*, *89*, 104575. Advance online publication. DOI: 10.1016/j.resourpol.2023.104575

Sun, Y., Rahman, M. M., Xinyan, X., Siddik, A. B., & Islam, M. E. (2024). Unlocking environmental, social, and governance (ESG) performance through energy efficiency and green tax: SEM-ANN approach. *Energy Strategy Reviews*, *53*, 101408. Advance online publication. DOI: 10.1016/j.esr.2024.101408

Tang, Y. E., Fan, R., Cai, A. Z., Wang, L. Y., Lin, R. M., Meng, X. Z., Chen, L., & Guo, R. (2023). Rethinking personal carbon trading (PCT) mechanism: A comprehensive review. *Journal of Environmental Management, 344*, 118478. Advance online publication. DOI: 10.1016/j.jenvman.2023.118478

Troshani, I., & Rowbottom, N. (2024). Corporate sustainability reporting and information infrastructure. *Accounting, Auditing & Accountability Journal, 37*(4), 1209–1237. DOI: 10.1108/AAAJ-01-2023-6244

Truant, E., Crocco, E., Corazza, L., & Borlatto, E. (2024). Life cycle thinking and carbon accounting in sustainable supply chains: A structured literature review and research agenda. *Sustainability Accounting, Management and Policy Journal.* Advance online publication. DOI: 10.1108/SAMPJ-09-2023-0708

Verde, S. F., & Borghesi, S. (2022). The international dimension of the EU Emissions Trading System: Bringing the pieces together. *Environmental and Resource Economics, 83*(3), 23–46. oaepublish.com+2mdpi.com+2researchgate.net+2DOI: 10.1007/s10640-022-00705-x

Wang, D., & Mei, J. (2024). An advanced review of climate change mitigation policies in the United States. *Resources, Conservation and Recycling, 208*, 107718. Advance online publication. DOI: 10.1016/j.resconrec.2024.107718

Wang, J. M., & Li, Y. Q. (2022). Soft economic incentives and soft behavioral interventions on the public's green purchasing behaviour: The evidence from China. *Psychology Research and Behavior Management, 15*, 2477–2499. DOI: 10.2147/PRBM.S373123

Wang, M., & Kuusi, T. (2024). Trade flows, carbon leakage, and the EU Emissions Trading System. *Energy Economics, 134*, 107556. Advance online publication. DOI: 10.1016/j.eneco.2024.107556

Wang, X., Khurshid, A., Qayyum, S., & Calin, A. C. (2022). The role of green innovations, environmental policies and carbon taxes in achieving the sustainable development goals of carbon neutrality. *Environmental Science and Pollution Research International, 29*(6), 1–15. DOI: 10.1007/s11356-021-16208-z

Wang, Y., Qamruzzaman, M., & Kor, S. (2023). Greening the future: Harnessing ICT, innovation, eco-taxes, and clean energy for sustainable ecology—Insights from dynamic seemingly unrelated regression. *Sustainability (Basel), 15*(23), 16417. Advance online publication. DOI: 10.3390/su152316417

Woo, J., Fatima, R., Kibert, C. J., Newman, R. E., Tian, Y., & Srinivasan, R. S. (2021). Applying blockchain technology for building energy performance measurement, reporting, and verification (MRV) and the carbon credit market: A review of the literature. *Building and Environment*, *205*, 108199. Advance online publication. DOI: 10.1016/j.buildenv.2021.108199

Wu, Z., Huang, X., Chen, R., Mao, X., & Qi, X. (2022). The United States and China on the paths and policies to carbon neutrality. *Journal of Environmental Management*, *320*, 115785. Advance online publication. DOI: 10.1016/j.jenvman.2022.115785

Xu, Y., Wen, S., & Tao, C. Q. (2023). Impact of environmental tax on pollution control: A sustainable development perspective. *Economic Analysis and Policy*, *79*, 89–106. DOI: 10.1016/j.eap.2023.06.006

Yang, K., Chen, G., & Chen, R. (2024). The dark side of climate policy uncertainty: Hindering energy transition by shaping environmental tax effectiveness. *Journal of Environmental Management*, *369*, 122314. Advance online publication. DOI: 10.1016/j.jenvman.2024.122314

Yu, H., Liao, L., Qu, S., Fang, D., Luo, L., & Xiong, G. (2021). Environmental regulation and corporate tax avoidance: A quasi-natural experiment study based on China's new environmental protection law. *Journal of Environmental Management*, *296*, 113160. Advance online publication. DOI: 10.1016/j.jenvman.2021.113160

Zeng, W., & Wang, G. (2025). On the obligations of states to respond to climate change and China's legal consequences: Based on the advisory opinion in Case No. 31 of the International Tribunal for the Law of the Sea. *Frontiers in Marine Science*, *11*, 1468210. Advance online publication. DOI: 10.3389/fmars.2024.1468210

Zhu, Y., Taylor, D., & Wang, Z. (2023). The role of environmental taxes on carbon emissions in countries aiming for net-zero carbon emissions: Does renewable energy consumption matter? *Renewable Energy*, *218*, 119239. Advance online publication. DOI: 10.1016/j.renene.2023.119239

Ziervogel, G., Enqvist, J., Metelerkamp, L., & van Breda, J. (2022). Supporting transformative climate adaptation: Community-level capacity building and knowledge co-creation in South Africa. *Climate Policy*, *22*(5), 607–622. DOI: 10.1080/14693062.2020.1863180

Chapter 4
Can Tax Incentives Act as Catalysts for a Circular Economy?
Modeling Tax Strategies to Drive Circular Innovation

Hrishikesh Desai
https://orcid.org/0000-0002-7945-3744
Arkansas State University, USA

ABSTRACT

This chapter investigates how tax incentives can influence firm-level investment in circular economy practices under environmental regulatory constraints. Motivated by the rising policy emphasis on fiscal instruments to support sustainable transitions, the study develops an analytical optimization model of a representative firm that faces a regulatory waste cap and may invest in circular practices to reduce environmental penalties. The model integrates production costs, environmental externalities, tax incentives, and the convex costs of sustainable investment. Through a constrained nonlinear optimization and numerical experiment simulation, the study identifies key behavioral patterns: (1) a critical activation threshold of tax incentives below which firms remain inactive; (2) a coupling effect whereby production and circular investment rise together to satisfy waste regulations; and (3) saturation and metastability effects as investment costs and waste-reduction returns flatten. A case study of the German packaging sector illustrates the model's real-world relevance.

DOI: 10.4018/979-8-3373-2492-0.ch004

1. INTRODUCTION

The transition to a circular economy (CE) has emerged as a strategic imperative for achieving long-term sustainability across industrial systems. By prioritizing resource efficiency, waste minimization, and the regeneration of materials, the CE model provides a viable alternative to the traditional linear take-make-dispose paradigm (Bocken et al., 2022; Elroi et al., 2023). Yet despite its environmental appeal, the economic viability of circular practices remains a major barrier to widespread adoption, particularly in resource-intensive sectors (Vermunt et al., 2019; Singh et al., 2020; Wang et al., 2022). Firms often encounter significant upfront costs, uncertain returns, and complex operational adjustments when implementing circular processes such as recycling, remanufacturing, or closed-loop supply chains (Asgari & Asgari, 2021; Grafström & Aasma, 2021; Takacs et al., 2022). In this context, fiscal policy, especially through tax-based instruments, has gained traction as a mechanism for lowering the financial hurdles associated with sustainable investment (Hart et al., 2019; Milios, 2021; Munteanu et al., 2024). This study examines how tax incentives influence a firm's decision to invest in circular economy practices under environmental regulatory constraints.

Tax incentives, such as credits, deductions, and investment subsidies, are increasingly employed to encourage firms to adopt circular technologies by effectively reducing their marginal cost of adoption. These instruments complement environmental regulations by enhancing firms' profitability from sustainable practices, thereby aligning private incentives with public environmental goals. However, empirical studies and policy evaluations have shown mixed results. While some firms respond actively to tax incentives, others remain inert, which suggests the presence of threshold effects and contextual constraints (Qi et al., 2023; Zhao et al., 2022). Moreover, the literature lacks robust analytical models that explain how tax incentives interact with regulatory frameworks to shape firm-level production and investment decisions. Few studies quantify the tipping points at which incentives become effective, or the saturation levels beyond which additional subsidies yield diminishing returns. This gap is especially important given the growing policy interest in using tax systems to facilitate circular economy transitions across sectors like manufacturing, packaging, and energy.

To address this gap, this chapter develops an analytical model of a representative firm operating under a waste regulation constraint and subject to a tax incentive program for circular investments. The model captures the interdependence between production decisions and investment in circular practices, factoring in production costs, waste penalties, fiscal subsidies, and diminishing marginal returns to investment. The firm seeks to maximize profit while complying with environmental limits. The model is operationalized using a constrained nonlinear optimization framework and validated through a numerical experiment simulating different tax incentive levels. The research questions guiding this study are (i) how do tax incentives influence a firm's decision to invest in circular economy practices?; (ii) under what conditions do firms simultaneously increase production and sustainable investment?; and (iii) what policy thresholds and saturation points characterize the fiscal effectiveness of tax incentives in driving circular transitions?.

The results of the model and simulation reveal several key insights. First, the firm remains inactive, producing nothing and investing nothing, until the tax incentive reaches a critical activation threshold. Once this threshold is crossed, both production and circular investment increase rapidly and in tandem. This coupling arises from a binding waste constraint, which forces any production expansion to be supported by proportional investments in waste-reducing circular technologies. Second, the simulation uncovers a saturation effect, i.e, beyond a certain tax incentive level, the benefits of additional subsidies diminish due to the quadratic nature of investment costs and the flattening gains from waste reduction. Third, at very high tax incentive rates, the model enters a metastable regime, where small parameter changes lead to significant shifts in optimal decisions. This highlights the complexity of decision-making under stringent environmental constraints and indicates the importance of calibrated policy design. Taken together, the findings indicate that fiscal incentives must be large enough to activate firm engagement but not so generous as to produce inefficient overinvestment or strategic volatility.

The contribution of this chapter is twofold. Theoretically, it provides an original optimization-based framework that integrates environmental constraints and fiscal instruments into firm-level decision modeling, which addresses a key gap in the circular economy and environmental economics literature. Methodologically, the study demonstrates how numerical experiments can validate and extend analytical predictions by providing insights for policymakers. Practically, the model highlights the conditions under which tax incentives become effective levers for circular innovation and identifies potential pitfalls in policy overdesign. As governments consider how to mobilize private investment toward sustainability goals, this study offers a quantitative foundation for aligning economic instruments with ecological imperatives.

2. THEORY

The circular economy (CE) is a model aimed at minimizing waste and reusing resources through recycling, remanufacturing, and extended product life cycles. In recent years, researchers have recognized that fiscal policy can be a powerful lever to drive this transition. Taxation strategies, ranging from tax credits for sustainable investment to environmental levies on resource use, are increasingly examined as tools to encourage firms in manufacturing, packaging, and other resource-intensive sectors to adopt circular practices. A robust policy mix is seen as important. Traditional environmental regulations alone may not sufficiently change corporate behavior, so complementing them with smart taxes and incentives is a key focus of academics and policymakers (Vence & López Pérez, 2021). However, extant research also highlights significant gaps, such as fragmented policies and a lack of integrated frameworks linking taxes, environmental regulations, and firm-level decision models (Losa, 2025).

2.1 Fiscal Instruments to Promote Circular Economy Practices

Recent research studies have explored how tax incentives and penalties can shift firms toward sustainable behavior. For instance, Munteanu et al. (2024) note that tax credits and subsidies for eco-innovation can *"stimulate investment in circular solutions and level the playing field between linear and circular business models."* Such incentives lower the cost of adopting circular practices (like recycling technologies or remanufacturing processes) and make them more financially attractive to firms. Munteanu et al. (2024) also highlight the role of government in creating an enabling environment through tax breaks and market mechanisms that encourage circular business models. Alongside carrots, there are also sticks as environmental levies and taxes directly price the negative externalities of linear models. Examples include pollution taxes, carbon pricing, and waste disposal fees, which are designed to push companies to reduce emissions and waste.

A notable study of Chinese firms showed that a general tax cut combined with environmental targets led to substantial pollution reductions (Qi et al., 2023). Specifically, the authors found that a value-added tax reform in China acting as an implicit incentive prompted firms to cut sulfur dioxide emissions intensity by ~16% on average, especially when paired with stricter emissions regulations. This indicates that tax policy can increase the effects of environmental regulations by freeing up resources or increasing returns for companies that invest in cleaner processes. On the other hand, direct green investment incentives (e.g. accelerated depreciation or credits for renewable energy, circular product design, or recycling facilities) have been adopted in various jurisdictions to spur corporate sustainability investments. Overall, recent research strongly suggests that a well-designed mix of tax incentives and environmental taxes can realign profit motives with circular economy goals and nudge firms toward sustainable materials management.

2.2 Sector-Specific Taxation Approaches

2.2.1 Manufacturing and Industrial Sectors

Manufacturing firms often face high upfront costs to switch from linear production to circular processes (such as redesigning products for reuse or investing in recycling technology). Fiscal tools are being explored to overcome these barriers. Several studies document that tax incentives have encouraged manufacturers to adopt circular economy (CE) practices. For example, evidence from Europe indicates that tax deductions for using recycled inputs or investing in resource-efficient equipment can positively influence firm behavior (Munteanu et al., 2024). Another empirical study of manufacturing companies in China found that investment tax incentives can promote pollution abatement strategies in factories, especially when combined with emissions regulations (Qi et al., 2023). However, not all manufacturing sub-sectors respond equally. Resource-intensive industries (e.g. metals, cement, chemicals) are often targeted by material or carbon taxes to drive efficiency.

Research on resource taxation in Europe shows that levies on raw material extraction can increase circularity. One analysis estimates that a €1 per ton increase in resource tax correlates with about an *"8-10% increase"* in the use of recycled materials on average (Deserno & Sterk, 2024). Yet these effects vary by country and industry, and some nations saw significant boosts in recycling from resource taxes, while others showed little change (Deserno & Sterk, 2024). The literature suggests that complementary measures (standards, technology support) are needed alongside taxes to ensure manufacturing firms actually invest in circular innovations rather than simply paying the tax. A major insight for industry is that predictable, well-calibrated taxation, for example, steadily rising levies on virgin material use can prompt firms to plan long-term investments in circular processes, especially when the tax revenue is recycled into supporting those transitions.

2.2.2 Packaging and Waste Management

The packaging sector, especially plastics, has seen high-profile fiscal measures aimed at waste reduction and recycling. Packaging taxes and extended producer responsibility (EPR) fees are increasingly used to discourage single-use packaging and fund recycling systems. For example, the UK's Plastic Packaging Tax (2022) imposes £200 per tonne on plastic packaging with less than 30% recycled content, explicitly to *"provide a clear economic incentive for businesses to use recycled plastic material"* and shift behavior toward recycled input (His Majesty's Revenue and Customs, 2021; Scott, 2022). At the European Union (EU) level, an innovative levy known as the "Plastics Own Resource" took effect in 2021 with each member state contributing €0.80 per kilogram of non-recycled plastic packaging waste to the EU budget (Eunomia, 2022). While not a direct consumer-facing tax, this mechanism pressures countries (and thereby producers) to cut down on unrecycled plastic. It is expected to *"encourage Member States to reduce packaging waste and stimulate the circular economy"* in line with the European Plastics Strategy (Eunomia, 2022). Some countries have responded by planning national plastic taxes (e.g. Spain and Italy are introducing their own levies on single-use plastics), or by strengthening EPR schemes to transfer the cost to producers. Early indications suggest these fiscal measures can drive design changes, for example, packaging firms increasing recycled content to qualify for tax exemptions (Eunomia, 2022).

In the waste management domain, landfill taxes have been a classic tool to promote recycling. The UK's landfill tax, steadily increased over two decades, is credited with diverting large volumes of waste from landfills to recycling. Evidence suggests that as the landfill tax rate climbed, recycling/composting tonnages rose sharply (Eunomia, 2022). This illustrates how a levy on disposal changed waste handling practices. Such taxes make disposal costlier and thereby improve the business case for waste reduction, reuse, and recycling infrastructure. That said, there could also be unintended effects as without parallel measures (like an incineration tax or robust enforcement), a landfill tax can lead to more incineration or even illegal dumping in some cases (Eunomia, 2022). To sum it up, the literature on packaging and waste emphasizes holistic policy design that combines taxes with recycling targets, take-back requirements, and reinvestment of tax revenues into circular systems to ensure that fiscal measures truly steer the sector toward a zero-waste circular model.

2.3 Firm-Level Decision Models under Environmental Constraints

Beyond empirical studies, researchers have developed analytical models to understand how firms make investment decisions when facing environmental taxes and regulations. These models, often drawing from operations research or environmental economics, help clarify the micro-level mechanisms by which fiscal policies influence firm behavior. A notable example is a dynamic optimization model of a manufacturing firm's pricing and recycling investment decisions (Schlosser et al., 2021). In this model, a firm can use both virgin and recycled materials in production, and it must decide how much to invest in recycling capabilities over time. Schlosser et al. (2021) formulate this as an optimal control problem and find that the *optimal interplay* between pricing strategy and recycling investment shifts as the firm increases its use of recycled inputs. Such models highlight that the profitability of circular practices (like using recycled material) can improve over time with investment, but firms need to account for diminishing returns and demand responses. Policy incentives can alter these calculations by effectively changing cost parameters in the model.

Real options analysis is another approach. Some studies determine the conditions (e.g. carbon price thresholds) at which it becomes optimal for a firm to invest in cleaner technology or more circular processes. Evidence from China's environmental protection tax law indicates that firms ramp up green innovation efforts when faced with pollution taxes, albeit with differences by firm type (Zhao et al., 2022). The general finding is thus that that moderate, well-timed taxes can induce optimal environmental investments (e.g. in emissions control or resource efficiency) that would not occur in the absence of such pricing. However, the literature also points out that if taxes are too high or poorly coordinated with other policies, they may either deter investment (by straining finances) or encourage only short-term compliance actions rather than long-term innovation (Zhao et al., 2022). Overall, integrated firm-level models are evolving to capture the complexities of decision-making under environmental constraints, but they remain a developing area. These models are kay for designing smart policies and helping predict how firms might adjust product design, supply chains, or technology strategy in response to a new tax credit or levy.

2.4 The Need for Integrated Frameworks

Despite the progress in research in this topic area, significant gaps remain in linking taxation, environmental regulation, and firm-level decision-making in a unified analytical framework. The prior studies cited earlier focus on individual policy instruments or single-country cases, but holistic analyses are scarce. Losa (2025) notes that *"there is little clarity as to the most effective public policies to push companies towards implementing [CE],"* partly because policies in regions like the EU have been fragmented and inconsistent. Integrated frameworks that consider the entire lifecycle, from resource extraction taxes to product use incentives and end-of-life levies, are still in their infancy. For example, Milios (2021) proposed a comprehensive circular economy taxation framework with taxes on raw materials, tax relief for product repair, and waste taxes at end-of-life. While conceptually robust, Milios (2021) acknowledged many implementation challenges and called for further research at both the individual instrument level and the system level to assess how such taxes would interact.

On similar lines, Vence & López Pérez (2021) argue that current tax systems are biased toward the linear economy (taxing labor heavily but under-taxing resource use), and they propose structural reforms to correct this bias. They advocate transforming *"environmentally harmful tax benefits into environmentally friendly tax measures"* and fundamentally redesigning fiscal architecture to support circular objectives.

However, these proposals remain mostly theoretical, and there is a lack of empirical evaluation of comprehensive tax-reform packages for circular economy outcomes.

There is also a dearth of cross-disciplinary models that tie together environmental science, economics, and management. Few firm-level optimization models incorporate policy constraints in a realistic way (e.g. considering uncertainty in future tax policy or the simultaneous effects of taxes and command-and-control regulations). The literature would benefit from integrated analytical frameworks that can evaluate, for instance, how a combination of a carbon tax, materials levy, and recycling subsidy together influence a firm's investment decision and environmental performance. Most research also isolates one policy instrument at a time. Additionally, sector-specific gaps exist. For packaging and consumer goods, long-term studies on how firms innovate in response to sustained packaging taxes or EPR fees are still limited (since many of these policies are quite new). In heavy industry, while we have data on carbon pricing, there is less research on materials taxes (like metal ore or mineral taxes) and how those might drive circular design or substitution. And in developing economies, high impact research on fiscal instruments for circular economy is sparse compared to Europe and China.

Bridging these gaps will likely involve collaborative research that combines economics, engineering, and management science, which is what I aim to achieve with the analytical model developed in this chapter. As the world moves toward ambitious sustainability targets, filling these knowledge gaps is important. Policymakers need guidance on designing tax systems that not only *internalize externalities* but actively propel companies toward circular business models for a more sustainable economy.

3. ANALYTICAL MODEL

3.1 Key Variables and Functional Relationships

I consider a representative firm that produces a quantity Q of goods. The firm has the option to invest in circular economy practices at an intensity x (with $x \geq 0$). Investment x reduces waste generation and may lower costs associated with environmental penalties. However, higher x increases upfront costs. In response, the government offers tax incentives (credits or deductions) that are a function of x. The firm's goal is to maximize its net profit, which is a function of revenue, production costs, environmental costs, and tax incentives.

In my model, the *production cost function* is formulated as follows:

$$C(Q,x) = Q\left(c_0 - c_1 h(x)\right)$$

Where Q denotes the production quantity and x represents the intensity of investment in circular economy practices. Here, c_0 is the base cost per unit without any circular investments, while c_1 quantifies the maximum potential reduction in cost achievable through such practices. The function $h(x)$ represents the efficiency gains derived from circular investments. Thus, the term $c_1 h(x)$ represents the cost reduction per unit that the firm achieves by investing in circular practices. Thus, the expression for $C(Q,x)$ represents the total production cost for producing Q units of a product.

The function $h(x)$ is defined as follows:

$$h(x) = 1 - e^{-kx}$$

Where $k > 0$. It is an increasing function that captures the idea of diminishing returns. As a firm increases its investment x in these sustainable practices, the value of $h(x)$ increases, which indicates that the investment is yielding benefits. Initially, small investments lead to significant improvements, but as x grows larger, the additional benefit starts to level off and approach a maximum benefit of 1. In this context, it means that as a firm increases its investment in circular practices, the cost savings accumulate; however, these savings eventually plateau as the investment reaches higher levels. This formulation thus indicates the trade-off inherent in circular investments.

The *waste generation function* is expressed as follows:

$$W(Q,x) = Q\left(w_0 e^{-\delta x}\right)$$

This expression integrates environmental considerations directly into the production process. In this expression, w_0 represents the baseline waste generated per unit of production in the absence of any mitigating investments. The exponential term, $e^{-\delta x}$, determines the effect of circular economy investments on waste reduction. Here, δ is a parameter that measures the efficiency of the circular practices in reducing waste.

As a firm increases its investment x, the exponential term diminishes and leads to a lower amount of waste produced per unit. This functional form effectively models the impact of investments aimed at recycling, reuse, or process optimization, all of which contribute to a reduced environmental footprint. The multiplicative structure with Q emphasizes that while waste generation scales with production volume, its intensity is moderated by the firm's efforts in implementing circular strategies. As x increases, the exponential term decreases, i.e., each unit generates less waste. Multiplying by Q then gives the overall waste produced by the firm. Thus, the expression for $W(Q,x)$ represents the total amount of waste generated by a firm when producing Q units of a product.

The *tax incentive function* in the model is represented by a linear formulation as follows:

$$T(x) = \tau x$$

Where τ denotes the tax credit rate per unit of investment in circular practices. This simple expression is designed to capture the role of fiscal policies in reducing the net cost of sustainability initiatives. For every unit of investment made, the firm gets a tax benefit calculated by multiplying that investment by the tax incentive rate τ. This linear relationship means that if a firm increases its investment, the tax benefit increases proportionally. By offering a tax credit that increases proportionally with the level of investment x, policymakers can directly influence the economic calculus of firms. This approach facilitates a straightforward integration of tax policy into the decision-making framework and highlights how fiscal measures can serve as a lever to promote environmental sustainability within the production process.

In contrast, the *investment cost function* is represented as follows:

$$I(x) = \alpha x^2$$

This expression highlights the inherent challenges of scaling circular economy practices. The quadratic nature of this function implies that as firms strive for higher levels of circularity, the incremental costs increase at an accelerating rate, i.e., as a firm increases its investment x, the cost rises at an accelerating rate, not just linearly. This suggests that while small investments might be relatively inexpensive, larger investments become increasingly costly because the expenses grow quadratically. The parameter $\alpha > 0$ scales this cost by setting how quickly the costs increase with x.

This simulates real-world conditions where initial investments are often subsidized by existing technologies and processes, but advancing beyond a certain threshold requires significant additional capital, innovation, and infrastructure development. The convexity captured in this formulation reinforces the need for a balanced approach in policy design, where tax incentives and other fiscal measures must be carefully calibrated to offset these increasing costs without leading to diminishing returns in environmental benefits.

To sum it up, the production cost function captures the reduction in per-unit costs achieved through circular investments, while the waste generation function quantifies the environmental benefits by reducing waste output. The tax incentive function serves to mitigate the financial burden of these investments by offering a direct fiscal benefit, and the investment cost function indicates the increasing marginal costs associated with scaling up circular practices. When viewed together, these four functions (production cost, waste generation, tax incentive, and investment cost) provide an integrated framework for analyzing the impact of tax incentives on the adoption of circular economy practices. The model incorporates the important trade-offs that firms face in pursuing sustainability, which involve the need to balance production efficiency, environmental impact, and the cost of investment, all within the context of policy-driven fiscal incentives. By adjusting parameters such as τ (the tax incentive rate) and α (the investment cost coefficient), decision makers can simulate various policy scenarios to identify the optimal conditions that encourage both economic viability and environmental stewardship.

3.2 Framework for Optimal Decision-making

The objective function in my model captures the comprehensive decision-making process of a firm as it balances revenue generation with production costs, environmental penalties, and the financial impacts of both investment and tax incentives. The profit function is formulated as follows:

$$\pi(Q,x) = pQ - Q\left(c_0 - c_1(1 - e^{-kx})\right) - \alpha x^2 - \gamma Q\left(w_0 e^{-\delta x}\right) + \tau x$$

In this expression, as explained in the previous section, the first term, pQ, represents the total revenue generated by the firm from producing Q units at a unit price p. The subsequent term, $Q\left(c_0 - c_1(1 - e^{-kx})\right)$, indicates the production cost. Here, c_0 is the baseline cost per unit in the absence of any circular economy investments, while c_1 represents the potential cost reduction achievable through such investments. The function $1 - e^{-kx}$ is a saturating function that increases with the investment level x and indicates the diminishing returns associated with further investments. The model further incorporates a quadratic investment cost term, αx^2, which highlights the convex nature of investments in circular economy practices. This component indicates that while initial investments may be relatively economical, the marginal cost of additional investments grows at an increasing rate. Such a structure is consistent with the idea that achieving higher levels of circularity often demands disproportionate additional resources and capital.

Environmental performance is integrated into the model through the penalty term, $\gamma Q\left(w_0 e^{-\delta x}\right)$. This term quantifies the cost imposed on the firm for waste generation, where w_0 denotes the baseline waste per unit and the exponential decay $e^{-\delta x}$ reflects the effectiveness of circular investments in reducing waste output. The penalty rate γ scales this environmental cost, which reinforces the economic imperative for firms to minimize waste in order to avoid higher regulatory costs. Finally, the tax incentive component, τx, is included to determine the fiscal benefits associated with investments in circular practices. This term acts as a counterbalance to the rising investment costs and provides a direct monetary offset that encourages firms to adopt sustainable practices.

Collectively, the objective function integrates these various elements into a single profit maximization framework. It provides a clear view of the trade-offs a firm faces that involves the need to boost revenue through increased production, the potential cost savings from circular investments, the rising marginal costs of such investments, and the dual impacts of environmental penalties and tax incentives. Appendix A provides a summary of key terms and definitions.

3.3 Regulatory and Feasibility Constraints

In developing the model, it is important to recognize the external regulatory and operational constraints that govern the firm's decision-making. The primary constraint in my analysis is the environmental, or waste, constraint. This constraint is formulated as follows:

$$Q\left(w_0 e^{-\delta x}\right) \leq \overline{w}$$

Here, Q is the production quantity, w_0 is the baseline waste per unit produced, and $e^{-\delta x}$ represents the reduction in waste due to the firm's investment x in circular practices. The parameter δ governs the efficiency with which investments reduce waste. Essentially, this constraint ensures that the total waste generated by the firm, which is directly proportional to the production volume but reduced by effective circular practices, does not exceed a prescribed regulatory limit $\overline{w}$. This reflects a real world requirement imposed by environmental regulations that compels firms to incorporate sustainable practices into their operations to avoid incurring additional costs or penalties.

In addition to the waste constraint, non-negativity constraints are imposed on both decision variables as follows:

$$Q \geq 0 \quad \text{and} \quad x \geq 0$$

These constraints are standard in optimization problems so that the production quantity and the level of investment in circular practices remain non-negative. In practical terms, these conditions prevent the model from considering infeasible solutions, such as negative production or negative investment, which do not have any meaningful interpretation in a real economic context.

3.4 Strategic Optimization Approach

The key challenge faced by the firm is to determine the optimal combination of production quantity Q and investment in circular practices x that maximizes its overall profit, while simultaneously adhering to the waste constraint imposed by environmental regulations. The optimization problem is thus to choose Q and x in order to maximize the profit function subject to the waste constraint (i.e., staying within environmental limits) and the non-negativity conditions. This can be formally stated as follows:

$$\max_{Q,x} \pi(Q,x) = pQ - Q\left(c_0 - c_1(1 - e^{-kx})\right) - \alpha x^2 - \gamma Q\left(w_0 e^{-\delta x}\right) + \tau x$$

Subject to:

$$Q\left(w_0 e^{-\delta x}\right) \leq \overline{w},$$

$$Q \geq 0 \quad \text{and} \quad x \geq 0$$

The solution to this optimization problem not only identifies the optimal levels of production and investment but also provides information on the trade-offs inherent in achieving both economic and environmental objectives. The key takeaway is that the firm must balance increasing production and investment to gain higher profit against the risk of producing too much waste, which could lead to higher penalties or non-compliance with environmental regulations.

4. NUMERICAL EXPERIMENT

To empirically validate the analytical framework developed in this study, following Anand et al. (2019) and Knox (2020), I conduct a numerical experiment simulation that captures the decision-making process of a representative firm under tax incentives and environmental constraints. The simulation solves the firm's profit-maximization problem, evaluates the impact of policy parameters, and quantifies trade-offs between production, investment in circular practices, and regulatory compliance. This section details the experimental setup, parameter selection, optimization methodology, and sensitivity analysis for reproducibility and alignment with real-world economic conditions.

4.1 Parameter selection

The model's parameters are calibrated to indicate plausible industrial scenarios while maintaining tractability for sensitivity analysis. The baseline production cost per unit, $c_0 = 50$, represents industry averages for conventional manufacturing. The maximum cost reduction achievable via circular practices, $c_1 = 15$, is estimated at 30% of c_0, which is consistent with resource efficiency gains from circular practices indicated in a research report by the Employer's Group of the European Economic and Social Committee (2016). The efficiency gain coefficient, $k = 0.5$, is chosen to indicate diminishing returns in circular investments. A smaller k (e.g., 0.1) would mean very slow efficiency gains and require extremely high investments to achieve meaningful cost reductions. A larger k (e.g., 1.0) would imply rapid initial gains but may overestimate the real-world feasibility of circular practices. A k of 0.5 strikes a balance by providing strong initial returns as early investments yield noticeable efficiency improvements but diminishing marginal gains as further investments provide progressively smaller benefits.

The baseline waste per unit, $w_0 = 0.8$ (or 80% waste per unit) indicates a conservative estimate for industries with moderate-to-high waste streams (Jackson, 2023). A waste reduction efficiency (δ) of 0.3 ensure investments yield measurable but saturating returns. A higher δ (e.g., 0.5) implies faster waste reduction, where small investments yield large waste cuts. A lower δ (e.g., 0.1) implies slower returns, which requires heavy investment to achieve modest reductions. A of 0.3 strikes a balance by providing measurable early gains as firms see tangible waste reduction from initial investments (e.g., process tweaks, basic recycling) but saturating returns as further investments (e.g., advanced sorting, closed-loop systems) face diminishing marginal benefits.

The penalty per unit waste (γ) is set to 20, which is large enough to affect decisions (e.g., reducing Q or increasing x to cut waste) and small enough to avoid making the constraint $W \leq \overline{w}$ the *only* driver of behavior. The value of γ represents a mid-tier penalty that is stringent enough to incentivize waste reduction but not so severe as to cripple firms financially. The tax credit per unit investment, $\tau = 30$, is selected to indicate a moderate but impactful fiscal incentive. At a lower τ (e.g., 10), firms underinvest (marginal cost > benefit), while at a higher τ (e.g., 50), there are risks of over-subsidizing with diminishing returns. The quadratic cost coefficient for investments, $\alpha = 0.8$, indicates escalating marginal costs of advanced circular technologies. This value of α ensures tax incentives (τ) are effective at moderate x but cannot fully offset costs at high x, which prevents overinvestment in impractical technologies. If α is too low, investments are too cheap, which can result in an overestimation of adoption. If α is too high, investments are prohibitively expensive, which can result in stalling circular transitions. However, there could be some sector variability here. Mature industries with low α face relatively modest cost escalation when scaling circular practices. For example, paper recycling, which is a well-established process, would require incremental investments in sorting or pulping equipment, where marginal costs rise gradually. However, emerging technologies with high α would experience steeper cost increases due to technical complexity and nascent infrastructure. Lithium-ion battery recycling is a good example of this, where advanced material recovery (e.g., hydrometallurgical processes) demands substantial R&D and specialized facilities, which can drive quadratic costs upward aggressively.

Finally, the unit price, $p = 100$, ensures profitability while allowing cost/penalty trade-offs. This price (p) is high enough so that firms can achieve positive profits after accounting for production costs ($c_0 = 50$), investments (αx^2), and penalties (γW), but low enough to force meaningful trade-offs between production volume (Q) and circular investments (x). For example, at $x = 0$, gross profit per unit is $p - c_0 = 50$, which leaves room for penalties/taxes to influence behavior. If p is too high (e.g., 200), firms would prioritize Q over x, which causes overproduction and ignores waste constraints. This is because even with high production costs or penalties, the marginal profit from increasing Q is so large that firms ignore other terms (as shown by the equation below). The tax credit (τx) and cost savings ($c_1 h(x)$) are dwarfed by the opportunity cost of not producing more Q. Firms would just rationally accept penalties as a "cost of doing business" to maximize Q. Investing in circular practices, x, to reduce waste would yield smaller profits due to high αx^2 and lower Q from reallocating resources. Thus, firms facing high prices are likely to focus on short-term output maximization (especially in competitive markets) and defer long-term investments like circular practices. This mirrors real-world scenarios where lucrative markets (e.g., plastics, mining) resist sustainability measures without strong regulatory interventions (Clube & Hazemba, 2024; Smith & Brisman, 2021).

$$\pi(Q,x) = \underbrace{200Q}_{\text{High revenue}} - \underbrace{Q\left(c_0 - c_1 h(x)\right)}_{\text{Production cost}} - \underbrace{\alpha x^2}_{\text{Investment cost}} - \underbrace{\gamma W(Q,x)}_{\text{Penalty}} + \underbrace{\tau x}_{\text{Tax credit}}$$

If p is too low (e.g., 50), profits would be too slim to justify any investment in circular practices.

The waste cap, $\overline{W} = 100$, simulates strict but achievable environmental regulations. It creates a hard limit that firms face, which makes investments (x) essential to grow production. At low Q, firms may tolerate penalties. But, at high Q, the cap becomes binding and forces investment even if penalties are economically bearable. With $w_0 = 0.8$ (baseline waste per unit), the cap $\overline{W} = 100$ implies,

$$Q_{max} = \frac{\overline{W}}{W_0} = \frac{100}{0.8} = 125 \text{ units}$$

This creates a binding constraint as firms must either limit production or invest in circular practices ($x > 0$) to exceed 125 units. To produce $Q > 125$, firms must increase x to reduce waste per unit, $W(Q,x) = Q\left(w_0 e^{-\delta x}\right) \leq 100$. This forces firms to balance production scale with circular investments.

4.2 Experiment design

The simulation is implemented in Python using the *scipy.optimize* library, which allows for constrained nonlinear optimization. The firm maximizes its profit function, $\pi(Q,x)$ subject to the waste constraint $Q\left(w_0 e^{-\delta x}\right) \leq \overline{w}$ and non-negativity constraints ($Q \geq 0, x \geq 0$). The optimization problem is solved using the Sequential Least Squares Programming (SLSQP) algorithm, which is well-suited for constrained nonlinear problems. The solver starts with an initial guess ($Q = 10$, ,$x = 1$) to avoid local minima. The waste constraint is implemented as an inequality ($Q\left(w_0 e^{-\delta x}\right) \leq 100$), while non-negativity bounds are enforced explicitly. The solver approximates gradients numerically, and the algorithm terminates when the change in profit falls below a tolerance threshold (10^{-6}) or when constraints are satisfied within a small margin.

To explore the impact of policy parameters, I conduct a sensitivity analysis on the tax incentive rate (τ). Thus, τ is varied linearly from 0 to 50 and systematically tested across 20 equally spaced values between its minimum ($\tau = 0$, no incentives) and maximum ($\tau = 50$, strong incentives). Fewer steps might miss critical inflection points, while more steps add noise without new insights. Policymakers typically test incentive rates in discrete increments (e.g., 5% changes), so making 20 steps seems to be a pragmatic choice. This can help identify threshold effects (what level of τ triggers significant adoption of x) and saturation points (what level of τ yields minimal additional investment). For each τ, the optimization problem is re-solved to compute the new optimal (Q,x). Lastly, the results are stored and plotted to visualize (i) *investment response* (how x varies with τ), and (ii) *production trade-offs* (how Q responds non-monotonically due to the waste constraint).

4.3 Simulation Results

The numerical experiment reveals a more complex and interdependent relationship between tax incentives, circular investment, and production than initially interpreted. Both Figureure 1 and Figureure 2 show nearly identical response patterns because the model's structure creates a fundamental coupling between investment and production decisions under the waste constraint.

For τ between 0 to 35, both circular investment (x) and production quantity (Q) remain at or near zero. This occurs because without sufficient tax incentives, the production cost exceeds the unit price when accounting for potential waste penalties. Firms cannot profitably operate at any scale without first investing in waste-reducing circular practices. The binding waste constraint makes any production impossible without some circular investment. The activation threshold for τ is around 37, which represents the point where tax incentives finally offset the combined costs of base production (c_0), initial circular investments (αx^2), and residual waste penalties (γW).

This creates a simultaneous emergence of both circular investment and production.

Figure 1. Impact of Tax Incentives on Circular Investment

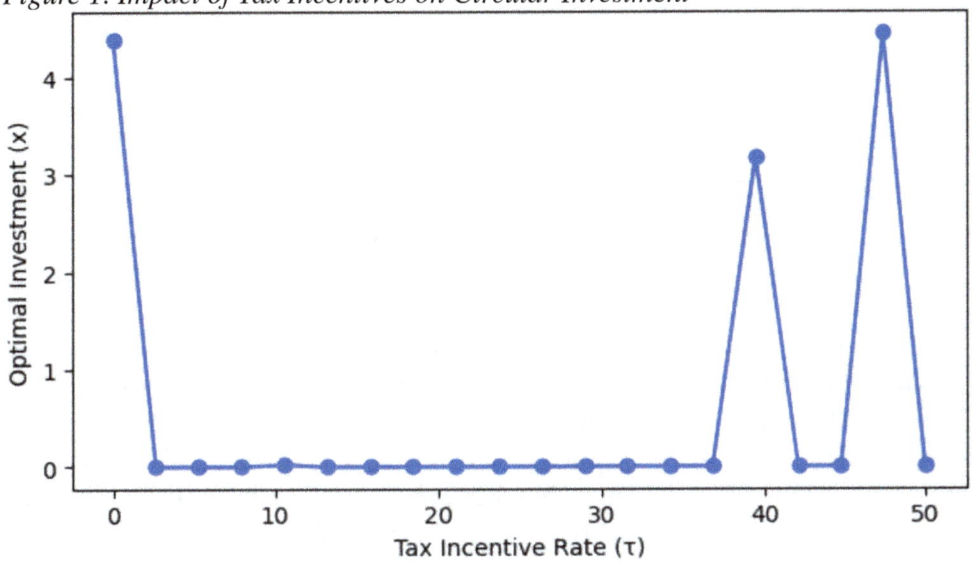

Figure 2. Impact of Tax Incentives on Production

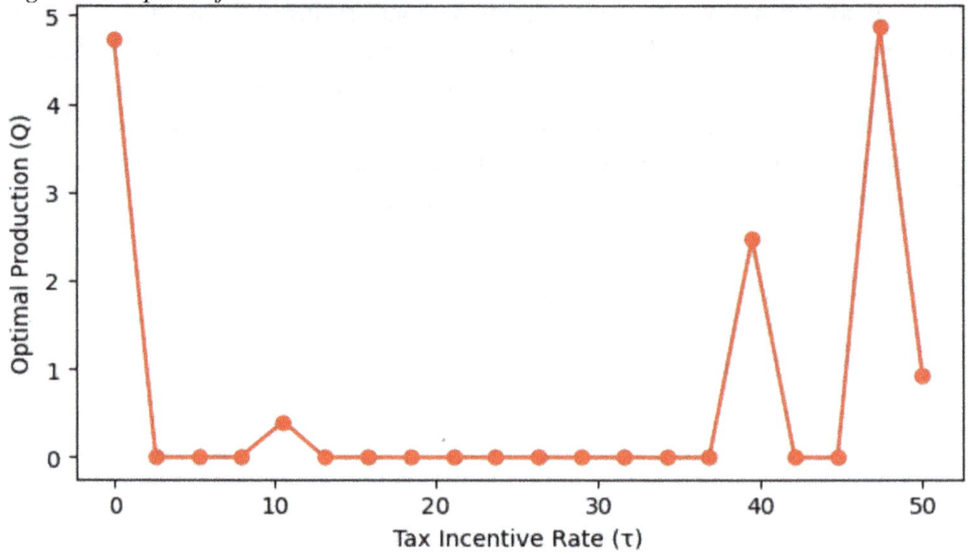

However, as τ approaches 40, firms dial back both x and Q. This is because reducing x cuts investment costs, while corresponding Q adjustment maintains $W(Q,x) \leq 100$. The parallel saturation patterns in both graphs occur because the waste constraint $W(Q,x)$ binds production (Q) and investment (x) together. This constraint forces a fixed proportional relationship between the two variables, and neither can increase independently without affecting the other. At higher τ values, while firms want to increase x further, the quadratic investment costs (αx^2) grow prohibitively large, and the exponential waste reduction ($e^{-\delta x}$) shows diminishing returns. This creates the same asymptotic approach in both variables - an initial rapid response when τ crosses the activation threshold, diminishing returns as x increases beyond a certain limit, and eventual flattening as the system approaches its mathematical limits (the waste constraint becomes strictly binding; marginal costs overwhelm marginal benefits; and further increases in τ yield negligible changes in x or Q).

As τ approaches 50, the optimization becomes increasingly complex. This is because the waste constraint ($\overline{w} = 100$) creates a razor-thin feasible region. Small changes in x generate disproportionate effects on allowable Q. The solver hunts for the precise (Q,x) combination that satisfies the $Q\left(w_0 e^{-\delta x}\right) \leq \overline{w}$, while maximizing $\pi(Q,x)$. The fluctuations represent tension between the linear benefit of τx (pushing x upward), the quadratic penalty of αx^2 (pushing x downward), and the exponential waste reduction $e^{-\delta x}$ (creating nonlinear production boundaries). The SLSQP solver exhibits this vacillating behavior because gradient calculations become unstable near constraint boundaries, the profit surface develops local maxima in this parameter region, and small numerical tolerances (10^{-6}) allow micro-adjustments that appear as oscillations. The system enters a metastable regime at this point where no dominant strategy exists, and policy effectiveness becomes unpredictable in this range.

4.4 Practical implications

The numerical results provide robust empirical validation of the analytical framework developed in this chapter. The simultaneous zero-output regime below $\tau = 37$ perfectly illustrates the analytical solution to the constrained optimization problem. It suggests that firms will remain inactive when incentives fail to offset the combined costs of production, investment, and penalties. The identical response patterns for x and Q validate the analytical relationship $W(Q,x) = Q\left(w_0 e^{-\delta x}\right) \leq \overline{w}$, which mathematically forces the observed coordination between production and investment decisions. This coupling explains why no partial adoption occurs, and why firms cannot marginally increase production without simultaneously implementing circular practices.

The results validate the necessity of including both threshold effects and constraint coupling in theoretical models of circular economy transitions. Traditional smooth response functions may fundamentally misrepresent firm behavior under stringent environmental regulations. The identified activation threshold provides an empirical benchmark for future modeling work and suggests that fixed costs of adoption must be explicitly incorporated in analytical frameworks. Policy instruments must be designed as coordinated packages, and isolated tax incentives below critical thresholds may have zero effect on both sustainability and economic outcomes. The tight coupling between production and circular investment implies that environmental regulations without adequate economic support mechanisms risk creating "no-go zones" where firms cannot operate profitably at any scale. The saturation effects suggest diminishing policy returns beyond certain investment levels, which highlights the need for balanced incentive structures that avoid over-subsidization. Firms should thus anticipate substantial upfront investments needed to simultaneously meet both economic and environmental objectives in constrained operating environments. To sum it up, my model provides a quantitative framework for evaluating the combined impact of regulatory costs and policy incentives on business viability.

These results advance circular economy theory by (i) demonstrating how environmental constraints fundamentally alter traditional production-investment decisions; (ii) quantifying the minimum policy intervention levels required to overcome adoption barriers; and (iii) revealing the nonlinear, threshold-driven nature of sustainable transitions.

5. LIMITATIONS

Despite the promising insights yielded by the analytical framework and numerical experiment simulation, several limitations warrant careful consideration. First, the analytical model is built on a representative-firm approach that abstracts from heterogeneity across different industries and firm sizes. This simplification, while useful for deriving general insights, limits the ability to capture sector-specific dynamics and market structures that may materially influence both cost structures and responsiveness to tax incentives. In practice, firms vary widely in their technological capabilities, access to capital, and regulatory environments. Future extensions of this research could incorporate firm-level heterogeneity or industry-specific case studies to more accurately reflect the diversity of responses to circular economy policies.

Another limitation arises from the functional forms used in the model. The production cost function, with its saturating cost-saving component $h(x) = 1 - e^{-kx}$, and the exponential decay model for waste reduction $W(Q,x) = Q\left(w_0 e^{-\delta x}\right)$, are both rooted in standard economic assumptions that imply diminishing returns. While these choices are theoretically justified and capture key trade-offs, they impose a specific non-linear structure that might not fully encompass the real-world complexity of circular investment returns. For example, there may be threshold effects or regime shifts, such as sudden changes in technological efficiency or cost reductions, that are not well-approximated by smooth exponential functions. Alternative functional forms or empirical calibration of these relationships could improve the model's realism and improve its predictive power.

The tax incentive function $T(x) = \tau x$ is modeled as a linear relationship, which simplifies the integration of fiscal benefits into the firm's decision-making process. However, real-world tax systems often exhibit non-linear features, such as tiered credit rates, phase-outs, or caps on subsidies. This linearity might overstate the efficacy of tax incentives at higher levels of investment, which may lead to an over-optimistic portrayal of their capability to drive circular transitions. Future research should consider incorporating more complex and realistic tax structures to evaluate how they might alter the optimal investment and production decisions.

Moreover, the investment cost function $I(x) = \alpha x^2$ is designed to capture the escalating marginal costs of additional circular investments. While the quadratic form is tractable and intuitively appealing, it may not fully capture cost dynamics in industries undergoing rapid technological innovation or shifts in capital intensity. In certain cases, economies of scale or learning-by-doing effects might lead to less convex cost structures, at least over an initial range of investment, while network effects or infrastructural bottlenecks could induce sharper cost escalations at later stages. The sensitivity of the model to the parameter α suggests that further empirical validation is needed to ensure that the cost function accurately reflects the economic realities faced by firms.

The numerical experiment simulation, which uses a constrained nonlinear optimization algorithm (SLSQP), also has its own set of limitations. One primary concern is the sensitivity of the optimization results to the choice of initial conditions and solver tolerances. As noted, the model exhibits regions of metastability, particularly near the binding waste constraint at high levels of the tax incentive rate (τ), where small numerical changes can lead to disproportionate shifts in the optimal solution. This instability indicates that the solution space may have multiple local optima, and the global optimum might not always be identified by the algorithm. While the SLSQP method is well-suited for the problem structure, future work might benefit from comparing different optimization strategies or employing global optimization techniques to ensure robustness.

Additionally, the simulation's parameter calibration is based on plausible industrial scenarios and draws from existing literature; however, the static nature of these parameters limits the dynamic interpretation of the model. The environment in which firms operate is subject to continuous change, from technological progress to evolving regulatory frameworks, and a static model may not fully reflect these temporal dynamics. Incorporating dynamic elements, such as time-varying parameters or a multi-period framework, could provide a richer understanding of how tax incentives affect firm behavior over time and how firms adjust their strategies in response to both internal learning and external shocks.

Finally, while the model successfully integrates production, investment, and waste constraints into a unified framework, it does not explicitly account for potential externalities or market feedback mechanisms. For example, the model assumes that firms act independently and that aggregate market effects, such as changes in supply and demand or shifts in competitive dynamics, are negligible. In practice, the broad adoption of circular practices may generate spillover benefits (or unintended consequences) that affect industry-wide pricing, resource availability, or innovation trajectories. Future research could extend the framework to a multi-firm setting or incorporate general equilibrium effects to capture these broader market interactions.

6. CASE STUDY

In this section, I present a case study that examines how targeted tax incentives can spur the adoption of circular economy practices within the context of the German packaging industry, a sector that is under increasing pressure to reduce waste and improve sustainability due to strict environmental regulations and growing consumer demand for sustainable products (Guikema, 2025).

Let's assume that the packaging industry currently faces high volumes of waste generation and stringent regulatory requirements aimed at curbing environmental impacts. In response, policymakers have introduced innovative tax incentive schemes designed to lower the effective cost of investing in circular practices such as improved recycling, improved resource recovery, and waste reduction technologies. Based on my findings from the analytical framework and the numerical experiment, it is possible that many firms in this sector found that the combined burdens of conventional production costs, high investment requirements for sustainable technologies, and steep waste penalties created a "no-go zone", where the prospect of profitability was negligible.

The analytical model developed in this chapter predicts that firms will remain largely inactive and maintain near-zero production and circular investment until tax incentives reach a critical activation threshold. Without policy reforms, companies are likely to report minimal investments in circular processes, as the net profit margins are eroded by high base production costs and punitive penalties for excessive waste. However, with the introduction of a tax credit scheme that provides a direct fiscal benefit proportional to the level of investment in circular practices, a marked shift can occur. Firms may begin to engage in simultaneous adjustments by both ramping up production and committing resources to circular investments. This concurrent emergence is consistent with my simulation findings, wherein both circular investment intensity and production quantity exhibited a sudden uptick once the tax incentive rate surpassed a critical level, which demonstrates that a threshold effect effectively mobilizes operational changes.

In practice, as firms increase their investments in circular practices, they would experience reductions in waste generation and associated penalties. This would enable them to operate at higher production levels within the limits imposed by strict waste caps. The tax incentive component of the policy would not only offset the upfront costs associated with these investments but also reinforce the interdependence of production decisions. Improvements in one area, such as improved recycling capabilities, may directly facilitate expansion in production by easing the regulatory burden, which substantiates the analytical prediction of a fixed proportional relationship between production quantity and circular investment.

While the initial response to the tax incentives could be robust, my numerical experiment simulation indicates that beyond a certain level of fiscal support, the benefits of additional tax incentives would begin to diminish. As firms increase their investment levels further, the quadratic nature of investment costs impose an accelerating cost penalty, and the marginal gains from waste reduction, modeled by the exponential decay function, would start to level off. Thus, several companies are likely to find that after surpassing a moderate level of circular investments, further enhancements in sustainable technology yield only marginal improvements in environmental performance. This saturation effect would align with my model's prediction and highlight a key policy implication - while tax incentives are key for overcoming initial adoption barriers, an overabundance of fiscal support may lead to diminishing returns and could potentially distort firms' strategic investments. As such, this case study serves as a cautionary tale that designing tax policies requires not only ensure sufficient fiscal support to trigger circular investments but also avoiding an oversupply of incentives that can lead to unstable operational strategies.

7. CONCLUSION AND FUTURE RESEARCH AGENDA

This chapter set out to explore a pressing question at the intersection of fiscal policy and sustainability: Can tax incentives act as catalysts for a circular economy? To address this, I developed a novel analytical model that captures how firms respond to environmental regulations and tax-based incentives when deciding whether and how much to invest in circular practices. The model integrates four key components, production costs, investment costs, environmental penalties, and tax credits, into a unified optimization framework, constrained by a regulatory waste limit. By solving this model through a numerical experiment and conducting a sensitivity analysis on tax incentive levels, I demonstrate how firms' production and investment decisions are simultaneously influenced by fiscal stimuli and environmental regulations.

The core findings of this study reaffirm the critical role of taxation in enabling circular transitions. First, the model reveals that firms face a threshold effect, i.e., below a certain tax incentive level, they find it unprofitable to produce at all, due to the combined burden of production costs, upfront investment requirements, and environmental penalties. Only when the tax credit rate crosses this activation threshold do firms simultaneously begin producing and investing in circular practices. Second, the results show that production and circular investment are tightly coupled under the waste constraint, i.e., firms cannot expand production without proportionally reducing waste per unit, which requires corresponding increases in circular investment. Third, the analysis identifies saturation effects, i.e., as tax incentives increase beyond a certain point, the marginal benefit of further investment declines due to the convex nature of investment costs and diminishing returns in waste reduction. This has important implications for policy design as the findings suggest that overly generous tax incentives may lead to inefficiencies or unintended strategic behaviors.

These findings contribute to the literature on circular economy transitions and environmental policy in several ways. The analytical model advances prior work by explicitly modeling firm-level decision making under the joint influence of fiscal and regulatory constraints, which is a gap identified in both theoretical and empirical studies (Milios, 2021; Losa, 2025). It builds on sector-specific insights from packaging and manufacturing industries (Deserno & Sterk, 2024; Scott, 2022) and extends them through generalizable mathematical formulations that can be applied across industries. Moreover, the numerical experiment provides important insights for policymakers, such as identifying minimum viable tax incentive levels and understanding where diminishing returns begin to set in. The results suggest that *a coordinated mix of fiscal and environmental policy tools* is necessary to overcome economic barriers to circular adoption while avoiding inefficient over-subsidization.

Nevertheless, this research is subject to several limitations. The model is based on a representative firm and does not account for heterogeneity in firm size, sectoral dynamics, or technological capabilities. The assumed functional forms, such as exponential decay in waste and quadratic investment costs, are stylized and, while theoretically justified, may not fully capture the complexity of real-world adoption trajectories. The tax incentive is modeled as a linear function, whereas actual policies may feature caps, thresholds, or regressivity. The numerical experiment, though carefully calibrated, is static and does not simulate dynamic adjustment over time, such as learning-by-doing or technological diffusion. Finally, the model does not account for general equilibrium effects or competitive responses in a multi-firm setting.

These limitations present valuable opportunities for future research. Future studies could extend the model to include firm heterogeneity, dynamic investment horizons, stochastic policy environments, and endogenous technological change. Empirical validation using firm-level panel data from sectors actively responding to green tax reforms, such as the EU's plastic levy or China's VAT reform, would also strengthen the policy relevance of such models. Moreover, future analytical frameworks could incorporate market feedbacks or simulate cross-firm strategic interactions to reflect real-world conditions more closely.

As governments around the world seek to meet ambitious climate and circularity targets, the insights from this chapter carry significant weight. The results suggest that simply introducing tax incentives is not enough; their magnitude, timing, and integration with environmental regulation determine whether firms can operate sustainably and profitably. If designed carefully, tax incentives can act as a catalytic mechanism, not only reducing barriers to adoption but also realigning profit motives with environmental objectives. However, poorly calibrated incentives risk either failing to trigger change or creating inefficiencies that erode fiscal and ecological outcomes. Thus, this study highlights that the transition to a more sustainable industrial system is not just a technological challenge, but also a *strategic economic optimization problem,* one in which the tax system can play a decisive role.

NOTE

During the preparation of this work the author used Anthropic's Claude AI in order to perform spelling and grammar checks and debug Python code. After using this tool/service, the author reviewed and edited the content as needed and takes full responsibility for the content of the publication.

REFERENCES

Anand, V. V., Balakrishnan, R., & Labro, E. (2019). A framework for conducting numerical experiments on cost system design. *Journal of Management Accounting Research*, *31*(1), 41–61. DOI: 10.2308/jmar-52057

Asgari, A., & Asgari, R. (2021). How circular economy transforms business models in a transition towards circular ecosystem: The barriers and incentives. *Sustainable Production and Consumption*, *28*, 566–579. DOI: 10.1016/j.spc.2021.06.020

Bocken, N. M., Harsch, A., & Weissbrod, I. (2022). Circular business models for the fastmoving consumer goods industry: Desirability, feasibility, and viability. *Sustainable Production and Consumption*, *30*, 799–814. DOI: 10.1016/j.spc.2022.01.012

Clube, R. K., & Hazemba, M. (2024). From waste to resource: Demystifying the policy challenges and identifying opportunities for a circular economy in Zambia. *Frontiers in Sustainability*, *5*, 1300904. DOI: 10.3389/frsus.2024.1300904

Deserno, L., & Sterk, E. (2024). Resource Taxes as an Instrument to Foster Circularity? Analysis of the Effects of Resource Taxation on Circular Economy Progress in Europe. *Circular Economy and Sustainability*, •••, 1–27.

Elroi, H., Zbigniew, G., Agnieszka, W. C., & Piotr, S. (2023). Enhancing waste resource efficiency: Circular economy for sustainability and energy conversion. *Frontiers in Environmental Science*, *11*, 1303792. DOI: 10.3389/fenvs.2023.1303792

Eunomia (2022). *Circular Taxation - A policy approach to reduce resource use and accelerate the transition to a circular economy.* European Environmental Bureau (EEB) Final Report. Retrieved from Link

European Economic and Social Committee. (2016). *The Circular Economy: Beneficial for All.* Employer's Group Report. Retrieved from Link

Grafström, J., & Aasma, S. (2021). Breaking circular economy barriers. *Journal of Cleaner Production*, *292*, 126002. DOI: 10.1016/j.jclepro.2021.126002

Guikema, A. J. (2025, February 11). *German Packaging Act (VerpackG): A 2025 Guide to International Packaging Laws (Part 1).* Sustainable-Markets.com. Retrieved from Link

Hart, J., Adams, K., Giesekam, J., Tingley, D. D., & Pomponi, F. (2019). Barriers and drivers in a circular economy: The case of the built environment. *Procedia CIRP*, *80*, 619–624. DOI: 10.1016/j.procir.2018.12.015

His Majesty's Revenue and Customs. (2021). *Introduction of Plastic Packaging Tax from April 2022.* Retrieved from Link

Jackson, A. (2023). *The Circular Built Environment Playbook.* World Green Building Council. Retrieved from Link

Knox, B. D. (2020). Semantic processing theory could help explain the effectiveness of creativity incentives: A numerical experiment. *Journal of Management Accounting Research*, *32*(3), 155–178. DOI: 10.2308/jmar-18-051

Losa, R. (2025). Public policies on circular economy: A systematic review. *Ecological Economics*, *228*, 108452. DOI: 10.1016/j.ecolecon.2024.108452

Milios, L. (2021). Towards a circular economy taxation framework: Expectations and challenges of implementation. *Circular Economy and Sustainability*, *1*(2), 477–498. DOI: 10.1007/s43615-020-00002-z

Munteanu, I., Ionescu-Feleagă, L., & Ionescu, B. . (2024). Financial Strategies for Sustainability: Examining the Circular Economy Perspective. *Sustainability (Basel)*, *16*(20), 8942. DOI: 10.3390/su16208942

Qi, Y., Zhang, J., & Chen, J. (2023). Tax incentives, environmental regulation and firms' emission reduction strategies: Evidence from China. *Journal of Environmental Economics and Management*, *117*, 102750. DOI: 10.1016/j.jeem.2022.102750

Schlosser, R., Chenavaz, R. Y., & Dimitrov, S. (2021). Circular economy: Joint dynamic pricing and recycling investments. *International Journal of Production Economics*, *236*, 108117. DOI: 10.1016/j.ijpe.2021.108117

Scott, C. (2022). *Plastic Packaging Tax: How you're affected and how we can help.* Green Economy. Retrieved from Link

Singh, R. K., Kumar, A., Garza-Reyes, J. A., & de Sá, M. M. (2020). Managing operations for circular economy in the mining sector: An analysis of barriers intensity. *Resources Policy*, *69*, 101752. DOI: 10.1016/j.resourpol.2020.101752

Smith, O., & Brisman, A. (2021). Plastic waste and the environmental crisis industry. *Critical Criminology*, *29*(2), 289–309. DOI: 10.1007/s10612-021-09562-4 PMID: 33746527

Takacs, F., Brunner, D., & Frankenberger, K. (2022). Barriers to a circular economy in small-and medium-sized enterprises and their integration in a sustainable strategic management framework. *Journal of Cleaner Production*, *362*, 132227. DOI: 10.1016/j.jclepro.2022.132227

Vence, X., & López Pérez, S. D. J. (2021). Taxation for a circular economy: New instruments, reforms, and architectural changes in the fiscal system. *Sustainability (Basel)*, *13*(8), 4581. DOI: 10.3390/su13084581

Vermunt, D. A., Negro, S. O., Verweij, P. A., Kuppens, D. V., & Hekkert, M. P. (2019). Exploring barriers to implementing different circular business models. *Journal of Cleaner Production*, *222*, 891–902. DOI: 10.1016/j.jclepro.2019.03.052

Wang, J. X., Burke, H., & Zhang, A. (2022). Overcoming barriers to circular product design. *International Journal of Production Economics*, *243*, 108346. DOI: 10.1016/j.ijpe.2021.108346

Zhao, X., Li, J., & Li, Y. (2022). Impact of environmental tax on corporate sustainable performance: Insights from high-tech firms in China. *International Journal of Environmental Research and Public Health*, *20*(1), 461. DOI: 10.3390/ijerph20010461 PMID: 36612778

KEY TERMS AND DEFINITIONS

Activation Threshold: The minimum level of tax incentive rate required to make circular economy investments economically viable for firms, below which firms remain inactive with zero production and investment

Circular Economy (CE): An economic model that prioritizes resource efficiency, waste minimization, and material regeneration as an alternative to the traditional linear take-make-dispose paradigm

Circular Investment Intensity: The level of investment a firm makes in circular economy practices such as recycling technologies, remanufacturing processes, or closed-loop supply chains

Constraint Coupling: The mathematical relationship where production quantity and circular investment are bound together by the waste constraint, which prevents independent optimization of either variable

Diminishing Returns: The economic principle where additional investments in circular practices yield progressively smaller benefits, modeled through exponential decay functions in waste reduction

Extended Producer Responsibility (EPR): A policy approach where producers bear responsibility for the environmental impacts of their products throughout the entire lifecycle, including end-of-life disposal costs

Fiscal Instruments: Economic policy tools including tax credits, deductions, subsidies, and levies used by governments to influence firm behavior toward desired outcomes

Investment Cost Function: A quadratic function representing the escalating marginal costs of scaling up circular economy practices

Metastable Regime: A state in the optimization model where small parameter changes lead to significant shifts in optimal decisions, indicating policy effectiveness becomes unpredictable

Production Cost Function: The total cost of producing units by incorporating both baseline costs and reductions achieved through circular investments

Quadratic Cost Structure: A mathematical representation where costs increase at an accelerating rate, which indicates the reality that advanced circular technologies become disproportionately expensive

Regulatory Arbitrage: The practice of firms relocating operations to regions with weaker environmental enforcement to avoid compliance costs rather than investing in sustainable practices

Saturation Effect: The point beyond which additional tax incentives yield diminishing returns due to quadratic investment costs and flattening gains from waste reduction

Sequential Least Squares Programming (SLSQP): A numerical optimization algorithm used to solve constrained nonlinear problems (employed in the simulation to find optimal production and investment levels)

Tax Credit Rate: The fiscal benefit per unit of circular investment, which represents the strength of government incentives to encourage sustainable practices

Tax Incentive Function: A linear function which represents the total tax benefits received based on the level of circular economy investment

Threshold Effect: The phenomenon where policy interventions show no impact below a critical level but trigger significant behavioral changes once that level is exceeded

Waste Constraint: The regulatory limit on total waste generation that firms must comply with, forcing trade-offs between production scale and circular investment

Waste Generation Function: An exponential function that models how total waste output depends on production quantity and the effectiveness of circular investments in reducing waste per unit

Zero-Output Regime: The operational state where firms find it unprofitable to produce at any scale due to insufficient tax incentives to offset combined production, investment, and penalty costs

Chapter 5
Does the Taxation of Plastic Bags Influence Consumption in the European Union?

Susana Raquel Patrão
https://orcid.org/0009-0004-2922-8460
University of Aveiro, Portugal

Sérgio Cruz
https://orcid.org/0000-0002-4454-2800
University of Aveiro, Portugal

Francisco Carreira
https://orcid.org/0000-0001-9913-4698
Polytechnic Institute of Setúbal, Portugal

ABSTRACT

This chapter aims to contribute to the analysis of the effectiveness of European environmental policy in reducing the consumption of plastic bags and to highlight the countries that have contributed most to mitigating environmental degradation. We analysed Eurostat data on the consumption of plastic bags per inhabitant and the taxation policies adopted by Member States of European Union between 2018 and 2022. The main conclusion of this study indicates that taxation of plastic bags has advantages for environmental protection, as it reduces consumption. Belgium, Poland, Portugal and Austria have lower values of bags per inhabitant and are seen as examples. Ireland stands out for having reduced consumption by 90% in

DOI: 10.4018/979-8-3373-2492-0.ch005

just one year. Lithuania and Latvia are far from reaching the target set by the EU of 40 bags per inhabitant by 2025. Awareness-raising campaigns and the use of reusable/recyclable alternatives are considered options for reducing consumption.

INTRODUCTION

The consumption of plastic bags and their environmental impact has been a pressing concern at a global level. The excessive use of these types of products and the lack of measures regarding their life cycle have contributed to the increase in pollution. Thompson et al. (2009) admit that humanity will become increasingly dependent on plastics in the coming decades.

Given this problem, it is crucial to adopt preventive measures to minimize and regulate the use of plastic bags.

The European Union (EU) has been dealing with this issue since 1975, when the first directive on waste was issued - Council Directive 75/442/EEC of 15 July 1975. Its regulatory role is to harmonise the legislation of each member state, with a view to protecting the environment and improving quality of life. This legislation is seen as a reference for countries to draw up management plans on these matters.

As regards the basic regulations in the field of plastics, we have the legal instrument on packaging and packaging waste - Directive 94/62/EC of the European Parliament and of the Council of 20 December 1994. This allows for a standardisation of the way in which EU countries can prevent and reduce the environmental impact of these materials, taking as a reference the principles of reuse, recycling and recovery of waste. The directive requires the disclosure and submission of information regarding its compliance, as well as the production of reports with the values at national level of each country. It was repealed in 2025 by Regulation (EU) 2025/40 of the European Parliament and of the Council of 19 December 2024, to clarify the requirements and rules for making all packaging reusable and recyclable by 2030.

Over the years, there has been a need to specifically regulate the consumption of plastic bags, and in 2015, a directive was introduced exclusively to reduce the consumption of these products - Directive (EU) 2015/720 of the European Parliament and of the Council of 29 April 2015. This directive defined for the first time the concept of lightweight plastic bags, with a thickness of less than 50 microns, considered the most polluting due to their propensity to become litter, given their lightness, with a low recycling rate. In addition to this fundamental concept, the notion of a very lightweight plastic bag, with a thickness of 15 microns, was also defined. We also highlight the importance of the targets set for reducing the consumption of plastic bags by each Member State, namely the annual limit of 90 bags per person by 2019, with consumption having to fall to 40 by 2025. The application of taxes and fees to these products is seen as an effective measure to reduce consumption.

The communication and dissemination of this information, for its comparability, is also defined by the EU in the following documents: Commission Decision 2005/270/EC of 22 March 2005 and Commission Implementing Decision (EU) 2018/896 of 19 June 2018. Both provide guidelines for the measurement and dissemination of statistics for each Member State. The first known data are from 2018.

Following the publication of European guidelines for reducing the consumption of plastic bags, there was a need to target measures for waste resulting from the end-of-life of plastics. In this context, Directive (EU) 2019/904 of the European Parliament and of the Council of 5 June 2019 on the reduction of the impact of certain plastic products on the environment was adopted, with the aim of protecting marine life and biodiversity and enabling the transition to a circular economy. In addition to providing for several bans, it refers to producer responsibility as part of the solution and highlights the importance of recycling. The EU aims for all member states to reduce plastic packaging waste by 5% by 2030, compared to 2018 figures, with a target of 10% by 2035 and 15% by 2040.

It is also important to mention, within the scope of the EU's guidelines, the European Green Deal, which aims to identify the following strategies to mitigate the environmental impacts caused by the consumption of plastics, to achieve climate neutrality. In summary, we highlight the main objectives regarding the issue under study: to strengthen the strategy so that by 2030 all plastics are recyclable or reusable, to increase the use of recycled products, to combat the use of single-use plastics and to promote more sustainable products.

Therefore, we consider it important to analyse the efficiency of European environmental policy in reducing the consumption of plastic bags, as well as to assess which countries have contributed to mitigating environmental degradation in this area. We also intend to verify whether taxation on plastic bags influences their consumption.

In addition to this introduction, this article is organized as follows: literature review; methodology; results and their analysis; conclusions with limitations and suggestions for future research.

VIEW OF PLASTIC BAG CONSUMPTION

"Plastic is a lightweight, hygienic and strong material that can be molded into different shapes and used in a wide range of applications" (United Nations Environment Programme 2018, p.2).

According to European legislation, plastic bags can be classified according to their thickness as follows: very light (thickness less than 15 microns) and light (thickness between 15 and 50 microns). Bags with a thickness greater than 50 microns, although they are expected and used, do not have an officially defined term. According to Gómez and Escobar (2022), plastic bags can also be categorized according to their use: transport bags and garbage bags. Those that represent the greatest concern, due to their environmental impact, are single-use plastic bags.

The excessive consumption of these products has contributed significantly to environmental degradation, with increased pollution. Every year, 300 million tons of plastic waste are produced, but only 9% is recycled worldwide (García-Marín et al., 2024). China, Indonesia, the Philippines, Vietnam and Sri Lanka are considered the largest plastic polluters, accounting for 56% of plastic waste worldwide, according to Rhodes (2018). The Philippines stands out with 356,371 tons of plastic recorded reaching the ocean in 2021, a fact mentioned by Fayshal (2024).

The consumption of these products has grown exponentially since 1970, the year in which they were introduced as an alternative to paper bags (O'Brien & Thondhlana, 2019). Clapp & Swanston (2009) report that it was only in 1977 that supermarkets began to offer plastic bags, which were promoted by the oil and gas industry in the United States of America. In the case of Western Europe, this behavior dates to the 1980s, and this practice reached developing countries ten years later.

Negative impacts on the environment are present throughout the life cycle of plastic bags, from the extraction of raw material, manufacturing and disposal. The main raw materials in the manufacturing process are crude oil and natural gas, with the emission of associated greenhouse gases (Li et al., 2022), with 4% of these materials allocated to the production of plastics, worldwide, highlighted by Hopewell et al. (2009). In 2019, the estimate of these gases was 1.8 gigatons, that is, 3.4% of global emissions that year (OECD, 2022).

Globally, plastic production could exceed 650 million tons by 2050, according to Fayshal (2024).

Although the scenario described is not desirable, European countries are the leaders in terms of regulations to minimize environmental impacts, according to the United Nations Environment Programme (2019).

Over the years, this issue has been investigated and analyzed to contribute to improving and preserving the environment, and to provide guidance for mitigating the effects of this type of pollution.

The consumption of single-use plastic bags in the United States in 2014 was approximately 103 billion. These figures have raised concerns among local governments. Measures have been taken to combat this excessive consumption, including bans on their use, taxes and fees, consumer education and mandatory take-back programs by retailers, according to a study by Wagner (2017).

Regarding Japan, there is evidence of a reduction in the consumption of plastic bags after the implementation of fees, because of a survey carried out by the Ministry of the Environment among consumers, with reductions of 40%. Nishijima & Nakatani (2024) found that the weekly consumption of plastic bags fell from 6 to 2 per inhabitant.

The United States of America and Japan are the countries that consume the most plastic packaging, according to Adeyanju et al. (2021). These authors also state that China is the country that wastes the most plastic bags.

A study by Tan et al. (2023) identifies the implementation of a ban on the use of single-use plastic bags in China, but they state that alternatives can trigger more significant environmental impacts throughout the life cycle of substitute products. This change could have a 1.4 to 22.6 times greater impact on the environment, as products that decompose after use will have to be disposed of in appropriate places. Wang et al. (2021) identified a 46% reduction in plastic bag consumption in China, with a 36% increase in reusable bags. However, not everyone follows the prohibitive measures imposed. Other measures will have to be found to combat this type of consumption.

The reality in South Africa shows that the use of plastic bags is still widespread, despite efforts to change these practices through taxes (O'Brien & Thondhlana, 2019). With the implementation of measures to reduce this consumption, there was an 80% reduction, as shown by Nielsen et al. (2019). This practice was not maintained over time, given that the tax levied was very low and the regulations did not provide for an increase in taxation on these products, thus contrasting with the reality in Botswana, which has been successful since 2007, according to the study by Dikgang & Visser (2012).

In the case of Australia, the regulation of plastic packaging has remained practically the same over the last two decades, as mentioned in the study by Johnson et al. (2025). This research brought together experts to assess new measures for new regulations in this area.

Serbia also falls short of what is desirable, as citizens' environmental awareness is not developed for the protection and preservation of the environment. Todorović et al. (2023) state that fees on plastic bags do not impact the reduction of consumption, as the low amount charged is considered income for traders without being allocated to environmental purposes. The lack of transparency and substitutes for plastic bags are cited as reasons for the failure to reduce consumption.

At European level, this issue was given relevance through the creation of specific regulations for plastic bags, with the aim of member states transposing the guidelines and policy instruments for reducing pollution into their regulations. Each country has adopted various measures over time to minimize the harmful effects on the environment caused by the consumption of plastic bags, with taxation being the cross-cutting approach found in managing this problem, as well as their prohibition. The study by Desalegn & Tangl (2022) analyzed both options, with prohibition being used more frequently in developing countries and taxation observed in developed countries. They also highlight that the role of governments and policymakers is essential in drafting legislation that promotes the reduction of environmental impacts.

For Uji et al. (2025), higher-income countries are more likely to adopt regulations to control pollution, but it is countries in the Global South that take the lead in regulating the consumption of plastic bags, through fees and bans. The perspective of Todorović et al. (2023) is consistent in the case of higher-income countries, however, the authors argue that lower-income countries do not highlight this issue enough due to economic and social problems.

Dove et al. (2025) assume that there are three forms of taxation available to combat the environmental impacts caused by plastics: 1) Taxation at the industrial level – in the initial phase of plastic use, which is crucial for researching and developing more sustainable products, but represents an increase in costs for companies; 2) Taxation at the consumer level – direct incidence on the consumption of non-recyclable bags, at the various points of sale. The possibility that consumers do not have plastic-free alternatives invalidates the change in behavior, so the revenue obtained does not minimize the number of plastics in circulation. While, on the one hand, taxing plastic directly at the end consumer allows for a similar distribution of the per capita tax burden among Member States, on the other hand, it proves to be more complex given the number of stakeholders involved and the difficulty in verifying all products containing plastic, emphasized by Ventosa et al. (2018); 3) Taxing the waste – only at the end of the plastic's life cycle is taxation introduced, in order to increase recycling, but there are no fees while the plastic is in circulation. Of all the options listed, the first is considered the most efficient.

Regarding the ban on the consumption of bags, this measure could jeopardize its purpose, given that the lack of suitable alternatives, the limited monitoring capacity for compliance and even the power of the plastics industry are conditions for the success of its implementation, as highlighted by Muposhi et al. (2022).

The study by Martinho et al. (2017) highlights some countries that have adopted taxation as a political instrument to mitigate the environmental damage caused by the consumption of these products and the results obtained. Spain has seen a 40% reduction in the consumption of plastic bags, Denmark 50%, and Belgium has seen a reduction between 60% and 80%. In the Spanish case, more specifically in the Community of Asturias, the revenue obtained from this type of taxation is allocated to environmental expenses, as highlighted by Gómez (2021).

In Portugal, consumption fell by 74% after the implementation of a fee of €0,10 per bag, accompanied by a 61% increase in the use of reusable plastic bags. Over the years, several bans have been implemented, as well as new fees on single-use plastic products and certain types of plastic bags, as reported by Patrão et al. (2025). Regarding plastic packaging recycling rates, Prata et al. (2022) report that Portugal has a rate of 34%, still far from the European targets of 42%.

Greece imposed a fee of €0,04, leading to an 80,3% reduction in consumption after 1 year, according to Milbreta et al. (2025). Charging this fee reinforced the adoption of pro-environmental behaviors, with marine pollution being a factor considered, according to the study by Mentis et al. (2022) through questionnaires analyses.

Convery et al. (2007) consider Ireland to be a success story, as it achieved a 90% reduction in the consumption of plastic bags. This was achieved due to the introduction of a fee of €0,15 per plastic bag, which was previously provided free of charge at points of sale. For Nielsen et al. (2019), Portugal is also considered an example of success in this reduction, as well as Germany, Denmark and Belgium. This author also highlights that most taxes on the consumption of plastic bags are passed on to the end consumer, however in Denmark the option was to charge producers directly. This country was a pioneer in imposing fees on these products in 1993, according to Abate & Elofsson (2024). The average amount charged per plastic bag for the year 2020 is around €0,54.

The option of charging fees directly to producers is seen as a mechanism to mitigate the effects of pollution caused by plastic bags, according to Pruess & Garrett (2025). The study by these authors showed that Germany, France and Belgium have shown effective results in this context, with producers being held responsible for managing the end-of-life of these products.

Sweden stands out as a country that is willing to continue its policies on plastic bags, supporting recycling, reuse and the development of waste management systems associated with these products. They are also in favor of deposit/refund systems, however, bans, taxes and stricter regulations are not as appealing to reduce the consumption of these products, as shown by Holmberg & Persson (2023) in their research on Swedish public opinion.

The environmental reasons associated with this cause mean that policies aimed at reducing the consumption of plastic bags are well accepted by society, and in the case of Portugal, there is agreement on the implementation of taxes and levies on these products. Taxation has resulted in a decrease in consumption, with a drop in the production and sale of plastic bags, leading to the adoption of reuse habits, as evidenced in the study by Luís et al. (2020). "The trend will be for the rate to approach zero, which is synonymous with the establishment of more responsible and sustainable consumption" (Patrão et al., 2025 p.21).

Despite the EU's efforts to harmonize with its member states on this issue, each country presents its own strategy regarding the use of plastic bags. Li et al. (2022) state that investment should be made in reusable alternatives to reduce pollution and associated energy consumption, accompanied by policy measures and other incentives.

Milbreta et al. (2025) state that the effectiveness of legislation to reduce plastic consumption depends on the involvement of the retail sector and not on the specific policies implemented to mitigate this problem. This sector is essential to disseminate more sustainable consumption, as they are aware of consumer consumption patterns and preferences. There must be coordination between these and governments to ensure the success of reducing plastic bag consumption.

Fayshal (2024) states that these efforts must be aligned with the Sustainable Development Goals, to ensure a cleaner and safer environment, namely sustainable consumption and production (SDG 12), and protect marine life (SDG 14).

Awareness campaigns are also considered a crucial tool for solving this problem, whether by governments, non-governmental organizations or companies, to promote a culture of responsible waste management and the reduction of plastic bag consumption, supported by Aare et al. (2024). To achieve sustainable development, it is essential to dissociate consumer behavior from the use of plastic bags, as stated by Ritch et al. (2009). These measures are essential to change consumption habits, as historical, cultural and behavioral factors continue to weigh on the results, for Kedzierski et al. (2020).

Chandra (2020) advocates a behavioral approach, given that the application of fee can lead to a reduction in guilt regarding environmental issues, requiring interventions that are not directly related to price. His research shows that it is possible to frame the issue in a way that motivates consumers by identifying the commitment, to use their plastic bags whenever necessary. This approach is as effective as the fee on plastic bags.

Still at a behavioral level, we find the study by Rivers et al. (2017) in which they state that the incidence of the fee on plastic bags influenced consumers of reusable bags, around 3.4%, however, no evidence was found of a change in the consumption pattern for those who did not have this habit. They also state that the fees applied have a low value to economically disincentivize consumers, with the desirable results being more visible in consumers with a higher socioeconomic status, not impacting those with a medium/low economic status.

Other behavioral studies highlight monetary incentives as an option to change consumption. Lange et al. (2021) tested an alternative way to encourage consumers to abandon plastic bags, namely by asking consumers to donate each bag they do not use in a restaurant's take-away to a charity. The results obtained were a reduction of the usual consumption of plastic bags by more than half, thus proving that pro-social incentives also contribute to a better environment.

In addition to the measures mentioned in the various studies presented, there was a paradigm shift in relation to the regulation of plastic bags, that is, measures were created aligned with the different phases of the life cycle of these products, instead of focusing only on the waste phase. There is a need for more regulation and strong political measures to move towards a circular plastic economy, according to Syberg et al. (2021). This transition has been gaining prominence in literature, given its relevance, being one of the ways found to change production and consumption patterns of plastic bags, as emphasized by Boeve & Waal (2024). For Eckert et al. (2024) and Milios (2018), political action is still very focused on the end of the life cycle of plastic bags.

With the change in focus regarding the management of plastic bag regulations and the associated environmental impacts, we find Chen et al. (2024) who highlight a greater interest in biodegradable products as substitutes for plastics. These are presented as being more advantageous in reducing emissions, whether in the production or waste disposal phase.

Biodegradable alternatives are more viable and environmentally friendly solutions for Gómez & Escobar (2022), given that they are produced with renewable and non-polluting raw materials. These products are seen as a better alternative, given consumers' aversion to fees on plastic bags, as evidenced in the study by Dunn et al. (2014).

For Ramachandruni & Ravi (2023), eco-friendly bags are the best solution, as they reduce plastic and contribute to a better environment.

Hopewell et al. (2009) argue that recycling allows for a reduction in greenhouse gas emissions, as well as a reduction in the amount of plastic waste that needs to be disposed of. They also warn that recycling varies geographically.

However, recycling is a costly process, given the high demand for economic and human resources to convert waste into useful products. For Iheukwumere et al. (2020), this option or the use of other alternatives does not have a zero environmental impact. The most advantageous way to prioritize the environment is to always consider the life cycle of plastic bags, from production to disposal. Reusable plastic bags are considered the best alternative in environmental terms, with a 60% lower impact than a single-use paper bag. Despite this fact, Iheukwumere et al. (2020) state that paper bags are a growing possibility with negative impacts on forests. An example of this practice is evidenced in the study by Frey & Cifuentes (2024), with a reduction in the consumption of plastic bags by replacing paper bags, in the Chilean case. They also identify an increase of more than 50% in garbage bags.

The cost of these processes and the lack of tax incentives to produce biodegradable products may in some cases be a barrier to their development. The conclusions of the study by Gómez (2021) highlight the lack of tax benefits in the Spanish case. In his opinion, if there were incentives of this nature, it would be possible to resort to the technological innovation needed to implement more efficient and ecological systems, as well as environmental investments.

Policies to mitigate this problem must be more rigorous, including the use of environmentally friendly taxation, consumer education, the promotion of industrial innovation and the application of extended producer responsibility. These are essential factors for encouraging more sustainable consumption, which together make it possible to achieve pollution reduction targets. The study by Dokl et al. (2024) indicates that the most successful countries are those that adopt these types of measures.

After analyzing trends in various countries to reduce the consumption of plastic bags, we highlight the main results of the most relevant studies in the table below – Table 1.

Table 1. Results of the most relevant studies on reducing plastic bag consumption

Country	Policy Instruments	Effects	References
United States of America	Ban/Fee	Largest plastic bag waste recorded Implementation of measures to reduce the recorded consumption of 103 billion plastic bags in 2014	Adeyanju et al. (2021) Wagner (2017)
Japan	Fee	40% reduction in plastic bag consumption	Nishijima & Nakatani (2023)
China	Ban	Largest waste of plastic bags recorded Use of alternatives that can impact the environment 46% reduction in the consumption of plastic bags, accompanied by a 36% increase in the use of reusable bags	Adeyanju et al. (2021) Tan et al. (2023) Wang et al. (2021)
South Africa	Fee	Widespread use of plastic bags 80% reduction in plastic bag consumption	O'Brien & Thondhlana (2019) Nielsen et al. (2019)
Botswana	Fee	50% reduction in the consumption of plastic bags has been recorded since 2007	Dikgang & Visser (2012)
Australia	Ban	Regulations unchanged over the last two decades	Johnson et al. (2025)
Indonesia	Pricing	Considered the biggest plastic polluters, along with China, representing 56% of plastic waste worldwide Philippines recorded 356,371 tons of plastic that reached the ocean	Rhodes (2018) Fayshal (2024) Nielsen et al. (2019)
Philippines			
Vietnam			
Sri Lanka			
Serbia	Fee	No impact on reducing consumption, as the fee is income for traders	Todorović et al. (2023)
Spain	Fee	40% reduction in plastic bag consumption	Martinho et al. (2017)

continued on following page

Table 1. Continued

Country	Policy Instruments	Effects	References
Denmark	Fee	50% reduction in the consumption of plastic bags Pioneering country in the implementation of this type of taxation, the rate of which is charged directly to producers and not to consumers as in most cases.	Martinho et al. (2017) Abate & Elofsson (2024)
Germany	Ban/Fee	Effective results in reducing consumption, as responsibility for the end of life of bags is attributed to producers	Pruess & Garrett (2025)
Belgium	Fee	Reduction of 60% to 80% in the consumption of plastic bags Effective results in reducing consumption, as responsibility for the end of life of bags is attributed to producers	Martinho et al. (2017) Pruess & Garrett (2025)
Portugal	Fee	74% reduction in plastic bag consumption, accompanied by a 61% increase in the use of reusable bags 34% plastic packaging recycling rat Adoption of reuse habits	Martinho et al. (2017) Prata et al. (2022) Luís et al. (2020)
France	Ban	Effective results in reducing consumption, as responsibility for the end of life of bags is attributed to producers	Pruess & Garrett (2025)
Greece	Fee	80,3% reduction in plastic bag consumption after 1 year Strengthening more sustainable practices, considering the marine environment	Milbreta et al. (2025) Mentis et al. (2022)
Ireland	Fee	90% reduction in plastic bag consumption	Convery et al. (2007)
Sweden	Fee	Consumers more in favor of recycling and reuse than taxes and bans	Holmberg & Persson (2023)

Source: own elaboration

DATA AND SAMPLE COLLECTION METHODOLOGY

Our study adopts a mixed methodology, given that we intend to analyze secondary quantitative and qualitative data. The combination of these data is in line with mixed secondary analysis. Our approach is supported by Bowen (2009), Chatfield (2020) and Creswell & Creswell (2018).

At a quantitative level, we have statistical data available from Eurostat, relating to the consumption of plastic bags per inhabitant in the countries of the European

Union. On a qualitative level, we have data from other scientific studies on European environmental policy, the effectiveness of implemented taxation and the European directives transposed by countries into their respective regulations. The data cited are considered secondary, as they were extracted from official sources and scientific literature.

At both levels highlighted we are faced with documentary analysis, which meets what Bowen (2009) defines as an analytical method that allows the analysis and interpretation of information from existing documents to develop empirical knowledge.

Chatfield (2020) reports that studies that use existing data, official statistics and other scientific investigations fall under mixed secondary analysis. This combination allows the integration of data on the consumption of plastic bags per inhabitant in the member states of the European Union and the scientific literature of other studies on European environmental policies, to assess which have contributed most to mitigating the degradation of the environmental problems underlying the topic under study. The effectiveness of taxation on plastic bags in the European Union is also evidence that we can measure with this type of methodology.

The data collected allows us to interpret and contextualize it, to verify trends and impacts, according to Creswell & Creswell (2018). This author argues that this triangulation of data contributes to strengthening the research, allowing a holistic view of the object under study. The data will be subject to a descriptive statistical analysis, through calculations of average values, minimum values, maximum values, standard deviation and coefficient of variation, identifying trends and dispersions in the annual consumption of plastic bags per inhabitant.

The dataset to be analysed is in accordance with Directive 94/62/EC of the European Parliament and of the Council of 20 December 1994 on packaging and packaging waste and Commission Directive 2015/720 of 22 March 2005 for lightweight plastic carrier bags (<50 microns thick) made available at points of sale to consumers and calculated based on applicable taxes and levies. The latter document obliges Member States to report information on the annual consumption of plastic carrier bags to the European Commission from 2018 onwards.

Given the requirement, Eurostat only has data available between 2018 and 2022. This condition was essential for us to define this period for analysis.

From the information available for the 27 member states, we chose to analyze the countries with data available for all years, excluding those with estimates or gaps in some years. In an initial analysis, our sample consists of 15 countries: Belgium, Bulgaria, Germany, Ireland, Spain, Italy, Cyprus, Latvia, Lithuania, Luxembourg, Austria, Slovenia, Slovakia, Finland and Sweden. In the second analysis, exclusively for the year 2022, we chose to include relevant countries in this context, namely Denmark, Estonia, Greece, France, Hungary, the Netherlands, Poland and Portugal.

In addition to expanding the sample to 23 countries, this period allows us to verify whether the policies adopted previously had an impact on the results reported.

RESULTS AND DISCUSSION

The initial information available on the consumption of plastic bags per inhabitant refers to the year 2018. However, EU member states had to develop preventive measures to reduce the consumption of plastic bags during 2017, in accordance with Article 4 of Directive 94/62/EC of the European Parliament and of the Council of 20 December 1994.

The presentation of the measures implemented by each member state is structured into three groups, considering the annual average of 77 plastic bags/inhabitant, for the last year with reported data. Therefore, we defined country ranges as follows: Countries below the average consumption [0;<60]; Countries within the average consumption [60;95]; and Countries above the average consumption [>95].

In Table 2 we can see the measures implemented by countries defined as below average consumption.

Table 2. Measures implemented by countries below the average for plastic bag consumption

Countries	Measures implemented
Belgium	Awareness campaigns and measures to promote alternatives to single-use plastics.
Germany	Awareness raising through campaigns carried out by the Ministry of the Environment and non-governmental organisations, but separately. Retailers can also do this with their customers and employees, and a voluntary agreement is foreseen for this.
Ireland	Active campaigns involving multiple entities such as the media, non-governmental organizations, retailers.
Luxembourg	The retail sector has been instructed to ban the free provision of bags. Public information campaigns have been carried out by the dedicated working group.
Austria	Agreements with retailers until 2020, replaced by a ban on plastic bags, accompanied by awareness campaigns.
Sweden	Retailers were required to inform consumers about the impacts of using plastic bags and ways to reduce consumption. Awareness-raising campaigns were carried out in conjunction with companies and trade organisations and consumer surveys were conducted.
Denmark	Press releases on measures to reduce the consumption of plastic bags between 2020 and 2021, as well as campaigns to combat waste.
France	Campaigns to ban single-use plastic bags at national level. Producers pay a reduced fee on biodegradable bags, as they are made available to consumers free of charge, ensuring consumer information campaigns.

continued on following page

Table 2. Continued

Countries	Measures implemented
Netherlands	Awareness raising and information are the responsibility of the Ministry of Infrastructure and Environment in conjunction with local authorities.
Poland	The implementation of the fee on plastic bags was widely publicized by all media outlets, with the Minister of the Environment being the leading figure in raising awareness among the population, with the distribution of reusable bags.
Portugal	Awareness and information campaigns carried out by economic operators, required by law. Involvement of the Ministry of the Environment and the Portuguese Environment Agency in actively promoting this cause.

Source: European Commission (2022)

As we can see, the member states listed have made a commitment to reducing the consumption of plastic bags. We have identified awareness-raising campaigns suggested by the EU across the board, as well as the adoption of bans in the case of France, Austria and Luxembourg. In addition to what has been proposed, Poland and France have presented alternative measures, namely reusable and recyclable products.

Table 3 explains the different measures implemented by the countries, in the second defined range, which are within the average consumption.

Table 3. Measures implemented by countries within the average consumption of plastic bags

Countries	Measures implemented
Spain	The Ministry of Agriculture and the autonomous communities are responsible for information/awareness campaigns. The law provides that economic operators must also carry out campaigns.
Slovenia	Involvement of the Ministry of Environment and Spatial Planning together with the National Institute of Education, non-governmental organizations, the Chamber of Commerce and the Chamber of Agriculture in carrying out information campaigns. Schools, retailers and the media joined in to promote sustainable consumption through reusable alternatives.
Slovakia	Information and awareness-raising initiatives carried out by the Ministry of the Environment in supermarket chains, with promotional materials to reduce the consumption of plastic bags. Retailers also carry out campaigns independently.
Greece	Awareness and information are provided through the Recycling Agency, independently or in conjunction with local authorities.
Hungary	State campaigns targeting purchases to promote a reduction in bag consumption. Initiatives at school and business level with recyclable materials.

Source: European Commission (2022)

In the group of countries mentioned, all implemented the necessary campaigns to change the consumption of plastic bags.

Below, we present in Table 4 the measures used by countries that are above the average in consumption, according to the last defined range.

Table 4. Measures implemented by countries above the average for plastic bag consumption

Countries	Measures implemented
Bulgaria	Public awareness and information campaigns, carried out on a mandatory basis, by economic operators.
Italy	The dissemination of information on reducing the consumption of plastic bags is the responsibility of a private non-profit consortium. This entity enables producers and consumers to meet recycling targets.
Cyprus	Campaigns to reduce plastic consumption across all media outlets, prepared by the Government.
Latvia	Legislation requires retailers to inform consumers about the need to reduce their consumption of plastic bags and to adopt alternatives at points of sale. Awareness-raising campaigns have involved schools and other organisations.
Lithuania	It changed the Waste Prevention Program to encourage the use of reusable bags and the negative effects of plastic bag consumption. There is no evidence that such campaigns have been put into practice.
Finland	Launch of the National Green Agreement by the Ministry of the Environment and retailers. Various campaigns marked by trade associations and retailers.
Estonia	Plastic bags must contain information about the damage they can cause to the environment, and awareness-raising is done through retailers at points of sale. There are non-governmental organizations that support and raise awareness about this cause.

Source: European Commission (2022)

We highlight the case of Lithuania, a country with above-average consumption and where there is no evidence that awareness-raising campaigns to reduce consumption have been carried out. This fact may explain the results obtained and demonstrated throughout our analysis, since success in achieving the targets and minimizing environmental impacts depends on the combination of the various measures proposed by the EU.

Below, Figure 1 presents the data for the first set of member states defined in the methodology. This considers the data reported and available on the Eurostat platform, with the time range from 2018 to 2022.

Figure 1. Annual consumption of plastic bags (<50 microns) per inhabitant

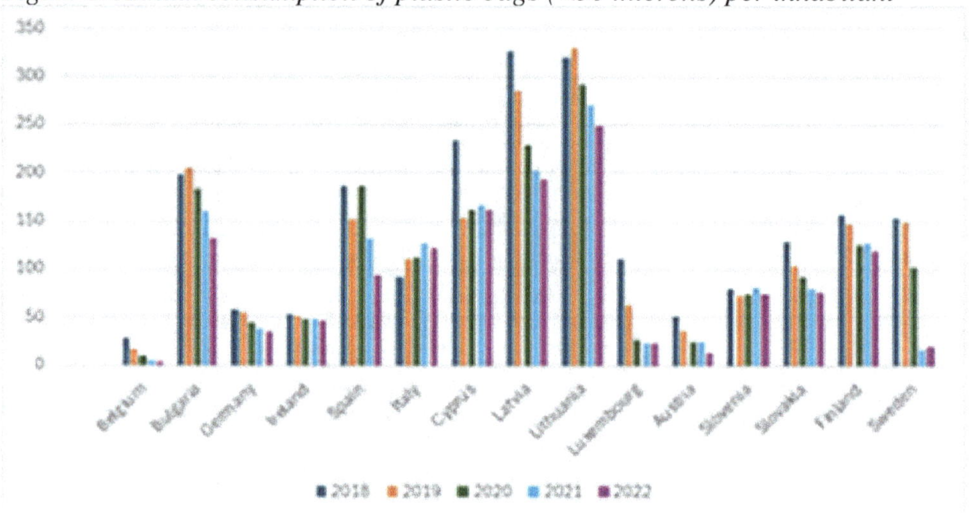

Source: Based on Eurostat (2024)

Figure 1 shows the evolution of consumption from 2018 to 2022, with a downward trend over time among the various countries. The first years show higher values, since the effects of the implementation of regulations were only felt later.

We highlight the countries with the highest average consumption values, namely Lithuania (292 bags/inhabitant), Latvia (247 bags/inhabitant) and Cyprus (176 bags/inhabitant). These values derive from the taxation policy applied to plastic bags, since there are no defined tax levels, which are at the discretion of retailers. According to the European Commission report (2022), Lithuania and Latvia apply rates of €0,01 and €0,02, respectively. This contrasts with countries such as Belgium (13 bags/inhabitant), Austria (31 bags/inhabitant) and Germany (46 bags/inhabitant), considered an environmental leader by Eckert et al. (2024). Latvia represents the steepest declines.

Regarding the variations in each country over the period under analysis, we highlight Ireland (5,77%) and Slovenia (5,00%), which have lower coefficients of variation, translating into more stable consumption. In 2018, 53 bags/ inhabitant and 79 bags/ inhabitant were recorded, respectively. In 2022, these countries had 46 bags/ inhabitant and 76 bags/ inhabitant, respectively.

On the other hand, Belgium (77,52%), Luxembourg (76,98%), and Sweden (76,27%) have higher coefficients, that is, with higher variations, so they fall below the target established for 2025. The values reported by these countries in 2018 were 28, 111, and 153 bags/inhabitant, respectively. However, in 2022, and justifying the high variations, these countries recorded 4, 24, and 18 bags/inhabitant consumed, respectively.

To provide a more comprehensive view of consumption in 2022, we have added relevant countries to our analysis, namely Denmark, Estonia, Greece, France, Hungary, the Netherlands, Poland and Portugal. The following figure (figure 2) identifies the 23 countries we considered and their respective consumption levels.

Figure 2. Consumption of plastic bags (<50 microns) per capita in 2022

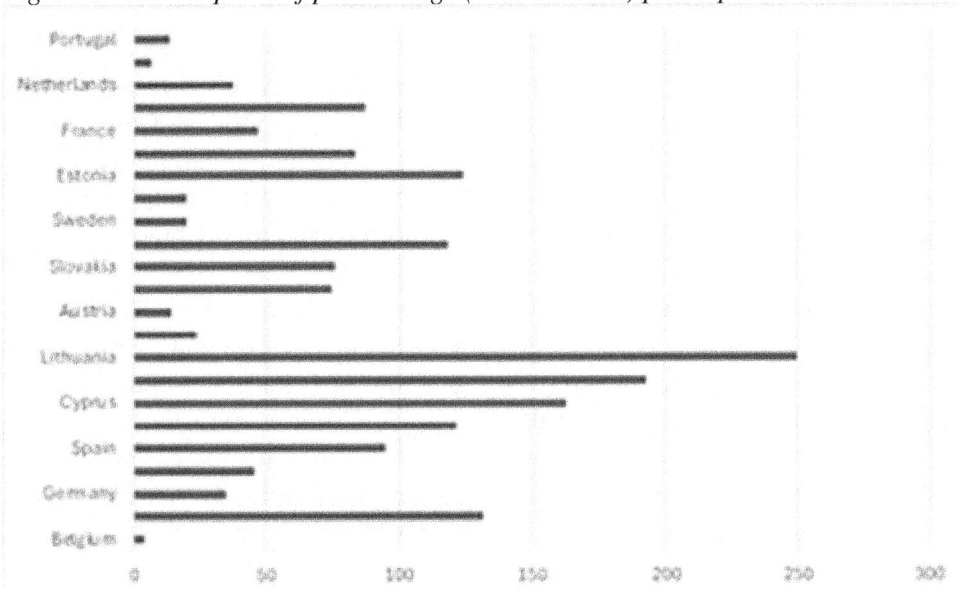

Source: Based on Eurostat (2024)

The group of 23 countries has an average plastic bag consumption of 77 bags/inhabitant in 2022, demonstrating a wide dispersion of values.

Poland and Belgium continue to stand out among all, recording annual consumption of 7 and 4 bags/inhabitant, respectively. This contrasts with Lithuania and Latvia, whose consumption figures are 249 and 193 bags/inhabitant, respectively.

Cyprus, Bulgaria, Italy, and Finland report consumption rates of 162, 132, 122, and 118 bags/inhabitant, values that remain constant throughout the period, translating into low and stable variations. The coefficients of variation for these countries are 18,78%, 17,06%, 11,72%, and 11.76%, respectively. These figures reflect an ingrained consumption pattern, and urgent measures beyond taxation are needed, including consumer awareness and the creation of incentives for more sustainable consumption.

Despite the European strategies, considered robust in combating the consumption of plastic bags, the implementation of regulations in this area varies between member states. Social, cultural, economic and environmental factors influence the effectiveness of the measures transposed into national regulations, with Nagtzaam et al. (2023) arguing that there are differences between countries, especially after the expansion of the EU in Central and Eastern Europe. This fact leads to the compromise of the established targets, an example of which is Hungary. Náhlik et al. (2022) and Kirchherr et al. (2018) highlight cultural barriers and consumer behavior as factors influencing the poor results of this country.

In economic terms, if the rate applied is higher in one country than in another, it may not be as effective, given the salaries charged, which influence purchasing power, according to the conclusions of the study by the European Commission (2022). Portugal, seen as a country that has been successful in measures to reduce consumption, as stated by Nielsen et al. (2019), could serve as an example to Lithuania for raising consumer awareness, implementing reusable/recyclable alternatives and increasing the rates charged.

Most countries allow retailers to set the level of rates, but we found countries such as Cyprus, Denmark, Greece, Ireland, Poland and Portugal that set minimum rates. The only country that only provides guidelines to retailers, without defined rates, is Spain (European Commission, 2022, p. 57). In our opinion, these practices may influence the effectiveness of reducing consumption. In the case of plastic packaging, the criterion is different, as taxes are levied at the production stage. This fact does not have the desired visibility among consumers, according to the Gómez (2021) study of the Spanish case.

Italy's high results are due to the failure of the fee on plastic bags, resulting from weak and unclear implementation. According to Scuderi (2021), this result is due to a lack of communication and awareness among consumers, as well as more sustainable alternatives. Incentives for economic agents to convert their activities to more sustainable production also represent measures to reduce consumption.

Poland's low consumption is because producers and consumers are increasingly focusing on the use of reusable materials and alternatives to plastic, highlighting the need to comply with European Union directives (Kasznik & Łapniewska, 2023).

We highlight the reductions in consumption in the cases of Greece and Portugal, resulting from the influence of economic culture and the crises that were felt, as they were subject to external support due to budgetary imbalances that influenced consumers' purchasing power.

The next figure - Figure 3 shows geographically the consumption of plastic bags/ inhabitants in the 23 countries analysed in the year 2022.

Figure 3. Geographical distribution of plastic bag consumption in 23 European countries (2022)

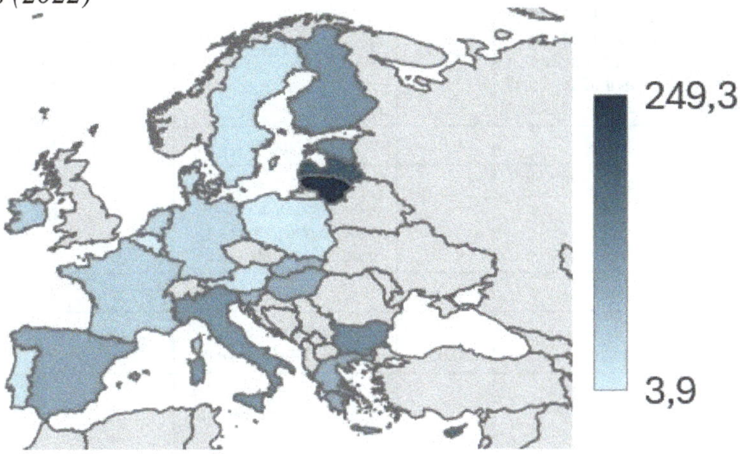

Source: Based on Eurostat (2024)

We then aggregate the relevant information from each member state country in Table 5 with the following parameters: type of policy implemented by each member state country, the minimum fees applied to each plastic bag consumed, the effects of this taxation in terms of reducing consumption, as well as the annual consumption per inhabitant reported in 2022.

Table 5. Policy, fees, effects of taxation and annual consumption per capita

Countries	Policy applied in accordance with Directive (EU) 2015/720 of the European Parliament and of the Council of 29 April 2015	Fee (€)	Effects Taxation	Annual consumption of plastic bags with a thickness of less than 50 microns/ inhabitant (2022)
Belgium	Fee	0,05/0,10	80% reduction in consumption in 10 years	3,9
Bulgaria	Fee	0,09	Reduction in consumption reported by the Government	131,6
Germany	Fee/ban	0,05/0,50	N/A	34,7
Ireland	Fee	0,22	90% reduction in consumption after 1 year	45,6
Spain	Fee/ban	0,05/0,10	N/A	94,6
Italy	Fee/ban	0,02/0,10	55% reduction in consumption since 2011	121,6

continued on following page

Table 5. Continued

Countries	Policy applied in accordance with Directive (EU) 2015/720 of the European Parliament and of the Council of 29 April 2015	Fee (€)	Effects Taxation	Annual consumption of plastic bags with a thickness of less than 50 microns/ inhabitant (2022)
Cyprus	Fee	0,06	N/A	162,4
Latvia	Fee	0,02	Reduction in consumption due to the use of reusable bags, stabilizing after 1 year	192,6
Lithuania	Fee	0,01	N/A	249,3
Luxembourg	Fee/ban	0,05	85% reduction in consumption in 9 years	23,5
Austria	Ban	-	Reduction in consumption overtime reported by the Government	14,2
Slovenia	Ban	-	N/A	74,5
Slovakia	Fee/ban	0,05	N/A	75,7
Finland	Fee	0,10/0,25	N/A	118,2
Sweden	Fee	0,57/0,67	Reduction in consumption in the first years of implementation of the fees	19,7
Denmark	Fee	0,54	800 million bags cut in half: 50% reduction in consumption after 2 years	19,6
Estonia	Fee	0,15/0,25	N/A	124
Greece	Fee	0,07	80% reduction in consumption after 1 month. Sales of reusable alternatives increased	83,7
France	Ban	-	N/A	46,8
Hungary	Fee		N/A	87,4
Netherlands	Fee	0,25	40% reduction after 1 year	37,5
Poland	Fee	0,23	N/A	6,6
Portugal	Fee	0,10	74% reduction in consumption after 4 months	13,2

Source: Adapted from United Nations Environment Programme (2018), European Commission (2022) and Nielsen et al. (2019).

As we can see, the implementation of the fees has resulted in a reduction in the consumption of plastic bags, with taxation being considered a tool to change consumption habits that are harmful to the environment, promoting its preservation and conservation.

Given the targets set by the EU, as defined in Directive (EU) 2015/720 of the European Parliament and of the Council of 29 April 2015, for the year 2025, to reduce the consumption of plastic bags to less than 40 bags per inhabitant, we can see that there are countries with a long way to go. In addition to Lithuania, countries such as Latvia, Cyprus, Bulgaria, Italy and Spain must review their consumption reduction policies. The average for all the countries analyzed in 2022 is 77 bags per inhabitant.

Naturally, countries must consider the targets, as well as the need to transition to a circular economy. In this context, the national legislation of each Member State must align with Directive (EU) 2019/904 of the European Parliament and of the Council of 5 June 2019, which aims to reduce the environmental impact of certain plastic products. This document arises due to the increase in pollution in marine environments resulting from the consumption of single-use plastic that is not recycled. It will be essential for everyone to collaborate to reduce marine pollution, as well as to achieve a sustainable and circular economy.

CONCLUSION

The plastic waste crisis is one of the most pressing environmental and ecological challenges. The consumption of plastic bags is still widespread, and it is essential to adopt strategies to mitigate the associated negative impacts, as stated by Fayshal (2024).

The European Union has made a long journey with its member states to change paradigms regarding this issue, whether through directives, regulations, awareness-raising campaigns and the establishment of environmental targets, as there is no single solution that is transversal to all countries, as stated by Kasidoni et al. (2015). The adoption of measures to mitigate negative environmental impacts must be based on technical, economic and environmental points of view, to select the most advantageous instrument, as concluded by Gómez (2021).

Our analysis focused on the consumption of plastic bags with a thickness <50 microns, since reporting for this category is mandatory and subject to taxation in some countries. Products with a thickness <15 microns and greater than 50 microns are optional in their disclosure, so statistics are scarce. The most effective strategy for reducing the consumption of these products, to mitigate environmental impacts, has been taxation on them. NAR (2019) states that taxation represents an average reduction of 70% in consumption.

We believe that awareness campaigns are essential to raise awareness of these issues, but they are not enough to reduce consumption. We have found that when a tax or duty is imposed on plastic bags, the observable trend is a reduction in consumption, with taxation serving the protection and conservation of the environment. Therefore, we highlight countries such as Belgium, Poland, Portugal and Austria where the consumption of plastic bags per inhabitant is 4, 7, 13 and 14, respectively.

Our results are in line with the study by Adeyanju et al. (2021), where they state that the use of higher taxation significantly reduces the consumption of plastic bags, with consumer behavior being influenced by public policies and regulations. Supported by Zainudin et al. (2021), we believe that this type of instrument is increasingly relevant in environmental policies adopted to control pollution and manage natural resources.

In the long term, these types of policies may not have a significant impact on the continued reduction of plastic bag consumption, as stated by Senturk & Dumludag (2021). This perception is worrying given that plastic pollution levels are rising in ecosystems, especially in the marine ecosystem, with a forecast doubling by 2030, according to the United Nations Environment Programme (2021) and, consequently, entering the food chain, as stated by Conti et al. (2021).

Although taxation has positive effects, the use of reusable alternatives is seen as one of the ways that causes the least environmental impact. Recycling also appears to be advantageous at the end of the life cycle of plastic bags, compared to composting, landfilling or incineration, according to the conclusions of the study by Gómez & Escobar (2022). Another alternative is paper bags, as Taylor and Villas-Boas (2015) state that this type of substitute has seen an increase of 10% to 40%.

Despite the success stories highlighted, the member states that are furthest from meeting the target set by the EU, of 40 bags per inhabitant by 2025, must analyse the failures in the implementation of environmental policies. This analysis must be carried out jointly with governments, producers, retailers and consumers.

Inertia around environmental policies could put future generations at risk, and it is essential that everyone, whether member states or not, align themselves. Concerns in this area are global, but some countries are not aligned with reducing the environmental impacts associated with the consumption of plastic bags.

Environmental preservation should be a priority for everyone, and taxation should be seen as a mechanism for environmental protection. When combined with strategies in education and innovation, taxation has the capacity to promote more responsible and sustainable consumption.

The limitations identified are related to the late provision of data by member states, as well as the existence of estimates from past years. The analysis of the effects of taxation on plastic bags cannot be considered in isolation, since awareness campaigns have an impact on consumer choices and, therefore, affect the results obtained.

Regarding future research perspectives, this study could be replicated covering more countries, including non-EU member states. Analyzing the differences before and after the transposition of directives and regulations associated with the reduction of plastic bag consumption, considering the economic and environmental impacts and consumption patterns, could be a clue for further research. Investigating the reasons for the poor performance of some countries could contribute to the implementation of in-depth and more effective reforms.

Evaluating the effectiveness of the use of reusable/recyclable alternatives and the environmental impacts associated with this paradigm shift, as well as analyzing the reduction in plastic bag consumption with the percentages of plastic recycling could enrich this line of research.

REFERENCES

Aare, F., Olorunfemi, O., & Ntor, G. (2024). Legal frameworks for single-use plastic management: Environmental challenges and solutions. *Kampala International University Law Journal*, *6*(1), 63–85. DOI: 10.59568/KIULJ-2024-6-1-04

Abate, T., & Elofsson, K. (2024). Environmental taxation of plastic bags and substitutes: Balancing marine pollution and climate change. *Journal of Environmental Management*, *359*, 120868. DOI: 10.1016/j.jenvman.2024.120868 PMID: 38692024

Adeyanju, G., Augustine, T., Volkmann, S., Oyebamiji, U., Ran, S., Osobajo, O., & Otitoju, A. (2021). Effectiveness of intervention on behaviour change against use of non-biodegradable plastic bags: A systematic review. *Discover Sustainability*, *2*(13), 13. Advance online publication. DOI: 10.1007/s43621-021-00015-0

Boeve, M., & Waal, I. M. (2024). Global Plastic Pollution and the Transition Towards a Circular Economy: Lessons from the EU's Legal Framework on Plastics. *Environmental Policy and Law*, *53*(5-6), 461–472. DOI: 10.3233/EPL-239016

Bowen, G. (2009). Document Analysis as a Qualitative Research Method. Qualitative Research Journal, 9, n. °2, 27-40. http://dx.doi.org/DOI: 10.3316/QRJ0902027

Chandra, G. (2020). Non-monetary intervention to discourage consumption of single-use plastic bags. *Behavioural Public Policy*, *7*(1), 143–156. DOI: 10.1017/bpp.2020.9

Chatfield, S. L. (2020). Recommendations for Secondary Analysis of Qualitative Data. *The Qualitative Report*, *25*(3), 833–842. DOI: 10.46743/2160-3715/2020.4092

Chen, G., Li, J., Sun, Y., Wang, Z., Leeke, G., Moretti, C., Cheng, Z., Wang, Y., Li, N., Mu, L., Li, J., Tao, J., Yan, B., & Hou, L. (2024). Replacing Traditional Plastics with Biodegradable Plastics: Impact on Carbon Emissions. *Engineering (Beijing)*, *32*, 152–162. DOI: 10.1016/j.eng.2023.10.002

Conti, I., Simioni, C., Varano, G., Brenna, C., Costanzi, E., & Neri, L. (2021). Legislation to limit the environmental plastic and microplastic pollution and their influence on human exposure. *Environmental Pollution*, *288*, 117708. DOI: 10.1016/j.envpol.2021.117708 PMID: 34256282

Creswell, J., & Creswell, J. (2018). *Research Design Qualitative, Quantitative, and Mixed Methods Approaches* (5th ed.). SAGE Publications., https://spada.uns.ac.id/pluginfile.php/510378/mod_resource/content/1/creswell.pdf

Desalegn, G., & Tangl, A. (2022). Banning Vs Taxing, Reviewing the Potential Opportunities and Challenges of Plastic Products. *Sustainability (Basel)*, *14*(12), 7189. DOI: 10.3390/su14127189

Dikgang, J., & Visser, M. (2012). Behavioural response to plastic bag legislation in Botswana. *The South African Journal of Economics*, *80*(1), 123–133. DOI: 10.1111/j.1813-6982.2011.01289.x

Dokl, M., Copot, A., Krajnc, D., Fan, Y., Vujanović, A., Aviso, K., Tan, R., Kravanja, Z., & Čuček, L. (2024). Global projections of plastic use, end-of-life fate and potential changes in consumption, reduction, recycling and replacement with bioplastics to 2050. *Sustainable Production and Consumption*, *51*, 498–518. DOI: 10.1016/j.spc.2024.09.025

Dunn, J., Caplan, A., & Bosworth, R. (2014). Measuring the value of plastic and reusable grocery bags. *Journal of Environmental Economics and Policy*, *3*(2), 125–147. DOI: 10.1080/21606544.2013.870052

Eckert, S., Karassin, O., & Steinebach, Y. (2024). A policy portfolio approach to plastics throughout their life cycle: Supranational and national regulation in the European Union. *Environmental Policy and Governance*, *34*(4), 427–441. DOI: 10.1002/eet.2092

European Commission. Directorate General for Environment, Sherrington, C., Watson, S., Marsh, P. and Bradley, C. (2022). Scoping study to assess the feasibility of further EU measures on waste prevention and implementation of the Plastic Bags Directive. Part II, Implementation of Plastic Bags Directive, Publications Office of the European Union https://data.europa.eu/doi/10.2779/304791

EUROSTAT (2024). Consumption of lightweight plastic carrier bags by their wall thickness. https://doi.org/DOI: 10.2908/env_waspcb

Fayshal, M. (2024). Current practices of plastic waste management, environmental impacts, and potential alternatives for reducing pollution and improving management. *Heliyon*, *10*(23), e40838. DOI: 10.1016/j.heliyon.2024.e40838 PMID: 39687131

Frey, M., & Cifuentes, L. (2024). Goodbye Plastic Bags? Lessons from the Shopping Plastic Bag Ban in Chile. *Sustainability (Basel)*, *16*(9), 3690. DOI: 10.3390/su16093690

García-Marín, L., & Rentería, M. (2024). Fighting plastic pollution with a circular economy roadmap and strategy: Addressed to the United Nations Environment Programme. *Journal of Science Policy & Governance*, *24*(1). Advance online publication. DOI: 10.38126/JSPG240107

Gómez, I., & Escobar, A. (2022). The dilemma of plastic bags and their substitutes: A review on LCA studies. *Sustainable Production and Consumption*, *30*, 107–116. DOI: 10.1016/j.spc.2021.11.021

Gómez, J. (2021). El impuesto sobre envases de plástico no reutilizables y outras medidas fiscales en el anteproyecto de ley de resíduos. Cronica Tributaria. Creative Commons Reconocimiento-NoComercial 4.0 Internacional, 178, 11-60. https://repositorio.comillas.edu/rest/bitstreams/438976/retrieve

Holmberg, K., & Persson, S. (2023). Keep plastics on a tight leash: Swedish public opinion on plastic policies. *Environmental Science & Policy*, *141*, 109–116. DOI: 10.1016/j.envsci.2023.01.005

Hopewell, J., Dvorak, R., & Kosior, E. (2009). Plastics recycling: Challenges and opportunities. *Philosophical Transactions of the Royal Society of London. Series B, Biological Sciences*, *364*(1526), 2115–2126. DOI: 10.1098/rstb.2008.0311 PMID: 19528059

Iheukwumere, S., Nkwocha, K., & Umeh, P. (2020). A Look at Plastic Bags and Alternatives. *Journal of Geography Meteorology and Environment*, *3*(1), 121–134. https://journals.unizik.edu.ng/index.php/jgme

Johnson, H., Keane, K., McGillivray, L., Akhtar-Khavari, A., Chambers, L., Barner-Kowollik, C., Lauchs, M., & Blinco, J. (2025). Reforming plastic packaging regulation: Outcomes from stakeholder interviews and regulatory analysis. *Sustainable Production and Consumption*, *54*, 52–63. DOI: 10.1016/j.spc.2024.12.017

Kasidoni, M., Moustakas, K., & Malamis, D. (2015). The existing situation and challenges regarding the use of plastic carrier bags in Europe. *Waste Management & Research*, *33*(5), 419–428. DOI: 10.1177/0734242X15577858 PMID: 25827845

Kasznik, D., & Łapniewska, Z. (2023). The end of plastic? The EU's directive on single-use plastics and its implementation in Poland. *Environmental Science & Policy*, *145*, 151–163. DOI: 10.1016/j.envsci.2023.04.005

Kedzierski, M., Frère, D., Le Maguer, G., & Bruzaud, S. (2020). Why is there plastic packaging in the natural environment? Understanding the roots of our individual plastic waste management behaviours. *The Science of the Total Environment*, *740*, 139985. DOI: 10.1016/j.scitotenv.2020.139985 PMID: 32563872

Kirchherr, J., Piscicelli, L., Bour, R., Kostense-Smit, E., Muller, J., Huibrechtse-Truijens, A., & Hekkert, M. (2018). Barriers to the Circular Economy: Evidence From the European Union (EU). *Ecological Economics*, *150*, 264–272. DOI: 10.1016/j.ecolecon.2018.04.028

Lange, F., & Weerdt, L. (2021). Reducing Plastic Bag Use Through Prosocial Incentives. *Sustainability (Basel), 13*(5), 2421. DOI: 10.3390/su13052421

Li, B., Lui, J., & Zheng, X. (2022). The Environmental Impact of Plastic Grocery Bags and Their Alternatives. *IOP Conference Series. Earth and Environmental Science, 1011*(1), 012050. DOI: 10.1088/1755-1315/1011/1/012050

Luís, S., Roseta-Palma, C., Matos, M., Lima, M., & Sousa, C. (2020). Psychosocial and economic impacts of a charge in lightweight plastic carrier bags in Portugal: Keep calm and carry on? *Resources, Conservation and Recycling, 161*, 104962. DOI: 10.1016/j.resconrec.2020.104962

Martinho, G., Balaia, N., & Pires, A. (2017). The Portuguese plastic carrier bag tax: The effects on consumers' behavior. *Waste Management (New York, N.Y.), 61*, 3–12. DOI: 10.1016/j.wasman.2017.01.023 PMID: 28131637

Mentis, C., Maroulis, G., Latinopoulos, D., & Kostas, B. (2022). The effects of environmental information provision on plastic bag use and marine environment status in the context of the environmental levy in Greece. *Environment, Development and Sustainability*. Advance online publication. DOI: 10.1007/s10668-022-02465-6 PMID: 35729922

Milbreta, U., Milich, L., Andze, L., & Gusca, J. (2025). Some Countries Can Say "No!" to Single-Use Plastics, Others Cannot: Why Do Seemingly Similar Policies Have Different Outcomes? *Journal of Sustainability Research, 7*(1), e250004. DOI: 10.20900/jsr20250004

Milios, L. (2018). Advancing to a Circular Economy: Three essential ingredients for a comprehensive policy mix. *Sustainability Science, 13*(3), 861–878. DOI: 10.1007/s11625-017-0502-9 PMID: 30147792

Muposhi, A., Mpinganjira, M., & Wait, M. (2022). Considerations, benefits and unintended consequences of banning plastic shopping bags for environmental sustainability: A systematic literature review. Waste Management & Research. *Waste Management & Research, 40*(3), 248–261. DOI: 10.1177/0734242X211003965 PMID: 33876669

Nagtzaam, G., Calster, G., Kourabas, S., & Karataeva, E. (2023). *Plastic regulation in the European Union. Global Plastic Pollution and its Regulation*. Edward Elgar Publishing., DOI: 10.4337/9781800373556

Náhlik, A., Pankotay, F. & Németh, N. (2022). Recycling of plastics in the European Union – exploring the potential domestic adaptation of best practices from other Member States. Gazdaság és Társadalom/ Journal of Economy & Society, 15(2), 90-110. https://doi.org/DOI: 10.21637/GT.2022.2.05

NAR, M. (2019). Plastic Bag Regulation for a Sustainable Environment. *International Journal of Contemporary Economics and Administrative Sciences*, *9*(2), 305–326. DOI: 10.5281/zenodo.3596081

Nielsen, T., Holmberg, K., & Stripple, J. (2019). Need a bag? A review of public policies on plastic carrier bags – Where, how and to what effect? *Waste Management (New York, N.Y.)*, *87*, 428–440. DOI: 10.1016/j.wasman.2019.02.025 PMID: 31109543

Nishijima, A., & Nakatani, J. (2024). Survey and analysis on the use and disposal of plastic shopping bags before and after the introduction of charges. *Journal of Material Cycles and Waste Management*, *26*(2), 741–754. DOI: 10.1007/s10163-023-01856-9

O'Brien, J., & Thondhlana, G. (2019). Plastic bag use in South Africa: Perceptions, practices and potential intervention strategies. *Waste Management (New York, N.Y.)*, *84*, 320–328. DOI: 10.1016/j.wasman.2018.11.051 PMID: 30691907

OECD. (2022). *Global Plastics Outlook: Economic Drivers, Environmental Impacts and Policy Options*. OECD Publishing., DOI: 10.1787/de747aef-

Official Journal of the European Communities. (1975). Council Directive 75/442/EEC of 15 July 1975 on waste. https://eurlex.europa.eu/legalcontent/EN/TXT/PDF/?uri=CELEX:31975L0442

Official Journal of the European Communities. (1994). Directive 94/62/EC of the European Parliament and of the Council of 20 December 1994 on packaging and packaging waste. https://eurlex.europa.eu/legalcontent/PT/TXT/PDF/?uri=CELEX:31994L0062&qid=1696722078331

Official Journal of the European Union. (2005). Commission Decision 2005/270/EC of the Commission of 22 March 2005. Establishing the forms relating to the database system under Directive 94/62/EC of the European Parliament and of the Council on packaging and packaging waste. https://eurlex.europa.eu/legalcontent/EN/TXT/PDF/?uri=CELEX:32005D0270

Official Journal of the European Union. (2015). Directive 2015/720 of the European Parliament and of the Council of 29 April 2015. Amending Directive 74/62/EC as regards the reduction of the consumption of plastic carrier bags. https://eurlex.europa.eu/legalcontent/EN/TXT/PDF/?uri=CELEX:32015L0720

Official Journal of the European Union. (2018). Commission Implementing Decision 2018/896 of 19 June 2018. Establishing the methodology for calculating the annual consumption of lightweight plastics and amending Decision 2005/270/EC. https://eurlex.europa.eu/legal-content/EN/TXT/PDF/?uri=CELEX:32018D0896

Official Journal of the European Union. (2019). Directive 2019/904 of the European Parliament and of the Council of 5 June 2019 on the reduction of the impact of certain plastic products on the environment. https://eurlex.europa.eu/legalcontent/EN/TXT/PDF/?uri=CELEX:32019L0904

Official Journal of the European Union. (2025). Regulation (EU) 2025/40 of the European Parliament and of the Council of 19 December 2024 on packaging and packaging waste, amending Regulation (EU) 2019/1020 and Directive (EU) 2019/904 and repealing Directive 94/62/EC. https://eur-lex.europa.eu/legal-content/EN/TXT/PDF/?uri=OJ:L_202500040

Patrão, S., Cruz, S., & Carreira, F. (2025). The evolution of green taxation in Portugal. 10th GECAMB/P-CSEAR & XXIV Grudis Conference and Doctoral Colloquium, EsACT-IPB, Mirandela. http://hdl.handle.net/10773/44024

Prata, J., Silva, A., Duarte, A., & Rocha-Santos, T. (2022). The road to sustainable use and waste management of plastics in Portugal. *Frontiers of Environmental Science & Engineering*, *16*(1), 5. DOI: 10.1007/s11783-021-1439-x PMID: 34697576

Pruess, J., & Garrett, R. (2025). Potential effectiveness of extended producer responsibility: An ex-ante policy impact analysis for plastic packaging waste in Belgium, France, and Germany. *Resources, Conservation and Recycling*, *219*, 108297. DOI: 10.1016/j.resconrec.2025.108297

Ramachandruni, U., & Ravi, H. (2023). Evolution of Plastic Bags: Reduced and Recycling Consumer Usage Level on Bags in Day-to-Day Life. *International Journal of Commerce and Management*, *3*(2), 253–259. DOI: 10.54368/qijcm.3.2.0022

Rhodes, C. (2018). Plastic pollution and potential solutions. *Science Progress*, *101*(3), 207–260. DOI: 10.3184/003685018X15294876706211 PMID: 30025551

Ritch, E., Brennan, C., & Macleod, C. (2009). Plastic bag politics: Modifying consumer behaviour for sustainable development. *International Journal of Consumer Studies*, *33*(2), 168–174. DOI: 10.1111/j.1470-6431.2009.00749.x

Rivers, N., Shenstone-Harris, S., & Young, N. (2017). Using nudges to reduce waste? The case of Toronto's plastic bag levy. *Journal of Environmental Management, 188*, 153–162. DOI: 10.1016/j.jenvman.2016.12.009 PMID: 27978442

Scuderi, E. (2021). Towards a Plastic-Free Economy: The Italian Plastic Tax Scuderi, Erika (2021). Towards a plastic-free economy: the Italian plastic tax. Rivista Telematica di Diritto Tributario. https://ssrn.com/abstract=3822296

Senturk, G., & Dumludag, D. (2021). An evaluation of the effect of plastic bag fee on consumer behavior: Case of Turkey. *Waste Management (New York, N.Y.), 120*, 748–754. DOI: 10.1016/j.wasman.2020.10.042 PMID: 33223247

Syberg, K., Nielsen, M., Westergaard Clausen, L., Calster, G., Wezel, A., Rochman, C., Koelmans, A., Cronin, R., Pahl, S., & Hansen, S. (2021). Regulation of plastic from a circular economy perspective. *Current Opinion in Green and Sustainable Chemistry, 29*, 100462. DOI: 10.1016/j.cogsc.2021.100462

Tan, Y., We, Z., Hu, Y., Zeng, X., Kosajan, V., Yin, G., & Zhang, T. (2023). Single-use plastic bag alternatives result in higher environmental impacts: Multi-regional analysis in country with uneven waste management. *Waste Management (New York, N.Y.), 171*, 281–291. DOI: 10.1016/j.wasman.2023.08.040 PMID: 37690403

Taylor, R. & Villas-Boas, S. (2015). Bans versus Fees: Disposable Carryout Bag Policies and Bag Usage. Agricultural and Applied Economics Association Conferences, Califórnia. https://doi.org.DOI: 10.22004/ag.econ.204783

Thompson, R., Swan, S., Moore, C., & Saal, F. (2009). Our plastic age. *Philosophical Transactions of the Royal Society of London. Series B, Biological Sciences, 364*(1526), 1973–1976. DOI: 10.1098/rstb.2009.0054 PMID: 19528049

Todorović, J., Đorđević, M., & Stojanović, M. (2023). The Impact of Environmental Taxes on the Reduction of Plastic Bag Consumption in the Republic of Servia. *TEME, XLVII*(4), 767–786. DOI: 10.22190/TEME220529048D

Uji, A., Song, J., Dolšak, N., & Prakash, A. (2025). Postmaterialism and Environmental Protection Revisited: Domestic Plastic Bag Regulations, 1992–2019. *Global Environmental Politics, 25*(1), 46–66. DOI: 10.1162/glep_a_00771

United Nations Environment Programme. (2018). Single-use Plastics: A Roadmap for Sustainability. UN Environment. https://www.unep.org/resources/report/single-use-plastics-roadmap-sustainability

United Nations Environment Programme. (2019). Legal limits on single-use plastics and microplastics: a global review of National Laws and Regulations. UN Environment. https://www.unep.org/resources/publication/legal-limits-single-use-plastics-and-microplastics-global-review-national

United Nations Environment Programme. (2021). From Pollution to Solution: A global assessment of marine litter and plastic pollution. UN Environment. https://www.unep.org/resources/pollution-solution-global-assessment-marine-litter-and-plastic-pollution

Ventosa, I., Sanz, S., & Sora, M. (2018) Research paper on a European tax on plastics, Zero Waste Europe. https://zerowasteeurope.eu/library/research-paper-on-a-european-tax-on-plastics/

Wagner, T. (2017). Reducing single-use plastic shopping bags in the USA. *Waste Management (New York, N.Y.)*, *70*, 3–12. DOI: 10.1016/j.wasman.2017.09.003 PMID: 28935376

Wang, B., Zhao, Y., & Li, Y. (2021). How do tougher plastics ban policies modify people's usage of plastic bags? A case study in China. *International Journal of Environmental Research and Public Health*, *18*(20), 10718. DOI: 10.3390/ijerph182010718 PMID: 34682464

Zainudin, Q., Qi, W. Y., Lau, J. L., Harun, Z., & Khalid, N. (2021). Determinants of Using Alternative to Single-Use Plastic Bags. *International Journal of Academic Research in Business & Social Sciences*, *11*(11), 1753–1766. DOI: 10.6007/IJARBSS/v11-i11/11659

KEY TERMS AND DEFINITIONS

Consumption: Acquisition of goods and/or services to satisfy the individual needs. Consumption must be sustainable to avoid environmental impacts.

European Union: A group of 27 member states united in economic and political terms, promoting stability for European citizens. They share common policies in the economic, commercial and environmental spheres, using transversal directives and regulations.

Fees: A service charged by the State or public institutions, bilateral in nature, in return for public service or use of public domain assets.

Plastic bags: Products produced using fossil fuels to package, store and transport goods and/or waste.

Pollution: Considered a negative externality caused by man, taking various forms, which degrades the environment and, consequently, human health.

Taxation: Mechanisms are used by governments, through taxes or fees, to collect revenue with the aim of financing public expenditure in various areas, such as social, health, education and infrastructure.

Taxes: Mandatory taxes paid by citizens and companies, unilateral in nature, to finance the State.

Chapter 6
Government Financial Mechanism Impacts on SDGs in Slovenia

Žiga Kotnik
https://orcid.org/0000-0003-2723-9364
Faculty of Public Administration, Univesity of Ljubljana, Slovenia

Maja Klun
https://orcid.org/0000-0002-1025-9134
Faculty of Public Administration, Univesity of Ljubljana, Slovenia

Tatjana Stanimirović
https://orcid.org/0000-0001-7407-7121
Faculty of Public Administration, Univesity of Ljubljana, Slovenia

ABSTRACT

Government mechanisms are vital for achieving Sustainable Development Goals (SDGs), with public spending accounting for nearly 50% of gross domestic product (GDP) in EU countries in 2022. This chapter analyses the impact of public financial instruments on SDG outcomes, using a structured literature review and linear regression in a Slovenian case study. Literature shows public spending promotes sustainable development by enabling green investments through tools like green procurement, subsidies, and tax incentives under stable governance. Empirical results indicate that Eco Fund loans and research and development (R&D) tax reliefs significantly reduce emissions intensity; subsidies lower CO_2 emissions from new vehicles, and government spending leads to a delayed decline in energy-related emissions. The strongest positive effects are seen for SDG 12.3, SDG 2.4, and SDG

DOI: 10.4018/979-8-3373-2492-0.ch006

12.2, reflecting improvements in sustainable production, food system resilience, and resource efficiency. These findings underscore the strategic importance of targeted public interventions in environmental sustainability.

INTRODUCTION

The global trend of several interconnected crises (environmental, migration, etc.) has put governments under severe pressure to provide sustainable solutions (OECD, 2017). Public administrations have concentrated on the challenges of environmental, economic, and social issues to provide services with no harm for future generations. These challenges of improving well-being and social equity, while significantly reducing environmental risks and ecological scarcities (United Nations, 2023) have been called the green economy. According to Eurostat (Eurostat, 2025), government spending presented, on average, almost 50% of economy measured by gross domestic product (GDP) in EU countries in the year 2023. In this context, this chapter is predominantly dealing with public spending impact on sustainability development goals (SDGs).

The fact that various government mechanisms and instruments can influence the achievement of SDGs – which include objectives such as economic growth, use of renewable energy sources, less pollution, innovation and digitalization, poverty reduction etc. – particularly through tax reductions and exemptions, has been known for a long time. As described by (Harris (2013), the integration of expansionary fiscal policy and environmental objectives—referred to as green Keynesianism—builds on earlier recovery strategies that frequently emphasized eco-friendly investments. However, international green investment implementation has so far insufficient, if positive, effects on the environment. Various kinds of tax instruments have been implemented in various countries, although there are very few studies that examine the direct link between tax policies and SDGs. Based on the literature review presented below, the main objective of this chapter is twofold: (i) to present international evidence on public spending and its impact on sustainable development outcomes, to offer insights into the promotion of green investment, and to provide case studies of selected strategic measures implemented in various countries; and (ii) to analyse the connection between public spending on green investments and the SDG indicators in Slovenia during the period between 2018 and 2022. To achieve this goal, the study focuses on three Research Questions, namely:

1. To what extent does public spending influence sustainable development outcomes, and which international policy instruments have been shown to effectively promote green investment?

2. To what extent do (i) loans and subsidies from the Eco Fund, (ii) tax relief for companies investing in research and development (R&D), and (iii) general government expenditures for environmental protection influence the achievement of the SDGs?
3. Which Sustainable Development Goal indicators have the highest proportion of positive impact from different government mechanisms, including green loans, subsidies, R&D tax reliefs, and budget expenditures?

In this manner, the theoretical background of the research is presented through a structured literature review. It is divided into three main subsections: the first examines international evidence on public spending and its impact on sustainable development outcomes; the second focuses on international insights into the promotion of green investment; and the third provides case studies of selected strategic measures implemented in various countries. Further, the following section presents the research framework, encompassing the study's conceptualization, data sources, and methodology used. The results are presented next, focusing on the relationship between selected green investment instruments and the achievement of SDGs using correlation and regression analysis based on Slovenian national data. The article concludes with a discussion and conclusion section that reflects on the implications of the findings for fiscal policy design and sustainable development strategies.

LITERATURE REVIEW

International Evidence on public spending and sustainable development outcomes

The United Nations report (2023) emphasizes that governments and the international community should intensify efforts to accelerate the achievement of the SDGs through integrated policies, strengthened institutions, increased investments—particularly in vulnerable countries—and an enhanced multilateral system. Empirical studies across a range of national contexts increasingly explore how such efforts, particularly in the form of targeted public expenditures, interact with and influence the complex and often non-linear pathways toward achieving the Sustainable Development Goals (SDGs). A growing body of evidence suggests that government financial resources—when mobilized strategically and allocated efficiently—can significantly influence development outcomes across multiple sectors. For instance, in Nigeria, Osuji & Nwani (2020) report that increased public expenditure contributed to improvements in education and health indicators; however, these gains were sometimes accompanied by persistent poverty and long-term environmental degradation, revealing tensions between short-term social investments and broader sustainability objectives. On a global scale, Schmidt-Traub (2015, 2018) highlights the scale of investment needed to meet the SDGs, estimating annual financing requirements of approximately 4% of global GDP, or US$1.3–1.4 trillion, with an annual funding gap of US$152–163 billion. These figures emphasize the importance of leveraging both public and private financing to address systemic development challenges.

In South Asia, national-level studies reinforce the critical role of education spending in advancing SDG outcomes. Ihsan et al. (2021), focusing on Pakistan, demonstrate that a 10% annual increase in education expenditure is strongly associated with improved enrollment rates, suggesting a direct link between fiscal inputs and educational access. In Southeast Asia, research from Indonesia by Mutiarani & Siswantoro (2020) and Permatasari et al. (2021) points to a positive relationship between local government financing—particularly from own-source revenues and Village Fund allocations—and progress across a wide range of SDG targets. These findings highlight the significance of fiscal decentralization and targeted local investments in driving sustainable development at the subnational level.

Similar trends are observed in Eastern Europe, where Martynenko (2023) finds that in Ukraine, 35% of local government budgets contributed to improvements in 41.2% of SDG indicators, including a notable 55% improvement in Goal 17, which relates to partnerships and institutional capacity. In Western Europe, Bisogno et al. (2024) analyse fiscal data from Italy and Spain, showing that stronger local fiscal sustainability—measured through indicators such as tax revenue capacity and per capita debt levels—is associated with higher performance across various SDGs. These studies collectively indicate that the quality and sustainability of public finance, not merely its volume, are central to effective SDG implementation. Meanwhile, Benedek & Tieman (2021) provide a cautionary perspective, showing that fiscal contractions during the COVID-19 pandemic significantly hindered progress in health, sanitation, and other core SDG areas, underlining the vulnerability of development gains to external fiscal shocks.

Taken together, these diverse empirical insights suggest that robust, well-designed, and context-sensitive public financial strategies are indispensable for advancing SDG targets. The evidence points especially to the importance of maintaining fiscal space for investment in critical sectors such as education, health, and local governance, while simultaneously ensuring the long-term sustainability of public finances.

Promoting sustainable development through green fiscal policy

A growing body of literature examines the relationship between fiscally incentivized green investments—particularly those supported through tax expenditures such as subsidies, tax credits, and relief measures—and their effectiveness in advancing environmental policy objectives and sustainable development goals. These studies highlight the importance of fiscal instruments in driving environmentally sustainable economic outcomes. One of the more comprehensive studies is by Eyraud et al. (2013), who assessed the macroeconomic and environmental impacts of green investments across a ten-year period in 35 developed and emerging countries. Their findings suggest that green investment increases with economic growth, low interest rates, and high fuel prices, while carbon pricing and feed-in tariffs also positively influence investment—unlike biofuel support, which shows no significant effect.

Other studies build on these insights by reinforcing the idea that green investments form one of the primary foundations for achieving sustainable development. For instance, studies (Dabyltayeva & Rakhymzhan, 2019; Dalevska et al., 2019; Miszczak et al., 2024; Raszkowski & Bartniczak, 2018) argue that green investments are instrumental in laying the financial groundwork for long-term sustainability. OECD (2015) frames green growth as an investment-led approach spanning sectors such as infrastructure, clean energy, and efficiency improvements. Achieving this vision depends on the strategic deployment of both fiscal tools and regulatory levers. Governments play a central role through mechanisms like tax breaks, conditional subsidies, and environmental standards that steer private sector behaviour toward sustainability while preserving ecological resources.

The environmental and economic outcomes of green investments are also corroborated by empirical analyses. For example, literature (Lyeonov et al., 2019; Ocal & Aslan, 2013; Priyan, 2023; Sadorsky, 2009), present evidence that such investments lead to reductions in greenhouse gas emissions and contribute to the mitigation of global warming. In addition to their direct environmental effects, green investments are associated with broader economic benefits, such as increased R&D expenditures, a higher proportion of GDP allocated to innovation activities, and overall improvements in sustainable economic growth and emissions productivity.

Within the policy landscape, market-based instruments are often highlighted for their efficiency advantages. Among these, environmental taxes (or levies) are the most widely applied fiscal tool. Their central mechanism lies in encouraging polluters to reduce emissions to a level where the marginal cost of abatement matches the tax rate. Such instruments offer firms a degree of flexibility in determining the most cost-effective method to achieve environmental compliance, as emphasized by Andrei et al. (2016). In contrast to command-and-control regulations, levies are generally less burdensome in terms of administrative costs. According to Kosonen & Nicodeme (2009), the administrative cost of implementing a tax levy is significantly lower—approximately 0.2% of tax revenue collected—compared to the five percent associated with managing subsidy programs.

The cost-effectiveness of market-based instruments is further substantiated by studies from the United States. Goulder & Parry (2008) demonstrate that market-based tools such as taxes and permit trading schemes can deliver equivalent pollution reductions at a fraction (40–95%) of the cost of direct regulatory interventions, depending on the regulatory scope. Additional evidence from Lu et al. 2010) suggests that carbon taxes can lead to meaningful reductions in CO_2 emissions with minimal adverse effects on economic growth. Besides influencing corporate behaviour, these levies indirectly affect consumer preferences by altering price structures, thereby nudging households towards cleaner and more sustainable consumption choices.

Research highlights the varied impacts of fiscal instruments used to promote the green transition, with notable distinctions between direct incentives, R&D-based measures, and market-based mechanisms. Evidence by Strand & Toman (2010) shows that incentives focused on research and development not only foster innovation but also contribute to productivity and employment—essential drivers of long-term sustainable growth. Similarly, Agrawala et al. (2020) compare a broad set of fiscal tools and conclude that tax incentives for clean energy and environmental R&D consistently deliver positive outcomes across emissions, economic growth, and environmental performance. Although interest subsidies tied to renewable energy credits show more limited effects, they remain part of a wider policy mix supporting the green transition.

Political and institutional dimensions of fiscal policy implementation

Fiscal policy implementation is increasingly understood through the lens of political economy, which emphasizes how governance quality and institutional dynamics shape policy outcomes (Umoh et al., 2018). The implementation of fiscal policy is often driven less by economic rationality and more by underlying political incentives and institutional dynamics (Auerbach, 2019; Keita & Turcu, 2022; Poterba, 1994). Key determinants of fiscal persistence include the quality of governance, levels of corruption, and the strength of the rule of law, all of which shape the consistency and credibility of fiscal actions (Umoh et al., 2018). In parallel, studies highlight that political configurations—such as stable governments, cohesive party systems, and strong institutional frameworks—can facilitate more effective and timely fiscal adjustments by enabling coordinated decision-making and reducing implementation delays (Addison et al., 2018; Carmichael, 2002; Fatas & Mihov, 2003)

Research on U.S. states and comparative international contexts shows that fiscal adjustments are more effective and timely when political power is concentrated—for example, when a single party controls both the executive and legislative branches or maintains consistent governance across election cycles (Lavigne, 2006). Cross-country evidence suggests that electoral cycles, political fragmentation, institutional instability, and social polarization systematically undermine fiscal responsiveness and macroeconomic stability. These conditions often delay necessary adjustments and weaken the effectiveness of fiscal interventions, particularly in politically volatile or governance-challenged contexts (Coutinho & Tsani, 2021; Woo, 2002). This pattern is also evident in advanced economies, where specific political configurations—such as fragmented legislatures and frequent electoral turnover—have been shown to bias fiscal decision-making toward short-term expenditure gains, often at the expense of long-term fiscal sustainability and SDG-aligned investments (Annett, 2002). Even in well-developed institutional contexts, political incentives can disrupt coherent long-term planning, underscoring the importance of aligning governance structures with sustainable fiscal objectives. A similar pattern is observed in parts of the Global South. For instance, studies from West Africa indicate that the continued reliance on outdated or ineffective fiscal policies—referred to as fiscal persistence—is less a result of economic reasoning and more a reflection of entrenched political interests, institutional fragility, and systemic corruption, which collectively hinder policy renewal and responsiveness. (Umoh et al., 2018).

Institutional mechanisms also play a crucial role in the context of fiscal policy. The design, credibility, and implementation of fiscal measures are closely tied to the strength, coherence, and accountability of public institutions, highlighting the importance of meaningful institutional engagement in achieving effective fiscal outcomes (Kotnik et al., 2020). According to Stoker (2006), poorly defined or fragmented institutional arrangements often result in limited authority, insufficient administrative capacity, and weak oversight mechanisms—all of which can significantly undermine the implementation of public policies. This perspective aligns with institutional theory, which views policy change as influenced by embedded rules, norms, routines, and environmental pressures that guide accepted behaviour. It also emphasizes normative, coercive, and mimetic forces that shape governmental decisions on policy adoption and execution (Toma et al., 2005). Institutional mechanisms, in this view, represent formal and legal structures that frequently outweigh market forces in shaping public organizations (DiMaggio & Powell, 2000; Kraft & Furlong, 2007). These institutional factors reveal how the actions of politicians and policymakers directly affect fiscal policy outcomes (Sadia et al., 2025). For instance, decentralization can improve fiscal performance when supported by strong party organization, while weak institutional quality—marked by corruption and low government effectiveness—is linked to fiscal policy persistence and inertia (Lin & Zhou, 2021). Additional evidence points to the limiting role of institutional weaknesses—particularly fragile regulatory systems and poor budget execution capacity—in undermining the implementation of fiscal policies aligned with the Sustainable Development Goals. An IMF study on Sub-Saharan Africa concluded that ambitious fiscal consolidation efforts frequently failed to materialize, especially in countries characterized by low institutional quality, weak governance structures, and overly optimistic macroeconomic assumptions (Lledó & Poplawski-Ribeiro, 2013). Moreover, the presence of corruption within fragile institutional frameworks can distort resource allocation and reduce productivity by altering incentive structures (Nawaz & Khawaja, 2019). Conversely, credible fiscal rules—such as no-deficit carryover provisions and limits on tax or expenditure discretion—are associated with faster fiscal adjustment and reduced volatility (Enikolopov & Zhuravskaya, 2003).

Based on the reviewed literature, it can be concluded that well-designed fiscal instruments—particularly green taxes and innovation-linked incentives—can effectively support sustainable investment. Taxes tend to outperform subsidies in terms of cost-efficiency, while market-based tools offer greater behavioural flexibility. Although levies may have inflationary side effects, targeted incentives remain essential for advancing long-term sustainability goals. These findings underscore the importance of aligning political authority with transparent and capable institutional frameworks to ensure that fiscal policy operates not only efficiently, but also delivers durable developmental and environmental outcomes.

Limits and challenges of fiscal incentives in achieving sustainable development goals

While fiscal instruments are widely promoted as key tools for advancing the Sustainable Development Goals (SDGs), a growing body of research emphasizes that their effectiveness is far from guaranteed. Evidence across sectors and national contexts highlights that design complexity, uneven regional implementation, and institutional weaknesses often undermine their intended outcomes. Already nearly four decades ago, Zodrow and Mieszkowski (1986) warned that competition among jurisdictions through tax incentives may trigger a "race to the bottom," leading to inefficient resource allocation. Recent studies show that fiscal incentives yield mixed results for SDGs in Indonesia, with their effectiveness largely dependent on policy context and institutional quality. In the environmental and energy sectors, they tend to perform better when clearly targeted and administratively simple; however, uptake is often hindered by design flaws, regressivity, and bureaucratic complexity—challenges that are particularly acute for SMEs (Sapar & Kusuma, 2025). This is further illustrated by a study showing that the absence of long-term regulatory predictability discouraged private investment in renewable energy, despite the presence of tax incentives (Sonjaya & Noch, 2024).Similarly, Peters & Fisher (2004) provide empirical evidence that many fiscal incentives are poorly targeted and ineffective, often rewarding firms for behaviour they would have adopted regardless. In sectors like forestry and manufacturing, large fiscal transfers and tax holidays have failed to generate the desired investment outcomes and have instead eroded public revenues vital for services such as education (Dasgupta & Srikanth, 2021).

Other scholars have highlighted the misuse of fiscal incentives, proposing alternatives that prioritize human capital and infrastructure investment over firm-based reliefs (Bartik, 2005). In Sub-Saharan Africa, Fowowe (2013) notes that poor targeting, lack of transparency, and weak governance frequently render incentives ineffective—findings echoed by Noombo & Mwange (2024), who show that weak policy coherence and fiscal leakages dilute the impact of green investment incentives. Toyin & Onanuga (2019) similarly report that in Nigeria, limited reach of green finance, inadequate administrative mechanisms, and poor contextual adaptation significantly constrained SDG progress. An earlier assessment of Ukraine's fiscal framework further reveals how poor coordination between tax and expenditure policies contributed to rising inequality and environmental degradation, undermining the country's SDG efforts (Lutsyk, 2021). Complementing these findings, Makhfudhah & Rasyid (2025) emphasize that heterogeneity in policy design, regional disparities, and data limitations further complicate implementation and weaken the transformative potential of fiscal tools.

Across these diverse studies, several critical policy design principles emerge as essential for improving effectiveness. Sapar & Kusuma (2025) emphasize that incentives must be sector- and context-specific, guided by clear objectives and eligibility criteria, and accompanied by streamlined administrative processes. Their effectiveness is greatly enhanced when embedded within broader regulatory, informational, and social policy frameworks. Nonetheless, common challenges persist. (Stausholm, 2017) further identify issues such as inefficient targeting, design flaws, insufficient equity focus, and a lack of compensatory mechanisms as key sources of failure. These shortcomings often result in suboptimal allocation of public funds, foregone revenues, and failure to achieve social or environmental goals.

Building on these challenges, Sapar & Kusuma (2025) highlight that high heterogeneity of outcomes and regressive fiscal effects remain widespread. To mitigate these risks, Sing et al. (2025) advocate for progressive tax structures, revenue recycling, and the inclusion of equity-sensitive safeguards. Additionally, ensuring long-term policy relevance requires the integration of robust monitoring, evaluation, and adaptive learning frameworks, as highlighted by Hammaker et al. (2022). These mechanisms are essential for detecting unintended effects, improving implementation, and refining policy design over time. Taken together, the literature strongly suggests that without context-sensitive design, regionally adapted implementation strategies, and institutional robustness, fiscal incentives are unlikely to deliver the inclusive and sustainable outcomes they are designed to achieve.

Coherent and just green fiscal reform through equity, institutions, and efficiency

Effective green fiscal policy (GFP) requires more than economic logic or environmental ambition—it demands a multi-dimensional framework that considers the social equity, institutional capacity, and economic efficiency of fiscal instruments. Recent literature highlights three interlinked dimensions critical to the design and implementation of green fiscal policies: equity and inclusiveness, institutional feasibility, and cost-effectiveness.

One of the most salient concerns in current research is the risk that GFPs may inadvertently exacerbate existing socio-economic and spatial disparities if they fail to incorporate principles of distributive justice. Urban green initiatives, for example, while beneficial in aggregate, have often marginalized vulnerable populations—particularly in ethnically diverse or low-income communities—leading to phenomena such as green gentrification, where climate resilience efforts raise property values and displace those most at risk (Anguelovski et al., 2019). In contrast, complementary insights from Heilongjiang Province in China further demonstrate the potential of localized, inclusive green finance to stimulate rural revitalization through investment in sustainable agriculture and infrastructure (Ma et al., 2023). These findings underscore the importance of incorporating equity-sensitive mechanisms—such as targeted subsidies, revenue recycling schemes, or participatory planning frameworks—into the fiscal policy design process.

However, the effectiveness of such redistributive instruments is heavily contingent upon the institutional context in which they are implemented. Green fiscal tools do not operate in a vacuum; their success hinges on administrative capacity, regulatory coherence, and the level of public trust. Evidence indicates that even technically robust instruments—such as carbon pricing mechanisms or green public investments—can falter when institutional arrangements are fragmented or when rebound effects neutralize anticipated environmental gains (Dafermos & Nikolaidi, 2019). For instance, dynamic simulation models from Myanmar show that fiscal reallocations aimed at inclusive development, such as expanding rural infrastructure, generate substantial benefits only when supported by strong governance structures and effective project oversight(Zuojun & Lynn, 2024). These observations highlight the importance of integrating institutional factor into the GFP design process, including thorough assessments of administrative capacity, inter-agency coordination mechanisms, and real-time implementation monitoring systems.

Finally, a growing body of literature calls for a broader interpretation of economic efficiency in evaluating GFPs—one that goes beyond the confines of traditional cost-benefit analysis. The field of institutional ecological economics, for example, posits that property rights regimes, actor-specific incentives, and governance arrangements may have a greater influence on policy effectiveness than conventional financial metrics (Slavikova, 2013). This perspective is echoed in recent comparative studies of green financial instruments, which reveal that features such as eligibility criteria, reporting obligations, and monitoring provisions play a decisive role in determining both uptake and ecological outcomes (Nozadze, 2024). Consequently, enhancing the analytical utility of fiscal evaluations requires attention not only to aggregate efficiency, but also to factors such as behavioural responsiveness, transaction costs, and adaptability to specific socio-economic contexts.

Taken together, these insights suggest that green fiscal policies are most likely to succeed when evaluated through a lens that jointly considers equity, institutional viability, and economic effectiveness. Embedding equity concerns, strengthening institutional conditions, and broadening efficiency criteria are not merely technical adjustments; they are essential components of a coherent and just green fiscal reform. Only by aligning these interrelated dimensions can policymakers design and implement GFPs that are not only environmentally effective and economically sound, but also socially inclusive and institutionally resilient.

Examples of selected strategic measures by country

There are several examples of policy packages implemented by individual countries to promote the green transition. Below, we focus on a few national measures from Sweden, the United Kingdom, France, Slovenia, Canada, Denmark, Japan, and the Netherlands that are related to the green transition. European Union member states are legally bound to implement a set of climate and energy laws that advance the green transition.

The Fit for 55 legislative package (European Council, 2025), in particular, directly shapes national measures by setting binding targets and revising key directives—such as the Renewable Energy Directive, Energy Efficiency Directive, and Emissions Trading System—which must be transposed into domestic policies. In contrast, non-EU countries are not subject to EU legislation and thus retain full autonomy in designing their own climate and energy strategies. In addition to the Fit for 55 package several other EU-level instruments guide member states in aligning national policies with sustainable development objectives. The European Green Deal (EGD) provides the overarching strategic vision for making Europe climate-neutral by 2050 and serves as the policy foundation for subsequent legislative initiatives targeting emissions, energy, and biodiversity (European Commission, 2019).

The COVID-19 pandemic had significant implications for green public spending in the 2018–2022 period. While early years reflect pre-pandemic investment patterns, the years following 2020 saw a pronounced shift due to emergency fiscal responses and the subsequent launch of green recovery frameworks. These developments were accompanied by substantial policy changes, most notably through the Recovery and Resilience Facility (RRF), introduced as part of the EU's response to the COVID-19 crisis. The RRF mandates that at least 37% of each member state's recovery plan directly supports climate objectives, thereby strengthening SDG alignment through targeted investments (European Commission, 2021b). The EU Taxonomy for Sustainable Activities establishes a common classification system to identify environmentally sustainable economic activities, aiming to steer both public and private capital flows toward projects that are consistent with climate and environmental goals (European Commission, 2020). Furthermore, National Energy and Climate Plans (NECPs) require each EU country to submit 10-year strategies detailing how they will meet common EU climate and energy targets, ensuring coherence between national planning and overarching European objectives, including the SDGs (European Commission, 2021a).

Sweden. Sweden implemented the "Miljöbilar 2020" program (Skatteverket, 2025; Swedish National Audit Office, 2025) to promote greener transport through subsidies for electric vehicle purchases and investments in charging infrastructure. Although Sweden introduced its transport subsidies before the Fit for 55 package, they support similar goals, such as reducing vehicle emissions and promoting cleaner transport. The "Miljöbilar 2020" program combined multiple fiscal measures, including purchase discounts for green and super-green vehicles, a bonus-malus system, CO_2-based vehicle tax differentiation, and reduced income tax for low-emission cars. Between 2007 and 2020, subsidies and tax expenditures amounted to €1.2 billion, while CO_2-based vehicle tax adjustments generated €0.4 billion in revenue. From 2013 to 2018, around 60,000 vehicle purchases were subsidized, resulting in an estimated 1.25 million tonnes of CO_2 reduction (Skatteverket, 2025; Sterner, 2012). However, the socio-economic cost per kilogram of CO_2 reduced averaged €0.35 and reached €0.54 specifically for green vehicle incentives—five times higher than the effectiveness of the Motor Vehicle Tax. The Swedish National Audit Office (2025) also noted several shortcomings: subsidies disproportionately benefited company cars used privately, were concentrated in urban areas, and had regressive effects under the bonus-malus system. It concluded that the program's overall cost-effectiveness and equity outcomes were limited, underscoring the challenges of balancing environmental goals with fiscal and social considerations.

United Kingdom. The United Kingdom implemented the "Non-Domestic Renewable Heat Incentive" (NDRHI) (Ofgem, 2025) program in 2011, aiming to accelerate the adoption of renewable and low-carbon heating technologies across businesses, public sector bodies, and non-profit organizations in England, Scotland, and Wales. Administered by Ofgem, the scheme provided financial incentives through quarterly payments over a 20-year period, calculated based on the amount of eligible heat generated by accredited installations. By supporting a substantial volume of renewable heat generation through thousands of accredited installations and biomethane injections into the gas grid, the NDRHI represented a major public investment in low-carbon heating technologies. Total payments under the scheme reached £5.94 billion by March 2024, reflecting the scale and sustained commitment to promoting renewable energy in the heating sector. Reports indicate that the program successfully increased the use of renewable energy sources and contributed to a significant reduction in greenhouse gas emissions. Overall, the scheme played a crucial role in helping the UK meet its renewable energy targets and advance decarbonization efforts within the non-domestic sector.

Although the United Kingdom is no longer required to comply with EU legislation following Brexit—including the Fit for 55 package (European Council, 2025)—its national climate strategy continues to reflect similar ambitions. The NDRHI and related measures demonstrate the UK's commitment to advancing renewable energy and decarbonization in line with broader European climate objectives.

France. France has implemented several initiatives to support the green transition, focusing on energy efficiency and the adoption of renewable energy sources. One of the key programs is the interest-free eco-loan (éco-prêt à taux zéro or eco-PTZ). The éco-PTZ program was first introduced in 2009 and has undergone several reforms, most recently in 2022, which increased the maximum loan amount to €50,000 and simplified eligibility criteria (Service-Public, 2025). The MaPrimeRénov' scheme was launched in 2020 as a consolidation of earlier energy renovation subsidies, aiming to enhance energy efficiency in residential buildings. Energy Saving Certificates (Certificats d'Économies d'Énergie, CEE) have been in place since 2006, requiring energy suppliers to promote energy savings among end-users. The "Plan de relance" (Recovery Plan) was announced in September 2020 in response to the economic fallout from the COVID-19 pandemic, with key green transition measures implemented from 2021 onwards (International Energy Agency, 2023; Ministère de l'Économie, des Finances et de la Souveraineté industrielle et numérique, 2025).

These programs are aligned with the objectives of the European Union's Fit for 55 legislative package, proposed by the European Commission in July 2021. The package aims to reduce greenhouse gas emissions by 55% by 2030 compared to 1990 levels. France's investments in energy efficiency, renewable energy, and industrial decarbonization under the "Plan de relance" (Recovery Plan) and other schemes support the national trajectory towards carbon neutrality by 2050 and contribute to fulfilling the EU's climate targets (European Commission, 2021b; European Council, 2025). The Recovery Plan allocates €30 billion to accelerate the ecological transition, with investments directed towards the thermal renovation of buildings, decarbonization of industry, development of green hydrogen, promotion of cleaner transport, and transformation of the agricultural sector. A part of the plan, that also includes various measures to stimulate the private sector, the country also introduced incentives for investments in renewable energy, energy efficiency, and green infrastructure. These initiatives reflect France's commitment to reducing greenhouse gas emissions and promoting sustainable development through substantial investments in energy efficiency and renewable energy projects.

Slovenia. The onset of the COVID-19 pandemic marked a turning point in public spending priorities, including in Slovenia, where fiscal strategies were reoriented to support both economic recovery and environmental objectives (Barbier, 2020; OECD, 2020). While the early years of the 2018–2022 period reflected pre-crisis investment patterns, the post-2020 phase was characterized by a strategic reallocation of resources toward green recovery measures. In Slovenia, this shift materialized through increased financing via the Environmental Public Fund (Eko sklad, 2024), which offered expanded subsidies and loans for energy-efficient renovations, renewable energy installations, and sustainable mobility projects. Additional fiscal support came from tax reliefs for research and development activities, including green innovation in the Information and Communication Technology (ICT) sector, and from increased public expenditures targeting environmental protection for companies and households (Eko sklad, 2024; FURS, 2024). A significant boost also came from the deployment of EU Recovery and Resilience Facility (RRF) resources aimed at advancing sustainable development (European Council, 2025). These developments contributed to the observed variation in green investment levels and SDG-related outcomes in 2021 and 2022. In particular, 2022 marked the operationalization of national reforms and investment initiatives linked to the RRF, with targeted emphasis on energy efficiency, low-carbon mobility, and green innovation (Muren & Franca, 2022). These priorities were closely aligned with the objectives of the Fit for 55 legislative package, which sets binding climate and energy targets for EU member states and thereby directly shaped the design and focus of Slovenia's post-pandemic green spending measures (European Council, 2025). Accordingly, the results for this period should be interpreted in light of these broader policy transformations driven by the pandemic context and the EU's climate policy framework.

Subsidy schemes in Canada, Denmark, and Japan. Several countries have adopted a range of targeted policy measures to promote the use of renewable energy sources, each tailored to their national contexts and energy transition goals. For example, Canada implemented the "ecoENERGY for Renewable Power" program (Government of Canada, 2025), which provides financial incentives to increase the production of electricity from renewable sources such as wind, solar, and biomass. Denmark introduced the "Energispareordningen" program (Green Power Denmark, 2025), focusing on energy savings and efficiency improvements across various sectors, particularly industry and buildings. Japan launched the "Feed-in Tariff" scheme (Ichigo, 2025), offering guaranteed pricing for renewable energy producers to encourage investment and stability in the sector. Similarly, the Netherlands established the

"SDE++" program (Rvo, 2025), which supports a wide range of sustainable energy technologies through a competitive subsidy system based on cost-effectiveness. All these initiatives are built around comprehensive subsidy frameworks designed to lower the financial barriers to green investments and accelerate the deployment of clean energy technologies. While Canada and Japan are not bound by EU legislation, Denmark's programs continue to evolve under the binding framework of Fit for 55, particularly in the energy efficiency and emissions trading sectors.

In response to Research Question 1: "To what extent does public spending influence sustainable development outcomes, and which international policy instruments have been shown to effectively promote green investment?", theoretical perspectives consistently underscore the significant influence of public spending on sustainable development by correcting market failures, internalizing negative externalities, and stimulating long-term investments that are often underprovided by the private sector. Keynesian economics emphasizes counter-cyclical public investment as a driver of economic stabilization and transformation, while ecological economics highlights the state's role in reorienting growth toward ecological limits and intergenerational equity. Public spending directed toward green infrastructure, renewable energy, environmental R&D, and subsidies for clean technologies reduces financial risk and creates enabling conditions for private sector engagement. Such expenditures can generate positive externalities, including technology spillovers, learning effects, and job creation in emerging green sectors. Empirical evidence from countries such as Sweden, the Netherlands, and Japan shows that specific policy instruments—such as green public procurement, targeted subsidies, feed-in tariffs, and comprehensive environmental tax reforms—have been effective in mobilizing green investment, particularly when embedded within coherent, long-term policy frameworks supported by robust institutional capacities. The success of these instruments, however, is contingent on national governance structures, policy credibility, administrative capacity, and alignment with broader regulatory, innovation, and industrial strategies.

RESEARCH FRAMEWORK AND METHODOLOGY

Research conceptualization

Green investments are among the most important drivers of sustainable development. Some studies (Dabyltayeva & Rakhymzhan, 2019; Dalevska et al., 2019; Kotnik et al., 2024; Raszkowski & Bartniczak, 2018) point out that green growth includes various investments in infrastructure, in renewable energy, and in energy efficiency. Those investments could be implemented using various financial and non-financial instruments, like subsidies or tax incentives for companies, government expenditures, various kinds of environmentally friendly business activities, etc.

A recent contribution emphasizes that despite constitutional provisions in Slovenia supporting state engagement in sustainable development, actual implementation has lagged, underscoring the need for a more active and coordinated role of the state in achieving the SDGs (Plicanic, 2020). This highlights that institutional commitment alone is insufficient without effective policy translation and sustained political will.

Furthermore, some studies (e.g. Ocal & Aslan (2013) and Sadorsky (2009) show that green investments cause higher spending on research and development, but at the same time have a positive impact on sustainable economic growth. It turns out that different government mechanisms aimed at reducing the economic risks associated with green innovations have different effects in different circumstances/countries. In some cases, they might be ineffective or statistically insignificant, or might even cause market distortions (Liang et al., 2022). As further contextual evidence, a public expenditure review of Slovenia highlights that, despite relatively high spending on health care, education, and social protection, the country exhibits limited performance gains due to structural inefficiencies and inflexible spending composition (Mattina & Gunnarsson, 2007). In light of these limitations, green development measures should be carefully designed to ensure that fiscal spending in the green economy yields maximum impact and avoids similar inefficiencies (Lin & Zhu, 2019).

Focusing specifically on each measure, Liang et al. (2022) proved that both subsidies and tax incentives have a positive effect on green innovation, while companies with longer traditions (older) and larger companies are more interested in such tax instruments, and consequently show greater interest in green innovation. Similar findings are reported by (Song et al., 2020), whereby the positive effect on green innovation is particularly evident in the case of tax incentives for research and development, which play an important role in promoting green product innovation.

The introduction of environmental taxes is also said to be more effective than other measures in developing countries (Andrei et al., 2016). Environmental taxes as the most common fiscal instrument encourage companies to reduce pollution to such an extent that the marginal cost of reducing pollution is equal to the tax. Additionally, tax compliance requires less administrative effort than direct regulation, which is why the administrative costs are lower (Kosonen & Nicodeme, 2009). As far as pollution reduction as a sustainable goal is concerned, the results of several studies in the US have shown that taxation or permit trading can achieve the same pollution reduction with significantly lower costs (from 40 to 95 percent) than direct regulatory measures, depending on the defined area of regulation (Goulder & Parry, 2008). Lu et al. (2010) revealed that environmental taxes reduce CO2 emissions with a small negative impact on economic growth and wages as labour market prices, which is reflected in higher social costs. (Houser et al., 2009) found that one billion US dollars spent on incentives for renewable energy sources (through subsidies and tax incentives) increased the number of jobs, reduced CO2 emissions, and lowered energy costs. Tax incentives for investments in the use of clean energy have a similar effect. A smaller effect was found when reviewing the impact of interest rate for loans on renewable energy investments (Agrawala et al., 2020). Several studies have explored the effects of various measures of green transition geared towards promoting economic growth, emission reduction, and other effects on the environment (for more details see Strand & Toman (2010). across EU countries (2010–2021) revealed complex dynamics between public spending and sustainability, showing that while fossil fuel consumption correlated positively with government environmental spending, financial development, innovation, and green energy use showed a negative association, pointing to tensions and competing priorities in advancing the SDGs. These findings highlight the difficulty of achieving coherent progress across multiple sustainability dimensions.

Indeed, most studies tend to focus on only a few selected goals, treating their effects in isolation, even though each policy measure often produces multiple—both desirable and undesirable—outcomes. This fragmentation poses a challenge for assessing the cumulative or cross-cutting effects of individual and combined interventions. Similarly, direct incentive measures may yield different results compared to regulatory or fiscal instruments

Database

To assess the impact of various green investment measures on the Sustainable Development Goals (SDGs) in Slovenia, we used multiple data sets in the empirical analysis. The input data were selected based on prior research and studies, with the aim of identifying which government measures influence progress toward the SDGs. Data collection was carried out in several phases, beginning with data gathering, followed by organisation, and concluding with statistical processing.

The selection of the 2018–2022 period for analysing public green spending is methodologically justified, as it encompasses both the pre-pandemic baseline and the significant fiscal interventions prompted by the COVID-19 crisis. This timeframe allows for an assessment of how green expenditures evolved in response to unprecedented external shocks and the implementation of major recovery initiatives, such as the European Union's RRF. The period is particularly pertinent for examining the effectiveness and orientation of green recovery strategies, a subject extensively explored in contemporary literature (e.g. Dafnomilis et al., 2022; Köppl & Schratzenstaller, 2024; Pigato et al., 2021).

Drawing on prior studies (Agrawala et al., 2020; Dabyltayeva & Rakhymzhan, 2019; Dalevska et al., 2019; Raszkowski & Bartniczak, 2018; Strand & Toman, 2010), government measures for promoting green investments can be broadly classified into four categories: (i) environmental or green taxes, as the most common fiscal instrument; (ii) incentive-based fiscal instruments, such as subsidies, allowances, and exemptions; (iii) emissions trading schemes; and (iv) direct foreign investment.

The data were sourced from the Slovenian Environmental Public Fund (Eko sklad, 2024), the Financial Administration of the Republic of Slovenia (FURS, 2024), the Statistical Office of the Republic of Slovenia (SURS, 2024), and the Ministry of Finance (MF, 2024). These data include the amounts of a) approved loans and subsidies from the Slovenian Environmental Public Fund, b) tax relief amounts for research and development that legal entities (under the Corporate Income Tax Act) and self-employed individuals (under the Personal Income Tax Act) can claim on up to 100% of their investment, and c) state expenditures for environmental protection in the national budget. Additionally, we collected data on sustainable development indicators prepared by the Statistical Office of the Republic of Slovenia based on Eurostat's methodology at the European Union level, which are aimed at monitoring the achievement of sustainable development goals.

Input data for the subsequent input-output regression analysis were collected on:

- sdg13_2: Emission intensity in energy consumption (index, 2000 = 100)
- sdg12_22: Disposal rate of waste excluding mineral waste (%)
- sdg12_21: Recycling rate of waste excluding mineral waste (%)
- sdg12_4: Average CO2 emissions per kilometre for new passenger cars (g CO2 per km)
- eco1: The amounts of granted loans for green investments made by the Slovenian Environmental Public Fund to companies and municipalities
- eko2: The percentage of approved loans relative to the total investment values made by Slovenian Environmental Public Fund to companies and municipalities
- eco3: The amounts of investments by Slovenian Environmental Public Fund
- eco4: The amounts of subsidies made by Slovenian Environmental Public Fund
- taxrel1: The number of taxpayers claiming tax reliefs, including for innovation or other activities.
- taxrel21: The amounts of tax relief for R&D (companies and self-entrepreneurs)
- taxrel3: The amount of tax relief for R&D for companies
- taxrel4: The amount of tax relief for R&D _ICT sector
- taxrel5: The amount of tax relief for R&D_ self-entrepreneur
- taxrel6: The amount of tax relief for R&D_ companies and self-entrepreneur

- envexp1: The amount of government expenditure on environmental protection
- envexp2: The amount of government expenditure on environmental protection for companies
- envexp3: The amount of government expenditure on environmental protection for households

The variable names used in the analysis refer to key environmental, economic, and policy indicators. For example, sdg13_2 represents emission intensity in energy consumption, expressed as an index with the base year 2000 set at 100. The variable sdg12_22 indicates the disposal rate of waste excluding mineral waste, while sdg12_21 reflects the recycling rate of such waste, both expressed in percentages. The variable sdg12_4 denotes the average CO_2 emissions per kilometre for new passenger cars, measured in grams of CO_2 per kilometre.

In the economic domain, eco1 captures the approved loan amounts for companies and municipalities, expressed in million euros. eco2 shows the approved loan amounts relative to investment values (as a percentage), and eco3 represents the total investment amounts by investors, also in million euros. The variable eco4 reflects the amount of subsidies or incentives granted, expressed in million euros.

Further, taxrel4 denotes tax reliefs for research and development (R&D) specifically for companies in the ICT sector, expressed as the total amount in euros per company. Environmental expenditures are represented by envexp2, which shows national expenditure on environmental protection (in million euros), and envexp3, which captures the total environmental protection investments by the entire economy, also in million euros.

To sum up, as inputs (independent variables), the following were used: eco1, eco2, eco3, eco4, taxrel4, envexp2, and envexp3. Indicators representing the achievement of the Sustainable Development Goals (SDGs) were selected as output (dependent) variables for inclusion in the analysis. Each SDG indicator is quantified using specific metrics designed to track progress toward the corresponding goals. The following variables were included as outputs: sdg13_2, sdg12_22, sdg12_21, and sdg12_4. A complete list of the included variables, along with their descriptive statistics, is presented in Table 1.

Table 1. The list of dependent variables and their descriptive statistics

Variables	Description of Variable	Mean	Std. Dev	Observations
sdg13_2	Emission intensity in energy consumption (index, 2000 = 100)	4.485	96.728	13
sdg12_22	Disposal rate of waste excluding mineral waste (%)	6.572	9.741	13
sdg12_21	Recycling rate of waste excluding mineral waste (%)	6.984	78.691	13

continued on following page

Table 1. Continued

Variables	Description of Variable	Mean	Std. Dev	Observations
sdg12_4	Average CO2 emissions per kilometre for new passenger cars (g CO2 per km)	16.343	135.905	13
eco1	Approved loan amounts for companies and municipalities (in mil. EUR)	14.077	34.806	13
eco2	Approved amounts relative to investment values (as %)	0.234	0.569	13
eco3	Investment amount by investors (in mil. EUR)	130.504	289.043	13
eco4	Amount of subsidies/incentives (in mil. EUR)	23.025603	51.420	13
taxrel4	Tax reliefs for R&D for companies, only ICT sector, total in EUR per company	12629.55022	30746.427	13
envexp2	National expenditure on environmental protection (in mil. EUR)	32.02718	189.860	13
envexp3	Environmental protection investments of the total economy (in mil. EUR)	103.659	360.762	13

Source: own elaboration.

Furthermore, this chapter examines seven selected Sustainable Development Goal (SDG) indicators (SDG 12.3, SDG 2.4, SDG 12.2, SDG 11.5, SDG 12.5, SDG 2.7, SDG 6.2) that show the highest positive impact proportions from budgetary environmental expenditure indicators (green investments).

Methodology

Pearson's bivariate correlation is a quantitative statistical measure of an association between variables. It measures the effect size and direction of the relationship between two variables. The effect size indicates the strength of the relationship between two variables. In practice, Pearson correlation values greater than ±0.20 are typically taken as indicative of a meaningful (though weak) correlation (Mondal & Mondal, 2017). The sign indicates the direction of the relationship: a positive sign (+) means that both variables increase or decrease together, while a negative sign (-) indicates that as one variable increases, the other decreases. In our case, the correlation analysis examines whether there is a connection between different kinds of expenditures1 (inputs) and indicators of individual Sustainable Development Goals (outputs). In the case of Slovenia, the indicators of individual Sustainable Development Goals were correlated with selected budget expenditure indicators (green investments) using a correlation matrix. The result of the analysis is the display of correlation using Pearson's bivariate correlations, which has been used instead of the Spearman matrix due to incomplete data and to incidences of missing values. The method used is more appropriate because it is less sensitive to extreme values and can capture nonlinear relationships between variables (Benesty et al., 2008; Hauke & Kossowski, 2011). Pearson values greater than ± 0.2 indicate a correlation between green investment expenditure and indicators of individual sustainable development goals. A positive correlation value represents synergy between input and output variables, while the negative correlation values represent compromise. The analysis was prepared in the form of a correlation matrix, in which the correlations do not show extreme correlations between pairs of variables, indicating the absence of obvious multicollinearity.[2]

In the regression analysis, the correlation of amounts of loans/tax reliefs/budget expenditures for green investments (inputs) with selected indicators of SDGs (outputs) was assessed. The analysis shows estimates of the impact of individual budget expenditure indicators on selected SDGs without lag, with a lag of 1 (one year), with a lag of 2 (two years), and with a lag of 3 (three years). For each pair of independent and dependent variables, three types of regressions were performed: linear OLS regression, robust regression, and Huber robust regression. To improve the reliability of results, we used different types of regression methods. Ordinary Least Squares (OLS) regression is a linear regression method that minimizes the sum of squared differences between observed and predicted values. It assumes normally distributed data and is highly sensitive to outliers, which can distort model estimates. Robust OLS regression addresses this limitation by reducing the influence of extreme or atypical values, thereby providing more stable and reliable estimates when anomalies are present in the dataset. A specific variant, Huber robust regression, combines the strengths of OLS and absolute error minimization. It applies squared loss to small residuals and absolute loss to larger ones, making it less sensitive to outliers while retaining efficiency under moderate violations of normality. The key distinction among these methods lies in how they treat influential data points—OLS fully incorporates them, whereas robust approaches limit or moderate their impact.

Due to the relatively large amount of input and output data, partial regression analysis was conducted for combination of each input variable (environmental investments) with each indicator of the selected sustainable development goals, although it could not be performed for some indicators due to the small number of observations. Careful interpretation is required because for some indicators, the lower and upper bounds of the confidence interval include both positive and negative values.

RESULTS

To clarify the complex empirical findings, the following conceptual framework illustrates how government financial mechanisms influence selected Sustainable Development Goals (SDGs). The Figure 1 demonstrates that loans for green investments with time lags have a decreasing effect on SDG12_22 (Disposal rate of waste excluding mineral waste (%)) but an increasing effect on SDG12_21 (Recycling rate of waste excluding mineral waste (%)). Green investments and green subsidies have a decreasing effect on SDG12_21. Tax relief for R&D in ICT companies with a time lag has a decreasing effect on SDG12_4 (Average CO2 emissions per kilometre for new passenger cars (g CO2 per km)). Environmental protection spending for households with a time lag has a decreasing effect on SDG13_2 (Emission intensity in energy consumption (index, 2000 = 100)), whereas total environmental spending for all sectors has an increasing effect on SDG13_2.

Figure 1. Relationship Between Government Financial Mechanisms and Their Impact on Sustainable Development Goals (SDGs)

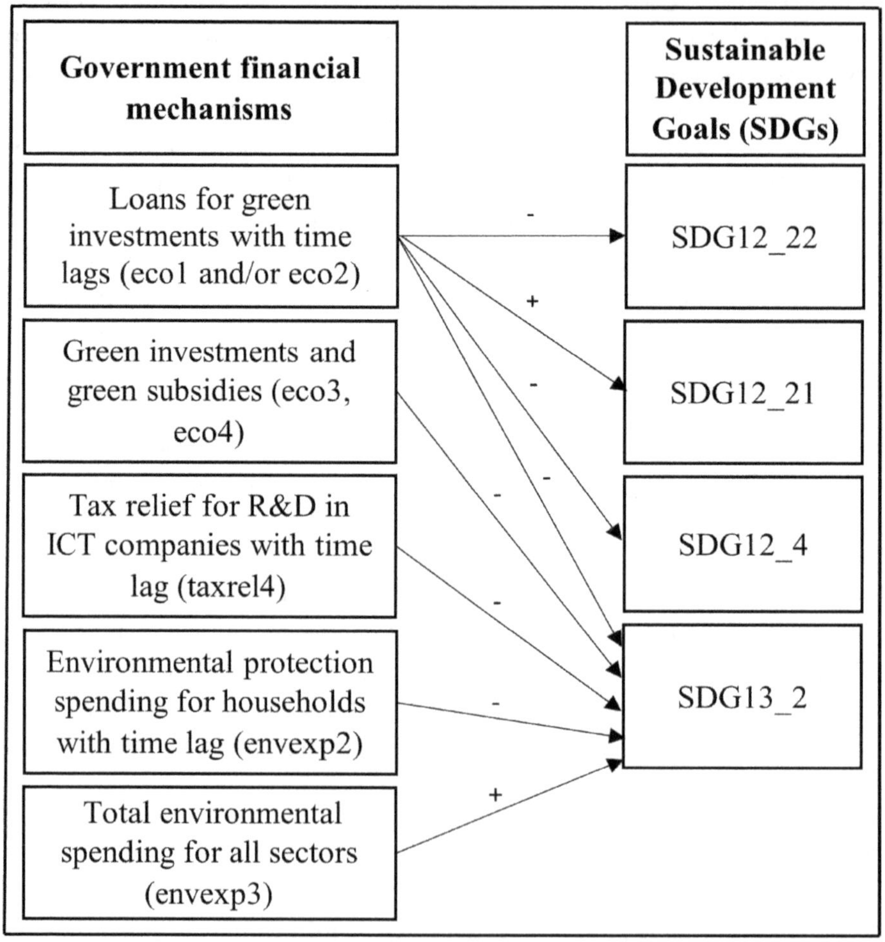

Source: own elaboration.

The results presented in Table 2 demonstrate statistically significant estimates of the impact of government mechanisms for green investments on selected Sustainable

Development Goals (SDGs), indicating that specific financial instruments—such as loans, subsidies, tax relief, and environmental spending—exert measurable effects on sustainability outcomes. These findings highlight the differentiated influence of various policy tools on individual SDG indicators, thereby contributing to a more nuanced understanding of their effectiveness.

Three different regression analyses were conducted—namely, ordinary least squares (OLS) regression, robust OLS regression, and Huber robust regression. Since the magnitude and direction of the effects do not vary substantially across these models, the OLS regression is considered the most appropriate for interpretation (Kotnik et al., 2014). The results of the OLS regression are presented in the following section .

Table 2. Estimations on Sustainable Development Goals (SDGs)

Explanatory variable	Dependent variable	Coefficients	OLS	Robust OLS	Huber robust regression
d2eco1	sdg12_22	β1	- 1.565*** (0.189)	-1.565*** (0.309)	-1.620*** (0.309)
d3eco2		β1	- 2.016*** (-0.252)	-2.016** (-0.317)	-2.654*** (-0.350)
d2eco2	sdg12_21	β1	1.557* (0.762)	1.557*** (0.560)	1.548** (0.434)
d3eco2		β1	2.108*** (0.853)	2.108** (0.591)	2.152* (0.771)
d3eco2	sdg12_4	β1	-1.1477* (0.260)	-1.147* (0.241)	-0.617* (0.832)

continued on following page

Table 2. Continued

Explanatory variable	Dependent variable	Coefficients	OLS	Robust OLS	Huber robust regression
d1eco1	sdg13_2	β1	-1.235 ** (0.226)	-1.235*** (0.258)	-1.246*** (0. 215)
d2eco2		β1	-1.109** (0.204)	-1.109** (0.9)	-1.299** (0.607)
eco3		β1	- 0.000*** (0.0)	-0.000*** (0.0)	-0.000*** (0.0)
eco4		β1	- 0.000*** (0.0)	-0.000** (0.0)	-0.000** (0.0)
d1taxrel4		β1	- 0.001*** (0.001)	-0.001*** (0.001)	-0.001** (0.001)
d2taxrel4		β1	- 0.001*** (0.001)	-0.001*** (0.001)	-0.001*** (0.001)
d3envexp2		β1	-0.113** (0.196)	-0.113** (0.187)	-0.113** (0.21)
envexp3		β1	0.032** (0.007)	0.032*** (0.013)	0.032** (0.005)

Notes: OLS, robust OLS, and robust Huber regression are used; dependent variable is x-th SDG; standard errors are reported in parentheses; ***, ** and * denote statistically significant values at 1.5% and 10% on a two-tailed test, respectively. A detailed description of the variables is provided in Table 1. In cases where a variable is preceded by the prefix d1 or d2, this indicates a one-year (d1) or two-year (d2) lag, respectively. For instance, d2eco1 refers to the approved loan amounts for companies and municipalities with a two-year lag.

The results in Table 2 show that a higher share of approved Eco Fund loans (eco2) helps lower emission intensity (SDG13_2) after one to two years. These loans also reduce waste disposal (SDG12_22) or increase recycling (SDG12_21) after two to three years.

A larger share of Eco Fund subsidies (eco5) lowers CO_2 emissions from new passenger cars (SDG12_4) after three years. However, another group of subsidies (eco4) has no meaningful effect on emission intensity (SDG13_2).

Tax relief for R&D in ICT companies (taxrel4) helps reduce emission intensity (SDG13_2) after one to two years, but this effect is not seen for self-employed individuals. Environmental protection spending for households (envexp2) lowers energy-related emission intensity after three years, while total environmental spending for all sectors (envexp3) unexpectedly shows an increase in emissions, which is difficult to explain.

The results for Research Question 2: "To what extent do (i) loans and subsidies from the Eco Fund, (ii) tax relief for companies investing in research and development (R&D), and (iii) general government expenditures for environmental protection influence the achievement of the Sustainable Development Goals (SDGs)?" show that Eco Fund loans contribute to reducing emission intensity (SDG13.2) and the waste disposal rate (SDG12.22). Subsidies are effective in lowering CO_2 emissions from new passenger cars (SDG12.4), though they do not significantly impact overall emission intensity. Tax reliefs for R&D in ICT companies also support reductions in emission intensity, while current household spending on environmental protection is associated with lower energy-related emissions — all with a certain time lag.

In addition to the previous analysis, a separate regression was conducted that focused on the seven environmentally related SDG indicators (SDG 1–17) most affected by green investments. As shown in Table 3, indicators with the highest share of positive impacts also had the most overall positive effects, suggesting that most green spending measures have at least some beneficial impact.

Table 3. The seven Sustainable Development Goals (SDGs) with the highest proportion of positive impacts.

SDG Indicator	Indicator Description	Proportion of Positive Impacts	Rank
SDG 12.3: Ensure sustainable production and consumption patterns	Indicator Description: Material productivity (EUR 2010/kg)	66.83%	1
SDG 2.4: End hunger, achieve food security and improved nutrition, and promote sustainable agriculture	Indicator Description: Share of agricultural land under organic or in conversion	66.67%	2
SDG 12.2: Ensure sustainable production and consumption patterns	Indicator Description: Recycling and waste disposal rate, excluding mineral waste - Recycling rate of waste, excluding mineral waste (%)	66.18%	3
SDG 11.5: Make cities and human settlements inclusive, safe, resilient, and sustainable	Indicator Description: Municipal waste recycling rate (%)	64.54%	4
SDG 12.5: Ensure sustainable production and consumption patterns	Indicator Description: Volume of goods transport relative to gross domestic product (index, 2010 = 100)	64.05%	5
SDG 2.7: Ensure access to affordable, reliable, sustainable, and modern energy for all	Indicator Description: Self-sufficiency rate - Self-sufficiency rate with vegetables (%)	63.56%	7
SDG 6.2: Ensure availability and sustainable management of water and sanitation for all	Indicator Description: Population connected to municipal wastewater treatment plants with at least secondary treatment (%)	63.56%	7

Source: own elaboration.

The analysis shows that government support for green investments affects different SDGs in different ways, with some showing more positive impacts than others. The highest share of positive impacts is seen for SDG 12.3, which focuses on sustainable production and consumption, with 66.83% (Rank 1). Close behind is SDG 2.4, targeting food security and sustainable agriculture, with 66.67% positive impacts. SDG 12.2, which promotes sustainable resource use and waste reduction, shows 66.18% positive impacts. SDG 11.5, related to making cities safer and more sustainable, has 64.54%. SDG 12.5, also focusing on sustainable consumption and production, reports 64.05%. Lastly, both SDG 2.7 (sustainable energy access) and SDG 6.2 (water and sanitation) show 63.56% positive impacts. These results suggest that budget expenditure indicators are particularly effective in supporting goals related to sustainability, food security, and resource management.

To sum up, in response to Research Question 3: "Which Sustainable Development Goal indicators have the highest proportion of positive impact from different government mechanisms, including green loans, subsidies, R&D tax reliefs, and budget expenditures?", the strongest positive impacts are seen for SDG 12.3 (66.83%), SDG 2.4 (66.67%), and SDG 12.2 (66.18%). These goals focus on sustainable production and consumption, food security, and resource management. The results show that budget spending and other green policy tools are especially effective in supporting these areas.

DISCUSSION WITH CONCLUSION

Sustainable development reflected in the SDGs has turned from a "trendy expression" into an existential necessity. Since companies are not motivated to adopt sustainable practices for altruistic reasons (Cimpoeru, 2012), governments bear responsibility for steering development through financial, fiscal, and regulatory tools. Public budgets are central to implementing policies that significantly impact the SDGs (Stanimirović et al., 2023). Yet complex questions remain about which stakeholders and which measures are most effective. Environmental technologies can foster innovation and competitiveness, while targeted tax reliefs may benefit specific industries.

Integrating environmental aims into fiscal stimulus—commonly referred to as 'green Keynesianism' (Harris, 2013)—has shaped many past recovery efforts. Public investment in low-carbon sectors has been promoted as a way to foster sustainable growth and competitiveness. Yet, implementation often lags, as green technologies are costly, uncertain, and slow to yield returns. Without strong incentives, firms tend to prefer cheaper conventional options. To address this, governments have employed subsidies, environmental taxes, and emissions trading to encourage greener investment. Further, research (Yong & Chang, 2023) suggests that tax-based policies outperform command-and-control approaches, prompting the adoption of various fiscal incentives to spur green transitions. Green growth depends on infrastructure investment, renewable energy, and energy efficiency (OECD, 2015). Alongside tax and regulatory tools, government expenditures and R&D spending also matter, particularly when measured relative to GDP (Ocal & Aslan, 2013; Zhang et al., 2021).

Our empirical results are consistent with global evidence showing that green innovations are key drivers of the green economy (OECD, 2015; Sadorsky, 2009).

Governments typically mitigate the investment risks associated with long-term, uncertain green technologies by employing fiscal tools such as subsidies and tax incentives. These green innovations—both technological and managerial—aim to reduce environmental impact while enhancing cost efficiency. This coherence between our findings and prior international research reinforces the importance of well-targeted fiscal support in accelerating sustainable industrial transformation.

While the theoretical and empirical foundations for green fiscal interventions are robust, their practical effectiveness—and the underutilization or limited impact of several instruments—stems from a combination of interrelated structural, administrative, and institutional constraints. Despite their theoretical soundness, fiscal instruments aimed at promoting green transitions often underperform in practice due to these overlapping barriers. Corruption, fragmented governance, and regulatory instability frequently undermine the intended impact of these tools, particularly in contexts where stable governance structures, inter-agency coordination, and institutional capacity are lacking (Chunyu et al., 2022; Keita & Turcu, 2022; Umoh et al., 2018). Even well-designed incentives may prove ineffective when deployed within weak institutional environments, resulting in limited or even counterproductive outcomes such as market distortions or the reinforcement of incumbent interests (Makhfudhah & Rasyid, 2025; Sapar & Kusuma, 2025). One of the most persistent challenges is inadequate targeting, whereby support is extended to firms that would have undertaken the investment irrespective of public assistance, thus undermining additionality and leading to inefficient fiscal spending (Peters & Fisher, 2004). Moreover, the absence of equity-sensitive mechanisms can result in regressive distributional outcomes, with benefits accruing disproportionately to higher-income households or urban populations, exacerbating existing social inequalities (Anguelovski et al., 2019; Swedish National Audit Office, 2025). High administrative complexity and limited absorptive capacity—especially among small and medium-sized enterprises (SMEs)—further hinder the uptake of relevant instruments such as R&D tax reliefs and targeted subsidies (Kotnik et al., 2024; Sapar & Kusuma, 2025). The lack of long-term regulatory predictability also weakens investor confidence and deters private sector engagement, particularly in capital-intensive sectors with long investment horizons such as renewable energy (Sonjaya & Noch, 2024). Finally, the limited integration of fiscal instruments into broader sustainability policy frameworks diminishes their systemic coherence and transformative potential, resulting in fragmented and isolated interventions that fail to deliver durable environmental outcomes (Dafermos & Nikolaidi, 2019; Nozadze, 2024). These multifaceted constraints underscore the critical importance of context-sensitive, equity-aware, and institutionally embedded fiscal policy design in advancing the developmental and environmental goals associated with green public finance.

Despite these challenges, empirical research from Slovenia indicates that targeted green fiscal instruments—such as loans, subsidies, and tax reliefs—can influence environmental SDG outcomes. Notably, the results show that Eco Fund loans effectively reduce emission intensity (SDG13.2) and improve waste management indicators (SDG12.22, SDG12.21), while tax reliefs for ICT-sector R&D similarly lower emissions over time. These outcomes align with broader findings from Eastern and post-socialist Europe, where institutionalized green public financing has increasingly become a lever for environmental modernization. For instance, Martynenko (2023) reports that 35% of local government budgets in Ukraine contributed to measurable improvements in SDG indicators, with particularly strong effects in institutional and environmental domains. Similarly, fiscal decentralization and targeted investments in regions like Eastern Poland or the Baltics have shown positive effects on local SDG indicators, especially those related to sustainable production and infrastructure (Bisogno et al., 2024). This parallels broader findings across EU low-carbon investment programs, where the impact of expenditures depends not only on the policy itself but also on the institutional capacity and cohesion among implementing bodies (Dueñas & Mandel, 2024).

The effectiveness of Slovenia's green fiscal instruments—particularly Eco Fund loans and R&D tax reliefs—must be understood within the broader context of its post-socialist transition. Compared to regional peers such as Croatia, Slovenia has benefited from stronger administrative capacity, policy coherence, and early alignment with EU sustainability norms (Babić & Lučev, 2019; Benedek & Tieman, 2021). These structural strengths have supported more consistent implementation of social and environmental policies, which helps explain the statistically significant outcomes observed for targeted fiscal tools, as opposed to broader, less-focused environmental expenditures.

Furthermore, Slovenia's experience exemplifies a wider pattern observed across post-socialist EU member states, where institutional quality and political coherence critically mediate the success of green fiscal reforms. As Wozniak-Jechorek (2024) notes, gradual economic reforms combined with effective public-sector capacity and European integration have created favorable conditions for implementing green fiscal measures. However, as Benedek & Tieman (2021) caution, even relatively advanced institutional settings remain vulnerable to external fiscal shocks—such as those induced by the COVID-19 pandemic—highlighting the need for adaptive, resilient policy frameworks.

Serving as more than a singular empirical illustration, the Slovenian case exemplifies how institutional quality, political coherence, and alignment with supranational EU governance frameworks jointly shape the success of green fiscal interventions. This reflects a broader lesson for post-socialist and transitioning economies: the effectiveness of fiscal tools is not solely determined by their design, but by the overall functionality and resilience of the institutional ecosystem in which they are embedded.

The findings clearly demonstrate that targeted green fiscal instruments—particularly Eco Fund loans and R&D tax reliefs for ICT companies—exert a measurable and statistically significant influence on selected Sustainable Development Goals (SDGs). Instruments with built-in return mechanisms, such as loans and tax incentives, appear more effective than undifferentiated public expenditures, reinforcing the case for strategic allocation and performance-based budgeting. Additionally, the observed time lags—often spanning one to three years—highlight the necessity of long-term planning horizons and consistent policy implementation. The results further emphasize the need to refine targeting frameworks, as inefficient allocation reduces policy impact and diminishes the added value of public intervention.

In 2022, Slovenia operationalized national reforms and investment initiatives tied to the EU's RRF, prioritizing energy efficiency, low-carbon mobility, and green innovation in alignment with the European Green Deal and the Fit for 55 legislative package—representing a marked shift toward structured and conditionally supported climate spending (European Council, 2025; Muren & Franca, 2022). These policy adjustments are mirrored in the empirical findings: regression analyses demonstrate that several green financial mechanisms, including loans, subsidies, and R&D tax reliefs, generated statistically significant effects on selected SDG indicators with time lags of one to three years—pointing to the delayed but measurable impact of strategic green recovery investments initiated in 2020–2021. For example, Eco Fund loans contributed to increased recycling rates (SDG 12.21) and reduced waste disposal (SDG 12.22), while R&D tax incentives and household-level environmental protection expenditures were associated with declines in emission intensity (SDG 13.2) (Kotnik et al., 2024).

Building on these findings, further evidence from 2022 illustrates a recalibration of Slovenia's green spending priorities, marked by a shift in the composition and targeting of public expenditures. Notably, general environmental spending across all sectors (envexp3) was found to correlate positively with emission intensity, whereas more targeted household environmental expenditures (envexp2) had a mitigating effect—highlighting the importance of specificity in fiscal design (Kotnik et al., 2024). This policy evolution is also consistent with broader EU governance reforms: the integration of criteria from the EU Taxonomy for Sustainable Activities (European Commission, 2020) and commitments outlined in NECPs (European Commission, 2021a) suggests that by 2022, Slovenia's public green spending had become more strategically aligned with supranational climate policy frameworks. Nonetheless, the persistence of institutional implementation gaps indicates that constitutional support alone has not sufficed, reinforcing calls for a more proactive and coordinated state role in advancing the SDGs (Plicanic, 2020).

Taken together, these insights underscore that the success of green public finance depends not only on the design of fiscal instruments but also on the broader governance context in which they are embedded. Effective green budgeting requires high administrative capacity, stable regulatory frameworks, and coherent cross-sectoral coordination. In countries such as Slovenia, where institutional fragmentation and implementation gaps persist despite formal policy commitments, building resilient and evidence-informed governance systems will be essential for sustaining long-term progress toward the SDGs.

FUTURE DIRECTION

While this book chapter provides a comprehensive analysis of government financial mechanisms and their impact on SDGs in Slovenia, it also highlights limited effectiveness of some instruments. Future research should examine why certain incentives are underused and how to improve their design. Cross-country comparisons could offer insights into what works best in similar economic contexts.

DECLARATION

The authors declare that the manuscript follows ethical standards and there are no potential conflicts of interest concerning the research, authorship, and/or publication of this chapter.

DISCLAIMER

The contents and views of this chapter are expressed by the authors in their personal capacities. It is not necessary for the Editor and the Publisher to agree with these viewpoints, and they are not responsible for any duty of care in this regard.

JEL Classification: H23, H50, Q01

CORRESPONDING AUTHOR

Žiga Kotnik, University of Ljubljana, Slovenia.

ACKNOWLEDGMENT

The authors extend sincere gratitude to

- The Editor and the International Editorial Advisory Board (IEAB) of this book who initially desk reviewed, arranged a rigorous double/triple-blind review process, and conducted a thorough, minute, and critical final review before accepting the chapter for publication.
- All anonymous reviewers who provided very constructive feedback for thorough revision, improvement, extension, and fine-tuning of the chapter.
- All colleagues, assistants, and well-wishers who assisted in completing this task.
- The Slovenian Research Agency for their financial support (Research Programme: Digital Transformation for Smart Public Governance, no. P2-0426, and Project: An Integrated Policy Approach to Simultaneously Address the Environmental and Economic Crisis, no. J5-4576).

REFERENCES

Addison, T., Niño-Zarazúa, M., & Pirttilä, J. (2018). Fiscal policy, state building and economic development. *Journal of International Development, 30*(2), 161–172. DOI: 10.1002/jid.3355

Agrawala, S., Dussaux, D., & Monti, N. (2020). What policies for greening the crisis response and economic recovery?: Lessons learned from past green stimulus measures and implications for the COVID-19 crisis. *OECD Environment Working Papers, No. 164*. DOI: 10.1787/19970900

Andrei, J., Mieila, P., Popescu, G. H., Nica, E., & Cristina, M. (2016). The impact and determinants of environmental taxation on economic growth communities in Romania. *Energies, 9*(11), 902. DOI: 10.3390/en9110902

Anguelovski, I., Connolly, J. J., Pearsall, H., Shokry, G., Checker, M., Maantay, J., Gould, K., Lewis, T., Maroko, A., & Roberts, J. T. (2019). Why green "climate gentrification" threatens poor and vulnerable populations. *Proceedings of the National Academy of Sciences of the United States of America, 116*(52), 26139–26143. DOI: 10.1073/pnas.1920490117

Annett, A. (2002). Politics, government size, and fiscal adjustment in industrial countries. IMF Working Paper No. 02/162. https://ssrn.com/abstract=880179

Auerbach, A. (2019). Fiscal policy. *Blanchard O. e Summers LH (a Cura Di), Evolution or Revolution*, 81–104. DOI: 10.7551/mitpress/11734.003.0010

Babić, Z., & Lučev, J. (2019). Comparative analysis of economic and social policy development in Croatia and Slovenia. *Problemy Polityki Społecznej. Studia i Dyskusje, 47 (4*, 47–71. https://doi.org/doi.org/10.31971/16401808.47.4.2019.3

Barbier, E. B. (2020). Greening the post-pandemic recovery in the G20. *Environmental and Resource Economics, 76*(4), 685–703. DOI: 10.1007/s10640-020-00437-w PMID: 32836827

Bartik, T. J. (2005). Solving the problems of economic development incentives. *Growth and Change, 36*(2), 139–166. DOI: 10.1111/j.1468-2257.2005.00272.x

Benedek, M. D., & Tieman, A. F. (2021). A post-pandemic assessment of the sustainable development goals. *IMF Staff Discussion Notes No. 2021/003, 21*(3), 6–24. DOI: 10.5089/9781498314909.006

Benesty, J., Chen, J., & Huang, Y. (2008). On the Importance of the Pearson Correlation Coefficient in Noise Reduction. *IEEE Transactions on Audio, Speech, and Language Processing, 16*(4), 4. Advance online publication. DOI: 10.1109/TASL.2008.919072

Bisogno, M., Cuadrado-Ballesteros, B., Manes-Rossi, F., & Peña-Miguel, N. (2024). Financial Sustainability and Sustainable Development in Local Governments: Empirical Insights. *Public Performance & Management Review, 47*(3), 784–811. DOI: 10.1080/15309576.2024.2340116

Carmichael, R. (2002). Measures of efficiency and effectiveness as indicators of quality: A systems approach. [JIRSEA]. *Journal of Institutional Research South East Asia, 1*(1), 3–14. https://api.semanticscholar.org/CorpusID:7713535

Chunyu, L., Ali, S. A., Tan, C., Yin, W., Kouser, R., & Gulzar, F. (2022). The Fiscal Hedging and Green Financing: Sustainability Challenges for Developing World. *Frontiers in Environmental Science, 9*. Crossref. DOI: 10.3389/fenvs.2021.807220

Cimpoeru, V.-M. (2012). An empirical study on key indicators of environmental quality: Green budgeting-a catalyst for sustainable economy and a factor for institutional change. *Amfiteatru Economic, 14*(32), 485–498. https://www.amfiteatrueconomic.ro/ArticolEN.aspx?CodArticol=1139

Coutinho, L., & Tsani, S. (2021). Fiscal policy, macroeconomic volatility and the role of institutions under resource abundance. *Handbook of Sustainable Politics and Economics of Natural Resources*, 261–290.

Dabyltayeva, N., & Rakhymzhan, G. (2019). The Green Economy Development Path: Overview of Economic Policy Priorities. *Journal of Security and Sustainability Issues, 8*(4), 643–651. DOI: 10.9770/jssi.2019.8.4(8)

Dafermos, Y., & Nikolaidi, M. (2019). Fiscal policy and ecological sustainability: A post-Keynesian perspective. In *Frontiers of heterodox macroeconomics* (pp. 277–322). Springer., DOI: 10.1007/978-3-030-23929-9_7

Dafnomilis, I., Chen, H.-H., den Elzen, M., Fragkos, P., Chewpreecha, U., van Soest, H., Fragkiadakis, K., Karkatsoulis, P., Paroussos, L., de Boer, H.-S., Daioglou, V., Edelenbosch, O., Kiss-Dobronyi, B., & van Vuuren, D. P. (2022). Targeted green recovery measures in a post-COVID-19 world enable the energy transition. *Frontiers in Climate*, *4*, 840933. DOI: 10.3389/fclim.2022.840933

Dalevska, N., Khobta, V., Kwilinski, A., & Kravchenko, S. (2019). A model for estimating social and economic indicators of sustainable development. *Entrepreneurship and Sustainability Issues*, *6*(4), 4. Advance online publication. DOI: 10.9770/jesi.2019.6.4(21)

Dasgupta, P., & Srikanth, K. (2021). Achieving the climate goal with intergovernmental transfers to the forestry sector: Insights from the Indian experience. *Climatic Change, 164*(3–4). Crossref. DOI: 10.1007/s10584-021-03016-0

de l'Économie, M. des Finances et de la Souveraineté industrielle et numérique. (2025, April 13). *France Relance – Le plan de relance économique*. https://www.economie.gouv.fr/plan-de-relance

DiMaggio, P. J., & Powell, W. W. (2000). The iron cage revisited institutional isomorphism and collective rationality in organizational fields. In *Economics meets sociology in strategic management* (pp. 143–166). Emerald Group Publishing Limited., DOI: 10.1016/S0742-3322(00)17011-1

Dueñas, M., & Mandel, A. (2024). Are EU low-carbon structural funds efficient in reducing emissions? *arXiv Preprint arXiv:2408.01782*. https://doi.org//arXiv.2408.01782DOI: 10.48550

Eko sklad. (2024). *Subvencije in ugodni krediti za okolju prijazne naložbe*. https://www.ekosklad.si/

Enikolopov, R., & Zhuravskaya, E. V. (2003). Decentralization and Political Institutions. SSRN *Electronic Journal*. Crossref. DOI: 10.2139/ssrn.408060

European Commission. (2019). *The European Green Deal*. https://commission.europa.eu/strategy-and-policy/priorities-2019-2024/european-green-deal_en

European Commission. (2020). EU Taxonomy Regulation. [EU]. *Regulation, 2020*(852). https://eur-lex.europa.eu/eli/reg/2020/852/oj/eng

European Commission. (2021a). *National energy and climate plans*. https://commission.europa.eu/energy-climate-change-environment/implementation-eu-countries/energy-and-climate-governance-and-reporting/national-energy-and-climate-plans_en

European Commission. (2021b). Recovery and Resilience Facility Regulation. [EU]. *Regulation, 2021*(241). https://eur-lex.europa.eu/eli/reg/2021/241/oj/eng

European Council. (2025). *Fit for 55*. https://www.consilium.europa.eu/en/policies/fit-for-55/

Eurostat. (2025). *Government expenditure by function – COFOG. Statistics Explained*. https://ec.europa.eu/eurostat/statistics-explained/index.php?title=Government_expenditure_by_function_%E2%80%93_COFOG

Eyraud, L., Clements, B., & Wane, A. (2013). Green investment: Trends and determinants. *Energy Policy*, *60*, 852–865. DOI: 10.1016/j.enpol.2013.04.039

Fatas, A., & Mihov, I. (2003). The Case for Restricting Fiscal Policy Discretion. *The Quarterly Journal of Economics, 118*(4), 1419–1447. Crossref. DOI: 10.1162/003355303322552838

Fowowe, B. (2013). Do Fiscal incentives promote investment?: Empirical evidence from Nigeria. *Journal of Developing Areas*, *47*(2), 17–35. DOI: 10.1353/jda.2013.0029

FURS. (2024). *Financial Administration of the Republic of Slovenia*. https://www.fu.gov.si/en/

Goulder, L. H., & Parry, I. W. (2008). Instrument choice in environmental policy. *Review of Environmental Economics and Policy*, *2*(2), 152–174. DOI: 10.1093/reep/ren005

Government of Canada. (2025, March 10). *ecoENERGY for Renewable Power*. https://natural-resources.canada.ca/corporate/planning-reporting/departmental-results-reports/departmental-performance-reports-2015%E2%80%9316/ecoenergy-renewable-power

Green Power Denmark. (2025, February 20). *Fakta om energispareordningen*. https://greenpowerdenmark.dk/udgivelser/fakta-om-energispareordningen

Harris, J. M. (2013). Green Keynesianism: Beyond standard growth paradigms. *Working Paper 13-02*. DOI: 10.22004/ag.econ.179111

Hauke, J., & Kossowski, T. (2011). Comparison of Values of Pearson's and Spearman's Correlation Coefficients on the Same Sets of Data. *Quaestiones Geographicae, 30*(2), 2. Advance online publication. DOI: 10.2478/v10117-011-0021-1

Houser, T., Mohan, S., & Heilmayr, R. (2009). *A green recovery? Assessing US economic stimulus and the prospects for international coordination*. Peterson Institute for International Economics., https://www.piie.com/publications/policy-briefs/green-recovery-assessing-us-economic-stimulus-and-prospects

Ichigo. (2025, March 11). *About Japan's Feed-In Tariff (FIT)*. https://www.ichigo-green.co.jp/en/operation/purchase/

Ihsan, A., Hureem, U., & Adil, S. (2021). Estimating the Financing Required to Fulfill the Education Targets Set by Sustainable Development Goals (SDGs): A Sample Study of Punjab, Pakistan. *Audit and Accounting Review, 1*(1), 82–97. DOI: 10.32350/aar.11.05

International Energy Agency. (2023). *France's "MaPrimeRénov" Programme*. https://www.iea.org/policies/17749-frances-maprimerenov-programme

Keita, K., & Turcu, C. (2022). Promoting counter-cyclical fiscal policy: Fiscal rules versus institutions. *Comparative Economic Studies, 1*. Advance online publication. DOI: 10.1057/s41294-022-00197-0 PMID: 36408198

Köppl, A., & Schratzenstaller, M. (2024). Macroeconomic effects of green recovery programs. *Eurasian Economic Review, 14*(1), 61–86. DOI: 10.1007/s40822-023-00250-y

Kosonen, K., & Nicodeme, G. (2009). The role of fiscal instruments in environmental policy. *CESifo Working Paper Series No. 2719*. DOI: 10.2139/ssrn.1437501

Kotnik, Ž., Klun, M., & Lah, L. M. (2024). Budget financing of sustainable development goals: The case of Slovenia. In *Modern Concepts and Practices of Climate Finance* (pp. 253–280). IGI Global., DOI: 10.4018/979-8-3693-2117-1.ch011

Kotnik, Ž., Maja, K., & Škulj, D. (2014). The effect of taxation on greenhouse gas emissions. *Transylvanian Review of Administrative Sciences, 10*(43), 43. https://rtsa.ro/tras/index.php/tras/article/view/407

Kotnik, Ž., Umek, L., Kovač, P., Stanimirović, D., & Vintar, M. (2020). Analysis of the key factors for successful public policy implementation: A qualitative study in Slovenia. *DANUBE, 11*(2), 2. Advance online publication. DOI: 10.2478/danb-2020-0007

Kraft, M. E., & Furlong, S. R. (2007). *Public policy: Politics, analysis, and alternatives.* CQ Press., https://questanbridge.com/wp-content/uploads/2024/11/Public-policy_-politics-analysis-and-alternatives.pdfhttps://questanbridge.com/wp-content/uploads/2024/11/Public-policy_-politics-analysis-and-alternatives.pdf

Lavigne, R. (2006). The Institutional and Political Determinants of Fiscal Adjustment. *Bank of Canada Staff Working Paper.* DOI: 10.34989/swp-2006-1

Liang, H., Li, G., Zhang, W., & Chen, Z. (2022). The impact of green innovation on enterprise performance: The regulatory role of government grants. *Sustainability (Basel), 14*(20), 13550. DOI: 10.3390/su142013550

Lin, B., & Zhou, Y. (2021). Does fiscal decentralization improve energy and environmental performance? New perspective on vertical fiscal imbalance. *Applied Energy, 302*, 117495. DOI: 10.1016/j.apenergy.2021.117495

Lin, B., & Zhu, J. (2019). Fiscal spending and green economic growth: Evidence from China. *Energy Economics, 83*, 264–271. DOI: 10.1016/j.eneco.2019.07.010

Lledó, V., & Poplawski-Ribeiro, M. (2013). Fiscal policy implementation in sub-Saharan Africa. *World Development, 46*, 79–91. DOI: 10.1016/j.worlddev.2013.01.030

Lu, C., Tong, Q., & Liu, X. (2010). The impacts of carbon tax and complementary policies on Chinese economy. *Energy Policy, 38*(11), 7278–7285. DOI: 10.1016/j.enpol.2010.07.055

Lutsyk, A. (2021). Substantiation of priority of achieving the goals of Sustainable Development (SDG) in the implementation of fiscal policy. *World of Finance, 1*(66), 89–101. DOI: 10.35774/sf2021.01.089

Lyeonov, S., Pimonenko, T., Bilan, Y., Štreimikienė, D., & Mentel, G. (2019). Assessment of green investments' impact on sustainable development: Linking gross domestic product per capita, greenhouse gas emissions and renewable energy. *Energies, 12*(20), 3891. DOI: 10.3390/en12203891

Ma, L., Zheng, B., Zhang, M., Zhu, X., & Wu, J. (2023). Research on Green Inclusive Finance to Promote Rural Revitalization under the Goals of Carbon Peaking and Carbon Neutrality—Take Heilongjiang Province as an Example. *Academic Journal of Business & Management, 5*(9). Advance online publication. DOI: 10.25236/AJBM.2023.050905

Makhfudhah, N. I. N., & Rasyid, M. (2025). Assessing the Effectiveness of Fiscal Incentives in Promoting Green Investments: A Stochastic Frontier Analysis (SFA) Approach. *KnE Social Sciences, 10*(5), 196–210. Crossref. DOI: 10.18502/kss.v10i5.18114

Martynenko, V. (2023). Strategic aspects of financial support for Sustainable Development Goals: The regional dimension. *Economy, Finances, Management. Topical Issues of Science and Practice*, *3*(65). Advance online publication. DOI: 10.37128/2411-4413-2023-3

Mattina, T. D., & Gunnarsson, V. (2007). Budget rigidity and expenditure efficiency in Slovenia (June 2007). *IMF Working Paper No. 07/131*. https://ssrn.com/abstract=995631 DOI: 10.5089/9781451866957.001

MF. (2024). *Ministry of Finance*. https://www.gov.si/drzavni-organi/ministrstva/ministrstvo-za-finance/

Miszczak, K., Krivins, A., & Kaze, V. (2024). Challenges and drivers of green and sustainable spatial development: A case study of Lower Silesia and Latvia. *Journal of Entrepreneurship & Sustainability Issues*, *12*(2), 85–98. DOI: 10.9770/b7283449476

Mondal, S., & Mondal, H. (2017). Value of r (2) in statistical analysis by Pearson correlation coefficient. *Journal of Clinical and Diagnostic Research : JCDR*, *11*(11), CL01. DOI: 10.7860/JCDR/2017/29763.10812

Muren, P. D., & Franca, V. (2022). National Recovery and Resilience Plan: Slovenia. *Italian Labour Law E-Journal*, *15*(1S). Advance online publication. DOI: 10.1016/j.repolx.2020.100008

Mutiarani, N. D., & Siswantoro, D. (2020). The impact of local government characteristics on the accomplishment of Sustainable Development Goals (SDGs). *Cogent Business & Management*, *7*(1), 1847751. DOI: 10.1080/23311975.2020.1847751

Nawaz, S., & Khawaja, M. I. (2019). Fiscal policy, institutions and growth: New insights. *The Singapore Economic Review*, *64*(05), 1251–1278. DOI: 10.1142/S0217590816500296

Noombo, C., & Mwange, A. (2024). The role of tax incentives in promoting sustainable investments in emerging economies in Sub-Saharan Africa: A legal and policy analysis. *International Journal of Multidisciplinary Research and Growth Evaluation*, *5*(6), 1225–1236. DOI: 10.54660/.IJMRGE.2024.5.6.1225-1236

Nozadze, I., Chelidze, M., Kapanadze, M., & Sesadze, N. (2024). „Green" Projects and Comparative Analysis of Related Financial Instruments. *Georgian Technical University*, *4*(534), 39–47. DOI: 10.36073/1512-0996-2024-4-39-47

Ocal, O., & Aslan, A. (2013). Renewable energy consumption–economic growth nexus in Turkey. *Renewable & Sustainable Energy Reviews*, *28*, 494–499. DOI: 10.1016/j.rser.2013.08.036

OECD. (2015). *Policy Framework for Investment, 2015 Edition*. DOI: 10.1787/9789264208667-en

OECD. (2017). *Government at a glance 2017*. OECD Publishing., DOI: 10.1787/gov_glance-2017-

OECD. (2020). *Building back better: A sustainable, resilient recovery after COVID-19* (OECD Policy Responses to Coronavirus (COVID-19); OECD Publishing). DOI: 10.1787/5b0fd8cd-en

Ofgem. (2025, March 15). *Renewable Heat Incentive*. https://www.ofgem.gov.uk/environmental-and-social-schemes/non-domestic-renewable-heat-incentive-rhi

Osuji, E., & Nwani, S. E. (2020). Achieving sustainable development goals: Does government expenditure framework matter? [IJMESS]. *International Journal of Management, Economics and Social Sciences*, *9*(3), 131–160. DOI: 10.32327/IJMESS/9.3.2020.8

Permatasari, P., Ilman, A. S., Tilt, C. A., Lestari, D., Islam, S., Tenrini, R. H., Rahman, A. B., Samosir, A. P., & Wardhana, I. W. (2021). The Village Fund Program in Indonesia: Measuring the Effectiveness and Alignment to Sustainable Development Goals. *Sustainability (Basel)*, *13*(21), 12294. Advance online publication. DOI: 10.3390/su132112294

Peters, A., & Fisher, P. (2004). The failures of economic development incentives. *Journal of the American Planning Association*, *70*(1), 27–37. DOI: 10.1080/01944360408976336

Pigato, M. A., Rafaty, R., & Kurle, J. (2021). *The COVID-19 Crisis and the Road to Recovery: Green or Brown?* World Bank., https://documents1.worldbank.org/curated/en/652851637126067927/pdf/The-COVID-19-Crisis-and-the-Road-to-Recovery-Green-or-Brown.pdf

Plicanic, S. (2020). The Role of State in Achieving Sustainable Development Goals in Slovenia. *Studia Iuridica Lublinensia*, *29*(4), 233–249. DOI: 10.17951/sil.2020.29.4.233-249

Poterba, J. M. (1994). State Responses to Fiscal Crises: The Effects of Budgetary Institutions and Politics. *Journal of Political Economy*, *102*(4), 799–821. Crossref. DOI: 10.1086/261955

Priyan, S. (2023). Effect of green investment to reduce carbon emissions in an imperfect production system. *Journal of Climate Finance*, *2*, 100007. DOI: 10.1016/j.jclimf.2023.100007

Raszkowski, A., & Bartniczak, B. (2018). Towards sustainable regional development: Economy, society, environment, good governance based on the example of Polish regions. *Transformations in Business & Economics*, *17*, 225–245.

Rvo. (2025). *Stimulation of sustainable energy production and climate transition (SDE++)*. https://english.rvo.nl/subsidies-financiering/sde

Sadia, H. S., Azeez, J. A., & Shehzadi, K. (2025). Driving Factors of Fiscal Stress: Panel Data Analysis for Emerging Countries. *Journal of Economic Sciences*, 91–104. https://jesciences.com/index.php/jes/article/view/116/51

Sadorsky, P. (2009). Renewable energy consumption, CO2 emissions and oil prices in the G7 countries. *Energy Economics*, *31*(3), 456–462. DOI: 10.1016/j.eneco.2008.12.010

Sapar, J. F., & Kusuma, E. R. H. (2025). Effectiveness of Tax Incentives in Increasing Investment in Green Technology and Green Energy. *Advances in Taxation Research*, *3*(1), 54–67. Crossref. DOI: 10.60079/atr.v3i1.459

Schmidt-Traub, G. (2015). Investment needs to achieve the Sustainable Development Goals: Understanding the billions and trillions. *SDSN Working Paper*. https://www.jstor.org/stable/resrep15864

Schmidt-Traub, G. (2018). On metrics and financing for the Sustainable Development Goals. *Sustainable Development*, *26*(1), 13–17. DOI: 10.1002/sd.1793

Service-Public. (2025). *Éco-prêt à taux zéro (éco-PTZ)*. https://www.service-public.fr/particuliers/vosdroits/F19905

Skatteverket. (2025). *Miljöbilar*. https://www.skatteverket.se/privat/skatter/arbeteochinkomst/formaner/bilforman/miljobilar.4.3f4496fd14864cc5ac9e89a.html

Slavikova, L. (2013). From cost-benefit to institutional analysis in the economics of the environment. *Contemporary Economics*, *7*(2), 67–75. DOI: 10.5709/ce.1897-9254.83

Song, M., Wang, S., & Zhang, H. (2020). Could environmental regulation and R&D tax incentives affect green product innovation? *Journal of Cleaner Production*, *258*, 120849. DOI: 10.1016/j.jclepro.2020.120849

Sonjaya, Y., & Noch, M. Y. (2024). Analysis of the Effectiveness of Tax Incentives on Energy Sector Investments. *Advances in Taxation Research*, *2*(2), 120–131. DOI: 10.60079/atr.v2i2.308

Stanimirović, T., Milan Lah, L., Kotnik, Ž., & Klun, M. (2023). Green budgeting implementation in financing of sustainable society-experience of Slovenia. *Management, 28*(Special Issue), 79–91. DOI: 10.30924/mjcmi.28.si.6

Stausholm, S. N. (2017). *Rise of ineffective incentives: New empirical evidence on tax holidays in developing countries*. Crossref. DOI: 10.31235/osf.io/4sn3k

Sterner, T. (2012). Distributional effects of taxing transport fuel. *Modeling Transport (Energy). Energy Policy, 41*, 75–83. DOI: 10.1016/j.enpol.2010.03.012

Stoker, G. (2006). Public value management: A new narrative for networked governance? *American Review of Public Administration, 36*(1), 41–57. DOI: 10.1177/0275074005282583

Strand, J., & Toman, M. (2010). Green stimulus, economic recovery, and long-term sustainable development. *World Bank Policy Research Working Paper Series 5163*. https://ideas.repec.org/p/wbk/wbrwps/5163.html

SURS. (2024). *SISTAT Database*. https://www.stat.si/statweb

Swedish National Audit Office. (2025, February 22). *Central government measures for more green cars*. https://www.riksrevisionen.se/en/audits/audit-reports/2020/central-government-measures-for-more-green-cars.html

Toma, J. D., Dubrow, G., & Hartley, M. (2005). The Uses of Institutional Culture: Strengthening Identification and Building Brand Equity in Higher Education. *ASHE Higher Education Report, 31*(2), 1–105. 1353/RHE.2005.0077

Toyin, O. O., & Onanuga, A. T. (2019). Carbon Fiscal Instruments and Green Finance: An Aid to the Success of SDGs in Nigeria? *Journal of Innovation in Business and Economics, 3*(02), 49–62. DOI: 10.22219/jibe.v3i02.7895

Umoh, O., Onye, K., & Atan, J. (2018). Political and institutional determinants of fiscal policy persistence in West Africa. *MPRA Paper No. 88452*. https://mpra.ub.uni-muenchen.de/88452/

United Nations. (2023). *The Sustainable Development Goals Report 2023*. https://sdgs.un.org/sites/default/files/2023-07/The-Sustainable-Development-Goals-Report-2023_0.pdf

Woo, J. (2002). Economic, Political and Institutional Determinants of Public Deficits. SSRN *Electronic Journal*. Crossref. DOI: 10.2139/ssrn.326520

Wozniak-Jechorek, B. (2024). Examining the European Transition: Central Eastern European Countries Two Decades Post-EU Accession. *Revista Economia e Políticas Públicas, 12*(1), 48–60. DOI: 10.46551/epp2024v12n0104

Yong, S. K., & Chang, Y. (2023). Emissions tax and executive compensation: A public–private joint mechanism to promote environmental and energy management. *The Singapore Economic Review*, *68*(02), 355–375. DOI: 10.1142/S0217590822500710

Zhang, W., Zhao, S., & Wan, X. (2021). Industrial digital transformation strategies based on differential games. *Applied Mathematical Modelling*, *98*, 90–108. DOI: 10.1016/j.apm.2021.05.001

Zodrow, G. R., & Mieszkowski, P. (1986). Pigou, Tiebout, property taxation, and the underprovision of local public goods. *Journal of Urban Economics*, *19*(3), 356–370. DOI: 10.1016/0094-1190(86)90048-3

Zuojun, F., & Lynn, T. Z. Z. (2024). Fiscal Policy for Inclusive Growth. A Case Study of Myanmar. *Journal of Economics. Finance and Management Studies*, *7*(4), 1914–1932. DOI: 10.47191/jefms/v7-i4-18

ADDITIONAL READING

Ajeigbe, K. B., Ganda, F., & Enowkenwa, R. O. (2024). Impact of sustainable tax revenue and expenditure on the achievement of sustainable development goals in some selected African countries. *Environment, Development and Sustainability*, *26*(10), 26287–26311. DOI: 10.1007/s10668-023-03730-y

Benito, B., Guillamón, M. D., & Ríos, A. M. (2023). The sustainable development goals: How does their implementation affect the financial sustainability of the largest Spanish municipalities. *Sustainable Development (Bradford)*, *31*(4), 2836–2850. DOI: 10.1002/sd.2551

Bisogno, M., Cuadrado-Ballesteros, B., Rossi, F. M., & Peña-Miguel, N. (2023). Sustainable development goals in public administrations: Enabling conditions in local governments. *International Review of Administrative Sciences*, *89*(4), 1223–1242. DOI: 10.1177/00208523221146458

Del-Aguila-Arcentales, S., Alvarez-Risco, A., & Yáñez, J. A. (2023). Innovation and its effects on compliance with Sustainable Development Goals and competitiveness in European Union countries. *Journal of Open Innovation*, *9*(3), 100127. DOI: 10.1016/j.joitmc.2023.100127

Li, C., Chen, Z., Jiang, Q., Yue, M., Wu, L., Bao, Y., Huang, B., Wang, A. B., Tan, Y., & Xu, Z. (2025). Impacts of government attention on achieving sustainable development goals: Evidence from China. *Geography and Sustainability*, *6*(2), 100233. DOI: 10.1016/j.geosus.2024.08.011

Saeed, M. M., Mohammed, S. S., Adeniyi, A., & Osei, M. (2025). The Impact of Corporate Governance on the Contribution of Listed Firms to Sustainable Development Goals (SDGs) Disclosures in Ghana. *Sustainable Development (Bradford), 33*(3), 4676–4688. DOI: 10.1002/sd.3367

Udeagha, M. C., & Muchapondwa, E. (2023). Striving for the United Nations (UN) sustainable development goals (SDGs) in BRICS economies: The role of green finance, fintech, and natural resource rent. *Sustainable Development (Bradford), 31*(5), 3657–3672. DOI: 10.1002/sd.2618

Yap, S., Shan Lee, H., & Xin Liew, P. (2023). The role of financial inclusion in achieving finance-related sustainable development goals (SDGs): A cross-country analysis. *Economic research-. Ekonomska Istrazivanja, 36*(3), 2212028. Advance online publication. DOI: 10.1080/1331677X.2023.2212028

Yousaf, T., Shahzad, M. F., & Ain, Q. U. (2025). Evaluating the environmental impacts of Chinese decentralization policies toward SDG 13. *Sustainable Development (Bradford), 33*(1), 939–956. DOI: 10.1002/sd.3160

KEY TERMS AND DEFINITIONS

Public spending: Public spending refers to the distribution of financial resources by government agencies and public institutions to provide goods and services that are important for social welfare and economic stability. It is the use of public funds to meet collective needs and improve the general welfare of the population. This spending includes areas such as education, healthcare, infrastructure, environmental protection and social welfare. In the context of sustainable development, public spending plays a crucial role in shaping market behaviour, correcting market failures and achieving long-term strategic goals such as climate change mitigation and social equity. It also reflects government priorities and can serve as a powerful tool for economic stabilisation, redistribution and structural transformation.

Green investments: Green investments are financial commitments or incentives that focus on environmentally sustainable projects, technologies or initiatives that counteract climate change, reduce ecological damage and promote long-term ecological resilience. These can include renewable energy investments, energy efficiency improvements, anti-pollution technologies, sustainable agricultural practises or circular economy initiatives. Green investments can take the form of direct budget allocations, low-interest loans, grants, tax breaks or public-private partnerships. They are designed to reconcile economic development with environmental integrity by incentivising behaviour that reduces carbon emissions, conserves natural resources and promotes long-term ecological resilience.

Environmental taxes: Environmental taxes are levies imposed on goods, services or practises that contribute to environmental degradation and aim to change behaviour towards more sustainable choices. These economic instruments, introduced by governments, target sources of pollution and resource consumption — such as greenhouse gas emissions, industrial waste and the overuse of finite natural resources — to internalise environmental costs and incentivise greener alternatives. Their main function is to internalise negative environmental externalities — costs that are not reflected in market prices — by making polluting or resource-intensive behaviour more expensive. In this way, environmental taxes aim to incentivise cleaner production and consumption patterns, support the transition to a low-carbon economy and generate public revenues that can be reinvested in sustainability-related projects. Well-designed environmental taxes can be economically efficient and administratively simple compared to direct regulation.

Sustainable Development Goals (SDGs): The Sustainable Development Goals (SDGs) are a universal framework of 17 interlinked goals adopted by all member states of the United Nations in 2015 as part of the 2030 Agenda for Sustainable Development. These goals cover a wide range of global challenges, including poverty, hunger, health, education, gender equality, clean water, clean energy, economic growth, infrastructure, reducing inequalities, responsible consumption and production, climate action and more. The SDGs serve as a blueprint for national and international development policy and require coordinated efforts by governments, the private sector and civil society to harmonise the social, economic and environmental dimensions of sustainability.

R&D tax incentives relief: R&D tax incentives refer to tax incentives offered by governments to encourage companies to invest in research and development activities. These incentives typically reduce taxable income or provide direct deductions or credits based on the amount or type of R&D expenditures. In the context of green innovation, such incentives are crucial for promoting technological progress in the areas of environmental protection, renewable energy and energy-efficient processes, particularly in the high-tech and ICT sectors. Tax breaks for R&D help to mitigate the financial risks associated with innovation, promote long-term competitiveness and accelerate the commercialisation of sustainable technologies that would otherwise be underfunded due to high uncertainties or limited short-term returns.

Environmental public fund: The Environmental Public Fund (Eko sklad) is Slovenia's national environmental financing institution established to promote environmentally friendly investments through financial support mechanisms. It offers a range of financial products, including low-interest loans, non-repayable grants and co-financing programmes aimed primarily at households, municipalities and companies that implement environmentally friendly projects. The Environmental Public Fund plays a central role in Slovenia's green transition strategy by supporting investments in renewable energy, energy efficiency, sustainable mobility and environmental protection. As a policy instrument, the fund operates at the interface between environmental objectives and fiscal instruments and aims to maximise the leverage of public funds to achieve measurable environmental results.

Emissions intensity: Emissions intensity is a metric used to quantify the amount of greenhouse gas (GHG) emissions generated per unit of economic activity or energy consumption. It is usually expressed in grammes of CO_2 equivalent per kilowatt hour (kWh) of energy or per euro of GDP. Emissions intensity serves as an indicator of the carbon efficiency of a country's or sector's production processes and energy systems. A lower emissions intensity indicates a cleaner, more efficient use of resources, while higher values indicate a greater environmental impact. Monitoring emissions intensity is essential for assessing the progress of environmental policy, particularly in relation to SDG 13 (climate action).

Material productivity: Material productivity measures the economic output (typically GDP) generated per unit of material input consumed in an economy. It reflects the efficiency with which natural resources such as minerals, fossil fuels, biomass, and construction materials are used to produce goods and services. High material productivity implies that more economic value is derived from fewer resources, contributing to sustainable consumption and production patterns (e.g., SDG 12). It is a key indicator for evaluating progress toward a circular economy and for identifying opportunities to decouple economic growth from environmental degradation.

Green Keynesianism: Green Keynesianism is a theoretical and policy framework that integrates Keynesian economic principles with environmental sustainability objectives. It advocates for proactive government intervention in the economy through increased public spending, particularly in times of economic downturn, to stimulate demand and simultaneously transition toward a low-carbon, sustainable economy. Green Keynesian policies prioritize investments in renewable energy, sustainable infrastructure, environmental technologies, and ecological restoration. The approach challenges traditional growth models by emphasizing that environmental constraints must be embedded into macroeconomic planning, asserting that public spending can be both economically stimulative and ecologically restorative.

Correlation analysis: Correlation analysis is a statistical method used to measure the strength and direction of a linear relationship between two variables. The result is typically expressed through a correlation coefficient, which ranges from -1 to 1. A value close to 1 indicates a strong positive relationship, while a value near -1 suggests a strong negative relationship. In sustainability research, correlation analysis helps identify whether variables such as environmental indicators and financial instruments move together, without implying causation.

Regression analysis: Regression analysis, in particular linear regression, is a statistical method for estimating the influence of one or more independent variables on a dependent variable. The focus is not only on identifying relationships, but also on quantifying the extent to which changes in predictors (e.g. public loans, subsidies or tax breaks) affect outcomes (e.g. SDG indicators). This method is widely used in sustainability studies to assess the impact of political or financial interventions on environmental and development goals and to support evidence-based decision-making.

ENDNOTES

1. The amounts of tax relief for R&D are not direct expenditures but they influence tax expenditures.

2. Since the table is very large, it is not included in the chapter. The table is available to interested researchers upon reasonable request.

Chapter 7
Reimagining Economic Prosperity for a Sustainable Future in the Global Context:
A Comparative Study of Developed and Developing Nations

Nishita Verma
https://orcid.org/0009-0003-7558-0206
Shri Mata Vaishno Devi University, India

Meenakshi Gupta
https://orcid.org/0000-0002-7866-4961
Shri Mata Vaishno Devi University, India

ABSTRACT

This study examines the variables that influence economic prosperity with a major focus on GDP per capita as dependent variable through comparative lens, by comparing 15 developed and 15 developing nations from 2009 to 2021. This study shows how trade openness, gender inequality index, government effectiveness, Gini coefficient and health & education spending influences prosperity. The study used econometric models such as Pooled OLS, Hausman test, Fixed effect and Random effect model. The findings of the study reveal that developed nations have high GDP as they frequently face environment degradation issues whereas developing nations

DOI: 10.4018/979-8-3373-2492-0.ch007

faces issues of weak governance and inadequate social equity. The findings shows that other than income, elements like health dimension and economic growth should be used to assess prosperity.

INTRODUCTION

Prosperity simply means overall well- being and it includes economic, emotional and social well -being. It describes a society's ability to offer its citizens a good standard of living, equitable opportunities, and a stable environment (Piketty, 2014; Wu et al., 2024). It occurs when people have the opportunity and freedom to thrive not just economically but also in all the aspects of life (Legathum Institute, 2023). It is a multidimensional idea which take both economic indicators (like Gross Domestic Product, GDP) and non –economic indicators such as social inclusion, distribution of resources (Infante-Amate et al., 2024). Accordingly, human development, sustainability, and social cohesion are examples of non-economic aspects of prosperity (Koch et al., 2012).

Economic Prosperity, a part of prosperity, mainly focusses on financial and economic conditions. It involves good economic conditions, stable economic growth and high income and employment levels. It is measured by the indicators such as GDP, Income per person etc. It reflects the ability of an economy to support high and rising standard of living (OECD, 2022). It has been associated with economic expansion, which is the increase in a nation's output of goods and services as indicated by GDP. GDP, however measures quantitative output; it does not account for inclusiveness or any environmental responsibility in growth (Jackson, 2009). It considers how economic benefits are shared across regions and populations and whether they contribute to quality life. The economic development often poses threat to environment resulting in climate change, which in turn impacts resource utilization and agricultural productivity (TF Choudhary and M Gupta, 2023; Nimisha et al., 2023; TF Choudhary and M Gupta, 2023; Bhat et al., 2024; Choudhary et al., 2022). Therefore, it becomes necessary to pursue sustainable development. Sustainability, meanwhile, refers to the ability to achieve socio-economic progress without harming sources and broadening inequity. It put more focus on ecological limits which are emissions, ecological footprints and inefficiency. Therefore, it is the integration of inclusiveness and equity United Nations. (2023).

It has been shown in many studies that prosperity often leads to income inequality and environment degradation. The traditional notation and existing structure of western prosperity are not only challenged by the level of inequality (Piketty, 2014) but also there is a lack of evidence for absolute decoupling of GDP growth, resource use and carbon emission (Jackson, 2009; Koch, 2012). Although global prosperity has increased in recent generations, progress has been uneven. The important nexus formed by economic, social and environment challenges, is addressed By SDGs (Wu & Roche, 2024).

Wu et al. (2024) basically prosperity is not merely a matter of growth but it shows how development is divided and distributed in long term prosperity in this research related to economic prosperity which is often works as a measure of a country's wealth output and large development however the effect of prosperity on income inequality and environment degradation can be both positive and negative depending on how prosperity is shared and maintained prosperity can boost sustainability generate jobs but if it is not handled properly it can also generate inequality and damage the environment

Economic growth which happens in nations without effective governance and integrated policies can leads nations towards high disparities and environmental issues (Lau et al., 2014) The need to highlights the understanding of prosperity, has shifted from narrow focus on income to equitable distribution and long-term growth. While the prosperity at global levels, has risen over recent decades and the need to reconsider traditional measurements is highlighted because of uneven progress which occurs across nations. The previous analysis of study indicates that in order to evaluate prosperity there is a need of paradigm shift that means moving beyond income which works as a sole proxy for this variable to addition of long-term equitable distribution. Wealth in recent decades is not properly distributed which become a main reason to assess conventional approach to measure economic indicators (Piketty et al., 2014)

According to literature, developed nations increased GDP per capita when it links human capital and infrastructure but sometimes it also coexists with significant ecological footprints (Infante-Amate et al., 2024) while in emerging nations economic growth helps to reduce poverty and leads economies towards long run growth and strong governance (Ahmad et al., 2021). The trends in GDP per capita in 15 developed and 15 developing nations, provide insights on ecological sustainability issues that each group faces.

Figure 1. GDP per Capita Trends in Developed Nations (2009–2021)

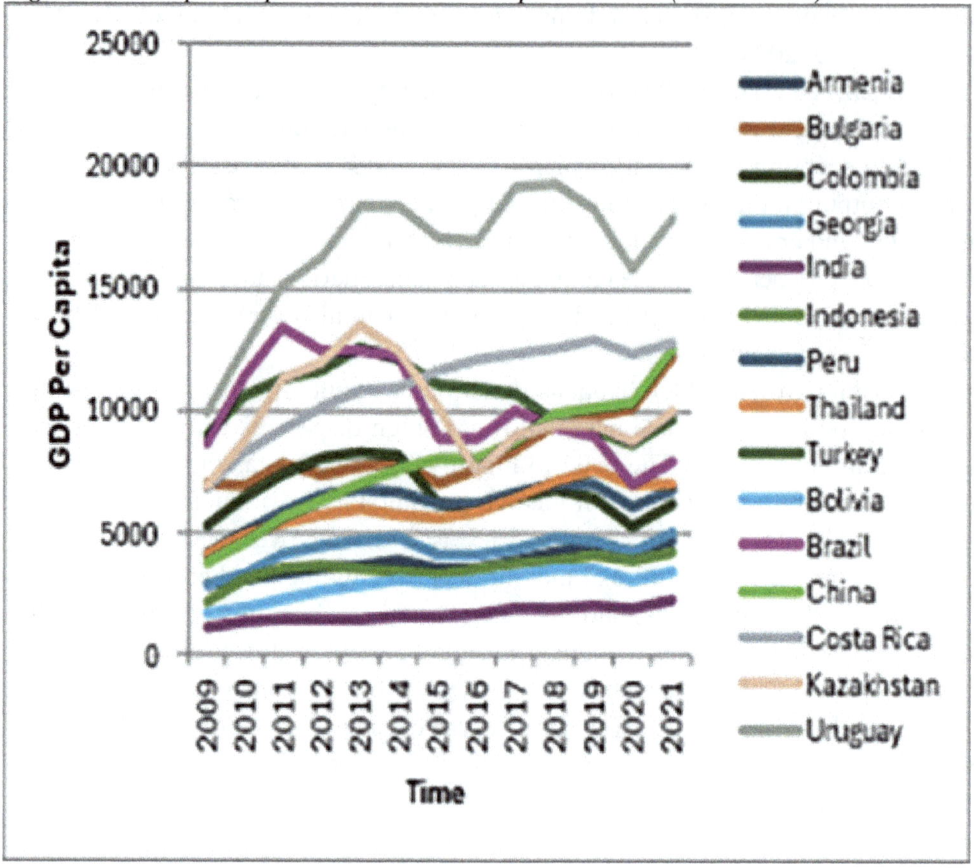

Figure 2: GDP per Capita Trends in Developing Nations (2009–2021)

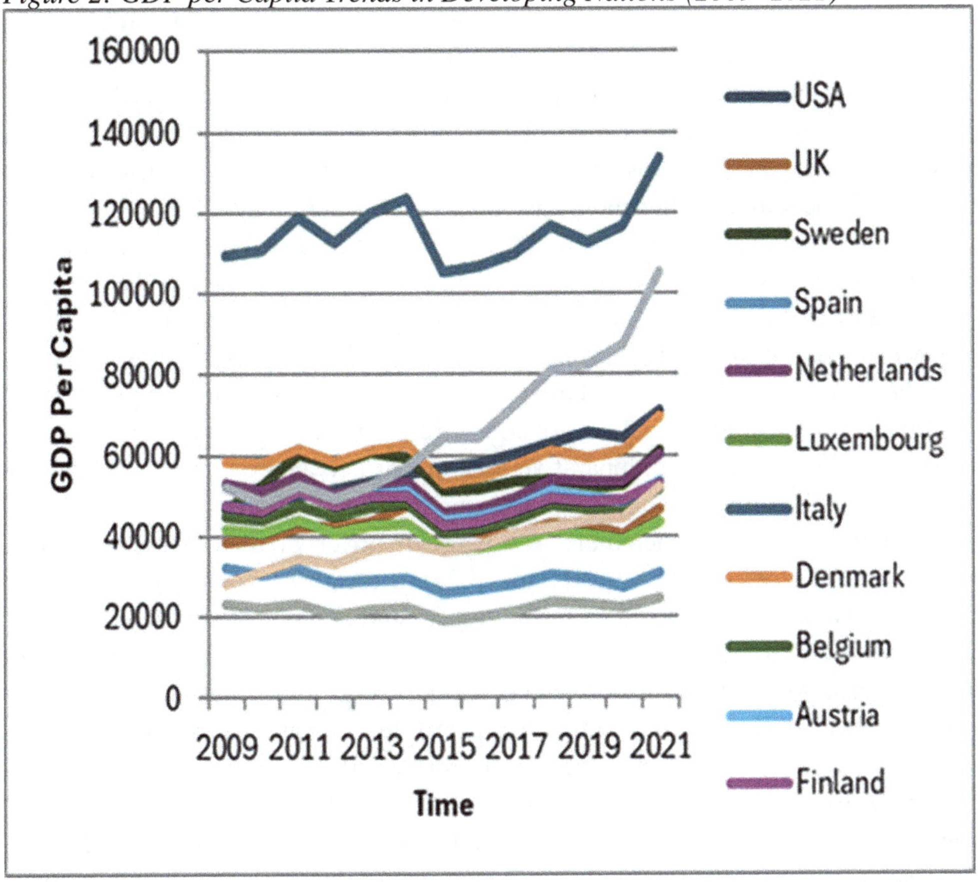

The GDP per capita trends for 15 developing nations from 2009 to 2021 are shown in this graph. Most nations like Kazakhstan, Uruguay and Costa Rica, Bolivia and India remain at lowest. The effect of shocks occurs in economy and Covid 19 is also seen from 2015 – 2016 and again in 202. The overall graph shows that inequalities in development of economy and wealth among developing nations.

This graph shows that USA has high GDP per capita between periods of 2009 – 2021. Since Luxembourg and Netherlands shows that there is increase in level after 2017. Some countries like UK, Sweden, Denmark and Germany shows moderate level of growth. Spain and Italy have low level of growth showing less increases over time. Although there is visible rise in growth after COVID 19 due to recovery policies. There are less proof where it shows that growth, CO_2 emissions and resource consumption are not related while it highlights the need to considerate prosperity using social and ecological factors (Koch et al., 2012). Some measures like Gini coefficient, Gender Inequality Index helps to access indicators of prosperity which refers to as an addition of Gross Domestic Product metrics. Since, these metrics help to determine the real value of sustainability or prosperity of a nation as per (Infante-Amate et al., 2024; Ahmad et al., 2021)

There is an urgent need for broader look out frameworks for nations which have Gross Domestic Product per capita like countries of US and Luxembourg which have faces huge consequences because of high carbon emissions and unsustainable patterns of spending. Furthermore, prosperity is not only measured and assessed by growth only, but it should look out how the wealth is distributed and divided in proportions and assess how it promotes sustainability in long run. (Piketty et al., 2014) states that the gap in income occurs in high income nations occurs due to inadequate wealth division and distribution mechanisms which creates concerns over the usefulness of metrics of Gross Domestic Product measures of prosperity.

The factors like trade openness, governance effectiveness, fair equity, and human capital metrics helps to a comparative assessment between countries in order to assess prosperity. For example the improvement of prosperity in developing countries usually can be seen when there are changes in poverty reduction measures and institutional changes as per (Ahmad et al., 2021) whereas in developed countries the more efforts to me made towards technological and ecological policies (Jackson, 2009; Wu et al., 2024). So, in view of this background discussion, this study aims to investigate the relationship between economic development and environmental sustainability, as well as income inequality, while comparing developed and developing nations. The remaining part of the study follows the following structure. Section 2 discuss the literature, Section 3 deals with the variable selection, data sources and methodology followed to achieve the objective, Section 4 deals with the results followed by discussion, conclusion, policy Implications and limitations.

REVIEW OF LITERATURE

Recent studies have explored the relationships between economic factors, GDP per capita emphasized on important determinants such as institutional quality, income inequality and financial development. A comprehensive summary of current research papers on the subject is provided in the section that follows, strictly put together summarizing the most important conclusions and insights derived from these studies.

1. Institutional governance, inequality, and prosperity

More and more research shows that inequality and governance systems cannot be separated from prosperity. In their investigation of the interrelated problems of prosperity, inequality, and environmental harm., Wu et al. (2024) claims that high economic expansion can result in environmental deterioration, particularly in nations with high levels of inequality. Using both static and dynamic research across 140 and 59 nations, their findings indicates that increased inequality ignore sustainability and environmental regulations. The inverted U-shaped relation was found between trade openness and common prosperity by Deng et al. (2025) in their analysis, underscoring the need of government regulation to maintaining a balance between economic openness and equitable growth. By looking at Sub-Saharan Africa, Gimba et al. (2023) shown that, in some circumstances, greater income disparity could lessen environmental deterioration.

2. Environmental Sustainability and Economic Growth

There has long been discussion about the relationship between economic growth and environmental sustainability, particularly in context of the Environmental Kuznets Curve (EKC) theory. The relationship between economic growth, well-being, and greenhouse gas emissions during a 150-year period was traced by Infante-Amate et al. (2024). They discovered that there is less environmental damage when GDP (economic growth) exceeds emissions or when AHDI (human development) exceeds income. Similar to this, Ahmad et al. (2021) shows EKC pattern in 11 developing nations while growth in GDP initially raises CO_2 emissions, it eventually helps the environment. By a comparative study of 138 nations by Fritz and Koch (2016), which shows that prosperity emphasize social inclusion and quality of life for enhancing environmental outcomes than GDP alone. Using data from 51 nations, Chaabouni and Saidi (2017) also noted that although economic expansion raises health spending and emissions, highlighting the need of region-specific sustainability strategies.

3. Technology, Energy Use, and Trade Openness

There is also evidence of the mediating effects of commerce, technology, and energy use on economic and environmental results. Sun & Abruzzian (2025) shows that how natural resources, trade openness, and innovation affected sustainability in the BRICS+T countries. Using econometric models like NARDL and DSUR, the results shows that trade openness has negative effect, whereas technological development and clean energy lower CO_2 emissions. In panel data research of G20 nations, Alakbarov et al. (2025) shows that pollution is increased by both economic growth and energy use, so there should be the need for cleaner energy policies. Using data from Denmark, the UK, and Spain, Bees and Kalayci et al. (2021) in developed economies their findings, shows no correlation between GDP and CO_2, imply that economic development alone is not enough to reduce emissions.

4. Human Capital and Financial Development

The impact of human capital and financial development on sustainability is also emphasized in the literature. Keswani et al. (2025) shows that industrial progress and financial development have a favourable correlation with economic growth, they also increase carbon emissions and ecological footprints. Similar study shows by Mashrur (2025) in Bangladesh, where their Granger and VECM causality tests shows that trade openness and foreign direct investment increased long-term economic growth. Varona and Gonzales (2025), on the other hand, conducted a study in Peru and shows if there is increase in the Human Development Index (HDI) it will have a direct impact on economic growth and productivity, Ngo et al. (2025) combined strategic governance tools with GNI forecasts to examine Vietnam from a forward-looking angle.

5. Well-being, Emissions, and Gender Equality

The relationship between environmental sustainability and gender equality is the subject of a new area of study. The Global Gender Gap Index, which measures gender equality, has been shown that it will lower CO_2 emissions (Sanchez-Olmedo et al., 2025). A 0.14-ton drop in per capita CO_2 emissions is linked to a 1% gain in gender equality, according to their panel study conducted across 49 nations. According to this, it is cleared that social structures can improve environmental performance and offer support for laws that combine environmental objectives with equity.

6. Evaluations of Developed and Developing Economies in Comparison

Numerous studies give comparisons between developed and developing nations regarding the ways in which sustainability is impacted by prosperity. Using data from 11 developing nations, Ahmad et al. (2021) shows that GDP expansion first makes emissions worse before lowering them at higher income levels. However, Bees and Kalayci et al. (2021), who examined Denmark, the UK, and Spain, could not find any evidence of this inverted-U relationship which claims that economic expansion in wealthy nations does not always leads to lower emissions. According to Fritz and Koch (2016), emerging and developing nations struggle to maintain balance between social and ecological inclusion and wealth. Their study, which classified 138 nations by income level, revealed that wealthy countries had bigger environmental footprints and stronger economic indices, highlighting the need of integrating ecological and redistributive policies.

Table 1. Summary of Selected Literature on Prosperity, Inequality, and Environmental Sustainability

S.No.	Author(s) & Year	Area of Study	Time Period	Methodology / Models Used	Key Findings
1	Wu et al. (2024)	140 countries	1995–2017	Static & dynamic analysis	Higher inequality worsens environmental degradation; EKC hypothesis partially supported.
2	Infante-Amate et al. (2024)	Global (150-year analysis)	Historical (150 yrs)	Decoupling, regional comparative analysis	Prosperity becomes sustainable when HDI > GDP growth; weak decoupling observed.
3	Sun & Abruzzian (2025)	BRICS+T nations	1990–2022	NARDL, DSUR, CUP-FM	Technological innovation reduces CO_2 and footprint; mixed impact of trade openness.
4	Alakbarov et al. (2025)	G20 countries	Not specified	Panel cointegration, causality analysis	Growth & energy use linked with pollution; urgent call for green policies.
5	Keswani et al. (2025)	India	1990–2022	VECM, Granger Causality, Cointegration	Financial development drives emissions; GDP growth increases ecological footprint.
6	Ngo et al. (2025)	Vietnam	Not specified	Mixed-method: CLA, AG, GNI forecast	Vietnam may reach high-income by 2050 with strategic governance.
7	Mashrur (2025)	Bangladesh	1999–2023	VECM, Granger Causality	FDI and trade openness positively affect economic growth.
8	Sanchez-Olmedo et al. (2025)	49 countries	2006–2020	Fixed effects regression	Gender equality reduces CO_2 emissions; strong negative correlation.
9	Fritz & Koch (2016)	138 countries (by income level)	Not specified	MFA, Correlation analysis	Inequality hinders growth; ecological trade-offs raise emissions.
10	Ahmad et al. (2021)	11 developing countries	1992–2014	EKC, Pearson, Unit Root	EKC hypothesis holds; bidirectional relationship between GDP, electricity & CO_2.
11	Gimba et al. (2023)	Sub-Saharan Africa	1995–2018	Westerlund cointegration, PML estimator	Income inequality may mitigate ecological footprint; pollution rises with urbanization.
12	Chaabouni & Saidi (2017)	51 countries	1995–2013	GMM model	Emissions raise health costs; GDP & emissions positively linked.
13	Asongu et al. (2016)	24 African countries	Not specified	Panel ARDL	Long-run link between EC, GDP, CO_2; no short-term causality.

Source: Author's own compilation

METHODS AND DATA

Objective:

This study's primary goal is to investigate the ways in which environmental sustainability, income inequality, and institutional quality affect economic prosperity in various nations. The study uses a panel dataset of 30 nations (15 developed and

15 developing) spanning the years 2009-2021 and uses GDP per capita as a stand-in for prosperity. The research attempts to offer a thorough and comparative analysis of prosperity determinants in various country contexts by combining socioeconomic and governance-related variables. The developed countries taken for this chapter includes United States, United Kingdom, Sweden, Spain, Netherland, Luxembourg, Italy, Denmark, Belgium, Austria, Finland, France, Ireland, Israel and Portugal while developing countries includes Armenia, Bulgaria, Colombia, Georgia, India, Indonesia, Peru, Thailand, Turkey, Bolivia, Brazil, China, Costa Rica, Kazakhstan and Uruguay.

Theoretical Justification and Selection of Variables

In the current study, we have used GDP per capita as a proxy of economic prosperity. There are some consequences which are linked to higher GDP per capita and lower GDP per capita. People when consume more products and services, it will raise carbon emissions and energy demand, particularly nations that rely on fossil fuels for energy production (Abbas, Sohail, & Rasheed, 2023). When manufacturing and production activities increase, industrial expansion follows economic growth and this greatly increases $C0_2$ emissions (Raupach et al., 2007). According to Grossman and Krueger (1995) the EKC reflects this link and shows that emissions rise at first, but then fall as economics develops sustainable practices (Ansari, Khan, & Ahmad, 2024). Conversely, Lower GDP per capita is linked with a different set of environmental consequences. In low-income nations limited industrial activity frequently leads to reduced C02 emissions but this doesn't mean that sustainable practices have been adopted. (World Bank, 2023). Furthermore, poor countries rely largely on resource intensive industries like agriculture, deforestation, and mining which seriously affect the environment (DE Decker, Radek, et al.). Lack of financing or environment protection, poor governance all of which make it difficult to manage emissions (Pastor et al., 2013). Economic prosperity is determined by a number of factors such as human capital, technological progress, institutional quality, macroeconomic stability, FDI, labour force participation etc. But for my current study we are using Gini coefficient, gender inequality index, Health & education, Govt. effectiveness and trade openness as independent variables.

1. Gini coefficient: It is a measure of income inequality ranging from 0 to 1. High income inequality limits access to health care, education, and employment, particularly for lower-income groups. Barro (2000) found that inequality harms growth in poorer countries by weakening human capital accumulation. Similarly, Ostry et al., (2011) concluded that equitable income distribution supports more stable and sustained growth. In highly unequal societies, spending levels drop

as wealth is concentrated in fewer hands, dampening both consumption and productivity. Therefore, a higher Gini coefficient is expected to have a negative effect on GDP per capita.

2. GII: It measures gender-based disparities in health. By limiting women's access to the workforce, gender disparity impedes economic growth, according to research by Klasen and Lamanna (2009). Furthermore, Seguino (2000) contends that closing the gender gap in education and employment greatly boosts growth and productivity, particularly in emerging nations. Thus, a higher GII score, indicating more gender inequality, is expected to negatively affect GDP per capita.
3. Govt spending on health & education: It refers to public investment in services that improve people's wellbeing and skills. According to Barro and Sala-i-Martin (1995), long-term economic growth and education spending are positively correlated. Investments in health and education are also essential for equitable growth in emerging nations, according to Baldacci et al. (2008). These expenditures promote sustainable development, increase worker productivity, and improve job performance. Accordingly, increased government spending on health and education is expected to positively affect GDP per capita.
4. Government effectiveness: It means how well a government executes policy, provides public services and upholds high quality institutions. Effective governance lowers corruption, enhances the quality of regulations, and establishes a stable environment for economic activity, according to Kaufmann et al. (2010). Stronger governance improves resource management and draws in more foreign investment. Therefore, government effectiveness is expected to have a positive impact on GDP per capita.
5. Trade openness: It is the degree at which a nation can freely exchange goods and services with other nations with less restrictions and taxes. Trade openness and income levels across nations were found to be significantly positively correlated by Frankel and Romer (1999). Similarly, Dollar and Kraay (2004) discovered that increased innovation and competitive efficiency lead to quicker growth in open economies. Therefore, increased trade openness is expected to have a favourable impact on GDP per capita.

Table 2. Choices of variables:

Variable	Description
GDP per capita (dependent Variable)	GDP per capita serves as an indicator of economic prosperity and average living standards. It is measured in constant 2015 United States dollars.
Gini coefficient (independent Variable)	Gini coefficient is a statistical measure which is used to assess income or wealth inequality within a population. Gini coefficient ranges from 0-1, where 0 represents perfect equality and 1 represents perfect inequality. Inequality is measured in terms of income before taxes and benefits.
Govt. spending on health and education (independent Variable)	Government spending on health and education (% of GDP) is the percentage of a nation's GDP that the government allots to public health care and educational institutions.
Population growth (independent Variable)	Population growth refers to the change in number of individuals over time. The number of births, deaths and migratory flows all affect this change. The growth in population is measured from percent increase or decrease in a year.
Trade openness (independent Variable)	Trade openness is defined as the total of a nation's imports and exports of goods and services, represented as a percentage of GDP. This indicator assesses the importance of international trade in a nation's economy.
Gender Inequality Index (GII) (independent Variable)	A composite indicator that assesses disparities in labour market participation, empowerment, and reproductive health depending on gender. Equality (zero) and inequality (one) are the range of values.
Government Effectiveness(independent Variable)	A governance indicator capturing perceptions of the quality of public services, civil service, policy formulation and implementation. Scaled from -2.5 (weak) to 2.5 (strong).

Source: Author's own compilation

SOURCE OF DATA: The data in this chapter has been collected from secondary sources. The details are presented in Table 3

Table 3. Data Sources

S. NO.	VARIABLE	SYMBOL	MEASURING UNIT	SOURCE	Expected Signs
1.	GDP per capita	GDP	Constant 2015 US$ per person	World Bank (2023). GDP per capita (constant 2015 US$). https://data.worldbank.org/indicator/NY.GDP.PCAP.KD	+
2.	Gender Inequality index	GII	0(perfect gender equality) no inequality between men and women - 1(extreme gender inequality) women experience the highest level of disadvantage.	United Nations Development Programme (UNDP) (2023). Human Development Reports – Gender Inequality Index. https://hdr.undp.org/data-center/thematic-composite-indices/gender-inequality-index	(+ / -)
3.	Govt spending on health and education	H&E	Dimensionless	World Bank (2023). Government expenditure on education and health (% of GDP). https://data.worldbank.org	-
4.	Gini Coefficient	GC	0 (perfect equality) everyone has the same income_ 1(perfect inequality) one person has all income and the other has none.	World Bank (2023). Gini index (World Bank estimate). https://data.worldbank.org/indicator/SI.POV.GINI	+
5.	Govt. Effectiveness	GE	Scale: -2.5 to +2.5Higher value shows better govt. effectiveness and lower values show weaker effectiveness.	World Bank (2023). Worldwide Governance Indicators – Government Effectiveness. https://info.worldbank.org/governance/wgi	–
6.	Trade openness	trade	(% of GDP) Higher percentage indicates more open economy and lower percentage indicates closed economy.	World Bank (2023). Trade (% of GDP). https://data.worldbank.org/indicator/NE.TRD.GNFS.ZS	(+ / -)

Source: Author's own compilation

Model Specification

Data and variables

This study employs Panel data analysis i.e. Pooled ordinary least square (POLS) which consists of several cross-sectional data collected over time. In addition to POLS, Fixed Effects (FE) and Random Effects (RE) models were applied to account for unobserved heterogeneity across countries. The Hausman specification test was conducted to determine the more appropriate model between FE and RE. The dependent variable is GDP per capita while independent variable includes Gini coefficient, health and education spending, government effectiveness and gender inequality index. Trade openness used as control variable. The data set uses a balanced panel of countries which is used over a specified period, ensuring robust and reliable estimations.

Initial Screenings of Data:

The methodology for this is below:

Economic prosperity model:

GDP per capita:

$$GDPpercapita_{it} = \alpha + \beta_1 GC_{it} + \beta_2 GII_{it} + \beta_3 HE_{it} + \beta_4 GE_{it} + \beta_5 trade_{it} + \varepsilon_{it}$$

Now we convert this equation into natural logarithmic form to estimate the effect of GDP Per Capita on both developed and developing countries. The equation can be written as:

$$LnGDPit = \alpha + \beta_{1LN} GC_{it} + \beta_{2LN} GII_{it} + \beta_{3LN} GE_{it} + \beta_{4LN} GE_{it} + \beta_{5LN} Trade_{it} + u_i + \varepsilon_{it}$$

Where:

CO_{2it} = C02 emission per capita

GC_{it} = Gini coefficient

Gii_{it} = Gender inequality index

He_{it} = Government spending on health and education

GDP_{it} = log of GDP per capita

Ge_{it} = Government effectiveness

$Trade_{it}$ = Trade openness

For Developed countries to examine the relationship between variables, we estimate the following fixed effect or random effect model and the choice is justified based on the Hausman test.

Economic Prosperity:

GDP per capita: Based on the Hausman test which yields a p value = 0.4977 which suggests that the Random effect model is preferred for our analysis. Accordingly random effect for lnGDP per capita is:

$$LnGDPit = a + ß1GCit + ß2GIIit + ß3GEit + ß4GEit + ß5Tradeit + ui + eit$$

Where:

LnGDPit = Natural log of GDP per capita for I country at time t
a= intercept term
ui= Unobserved individual specific results
eit= Error term

For Developing countries to examine relationships between variables, we estimate the following fixed effect or Random effect and the choice is based on the Hausman test.

Economic prosperity:

GDP $_{it}$ ***per capita:*** Based on the Hausman test yields P value = 0.2252 which suggests that the Random effect model is preferred for our analysis. Accordingly random effect model for lnGDPit is:

$$LnGDPit=a+\beta1GCit+\beta2GIIit+\beta3HEit+\beta4GEit+\beta5Tradeit+ui+\varepsilon it$$

Where:

LnGDPit = Natural log of GDP per capita for I country at time t
a= intercept term
u_i= Unobserved individual specific results
e_{it} = Error term

Results:

DEVELOPED NATIONS RESULTS

The developed nations considered in the analysis are the United States, United Kingdom, Sweden, Spain, Netherlands, Luxembourg, Italy, Denmark, Belgium, Austria, Finland, France, Ireland, Israel and Portugal. These nations were chosen on the basis of their strong economic development, high income status and accessibility to data.

Initial Screening Tests

Measures such as the mean, median, standard deviation, skewness and Kurtosis are examples of descriptive statistics that highlight and describe a dataset's salient characteristics. Researchers and analysts can use these techniques to derive insights from data distributions. Sir Francis Galton made significant contributions in statistical science during the 19th century, especially in the creation of techniques for characterising, summarizing and describing.

The dataset's descriptive results of developed nations which comprise 195 observations, offers an insightful overview of various indicators. The GDP per capita shows that The LNGDP respective mean is 10.834 indicates GDP is high across nation, Skewness is 0.3116 which shows positive skew, means that few countries have very high-income levels, SD is 0.4304 shows low variability across country and Kurtosis is 3.1305 which indicates equal distribution Refer Appendix).

Before applying the regression models, the selected independent variables were checked for multicollinearity. To ensure there is no significant multicollinearity among independent variables, Variance Inflation Factor (VIF) tests were conducted. All VIF values were found to be below the acceptable threshold of 5, indicating no multicollinearity concerns. Detailed results are provided in Appendix A.

Based on this validation; the models were estimated using panel data analysis methods such as Pooled OLS, Fixed Effects, and Random Effects. The coefficients of the association between the selected variables are presented in Table 6.

Table 4. Estimates of Parameters for Panel Regression Model

Variables	Pooled OLS	P-value	Random Effect	P-value
GC	0.7159	0.5836	–3.8151	0.0000
GII	0.2967	0.7360	–1.12070	0.0053
GE	–0.2183	0.0097	–0.0446	0.4242
HE	0.0444	0.0273	–0.0189	0.0121
Trade Openness	0.0036	0.0000	0.00080	0.1801
Constant	9.9173	0.0000	12.3869	0.0000
R-squared	0.270980		0.335886	
F-statistic	14.05043	0.0000	19.11797	0.0000

Source: Author Estimation Software E- Views 12

Mixed results are shown by the Pooled OLS model. GDP per capita is significant but negatively impacted by government effectiveness (p = 0.0097), because of wasteful spending. Spending on health and education is positively significant (p = 0.0273), indicating that prosperity is supported by social investment. However, Trade Openness have a positive and significant, impact whereas Gini and GII are negligible. Durbin-Watson = 0.05 and R2 = 0.2709 for the model show high autocorrelation and not good fit model. On the other hand, the Random Effects model reveals that both Gini and GII are significant, shows the negative impact of inequality on economic growth. Trade openness is still negligible. The model still consists of autocorrelation with low fits model with R2 = 0.3356 and Durbin-Watson = 0.83. In conclusion, the RE model identifies inequality (GC and GII) as a major drawback, whereas social investment exhibits inconsistent results across models.

Table 5. Random Effect - Hausman Test having Primary GDP:

Test Summary		**Chi-sq. Statistic**	**Chi-sq. d.f.**	**Prob.**
Cross-section random		**4.368114**	**5**	**0.4977**
Variable	**Fixed**	**Random**	**Var (Diff.)**	**Prob.**
GC	-3.944552	-3.815157	0.03222	0.4711
GE	-0.034610	-0.044641	0.00015	0.4151
GII	-1.220635	-1.120750	0.00718	0.2388
HE	-0.019016	-0.018999	0.00000	0.9912
Trade Openness	0.000643	0.000804	0.00000	0.5102

Source: Author Estimation Software E- Views

Hausman test results indicate a Chi-Square statistic of 4.368 with a p-value of 0.4977. Since $p > 0.05$, the null hypothesis cannot be rejected, thus confirming that the Random Effects (RE) model is more appropriate for interpreting the relationship between GDP per capita and the independent variables in this study (Hausman, 1978; Săvoiu & Manea, 2013). Since, GII are both significantly and negatively associated with GDP per capita. H&E spending has a little but significant negative impact on GDP. GE shows negative and not statistically significant impact. Lastly, trade openness is negative but not statistically significant whereas no clear effect on GDP per capita in this model. The high R squared Value (0.965) confirms a strong model fit. The D-W value is 0.9082 whose value is less than 2 suggests the presence of positive autocorrelation.

DEVELOPING NATIONS RESULTS:

This section includes, Descriptive statistics, VIF test results for developing countries. The developing nations taken are Armenia, Bulgaria, Colombia, Georgia, India, Indonesia, Peru, Thailand, Turkey, Bolivia, Brazil, China, Costa Rica, Kazakhstan and Uruguay. These nations were selected on the basis of lower- or middle-income status, emerging characteristics and availability of consistent data over the period.

The dataset's descriptive findings (Ref Appendix) of developing nations, which include 195 observations, gives a useful summary of metric economic prosperity. The GDP mean is 10.834 which indicates average GDP across countries, SD is 0.4304 indicates low variability in income, Skewness is 0.3116 shows distribution is mostly symmetrical and Kurtosis is very close to 3 the distribution is mesokurtic. The Trade mean is 108.82 shows countries are highly trade dependant, SD is 78.021 have high variability - showing that trade openness differs significantly, Skewness is 1.8619 shows strong positive skew distribution I-e some countries are extremely open to trade and kurtosis is 3.1632 indicates distribution is leptokurtic and has heavy tails with sharp peak.

Before applying the regression models, the selected independent variables were checked for multicollinearity. To ensure there is no significant multicollinearity among independent variables, Variance Inflation Factor (VIF) tests were conducted. All VIF values were found to be below the acceptable threshold of 5, indicating no multicollinearity concerns. Detailed results are provided in Appendix B. Based on this validation; the models were estimated using panel data analysis methods such as Pooled OLS, Fixed Effects, and Random Effects.

Table 6. Estimates of Parameters for Panel Regression Model

Variables	Pooled OLS	P-value	Random Effects	P-value
GC	2.0041	0.0000	0.08774	0.7830
GII	–4.2199	0.0000	–2.2926	0.0000
GE	0.32801	0.0001	0.07414	0.0001
HE	0.0503	0.0002	0.04080	0.0129
Trade Openness	–0.0041	0.0001	–0.0017	0.0000
Constant	9.2784	0.0000	31.3224	0.0000
R-squared	0.64614		0.32886	
F-statistic	69.02323	0.0000	18.5226	0.0000

Source: Author Estimation Software E- Views 12

According to the Pooled OLS model, GDP per capita is positively and significantly impacted Gini coefficient (Coefficient = 2.004, p = 0.000), suggesting a relationship between increased output and rising inequality. Spending on health and education (0.0502, p = 0.0002) and government effectiveness (0.328, p = 0.0001) also have favourable and noteworthy effects, underscoring the significance of human capital and governance. The Gender Inequality Index (GII) indicates that gender inequality slows growth because it is negative (–4.2199, p = 0.0000). Additionally significant but negative (-0.0041, p = 0.0001) is trade openness, which may be the result of trade structural inefficiencies. Although the model has a good fit (R2 = 0.6461), it has a high level of autocorrelation (Durbin-Watson = 0.2018). GII's negative influence in growth is reaffirmed in the Random Effects model, where it is still significant and negative (–2.3926, p = 0.0000). Investment in social development is supported by the positive significance of Health & Education (0.0480, p = 0.0129) once more. However, the Gini Coefficient drops to negligible (0.0857, p = 0.7830), indicating that this model does not use income inequality to explain growth. Trade Openness is negligible (p = 0.2731), while Government Effectiveness is still positive and substantial (0.2104, p = 0.0296). The model exhibits positive autocorrelation (D-W = 0.5513) despite having a weaker explanatory power (R2 = 0.3288).

Table 7. Correlated Random Effect - Hausman Test having Primary GDP PER CAPITA

Test Summary	Chi-sq. Statistic	Chi-sq. d.f.		Prob.
Cross-section random	6.939213	5		0.2552
Variable	Fixed	Random	Var (Diff.)	Prob.
GC	–0.038712	0.087746	0.00477	0.0667
GE	0.282696	0.290185	0.00038	0.6794
HE	0.034862	0.040801	0.00000	0.4004
GII	–2.169207	–2.292605	0.01368	0.2909
Trade Openness	–0.001508	–0.001724	0.00001	0.7644

Source: Author Estimation Software E- Views 12

The Hausman test was applied to determine the appropriate model between fixed effects and random effects. The p-value (0.2552) is greater than 0.05, indicating that the null hypothesis of no correlation cannot be rejected. Therefore, the Random Effects (RE) model is preferred over the Fixed Effects (FE) model for estimating GDP per capita. (Hausman, 1978; Săvoiu & Manea, 2013). Since, GII and GE are significant predictors, GDP per capita is significantly impacted negatively by gender inequality indicating that greater levels of gender inequality are linked to strong economies. However, there is a strong positive correlation between GE and GDP suggesting that improved governance raises GDP. Spending on HE has a significant positive impact, suggesting that the effect is not very large. GC and trade openness don't show statistically significant effects in this model.

Inconsistent Results in Developed Countries

(Supported by: Abbas et al., 2021; Barro & Sala-i-Martin, 1995; Baldacci et al., 2008; Pastor et al., 2013; Sun & Abruzzian, 2025)

1. Government Effectiveness: This variable had a statistically significant negative correlation (coefficient = -0.218, p = 0.0097) with GDP per capita. This result holds that good governance increases institutional quality, lowers corruption, and encourages investment—all of which are elements commonly linked to economic growth. However, such advancements can result in decreasing returns in highly developed economies with robust governance structures. Therefore, rather than administrative reforms, growth might be more reliant on innovation, technological advancement, and market efficiency.
2. Health and Education Spending: This variable had a significant but negative effect on GDP per capita (coefficient = –0.01899, p = 0.0121), which was in contrast human capital theory. It can happen due to delays in the returns on investments in health and education or inefficiencies. Further social spending may be less effective in well-developed systems due to the resource misallocation.
3. Trade Openness: The model showed a statistically negative effect (p = 0.1801, coefficient = 0.00080). This is against traditional trade theory, which contends that more market access and competitiveness lead to growth. Most of the benefits of trade may already have been achieved in developed economies. Furthermore, the overall advantages of openness may be limited by sensitivity to trade imbalances and global shocks.

Inconsistent Results in Developing Countries

(Supported by: Piketty, 2014; Ansari, Khan, & Ahmad, 2021; Gimba et al., 2023; World Bank, 2025)

1. Gini Coefficient: Contrary this shows that inequality has a positive impact on long-term economic performance, with GDP per capita (coefficient = 2.004189, p = 0.000). This could be as a result of early development's growth on particular high-growing industries, such manufacturing or information technology. Even if inequality increases, these industries might have high GDP growth, which would reflect short-term advantages rather than inclusive growth.

2. Trade Openness: The traditional economic theory that links trade openness to growth was contradicted by this variable's negative but statistically insignificant effect (coefficient = –0.0017, p = 0.2760). Poor infrastructure, less trade regulations, may be the cause of this in emerging nations. Trade openness might not produce favourable gains in economic growth.

All things considered, these results highlight how crucial context-specific policy approaches are. They also emphasize the need to exercise caution when assuming that governance, inequality, and economic growth have a linear relationship, particularly when considering various developmental stages.

Cross – Study Evaluation of Fixed, Random, Pooled Model Results against Prior Studies:

The results of this study usually link with several studies which highlights variations between developed and developing countries. By comparing results with earlier research, the evidence gives a wider context to validate. The results of random effect shows that Gini coefficient reduces GDP per capita in both developed and developing nations. This results also validates in Piketty et al. 2014 which claims that when there is growing inequality it will reduces long term growth. Infante – Amante et al. 2024 shows that when there is inequality it will slow down prosperity for sustainable practices. Since the model in our study shows that the inequality reduces prosperity if redistribution is weak in nations.

1. Gender Inequality Index: In developing nations, GII has negative effect on GDP per capita which indicates that inequality of gender limits the productive growth of economy. Wu et al. 2024 claims that nations which has unequal and less sustainable growth reduces GDP per capita whereas Ahmad et al. 2021 demonstrate that gender inequality reduces the participation of labour.
2. Health & Education expenditure: The spending shows positive effect on GDP per capita in developing nations but has small impact on developed nations. The findings are supported by Asongu et al. 2016 and Deng et al. 2025 claims that role of spending plays a crucial role in increasing productivity and output especially in developed nations. In contrast to developing nations when level of investment is high there is minimum marginal impact on levels.
3. Government Effectiveness: Ahmad et al. 2021 and Chaabouni & Saidi 2017 shows that institutions are essential for sustainable development as there is positive relation between GDP per capita in developing nations, however the effect in developed nations have negative effect. It suggests that high income

nations have less changes in quality of government which may reduce the impact of growth.

4. Trade Openness: The results of random effect model have negative effect on GDP per capita in both developed and developing nations which have contrary impact on trade growth. Gimba et al. 2023 shows that trade has uneven impact on global market and industries of domestic. The contrast studies of Sun & Abruzzian, 2025 which seen as that trade promotes technological and innovation ideas.

Table 8. Cross study evaluation

VARIABLE	MODEL FINDINGS	CONSISTENCY WITH PRIOR STUDIES
GINI COEFFECIENT	Negative impact on GDP per capita	The results are similar to Infante-Amante et al.2024 & Piketty et al. 2014: Growth reduces inequality
GENDER INEQUALITY INDEX	Negative effect in developing nations	Similar with Ahmad et al. 2021 and Wu et al. 2024: Gaps in gender reduces growth.
HEALTH & EDUCATION SPENDING	Positive effect in developing nations: But low effect in developed nations	Aggress with Deng et al. 2025& Asongu et al. 2016: Human capital limits prosperity in developing nations
GOVERNMENT EFFECTIVENESS	Mixed effect: Positive effect in developing and Negative effect in developed nations	Supports by Ahmad et al. 2021and Kesawani et al.2025 IT boosts growth in developing nations
TRADE OPENESS	In both has negative effect	Contrast with Sun & Abruzzian, 2025 and Gimba et al. 2023 which shows that trade increase sustainability and trade have mixed effect in developing nations.

Source: Author Estimation

Integrating Environmental Sustainability and Strategies for Achieving Prosperity

While in this study, GDP per capita is used as proxy for prosperity but it cannot remain separated from sustainability. The costs of environment such as carbon emissions, depletion of resources are focussed in traditional models. In the study of (Infante – Amate et al.,2024) it shows that even if there are strong regulations in high income nations, the nation's exceeds high CO_2 emissions and ecological footprints.

These limits can be corrected by putting emphasis on prosperity which act as a state of equitable and ecological development with environment related frameworks.

One major area of concern is carbon emissions. When nations are prosperous, it relies heavily on fossil fuels and it faces pressure in order to make it decarbonize. According to framework of climate linked prosperity; carbon neutrality is the ultimate goal. Adopted by European Union in 2019, European green deal aims at to invest in renewable energy, more practices in circular economy and agriculture system to be sustainable to achieve European Climate neutral by 2050. Similarly, China aims to reduce emissions and sustain growth in 2060 with target of Carbon Neutrality. It recognizes that long term prosperity depends on balancing economic growth with some responsibility towards environment. These two frameworks clearly show that in order to achieve prosperity today there is need for long term environment resilience not only rising incomes.

Another framework like SDG goals like Goal 7 (Affordable and Clean energy), Goal 13 (Climate action) shows that there is need to sync growth with sustainability. Regional initiatives like National Action Plan on Climate Change (NAPCC) of India and Canada Clean Growth and Climate Action Plan has their vision of low carbon strategies, renewable energy with green infrastructure. These policies show that achieving long term growth by remaining in limits of economy give way out to attain prosperity. Thus, prosperity when link with sustainability shows the dimensions of equitability, inclusiveness and sustainability.

These Policy changes are necessary to integrate prosperity with sustainability as used in frameworks like Sustainable development goals and European Green Deal. These recommendation work on criteria for renewable energy, green infrastructure and green taxation particularly in developing and high-income nations. As per study of Wu et al. 2024 and Sun & Abruzzian, 2025 they show that the dependency of carbon and degradation of environment should get separated from prosperity. Thus, in order to prove that economic gains to be long term and sustainable, prosperity models include more environmental variable such as emissions, carbon intensity and ecological footprints.

CONCLUSION

This study examined the effects of important institutional, social, and economic factors on economic prosperity, including the Gini coefficient, gender inequality index, government efficacy, public spending on health and education, and trade openness. Between 2009 and 2021, a panel data technique was used for both developed and developing nations. The results show that these factors and economic outcomes have a complicated and perhaps illogical relationship. Developed countries have strong wealth success as seen because of increase in GDP per capita. However if fair distribution and ecological consideration are not taken into account prosperity coexists with income inequality and environment issue decoupling economic growth from inequality GDP per capita in emerging nations is comparatively low because of lack of development and technological innovation.

This study's primary contributions include comparing industrialized and developing nations, incorporating institutional and environmental elements into the analysis of prosperity, and revealing the complex relationships between socioeconomic determinants and GDP per capita. These revelations emphasize the significance of context-specific policy design and advance our understanding of inclusive and sustainable prosperity.

Future studies should think at implementing more thorough measures that will take environmental sustainability and well-being into account. Deeper understanding of causation may also be possible through mixed-method approaches or longitudinal case studies. Furthermore, investigating the function of technological innovation, digital infrastructure, and regional governance frameworks may add more levels of insight into the relationship between prosperity and progress.

Policy Suggestions

The policy suggestions for GDP per capita as a dependent variable in this study include a number of targeted strategies. For developed countries, modernizing e-vehicles, transport, and digital infrastructure will lower operational costs and increase firm output, thereby boosting economic growth. Increasing R&D expenditures by boosting funds for public and private research will improve long-term productivity growth. It is also important to transfer the tax burden towards consumption and environmental levies by replacing labour and capital taxes with carefully implemented taxes on carbon and recycling the funds to protect low-income households. R&D spending should be increased to more than 3% of GDP, as meeting this target for public and private research investment will increase productivity growth over the long term by increasing innovation. For developing countries, encouraging mobilisation of domestic resources through value-added taxes and combining income with transfers can finance social services without discouraging investment. Boosting institutional capacity and governance by improving anti-corruption measures and domestic tax administration will reduce operational costs and increase revenue for public services. Exports should be diversified into high-value goods and services, as larger exports are linked with higher per capita income and more economic stability among low-income countries and also lessen vulnerability to price shocks. Finally, investing widely in human capital is crucial, as global GDP per capita might increase by 12% by 2050, and for this, key initiatives include universal primary education, some nutrition programs, and access to health care.

Future Research

Future research can be broadened by include additional variables that better capture complex aspects, like ecological footprint, environmental sustainability, innovation indicators, and digital infrastructure. These would make it possible to examine the connection between prosperity and sustainability in greater detail. Moreover, econometric techniques like the Generalized Method of Moments (GMM) and dynamic panel data models can be used to address endogeneity problems. By expanding the regional focus to include other economic blocs like ASEAN, the African Union, or MENA, comparative insights can be gained beyond the developed-developing divide. Future research could examine governance effectiveness, country-specific policies, and technology adoption to examine intra-group differences among the BRICS nations. Last but not least, mixed-method approaches that include qualitative data—like policy case studies can enhance quantitative findings and offer deeper aware insights.

Limitations

This study is not free from limitations. Firstly, the study uses GDP per capita as a proxy of economic prosperity, which cannot capture factors like quality life, well-being and sustainability which can lead to incomplete evaluation of development outcome results. Secondly, the study uses only 30 countries and 13-year time period. This limited sample may not cover wider range of global economies. More diverse data could improve generalizability. Thirdly, there is possibility of endogeneity which indicates model inefficiency and affect reliability of estimates. Some other models like GMM or dynamic panel models can be used in order to improve accuracy and control biasedness in panel data. Finally, despite discussion of sustainability in conceptual manner, environment variables like carbon emissions and ecological footprint are not included in empirical model. This restricts the study to assess environment dimension of prosperity

REFERENCES

Abbas, S., Hassan, S. T., Muhammad, A., & Xia, E. (2021). Effects of energy consumption and ecological footprint on CO_2 emissions: Empirical evidence from Pakistan. *Environment, Development and Sustainability, 23*(9), 13364–13381. DOI: 10.1007/s10668-020-01216-9

Ahmad, M., Zhao, Z. Y., Irfan, M., & Mukeshimana, M. C. (2021). Does economic prosperity lead to environmental sustainability in developing economies? Environmental Kuznets curve theory. *Environmental Science and Pollution Research International, 28*(18), 22588–22601. DOI: 10.1007/s11356-020-12276-9 PMID: 33420933

Alakbarov, N., Mammadova, A., & Hasanli, Y. (2025). Exploring the link between economic growth, energy consumption, and environmental pollution in G20. *Natural Resources Forum, 49*(2), 1445–1461. DOI: 10.1111/1477-8947.12440

Asongu, S., le Roux, S., & Biekpe, N. (2016). Testing the relationships between energy consumption, CO_2 emissions, and economic growth in 24 African countries: A panel ARDL approach. *Environmental Science and Pollution Research International, 23*(7), 6563–6573. DOI: 10.1007/s11356-015-5883-7 PMID: 26635224

Baldacci, E., Clements, B., Gupta, S., & Cui, Q. (2008). Social spending, human capital, and growth in developing countries. *World Development, 36*(8), 1317–1341. DOI: 10.1016/j.worlddev.2007.08.003

Barro, R. J., & Sala-i-Martin, X. (1995). *Economic growth*. McGraw-Hill.

R Bhat, M Gupta, TF Choudhary, and AK Singh (2024) Modelling the Effects of Climatic Variables and Political Instability on the Agricultural Sector in South Asian Countries Building Climate Neutral Economies through Digital Business and Green Skills DOI: DOI: 10.4018/979-8-3693-5673-9.ch001

Chaabouni, S., & Saidi, K. (2017). The dynamic links between carbon dioxide (CO_2) emissions, health spending and GDP growth: A case study for 51 countries. *Environmental Research, 158*, 137–144. DOI: 10.1016/j.envres.2017.05.041 PMID: 28624630

Choudhary, T. F., & Gupta, M. (2023). Analyzing the long-run and short-run impacts of climate change on Wheat and Maize Yield in Western Himalayan Region of India. *Climate Change Economics (Singapore)*. Advance online publication. DOI: 10.1142/S2010007823500197

Choudhary, T. F., Gupta, M., & Mavi, H. K. (2022). Modelling the Relationship between Climate Change and Rice Yield: Evidence from Indian Agriculture. *Indian Journal of Economics and Development*, *18*(2), 495–500.

Deng, Y., Li, M., Zhang, T., & Zhao, Y. (2025). The impact of economic openness on common prosperity: Insights from provincial panel data. *International Review of Economics & Finance*, *98*, 103908. DOI: 10.1016/j.iref.2025.103908

Dollar, D., & Kraay, A. (2004). Trade, growth, and poverty. *Economic Journal (London)*, *114*(493), F22–F49. DOI: 10.1111/j.0013-0133.2004.00186.x

Frankel, J. A., & Romer, D. (1999). Does trade cause growth? *The American Economic Review*, *89*(3), 379–399. DOI: 10.1257/aer.89.3.379

Fritz, M., & Koch, M. (2016). Economic development and prosperity patterns around the world: Structural challenges for a global steady-state economy. *Global Environmental Change*, *38*, 41–48. DOI: 10.1016/j.gloenvcha.2016.02.007

Gimba, O. J., Bekun, F. V., & Gyamfi, B. A. (2023). Towards low carbon and sustainable environment: Does income inequality mitigate ecological footprints in Sub-Saharan Africa? *Environment, Development and Sustainability*, *25*(9), 10425–10445. DOI: 10.1007/s10668-023-03580-8

Gini coefficient: World Bank. (2023). Gini index (World Bank estimate) https://data.worldbank.org/indicator/SI.POV.GINI

Government Effectiveness. World Bank. (2023). Worldwide Governance Indicators: Government Effectiveness https://info.worldbank.org/governance/wgi

Government spending on health and education (% of GDP): World Bank. (2023). Government expenditure on education, total (% of GDP); Current health expenditure (% of GDP). https://data.worldbank.org

Grossman, G. M., & Krueger, A. B. (1995). Economic growth and the environment. *The Quarterly Journal of Economics*, *110*(2), 353–377. DOI: 10.2307/2118443

Hausman, J. A. (1978). Specification tests in econometrics. *Econometrica*, *46*(6), 1251–1271. DOI: 10.2307/1913827

Index, G. I. (GII): United Nations Development Programme. (2023). Gender Inequality Index (GII) https://hdr.undp.org/data-center/thematic-composite-indices/gender-inequality-index

Infante-Amate, J., Gálvez, R. A., Aguilera, E., & González de Molina, M. (2024). Unsustainable prosperity? Decoupling wellbeing, economic growth, and greenhouse gas emissions over the past 150 years. *World Development, 184*, 106754. DOI: 10.1016/j.worlddev.2024.106754

Jackson, T. (2009). *Prosperity without growth: Economics for a finite planet* (1st ed.). Routledge. [e-book], DOI: 10.4324/9781849774338

Kaufmann, D., Kraay, A., & Mastruzzi, M. (2010). *The Worldwide Governance Indicators: Methodology and analytical issues*. World Bank. https://doi.org/DOI: 10.1596/1813-9450-5430

Keswani, S., Sharma, M., Chauhan, N. S., & Bansal, M. (2025). Association among financial development, economic growth, ecological footprint, and carbon emissions in India: A VECM analysis. *Cogent Social Sciences, 11*(1), 2448769. DOI: 10.1080/23311886.2024.2448769

Klasen, S., & Lamanna, F. (2009). The impact of gender inequality in education and employment on economic growth: New evidence for a panel of countries. *Feminist Economics, 15*(3), 91–132. DOI: 10.1080/13545700902893106

Koch, M. (2012). *Capitalism and climate change: Theoretical discussion, historical development and policy responses*. Palgrave Macmillan. DOI: 10.1057/9780230355088

Lau, L.-S., Choong, C.-K., & Eng, Y.-K. (2014). Carbon dioxide emission, institutional quality, and economic growth: Empirical evidence in Malaysia. *Renewable Energy, 68*, 276–281. DOI: 10.1016/j.renene.2014.02.013

Mashrur, F. A. (2025). Foreign direct investment, trade openness, financial development, and economic growth dynamics: Empirical evidence from Bangladesh. *European Journal of Development Studies, 5*(1), 43–51. DOI: 10.24018/ejdevelop.2025.5.1.409

Ngo, Q. D., Phan, V. H., & Le, T. M. (2025). Anticipating prosperity: A systemic analysis of long-term economic trajectories. *Journal of Economic Development, 27*(1), 4–21. DOI: 10.1108/JED-08-2024-0299

Organisation for Economic Co-operation and Development. (2022). Economic Outlook. https://www.oecd.org/economic-outlook/

Ostry, J. D., Berg, A., & Tsangarides, C. G. (2011). Inequality and unsustainable growth: Two sides of the same coin? *IMF Staff Discussion Notes, 11*(08), 1–25. DOI: 10.5089/9781463926564.006

Pastor, J. M., Pérez, F., & Fernández de Guevara, J. (2013). Measuring the local economic impact of universities: An approach that considers uncertainty. *Higher Education*, *65*(5), 539–564. DOI: 10.1007/s10734-012-9562-z

Sanchez-Olmedo, D., Navarro-Pedreño, J., & Rocamora, I. (2025). Bridging the gap: The impact of gender equality on CO_2 emissions across countries. *WORLD (Oakland, Calif.)*, *6*(1), 26. DOI: 10.3390/world6010026

Săvoiu, G., & Manea, D. (2013). Comparing Fixed and Random Effects Models using Hausman Test in a Panel Data Analysis. Theoretical and Applied Economics, 20(6), 5–20. https://rtsa.ro/tras/index.php/tras/article/view/407

Sun, J., & Abruzzian, M. (2025). Technological innovation, trade openness, natural resources, clean energy on environmental sustainability: A competitive assessment between CO_2 emission, ecological footprint, load capacity factor and inverted load capacity factor in BRICS+T. *Frontiers in Environmental Science*, *12*, 1520562. DOI: 10.3389/fenvs.2024.1520562

Trade openness (Exports + Imports as % of GDP): World Bank. (2023). Trade (% of GDP) https://data.worldbank.org/indicator/NE.TRD.GNFS.ZS

Varona, L., & Gonzales, J. R. (2025). Human development, productivity, and economic growth. *Journal of Human Development and Capabilities*, *26*(1), 33–58. DOI: 10.1080/19452829.2024.2439947

World Bank. (2023). GDP per capita (current US$). https://data.worldbank.org

World Bank. (2025). GDP per capita (constant 2015 US$). World Development Indicators https://data.worldbank.org/indicator/NY.GDP.PCAP.KD

Wu, T., & Roche, J. C. (2024). Triple bottom line or trilemma? Global trade-offs between prosperity, inequality, and the environment. *World Development*, *178*, 106595. DOI: 10.1016/j.worlddev.2024.106595

Zhao, T., Liang, X., & Hu, B. (2023). Digital economy, entrepreneurial activity, and common prosperity: Evidence from China. *Journal of Information Economics*, *1*(1), 5. DOI: 10.58567/jie01010005

APPENDICES

Table A1. Descriptive Statistics of Developed Nations

GDP Percapita	Mean	Median	Max	Min	Skewness	Kurtosis	JB	Prob.	Std Dev	Observ.
	10.8343	10.8079	11.8034	9.8634	0.3316	3.1305	3.9253	0.1924	0.4304	195

Source: Author Estimation Software E- Views 12

Table A2. Descriptive Statistics of developing Nations

GDP Per capita	Mean	Median	Max	Min	Skewness	Kurtosis	JB	Prob.	Std Dev	Observ.
	8.7268	8.82863	9.8652	8.7268	6.9984	2.7479	*8.4158*	*0.01487*	*0.6189*	***195***

Table A3. VIF Results for Developed Nations (GDP per Capita Model)

Variable	VIF	1/VIF
GC	4.27	0.234408
HE	2.91	0.3435545
GII	2.70	0.370056
Trade Openness	2.17	0.459884
GE	1.62	0.615751
Mean VIF	2.74	

Source: Author Estimation Software E- Views 12

Interpretation: All VIF values are below the threshold of 5, confirming that multicollinearity is not a significant issue in the model for developed nations.

Table A4. VIF Results for Developing Nations (GDP per Capita Model)

Variable	VIF	1/VIF
GC	1.97	0.508569
HE	1.78	0.561763
GII	1.37	0.732186

continued on following page

Table A4. Continued

Variable	VIF	1/VIF
Trade Openness	1.25	0.802930
GE	1.14	0.879049
Mean VIF	1.51	

Source: Author Estimation Software E- Views 12

Compilation of References

Aare, F., Olorunfemi, O., & Ntor, G. (2024). Legal frameworks for single-use plastic management: Environmental challenges and solutions. *Kampala International University Law Journal*, *6*(1), 63–85. DOI: 10.59568/KIULJ-2024-6-1-04

Abate, T., & Elofsson, K. (2024). Environmental taxation of plastic bags and substitutes: Balancing marine pollution and climate change. *Journal of Environmental Management*, *359*, 120868. DOI: 10.1016/j.jenvman.2024.120868 PMID: 38692024

Abbas, S., Hassan, S. T., Muhammad, A., & Xia, E. (2021). Effects of energy consumption and ecological footprint on CO_2 emissions: Empirical evidence from Pakistan. *Environment, Development and Sustainability*, *23*(9), 13364–13381. DOI: 10.1007/s10668-020-01216-9

Acar, E., Tunca Çalıyurt, K., & Zengin-Karaibrahimoglu, Y. (2021). Does ownership type affect environmental disclosure? *International Journal of Climate Change Strategies and Management*, *13*(2), 120–141. DOI: 10.1108/IJCCSM-02-2020-0016

Adanma, U. M., & Ogunbiyi, E. O.Uwaga Monica AdanmaEmmanuel Olurotimi Ogunbiyi. (2024). A comparative review of global environmental policies for promoting sustainable development and economic growth. *International Journal of Applied Research in Social Sciences*, *6*(5), 954–977. DOI: 10.51594/ijarss.v6i5.1147

Addison, T., Niño-Zarazúa, M., & Pirttilä, J. (2018). Fiscal policy, state building and economic development. *Journal of International Development*, *30*(2), 161–172. DOI: 10.1002/jid.3355

Adeyanju, G., Augustine, T., Volkmann, S., Oyebamiji, U., Ran, S., Osobajo, O., & Otitoju, A. (2021). Effectiveness of intervention on behaviour change against use of non-biodegradable plastic bags: A systematic review. *Discover Sustainability*, *2*(13), 13. Advance online publication. DOI: 10.1007/s43621-021-00015-0

Adula, M., Kant, S., Badi, S., & Kumari, M. (2025). Abusive Work Environment Effect on Female Entrepreneurs' Emotional Wellbeing by Mediation of Social and Moral Values in the Horn of Africa. In *Supporting Psychological and Emotional Wellbeing Among Entrepreneurs* (pp. 1-22). IGI Global Scientific Publishing.

Agrawala, S., Dussaux, D., & Monti, N. (2020). What policies for greening the crisis response and economic recovery?: Lessons learned from past green stimulus measures and implications for the COVID-19 crisis. *OECD Environment Working Papers, No. 164*. DOI: 10.1787/19970900

Ahmad, M., Zhao, Z. Y., Irfan, M., & Mukeshimana, M. C. (2021). Does economic prosperity lead to environmental sustainability in developing economies? Environmental Kuznets curve theory. *Environmental Science and Pollution Research International*, *28*(18), 22588–22601. DOI: 10.1007/s11356-020-12276-9 PMID: 33420933

Ajzen, I. (1991). The theory of planned behavior. *Organizational Behavior and Human Decision Processes*, *50*(2), 179–211. DOI: 10.1016/0749-5978(91)90020-T

Alakbarov, N., Mammadova, A., & Hasanli, Y. (2025). Exploring the link between economic growth, energy consumption, and environmental pollution in G20. *Natural Resources Forum*, *49*(2), 1445–1461. DOI: 10.1111/1477-8947.12440

Aldy, J. E., & Stavins, R. N. (2023). Rolling the dice in the corridors of power: Firm lobbying and carbon pricing policies. *Environmental and Resource Economics*, *86*(3), 425–451. DOI: 10.1007/s10640-023-00789-y

Almström, P., Anderstig, C., & Sundberg, M. (2024). Effects on sectors and regions of a carbon tax increase in Sweden: Analysis with an SCGE model. *The Annals of Regional Science*, *73*(2), 731–756. DOI: 10.1007/s00168-024-01269-y

Anand, V. V., Balakrishnan, R., & Labro, E. (2019). A framework for conducting numerical experiments on cost system design. *Journal of Management Accounting Research*, *31*(1), 41–61. DOI: 10.2308/jmar-52057

Andrades, J., Martinez-Martinez, D., & Larrán, M. (2024). Sustainability reporting, institutional pressures and universities: Evidence from the Spanish setting. *Sustainability Accounting. Management and Policy Journal*, *16*(4), 1045–1071. DOI: 10.1108/SAMPJ-07-2023-0455

Andrei, J., Mieila, P., Popescu, G. H., Nica, E., & Cristina, M. (2016). The impact and determinants of environmental taxation on economic growth communities in Romania. *Energies*, *9*(11), 902. DOI: 10.3390/en9110902

Anguelovski, I., Connolly, J. J., Pearsall, H., Shokry, G., Checker, M., Maantay, J., Gould, K., Lewis, T., Maroko, A., & Roberts, J. T. (2019). Why green "climate gentrification" threatens poor and vulnerable populations. *Proceedings of the National Academy of Sciences of the United States of America, 116*(52), 26139–26143. DOI: 10.1073/pnas.1920490117

Annett, A. (2002). Politics, government size, and fiscal adjustment in industrial countries. IMF Working Paper No. 02/162. https://ssrn.com/abstract=880179

Asante-Darko, D., Dadzie, S. A., Kwarteng, A., Agbodjah, S., & Aryee, T. E. (2024). Influences of Circular Economy Practices and Accounting Innovations on Sustainable Development Goals. *Circular Economy and Sustainability*, *4*(4), 1–34.

Asgari, A., & Asgari, R. (2021). How circular economy transforms business models in a transition towards circular ecosystem: The barriers and incentives. *Sustainable Production and Consumption*, *28*, 566–579. DOI: 10.1016/j.spc.2021.06.020

Ashuro, T., Kant, S., Alemu, Z. K., & Takaro, G. S. (2025). Effect of Tax Solidarity on the Taxpayer's Sense of Civic Duty by Mediation of Tax Morality in the Horn of Africa. In *Modeling and Profiling Taxpayer Behavior and Compliance* (pp. 207–164). IGI Global Scientific Publishing. DOI: 10.4018/979-8-3373-0422-9.ch006

Asongu, S., le Roux, S., & Biekpe, N. (2016). Testing the relationships between energy consumption, CO_2 emissions, and economic growth in 24 African countries: A panel ARDL approach. *Environmental Science and Pollution Research International*, *23*(7), 6563–6573. DOI: 10.1007/s11356-015-5883-7 PMID: 26635224

Auerbach, A. (2019). Fiscal policy. *Blanchard O. e Summers LH (a Cura Di), Evolution or Revolution*, 81–104. DOI: 10.7551/mitpress/11734.003.0010

Australian Government. (2014). *Repeal of the carbon tax*. https://www.australia.gov.au/about-government/how-government-works/repeal-carbon-tax

Babić, Z., & Lučev, J. (2019). Comparative analysis of economic and social policy development in Croatia and Slovenia. *Problemy Polityki Społecznej. Studia i Dyskusje, 47 (4*, 47–71. https://doi.org/doi.org/10.31971/16401808.47.4.2019.3

Baldacci, E., Clements, B., Gupta, S., & Cui, Q. (2008). Social spending, human capital, and growth in developing countries. *World Development*, *36*(8), 1317–1341. DOI: 10.1016/j.worlddev.2007.08.003

Barbier, E. B. (2020). Greening the post-pandemic recovery in the G20. *Environmental and Resource Economics*, *76*(4), 685–703. DOI: 10.1007/s10640-020-00437-w PMID: 32836827

Barro, R. J., & Sala-i-Martin, X. (1995). *Economic growth.* McGraw-Hill.

Bartik, T. J. (2005). Solving the problems of economic development incentives. *Growth and Change, 36*(2), 139–166. DOI: 10.1111/j.1468-2257.2005.00272.x

Beerbaum, D., & Puaschunder, J. M. (2019). A behavioral market places approach to sustainability reporting. *Julia M., A Behavioral Market places Approach to Sustainability Reporting (May 2, 2019).*

Benedek, M. D., & Tieman, A. F. (2021). A post-pandemic assessment of the sustainable development goals. *IMF Staff Discussion Notes No. 2021/003, 21*(3), 6–24. DOI: 10.5089/9781498314909.006

Benesty, J., Chen, J., & Huang, Y. (2008). On the Importance of the Pearson Correlation Coefficient in Noise Reduction. *IEEE Transactions on Audio, Speech, and Language Processing, 16*(4), 4. Advance online publication. DOI: 10.1109/TASL.2008.919072

Bhope, A., Varimani, S., & Manjunath, T. C. (2025). Financial strategies. In *AI Methods for Environmental Protection and Resource Conservation* (Vol. 187, pp. 45–67). Springer., DOI: 10.1007/978-3-031-590XX-X_7

Bibri, S. E., Huang, J., Jagatheesaperumal, S. K., & Krogstie, J. (2024). The synergistic interplay of artificial intelligence and digital twin in environmentally planning sustainable smart cities: A comprehensive systematic review. *Environmental Science and Ecotechnology, 100433*, 100433. Advance online publication. DOI: 10.1016/j.ese.2024.100433

Bisogno, M., Cuadrado-Ballesteros, B., Manes-Rossi, F., & Peña-Miguel, N. (2024). Financial Sustainability and Sustainable Development in Local Governments: Empirical Insights. *Public Performance & Management Review, 47*(3), 784–811. DOI: 10.1080/15309576.2024.2340116

Bocken, N. M., Harsch, A., & Weissbrod, I. (2022). Circular business models for the fastmoving consumer goods industry: Desirability, feasibility, and viability. *Sustainable Production and Consumption, 30*, 799–814. DOI: 10.1016/j.spc.2022.01.012

Boeve, M., & Waal, I. M. (2024). Global Plastic Pollution and the Transition Towards a Circular Economy: Lessons from the EU's Legal Framework on Plastics. *Environmental Policy and Law, 53*(5-6), 461–472. DOI: 10.3233/EPL-239016

Böhringer, C., Fischer, C., & Rosendahl, K. E. (2022). Carbon pricing and global trade. *Journal of Environmental Economics and Management, 45*(3), 123–140. DOI: 10.1016/j.jeem.2022.100000

Bonilla, D., Banister, D., & Nieto, U. S. (2022). Tax or clean technology? Measuring the true effect on carbon emissions mitigation for Sweden and Norway. *Energies*, *15*(11), 3885. Advance online publication. DOI: 10.3390/en15113885

Bowen, G. (2009). Document Analysis as a Qualitative Research Method. Qualitative Research Journal, 9, n. °2, 27-40. http://dx.doi.org/DOI: 10.3316/QRJ0902027

Brazil Ministry of Environment. (2024). *Carbon tax pilot program report 2023*. https://www.gov.br/meioambiente/en/topics/climate-policy

Bureau of Energy Efficiency. (2023). *PAT scheme annual report 2022*. Government of India. https://beeindia.gov.in/content/pat-scheme

Cai, W., Bai, M., & Davey, H. (2022). Implementing environmental protection tax in China: An alternative framework. *Pacific Accounting Review*, *34*(5), 671–690. DOI: 10.1108/PAR-02-2021-0021

Carmichael, R. (2002). Measures of efficiency and effectiveness as indicators of quality: A systems approach. [JIRSEA]. *Journal of Institutional Research South East Asia*, *1*(1), 3–14. https://api.semanticscholar.org/CorpusID:7713535

Castelblanco, G., Narbaev, T., Osei-Kyei, R., Serikbay, D., Mukashev, Y., & Guevara, J. (2025). Pandemic risks in PPPs: Comparative analysis within developing countries. *International Journal of Construction Management*, *25*(4), 456–468. DOI: 10.1080/15623599.2024.2336660

Chaabouni, S., & Saidi, K. (2017). The dynamic links between carbon dioxide (CO_2) emissions, health spending and GDP growth: A case study for 51 countries. *Environmental Research*, *158*, 137–144. DOI: 10.1016/j.envres.2017.05.041 PMID: 28624630

Chandra, G. (2020). Non-monetary intervention to discourage consumption of single-use plastic bags. *Behavioural Public Policy*, *7*(1), 143–156. DOI: 10.1017/bpp.2020.9

Chatfield, S. L. (2020). Recommendations for Secondary Analysis of Qualitative Data. *The Qualitative Report*, *25*(3), 833–842. DOI: 10.46743/2160-3715/2020.4092

Chen, G., Li, J., Sun, Y., Wang, Z., Leeke, G., Moretti, C., Cheng, Z., Wang, Y., Li, N., Mu, L., Li, J., Tao, J., Yan, B., & Hou, L. (2024). Replacing Traditional Plastics with Biodegradable Plastics: Impact on Carbon Emissions. *Engineering (Beijing)*, *32*, 152–162. DOI: 10.1016/j.eng.2023.10.002

Chen, X., Weerathunga, P. R., Nurunnabi, M., Kulathunga, K. M. M. C. B., & Samarathunga, W. H. M. S. (2020). Influences of behavioral intention to engage in revenue collection accounting practices for corporate sustainability: Managerial perspectives from a developing country. *Sustainability (Basel), 12*(13), 5266. DOI: 10.3390/su12135266

Chen, Y., Masron, T. A., & Mai, W. (2024). Role of investor attention and executive green awareness on environmental information disclosure of Chinese high-tech listed companies. *Journal of Environmental Management, 365*, 121552. Advance online publication. DOI: 10.1016/j.jenvman.2024.121552

Chopra, S. S., Senadheera, S. S., Dissanayake, P. D., Withana, P. A., Chib, R., Rhee, J. H., & Ok, Y. S. (2024). Navigating the challenges of environmental, social, and governance (ESG) reporting: The path to broader sustainable development. *Sustainability (Basel), 16*(2), 606. Advance online publication. DOI: 10.3390/su16020606

Choudhary, T. F., & Gupta, M. (2023). Analyzing the long-run and short-run impacts of climate change on Wheat and Maize Yield in Western Himalayan Region of India. *Climate Change Economics (Singapore)*. Advance online publication. DOI: 10.1142/S2010007823500197

Choudhary, T. F., Gupta, M., & Mavi, H. K. (2022). Modelling the Relationship between Climate Change and Rice Yield: Evidence from Indian Agriculture. *Indian Journal of Economics and Development, 18*(2), 495–500.

Chunyu, L., Ali, S. A., Tan, C., Yin, W., Kouser, R., & Gulzar, F. (2022). The Fiscal Hedging and Green Financing: Sustainability Challenges for Developing World. *Frontiers in Environmental Science, 9*. Crossref. DOI: 10.3389/fenvs.2021.807220

Cimpoeru, V.-M. (2012). An empirical study on key indicators of environmental quality: Green budgeting-a catalyst for sustainable economy and a factor for institutional change. *Amfiteatru Economic, 14*(32), 485–498. https://www.amfiteatrueconomic.ro/ArticolEN.aspx?CodArticol=1139

Clube, R. K., & Hazemba, M. (2024). From waste to resource: Demystifying the policy challenges and identifying opportunities for a circular economy in Zambia. *Frontiers in Sustainability, 5*, 1300904. DOI: 10.3389/frsus.2024.1300904

Conti, I., Simioni, C., Varano, G., Brenna, C., Costanzi, E., & Neri, L. (2021). Legislation to limit the environmental plastic and microplastic pollution and their influence on human exposure. *Environmental Pollution, 288*, 117708. DOI: 10.1016/j.envpol.2021.117708 PMID: 34256282

Convery, F., McDonnell, S., & Ferreira, S. (2007). The most popular tax in Europe? Lessons from the Irish plastic bags levy. *Environmental and Resource Economics*, *38*(1), 1–11. DOI: 10.1007/s10640-006-9059-2

Correia, C. R., & Roseland, M. (2022). Addressing negative externalities of urban development: Toward a more sustainable approach. *Urban Science (Basel, Switzerland)*, *6*(2), 38. DOI: 10.3390/urbansci6020038

Costa, F., Frecassetti, S., Rossini, M., & Portioli-Staudacher, A. (2023). Industry 4.0 digital technologies enhancing sustainability: Applications and barriers from the agricultural industry in an emerging economy. *Journal of Cleaner Production*, *408*, 137208. Advance online publication. DOI: 10.1016/j.jclepro.2023.137208

Coutinho, L., & Tsani, S. (2021). Fiscal policy, macroeconomic volatility and the role of institutions under resource abundance. *Handbook of Sustainable Politics and Economics of Natural Resources*, 261–290.

Creswell, J., & Creswell, J. (2018). *Research Design Qualitative, Quantitative, and Mixed Methods Approaches* (5th ed.). SAGE Publications., https://spada.uns.ac.id/pluginfile.php/510378/mod_resource/content/1/creswell.pdf

D'Orazio, P. (2025). Addressing climate risks through fiscal policy in emerging and developing economies: What do we know and what lies ahead? *Energy Research & Social Science*, *119*(2), 103852. Advance online publication. DOI: 10.1016/j.erss.2024.103852

Dabyltayeva, N., & Rakhymzhan, G. (2019). The Green Economy Development Path: Overview of Economic Policy Priorities. *Journal of Security and Sustainability Issues*, *8*(4), 643–651. DOI: 10.9770/jssi.2019.8.4(8)

Dafermos, Y., & Nikolaidi, M. (2019). Fiscal policy and ecological sustainability: A post-Keynesian perspective. In *Frontiers of heterodox macroeconomics* (pp. 277–322). Springer., DOI: 10.1007/978-3-030-23929-9_7

Dafnomilis, I., Chen, H.-H., den Elzen, M., Fragkos, P., Chewpreecha, U., van Soest, H., Fragkiadakis, K., Karkatsoulis, P., Paroussos, L., de Boer, H.-S., Daioglou, V., Edelenbosch, O., Kiss-Dobronyi, B., & van Vuuren, D. P. (2022). Targeted green recovery measures in a post-COVID-19 world enable the energy transition. *Frontiers in Climate*, *4*, 840933. DOI: 10.3389/fclim.2022.840933

Daiyabu, Y. A., Manaf, N. A. A., & Mohamad Hsbollah, H. (2023). Extending the theory of planned behaviour with application to renewable energy investment: The moderating influence of tax incentives. *International Journal of Energy Sector Management*, *17*(2), 333–349. DOI: 10.1108/IJESM-11-2021-0011

Dalevska, N., Khobta, V., Kwilinski, A., & Kravchenko, S. (2019). A model for estimating social and economic indicators of sustainable development. *Entrepreneurship and Sustainability Issues*, *6*(4), 4. Advance online publication. DOI: 10.9770/jesi.2019.6.4(21)

Darrah, T., Herbert, S., & Chambers, T. (2024). A thematic analysis of alcohol and alcohol-related harm across health and social policy in Aotearoa New Zealand. *Australian and New Zealand Journal of Public Health*, *48*(2), 100143. Advance online publication. DOI: 10.1016/j.anzjph.2024.100143

Dasgupta, P., & Srikanth, K. (2021). Achieving the climate goal with intergovernmental transfers to the forestry sector: Insights from the Indian experience. *Climatic Change, 164*(3–4). Crossref. DOI: 10.1007/s10584-021-03016-0

Davis, F. D. (1989). Perceived usefulness, perceived ease of use, and user acceptance of information technology. *Management Information Systems Quarterly*, *13*(3), 319–340. DOI: 10.2307/249008

Dayani, N. W. Y. P., & Budiasih, I. (2024). BEHAVIORAL ACCOUNTING AS A CATALYST IN THE ORGANIZATIONAL TRANSFORMATION PROCESS TOWARD SUSTAINABILITY. *Jurnal Akuntansi dan Keuangan Indonesia, 21*(2), 6.

de l'Économie, M. des Finances et de la Souveraineté industrielle et numérique. (2025, April 13). *France Relance – Le plan de relance économique*. https://www.economie.gouv.fr/plan-de-relance

Delgado, F. J., Freire-González, J., & Presno, M. J. (2022). Environmental taxation in the European Union: Are there common trends? *Economic Analysis and Policy*, *73*, 670–682. DOI: 10.1016/j.eap.2021.12.019

Delmas, M. A., & Burbano, V. C. (2011). The drivers of greenwashing. *California Management Review*, *54*(1), 64–87. DOI: 10.1525/cmr.2011.54.1.64

Deng, Y., Li, M., Zhang, T., & Zhao, Y. (2025). The impact of economic openness on common prosperity: Insights from provincial panel data. *International Review of Economics & Finance*, *98*, 103908. DOI: 10.1016/j.iref.2025.103908

Desalegn, G., & Tangl, A. (2022). Banning Vs Taxing, Reviewing the Potential Opportunities and Challenges of Plastic Products. *Sustainability (Basel)*, *14*(12), 7189. DOI: 10.3390/su14127189

Deserno, L., & Sterk, E. (2024). Resource Taxes as an Instrument to Foster Circularity? Analysis of the Effects of Resource Taxation on Circular Economy Progress in Europe. *Circular Economy and Sustainability*, •••, 1–27.

Dhahri, S., Slimani, S., & Omri, A. (2021). Behavioral entrepreneurship for achieving the sustainable development goals. *Technological Forecasting and Social Paradigm shift, 165*, 120561.

Dikgang, J., & Visser, M. (2012). Behavioural response to plastic bag legislation in Botswana. *The South African Journal of Economics, 80*(1), 123–133. DOI: 10.1111/j.1813-6982.2011.01289.x

DiMaggio, P. J., & Powell, W. W. (2000). The iron cage revisited institutional isomorphism and collective rationality in organizational fields. In *Economics meets sociology in strategic management* (pp. 143–166). Emerald Group Publishing Limited., DOI: 10.1016/S0742-3322(00)17011-1

Dokl, M., Copot, A., Krajnc, D., Fan, Y., Vujanović, A., Aviso, K., Tan, R., Kravanja, Z., & Čuček, L. (2024). Global projections of plastic use, end-of-life fate and potential changes in consumption, reduction, recycling and replacement with bioplastics to 2050. *Sustainable Production and Consumption, 51*, 498–518. DOI: 10.1016/j.spc.2024.09.025

Dollar, D., & Kraay, A. (2004). Trade, growth, and poverty. *Economic Journal (London), 114*(493), F22–F49. DOI: 10.1111/j.0013-0133.2004.00186.x

Drumond, P.Jr, de Castro, R. D., & Seabra, J. A. E. (2021). Impact of tax and tariff incentives on the economic viability of residential photovoltaic systems connected to energy distribution network in Brazil. *Solar Energy, 227*, 3784. Advance online publication. DOI: 10.1016/j.solener.2021.06.034

Dueñas, M., & Mandel, A. (2024). Are EU low-carbon structural funds efficient in reducing emissions? *arXiv Preprint arXiv:2408.01782*. https://doi.org//arXiv.2408 .01782DOI: 10.48550

Du, J., Li, Z., Shi, G., & Wang, B. (2024). Can "environmental protection fee to tax" reduce carbon emissions? Evidence from China. *Finance Research Letters, 62*, 103270. Advance online publication. DOI: 10.1016/j.frl.2024.105184

Dunn, J., Caplan, A., & Bosworth, R. (2014). Measuring the value of plastic and reusable grocery bags. *Journal of Environmental Economics and Policy, 3*(2), 125–147. DOI: 10.1080/21606544.2013.870052

Eckert, S., Karassin, O., & Steinebach, Y. (2024). A policy portfolio approach to plastics throughout their life cycle: Supranational and national regulation in the European Union. *Environmental Policy and Governance, 34*(4), 427–441. DOI: 10.1002/eet.2092

EIA. (2024). *U.S. energy outlook 2023*. U.S. Energy Information Administration. https://www.eia.gov/outlooks/aeo/

Eko sklad. (2024). *Subvencije in ugodni krediti za okolju prijazne naložbe*. https://www.ekosklad.si/

Elkington, J. (1997). *Cannibals with Forks: The Triple Bottom Line of 21st Century Business*. Capstone.

Elroi, H., Zbigniew, G., Agnieszka, W. C., & Piotr, S. (2023). Enhancing waste resource efficiency: Circular economy for sustainability and energy conversion. *Frontiers in Environmental Science*, *11*, 1303792. DOI: 10.3389/fenvs.2023.1303792

Elsässer, J. P., Hickmann, T., Jinnah, S., Oberthür, S., & Van de Graaf, T. (2022). Institutional interplay in global environmental governance: Lessons learned and future research. *International Environmental Agreement: Politics, Law and Economics*, *22*(2), 373–391. DOI: 10.1007/s10784-022-09569-4

Enikolopov, R., & Zhuravskaya, E. V. (2003). Decentralization and Political Institutions. SSRN *Electronic Journal*. Crossref. DOI: 10.2139/ssrn.408060

Equinor. (2023). Sustainability Report 2022. Equinor ASA. https://www.equinor.com/

Equinor. (2025). *Sustainability report 2024*. https://www.equinor.com/en/sustainability.html

Esen, Ö., Yıldırım, D. Ç., & Yıldırım, S. (2021). Pollute less or tax more? Asymmetries in the EU environmental taxes–Ecological balance nexus. *Environmental Impact Assessment Review*, *91*, 106662. Advance online publication. DOI: 10.1016/j.eiar.2021.106662

Eunomia (2022). *Circular Taxation - A policy approach to reduce resource use and accelerate the transition to a circular economy*. European Environmental Bureau (EEB) Final Report. Retrieved from Link

European Commission. (2019). *The European Green Deal*. https://commission.europa.eu/strategy-and-policy/priorities-2019-2024/european-green-deal_en

European Commission. (2020). EU Taxonomy Regulation. [EU]. *Regulation*, *2020*(852). https://eur-lex.europa.eu/eli/reg/2020/852/oj/eng

European Commission. (2021a). *National energy and climate plans*. https://commission.europa.eu/energy-climate-change-environment/implementation-eu-countries/energy-and-climate-governance-and-reporting/national-energy-and-climate-plans_en

European Commission. (2021b). Recovery and Resilience Facility Regulation. [EU]. *Regulation, 2021*(241). https://eur-lex.europa.eu/eli/reg/2021/241/oj/eng

European Commission. (2023a). *CBAM*. https://ec.europa.eu/clima/policies/cbam_en

European Commission. (2023b). *Corporate Sustainability Reporting Directive (CSRD)*. https://finance.ec.europa.eu/capital-markets-union-and-financial-markets/company-reporting-and-auditing/company-reporting/corporate-sustainability-reporting_en

European Commission. Directorate General for Environment, Sherrington, C., Watson, S., Marsh, P. and Bradley, C. (2022). Scoping study to assess the feasibility of further EU measures on waste prevention and implementation of the Plastic Bags Directive. Part II, Implementation of Plastic Bags Directive, Publications Office of the European Union https://data.europa.eu/doi/10.2779/304791

European Council. (2025). *Fit for 55*. https://www.consilium.europa.eu/en/policies/fit-for-55/

European Economic and Social Committee. (2016). *The Circular Economy: Beneficial for All.* Employer's Group Report. Retrieved from Link

EUROSTAT (2024). Consumption of lightweight plastic carrier bags by their wall thickness. https://doi.org/DOI: 10.2908/env_waspcb

Eurostat. (2025). *Government expenditure by function – COFOG. Statistics Explained*. https://ec.europa.eu/eurostat/statistics-explained/index.php?title=Government_expenditure_by_function_%E2%80%93_COFOG

Eyraud, L., Clements, B., & Wane, A. (2013). Green investment: Trends and determinants. *Energy Policy*, *60*, 852–865. DOI: 10.1016/j.enpol.2013.04.039

Famulska, T., Kaczmarzyk, J., & Grząba-Włoszek, M. (2022). Environmental taxes in the member states of the European Union—Trends in energy taxes. *Energies*, *15*(22), 8718. Advance online publication. DOI: 10.3390/en15228718

Fatas, A., & Mihov, I. (2003). The Case for Restricting Fiscal Policy Discretion. *The Quarterly Journal of Economics, 118*(4), 1419–1447. Crossref. DOI: 10.1162/003355303322552838

Fayshal, M. (2024). Current practices of plastic waste management, environmental impacts, and potential alternatives for reducing pollution and improving management. *Heliyon*, *10*(23), e40838. DOI: 10.1016/j.heliyon.2024.e40838 PMID: 39687131

Fowowe, B. (2013). Do Fiscal incentives promote investment?: Empirical evidence from Nigeria. *Journal of Developing Areas*, *47*(2), 17–35. DOI: 10.1353/jda.2013.0029

Frankel, J. A., & Romer, D. (1999). Does trade cause growth? *The American Economic Review*, *89*(3), 379–399. DOI: 10.1257/aer.89.3.379

Frederick, S., Loewenstein, G., & O'Donoghue, T. (2002). Time discounting and time preference: A critical review. *Journal of Economic Literature*, *40*(2), 351–401. DOI: 10.1257/jel.40.2.351

Frey, M., & Cifuentes, L. (2024). Goodbye Plastic Bags? Lessons from the Shopping Plastic Bag Ban in Chile. *Sustainability (Basel)*, *16*(9), 3690. DOI: 10.3390/su16093690

Fritz, M., & Koch, M. (2016). Economic development and prosperity patterns around the world: Structural challenges for a global steady-state economy. *Global Environmental Change*, *38*, 41–48. DOI: 10.1016/j.gloenvcha.2016.02.007

Fu, C., Lu, L., & Pirabi, M. (2024). *Advancing green finance: A review of climate change and decarbonization*. Digital Economy and Sustainable Development., DOI: 10.1007/s44265-023-00026-x

FURS. (2024). *Financial Administration of the Republic of Slovenia*. https://www.fu.gov.si/en/

García-Marín, L., & Rentería, M. (2024). Fighting plastic pollution with a circular economy roadmap and strategy: Addressed to the United Nations Environment Programme. *Journal of Science Policy & Governance*, *24*(1). Advance online publication. DOI: 10.38126/JSPG240107

Gazzani, F. (2021). Transition to social-ecological sustainability using the environmental fiscal reform. *International Journal of Social Economics*, *48*(5), 675–692. Advance online publication. DOI: 10.1108/IJSE-09-2020-0656

Gillingham, K., & Palmer, K. (2014). Bridging the energy efficiency gap: Policy insights from economic theory and empirical evidence. *Review of Environmental Economics and Policy*, *8*(1), 18–38. DOI: 10.1093/reep/ret021

Gimba, O. J., Bekun, F. V., & Gyamfi, B. A. (2023). Towards low carbon and sustainable environment: Does income inequality mitigate ecological footprints in Sub-Saharan Africa? *Environment, Development and Sustainability*, *25*(9), 10425–10445. DOI: 10.1007/s10668-023-03580-8

Gini coefficient: World Bank. (2023). Gini index (World Bank estimate) https://data.worldbank.org/indicator/SI.POV.GINI

Gómez, J. (2021). El impuesto sobre envases de plástico no reutilizables y outras medidas fiscales en el anteproyecto de ley de resíduos. Cronica Tributaria. Creative Commons Reconocimiento-NoComercial 4.0 Internacional, 178, 11-60. https://repositorio.comillas.edu/rest/bitstreams/438976/retrieve

Gómez, I., & Escobar, A. (2022). The dilemma of plastic bags and their substitutes: A review on LCA studies. *Sustainable Production and Consumption*, *30*, 107–116. DOI: 10.1016/j.spc.2021.11.021

Gonzalez, C. C., & Peña-Vinces, J. (2023). A framework for a green accounting system: Exploratory study in a developing country context, Colombia. *Environment, Development and Sustainability*, *25*(9), 9517–9541. DOI: 10.1007/s10668-022-02445-w

Goulder, L. H., & Parry, I. W. (2008). Instrument choice in environmental policy. *Review of Environmental Economics and Policy*, *2*(2), 152–174. DOI: 10.1093/reep/ren005

Government Effectiveness. World Bank. (2023). Worldwide Governance Indicators: Government Effectiveness https://info.worldbank.org/governance/wgi

Government of Canada. (2023). Carbon pricing: How it works (2023 update). Environment and Climate Change Canada. https://www.canada.ca/

Government of Canada. (2025). *Carbon pricing impact report*. https://www.canada.ca/en/environment-climate-change/services/climate-change/pricing-pollution-how-it-will-work.html

Government of Canada. (2025, March 10). *ecoENERGY for Renewable Power*. https://natural-resources.canada.ca/corporate/planning-reporting/departmental-results-reports/departmental-performance-reports-2015%E2%80%9316/ecoenergy-renewable-power

Government of India. (2023). *Trade and climate statement*. Ministry of Commerce. https://www.commerce.gov.in/trade-climate-statement

Government of Norway. (2023). Climate policy and use of carbon tax revenues—2023 update. Royal Norwegian Ministry of Climate and Environment. https://www.regjeringen.no/

Government of Norway. (2025). *Climate policy and carbon tax revenue use*. https://www.regjeringen.no/en/topics/climate-and-environment/climate/climate-policy/id2006123/

Government of Sweden. (2023). Sweden's carbon tax and climate policy—overview (2023 update). Government Offices of Sweden. https://www.government.se/

Government of Sweden. (2025). *Climate policy framework*. https://www.government.se/topics/climate-and-environment/climate-policy

Government spending on health and education (% of GDP): World Bank. (2023). Government expenditure on education, total (% of GDP); Current health expenditure (% of GDP). https://data.worldbank.org

Grafström, J., & Aasma, S. (2021). Breaking circular economy barriers. *Journal of Cleaner Production*, *292*, 126002. DOI: 10.1016/j.jclepro.2021.126002

Green Power Denmark. (2025, February 20). *Fakta om energispareordningen*. https://greenpowerdenmark.dk/udgivelser/fakta-om-energispareordningen

Greenpeace. (2024). *Shell's tax avoidance and environmental impact*. https://www.greenpeace.org/international/story/60545/shell-tax-avoidance-environmental-impact/

GRI. (2025). *Global Reporting Initiative standards*. https://www.globalreporting.org/standards/

Grossman, G. M., & Krueger, A. B. (1995). Economic growth and the environment. *The Quarterly Journal of Economics*, *110*(2), 353–377. DOI: 10.2307/2118443

Grubb, M., Jordan, N. D., Hertwich, E., Neuhoff, K., Das, K., Bandyopadhyay, K. R., van Asselt, H., Sato, M., Wang, R., Pizer, W. A., & Oh, H. (2022). Carbon leakage, consumption, and trade. *Annual Review of Environment and Resources*, *47*, 753–795. DOI: 10.1146/annurev-environ-120820-053625

Guikema, A. J. (2025, February 11). *German Packaging Act (VerpackG): A 2025 Guide to International Packaging Laws (Part 1)*. Sustainable-Markets.com. Retrieved from Link

H&M Group. (2023). Sustainability Disclosure 2023. H & M Hennes & Mauritz AB. https://hmgroup.com/

H&M Group. (2025).. . *Sustainability Report*, *2024*, •••. https://hmgroup.com/sustainability/sustainability-reporting/

Hamid, R. S. (2024). Behavioral Accounting: Evaluating Policy and Academic Support Influence on Sustainable Green Mining Practices. *Jurnal Kajian Akuntansi*, *8*(1), 94–120. DOI: 10.33603/jka.v1i1.9554

Hanley, N. (2021). Economic incentives for sustainability. *Environmental Economics Journal*, *12*(4), 89–104. DOI: 10.1007/s10640-021-00567-8

Harris, J. M. (2013). Green Keynesianism: Beyond standard growth paradigms. *Working Paper 13-02*. DOI: 10.22004/ag.econ.179111

Harrison, M. T., Cullen, B. R., Mayberry, D. E., Cowie, A. L., Bilotto, F., Badgery, W. B., Liu, K., Davison, T., Christie, K. M., Muleke, A., & Eckard, R. J. (2021). Carbon myopia: The urgent need for integrated social, economic and environmental action in the livestock sector. *Global Change Biology*, *27*(22), 5726–5761. Advance online publication. DOI: 10.1111/gcb.15816

Hart, J., Adams, K., Giesekam, J., Tingley, D. D., & Pomponi, F. (2019). Barriers and drivers in a circular economy: The case of the built environment. *Procedia CIRP*, *80*, 619–624. DOI: 10.1016/j.procir.2018.12.015

Hauke, J., & Kossowski, T. (2011). Comparison of Values of Pearson's and Spearman's Correlation Coefficients on the Same Sets of Data. *Quaestiones Geographicae*, *30*(2), 2. Advance online publication. DOI: 10.2478/v10117-011-0021-1

Hausman, J. A. (1978). Specification tests in econometrics. *Econometrica*, *46*(6), 1251–1271. DOI: 10.2307/1913827

Hikmah, H., Adi, P. H., Supramono, S., & Damayanti, T. W. (2021). The nexus among attitude, social norms, intention to comply, financial performance, mental accounting and tax compliance behavior. *Asian Market place and Financial Review*, *11*(12), 938.

His Majesty's Revenue and Customs. (2021). *Introduction of Plastic Packaging Tax from April 2022*. Retrieved from Link

Holmberg, K., & Persson, S. (2023). Keep plastics on a tight leash: Swedish public opinion on plastic policies. *Environmental Science & Policy*, *141*, 109–116. DOI: 10.1016/j.envsci.2023.01.005

Hopewell, J., Dvorak, R., & Kosior, E. (2009). Plastics recycling: Challenges and opportunities. *Philosophical Transactions of the Royal Society of London. Series B, Biological Sciences*, *364*(1526), 2115–2126. DOI: 10.1098/rstb.2008.0311 PMID: 19528059

Houser, T., Mohan, S., & Heilmayr, R. (2009). *A green recovery? Assessing US economic stimulus and the prospects for international coordination*. Peterson Institute for International Economics., https://www.piie.com/publications/policy-briefs/green-recovery-assessing-us-economic-stimulus-and-prospects

Hu, S., Wang, A., & Du, K. (2023). Environmental tax reform and greenwashing: Evidence from Chinese listed companies. *Energy Economics*, *124*, 106873. Advance online publication. DOI: 10.1016/j.eneco.2023.106873

Ichigo. (2025, March 11). *About Japan's Feed-In Tariff (FIT)*. https://www.ichigo-green.co.jp/en/operation/purchase/

IEA. (2021). Denmark 2021: Energy Policy Review. International Energy Agency. https://www.iea.org/

IEA. (2024). *Energy efficiency report*. International Energy Agency. https://www.iea.org/reports/energy-efficiency-2024

Iheukwumere, S., Nkwocha, K., & Umeh, P. (2020). A Look at Plastic Bags and Alternatives. *Journal of Geography Meteorology and Environment*, *3*(1), 121–134. https://journals.unizik.edu.ng/index.php/jgme

Ihsan, A., Hureem, U., & Adil, S. (2021). Estimating the Financing Required to Fulfill the Education Targets Set by Sustainable Development Goals (SDGs): A Sample Study of Punjab, Pakistan. *Audit and Accounting Review*, *1*(1), 82–97. DOI: 10.32350/aar.11.05

IMF. (2025). *Fiscal policies for sustainability*. International Monetary Fund. https://www.imf.org/en/Publications/fiscal-monitor

Index, G. I. (GII): United Nations Development Programme. (2023). Gender Inequality Index (GII) https://hdr.undp.org/data-center/thematic-composite-indices/gender-inequality-index

Indriastuti, M., & Mutamimah, M. (2023). Green accounting as well as sustainable performance of micro, small, and medium enterprises: The role of financial performance as mediation. *The Indonesian Journal of Accounting Investigation*, *26*(2), 249–272.

Infante-Amate, J., Gálvez, R. A., Aguilera, E., & González de Molina, M. (2024). Unsustainable prosperity? Decoupling wellbeing, economic growth, and greenhouse gas emissions over the past 150 years. *World Development*, *184*, 106754. DOI: 10.1016/j.worlddev.2024.106754

International Energy Agency. (2023). *France's "MaPrimeRénov" Programme.* https://www.iea.org/policies/17749-frances-maprimerenov-programme

International Monetary Fund. (2016, April 21). *Leaders set landmark global goals for pricing carbon pollution.* https://www.imf.org

IRS. (2023). *Clean energy tax credit guidelines.* U.S. Internal Revenue Service. https://www.irs.gov/credits-deductions/renewable-electricity-production-tax-credit-information

Izzo, T., Russo, A., & Risaliti, G. (2025). Integrated reporting, stakeholders' perspective and sustainable disclosure: Systematic insights from empirical research. *Corporate Social Responsibility and Environmental Management.* ideas.repec.org+4dokumen.pub+4journals.indexcopernicus.com+4DOI: 10.1002/csr.3212

Jackson, A. (2023). *The Circular Built Environment Playbook.* World Green Building Council. Retrieved from Link

Jackson, T. (2009). *Prosperity without growth: Economics for a finite planet* (1st ed.). Routledge. [e-book], DOI: 10.4324/9781849774338

Jiang, X., Li, G., & Fan, X. (2023). Environmental protection fee-to-tax and corporate environmental social responsibility: A test based on corporate life cycle theory. *Sustainability (Basel), 15*(3), 2128. Advance online publication. DOI: 10.3390/su15032128

Johnson, H., Keane, K., McGillivray, L., Akhtar-Khavari, A., Chambers, L., Barner-Kowollik, C., Lauchs, M., & Blinco, J. (2025). Reforming plastic packaging regulation: Outcomes from stakeholder interviews and regulatory analysis. *Sustainable Production and Consumption, 54*, 52–63. DOI: 10.1016/j.spc.2024.12.017

Kahneman, D., & Tversky, A. (1979). Prospect theory: An analysis of decision under risk. *Econometrica, 47*(2), 263–291. DOI: 10.2307/1914185

Kant, S., Niguse, T., Adula, M., & Terefe, A. (2025). Sustainable Finance's Effect on the Green Economy by the Mediation of Corporate Governance in the Horn of Africa. In *Behavioral Finance and AI Tools for Sustainability* (pp. 301–320). IGI Global Scientific Publishing. DOI: 10.4018/979-8-3693-9684-1.ch012

Kasidoni, M., Moustakas, K., & Malamis, D. (2015). The existing situation and challenges regarding the use of plastic carrier bags in Europe. *Waste Management & Research, 33*(5), 419–428. DOI: 10.1177/0734242X15577858 PMID: 25827845

Kasznik, D., & Łapniewska, Z. (2023). The end of plastic? The EU's directive on single-use plastics and its implementation in Poland. *Environmental Science & Policy, 145*, 151–163. DOI: 10.1016/j.envsci.2023.04.005

Kaufmann, D., Kraay, A., & Mastruzzi, M. (2010). *The Worldwide Governance Indicators: Methodology and analytical issues*. World Bank. https://doi.org/DOI: 10.1596/1813-9450-5430

Kedzierski, M., Frère, D., Le Maguer, G., & Bruzaud, S. (2020). Why is there plastic packaging in the natural environment? Understanding the roots of our individual plastic waste management behaviours. *The Science of the Total Environment, 740*, 139985. DOI: 10.1016/j.scitotenv.2020.139985 PMID: 32563872

Keita, K., & Turcu, C. (2022). Promoting counter-cyclical fiscal policy: Fiscal rules versus institutions. *Comparative Economic Studies, 1*. Advance online publication. DOI: 10.1057/s41294-022-00197-0 PMID: 36408198

Kelling, N. K., Sauer, P. C., Gold, S., & Seuring, S. (2021). The role of institutional uncertainty for social sustainability of companies and supply chains. *Journal of Business Ethics, 173*(4), 813–833. DOI: 10.1007/s10551-020-04423-6

Keswani, S., Sharma, M., Chauhan, N. S., & Bansal, M. (2025). Association among financial development, economic growth, ecological footprint, and carbon emissions in India: A VECM analysis. *Cogent Social Sciences, 11*(1), 2448769. DOI: 10.1080/23311886.2024.2448769

Khan, S. A. R., Sheikh, A. A., & Ahmad, Z. (2023). Developing the interassociation among green employee behavior, tax avoidance, green capability, as well as sustainable performance of SMEs through corporate social responsibility. *Journal of Cleaner Production, 419*, 138240. DOI: 10.1016/j.jclepro.2023.138236

Kim, H. (2025). A real-time lifecycle analysis model with digital twin and novel control method for enhancing the environmental performance of electric/hybrid propulsion ships. *Ocean Engineering, 292*, 114215. Advance online publication. DOI: 10.1016/j.oceaneng.2025.121195

Kirchherr, J., Piscicelli, L., Bour, R., Kostense-Smit, E., Muller, J., Huibrechtse-Truijens, A., & Hekkert, M. (2018). Barriers to the Circular Economy: Evidence From the European Union (EU). *Ecological Economics, 150*, 264–272. DOI: 10.1016/j.ecolecon.2018.04.028

Klasen, S., & Lamanna, F. (2009). The impact of gender inequality in education and employment on economic growth: New evidence for a panel of countries. *Feminist Economics, 15*(3), 91–132. DOI: 10.1080/13545700902893106

Kliskey, A., Williams, P., Griffith, D. L., Dale, V. H., Schelly, C., Marshall, A.-M., Gagnon, V. S., Eaton, W. M., & Floress, K. (2021). Thinking big and thinking small: A conceptual framework for best practices in community and stakeholder engagement in food, energy, and water systems. *Sustainability (Basel), 13*(4), 2160. Advance online publication. DOI: 10.3390/su13042160

Knox, B. D. (2020). Semantic processing theory could help explain the effectiveness of creativity incentives: A numerical experiment. *Journal of Management Accounting Research, 32*(3), 155–178. DOI: 10.2308/jmar-18-051

Koch, M. (2012). *Capitalism and climate change: Theoretical discussion, historical development and policy responses.* Palgrave Macmillan. DOI: 10.1057/9780230355088

Köppl, A., & Schratzenstaller, M. (2024). Macroeconomic effects of green recovery programs. *Eurasian Economic Review, 14*(1), 61–86. DOI: 10.1007/s40822-023-00250-y

Kosonen, K., & Nicodeme, G. (2009). The role of fiscal instruments in environmental policy. *CESifo Working Paper Series No. 2719.* DOI: 10.2139/ssrn.1437501

Kotnik, Ž., Klun, M., & Lah, L. M. (2024). Budget financing of sustainable development goals: The case of Slovenia. In *Modern Concepts and Practices of Climate Finance* (pp. 253–280). IGI Global., DOI: 10.4018/979-8-3693-2117-1.ch011

Kotnik, Ž., Maja, K., & Škulj, D. (2014). The effect of taxation on greenhouse gas emissions. *Transylvanian Review of Administrative Sciences, 10*(43), 43. https://rtsa.ro/tras/index.php/tras/article/view/407

Kotnik, Ž., Umek, L., Kovač, P., Stanimirović, D., & Vintar, M. (2020). Analysis of the key factors for successful public policy implementation: A qualitative study in Slovenia. *DANUBE, 11*(2), 2. Advance online publication. DOI: 10.2478/danb-2020-0007

Kraft, M. E., & Furlong, S. R. (2007). *Public policy: Politics, analysis, and alternatives.* CQ Press., https://questanbridge.com/wp-content/uploads/2024/11/Public-policy_-politics-analysis-and-alternatives.pdfhttps://questanbridge.com/wp-content/uploads/2024/11/Public-policy_-politics-analysis-and-alternatives.pdf

Kumar, R., & Sharma, A. (2021). Energy efficiency in Indian cement industry: The role of PAT scheme. *Journal of Cleaner Production, 312*, 127689. DOI: 10.1016/j.jclepro.2021.127689

Kurbatova, T., Sotnyk, I., Prokopenko, O., Bashynska, I., & Pysmenna, U. (2023). Improving the feed-in tariff policy for renewable energy promotion in Ukraine's households. *Energies, 16*(19), 6773. Advance online publication. DOI: 10.3390/en16196773

Lange, F., & Weerdt, L. (2021). Reducing Plastic Bag Use Through Prosocial Incentives. *Sustainability (Basel), 13*(5), 2421. DOI: 10.3390/su13052421

Lau, L.-S., Choong, C.-K., & Eng, Y.-K. (2014). Carbon dioxide emission, institutional quality, and economic growth: Empirical evidence in Malaysia. *Renewable Energy, 68*, 276–281. DOI: 10.1016/j.renene.2014.02.013

Lavigne, R. (2006). The Institutional and Political Determinants of Fiscal Adjustment. *Bank of Canada Staff Working Paper*. DOI: 10.34989/swp-2006-1

Lehner, O. M., Harrer, T., Silvola, H., & Weber, O. (2023). *The Routledge handbook of green finance* (1st ed.). Routledge., DOI: 10.4324/9781003345497

Liang, H., Li, G., Zhang, W., & Chen, Z. (2022). The impact of green innovation on enterprise performance: The regulatory role of government grants. *Sustainability (Basel), 14*(20), 13550. DOI: 10.3390/su142013550

Li, B., Lui, J., & Zheng, X. (2022). The Environmental Impact of Plastic Grocery Bags and Their Alternatives. *IOP Conference Series. Earth and Environmental Science, 1011*(1), 012050. DOI: 10.1088/1755-1315/1011/1/012050

Lin, B., & Zhou, Y. (2021). Does fiscal decentralization improve energy and environmental performance? New perspective on vertical fiscal imbalance. *Applied Energy, 302*, 117495. DOI: 10.1016/j.apenergy.2021.117495

Lin, B., & Zhu, J. (2019). Fiscal spending and green economic growth: Evidence from China. *Energy Economics, 83*, 264–271. DOI: 10.1016/j.eneco.2019.07.010

Li, Y., Al-Sulaiti, K., Dongling, W., Abbas, J., & Al-Sulaiti, I. (2022). Tax avoidance culture and employees' behavior influence sustainable business performance: The moderating role of corporate social responsibility. *Frontiers in Revenue collection. Science, 10*, 964410.

Lledó, V., & Poplawski-Ribeiro, M. (2013). Fiscal policy implementation in sub-Saharan Africa. *World Development, 46*, 79–91. DOI: 10.1016/j.worlddev.2013.01.030

Losa, R. (2025). Public policies on circular economy: A systematic review. *Ecological Economics, 228*, 108452. DOI: 10.1016/j.ecolecon.2024.108452

Lu, C., Tong, Q., & Liu, X. (2010). The impacts of carbon tax and complementary policies on Chinese economy. *Energy Policy*, *38*(11), 7278–7285. DOI: 10.1016/j.enpol.2010.07.055

Luís, S., Roseta-Palma, C., Matos, M., Lima, M., & Sousa, C. (2020). Psychosocial and economic impacts of a charge in lightweight plastic carrier bags in Portugal: Keep calm and carry on? *Resources, Conservation and Recycling*, *161*, 104962. DOI: 10.1016/j.resconrec.2020.104962

Lutfi, A., Al-Hiyari, A., Elshaer, I. A., Alrawad, M., & Almaiah, M. A. (2024). Green environmental management system and environmental performance: Results from PLS-SEM and fsQCA. *Sustainable Futures : An Applied Journal of Technology, Environment and Society*, *8*, 100276. Advance online publication. DOI: 10.1016/j.sftr.2024.100276

Lutsyk, A. (2021). Substantiation of priority of achieving the goals of Sustainable Development (SDG) in the implementation of fiscal policy. *World of Finance*, *1*(66), 89–101. DOI: 10.35774/sf2021.01.089

Lyeonov, S., Pimonenko, T., Bilan, Y., Štreimikienė, D., & Mentel, G. (2019). Assessment of green investments' impact on sustainable development: Linking gross domestic product per capita, greenhouse gas emissions and renewable energy. *Energies*, *12*(20), 3891. DOI: 10.3390/en12203891

Makhfudhah, N. I. N., & Rasyid, M. (2025). Assessing the Effectiveness of Fiscal Incentives in Promoting Green Investments: A Stochastic Frontier Analysis (SFA) Approach. *KnE Social Sciences*, *10*(5), 196–210. Crossref. DOI: 10.18502/kss.v10i5.18114

Ma, L., Zheng, B., Zhang, M., Zhu, X., & Wu, J. (2023). Research on Green Inclusive Finance to Promote Rural Revitalization under the Goals of Carbon Peaking and Carbon Neutrality—Take Heilongjiang Province as an Example. *Academic Journal of Business & Management*, *5*(9). Advance online publication. DOI: 10.25236/AJBM.2023.050905

Mardones, C., & Ortega, J. (2023). The individual and combined impact of environmental taxes in Chile: A flexible computable general equilibrium analysis. *Journal of Environmental Management*, *325*(Pt A), 116508. DOI: 10.1016/j.jenvman.2022.116508

Martinho, G., Balaia, N., & Pires, A. (2017). The Portuguese plastic carrier bag tax: The effects on consumers' behavior. *Waste Management (New York, N.Y.)*, *61*, 3–12. DOI: 10.1016/j.wasman.2017.01.023 PMID: 28131637

Martynenko, V. (2023). Strategic aspects of financial support for Sustainable Development Goals: The regional dimension. *Economy, Finances, Management. Topical Issues of Science and Practice, 3*(65). Advance online publication. DOI: 10.37128/2411-4413-2023-3

Mashrur, F. A. (2025). Foreign direct investment, trade openness, financial development, and economic growth dynamics: Empirical evidence from Bangladesh. *European Journal of Development Studies, 5*(1), 43–51. DOI: 10.24018/ejdevelop.2025.5.1.409

Masoud, N. (2024). Integrating theories for insight: Corporate governance and environmental disclosure practices in the UAE. *Corporate Governance (Bradford)*. Advance online publication. DOI: 10.1108/CG-03-2024-0168

Mattina, T. D., & Gunnarsson, V. (2007). Budget rigidity and expenditure efficiency in Slovenia (June 2007). *IMF Working Paper No. 07/131*. https://ssrn.com/abstract=995631 DOI: 10.5089/9781451866957.001

Mehling, M. A., van Asselt, H., Das, K., & Droege, S. (2022). Designing border carbon adjustments for enhanced climate action. *The American Journal of International Law, 116*(4), 763–810. DOI: 10.1017/ajil.2022.46

Mentis, C., Maroulis, G., Latinopoulos, D., & Kostas, B. (2022). The effects of environmental information provision on plastic bag use and marine environment status in the context of the environmental levy in Greece. *Environment, Development and Sustainability*. Advance online publication. DOI: 10.1007/s10668-022-02465-6 PMID: 35729922

Merlo, A. L., Mendonça, D. S., Santos, J., Carvalho, S. T., Guerra, R., & Brandão, D. (2025). Blockchain for the carbon market: A literature review. *Discover Environment, 3*(1), 1–21. DOI: 10.1007/s44274-025-00260-4

Meshack, A., Orji, M. G., Nworie, G. O., & Aggreh, M. S. (2022). Achieving sustainable development agenda of 2030: The role of accountants. *Britain International of Humanities and Social Sciences (BIoHS). Journal, 4*(3), 493–556.

MF. (2024). *Ministry of Finance*. https://www.gov.si/drzavni-organi/ministrstva/ministrstvo-za-finance/

Milbreta, U., Milich, L., Andze, L., & Gusca, J. (2025). Some Countries Can Say "No!" to Single-Use Plastics, Others Cannot: Why Do Seemingly Similar Policies Have Different Outcomes? *Journal of Sustainability Research, 7*(1), e250004. DOI: 10.20900/jsr20250004

Milios, L. (2018). Advancing to a Circular Economy: Three essential ingredients for a comprehensive policy mix. *Sustainability Science*, *13*(3), 861–878. DOI: 10.1007/s11625-017-0502-9 PMID: 30147792

Milios, L. (2021). Towards a circular economy taxation framework: Expectations and challenges of implementation. *Circular Economy and Sustainability*, *1*(4), 737–756. DOI: 10.1007/s43615-020-00002-z

Miller, T., Durlik, I., Kostecka, E., Łobodzińska, A., & Matuszak, M. (2024). The emerging role of artificial intelligence in enhancing energy efficiency and reducing greenhouse gas emissions in transport systems. *Energies*, *17*(24), 6271. Advance online publication. DOI: 10.3390/en17246271

Milne, J. E. (2024). Environmental taxation and ESG: Silent partners. In *Sustainable Finances and the Law: Between Public and Private Solutions* (pp. 253–279). Springer Nature Switzerland. DOI: 10.1007/978-3-031-49460-4_11

Miszczak, K., Krivins, A., & Kaze, V. (2024). Challenges and drivers of green and sustainable spatial development: A case study of Lower Silesia and Latvia. *Journal of Entrepreneurship & Sustainability Issues*, *12*(2), 85–98. DOI: 10.9770/b7283449476

Mondal, S., & Mondal, H. (2017). Value of r (2) in statistical analysis by Pearson correlation coefficient. *Journal of Clinical and Diagnostic Research : JCDR*, *11*(11), CL01. DOI: 10.7860/JCDR/2017/29763.10812

Morris, A. (2022). *Equity in U.S. energy policy*. Brookings Institution Report. https://www.brookings.edu/research/equity-in-u-s-energy-policy/

Mpofu, F. Y. (2022). Green taxes in Africa: Opportunities and challenges for environmental protection, sustainability, and the attainment of sustainable development goals. *Sustainability (Basel)*, *14*(3), 1234. DOI: 10.3390/su141610239

Munteanu, I., Ionescu-Feleagă, L., & Ionescu, B. . (2024). Financial Strategies for Sustainability: Examining the Circular Economy Perspective. *Sustainability (Basel)*, *16*(20), 8942. DOI: 10.3390/su16208942

Muposhi, A., Mpinganjira, M., & Wait, M. (2022). Considerations, benefits and unintended consequences of banning plastic shopping bags for environmental sustainability: A systematic literature review. Waste Management & Research. *Waste Management & Research*, *40*(3), 248–261. DOI: 10.1177/0734242X211003965 PMID: 33876669

Muren, P. D., & Franca, V. (2022). National Recovery and Resilience Plan: Slovenia. *Italian Labour Law E-Journal*, *15*(1S). Advance online publication. DOI: 10.1016/j.repolx.2020.100008

Mustaffa, N. K., Isa, C. M. M., & Ibrahim, C. K. I. C. (2021). Top-down bottom-up strategic green building development framework: Case studies in Malaysia. *Building and Environment, 203*, 108052. Advance online publication. DOI: 10.1016/j.buildenv.2021.108052

Mutiarani, N. D., & Siswantoro, D. (2020). The impact of local government characteristics on the accomplishment of Sustainable Development Goals (SDGs). *Cogent Business & Management, 7*(1), 1847751. DOI: 10.1080/23311975.2020.1847751

Nagtzaam, G., Calster, G., Kourabas, S., & Karataeva, E. (2023). *Plastic regulation in the European Union. Global Plastic Pollution and its Regulation*. Edward Elgar Publishing., DOI: 10.4337/9781800373556

Náhlik, A., Pankotay, F. & Németh, N. (2022). Recycling of plastics in the European Union – exploring the potential domestic adaptation of best practices from other Member States. Gazdaság és Társadalom/ Journal of Economy & Society, 15(2), 90-110. https://doi.org/DOI: 10.21637/GT.2022.2.05

NAR, M. (2019). Plastic Bag Regulation for a Sustainable Environment. *International Journal of Contemporary Economics and Administrative Sciences, 9*(2), 305–326. DOI: 10.5281/zenodo.3596081

Nawaz, S., & Khawaja, M. I. (2019). Fiscal policy, institutions and growth: New insights. *The Singapore Economic Review, 64*(05), 1251–1278. DOI: 10.1142/S0217590816500296

Ngo, Q. D., Phan, V. H., & Le, T. M. (2025). Anticipating prosperity: A systemic analysis of long-term economic trajectories. *Journal of Economic Development, 27*(1), 4–21. DOI: 10.1108/JED-08-2024-0299

Nielsen, T., Holmberg, K., & Stripple, J. (2019). Need a bag? A review of public policies on plastic carrier bags – Where, how and to what effect? *Waste Management (New York, N.Y.), 87*, 428–440. DOI: 10.1016/j.wasman.2019.02.025 PMID: 31109543

Nishijima, A., & Nakatani, J. (2024). Survey and analysis on the use and disposal of plastic shopping bags before and after the introduction of charges. *Journal of Material Cycles and Waste Management, 26*(2), 741–754. DOI: 10.1007/s10163-023-01856-9

Noombo, C., & Mwange, A. (2024). The role of tax incentives in promoting sustainable investments in emerging economies in Sub-Saharan Africa: A legal and policy analysis. *International Journal of Multidisciplinary Research and Growth Evaluation, 5*(6), 1225–1236. DOI: 10.54660/.IJMRGE.2024.5.6.1225-1236

Nordhaus, W. (2023). The economics of climate change mitigation: Policy instruments and global coordination. *The Journal of Economic Perspectives*, *37*(1), 45–68. DOI: 10.1257/jep.37.1.45

Nozadze, I., Chelidze, M., Kapanadze, M., & Sesadze, N. (2024). „Green" Projects and Comparative Analysis of Related Financial Instruments. *Georgian Technical University*, *4*(534), 39–47. DOI: 10.36073/1512-0996-2024-4-39-47

Nyakuwanika, M., van der Poll, H. M., & van der Poll, J. A. (2021). A conceptual framework for greener goldmining through environmental management accounting practices (EMAPs): The case of Zimbabwe. *Sustainability (Basel)*, *13*(18), 10466. DOI: 10.3390/su131810466

O'Brien, J., & Thondhlana, G. (2019). Plastic bag use in South Africa: Perceptions, practices and potential intervention strategies. *Waste Management (New York, N.Y.)*, *84*, 320–328. DOI: 10.1016/j.wasman.2018.11.051 PMID: 30691907

Ocal, O., & Aslan, A. (2013). Renewable energy consumption–economic growth nexus in Turkey. *Renewable & Sustainable Energy Reviews*, *28*, 494–499. DOI: 10.1016/j.rser.2013.08.036

OECD. (2015). *Policy Framework for Investment, 2015 Edition*. DOI: 10.1787/9789264208667-en

OECD. (2017). *Government at a glance 2017*. OECD Publishing., DOI: 10.1787/gov_glance-2017-

OECD. (2020). *Building back better: A sustainable, resilient recovery after COVID-19* (OECD Policy Responses to Coronavirus (COVID-19); OECD Publishing). DOI: 10.1787/5b0fd8cd-en

OECD. (2022). *Base erosion and profit shifting (BEPS) framework*. https://www.oecd.org/tax/beps/

OECD. (2022). *Global Plastics Outlook: Economic Drivers, Environmental Impacts and Policy Options*. OECD Publishing., DOI: 10.1787/de747aef-

OECD. (2023). *Effective Carbon Rates 2023: Pricing carbon emissions through taxes and emissions trading*. Organisation for Economic Co-operation and Development.

OECD. (2024). Effective Carbon Rates 2024: Pricing carbon emissions through taxes and emissions trading. Organisation for Economic Co-operation and Development. https://www.oecd.org/

OECD. (2025). *Carbon pricing trends*. Organisation for Economic Co-operation and Development. https://www.oecd.org/environment/tools-evaluation/carbon-pricing.htm

Official Journal of the European Communities. (1975). Council Directive 75/442/EEC of 15 July 1975 on waste. https://eurlex.europa.eu/legalcontent/EN/TXT/PDF/?uri=CELEX:31975L0442

Official Journal of the European Communities. (1994). Directive 94/62/EC of the European Parliament and of the Council of 20 December 1994 on packaging and packaging waste. https://eurlex.europa.eu/legalcontent/PT/TXT/PDF/?uri=CELEX:31994L0062&qid=1696722078331

Official Journal of the European Union. (2005). Commission Decision 2005/270/EC of the Commission of 22 March 2005. Establishing the forms relating to the database system under Directive 94/62/EC of the European Parliament and of the Council on packaging and packaging waste. https://eurlex.europa.eu/legalcontent/EN/TXT/PDF/?uri=CELEX:32005D0270

Official Journal of the European Union. (2015). Directive 2015/720 of the European Parliament and of the Council of 29 April 2015. Amending Directive 74/62/EC as regards the reduction of the consumption of plastic carrier bags. https://eurlex.europa.eu/legalcontent/EN/TXT/PDF/?uri=CELEX:32015L0720

Official Journal of the European Union. (2018). Commission Implementing Decision 2018/896 of 19 June 2018. Establishing the methodology for calculating the annual consumption of lightweight plastics and amending Decision 2005/270/EC. https://eurlex.europa.eu/legal-content/EN/TXT/PDF/?uri=CELEX:32018D0896

Official Journal of the European Union. (2019). Directive 2019/904 of the European Parliament and of the Council of 5 June 2019 on the reduction of the impact of certain plastic products on the environment. https://eurlex.europa.eu/legalcontent/EN/TXT/PDF/?uri=CELEX:32019L0904

Official Journal of the European Union. (2025). Regulation (EU) 2025/40 of the European Parliament and of the Council of 19 December 2024 on packaging and packaging waste, amending Regulation (EU) 2019/1020 and Directive (EU) 2019/904 and repealing Directive 94/62/EC. https://eur-lex.europa.eu/legal-content/EN/TXT/PDF/?uri=OJ:L_202500040

Ofgem. (2025, March 15). *Renewable Heat Incentive*. https://www.ofgem.gov.uk/environmental-and-social-schemes/non-domestic-renewable-heat-incentive-rhi

Organisation for Economic Co-operation and Development. (2022). Economic Outlook. https://www.oecd.org/economic-outlook/

Ostry, J. D., Berg, A., & Tsangarides, C. G. (2011). Inequality and unsustainable growth: Two sides of the same coin? *IMF Staff Discussion Notes*, *11*(08), 1–25. DOI: 10.5089/9781463926564.006

Osuji, E., & Nwani, S. E. (2020). Achieving sustainable development goals: Does government expenditure framework matter? [IJMESS]. *International Journal of Management, Economics and Social Sciences*, *9*(3), 131–160. DOI: 10.32327/IJMESS/9.3.2020.8

Othman, R., & Ameer, R. (2024). Rethinking accounting education for a sustainable future: Charting a course for sustainable development goals 2030. *Meditari Accountancy Investigation*, *32*(5), 1809–1840. DOI: 10.1108/MEDAR-05-2023-2009

Pan, J., Cross, J. L., Zou, X., & Zhang, B. (2024). To tax or to trade? A global review of carbon emissions reduction strategies. *Energy Strategy Reviews*, *55*, 101508. Advance online publication. DOI: 10.1016/j.esr.2024.101508

Parry, I. W. H., Veung, C., & Heine, D. (2017). How much carbon pricing is in countries' own interests? The critical role of co-benefits. *Climate Change Economics (Singapore)*, *8*(2), 1740009. DOI: 10.1142/S2010007817400096

Pastor, J. M., Pérez, F., & Fernández de Guevara, J. (2013). Measuring the local economic impact of universities: An approach that considers uncertainty. *Higher Education*, *65*(5), 539–564. DOI: 10.1007/s10734-012-9562-z

Patrão, S., Cruz, S., & Carreira, F. (2025). The evolution of green taxation in Portugal. 10th GECAMB/P-CSEAR & XXIV Grudis Conference and Doctoral Colloquium, EsACT-IPB, Mirandela. http://hdl.handle.net/10773/44024

Permatasari, P., Ilman, A. S., Tilt, C. A., Lestari, D., Islam, S., Tenrini, R. H., Rahman, A. B., Samosir, A. P., & Wardhana, I. W. (2021). The Village Fund Program in Indonesia: Measuring the Effectiveness and Alignment to Sustainable Development Goals. *Sustainability (Basel)*, *13*(21), 12294. Advance online publication. DOI: 10.3390/su132112294

Peters, A., & Fisher, P. (2004). The failures of economic development incentives. *Journal of the American Planning Association*, *70*(1), 27–37. DOI: 10.1080/01944360408976336

Petrie, M. (2021). *Environmental governance and the greening of fiscal policy*. Palgrave Macmillan. orcid.org+9ideas.repec.org+9scholar.unand.ac.id+9DOI: 10.1007/978-3-030-83796-9

Pigato, M. A., Rafaty, R., & Kurle, J. (2021). *The COVID-19 Crisis and the Road to Recovery: Green or Brown?* World Bank., https://documents1.worldbank.org/curated/en/652851637126067927/pdf/The-COVID-19-Crisis-and-the-Road-to-Recovery-Green-or-Brown.pdf

Plicanic, S. (2020). The Role of State in Achieving Sustainable Development Goals in Slovenia. *Studia Iuridica Lublinensia, 29*(4), 233–249. DOI: 10.17951/sil.2020.29.4.233-249

Poterba, J. M. (1994). State Responses to Fiscal Crises: The Effects of Budgetary Institutions and Politics. *Journal of Political Economy, 102*(4), 799–821. Crossref. DOI: 10.1086/261955

Prata, J., Silva, A., Duarte, A., & Rocha-Santos, T. (2022). The road to sustainable use and waste management of plastics in Portugal. *Frontiers of Environmental Science & Engineering, 16*(1), 5. DOI: 10.1007/s11783-021-1439-x PMID: 34697576

Priyan, S. (2023). Effect of green investment to reduce carbon emissions in an imperfect production system. *Journal of Climate Finance, 2*, 100007. DOI: 10.1016/j.jclimf.2023.100007

Pruess, J., & Garrett, R. (2025). Potential effectiveness of extended producer responsibility: An ex-ante policy impact analysis for plastic packaging waste in Belgium, France, and Germany. *Resources, Conservation and Recycling, 219*, 108297. DOI: 10.1016/j.resconrec.2025.108297

Qi, Y., Zhang, J., & Chen, J. (2023). Tax incentives, environmental regulation and firms' emission reduction strategies: Evidence from China. *Journal of Environmental Economics and Management, 117*, 102750. DOI: 10.1016/j.jeem.2022.102750

R Bhat, M Gupta, TF Choudhary, and AK Singh (2024) Modelling the Effects of Climatic Variables and Political Instability on the Agricultural Sector in South Asian Countries Building Climate Neutral Economies through Digital Business and Green Skills DOI: DOI: 10.4018/979-8-3693-5673-9.ch001

Rahman, M. M. (2023). Influence of taxes on the 2030 agenda for sustainable development: Evidence from organization for market place co-operation and development (OECD) countries. *Regional Sustainability, 4*(3), 235–248. DOI: 10.1016/j.regsus.2023.07.001

Ramachandruni, U., & Ravi, H. (2023). Evolution of Plastic Bags: Reduced and Recycling Consumer Usage Level on Bags in Day-to-Day Life. *International Journal of Commerce and Management, 3*(2), 253–259. DOI: 10.54368/qijcm.3.2.0022

Rao, M., Vasa, L., Xu, Y., & Chen, P. (2023). Spatial and heterogeneity analysis of environmental taxes' impact on China's green economy development: A sustainable development perspective. *Sustainability (Basel)*, *15*(12), 9332. Advance online publication. DOI: 10.3390/su15129332

Raszkowski, A., & Bartniczak, B. (2018). Towards sustainable regional development: Economy, society, environment, good governance based on the example of Polish regions. *Transformations in Business & Economics*, *17*, 225–245.

Rhodes, C. (2018). Plastic pollution and potential solutions. *Science Progress*, *101*(3), 207–260. DOI: 10.3184/003685018X15294876706211 PMID: 30025551

Ritch, E., Brennan, C., & Macleod, C. (2009). Plastic bag politics: Modifying consumer behaviour for sustainable development. *International Journal of Consumer Studies*, *33*(2), 168–174. DOI: 10.1111/j.1470-6431.2009.00749.x

Rivers, N., Shenstone-Harris, S., & Young, N. (2017). Using nudges to reduce waste? The case of Toronto's plastic bag levy. *Journal of Environmental Management*, *188*, 153–162. DOI: 10.1016/j.jenvman.2016.12.009 PMID: 27978442

Rövekamp, P., Schöpf, M., Wagon, F., Weibelzahl, M., & Fridgen, G. (2021). Renewable electricity business models in a post feed-in tariff era. *Energy*, *216*, 119228. Advance online publication. DOI: 10.1016/j.energy.2020.119228

Rvo. (2025). *Stimulation of sustainable energy production and climate transition (SDE++)*. https://english.rvo.nl/subsidies-financiering/sde

Sadia, H. S., Azeez, J. A., & Shehzadi, K. (2025). Driving Factors of Fiscal Stress: Panel Data Analysis for Emerging Countries. *Journal of Economic Sciences*, 91–104. https://jesciences.com/index.php/jes/article/view/116/51

Sadorsky, P. (2009). Renewable energy consumption, CO2 emissions and oil prices in the G7 countries. *Energy Economics*, *31*(3), 456–462. DOI: 10.1016/j.eneco.2008.12.010

Sanchez-Olmedo, D., Navarro-Pedreño, J., & Rocamora, I. (2025). Bridging the gap: The impact of gender equality on CO_2 emissions across countries. *WORLD (Oakland, Calif.)*, *6*(1), 26. DOI: 10.3390/world6010026

Sapar, J. F., & Kusuma, E. R. H. (2025). Effectiveness of Tax Incentives in Increasing Investment in Green Technology and Green Energy. *Advances in Taxation Research*, *3*(1), 54–67. Crossref. DOI: 10.60079/atr.v3i1.459

Sarpong, K. A., Xu, W., Gyamfi, B. A., & Ofori, E. K. (2023). A step towards carbon neutrality in E7: The role of environmental taxes, structural change, and green energy. *Journal of Environmental Management, 337*, 117556. Advance online publication. DOI: 10.1016/j.jenvman.2023.117556

Sartor, O., & Bataille, C. (2019). Decarbonising basic materials in Europe. *Climate Policy, 19*(7), 875–891. DOI: 10.1080/14693062.2019.1623985

Sasol. (2023). Integrated Report 2023. Sasol Ltd. https://www.sasol.com/

Săvoiu, G., & Manea, D. (2013). Comparing Fixed and Random Effects Models using Hausman Test in a Panel Data Analysis. Theoretical and Applied Economics, 20(6), 5–20. https://rtsa.ro/tras/index.php/tras/article/view/407

Schlosser, R., Chenavaz, R. Y., & Dimitrov, S. (2021). Circular economy: Joint dynamic pricing and recycling investments. *International Journal of Production Economics, 236*, 108117. DOI: 10.1016/j.ijpe.2021.108117

Schmidt-Traub, G. (2015). Investment needs to achieve the Sustainable Development Goals: Understanding the billions and trillions. *SDSN Working Paper*. https://www.jstor.org/stable/resrep15864

Schmidt-Traub, G. (2018). On metrics and financing for the Sustainable Development Goals. *Sustainable Development, 26*(1), 13–17. DOI: 10.1002/sd.1793

Scott, C. (2022). *Plastic Packaging Tax: How you're affected and how we can help.* Green Economy. Retrieved from Link

Scuderi, E. (2021). Towards a Plastic-Free Economy: The Italian Plastic Tax Scuderi, Erika (2021). Towards a plastic-free economy: the Italian plastic tax. Rivista Telematica di Diritto Tributario. https://ssrn.com/abstract=3822296

Senturk, G., & Dumludag, D. (2021). An evaluation of the effect of plastic bag fee on consumer behavior: Case of Turkey. *Waste Management (New York, N.Y.), 120*, 748–754. DOI: 10.1016/j.wasman.2020.10.042 PMID: 33223247

Serafeim, G. (2020). Social-impact efforts that create real value. *Harvard Business Review, 98*(5), 38–48. https://hbr.org/2020/09/social-impact-efforts-that-create-real-value

Service-Public. (2025). *Éco-prêt à taux zéro (éco-PTZ).* https://www.service-public.fr/particuliers/vosdroits/F19905

Shaikh, A. A., Alamoudi, H., Alharthi, M., & Glavee-Geo, R. (2022). Advances in mobile financial services: A review of the literature and future research directions. *International Journal of Bank Marketing*, *41*(1), 1–33. DOI: 10.1108/IJBM-06-2021-0230

Shen, Y., & Zhang, X. (2022). Study on the impact of environmental tax on industrial green transformation. *International Journal of Environmental Research and Public Health*, *19*(24), 16749. Advance online publication. DOI: 10.3390/ijerph192416749

Singhania, M., & Saini, N. (2023). Institutional framework of ESG disclosures: Comparative analysis of developed and developing countries. *Journal of Sustainable Finance & Investment*, *13*(1), 516–559. DOI: 10.1080/20430795.2021.1964810

Singh, R. K., Kumar, A., Garza-Reyes, J. A., & de Sá, M. M. (2020). Managing operations for circular economy in the mining sector: An analysis of barriers intensity. *Resources Policy*, *69*, 101752. DOI: 10.1016/j.resourpol.2020.101752

Singun, A. J. (2025). Unveiling the barriers to digital transformation in higher education institutions: A systematic literature review. *Discover Education*, *4*(1), 37. Advance online publication. DOI: 10.1007/s44217-025-00430-9

Skatteverket. (2025). *Miljöbilar*. https://www.skatteverket.se/privat/skatter/arbeteochinkomst/formaner/bilforman/miljobilar.4.3f4496fd14864cc5ac9e89a.html

Slavikova, L. (2013). From cost-benefit to institutional analysis in the economics of the environment. *Contemporary Economics*, *7*(2), 67–75. DOI: 10.5709/ce.1897-9254.83

Smith, O., & Brisman, A. (2021). Plastic waste and the environmental crisis industry. *Critical Criminology*, *29*(2), 289–309. DOI: 10.1007/s10612-021-09562-4 PMID: 33746527

Soares, E. C., Lima, N. C., & Coelho, A. F. M. (2024). Towards sustainability engaged accounting: A behavioral approach. *Revista Contabilidade & Finanças*, *35*(95), e2019. DOI: 10.1590/1808-057x20242019.pt

Song, M., Wang, S., & Zhang, H. (2020). Could environmental regulation and R&D tax incentives affect green product innovation? *Journal of Cleaner Production*, *258*, 120849. DOI: 10.1016/j.jclepro.2020.120849

Sonjaya, Y., & Noch, M. Y. (2024). Analysis of the Effectiveness of Tax Incentives on Energy Sector Investments. *Advances in Taxation Research*, *2*(2), 120–131. DOI: 10.60079/atr.v2i2.308

Stanimirović, T., Milan Lah, L., Kotnik, Ž., & Klun, M. (2023). Green budgeting implementation in financing of sustainable society-experience of Slovenia. *Management, 28*(Special Issue), 79–91. DOI: 10.30924/mjcmi.28.si.6

Stausholm, S. N. (2017). *Rise of ineffective incentives: New empirical evidence on tax holidays in developing countries*. Crossref. DOI: 10.31235/osf.io/4sn3k

Stern, N. (2022). Towards a carbon neutral economy: How government should respond to market failures and market absence. *Journal of Government and Economics*. Advance online publication. https://doi.org/DOI: 10.1016/j.jgoe.2022.101029

Sterner, T. (2012). Distributional effects of taxing transport fuel. *Modeling Transport (Energy). Energy Policy, 41*, 75–83. DOI: 10.1016/j.enpol.2010.03.012

Sterner, T. (2024). Environmental taxation and economic growth: Balancing incentives and impacts. *Ecological Economics, 218*, 108093. DOI: 10.1016/j.ecolecon.2023.108093

Stoker, G. (2006). Public value management: A new narrative for networked governance? *American Review of Public Administration, 36*(1), 41–57. DOI: 10.1177/0275074005282583

Strand, J., & Toman, M. (2010). Green stimulus, economic recovery, and long-term sustainable development. *World Bank Policy Research Working Paper Series 5163*. https://ideas.repec.org/p/wbk/wbrwps/5163.html

Suncor. (2025). *Sustainability report 2024*. https://www.suncor.com/en-ca/sustainability

Sun, J., & Abruzzian, M. (2025). Technological innovation, trade openness, natural resources, clean energy on environmental sustainability: A competitive assessment between CO_2 emission, ecological footprint, load capacity factor and inverted load capacity factor in BRICS+T. *Frontiers in Environmental Science, 12*, 1520562. DOI: 10.3389/fenvs.2024.1520562

Sun, J., Li, P., & Wang, Y. (2024). Policy tools for sustainability: Evaluating the effectiveness of fiscal measures in natural resource efficiency. *Resources Policy, 89*, 104575. Advance online publication. DOI: 10.1016/j.resourpol.2023.104575

Sun, Y., Rahman, M. M., Xinyan, X., Siddik, A. B., & Islam, M. E. (2024). Unlocking environmental, social, and governance (ESG) performance through energy efficiency and green tax: SEM-ANN approach. *Energy Strategy Reviews, 53*, 101408. Advance online publication. DOI: 10.1016/j.esr.2024.101408

SURS. (2024). *SISTAT Database*. https://www.stat.si/statweb

Su, S., Qamruzzaman, M., & Karim, S. (2023). Charting a sustainable future: The impact of economic policy, environmental taxation, innovation, and natural resources on clean energy consumption. *Sustainability (Basel), 15*(6), 4789. Advance online publication. DOI: 10.3390/su151813585

Swedish National Audit Office. (2025, February 22). *Central government measures for more green cars.* https://www.riksrevisionen.se/en/audits/audit-reports/2020/central-government-measures-for-more-green-cars.html

Syberg, K., Nielsen, M., Westergaard Clausen, L., Calster, G., Wezel, A., Rochman, C., Koelmans, A., Cronin, R., Pahl, S., & Hansen, S. (2021). Regulation of plastic from a circular economy perspective. *Current Opinion in Green and Sustainable Chemistry, 29*, 100462. DOI: 10.1016/j.cogsc.2021.100462

Takacs, F., Brunner, D., & Frankenberger, K. (2022). Barriers to a circular economy in small-and medium-sized enterprises and their integration in a sustainable strategic management framework. *Journal of Cleaner Production, 362*, 132227. DOI: 10.1016/j.jclepro.2022.132227

Tang, Y. E., Fan, R., Cai, A. Z., Wang, L. Y., Lin, R. M., Meng, X. Z., Chen, L., & Guo, R. (2023). Rethinking personal carbon trading (PCT) mechanism: A comprehensive review. *Journal of Environmental Management, 344*, 118478. Advance online publication. DOI: 10.1016/j.jenvman.2023.118478

Tan, Y., We, Z., Hu, Y., Zeng, X., Kosajan, V., Yin, G., & Zhang, T. (2023). Single-use plastic bag alternatives result in higher environmental impacts: Multi-regional analysis in country with uneven waste management. *Waste Management (New York, N.Y.), 171*, 281–291. DOI: 10.1016/j.wasman.2023.08.040 PMID: 37690403

Taylor, R. & Villas-Boas, S. (2015). Bans versus Fees: Disposable Carryout Bag Policies and Bag Usage. Agricultural and Applied Economics Association Conferences, Califórnia. https://doi.org.DOI: 10.22004/ag.econ.204783

Thaler, R. H., & Sunstein, C. R. (2008). *Nudge: Improving decisions about health, wealth, and happiness.* Yale University Press.

Thompson, R., Swan, S., Moore, C., & Saal, F. (2009). Our plastic age. *Philosophical Transactions of the Royal Society of London. Series B, Biological Sciences, 364*(1526), 1973–1976. DOI: 10.1098/rstb.2009.0054 PMID: 19528049

Todorović, J., Đorđević, M., & Stojanović, M. (2023). The Impact of Environmental Taxes on the Reduction of Plastic Bag Consumption in the Republic of Servia. *TEME, XLVII*(4), 767–786. DOI: 10.22190/TEME220529048D

Toma, J. D., Dubrow, G., & Hartley, M. (2005). The Uses of Institutional Culture: Strengthening Identification and Building Brand Equity in Higher Education. *ASHE Higher Education Report*, *31*(2), 1–105. 1353/RHE.2005.0077

Toyin, O. O., & Onanuga, A. T. (2019). Carbon Fiscal Instruments and Green Finance: An Aid to the Success of SDGs in Nigeria? *Journal of Innovation in Business and Economics*, *3*(02), 49–62. DOI: 10.22219/jibe.v3i02.7895

Toyota. (2023). *Sustainability data book 2022*. https://global.toyota/en/sustainability

Trade openness (Exports + Imports as % of GDP): World Bank. (2023). Trade (% of GDP) https://data.worldbank.org/indicator/NE.TRD.GNFS.ZS

Troshani, I., & Rowbottom, N. (2024). Corporate sustainability reporting and information infrastructure. *Accounting, Auditing & Accountability Journal*, *37*(4), 1209–1237. DOI: 10.1108/AAAJ-01-2023-6244

Truant, E., Crocco, E., Corazza, L., & Borlatto, E. (2024). Life cycle thinking and carbon accounting in sustainable supply chains: A structured literature review and research agenda. *Sustainability Accounting, Management and Policy Journal*. Advance online publication. DOI: 10.1108/SAMPJ-09-2023-0708

Uji, A., Song, J., Dolšak, N., & Prakash, A. (2025). Postmaterialism and Environmental Protection Revisited: Domestic Plastic Bag Regulations, 1992–2019. *Global Environmental Politics*, *25*(1), 46–66. DOI: 10.1162/glep_a_00771

Umoh, O., Onye, K., & Atan, J. (2018). Political and institutional determinants of fiscal policy persistence in West Africa. *MPRA Paper No. 88452*. https://mpra.ub.uni-muenchen.de/88452/

UNEP. (2023). Kenya's plastic bag ban: Progress and lessons (2023 brief). United Nations Environment Programme. https://www.unep.org/

UNEP. (2025). *Kenya plastic ban impact*. United Nations Environment Programme. https://www.unep.org/resources/report/kenya-plastic-ban-impact

UNFCCC. (2015). *Paris Agreement*. United Nations Framework Convention on Climate Change. https://unfccc.int/process-and-meetings/the-paris-agreement/the-paris-agreement

United Nations Development Programme. (2021). *Tax for Sustainable Development Goals (Tax for SDGs)*. About. United Nations Development Programme.

United Nations Development Programme. (n.d.). *Tax for Sustainable Development Goals (Tax for SDGs): About*. https://www.taxforsdgs.org/about

United Nations Environment Programme. (2018). Single-use Plastics: A Roadmap for Sustainability. UN Environment. https://www.unep.org/resources/report/single-use-plastics-roadmap-sustainability

United Nations Environment Programme. (2019). Legal limits on single-use plastics and microplastics: a global review of National Laws and Regulations. UN Environment. https://www.unep.org/resources/publication/legal-limits-single-use-plastics-and-microplastics-global-review-national

United Nations Environment Programme. (2021). From Pollution to Solution: A global assessment of marine litter and plastic pollution. UN Environment. https://www.unep.org/resources/pollution-solution-global-assessment-marine-litter-and-plastic-pollution

United Nations. (1987). *Report of the World Commission on Environment and Development: Our common future*. https://www.un.org/en/ga/documents/our-common-future

United Nations. (2015). *Transforming our world: The 2030 agenda for sustainable development*. https://sdgs.un.org/2030agenda

United Nations. (2023). *The Sustainable Development Goals Report 2023*. https://sdgs.un.org/sites/default/files/2023-07/The-Sustainable-Development-Goals-Report-2023_0.pdf

Varona, L., & Gonzales, J. R. (2025). Human development, productivity, and economic growth. *Journal of Human Development and Capabilities*, *26*(1), 33–58. DOI: 10.1080/19452829.2024.2439947

Vasilyeva, O., Libman, A., & Zaytsev, Y. (2023). Tax policy and environmental governance. *Public Policy Research*, *29*(3), 301–322. DOI: 10.1111/padm.12890

Vence, X., & López Pérez, S. D. J. (2021). Taxation for a circular economy: New instruments, reforms, and architectural changes in the fiscal system. *Sustainability (Basel)*, *13*(8), 4581. DOI: 10.3390/su13084581

Ventosa, I., Sanz, S., & Sora, M. (2018) Research paper on a European tax on plastics, Zero Waste Europe. https://zerowasteeurope.eu/library/research-paper-on-a-european-tax-on-plastics/

Verde, S. F., & Borghesi, S. (2022). The international dimension of the EU Emissions Trading System: Bringing the pieces together. *Environmental and Resource Economics, 83*(3), 23–46. oaepublish.com+2mdpi.com+2researchgate.net+2DOI: 10.1007/s10640-022-00705-x

Vermunt, D. A., Negro, S. O., Verweij, P. A., Kuppens, D. V., & Hekkert, M. P. (2019). Exploring barriers to implementing different circular business models. *Journal of Cleaner Production, 222*, 891–902. DOI: 10.1016/j.jclepro.2019.03.052

Wagner, T. (2017). Reducing single-use plastic shopping bags in the USA. *Waste Management (New York, N.Y.), 70*, 3–12. DOI: 10.1016/j.wasman.2017.09.003 PMID: 28935376

Wang, B., Zhao, Y., & Li, Y. (2021). How do tougher plastics ban policies modify people's usage of plastic bags? A case study in China. *International Journal of Environmental Research and Public Health, 18*(20), 10718. DOI: 10.3390/ijerph182010718 PMID: 34682464

Wang, D., & Mei, J. (2024). An advanced review of climate change mitigation policies in the United States. *Resources, Conservation and Recycling, 208*, 107718. Advance online publication. DOI: 10.1016/j.resconrec.2024.107718

Wang, J. M., & Li, Y. Q. (2022). Soft economic incentives and soft behavioral interventions on the public's green purchasing behaviour: The evidence from China. *Psychology Research and Behavior Management, 15*, 2477–2499. DOI: 10.2147/PRBM.S373123

Wang, J. X., Burke, H., & Zhang, A. (2022). Overcoming barriers to circular product design. *International Journal of Production Economics, 243*, 108346. DOI: 10.1016/j.ijpe.2021.108346

Wang, M., & Kuusi, T. (2024). Trade flows, carbon leakage, and the EU Emissions Trading System. *Energy Economics, 134*, 107556. Advance online publication. DOI: 10.1016/j.eneco.2024.107556

Wang, X., Khurshid, A., Qayyum, S., & Calin, A. C. (2022). The role of green innovations, environmental policies and carbon taxes in achieving the sustainable development goals of carbon neutrality. *Environmental Science and Pollution Research International, 29*(6), 1–15. DOI: 10.1007/s11356-021-16208-z

Wang, Y., Qamruzzaman, M., & Kor, S. (2023). Greening the future: Harnessing ICT, innovation, eco-taxes, and clean energy for sustainable ecology—Insights from dynamic seemingly unrelated regression. *Sustainability (Basel), 15*(23), 16417. Advance online publication. DOI: 10.3390/su152316417

Weber, J., Fooken, J., & Herrmann, B. (2022). Behavioural economics in tax policy. *Fiscal Studies, 43*(2), 145–162. DOI: 10.1111/1475-5890.12289

Woo, J. (2002). Economic, Political and Institutional Determinants of Public Deficits. SSRN *Electronic Journal*. Crossref. DOI: 10.2139/ssrn.326520

Woo, J., Fatima, R., Kibert, C. J., Newman, R. E., Tian, Y., & Srinivasan, R. S. (2021). Applying blockchain technology for building energy performance measurement, reporting, and verification (MRV) and the carbon credit market: A review of the literature. *Building and Environment, 205*, 108199. Advance online publication. DOI: 10.1016/j.buildenv.2021.108199

World Bank. (2023). GDP per capita (current US$). https://data.worldbank.org

World Bank. (2023). *State and Trends of Carbon Pricing 2023*. World Bank Group.

World Bank. (2024). State and Trends of Carbon Pricing 2024. World Bank Group. https://carbonpricingdashboard.worldbank.org/

World Bank. (2025). *Carbon pricing dashboard*. https://carbonpricingdashboard.worldbank.org/

World Bank. (2025). GDP per capita (constant 2015 US$). World Development Indicators https://data.worldbank.org/indicator/NY.GDP.PCAP.KD

World Values Survey. (2023). Wave 7 & 2023 cross-national trends: Climate policy attitudes. World Values Survey Association. https://www.worldvaluessurvey.org/

World Values Survey. (2025). *Public opinion on climate policies*. https://www.worldvaluessurvey.org/WVSContents.jsp

Wozniak-Jechorek, B. (2024). Examining the European Transition: Central Eastern European Countries Two Decades Post-EU Accession. *Revista Economia e Políticas Públicas, 12*(1), 48–60. DOI: 10.46551/epp2024v12n0104

Wu, T., & Roche, J. C. (2024). Triple bottom line or trilemma? Global trade-offs between prosperity, inequality, and the environment. *World Development, 178*, 106595. DOI: 10.1016/j.worlddev.2024.106595

Wu, Z., Huang, X., Chen, R., Mao, X., & Qi, X. (2022). The United States and China on the paths and policies to carbon neutrality. *Journal of Environmental Management, 320*, 115785. Advance online publication. DOI: 10.1016/j.jenvman.2022.115785

Xu, Y., Wen, S., & Tao, C. Q. (2023). Impact of environmental tax on pollution control: A sustainable development perspective. *Economic Analysis and Policy, 79*, 89–106. DOI: 10.1016/j.eap.2023.06.006

Yang, K., Chen, G., & Chen, R. (2024). The dark side of climate policy uncertainty: Hindering energy transition by shaping environmental tax effectiveness. *Journal of Environmental Management, 369*, 122314. Advance online publication. DOI: 10.1016/j.jenvman.2024.122314

Yong, S. K., & Chang, Y. (2023). Emissions tax and executive compensation: A public–private joint mechanism to promote environmental and energy management. *The Singapore Economic Review, 68*(02), 355–375. DOI: 10.1142/S0217590822500710

Yu, H., Liao, L., Qu, S., Fang, D., Luo, L., & Xiong, G. (2021). Environmental regulation and corporate tax avoidance: A quasi-natural experiment study based on China's new environmental protection law. *Journal of Environmental Management, 296*, 113160. Advance online publication. DOI: 10.1016/j.jenvman.2021.113160

Zainudin, Q., Qi, W. Y., Lau, J. L., Harun, Z., & Khalid, N. (2021). Determinants of Using Alternative to Single-Use Plastic Bags. *International Journal of Academic Research in Business & Social Sciences, 11*(11), 1753–1766. DOI: 10.6007/IJARBSS/v11-i11/11659

Zeng, W., & Wang, G. (2025). On the obligations of states to respond to climate change and China's legal consequences: Based on the advisory opinion in Case No. 31 of the International Tribunal for the Law of the Sea. *Frontiers in Marine Science, 11*, 1468210. Advance online publication. DOI: 10.3389/fmars.2024.1468210

Zhang, W., Zhao, S., & Wan, X. (2021). Industrial digital transformation strategies based on differential games. *Applied Mathematical Modelling, 98*, 90–108. DOI: 10.1016/j.apm.2021.05.001

Zhao, T., Liang, X., & Hu, B. (2023). Digital economy, entrepreneurial activity, and common prosperity: Evidence from China. *Journal of Information Economics, 1*(1), 5. DOI: 10.58567/jie01010005

Zhao, X., Li, J., & Li, Y. (2022). Impact of environmental tax on corporate sustainable performance: Insights from high-tech firms in China. *International Journal of Environmental Research and Public Health, 20*(1), 461. DOI: 10.3390/ijerph20010461 PMID: 36612778

Zhu, Y., Taylor, D., & Wang, Z. (2023). The role of environmental taxes on carbon emissions in countries aiming for net-zero carbon emissions: Does renewable energy consumption matter? *Renewable Energy, 218*, 119239. Advance online publication. DOI: 10.1016/j.renene.2023.119239

Ziervogel, G., Enqvist, J., Metelerkamp, L., & van Breda, J. (2022). Supporting transformative climate adaptation: Community-level capacity building and knowledge co-creation in South Africa. *Climate Policy, 22*(5), 607–622. DOI: 10.1080/14693062.2020.1863180

Zodrow, G. R., & Mieszkowski, P. (1986). Pigou, Tiebout, property taxation, and the underprovision of local public goods. *Journal of Urban Economics*, *19*(3), 356–370. DOI: 10.1016/0094-1190(86)90048-3

Zuojun, F., & Lynn, T. Z. Z. (2024). Fiscal Policy for Inclusive Growth. A Case Study of Myanmar. *Journal of Economics. Finance and Management Studies*, *7*(4), 1914–1932. DOI: 10.47191/jefms/v7-i4-18

About the Contributors

Albertina Paula Moreira Monteiro holds a PhD in Economics and Business, specialising in accounting (University of Santiago de Compostela) and a PhD in Marketing and Strategy (University of Minho). Coordinating Professor at Porto Accounting and Business School of the Polytechnic Institute of Porto (ISCAP.IPP) in the scientific area of Accounting. Researcher at Centre for Organisational and Social Studies of the Polytechnic Institute of Porto (CEOS.PP) and CICF (Polytechnic Institute of Cávado and Ave) and OSEAN (University of Madeira). Author of several publications (papers and book chapters) indexed to the main bibliographic databases.

Ana Pinto Borges holds a PhD in Economics at Faculty of Economics, University of Porto and the Economic Degree in Lusíada University - North. She is coordinating Professor at ISAG - European Business School (ISAG) since 2010, President of the Pedagogical Council since 2015 and has been the Executive Coordinator of the ISAG Research Center (NIDISAG) since 2014. She is one of the founding members of the Research Center in Business Sciences and Tourism (CICET). She is the author of more than 40 publications in scientific journals with peer review and indexed in the various international databases. The researcher has been participating in various national and international congresses and member of the Scientific Commissions and Organizing Committees in academic events. Editor and one of the founding members of the academic journal European Journal of Applied Business and Management (EJABM). She was consultant at Accenture in the financial area. Economist at the Portuguese Healthcare Regulation Authority since 2010.

Elvira Vieira holds a PhD in Applied Economics, University of Santiago de Compostela. Professor, member of the Scientific Council at Institute of Marketing Management between 2007-2009 and Invited Professor at Minho University between 2009-2012. Professor at Polytechnic Institute of Viana do Castelo and Coordinating Professor at ISAG - European Business School since 2009. General

Director at ISAG - European Business School since 2012, researcher in UNIAG, scientific coordinator of NIDISAG Research Center (between 2014 - 2021) and of Center in Business Sciences and Tourism (CICET - FCVC) since 2021. Author of several publications (papers and book chapters) indexed to the main bibliographic databases. Editor and one of the founding members of the European Journal of Applied Business and Management (EJABM). 2009 1st prize winner for research of the "Catedra da Euroregión Galicia – Norte of Portugal" and President of the European Grouping of Territorial Cooperation Galicia – North of Portugal, from 2010-2012.

***

Francisco Alegria Carreira holds a degree Habilitation and a PhD in business sciences, with a thesis in accounting. He is Principal Coordinating Professor at the Polytechnic Institute of Setúbal, Portugal, where he teaches courses in the areas of financial accounting, auditing and taxation and was, for ten years, director of the accounting and finance department and director of the accounting and finance course. He develops his research activity at the Centre for Research in Accounting and Taxation (CICF) and his area of research includes accounting, taxation, auditing and social responsibility. He is the author of several scientific articles, in journals and conferences, and book chapters, as well as a reviewer for various scientific events and journals, and has also been an expert assessor at the Higher Education Assessment and Accreditation Agency since 2010, in the areas of management, accounting, taxation and auditing. He was vice-president of the Setúbal Polytechnic Institute for 10 years, deputy director of the School of Business Sciences for two years, and was financial director and management, accounting, tax and auditing consultant in private organizations for 12 years

I Nyoman Darmayasa is a lecturer (Professor on Accounting and Tax) and researcher in the Accounting Department, Bali State Polytechnic, Indonesia. He holds a doctoral degree in accounting, specializing in taxation, from Brawijaya University, and honored cum laude grade. His research expertise relates to green taxation, green accounting, and green auditing. He also appointed be a reviewer in the international reputable journals published by Elsevier, European Academy of Management and Business Economics, EnPress Publisher, LLC, and Cogent. I Nyoman Darmayasa is also a certified specialist in Chartered Accountant (CA), Bersertifikat Konsultan Pajak (BKP), Certified Professional Management Accountant (CPMA), Certified Public Accountant (CPA), and ASEAN CPA. He is a partner in the Public Accounting Firm and handle numerous of international tax clients.

Hrishikesh Desai is an Assistant Professor of Accounting at Arkansas State University. He is also the Director of the Master of Accountancy with Data Analytics Program at the university.

Meenakshi Gupta is working as an Associate Professor in the School of Economics, at Shri Mata Vaishno Devi University, Katra. She has teaching and research experience of almost 16 years. She has been a part of many academic and non- academic committees of the university since 2007. Her main areas of interest are Agricultural Economics, Environmental Economics and Development Economics. Her research work has been published in various national and international journals. She has contributed to various books also. She has also presented various articles at National and International Conferences. She is also awarded with many prestigious national and international awards. She is a life Member of Indian Economic Association, Indian Society of Agri- business and Management, Indian Society of Agricultural Economics, TIES, AERA, etc.

Maja Klun is a Full Professor in the Department of Economics and Public Sector Management at the Faculty of Public Administration, University of Ljubljana, Slovenia. She currently acts as Vice-Rector at the University of Ljubljana. Her areas of research interest encompass Public Sector Economics, Public Finance and International Economics. She has actively participated in more than thirty international conferences and published many professional and scientific articles in various domestic and international publications (International Review of Administrative Sciences, FinanzArchiv, Transylvanian Review of Administrative Sciences, etc.), recently. Since 2007 she has been a contracting partner for government activities in the field of better regulation, especially in measurement of administrative costs.

Žiga Kotnik is a researcher and associate professor in the Department of Economics and Public Sector Management at the Faculty of Public Administration, University of Ljubljana, Slovenia. He earned his PhD in Statistics from the University of Ljubljana in 2014 and received the Faculty of Social Sciences' Best PhD Thesis Award in 2015. His research interests include Public Administration, Public Sector Economics, and Environmental Economics. Since 2009, he has presented at international conferences and published articles and monographic chapters. His primary teaching areas are Statistics, Quantitative Methods, Environmental Policy Evaluation, European Tenders, and Project Management. He has been recognized for his teaching excellence with awards from the University's Student Council (2012) and the Faculty of Public Administration (2019 and 2021).

Indra Pahala is Senior Lecturer (Lektor Kepala) at State University of Jakarta (UNJ). He is Expertise in Accounting, Taxation, Corporate Governance. Dr. Indra Pahala completed his undergraduate studies in Accounting before pursuing master's and doctoral degrees. Currently serving as a Senior Lecturer at UNJ with the rank of Penata (Grade III D), demonstrating his significant dedication and contributions to academia. Research focuses include: Corporate governance and accountability; Taxpayer behavior and taxation systems; Financial reporting and accounting standards; All research projects funded by BLU UNJ. Actively contributes to the development of accounting and taxation knowledge in Indonesia. His research has been applied in policy-making and business practices.

Rismawati is a distinguished academic and consultant with a robust focus on sustainability reporting. She currently holds the position of lecturer and Head of the Quality Assurance Institute at Universitas Muhammadiyah Palopo, where she has been pivotal in ensuring the quality of university processes and outputs since February 2020. Additionally, she serves as an Assurer for Sustainability Reporting at the National Center for Sustainability Reporting in Jakarta, specializing in the evaluation of sustainability reports for mining companies across Indonesia. Her academic qualifications are extensive, comprising a Bachelor's degree in Economics and Accounting, a Master's degree in Accounting Science, and a Doctorate in Accounting from Universitas Brawijaya, Malang. Rismawati is also a certified specialist in sustainability reporting, risk management, and tax planning, holding several prestigious certifications including Certified Sustainability Reporting Specialist (CSRS), Certified Risk Management Practitioner (CRMP), Certified Management Accountant (CMA) and Certified Enterprise Risk Analysis (CERA). In her professional capacity, she has provided consultancy services in financial management and tax compliance for companies such as PT. Reski Barito Timur and PT. Helay Raya. Furthermore, she has authored multiple publications on Social Accounting, Sustainability Accounting, Management Accounting and CSR, contributing significantly to the academic community. Her interests in reading, writing, and travel reflect her commitment to lifelong learning and professional growth in her field.

Harikrishnan S is an expert in tax law and public finance, holding a Master's degree in Tax Laws. Currently, they serve as a key contributor at the Centre of Excellence in Public Policy, Sustainability, and ESG Research at Alliance University, where they specialise in crafting policy papers on public finance and related domains.

Mukul Saxena Professor & Director- Centre for PG and Legal Studies and Centre of Excellence in Public Policy, Sustainability and ESG Research He holds a

Ph.D. from the Tata Institute of Social Sciences, Mumbai, and is a Master's in Public Administration (Edward Mason Fellow), Harvard University, USA. During this period, he was awarded the John Kenneth Galbraith Public Service fellowship and was the only Indian in the Diversity Committee. He is also an LL. M. in International Human Rights Law, University of Essex, UK, a Draper Hills Democracy Fellow, Stanford University, a Chevening Gurukul Fellow for Leadership and Excellence, London School of Economics and Political Science, United Kingdom.

Salmah Sharon holds a Doctorate in Accounting from Brawijaya University Malang, and I am currently an associate professor at Ciputra College of Economics Makassar. She specializes in accounting, with a research focus on public sector accounting, accountability, and financial management. As an academic, St. Salmah Sharon plays an active role in developing accounting science by publishing books and contributing to various scientific publications. In addition, she is also active in national and international seminars and conferences and often wins awards as the best presenter. Her contribution to the academic world is limited to research and community service, and she has been recognized with the Best Lecturer in Community Development Excellence award. His teaching has positively impacted the scientific development in accounting, especially in public sector accounting, which continues to inspire and guide students and the community to contribute more in the field.

Tatjana Stanimirović holds a PhD in Public Administration from the University of Ljubljana, Slovenia. She is an associate professor in the Department of Economics and Public Sector Management at the Faculty of Public Administration. Her research focuses on public sector economics, with particular emphasis on taxation and accounting. She is actively engaged in academic and professional activities, participating in both domestic and international conferences and projects.

Index

S

T

www.ingramcontent.com/pod-product-compliance
Lightning Source LLC
LaVergne TN
LVHW080856300926
849162LV00003B/433